Margaret Atwood

a reference guide

A
Reference
Guide
to
Literature

Margaret Atwood

a reference guide

Judith McCombs

and

Carole L. Palmer

G.K.HALL&CO.
70 LINCOLN STREET, BOSTON, MASS.

First published 1991
by G.K. Hall & Co.
70 Lincoln Street
Boston, Massachusetts 02111

10 9 8 7 6 5 4 3 2 1

Library of Congress Cataloging-in-Publication Data

McCombs, Judith.
    Margaret Atwood: a reference guide / Judith McCombs
and Carole L. Palmer.
      p. cm. – (Reference guides to literature)
    Includes bibliographical references and index.
    ISBN 0-8161-8940-4
    1. Atwood, Margaret Eleanor, 1939- – Bibliography. I. Palmer,
Carole L.
II. Title. III. Series: Reference guide to literature.
Z8046.947.M24 1991
[PR9199.3.A8]
016.818'5409 – dc20   91-11385
                                            CIP

Contents

Preface

Over a period of less than thirty years, Margaret Atwood's prolific writing has generated a monumental amount of diverse scholarly and popular commentary. Her work has reached beyond Canada and the United States to a wide international audience, including Great Britain, the British Commonwealth, European, and Scandinavian countries, and the Soviet Union. As coauthors, we have worked together to collect, organize, annotate, and index the accelerating amount of material written about Margaret Atwood. Judith McCombs, a poet and widely published Atwood scholar, has contributed her knowledge of Atwood and Canadian Studies, and her writing skills; and is primarily responsible for the literary introduction, the English-language annotations, and the subject index, which follows that of her 1988 *Critical Essays on Margaret Atwood*. As an academic librarian, I have contributed bibliographic knowledge and research skills; and am primarily responsible for the research activities, bibliographic verification, the overall compilation of the bibliography, the author index, the primary bibliography, and coordination of the research assistants and translators. Our goal has been to combine our research and writing efforts to prepare a useful and comprehensive reference tool for students and scholars, and to create a text that serves to document accurately the critical reputation of Margaret Atwood.

Our starting point for this project was Alan J. Horne's essential "Margaret Atwood: An Annotated Bibliography," covering publications by and about Atwood's prose and poetry in volumes 1 and 2 (1979 and 1980) of *The Annotated Bibliographies of Canada's Major Authors*. Horne's updated checklist of this important work appeared in the 1981 *The Art of Margaret Atwood: Essays in Criticism*, edited by Arnold E. and Cathy N. Davidson.

Alan J. Horne's works, supplemented by Carol J. Fairbanks's 1979 bibliography of Atwood criticism in *The Bulletin of Bibliography*, which made progress in documenting much of the U.S. writing, have stood as the major resources for Atwood research to date. With Alan J. Horne's permission, we have expanded and updated the earlier lists, bringing together into a single volume over 2000 items about Margaret Atwood, nearly seven times the material in Horne's or Fairbanks's previous bibliographies. Beginning with the reviews of *Double Persephone* in 1962, *Margaret Atwood: A Reference Guide* covers writing through 1987, with a short list of 1988 publications, primarily the work from two books of criticism: *Critical Essays on Margaret Atwood*, edited by Judith McCombs, and *Margaret Atwood: Vision and Forms*, edited by Kathryn VanSpanckeren and Jan Garden Castro. A more comprehensive 1988 listing, and updates for subsequent years, can be found in my "Current Atwood Checklist," published annually since 1986 in *The Newsletter of the Margaret Atwood Society*, currently edited by Jerome Rosenberg at Miami University, Ohio.

The search for material, spanning more than four years and utilizing major research library collections in Canada and the United States, produced a wealth of material and many important leads to additional sources; but the scope and depth of this bibliography was enhanced most by Margaret Atwood, who graciously allowed access to her private archive in Toronto for this project. Atwood's extensive files included newspaper and magazine clippings from Canada and the United States, and an array of foreign language materials, not previously uncovered by our research.

The task of bibliographic verification is complicated when working with collections of clippings, since complete publication information is not always readily accessible. During the course of this project, the task of identifying, locating, and examining a library copy of each item often proved to be difficult. In some cases, all efforts to track down a publication failed. Regretfully, there are a number of items, primarily clippings of book reviews from foreign language newspapers and a small collection of Dutch items, that have not been added due to major verification and translation problems. Entries with minor verification problems have been included and are noted with an asterisk (*).

It is likely that some of the more obscure publications cited in this bibliography may be difficult to locate or to obtain through interlibrary loan. Despite this drawback, we have included as much material as possible, from a variety of countries and in many types of publications. Little magazines, trade publications, popular magazines, newsletters, an occasional university publication, and large and small newspapers are represented, in addition to scholarly journals and books. It is hoped that this broad guideline for inclusion will encapsulate a wide perspective, making it easy to identify scholarly criticism and reviews of Atwood's work, as well as popular writing about Atwood.

The city of publication has been added after journal, magazine, and newspaper titles when there is a possibility of confusion with another publication, and on foreign language entries to clarify country of publication. Widely known U.S. and Canadian titles, such as Toronto's *Globe and Mail*, are generally not qualified by city. Newspaper collation (numbers, letters, titles of sections, and page numbers) has been cited to match the usage of the individual newspaper. Due to the complications of obtaining copies of smaller circulation newspapers, page numbers are still missing from some citations. To increase access to U.S. newspaper material, many citations contain information for Newsbank's *Review of the Arts: Literature*, an index with microfiche that reprints newspaper articles from cities throughout the United States.

Selected biographical sources are included, particularly those that are widely available and fairly extensive. Interviews (with the interviewer cited as author) are listed, including many from Atwood's travels around the world. Works by Atwood discussing her writing, or responding to criticism of her writing, are also listed. Encyclopedia entries and brief biographies have generally been omitted. Treatment in textbooks, anthologies, and general literary histories, and short mentions in books or articles have not been added, unless they have been written by a key critic, contradict a major trend in criticism, or appear to be significant within the entire body of criticism. Reviews of books about Margaret Atwood are not included.

The arrangement of this book matches that of other volumes in the Reference Guides to Literature Series. The preliminary "Writings by Margaret Atwood" is a basic, chronological list of books of poetry, prose, and criticism written by Atwood. Selected translations, essays, and other works that complement the content of the secondary material have also been included in this primary list. Alan J. Horne's bibliographies in *The Annotated Bibliographies of Canada's Major Authors* may be consulted for additional primary writings published before 1980. The bibliography of material about Margaret Atwood follows, and is fully annotated. Citations are grouped by year of publication and alphabetically by author within each year. Dissertations are listed in the year the degree was obtained. There are two indexes, one that lists the authors, and one that classifies key literary subjects and the criticism of Atwood's works. A combination of the year and entry number (i.e., 1980.60), not the page number, is used to identify citations in the index and to indicate cross references in the annotations.

Having striven to be as comprehensive and accurate as possible, we are keenly aware that significant items may have been missed and errors may have occurred. We welcome notification of omissions, corrections, and information on other oversights.

We are indebted to Margaret Atwood for her cooperation on this project, and to her assistant, Melanie Dugan, for her aid with the archival material. We also wish to thank Marian Burghardt for her long hours of work in Toronto libraries.

I would like to thank Sarah Zimmerman, David Braasch, and Zse Tho Siew Yoke for their research assistance and work on the manuscript, and the staff of the outstanding Interlibrary Loan departments at Southern Illinois University and Northern Illinois University for their endurance and hard work. I wish to acknowledge the many individuals who contributed their translating skills to this project: Christl Giggenbach for German; Peggy Lietz, Barbara Marcetich, and Bill Levelsmier for French; Jerilyn Marshall for Italian and Russian; Larry Palmquist for the Scandinavian languages; Annie Woodbridge for Spanish; and others; and Judith McCombs for editing the foreign language annotations to maintain a consistent voice throughout the volume. With great respect, I must recognize the late master bibliographer, Alan Cohn, for his years of guidance and encouragement.

I am grateful to Southern Illinois University for the Special Research Project award that provided funding for research assistants. Finally, I wish to express my gratitude for the Canadian Studies Faculty Research Grant from the Canadian Embassy that supported my research activities in Toronto and the United States, and, in turn, greatly advanced this project.

Carole L. Palmer

Literary Introduction

This introduction supplements the bibliographic introduction to my 1988 *Critical Essays on Margaret Atwood*, that traced the patterns of almost all the key English-language criticism from Canada, and the scholarly criticism from the United States; assessed her reputation as a poet, fiction writer, and critic through much of 1987; and discussed in detail the first three collections of Atwood essays and the first three Atwood books, from Linda Sandler 1977, Sherrill [E.] Grace 1980, Arnold E. Davidson and Cathy N. Davidson 1981, Sherrill E. Grace and Lorraine Weir 1983, Frank Davey 1984, and Jerome H. Rosenberg 1984.

The updated, supplementary bibliographic guide here discusses more fully the three Atwood books that could barely be mentioned before – Barbara Hill Rigney's 1987 *Margaret Atwood*, and key essays in Beatrice Mendez-Egle's 1987 *Margaret Atwood: Reflection and Reality* and Kathryn VanSpanckeren and Jan Garden Castro's 1988 *Margaret Atwood: Vision and Forms*; the Canadian criticism written *en français*, plus omitted and recent Canadian work in English; certain of the U.S. trade and library reviews that, especially in *Publishers Weekly* and *Library Journal*, provide an essential portion of the poetry criticism, and a capsule history of the popular and critical success of Atwood's fiction here; the U.S. newspaper coverage, which is particularly relevant to the credibility of *The Handmaid's Tale*'s scenario; the British coverage, which becomes increasingly important with *Life Before Man*; and salient works from Australia, India, Italy, France, German-speaking Europe, Scandinavia, and other Commonwealth and European countries.

The annotations here attempt to create a faithful abstract of the essays and the important (or hard-to-obtain) reviews; a surprising proportion of Atwood's reviews, in newspapers as well as in literary journals, have been quite serious, or foreshadowed later work. Particular care has been taken to preserve the critic's exact terms, preferred spellings, and tone, especially with intense, elusive, or ambivalent responses. For most of the reviews, topic and evaluation are summarized in the first clause of the annotation, so that the annotation can be quickly skimmed, or tabulated as extremely positive, positive, mixed or noncommittal, negative, or extremely negative. (So many of the praises were high praises that an additional category could be made for that.)

Key interviews, that illuminate Atwood's works, have been annotated in detail, as have the key essays, books, and reviews; biographical aspects, however, have been only briefly indicated. Because the book-promotion tours for Atwood's later novels have generated a number of overlapping interviews, the annotations for those are usually lists of topics covered. Interviews annotated as "Atwood explains" offer her direct explanations of key matters. "Atwood discusses" indicates answers of some length; "talks about" and "comments on" refer to less formal and briefer responses.

Dissertations have been annotated from *Dissertations Abstracts International*, if available, and cross-referenced to later publications. The very small proportion of cursory, redundant, or misleadingly Atwood-titled items has been annotated accordingly. From the reader's point of view, it is easier to discount such annotations than to track down excluded material, or to wonder whether the bibliographers were aware of it.

In discussing certain now-salient works and patterns not fully covered in the 1988 *Critical Essays* introduction, the guide here follows primarily the first-publication chronology of Atwood's writings. Skipped Atwood books mean that no additions are needed; the *Critical Essays* introduction, which has been painstakingly reexamined, suffices.[1] In comparing criticism from various countries, the guide and index here define country as the place of publication, which is not necessarily the passport, residence, or orientation of the critic: given the border-crossing habits of academics, criticism, and reprints, something published in Australia, India, Texas, or Wales may well be written by a citizen of Canada or elsewhere. Most of the essays included here as published in India, thus, come from critics closely identified with Canada; see, for example, Susan Gingell's 1984/1985 *Survival*-oriented reading of Atwood's poetry.

It is now clear that the pattern of Atwood's development as a writer has several stages: an apprentice, allegorical period; the first creative stage, of gothic realism, that extends from the 1966 *Circle Game* to the 1977 *Dancing Girls*; and the second creative stage, of political and didactic realism, that extends from the 1978 *Two-Headed Poems* through at least the 1984 *Interlunar* poems and the 1985 *Handmaid's Tale*; note that the 1990 *Selected Poems 1966-1984* stops with the *Interlunar* poems.[2] The post-*Interlunar* poems, which appear in the 1986 Canadian *Selected Poems II: Poems Selected and New*, and the kindred 1988 *Cat's Eye*, with its mystic realism and its portrait of the aging artist in Toronto, may well begin a third parallel and mirroring creative stage; in which, one predicts, Atwood's image-laden, resonant, collage- and mirror-structured fiction will increasingly be called postmodern, and may continue to incorporate more and more of what became lyric poetry in the first creative stage.

Meanwhile, for the emerging archival scholarship, see Barbara Godard's 1987 feminist, Canadian, and postmodern interpretation of the 1961 *Double Persephone* chapbook and other apprentice writings; Judith McCombs 1988 on poetic development in apprentice manuscripts and later sequences; and, beyond the cut-off dates for these annotations, W. J. Keith's detailed 1989 guide to *The Edible Woman*'s comedy, which is the first to include manuscript evidence; Carol L. Beran's key 1990 archival analysis of Atwood's much-debated affirmations in *Life Before Man*; and Marilyn Patton's germinal forthcoming analysis of the politics of the *Life, Bodily Harm*, and earlier manuscripts.[3]

For Atwood's first-stage poetry, see Gillian Porter-Ladousse 1976, in France, on Atwood's Protean and Circean metamorphosis from imprisoning form; pioneering Italian Canadianist Giovanna Capone 1978 on woman, earth, and water themes; and, in Quebec 1979 and Toronto 1983, Clément Moisan's comparison of Atwood's and Michèle Lalonde's kindred identity themes. In the United States, where critics of Atwood's first-stage poetry have mostly focused on its sexual politics, Alicia Ostriker 1986 placed the 1966 *Circle Game*'s opening poem, "This Is a Photograph of Me," in an invisible woman tradition; similarly, for another Atwood medium, Sharon R. Wilson's 1988 "Sexual Politics" discussed, and reproduced, eight of Atwood's unpublished 1969-1974 watercolors, including the original Tarot-based cover for *Power Politics*. Jes Simmons 1987, however, traced Jungian individuation in the Canadian-acclaimed 1970 wilderness *Journals of Susanna Moodie*; David Buchbinder 1988 decoded a Homeric gender politics in the 1976 *Selected Poems*; and, in England and the States, Coral Ann Howells 1987 found a feminized wilderness myth in the *Journals* and *Surfacing*.

For Atwood's first- and second-stage poetry, Christina Strobel 1987, in Germany, examined woman's relationship to man from *The Circle Game* through *Murder in the Dark*; and Kathryn VanSpanckeren 1988, in the States, explicated most thoroughly Atwood's shamanic linking of death and creativity, from *Double Persephone* and the watery Inuit spirit realm of *The Circle Game* through the 1984 *Interlunar* poems and the 1981 *Bodily Harm* novel.

For Atwood's first novel, the 1969 *Edible Woman*, Kim Chernin 1981 provided the first full-length treatment of its protagonist's anorexia; Raffaele Cocchi 1981, in Italy, analyzed its triadic structures, and Gayle Greene 1988 its two-suitor convention and lyric structure; Pamela S. Bromberg 1988, which is part of the 1980s focus on French feminist theory, read both *The Edible Woman* and *Lady Oracle* as exemplifying Luce Irigaray's subversions and deconstructions.

The 1972 *Surfacing* remains Atwood's most studied novel, and a number of key works should be added here. In Canada, Allison Micham 1974 pioneered in placing *Surfacing* in a tradition of French Canadian northern wilderness quest novels, and is one of the small number of much-needed studies of French Canadian links to Atwood's prose and poetry. In the United States, Cathy N. Davidson's 1975 comparison of Kate Chopin's *The Awakening* and Atwood's *Surfacing*, as equivalently realistic, incompletely resolved feminist novels of revolt, is part of the 1970s feminist rediscovery and recognition of women's literature.

A good number of major Canadian-oriented literary essays have appeared in France, and especially from the University of Bordeaux III: founding Canadianist Pierre Spriet 1974 defined essential English Canadian myths in *Surfacing*, *Survival*, *The Edible Woman*, and Atwood's poetry; Kathleen Hulley 1975 examined *Surfacing*'s language as enabling yet colonizing and patriarchal, in the first extended analysis of the politics of language and silence in Atwood's books; and Marcienne Rocard 1977 discussed *Surfacing*'s Anglo-Canadian identity and French Canadian northern pilgrimage. Compare also the perceptive 1978 reviews of *Faire surface*, the French translation of *Surfacing*, from Dominique Autrand in France and Jacques Godbout in Quebec.

In the United States, poet Adrienne Rich's germinal 1976 *Of Woman Born* recognized *Surfacing* as a strange, complex version of the Demeter-Kore myth. Among the later Demeter-Kore and mother-daughter studies, see Nancy C. Carter 1979 on Atwood's first three novels, and especially *Surfacing*, in relation to the matriarchal Demeter-Persephone (Kore) myth; and, much later, Sherrill E. Grace 1988 on *Surfacing* as a muted, altered story of a Persephone searching for Demeter, within a dominant story of a quest for a father.

Among the other mythic and kindred studies of *Surfacing*, see particularly Evelyn J. Hinz and John J. Teunissen 1979 on an apolitical Grieving Mother archetype; Kathleen Wall 1988 on a matriarchal Callisto myth; Kathryn VanSpanckeren 1987 on Western magic in Atwood's first three novels, and alchemy in *Surfacing*; Elizabeth R. Baer 1988 on transformed *loup-garou* and "Fitcher's Bird" motifs; David Carpenter 1985 on geopiety; and, beyond the cut-off dates for these annotations, George Woodcock's 1990 guide to *Surfacing*, which uses Atwood's 1982 *Second Words*, and key 1973 criticism from Canada and the United States, to trace Atwood's pressingly relevant ecological vision.[4]

Surfacing's often comparative Commonwealth- or postcolonial-oriented studies, from Commonwealth and other countries, have been literary, feminist, and political. In one of the earliest feminist approaches, Lois G. Gottlieb and Wendy Keitner 1979 followed Simone de Beauvoir to explore *Surfacing*'s sexual colonialism; more recently, Sushila Singh 1987 discussed *Surfacing*'s New World feminism, and Sylvia Söderlind 1984 focused on its postcolonial anglophone Canadian identity and metamorphosis. Three mid-1980s essays compare *Surfacing* with Australian Patrick White's *A Fringe of Leaves*: Diana Brydon 1984 followed Commonwealth and structuralist theories to find subversive rewritings of Conrad's Eurocentric *Heart of Darkness*; Jeanne Delbaere-Garant 1985 found decolonizings of the self; and Manfred Mackenzie 1986 discussed a postcolonial naturalization of alien place.

German-speaking European responses have often focused on the nature themes and political feminism of Atwood's books: Arno Heller 1984 examined *Surfacing*'s eco-feminist themes, and Brunhild de la Motte-Sherman 1987 the political-economic feminism of *Surfacing* and *Bodily Harm*. Compare also the scholarly reviews of the German and East German translations of *Surfacing*, from Norbert Schachtsiek-Freitag 1979 and Marianne Müller 1981; and see Leif Tufte 1979 on the Norwegian translation.

Had space permitted in the *Critical Essays* introduction, another paragraph on the 1972 *Survival* should have cited Rick Salutin's 1977 proto-Marxist reading, which offered a creative alternative to the late 1970s ideological critiques and denunciations of *Survival*; Joanne Hedenstrom's germinal 1978 essay, which followed *Survival* in defining feminine and masculine traditions in English Canadian literature, including Atwood's first three novels; Donna Bennett's 1983 assessment, which confirms Eli Mandel's 1977 gothic readings; and Gaile McGregor's 1985 *The Wacousta Syndrome*, which is the most extensive reworking of *Survival*'s concepts. See also the reviews from founding German Canadianist Walter Pache 1973, and from Marie-Christine Pioffet 1987, in Quebec, on the fifteen-years-late translation of *Survival* into French.

For *Lady Oracle*'s 1976 reviews, see novelist Mordecai Richler's *Book-of-the-Month Club News* acclaim, and J. R. Struthers on *Oracle*'s upside-down Frygian romance; see, more recently, Gunther Schloz 1985 on the German translations of Atwood's satiric first and third novels. *Lady Oracle*'s many key essays, from diverse countries, have focused on genre, psychology, and myth: Claudio Gorlier 1978 on its gothic comedy and Ann McMillan 1988 on its mixed gothic fantasy and gothic naturalism; see also the 1978 interview with the pioneering Italian Canadianist and translator, Amleto Lorenzini. Sherrill E. Grace 1984 provided a Jungian fairy-tale analysis of *Oracle*'s Bluebeard theme; Emily Jensen 1986 read *Oracle* as a professional woman's – more than an artist's – parable of work versus love; and Mary Jean Green 1987 affirmed *Oracle*'s Canadian and feminine mother-daughter ties; its Great Mother myths are discussed in Cathrine Martens's 1984 Oslo interview and Roberta Sciff-Zamaro's 1987 essay.

The reviews of the retrospective 1977 Canadian *Dancing Girls* were mostly praises: I. M. Owen 1977 acclaimed its haunting comedy, and Patricia Morley 1978 appreciated its framing *doppelgänger* stories; much later, Frank Davey 1986 examined secret and inherited, iconic stories in its seldom-reviewed "Resplendent Quetzal." The 1982 *Dancing Girls*, which replaces two of the 1977 Canadian collection's stories with newer work, was published after *Bodily Harm* in the United States and Britain, and given mostly praise and higher praise in both countries. In the 1982 United States reviews of *Dancing Girls*, novelist Anne Tyler especially appreciated its poet's prose, singling out, as others in both countries did, its opening story of "The Man from Mars"; Joe Coomer identified with its very real characterizations of men and women; Constance Buchanan, in one of the few critiques, faulted its characters' passivity. In the British 1982 reviews, Cara Chanteau found the stories' strangeness fantastic, yet recognizable and compelling, as in "The Man from Mars"; and writer Victoria Glendinning was one of several who read "When It Happens" as our shared apocalyptic nightmare.

The Canadian reviews of the 1978 *Two-Headed Poems* that began Atwood's second creative stage were mostly praises; see Tom Henighan 1978 on Atwood's bleak, honest themes, Wendy Keitner 1979 on her feminist and mother-daughter affirmations, and the detailed appreciation from Edward Prato 1979/George Bowering 1981. *Two-Headed Poems* was published in the United States in 1981, and except for a few men's literary reviews, mostly praised; see, in 1981, Josephine Jacobsen, Stephen Knight, Vernon Young, and the revealing interview by Christine Mack Gordon. For later work, see Lorraine Weir's 1983 cosmological reflections, Shannon Hengen's 1986 feminist and Lacanian psychotherapeutic reading, and Cheryl Walker's 1987 postmodern interpretation.

For diverse Canadian views of the mostly praised *Life Before Man*'s ethics, genre, and politics, see, in 1979, novelist Adele Wiseman's acclaim for its moral humanism, Barbara Amiel's high praise of *Life* as a women's novel, and Sam Solecki's mixed response to its pessimism; for counter arguments on its genre and political realism, see, in 1980, Rick Salutin and the *Atlantis* interview (which casts some light on Atwood's "Women's Novels," in *Murder in the Dark* 1983), and the 1979/81 Alan Twigg interview. Compare Bruce King's 1980 appreciation, in Australia, of social class and ethnicity in *Life Before Man*; and see Diane Almeras's 1982 praise of *La vie avant l'homme*, the French-Canadian translation of *Life*.

In the States, where in 1980 Atwood was, for the first time, acclaimed on the *New York Times Book Review*'s front page, by novelist Marilyn French, *Life Before Man* became Atwood's first novel to get significantly more reviews there than it had in Canada. The most serious of the general 1980 praises include poet Rosellen Brown and critic John A. Weigel on *Life*'s uncompromising and tragic realism; see also the 1980 Carolyn Clay interview-review. For varying responses to *Life*'s poetic elements, see the ambivalent 1979 *Kirkus* review, novelist Anne Tyler's 1980 mixed praise for *Life*'s cosmic dreams (which anticipates Greene 1988), and Elizabeth Johnston Lipscomb's 1981 appreciation of its haunting images; and compare Sergei Belov 1981, in Moscow, on its poet's prose and fragmented structure.

In 1980 *Life Before Man* also became Atwood's first book to be widely – and appreciatively – reviewed in Britain. Julian Symons 1969 had seriously praised *The Edible Woman*'s psychological rebellion against consumer society; but the few other British reviews did not. *Surfacing* had a handful of brief and multi-book 1973 reviews, complimentary and otherwise, with Elaine Glover admiring it most thoroughly, and the reissued *Surfacing* had a small number of 1979 praises: in contrast to the North American acclaim, however, British reviewers mostly kept a certain distance, treating *Surfacing*'s nationalist, wilderness, and female elements intellectually or psychologically. *Lady Oracle* was more enjoyed, for its fun and wit, in the handful of mostly multi-book 1977 reviews; Jane Miller's full-length appreciation caught the John Stonehouse precedent for its staged drowning.

Life Before Man had in 1980 over twice as many English and Scots reviews as had the original *Surfacing* or *Lady Oracle*: Philip Howard, Peter Kemp, Herbert Michael, and almost everyone gave praise and higher praise to Atwood's psychological and evolutionary acuity, wit, and symbols; see also the detailed Ronald Hayman interview. The British reviews, which came mostly from men, seemed generally not to expect the sympathetic characters, strong men, or happy endings that a significant minority of the more numerous Canadian and United States reviews, from both genders, had wanted; perhaps *Life*'s intellectual appeal, characterization, and themes were closer to British than to North American traditions.

Fewer essays have since been written on *Life* than on any of Atwood's first six novels; but see especially John Woodcock 1986 on its pervasive science, M. Sharon Jeannotte 1981 and Gayle Greene 1988 on its use of time, and German critic Paul Goetsch 1985 on *Life* as a novel of manners. *Life*'s connection to George Eliot's *Middlemarch*, cited in various interviews, might be worth further exploring; certainly more could be done to compare *Life*, and Atwood's other novels, to the Victorian literature she studied, taught, and cites.

Atwood's fifth novel, the overtly political *Bodily Harm*, was published in spring 1982 in the United States, where, as in Canada, it received a good number of mainly favorable reviews, though somewhat fewer than for *Life Before Man*, and often with reservations.[5] As the annotations indicate, the varying evaluations, from all countries, of *Bodily Harm*'s affirmations, realism, and pessimism correlate with the varying interpretations of its climactic prison scene and final flight, as a prison pietà, rebirth, real or wished-for release, moral or political conversion, survival, or not.

Among the 1982 United States reviews, Janice MacKinnon fully appreciated Rennie's transfiguring rebirth; Susan Ager found *Bodily Harm* finally and shockingly powerful but, like others, wanted a sympathetic heroine; and Newton Koltz saw *Harm* as a classic misanthropic novel, Canadian version; but the influential *Publishers Weekly* and *New York Times Book Review* responses, from [Barbara A. Bannon] and John Leonard, were not pleased.

The 1982 *Bodily Harm* received, in Britain, about as many reviews as *Life Before Man* had; mostly these were favorable, and saw *Harm* as a skillful, satiric, realistic novel. Among the 1982 reviews, Sally Emerson featured *Bodily Harm* as a sharp, funny, profound thriller; John Mellors valued its authentic, witty portrayal of Canadians and women; and Peter Kemp admired its mordant, exhilarating satire; see also the comprehensive 1982 Adam Hopkins interview. In German-speaking Europe, where the *Verletzungen* translation of *Bodily Harm* received a good number of reviews, see the serious praises from Kyra Stromberg 1982 and Angela Praesent 1983, I[lse] L[eitenberger]'s 1982 rave review, and M[agdalena] V[ogel]'s mixed 1983 consideration.

As with *Surfacing*, later *Bodily Harm* essays have been literary, religious, Commonwealth, political, and international. Geraldine Finn 1983 found a representative but politically limited awareness; Dorothy Jones 1984, a secular pilgrimage and luck equivalent to grace; Elaine Tuttle Hansen 1985, a consciousness-raising structure of women's stories; Louise Milot 1985, a feminist realist discourse; and Mary K. Kirtz 1987, didactic and often triadic characterizations. Two 1987 Australian essays debated *Bodily Harm*'s Third World politics: Jennifer Strauss appreciated its humanist use of Third World confrontations to examine the Canadian consciousness; but Helen Tiffin critiqued its universalist and inadequate representation of the '"other"' culture. Compare also the political assessments in the earlier reviews from Joanne Kates 1981, Kathryn Kilgore 1982, Paul Skenazy 1983, and Jaidev 1984; and the social concern in Elaine Dewar 1982. Other work on *Bodily Harm* and *The Handmaid's Tale* is cited under the later novel.

True Stories, like the altered *Dancing Girls*, appeared in the United States and in Britain (as Atwood's first poetry book published there) in 1982, after *Bodily Harm*. The mainly favorable U.S. reviews divided on its political and feminist assertions, with Joseph Parisi 1982 and Eve Siegel 1982 acclaiming its political honesty and commitment, and M. L. Rosenthal 1983 faulting its confessional and polemical parts. In Wales and England, where the poems were mostly praised, Tony Curtis 1982 enthusiastically affirmed the true political commitment of *True Stories* and *Bodily Harm*; and Fleur

Adcock's more qualified 1983 praise found the poems good, but inferior to *Bodily Harm*.

Meanwhile, in Canada, the 1982 *New Oxford Book of Canadian Verse in English* was generally welcomed as a national literary milestone; see, in 1982, scholar Leon Edel's survey of the evolving Canadian tradition, poet Patrick Lane's lively and pointed appreciation, and W. J. Keith's critical assessment.

Second Words appeared in Canada in 1982, and in the United States in 1984, and was mostly welcomed, in both countries, as a portrait of the writer. Canadian reviews, which saw *Second Words* in relation to *Survival*, focused more on Atwood's Canadian work; the U.S. reviews, which were less numerous and less prestigious, focused more on Atwood's feminism. See, for a spectrum of responses to Atwood's politics and feminism: in Canada, in 1983, John Hofsess on compassionate commitment and Mary Meigs on self-made feminism; in the United States, in 1984, Valerie Miner on resistance to feminism and Karen Rosenberg on realistic literary feminism. Though *Second Words* has not had *Survival*'s impact, certain of its essays have since been used as keys to Atwood's work; "An End to Audience?," which is one of the most often cited, profoundly shapes Barbara Hill Rigney's 1987 *Margaret Atwood*.

Bluebeard's Egg was published in Canada in 1983; and in the United States in 1986, and Britain in 1987, after *The Handmaid's Tale*, and with two of the 1983 Canadian collection's stories replaced by newer work. Reviews in all three countries were mostly praises, of somewhat different kinds. The Canadian warm appreciations of Atwood's compassionate realism and humour countered earlier and still occasional Canadian complaints of lack of warmth; see Christopher Defoe 1983 and Elizabeth Bradley 1985, who praised also Atwood's underpainting and fabrications. In the States, *Bluebeard's Egg* was generally praised for its studies of characters and relationships, but not perceived as having the power of *The Handmaid's Tale*; among the 1986 reviews, Gail Caldwell and Michiko Kakutani particularly appreciated Atwood's diminutive explosions and luminous imagery and metaphors. In Britain, where *The Handmaid's Tale* had less impact, *Bluebeard's Egg* was praised and highly praised, as expert, perceptive, comic, and ironic; novelist Emma Tennant 1987 particularly enjoyed the strong women characters.

In all three countries, the often-parallel reviews that focused on political themes and "The Salt Garden" found a more unified collection. In Canada, Barbara Black 1983 and Barbara Leckie 1984 saw a nuclear-threatened future and a despairing modern generation. In the States, Sherie Poseorski 1986 found characters trapped in history's pressures; and in 1987 Carolyn See, who had written a nuclear novel, contrasted the mother's now-obsolete stories to those of the daughter's nuclear-threatened generation. In

Britain, in 1987, Sally Laird saw the pathos of contemporary estrangements; John Clute traced *Survival* themes in Atwood's and other Canadian stories; and Leslie-Ann Hales assessed Atwood's nuclear-threatened characters as psychological casualties.

Nancy J. Peterson's 1987 essay on *Bluebeard's Egg*'s title story is part of the Canadian and United States feminist reclaiming and critiquing of folklore, in Atwood's work and elsewhere; compare the Bluebeard essays from Sherrill E. Grace 1984 and Sharon R. Wilson 1986. See also Marion Halligan's 1987 celebration of Atwood's style, which is part of the growing Australian appreciation.

Atwood's sixth novel, *The Handmaid's Tale*, soon became her most honored: published in fall 1985 in Canada, it won the nationally prestigious Governor General's Award; in the United States, it won the *Los Angeles Times* Book Award, and both the spring 1986 hardcover and the spring 1987 paperback became Atwood's first U.S. best sellers; published in Britain in spring 1986, *The Handmaid's Tale* won the Arthur C. Clarke science fiction award and was short-listed for the internationally prestigious Booker Prize. Atwood's other major awards, reported by Ellen Vanstone 1987, include the 1987 Humanist of the Year and a *Ms.* magazine Woman of the Year.

Reviews in all three countries were predominantly praises, high praises, and acclaim, with few negatives. In Canada, *The Handmaid's Tale* was hailed as a compelling read and a chillingly plausible satire, anti-Utopia, or speculative fiction; some thought it Atwood's best novel. See Robert Fulford 1985 on its realism and nostalgic pleasures; Michele Belling 1986 on its humanist feminism; and, in 1987, Ildikó de Papp Carrington and W. J. Keith on its cautionary satire. The key interviews by Katherine Govier 1985 and Sue Matheson 1986 detail historic and literary sources for Atwood's dystopia, as does the somewhat later 1986 interview by Mary Battiata, printed in both the United States and Canada. For the two germinal images behind *The Handmaid's Tale*, see Kenneth McGoogan's 1985 "Varied Images"; and, in the States, Le Anne Schreiber's revealing 1986 interview.

The Handmaid's Tale is Atwood's first book to receive far, far more reviews in the United States than in Canada[6] – and the appreciation and acclaim, though similar, had a more intense and personal tone here. Atwood's repressive fundamentalist Republic of Gilead was, for most reviewers, a quite plausible near-future scenario for the United States, and particularly frightening on this side of the border; most found the entrapped handmaid narrator, Offred, sympathetic, perceptive, and engaging; many identified with her. The most influential U.S. acclaim began with [Sybil Steinberg's] December 1985 *Publishers Weekly* rave, that placed Atwood's all-too-plausible anti-Utopia beside *Brave New World* and *Nineteen Eighty-Four*, and Christopher Lehmann-Haupt's January 1986 *New York Times* accolades for Atwood's anti-Utopian heroine; Sharan Gibson's "Read it while it's still allowed,'" in the January *Houston Chronicle*, was much quoted in book advertisements.

Throughout February 1986 *The Handmaid's Tale* received extraordinary nation-wide praise and acclaim in the literary and popular press: Joyce Johnson in the *Washington Post Book World*, Elaine Kendall in the *Los Angeles Times Book Review* and *Miami Herald*, and Jerome Rosenberg in the *Philadelphia Inquirer* lauded the novel's humanity and Gilead's terrifying realism; and Peter S. Prescott in *Newsweek* acclaimed its literary dystopia. The one prominent exception, from writer Mary McCarthy, 9 February on the front page of the *New York Times Book Review*, found Atwood's fundamentalist rulers incredible: then, as a number of reviews pointed out, on 17 February *Time*'s cover story starred right-wing television evangelist Pat Robertson as potential Presidential candidate.[7] *The Handmaid's Tale*'s breakthrough successes were well reported in Canada: in January 1986 Beverley Slopen quoted [Steinberg's] December rave review, and in February Larry Black detailed Atwood's new literary stardom and the McCarthy-Robertson story.

Almost all the later 1986 responses confirmed *The Handmaid's Tale*'s powerful realism. Virginia Low, Elaine Melson Madsen, and Annie Laurie Gaylor, among others, identified specific United States developments that could lead to–or were leading to–a Gilead here. Anticipating later work, Ann Snitow and Stephen McCabe praised Atwood's history-creating narrator and responsible message; see also the fundamentalist protest from historian James J. Thompson, Jr. Later, in March 1987, concurrent with *The Handmaid's Tale*'s paperback publication, events again highlighted what one reporter called Atwood's "fictional nightmare" of surrogacy when, after bitter national controversy, surrogate mother Mary Beth Whitehead lost custody of her daughter in the Baby M case.[8]

The probing 1986 analyses of the sexual and feminist politics of Atwood's dystopia, from Barbara Ehrenreich, Pam Rosenthal, and Gayle Greene, made it clear that *The Handmaid's Tale*, like earlier Atwood work, upheld yet challenged both left and feminist politics. Mary Wilson Carpenter 1986 followed feminist literary theory to argue that the final "Historical Notes" redefined the novel; similarly, Janet Karsten Larson 1987 celebrated *The Handmaid's Tale*'s empowering textual reconstruction of women's scriptural stories. The 1988 VanSpanckeren and Castro *Margaret Atwood* has two key essays on *The Handmaid's Tale*: Arnold E. Davidson followed Carpenter 1986 to analyze sexism and history in the concluding "Historical Notes"; and Roberta Rubenstein, whose 1987 book had traced gender boundary issues in Atwood's first six novels, explicated inversions of nature and nurture in Atwood's dystopia.

In Britain, where *The Handmaid's Tale* was Atwood's first short-listing for the Booker Prize, Atwood received significantly more reviews, and more one-book reviews, than ever before. Some confirmed *The Handmaid's Tale*'s parallels to contemporary America or Iran; most focussed on its system, feminism, and genre, reading the novel as a feminist dystopia, satire, science fiction, fantasy, etc. See especially, in 1986, Patrick Parrinder's celebration of Atwood's science fiction fable of survival and Jane Gardam's high praise of *The Handmaid's Tale*'s terrible beauty; in 1987, Rik Scarce on its alternative futures, Brian Stableford on its Orwellian feminist dystopia, and Lorna Sage on its contemporary political referents.

In Europe, the most thoughtful reviews of *The Handmaid's Tale* include the anonymous Spanish 1986.231, Antti Majander 1986 on the Finnish translation, and Ingrid Strobl 1987 on the German; see also the 1986 Kristina Carlson interview. Two European essays, from Jacques LeClaire 1986 in France and key Canadianist Reingard M. Nischik 1987 in Germany, further examined *The Handmaid's Tale*'s ironic feminism and dystopian genre.

Other 1987 work, in Britain, linked *Bodily Harm* and *The Handmaid's Tale*: Leslie-Ann Hales saw society's too-real dangers precluding the positive descent and rebirth of earlier fiction; Coral Ann Howells, in contrast, saw moral rebirth in *Bodily Harm*, and resistance, love, and survival in *The Handmaid's Tale*. Barbara Hill Rigney's 1987 *Margaret Atwood*, which found a redemptive rebirth in *Bodily Harm*, but a limited heroine in *The Handmaid's Tale*, assessed the protagonists of the first six novels as, in varying degrees, failed artists who must recognize their responsibility to bear witness.

Selected Poems II: Poems Selected and New 1976-1986 appeared in Canada in late 1986, and was mostly praised, but not so often, or so highly, as Atwood's first *Selected Poems* had been; the difference may well reflect not only a change in the primary focus of Atwood's writing, but also a change in the culture, a turning away from the consciousness-raising, nationalistic, flourishing Canadian poetry scene of the 1960s and early 1970s. Robert M. Seiler 1986 was one of several 1986-1987 Canadian reviewers who found control and power, but also gloom, in *Selected Poems II*. A different *Selected Poems II*, without the concluding newer work, appeared in the United States in 1987; see the concise 1987 praise from poet Ivan Argüelles. A *Selected Poems 1966-1984*, that also omits the newer, post-*Interlunar* work, appeared in Canada in 1990.

The *Oxford Book of Canadian Short Stories in English*, co-edited by Atwood and Robert Weaver, was published in Canada in late 1986, in Britain in 1987, and was generally appreciated in Canada, more briefly in Britain; see especially the historic overview from Michael Smith 1987.

Cat's Eye, Atwood's seventh novel, appeared in Canada fall 1988, with, for the first time, no new book of poetry between it and the previous novel, though several of the new, post-*Interlunar* poems in the 1986 Canadian

Selected Poems II, and parts of the 1983 *Murder in the Dark*, anticipate *Cat's Eye*. Published in 1989 in the States, *Cat's Eye* became Atwood's second best seller here, both in hard cover and paperback, albeit for fewer weeks than *The Handmaid's Tale*; in Britain, the 1989 *Cat's Eye* became Atwood's second Booker Prize short-listing. Many of the 1988-1989 Canadian and U.S. reviews (which fall outside these annotations' cut-off dates) appreciated *Cat's Eye* as a realistic, or all-too-realistic, novel about girlhood; some found the book, or its hero, anti-feminist: see Douglas Glover 1988 on *Cat's Eye*'s metastacizing imagery, Caryn James and Alice McDermott in 1989 on its realism and anti-feminism, and this author's forthcoming 1991 essay on the creative self and feminism in *Cat's Eye*.[9]

As Carole L. Palmer's indispensable annual checklists indicate, Atwood translations and secondary work are flourishing internationally; see, for example, the seven essays on Atwood in the 1988 Yugoslavian *Cross-Cultural Studies*, edited by Mirko Jurak; and the six more, which include European and British critics, in the Spring 1989 French *Commonwealth Essays and Studies*.[10] A film of *The Handmaid's Tale*, directed by Volker Schlondorff with a screenplay by Harold Pinter, was released spring 1990 with international publicity, and received mixed reviews; a videotape also appeared in 1990.[11] Although, in the 1989 checklist, much work still focuses on *Surfacing*, there is a remarkable surge of work on *The Handmaid's Tale* – some twenty secondary items, including at least twelve essays, on that novel's various genres, postmodern form, and feminist politics. In the 1990 checklist, some twenty-four secondary items on *The Handmaid's Tale* as novel and film, including at least a dozen essays on the novel, with only three essays on *Surfacing*, strongly suggest that Atwood's sixth novel is already becoming her most important one.

Meanwhile, more books of Atwood criticism are published, in process, and begun. Earl G. Ingersoll's comprehensive 1990 *Margaret Atwood: Conversations* reprints twenty-one 1972-1990 literary interviews from Canada, the United States, and Australia, including Linda Sandler 1977 and other key interviews; Reingard M. Nischik's forthcoming stylistic and narrative theory approach to Atwood's fiction will be the first critical Atwood book in German.[12] Colin Nicholson's *Margaret Atwood: New Critical Essays*, a second essay collection, and several reading and teaching guides, are in preparation in Canada, the United States, and Britain.[13] Given the exponential growth of Atwood criticism, and her growing reputation in these and other countries, it can only be an understatement to say that much, much other Atwood work is yet to come.

Judith McCombs

Notes

1. As pages xxxvii-xlii indicate, Atwood's work is often published first in Canada, and some books have been published only in Canada.

Two statements in the 1988 *Critical Essays* introduction should be corrected here. Contrary to the fourth paragraph on page 19, *Murder in the Dark* did draw a small number of reviews in England, the United States, and elsewhere; these are annotated here. The penultimate sentence on page 19 should indicate that, when *Interlunar* was published in Canada in 1984, most reviews from both genders affirmed Atwood's characteristic voice, world view, and new humanity, though several of the men's reviews found Atwood's poems too bleak, dark, and cold.

2. Margaret Atwood, *Selected Poems 1966-1984* (Toronto: Oxford University Press, 1990).

3. W. J. Keith, *Introducing Margaret Atwood's The Edible Woman*, Canadian Fiction Studies No. 3 (Toronto: ECW Press, 1989; General Paperbacks, 1990); Carol L. Beran, "The Canadian Mosaic: Functional Ethnicity in Margaret Atwood's *Life Before Man*," *Essays on Canadian Writing*, no. 41 (Summer 1990):59-73; and Marilyn Patton, "Tourists and Terrorists: The Creation of *Bodily Harm*," *Papers on Language and Literature,* Southern Illinois University at Edwardsville, forthcoming c. Fall 1991.

4. George Woodcock, *Introducing Margaret Atwood's Surfacing*, Canadian Fiction Studies No. 4 (Toronto: ECW Press, 1990; General Paperbacks, 1991).

5. As with most of Atwood's novels, the Canadian as well as the United States reviews for *Bodily Harm* ranged from extremely positive to extremely negative.

6. From *Surfacing* on, this bibliography has found a few, or some, more reviews for Atwood's novels in the States than in Canada. The thirty or so Canadian reviews tend to be more knowledgeable about Atwood's earlier work, and more nationally prestigious; the United States reviews are more limited to general newspapers. *Life Before Man* received some three dozen Canadian reviews, and some fifty United States ones. *The Handmaid's Tale* is the dramatic change, with some three dozen Canadian reviews, and almost a hundred U.S. reviews, annotated here.

7. Richard N. Ostling, "Power, Glory–and Politics," *Time* 127, no. 7 (17 February 1986), pp. 62-69; see also cover and p. 3.

8. Susan G. Cole, "Pondering the Problems of Paid Female Fertility," *NOW* (Toronto), 21-27 May, 1987, pp. 7-8, quoted p. 8. When Baby M was

born on 27 March 1986, Mary Beth Whitehead, who had been artificially inseminated with William Stern's sperm, changed her mind about the surrogacy contract; in March 1987, after a bitter and widely publicized trial, the New Jersey Bergen County Superior Court denied Whitehead's claims, upheld the surrogacy contract, and allowed William Stern's wife, Elizabeth, to adopt Baby M immediately. Whitehead appealed, and on 3 February 1988, the New Jersey Supreme Court invalidated the Stern-Whitehead surrogacy contract, but awarded custody to the Sterns. Marianne Yen, "High State Court Invalidates Baby M Surrogacy Contract," *Washington Post*, 4 February 1988, p. A3. As of late 1990, controversy over the legality of surrogacy contracts continues, state by state.

9. Douglas Glover, "Her Life Entire," *Books in Canada* 17, no. 7 (October 1988):11-14; Caryn James, "Ambiguity between Best Girlfriends," *New York Times*, 28 January 1989, p. 16; Alice McDermott, "What Little Girls Are Really Made of," *New York Times Book Review*, 5 February 1989, pp. 1, 35; and Judith McCombs, "Contrary Re-memberings: The Creating Self and Feminism," *Canadian Literature*, forthcoming 1991.

10. Carole L. Palmer, "Current Annual Checklist, 1988," *Newsletter of the Margaret Atwood Society*, no. 5 (1988):[5-11]; "Current Annual Checklist, 1989," *Newsletter*, no. 6 (1989):[7-13]; and "Current Annual Checklist, 1990," *Newsletter*, no. 7 (1990):[6-11]; see the annotations of the 1986 and 1987 checklists. The *Newsletter* is edited by Jerome Rosenberg, Department of English, Miami University, Oxford, Ohio 45056, and available for a modest sum. The Margaret Atwood Society, founded in 1983 and recognized as an Allied Organization by the Modern Language Association in 1990, conducts meetings and sessions at the annual MLA conventions. Mirko Jurak, ed., *Cross-Cultural Studies: American, Canadian, and European Literatures: 1945-1985* (Ljubljana, Yugoslavia: English Department, Filozofka Fakulteta, Edvard Kardelj University of Ljubljana, 1988); and *Commonwealth Essays and Studies* 11, no. 2 (Spring 1989), Dijon, France.

11. Natasha Richardson played the handmaid, and Robert Duvall the Commander; when the movie was released, the paperback *Handmaid's Tale* then returned, for a few weeks, to the *New York Times Book Review*'s best seller list. See Laura Flanders, "*The Handmaid's Tale*'s Near Futurism Misses Chill Factor," *In These Times* 14, no. 18 (28 March-3 April 1990), p. 20; the HBO videotape was similarly reviewed by Rita Kempley, *Washington Post*, 13 September 1990, p. D7.

12. Earl G. Ingersoll, ed., *Margaret Atwood: Conversations*, Ontario Review Press Critical Series, ed. Raymond J. Smith (Willowdale, Ontario: Firefly Books Ltd. and Ontario Review Press, 1990); and Reingard M.

Nischik, *Mentalstilistik: Ein Beitrag zu Stiltheorie und Narrativik dargestellt am Erzählwerk Margaret Atwoods* (Tübingen: Narr, forthcoming 1991).

13. In the forthcoming ECW *Introductions* to Atwood's novels, Carol L. Beran's much-needed guide to *Life Before Man* and Lorna Irvine's germinal re-interpretation of *Bodily Harm* are now in press; and the Modern Language Association has just approved a proposal for *Approaches to Teaching Margaret Atwood*, to be edited by Sharon R. Wilson and Thomas B. Friedman, with Shannon Hengen as editorial assistant.

Writings by Margaret Atwood

Double Persephone. Toronto: Hawkshead Press, 1961.

The Circle Game. Toronto: Contact Press, 1966; House of Anansi Press, 1967, 1978.

The Animals in That Country. Toronto: Oxford University Press, 1968; Boston: Little, Brown, [1969].

The Edible Woman. Toronto: McClelland and Stewart, 1969; Boston: Little, Brown, 1969; London: André Deutsch, 1969.

> *La donna da mangiare*. Translated by Mario Manzari. Milan: Longanesi, 1976.
>
> *Den ätbara kvinnan*. Translated by Vanja Lantz. Stockholm: Prisma, 1980.
>
> *La femme comestible*. Translated by Hélène Filion. Montréal: Quinze, 1984.
>
> *Die eßbare Frau*. Translated by Werner Waldhoff. Düsseldorf: Claassen, 1985.

The Journals of Susanna Moodie. Toronto: Oxford University Press, 1970.

Procedures for Underground. Toronto: Oxford University Press, 1970; Boston: Little, Brown, 1970.

Power Politics. Toronto: House of Anansi Press, 1971; New York: Harper & Row, 1973.

Surfacing. Toronto: McClelland and Stewart, 1972; New York: Simon & Schuster, 1973; London: André Deutsch, [1973].

> *Faire surface.* Translated by Marie-France Girod. Montréal: Éditions l'Étincelle, 1978; Paris: Grasset, 1978.

> *Gjenkjennelsen.* Translated by Inger Elisabeth Hansen. Oslo: Gyldendal, 1978.

> *Der lange Traum.* Translated by Reinhild Böhnke. Düsseldorf: Claassen, 1979.

> *Strömung.* Translated by Gabriele Bock. Leipzig: Verlag Philipp Reclam, 1979.

> *Upp till ytan.* Translated by Vanja Lantz. Stockholm: Prisma, 1979.

Survival: A Thematic Guide to Canadian Literature. Toronto: House of Anansi Press, 1972.

> *Essai sur la littérature canadienne.* Translated by Hélène Filion. Montréal: Boréal, 1987.

You Are Happy. Toronto: Oxford University Press, 1974; New York: Harper & Row, 1974.

"Don't Expect the Bear to Dance." *Maclean's* 88, no. 6 (June 1975):68-71.

Lady Oracle. Toronto: McClelland and Stewart, 1976; New York: Simon & Schuster, 1976; London: André Deutsch, 1977.

> *Dronning Orakel.* Translated by Ingebjorg Nesheim. Oslo: Gyldendal, 1979.

> *Lady Oracle.* Translated by Marlyse Piccand. Montréal: Éditions L'Étincelle, 1980.

> *Lady Orakel.* Translated by Werner Waldhoff. Düsseldorf: Claassen, 1984.

> *Lady Oracolo.* Translated by Fausta Alberta Libardi. Florence: Giunti, 1986.

Selected Poems. Toronto: Oxford University Press, 1976; New York: Simon & Schuster, 1978.

Dancing Girls and Other Stories. Toronto: McClelland and Stewart, 1977; New York: Simon & Schuster, 1982; London: Jonathan Cape, 1982.

> *Les danseuses et autres nouvelles*. Translated by Jean Bernier. Montréal: Quinze, 1986.

> *Unter Glas*. Translated by Helga Pfetsch. Düsseldorf: Claassen, 1986.

"Canadian Monsters: Some Aspects of the Supernatural in Canadian Fiction." In *The Canadian Imagination: Dimensions of a Literary Culture*. Edited by David Staines. Cambridge, Mass. and London: Harvard University Press, 1977, pp. 97-122. Reprinted in *Second Words: Selected Critical Prose*, 1984, pp. 229-53.

Days of the Rebels: 1815-1840. Canada's Illustrated Heritage. Toronto: Natural Science of Canada, 1977.

Two-Headed Poems. Toronto: Oxford University Press, 1978; New York: Simon & Schuster, 1980.

Up in the Tree. Toronto: McClelland & Stewart, 1978.

> *Sur l'arbre perchés*. Translated by Michel Caillol. Montréal: Tisseyre, 1979.

Life Before Man. Toronto: McClelland & Stewart, 1979; New York: Simon & Schuster, 1979; London: Jonathan Cape, 1980.

> *Die Unmöglichkeit der Nähe*. Translated by Werner Waldhoff. Düsseldorf: Claassen, 1980.

> *När livet var ungt*. Translated by Vanja Lantz. Stockholm: Prisma, 1981.

> *La vie avant l'homme*. Translated by Marianne Véron. Montréal: Quinze, 1981; Paris: Laffont, 1981.

Anna's Pet, by Margaret Atwood and Joyce Barkhouse. Toronto: Lorimer, 1980.

Introduction to *To See Our World*, [photographs] by Catherine M. Young. New York: Morrow, 1980, pp. 18-23.

Bodily Harm. Toronto: McClelland & Stewart, 1981; New York: Simon & Schuster, 1982; London: Jonathan Cape, 1982.

> *Verletzungen*. Translated by Werner Waldhoff. Düsseldorf: Claassen, 1982.

> *Ingreppet*. Translated by Vanja Lantz. Stockholm: Prisma, 1983.

> *Marquée au corps*. Translated by Hélène Filion. Montréal: Quinze, 1983.

True Stories. Toronto: Oxford University Press, 1981; New York: Simon & Schuster, 1981; London: Jonathan Cape, 1982.

> *Wahre Geschichten: Gedichte*. Translated by Astrid Arz. Düsseldorf: Claassen, 1984.

The New Oxford Book of Canadian Verse in English. Edited by Margaret Atwood. Toronto and London: Oxford University Press, 1982.

Second Words: Selected Critical Prose. Toronto: House of Anansi Press, 1982; Boston: Beacon Press, 1984.

Bluebeard's Egg. Toronto: McClelland & Stewart, 1983; Boston: Houghton Mifflin, 1986; London: Jonathan Cape, 1987.

> *L'Oeuf de Barbe-Bleue*. Translated by Hélène Filion. Montréal: Libre Expression, 1985.

Murder in the Dark: Short Fictions and Prose Poems. Toronto: Coach House Press, 1983; London: Jonathan Cape, 1984.

> *Die Giftmischer: Horror-Trips und Happy Ends*. Translated by Anna Kamp. Düsseldorf: Claassen, 1985.

> *Meurtre dans la nuit*. Translated by Hélène Filion. Montréal: Éditions du Remue-ménage, 1987.

Interlunar. Toronto: Oxford University Press, 1984.

The Handmaid's Tale. Toronto: McClelland & Stewart, 1985; Boston: Houghton Mifflin, 1986; London: Jonathan Cape, 1986.

> *Orjattaresi*. Translated by Matti Kannosto. Helsinki: Kirjayhtymä, 1986.

> *Tjänarinnans berättelse*. Translated by Maria Ekman. Stockholm: Prisma, 1986.

> *El cuento de la criada*. Translated by Elsa Mateo Blanco. Barcelona: Seix Barral, 1987.

> *Der Report der Magd*. Translated by Helga Pfetsch. Düsseldorf: Claassen, 1987.

> *La Servante écarlate*. Translated by Sylviane Rué. Paris: Laffont, 1987.

Introduction to *Roughing It in the Bush, or, Life in Canada*, by Susanna Moodie. London: Virago, 1986.

The Oxford Book of Canadian Short Stories in English. Selected by Margaret Atwood and Robert Weaver. Toronto and New York: Oxford University Press, 1986.

The CanLit Foodbook. Edited by Margaret Atwood. Toronto: Totem Books, 1987.

Selected Poems II: Poems Selected and New, 1976-1986. Toronto: Oxford University Press, 1986; Boston: Houghton Mifflin, 1987.

Cat's Eye. Toronto: McClelland & Stewart, 1988; New York: Doubleday, 1989; London: Bloomsbury, [1989].

Selected Poems: 1966-1984. Toronto: Oxford University Press, 1990.

Writings about Margaret Atwood

1962

1 MANDEL, ELI. "Seedtime in Dark May." *Alphabet*, no. 4 (June), pp. 69-70.

    Reviews *Poems* by David A. Donnell, *Double Persephone* by M.E. Atwood, and *The Drunken Clock* by Gwendolyn MacEwen. Praises the paradoxically opposed "metamorphic metaphors" of a "haunted and haunting" *Double Persephone*, but notes the borrowing of poet Jay Macpherson's "good muse." Prefers MacEwen.

2 SCOTT, PETER DALE. "Turning New Leaves." *Canadian Forum* 41 (February):259-60.

    Brief note in a round-up review. Finds *Double Persephone* serious and thoughtful, with powerful understatements; but "Miss Atwood borrows too much, or not enough"; her "archetypal menagerie" and meditations seem contrived.

3 WILSON, MILTON. "Letters in Canada, 1961: Poetry." *University of Toronto Quarterly* 31, no. 4 (July):448-49.

    Briefly reviews *Double Persephone* and other 1961 pamphlets; prefers Gwendolyn MacEwen's poems. Finds *Double Persephone* precocious, startling, and poised, but brittle and "a bit lifeless," with its gorgon's glance. Quotes its "admirable" shepherdess poem, and concludes that Miss Atwood need only learn "to be really gay or really elegiac."

1966

1 MacCALLUM, HUGH. "Letters in Canada, 1965: Poetry." *University of Toronto Quarterly* 35, no. 4 (July):383.
    Briefly praises, as the year's "most handsome work," Charles Pachter's fifteen-copy illustrated edition of the seven poems of *The Circle Game*. Atwood's interesting poems combine realism, ritual, and a Robert Gravesian lightness of touch; Pachter's well-matched lithographs unite icon, whimsy, and a Rorschach-blot suggestiveness.

1967

1 GIBBS, ROBERT. Review of *The Circle Game*. *Fiddlehead*, no. 71 [sic 70] (Winter), pp. 69-71.
    Comparative review of Margaret Avison's *The Dumbfounding*, and *The Circle Game*. Like Avison, Atwood has a unique sensibility, and is complex and disciplined. In contrast to Avison's great, centered, and profound religious poetry, Atwood writes of a dissolving, tense, ironic world that is "at once over-civilized and savage"; its affirmations are human, and infrequent, but strengthened by the irony's negative energy.

2 HARRISON, KEITH. "Poetry Chronicle." *Tamarack Review*, no. 42 (Winter), pp. 73-74.
    Praises *The Circle Game* highly in a round-up review. Miss Atwood's light touch acts as foil for a darker undertone; the playful games articulate disturbing experiences with wit and control. "This Is a Photograph of Me" and "Camera" are fascinating: "Strange pieces–which resonate hauntingly in the mind long after one has read them. Something important is being said, but it resists analysis."

3 HELWIG, DAVID. "Canadian Poetry: Seven Recent Books." *Queen's Quarterly* 74, no. 4 (Winter):758.
    Praises *The Circle Game*'s imagination, wit, seriousness, and startling confrontations, but finds its love poems singularly loveless, and reacts against its tone of "tired acceptance or tired denial." The excitements come from ways of seeing things; there's little passion, no gaiety. Much talent here expresses an invalid sensibility; though the reviewer respects and enjoys *The Circle Game*, he turns to Irving

Layton's outrageous boasts for relief, and "can't believe it's that awful to be a woman."

4 MacCALLUM, HUGH. "Letters in Canada, 1966: Poetry." *University of Toronto Quarterly* 36, no. 4 (July):357-59.

   Praises *The Circle Game* highly, featuring it, after Margaret Avison's *The Dumbfounding*, in the annual round-up. Atwood's fastidious, evocative poetry focuses on the forms of imagination and myth. Here "[a]n ancient world of totems, floods, and pre-historic landscapes lies just behind the familiar world"; here myth can overwhelm reality, or retreat before it. Sleep may be fearful, games may tyrannize, art may imprison, as Atwood adeptly moves between myth and fact, inner and outer reality. Briefly praises Atwood's dramatic parable of creation, *Speeches for Doctor Frankenstein*, printed and illustrated by Charles Pachter in a fifteen-copy edition.

5 ONDAATJE, MICHAEL. Review of *The Circle Game. Canadian Forum* 47 (April):22-23.

   Acclaims *The Circle Game* as a fully imagined world of Atwood's personal mythologies, which at times re-create traditional myths. Like an arsonist, or a mysterious Mata Hari, Margaret Atwood opposes the too-clean and ordered, and "brings all the violence of mythology into the present world." Her "cannibalistic speaker . . . demands to know everything," and reveals it to us. The last two survivor poems are the best. Reprinted: 1988.36. Excerpted 1975.18.

6 RUTSALA, VERN. "An Authentic Style." *Kayak*, no. 12, pp. 63-65.

   Acclaims Atwood's rare, authentic style and welcomes *The Circle Game's* realistic, "unrelenting clarity." *Circle's* people are separated "by the apparatus of daily life," or by something else, an inner aversion or animal fear. Both awareness and ignorance serve to wedge distances between these people; closeness becomes an invasion. A skillful, authentic book.

7 SEAMAN, ROGER. Review of *The Circle Game. Quarry* 16, no. 4 (Summer):40-42.

   Appreciatively reviews both *The Circle Game* and Phyllis Webb's *Naked Poems*. Atwood's language pursues experience; her wanting the circle broken gives energy to the poems, the best of which "struck me

1967

in the way that I was struck when I heard that the continents floated, that the atmosphere was a sea . . . ." *Circle*'s "transformations are touched by horror"; its metamorphoses frighten by suggesting that there is no final form.

8 STEVENS, PETER. "On the Edge, on the Surface." *Canadian Literature*, no. 32 (Spring), pp. 71-72.
    Acclaims *The Circle Game*; identifies closely with its poetic vision of our tentative, edgy world, where "[d]angerous evolutionary menace lurks under the surface," little hope or real communication surfaces, and yet we must make the journeys that may mean our survival, or may be only pointless circlings. A two-book review focussed on *The Circle Game*.

9 WEAVER, ROBERT. "An Alternate Selection: *The Circle Game*." *Canadian Reader* 8, no. 8 [1967]:4-5.
    Commends *The Circle Game*, which won the 1967 Governor General's Award, Weaver being one of the judges choosing *Circle*. Atwood belongs, with John Newlove, Gwendolyn MacEwen, and George Bowering, to a new generation of young Canadian poets portraying their (or our) "world on the knife-edge of public and private disaster." "Journey to the Interior" suggests Atwood's already "astonishing authority."

1968

1 BARBOUR, DOUGLAS. Review of *The Animals in That Country*. *Dalhousie Review* 48, no. 4 (Winter):568-70.
    Commends, in a round-up review, the wider, more public voice of *The Animals in That Country*, as "a real progression from the severely personal" first book. Although "A night in the Royal Ontario Museum" has the too-familiar isolated, marooned Atwood persona, the "Progressive insanities of a pioneer" brilliantly widens her inner/outer struggle, and the final love poems set a new tone, distinct from *The Circle Game's* ever-present dangers.

2 GASPARINI, LEN. Review of *The Animals in That Country*. *Canadian Forum* 48 (December):212.

Atwood's animals play a losing, predestined, human game. Though occasionally Atwood lapses into "feminine conceit" and "close-phrase-cultism," the best poems, which include "It is dangerous to read newspapers" and "Progressive insanities of a pioneer," are serious, powerful, and true, outweighing the faulty ones.

3 GILLER, DORIS. "Prizewinner Praises Canadian Government Response to Poets." *Montreal Star*, 16 September, p. 32.
Quotes Atwood, whose Centennial Commission prize-winning *The Animals in That Country* has just appeared, on Canada's poetry consciousness; her forthcoming first novel and current novel in progress; being a Canadian versus a U.S. writer; and Canada as home.

4 MANDEL, ELI. "The Poet as Animal – of Sorts." *Globe and Mail Magazine*, 12 October, p. 17.
A four-book review featuring Alfred Purdy and Joe Rosenblatt, followed by Atwood's *The Animals in That Country*, and John Newlove; finds Atwood's animals, whatever they are, not Purdy's nor Rosenblatt's. Atwood's method "consistently takes the image for the reality"; she journeys, like Stanley Kubrick's *2001* voyager, towards a perception-shaping space-time warp. With beautiful control, she faces the mysteries of things and of self.

5 "Margaret Atwood: Her Cells Are Always Changing." *Toronto Life* 2, no. 12 (October):70.
Reprints a college self-portrait of M.E.A., and profiles an elusive, mutable Atwood, like that of "This Is a Photograph of Me." Her elusive lyrics and astonishingly original metaphors are mainly foreboding, or occult and bizarre, as in "Speeches for Dr. Frankenstein." Her images are uncannily right, as in "[A] Foundling." "'Her cells are always changing,'" according to Charles Pachter, who illustrated and published limited editions of her poetry. Atwood is a nature expert and a perceptive fortuneteller. The heroine of her forthcoming *The Edible Woman* resembles an Atwood ex-acquaintance now living in ultra-foreign parts.

6 MOON, SAMUEL. "Canadian Chronicle." *Poetry* 112, no. 3 (June):204-5.

1968

Features *The Circle Game* at end of Canadian round-up review. The circle game of the title poem is a symbol accruing meaning throughout the book: a symbol first of regional conventionality, then of propriety in marriage; then of inherited allegories of tradition. The final liberating, moving poems of a selfless search for the other come close to Buber's understanding. A book of "ultimate honesty." Excerpted 1977.21.

*7 PEARSON, ALAN. "The Poetry of Margaret Atwood, Anne Wilkinson." *Montreal Star*, 2 November.
    Praises, in a two-book review, *The Animals in That Country*'s unboring and very Canadian-sounding poetry, where snow and landscape provide objective correlatives for haunted emotions. Atwood writes with spare passion and pure language. The *Animals in That Country*'s poetic range, from *aboulia* to satirized cowboy to Dr. Frankenstein, goes beyond that of her first book of poetry.

8 THOMPSON, ERIC. Review of *The Circle Game. Fiddlehead*, no. 75 (Spring), pp. 76-77.
    A two-book review, of *The Circle Game* and Dennis Lee's *Kingdom of Absence*. Finds Miss Atwood "something of a darling of the literary Establishment," having won the Governor General's Award and now, for *The Animals in That Country*, the Centennial Poetry prize. Finds in *The Circle Game* a clear, mythopoetic poet, but of limited experience, yet inferior to Emily Dickinson. The centerless, passive conclusion disappoints; a facile but minor poet. Excerpted 1975.18.

1969

1 BROWN, MARILYN. "As a First Novel – Very Digestible." *Edmonton Journal*, 26 September, p. 70.
    Praises *The Edible Woman* as an excellent first novel of the conservative, Dullsville, prehippie sixties; "a real Canadian novel," and a statement about young adults. There are many fine and representative characterizations, of Ainsley, Clara and her family, and best, of course, Duncan. The reviewer could do without some of the mouldy pots, dust swirls, and pubic hair. The final cake bit is marvelous.

1969

2 COHEN, ANNETTE. "Superbly This Side of Important." *Globe and Mail Magazine*, 11 October, p. 18.

Gives mixed praise to *The Edible Woman* as a charming and good first novel that falls short of importance, and of Atwood's poetry. Superb description, brilliant observation, witty irony; but the major characters need to be developed, with a consistent tone.

3 CUSHMAN, JEROME. Review of *The Animals in That Country*. *Library Journal* 94, no. 5 (1 March):1000.

Briefly recommends, in a four-book review, these deeply-rooted Canadian poems of man's dehumanization and of the spoilers of the forests; praises the uncomfortably true, compellingly valid themes.

4 GIBBS, ROBERT. Review of *The Animals in That Country*. *Fiddlehead*, no. 79 (March-April), pp. 117-18.

Praises the distinct, hardening, intensifying "turn of the screw" that makes *The Animals in That Country* even better than *The Circle Game*. A mythologizer and maker of landscapes, Atwood twists the poems to a very high pitch, followed by a deliberate falling off; the whole book moves deliberately "toward a centre of horror, then away"; see especially "Speeches for Dr. Frankenstein" and "A night in the Royal Ontario Museum." The final poems, of possible love and self-discovery, provide release. Not a comfortable book–perhaps more to admire than to love–but "certainly poetry of a high order." Excerpted 1975.18.

5 HELWIG, DAVID. Review of *The Animals in That Country*. *Queen's Quarterly* 76, no. 1 (Spring):161-62.

Finds Atwood's second book, like her first, exciting, highly disciplined, centered on obsessive images, cerebrally violent. The poems "multiply paradoxes into a surreal country," as in "Progressive insanities of a pioneer." Form oppresses, encircles, traps, as in "The reincarnation of Captain Cook." Helwig respects Atwood's poetry more than he can like it and, sentimentalist or not, prefers *The Animals in That Country* for its warmer love poems. Reprinted: 1988.23.

6 MacCALLUM, HUGH. "Letters in Canada, 1968: Poetry." *University of Toronto Quarterly* 38, no. 4 (July):343-44.

Finds, in the annual round-up review, that *The Animals in That Country* continues Atwood's disquieting exploration of identity. In her world the human psyche divides, disintegrates, or freezes; reality dissolves, or suffocates; alienation, as in "A fortification," pervades; the satisfactory human responses are denied. Though such precariously poised poetry can be disturbing, on the whole it is vital and admirable.

7 MARSHALL, TOM. Review of *The Animals in That Country*. *Quarry* 18, no. 3 (Spring):53-54.

Wonders, in a four-book review of Atwood, Margaret Avison, Joe Rosenblatt, and Dennis Lee, whether "Atwood's by-now-characteristic cool . . . is not likely to harden soon into a mannerism. Her poems are beautifully made and always intelligent, but a little inhuman." But in her best, such as "Progressive insanities of a pioneer," there is intellectual excitement, a search for identity, genuine pioneering, an illumination of the Canadian experience. Prefers Margaret Avison and Al Purdy.

8 MILLAR, GAVIN. "She and He." *Listener* 82 (28 August):287.

Briefly reviews *The Edible Woman* in a four-book review of women writers. Seems to find sexual-identity elements of interest; finds some of the language overworked.

9 MONTAGNES, ANNE. "Two Novels That Unveil, Maybe, a Coming Phenomenon, the Species Torontonensis." *Saturday Night* 84, no. 11 (November):54, 56, 58.

Reviews *The Edible Woman* and James Bacque's *The Lonely Ones*, naming the uncannily shared Toronto elements in both, and in Montagnes' own nearly-completed novel, suggesting these seventy-seven coincidences may be "the inception of a Canadian national identity, *Species Torontonensis*." Notes also the eerily coincidental camera-terror scenes in Atwood and Bacque. Identifies Atwood's heroine's *anorexia nervosa*, and praises *The Edible Woman's* startling images and deadpan humour, but not its unimpassioned superficiality.

10 PURDY, A[L] W. "Poet Besieged." *Canadian Literature*, no. 39 (Winter), pp. 94-96.

Responds to *The Animals in That Country* not as "'women's poems'" but as "tremendous, soul-stirring, awesomely analytical, penetrating," complicatedly simple poems from a writer besieged, inside and out, or, in "Arctic syndrome," a metamorphosed Peggy-animal who "attacks the man-animal . . . . Perhaps she is too terrified of the Indians (animals, damnit!) on the outside of her stockade (skin)."

11 "Self-Deprecating." *TLS*, 2 October, p. 1122.
     Brief, anonymous review of *The Edible Woman*, which complains that some embarrassment, or failure of nerve, has made Atwood trim an otherwise sensitive and serious novel with "that self-deprecating humour lady columnists use," weird caricatures, and an "excruciating" end. Excerpted: 1977.21.

12 SHEPPARD, JUNE. "Poet Often Lurks Inside." *Edmonton Journal*, 27 September, p. 22.
     Interviews and quotes Atwood, whose first novel has just appeared, on teaching poetry and encouraging the poet inside the student to emerge; on being a "'rabid'" conservationist; on books versus television for children; on critics' discoveries versus a male review of her "feminine subjects like life, love and death"; on the occult; and on storytelling versus a message in *The Edible Woman*.

13 SYMONS, JULIAN. "An Extremely Funny First Novel." *Sunday Times* (London), 31 August, p. 27.
     Praises *The Edible Woman* highly, in a four-book review of first novels, as the best first novel read that year. Novels on dropouts from consumer society are common; this one's originality rests in its central character's conscious attempts to conform, while her thoughts and body refuse to conform. Though minor faults exist, including the somehow unsatisfactory end, overall this book shows a most unusual and inventive comic imagination.

14 Van STEEN, MARCUS. "Precise, Figurative Poetry: Well Disciplined, Powerful." *Ottawa Citizen*, 6 September, p. 29.
     Compliments *The Animals in That Country*, which like *The Circle Game* portrays men and women's inter-relationships subtly and sensitively, with striking metaphors, and probes life's mysteries in an original way. Though *Double Persephone* "deservedly attracted little attention," Miss Atwood's later poetry has an impressive power and discipline. Her range, which slightly extends that of *The Circle Game*,

1969

"is still bound within the traditional feminine limits of life and love and death, of which she treats in the highly subjective manner that is also traditionally feminine," as in ["A pursuit"]. Her poetry is profoundly moving.

15 WHITE, ALISON. "Poems That Will Take Years to Explore." *Edmonton Journal*, 7 February, p. 31.

Appreciates highly Atwood's Canadian-centered, Centennial Commission award-winning *The Animals in That Country*: "Luckily for Canada, it is the large Canadian corner of the map that engrosses the poet," who, very luckily for Edmonton, lives here. These poems are Atwood's Rosetta Stone; she traces and deciphers "the meanings strewn like hieroglyphs about" this planet. Her Canadian-centered verse evokes, fascinatingly, our English heritage, with echoes of [Algernon Charles] Swinburne, [Gerard Manley] Hopkins, and Stevie Smith. For "Atwood an incomprehensible X equals" a ceremonial, picture-book animal.

16 WOODCOCK, GEORGE. "Are We All Emotional Cannibals?" *Toronto Star*, 13 September, p. 13.
       See 1969.17.

17 ____. "The Symbolic Cannibals." *Canadian Literature*, no. 42 (Autumn), pp. 98-100.

Acclaims *The Edible Woman* and praises Atwood's poetry; as with Siamese twins, her fictional and poetic talents are inextricably connected. Like *The Circle Game*, *The Edible Woman* is about human distances and defences. It is really about emotional cannibalism; its predatory or parasitic characters feed on one another, while its heroine becomes, plausibly if improbably, unable to eat. Commends Atwood's handling of fantasy, over Mordecai Richler's in *Cocksure*. As a highly perceptive social novelist, Atwood has done what Jane Austen similarly did, for the "ordinary" people of her time. Slightly expanded version of 1969.16. Slightly revised, as part of 1972.40 and 1975.52.

1970

1 AVANT, JOHN ALFRED. Review of *The Edible Woman*. *Library Journal* 95, no. 16 (15 September):2934.

Rejects Atwood's novel as much too tediously and irrelevantly padded. Though the title seems deliciously awful, and the style can be nicely perverse, like Muriel Spark's, the plot is inadequate and the characters essentially uninteresting. Though first novelists are seldom "promising," maybe someday Atwood will write a book worth reading.

2 [BANNON, BARBARA A.]. Review of *The Edible Woman*. *Publishers Weekly* 198, no. 4 (27 July):67.

Likes and recommends *The Edible Woman*; finds Atwood genuinely witty and highly original, though not yet in Margaret Laurence's class. *The Edible Woman*'s style and dry, infectious humor are so good that you'll forgive the only fault – which is the end just dribbling off – and eagerly await Atwood's next novel.

3 BARBOUR, DOUGLAS. Review of *Procedures for Underground*. *Dalhousie Review* 50, no. 3 (Autumn):437, 439.

Finds in *Procedures for Underground* unsentimental poems, "carved out of stone," hard-edged, finely crafted, preoccupied with loneliness, fear, and place; finds also a new, subtle reaching out to an other. Atwood's consistent form has a variety of contents, often mythic; praises and quotes entire "Game After Supper."

4 ____. Review of *The Journals of Susanna Moodie* and the CBC Canadian Poets Series LP read by Mia Anderson. *Canadian Forum* 50 (September):225-26.

Praises highly this subtle, brilliant sequence that establishes Atwood as a most important young Canadian poet. The voice of Atwood's mythic Canadian Moodie adapts and changes, "coming to uncertain terms" with our land. Atwood's Moodie may not match the historic character, but is a very real woman, entirely believable, a pleasing intelligence. Mia Anderson's reading interferes with these marvelous poems; get the book, not the record.

5 BELL, MILLICENT. "The Girl on the Wedding Cake." *New York Times Book Review*, 18 October, p. 51.

Praises *The Edible Woman* highly as a work of "feminist black humor" on the consumer society, with woman as edible product, and man as media-programmed *Playboy* consumer. Atwood's situation-comedy elements serve wacky, sinister, surreal ends; the heroine's inability to eat becomes a "truth-telling dementia that is a symbolic answer to lying sanity." Excerpted: 1974.37.

6 BOWERING, GEORGE. "To Share the World or Despair of It." *Globe Magazine*, 2 May, p. 16.

A two-book review, praising *The Journals of Susanna Moodie* and contrasting it with George Jonas's *The Happy Hungry Man*. Atwood works not in fragments but in pieces we can connect; she shares the world. These are not found poems, but detached from their events, as her "Afterword" says. Journal I connects with Susanna Moodie's *Roughing It in the Bush*, Journal II with her *Life in the Clearings*. This is the myth where "man enters the forest and finds that it has entered him." Atwood masks her own voice a bit too much, save in moments like the lovely, clear "Wereman," quoted entire. The Atwood portion is reprinted, slightly revised, as part of 1981.9.

7 BREWSTER, ELIZABETH. "Dream Gave Life to Atwood Poems." *Edmonton Journal*, 10 April, p. 61.

Praises highly *The Journals of Susanna Moodie*, as real but dreamlike, sometimes nightmare; not primarily historic, which could have ended before most or all of Journal III, where Moodie becomes more a natural force than a person. If, as the "Afterword" suggests, we Canadians are like Moodie, we can hope to survive threats from outside and inside; we share Moodie's double vision, obsessions, struggle – do we share her toughness? Moodie and her struggle, and the recurrent light imagery, unify the sequence; the precise language and cool style are admirable. Atwood is certainly one of the best Canadian poets writing now.

8 ____. "Poetic Dreams in a City Park." *Edmonton Journal*, 4 September, p. 55.

Praises *Procedures for Underground*, which juxtaposes the underground world of dreams and subconscious with the aboveground world of ordinary realities; praises Atwood's understated, cool, controlled poems; and notes the slightly warmer, more human tone here, not sentimental, but "learning to make fire."

9 CALLAGHAN, BARRY. "Atwood: 'We Are All Immigrants to This Place.'" *Telegram* (Toronto), 14 March, p. 59.

Appreciates Atwood's grim, cold, Canadian *The Journals of Susanna Moodie*, which evokes the reviewer's childhood memory of the strange madness of [Robert Service's "The Cremation of Sam McGee"]. The pioneer gentlewoman Moodie has, underneath her rambling anecdotes, a hard core "made queer by the jack knife cold nights," bitter by hunger, and disconcerted. Atwood, whose own poetry has a kind of madness, of despair, edges, shattered memories, impermanence, and a missing centre, has found in Moodie's thick prose a kindred, split-apart soul. The grim Moodie-Atwood reflects "an obsession that is in our veins," which the "Afterword" calls a Canadian paranoid schizophrenia. Perhaps a blood-chilling Sam McGee lurks in all of us – and Atwood takes us "close to the coldness of the bone."

10 DUNCAN, CHESTER. "Truth in a Glass Bell." *Winnipeg Free Press*, 21 November, New Leisure sec., p. 20.

Admires Atwood's very serious, brilliant, laconic *Procedures for Underground*, but has misgivings about its difficulty and tense, dark truths. "Her eye is brilliant but at times horror-struck"; "Game after supper" recalls Paul Almond's very frightening film, *Isabel* – maybe Canadians have a talent for this. The excellently-titled and well-arranged *Procedures for Underground* shows how such procedures eat up one's cheerfulness: dark truths, sad facts, solipsism's pathos, a haunting past give an enormous excitement that could be hysteria. What is most striking is Atwood's delicate capture of sad, ecstatic, or disturbing moments.

11 EASTON, ELIZABETH. Review of *The Edible Woman*. *Saturday Review* 53, no. 40 (3 October):40.

Does not recommend this novel, where "what might be briefly amusing becomes tedious" in rambling length. Atwood's sharp imagery can't compensate for the trite characters and the lack of a plot. But if the book's summarized contents attract you, do try it; if not, find a livelier book.

12 ELLIOTT, GORDON R. Review of *The Edible Woman*. *West Coast Review* 5, no. 2 (October):68-69.

A comparative review which starts to praise, then criticizes, Atwood's first novel, while acclaiming Margaret Laurence's *A Bird in the House*. Atwood sees a male-dominated consumer society, where

1970

women are consumed by men; scenes and background world are perceptively detailed. The idea is good for a Status of Women brief, but somewhere a reader gets enough. Despite all the humour, wit, and astute background, the characters are dull, lifeless, and boring. Almost nothing works; Atwood squanders her talents and seemingly forgets the reader. Unlike Laurence, Atwood explains too much and details too much, perhaps because she doesn't know what she wants to say, and doesn't trust her readers.

13 EWART, GAVIN. "Laureate Versus the Rest." *Ambit*, no. 43, pp. 41-42.

Gives mixed praise to *The Animals in That Country* in a six-book review; finds short, unrhymed dream-poems, like "Progressive insanities of a pioneer," with Canadian backgrounds. Though some poems are "a bit wishy-washy," the best, which include the Sylvia Plath-influenced "Chronology" and "The green giant murder," are truly original. A talented, but overpriced, book.

14 GARDNER, RAYMOND. "In a Strange Land: Raymond Gardner Talks to Margaret Atwood." *Guardian* (Manchester), 14 October, p. 9.

Remarks on Atwood, *The Edible Woman*, the historic Susanna Moodie, and Atwood's haunting *Journals of Susanna Moodie*; quotes Atwood on being a writer and Canadian. The novel is about a girl who tries to "make it" in her society–does Atwood see that as desirable? Atwood says it's what she sees, in a lot of people. Isn't the novel autobiographical? Atwood says no, it's "about someone who does not know what to do with her life and that has never been my predicament."

15 GARNET, ELDON. "For the Poets, the Landscape Is the Great Canadian Myth." *Saturday Night* 85, no. 2 (February):31-33.

Canada lacks neither mythology nor ghosts; our wilderness is our myth and our identity. Our poets humanize our wilderness and speak for Canada, as Atwood does in *The Circle Game*; as also do Alden Nowlan, Ian Young, and Barry Charles.

16 GEDDES, GARY. "Poets in Residence." *Globe and Mail Magazine*, 10 October, p. 20.

Concludes a six-book review by praising *Procedures for Underground's* "eerie, sometimes ghoulish voice" and "fine skeletons." This book continues Atwood's space-time explorations, with her usual fascinating science-fiction inventiveness, and adds a new, more personal tone.

17 GEDDES, GARY, and BRUCE, PHYLLIS, eds. "Notes on the Poets: Margaret Atwood." *15 Canadian Poets*. Toronto: Oxford University Press, pp. 265-66.

Atwood's poems pioneer in uncharted consciousness, with a Cartesian "'I think, therefore I am in trouble.'" There is always fear. Perception produces alienation or isolation. "Atwood's poems reveal an obsession with space – the spaces within, around, and between men and objects. . . . She is both the archetypal first Canadian . . . and the archetypal first human walking [sic, but corrected to waking in 1978.29] from the unconscious sleep of evolution." Her startlingly surreal images can be presented in a dislocatingly prosaic manner. She experiments; her seemingly haphazard line-lengths can be seen as unexpected springboards to meaning. Revised: 1978.29.

18 GELLATLY, PETER. Review of *The Journals of Susanna Moodie*. *Library Journal* 95, no. 19 (1 November):3784-85.

Recommends this book, despite the regional setting, for all poetry collections. Clearly Atwood dislikes but is fascinated by Moodie, whose recollections are astonishing, sometimes bizarre. Atwood uses Moodie's Canadian-English ambivalence for her own musings; this is a Moodie transformed with modernity and cryptic grace. Atwood's semi-abstract collages are charming. Reproduces collage for "Alternate Thoughts from Underground."

19 GIBBS, JEAN. Review of *Procedures for Underground*. *Fiddlehead*, no. 87 (November-December), pp. 61-65.

Explicates structure and poems to reveal this book's progressively maturing poetic vision and aesthetic whole; the three parts move from inner self to outer world to a precarious but transcendent reconciliation of inner and outer. The first section tries to exorcise our sometimes nightmare myths of childhood, family, deaths, and the Romantic journey underground. The second section tries to survive a wasteland world stripped of myths; panic lies under the surface. The final section reaches tenuous but primal affirmations, through the lovers and through love, as in "Fragments: Beach," "Woman Skating," and "Dancing Practice," which reveal life's cosmic rhythms and patterns.

20 IRVING, JUDY. "Margaret Atwood Stirs a Literary Storm." *Montreal Star*, 27 May, p. 89.

Profiles Atwood as prize-winning poet, internationally praised novelist, script writer, and a rain-maker in the new wave of Canadians portraying Canadians. Atwood discusses writing the film script for *The Edible Woman* with producer Oscar Lewenstein and director George Kaczender; Americans versus Canadians; her childhood and jobs; the imperilled future; her luck, Scorpio sign, and the occult; and her writing plans.

21 JACKSON, MARNI. "A Poet and the Membrane of Mystery." *Toronto Star*, 22 August, p. 45.

Praises *Procedures for Underground*, in a round-up of recent titles, as work from one of Canada's best poets, albeit weaker than *The Journals of Susanna Moodie*. Atwood's deceptively simple words and clear images evoke strange refractions, memory and emotions; as in "Two Gardens," a thin membrane divides the familiar and the mysterious.

22 JOHNSON, JANE. Review of *Procedures for Underground*. *Other Voices* 6, no. 3 (November):[17].

Admires *Procedures for Underground* and Nancy-Lou Patterson's *Sugar Bush*. Both writers, like Joyce Carol Oates, wear pokerfaced masks. Atwood's words jump off the page, almost too excitingly; her world is Oates's nightmare world, claimed as real.

23 JONAS, GEORGE. "A Choice of Predators." *Tamarack Review*, no. 54, pp. 75-77.

Praises the playful and sardonic realism with which *The Edible Woman* examines our predatory, less-than-endearing natures; identifies the heroine's cake-woman as a substitute sacrifice; praises the poet's use of symbols. But the late-fifties Toronto realism could date, the self-centered characters could bother some readers, and the book could be misread as a women's rights crusade. But certainly *The Edible Woman* is entertaining fun.

24 KATTAN, NAIM. "Le goût de ressembler à tout le monde." *Devoir* (Montréal), 14 February, p. 12.

   The Edible Woman makes a successful transition, allowing Atwood's poetry to come alive through fiction. Atwood shares with the reader her detachment toward the protagonist who struggles, but never succeeds in conforming to the role expected of her by society. Atwood avoids sentimentality by building the story around a facade of desperate and absurd situations. Expanded 1976.52.

25 MADDOCKS, MELVIN. "That Consuming Hunger." *Time* 96, no. 17 (26 October):116; (p. 82 in Canadian edition).

   Praises *The Edible Woman* and *Procedures for Underground* for going beyond the Woman Writer sensibility of Katherine Mansfield's "The Garden Party." Atwood, like Joan Didion and Anne Sexton, belongs to a new sisterhood; *The Edible Woman*, with its comic surface and all-consuming metaphor of cannibalism, "conceals the kick of a perfume bottle converted into a Molotov cocktail." *Procedures for Underground* compresses Atwood's evolutionary terrors, and shows that the barbarous and the overcivilized are one. Atwood's new sensibility is natural, honest, and tough. Excerpted:1975.18.

26 MANDEL, ELI. "Modern Canadian Poetry." *Twentieth Century Literature* 16, no. 3 (July):177.

   Briefly comments on Atwood's use of space and time in three poems from *The Animals in That Country* ("A night in the Royal Ontario Museum," "Progressive insanities of a pioneer," and "Astral traveller"), as part of an essay defining national and modern elements in some twenty-seven Canadian poets. Reprinted 1977.54.

27 MARSHALL, TOM. "Les animaux de son pays: Notes sur la poésie de Margaret Atwood." *Ellipse* (Sherbrooke, Québec), no. 3 (Spring), pp. 81-86.

   A review article on *The Animals in That Country* that sees similarities between Atwood's lucid and macabre images and Marie-Claire Blais's ideas and work; both writers share the same Canadian universe. The problems presented in *The Circle Game* find some

1970

possible solutions in *The Animals in That Country*. "A voice" shows optimism, but "The green giant murder" is pessimistic. "Speeches for Dr. Frankenstein" infers that we may have created a dangerous monster. "Backdrop addresses cowboy" claims we prostitute what should be sanctified. Atwood's poems utilize an intellectual formula, like that of Northrop Frye, and feature rhythmic precision and a distinct mythology. Her supple words are bonded in sentences that convey strong, nearly clairvoyant emotions, sharing with the reader a new, personal research.

28 _____. "Canpo: A Chronicle." *Quarry* 19, no. 4 (Summer):51.
        Comments on the young Canadian poets' nationalism, in a ten-poet review; praises *The Journals of Susanna Moodie* as Atwood's best, finding it both personal and objective, and movingly human, unlike the earlier fables of green giants, Frankenstein, and space-men. Moodie's own *Roughing It in the Bush* has the almost archetypal Canadian experience. Atwood's Moodie becomes Canadian myth, a ghostly ancestor showing us the beauty and terror of the wilderness, inner and outer.

29 _____. Review of *The Edible Woman*. *Quarry* 19, no. 3 (Spring):55-56.
        Praises *The Edible Woman* highly, in a three-novel review, along with Graeme Gibson's *Five Legs* and over Margaret Laurence's *The Fire-Dwellers*. Atwood's satire is wickedly funny, and Duncan impossibly true; the end is ambivalent but intriguing. Not a poet's novel like Leonard Cohen's *Beautiful Losers*, but carefully plotted, with a beautiful shift in narrative person, and a shrewd understanding of how absurdly Canadian men and women live in their absurd and predatory consumer society.

30 [MEZEI, STEPHEN]. Review of *The Edible Woman*. *Performing Arts in Canada* 7, no. 1:47.
        A mini-review that finds *The Edible Woman's* "Silent Majority" characters, except for Duncan, too ordinary and dull.

31 PURDY, AL [W.]. Review of *The Journals of Susanna Moodie*. *Wascana Review* 5, no. 2:57-58.
        Based on Susanna Moodie's "grotesque classic" of *Roughing It in the Bush*, and generated by a dreamt opera, *The Journals of Susanna*

Moodie are in a way a libretto for "a very female opera," albeit in Atwood's cold logic. These poems are "legitimately female," but lack the male half of the human viewpoint, which may be inevitable in life and art. The book is "close to great," though it excludes love and misses that double viewpoint.

32 Review of *The Edible Woman*. *Best Sellers* 30, no. 16 (15 November):335-36.

Attacks *The Edible Woman* as worthless, starting nowhere and ending nowhere. The male characters are jellyfish, the women self-devouring. "What a pity that an author who writes so well cannot produce a plot worthy of her talent." Everyday lives, even the reviewer's own, are just not interesting!

33 Review of *The Edible Woman*. *Kirkus Reviews* 38, no. 15 (1 August):817.

Pleased; "genuine style applied to the most ordinary circumstances . . . disconcerting, faintly ominous, and moving with the greatest of ease from the expected to the unexpected." An original talent, something like Penelope Mortimer's; sympathetic intelligence, telltale details, and humor ranging from wit to wayward fun.

34 ROPER, GORDON. "Letters in Canada, 1969: Fiction." *University of Toronto Quarterly* 39, no. 4 (July):341.

Briefly praises *The Edible Woman* as the richest, in characterization, language, and wit, of three first novels from McClelland and Stewart: "a refreshingly human comedy. . . . These young people may dramatize themselves as cannibalizing each other, but in the end they all eat cake," baked by Marian.

35 SIMON, MARJORIE. "An Astonishing, Near-Flawless First Novel." *Courier-Journal and Times* (Louisville, Ky.), 27 December, p. E5.

Recommends highly the astonishing and near-flawless *The Edible Woman*, which "magnetically hold[s] the reader to each page." The outwardly solid Marian feels inwardly drained by the obligations, demands, and caprices surrounding her. There are unexplainable, almost mystic encounters with [Duncan]. In her increasingly disturbing fantasies, an inanimate steak and a carrot acquire life. This "very meaty book" will have many interpretations.

1970

36 S[KELTON], R[OBIN]. Review of *The Edible Woman*. *Malahat Review*, no. 13 (January), pp. 108-9.

Praises Atwood's novel seriously, as a fable and a Swiftian sexual satire, and therefore entitled to unreal characters; but finds it disquieting. The protagonist is shadowy and oddly obsessed, the men totally lack human presence, the love and sex are totally without tenderness. How can we condemn trivial appetites if no serious values exist? Still, *The Edible Woman* is engaging, well written, shrewd, and witty; but it lacks the deep feeling and human dignity of Atwood's poetry.

37 STEDMOND, JOHN. Review of *The Edible Woman*. *Canadian Forum* 49 (February):267.

Complains that this poet's novel doesn't live up to its possibilities. The cleverly sketched characters don't jell, the plot creaks a bit, the point-of-view switch has little effect. Marian isn't up to a Margaret Drabble heroine, Duncan can't be taken seriously, the juju-cake-woman is a crumby end. The other characters – the "new woman" roommate, pregnant friend, "office virgins," and prying landlady, are stock. The potentialities of the "woman" question are unrealized.

38 Van DUYN, MONA. "Seven Women." *Poetry* 115, no. 6 (March):432-33.

Finds, in a group review, "nothing 'feminine'" and nothing trite in *The Animals in That Country*, and tries to empathize with the writer's fears: "What interests me is the compulsive subject of these poems: a distrust of the mind of man, the word, the imagination, even the poem." The ambivalence, in the love poems also, fascinates; "as one guilty trapper to another, one hopes for her, in her country, her poetry, her love, something she can see as both a solid and a benevolent fullness of creation." Excerpted: 1974.37; 1977.21.

39 Van STEEN, MARCUS. "Voice of Pioneer Women." *Ottawa Citizen*, 20 June, p. 27.

Celebrates *The Journals of Susanna Moodie* as, amazingly, "the voice of Mrs. Moodie speaking directly to us"; the voice of all Canada's pioneer women; and a testament to survival. Atwood, who identifies completely with the indomitable pioneer and writer, Mrs. Moodie, complains unfairly, in the prose notes, of Moodie's shapeless journals and difficulties in adjusting. But "in the poems Mrs. Moodie strides forth," determined but sensitive, intelligent but bravely persevering. "And in a subtly inexorable way, the one woman becomes all pioneer women, and inevitably merges with us as we face the hardships, the losses and griefs, the radioactive wilderness of the twentieth century." This is another Atwood prizewinner, enhanced with her evocative collages.

40 WAINWRIGHT, ANDY. "Margaret Atwood's Drowned World." *Saturday Night* 85, no. 12 (December):33, 35.

The Circle Game's violence and claustrophobia have now changed to *Procedure for Underground's* wiser acceptance of Atwood's drowned, under-surface world. With the circle game broken, Atwood sees more clearly her startling, Dali-like, sinister yet beautiful world. Now men are seen more calmly, as mythical, or inhabiting their own dream worlds. *The Journals of Susanna Moodie*, which deal with ordered, almost gentle reflections, is worth reading, though its history seems more mood than conviction. Atwood "will never be a popular poet," because she deals too much with vortexes and with what we deny.

1971

1 ANDERSON, J.L. Review of *The Journals of Susanna Moodie*. *Poet and Critic* 6, no. 2:44-45.

Finds *The Journals of Susanna Moodie* an interesting and well-written linking of past and present. Based on the historic Moodie's writings, the poems follow her through alienation and fear in the bush, to the immigrant's mixed love and hate for the new country, through madness and death. The final poems, where Atwood tries to make Moodie a "'spirit of the land,'" verge on a sentimentality that "the strength of the poems" carries quite well.

2 BREWSTER, ELIZABETH. "Powerful Poetry." *Edmonton Journal*, 16 April, p. 60.

Finds *Power Politics* somewhat disturbing, but unified and powerful; discusses characters and theme. The "you," if individual, is very strange, a Superman, Christ, everyman, and seemingly also a male muse, such as Atwood found in Gwendolyn MacEwen. The "I" represents all females, and perhaps the earth, but like the "you," fails with love. The world they inhabit is sterile, loveless, hostile to creative art, preoccupied with disastrous power struggles. An important book from a major Canadian poet, though not at first glance as attractive as *The Journals of Susanna Moodie* or *Procedures for Underground*. Reprinted: 1988.6.

3 BROWN, ROSELLEN. "The Poetry of Margaret Atwood." *Nation* 212, no. 26 (28 June):824-26.

Appreciates Atwood's simple language, transforming vision, and rational but haunted voice in *Procedures for Underground*, *The Journals of Susanna Moodie*, *The Animals in That Country*, and *The Circle Game*. In "Midwinter, Presolstice," the matter-of-fact becomes dream and nightmare; the transparent language of "Game after supper" moves through memory's dark filter into terror. Stone, water, animals fill Atwood's totemic world; in her transforming vision "[e]verything wavers, nothing is stable." Yet her voice is rational and reticent, unlike Sylvia Plath's; though some *Circle Game* poems can be read as "feminist" or "feminine," the anger is muted, not confessional. Similarly, the Canadian identity poems are not "nationalist," but searching for an elusive essence.

4 EDWARDS, MARY JANE. "Hook and Eye." *Ottawa Journal*, 10 April, p. 52.

Values *Power Politics*. The dramatic, witty "'you fit into me'" displays Atwood's characteristic conversational tone, simple structure, domestic imagery, and macabre metamorphosis; and suggests paradoxes of feminine/masculine relationship, and mythical connections of opposites. After exploring these themes, and after several transformations of both personae, *Power Politics* ends with "He is last seen," where he is the fish bringing death, which deepens the paradox of the feminine/masculine relationship, of the poet and her poetry or muse, and of life's creating and destroying forces. Though *Power Politics* "is not easy to hook," with its difficult tight construction, archetypal imagery, confusingly untitled poems, and tough humor, it is "worth hooking," for its clear, searching woman's eye.

5 GELLATLY, PETER. Review of *Procedures for Underground*. *Library Journal* 96, no. 1 (1 January):82.

Enthusiastically recommends this book, and Atwood's earlier *The Journals of Susanna Moodie* and *The Edible Woman*, for all collections. Atwood is not just "'a poet to watch,'" but an astonishing writer, of enormous, burgeoning artistry. Her surfaces conceal mysteries; the strikingly clear diction conveys omens and paradoxes. Humans are incurably lonely, with their best hope being, as "Procedures for Underground" suggests, "a Tenniel-like earth change."

6 HARCOURT, JOAN. Review of *Power Politics*. *Quarry* 20, no. 4:70-73.
Quarrels not with what is here, but with what is left out. In a no man's land most of us have visited, Atwood's prototypical couple struggle for psychic superiority. Love is a weapon; fantasy and reality collide, merge, separate; the images are violent, cannibalistic, paranoid, but always controlled. Even hysteria would be a relief here. *Power Politics'* very lopsided, narrowed vision shuts out hope, compassion, and joy; in this desolating terrain, a grim endurance is the only positive left.

7 ____. Review of *Procedures for Underground*. *Quarry* 20, no. 1 (Winter):52-53.
Praises poetry "as compelling as a nightmare." Atwood's sinister, bleak, otherworldly images intertwine with calm physical realities. Here the human psyche's dinosaurs seek less for light than for survival in a hostile, uncertain world. Atwood's eerie experiments with shifting time, persona, and souls as geological fragments, create dark brilliances in desolate terrain. Her nihilism ends not in silence, but in "a cry for help," and questioning.

8 HELWIG, SUSAN. "Margaret Atwood's Poetry: The Struggle for Dominance: Painful Politics." *Toronto Citizen* 2, no. 5 (11 March):12.
Defends *Power Politics* as far too perceptive and imaginative to be dismissed as bitter in superficial or anti-feminist reactions. The linking of seemingly unconnected ideas and the twisting of lines into logic, as in "'you fit into me,'" recalls John Donne; but Atwood is very much of this century, hooked by and alienated from her man, yet "making images to which he must conform." This reviewer has never seen the destructiveness of the male-female struggle for dominance so clearly defined as here. Bitter, or clear-seeing? Lovers should decide, in bed. See also 1971.9 and 21.

9 HODGSON, PAMELA. "Margaret Atwood's Poetry: The Struggle for Dominance: Searing Vision." *Toronto Citizen* 2, no. 5 (11 March):12.

1971

Praises *Power Politics*'s searing, powerful, wonderfully magic poetry that "clutches at the heart, destroying our minds' illusions," and communicates underlying, unexpressed feelings. See also 1971.8 and 21.

10 HORNYANSKY, MICHAEL. "Letters in Canada, 1970: Poetry." *University of Toronto Quarterly* 40, no. 4 (Summer):378-79.

Acclaims *Procedures for Underground*, and Atwood; her exact imagination pinpoints the everyday, and moves through it to the unknown. The few, precise, always controlled words fall oracularly, making the title poem more terrifying than Susan Musgrave's visionary animism. Worlds collide, mirror, seep together. Tension comes from oppositions, queer inversions, shifting perspectives. One remembers not lines but the whole, as with "The Creatures of the Zodiac," quoted entire. "[A] foreign cosmos that compels" the reviewer's assent and, reluctantly, superlatives – has he been had?

11 JONAS, GEORGE. "Cool Sounds in a Minor Key." *Saturday Night* 86, no. 5 (May):30-31.

Reads *Power Politics* as a unified whole, like an orchestral suite; the theme is sounded in the four opening lines, and then, "with cool sounds and in a minor key," precisely developed. The lines work best as part of the whole, not as epigrams. This study of love and aggression in a man-woman relationship is done from only one angle, which is fine. *Power Politics* is controlled, revealing, and totally free of self-pity, stridency, and mental vulgarity; not particularly a woman's book, but one very few poets, men or women, could have written. Excerpted 1975.39.

12 P[IFFER], P[HIL]. Review of *Power Politics*. *Vigilante*, no. 3 (April), p. 44.

Disliked Atwood's early books, which seemed exercises in camouflage, and her controlled 1969 reading voice; was forced to reconsider with *The Journals of Susanna Moodie*; now "shocked/moved" by her superb and terrifying *Power Politics*. Still thinks many early poems use surfaces to avoid emotions, but they do get stronger in each reading. *Power Politics* understands with her emotions and language. The tension that starts with "you fit into me" becomes a cumulative structure. Are these love poems? She cares about what places are possible, and sees herself as weak and strong, exploiter and exploited.

13 POWELL, DEBORAH. "A Poetess' Reflections: Margaret Atwood's Visions of Life." *Detroit Free Press*, 17 January, p. B5.

Appreciates Atwood's strong, clear voice and sixth, foreboding sense in *Procedures for Underground*: her images are sound and precise, yet cast multiple reflections, like a broken mirror, as in ["Dancing Practice"]. Her eye catches a "penumbral light . . . in the simplest experience": characteristically, in ["Carrying Food Home in Winter"], the quiet image of carrying groceries becomes an intense, all-encompassing involvement and love. "'Precise as crystals' her words move to the passionate rhythm of life itself."

14 PURDY, A[L] W. "Atwood's Moodie." *Canadian Literature*, no. 47 (Winter), pp. 80-84.

Wrestles with issues of voice, gender, history, and a dearth of love in author or character of *The Journals of Susanna Moodie*; concludes with high praise. The voice is not Moodie's, but Atwood's, with her own schizophrenic duality of "an entirely subjective Martian." The reviewer sees no humour except satire, and very little love, except perhaps for the dead Atwood-Moodie children; only solipsism and "a hard cold look at the human condition." Yet, like Yeats and Eliot, Atwood as poet is marvellous without joy. Atwood's Moodie is "scared to death of life," but real; an uncaring "bitch," but seen as ghostly, and solipsistic, which is one of Atwood's strengths. Atwood's Moodie comes to love the country, finally, as a primitive corn-mother-spirit. Though the reviewer disagrees with many Atwood ideas, the book as a whole is magnificent. Reprinted: 1988.40.

15 Review of *Procedures for Underground. Booklist* 67, no. 13 (1 March):540-41.

A two-sentence description of Atwood's penetrating discernment, science-fiction metaphors, despairing individuals, highly original vision, and publishing credits.

16 Review of *The Edible Woman. Booklist* 67, no. 9 (1 January):354.

Finds "a light psychological novel of especial interest to women"; briefly summarizes the plot and explains the shift in narrative person.

1971

17 S[KELTON], R[OBIN]. Review of *The Journals of Susanna Moodie* and *Procedures for Underground. Malahat Review*, no. 17 (January), pp. 133-34.

Acclaims both books as the "Canadian experience" made universal, and Atwood as one of a very few important English-language poets under forty. Atwood's Canada is a haunted and wary "vision of the human condition." These books come from Canada as *Candide* comes from France; their gothic is a spiritual environment, like Kafka's *Castle* and Walpole's *Otranto*. With spare language, acute perceptions, and often profound thought, Atwood has created the coherent poetic system of a major talent, as have Wallace Stevens and Robert Lowell. Reprinted: 1988.47.

18 STEVENS, PETER. "Dark Mouth." *Canadian Literature*, no. 50 (Autumn), pp. 91-92.

Welcomes *Procedures for Underground*, which presents Atwood's familiar *Circle Game* world, but in its second half promises a new breaking out. People still live on the edge, haunted and menaced, but now at least we are evolving in our human relationships; art may connect the buried and upper worlds; man may fear, but also creates. This is Atwood's best poetry, progressing from its initial fantasied entrapment to the finally transformed dance. Atwood has broken the circle, and shaken off the restricting Moodie persona. Reprinted: 1988.48. Excerpted: 1975.40.

19 ____. "Deep-Freezing a Love's Continual Small Atrocities." *Globe Magazine*, 24 April, p. 16.

Finds a probing, Laingian *Power Politics*, where love breaks down, and the ordinary becomes frightening, violent, cannibalistic, alienated; "the whole book seethes with cool outrage." But the hard, cool language diminishes situations, and this reader's interest; though image and language are sharp, memorable, and admirable, still the chilly, cruel diction seems at times contrived and repetitious. A two-book review focussed on *Power Politics*.

20 STUBBS, ROY St. GEORGE. "Poet for Today." *Winnipeg Free Press*, 10 July, p. 21.

Disapproves, in a review of *Power Politics*, of the current publish-or-perish Canadian poetry scene, which forces quantity over quality.

1971

Power Politics, though less alive and inspiring than *The Circle Game*, which "flashed across the Canadian literary scene like a comet," still shows Atwood to be one of the brightest stars in Canadian poetry. But *Power Politics* "sometimes strikes a tired, brittle, cynical note, as witness these two exhibits" from ["Their attitudes differ" and "Small tactics"], which are clever, in an unhealthy contemporary way—but are they poetry? Poets must not sin "against their own better poetic selves." We need Miss Atwood "at her own supreme best."

21 TOPPINGS, EARLE. "Margaret Atwood's Poetry: The Struggle for Dominance: Jagged Truths." *Toronto Citizen* 2, no. 5 (11 March):12
    Praises *Power Politics*'s jagged truths about humans and love, which "you have to be in good psychological shape to take"; these poems are chillingly forthright and honest about "the terrible distances between even lovers. . . . [E]ven in life's dream sequences man never belongs," yet struggles for self-preservation. "In the violent crucible of life and love, we reap but one certain benefit: the raw material of poetry," as in ["Their attitudes differ"]. See also 1971.8 and 9.

1972

1 ALLEN, DICK. "Shifts." *Poetry* 120, no. 4 (July):239-40.
    Praises and quotes *Power Politics*, in a group review. Written with intense feeling, careful skill, and harrowing imagery, this honest and deeply moving book gets as close to the love struggle as did the very best of Sylvia Plath; we emerge shaken. The unnamed "he" makes us want more facts. Excerpted: 1974.37.

2 ALSOP, KAY. "She Builds a House with Words." *Province* (Vancouver, B.C.), 2 November, p. 41.
    Interviews Atwood, who is a major talent, and whose words do not lack love. Atwood comments on failure and on growing up in the bush, where *Surfacing* is set; and discusses cardboard-box images of writers versus her idol Beatrix Potter, and her writing: "When I write, I'm making a place for the reader to go into. It's not furnished. That comes out of the reader's own experiences, his background. Writers sometimes get suckered into believing they're writing the Bible, but it's a house."

1972

3 AYRE, JOHN. "Margaret Atwood and the End of Colonialism." *Saturday Night* 87, no. 11 (November):23-26.

Profiles Atwood as one of the young nationalist radicals: publicizing Canadian literature, along with Graeme Gibson and Dave Godfrey; Ontario readings and York University teaching, out of which her just-written *Survival* came; editing experimentalist Bill Bissett for House of Anansi, which leads in publishing new Canadian writers; nature knowledge; Canada versus America in her education. Nationalists like Atwood see older writers like Morley Callaghan and Mordecai Richler as alienated and colonialist expatriates; like Ronald Sutherland, Atwood sees colonial inferiority in both French and English Canadian literature. A psychic iconoclast, Atwood "demands uncomfortable mental confrontations" and renunciation of our colonialist mentalities; like women's liberation, *Survival*'s approach is psychological, attacking mental barriers first.

4 BARBOUR, DOUGLAS. "The Search for Roots: A Meditative Sermon of Sorts." *Literary Half-Yearly* 13, no. 2 (July):1-14.

Discusses the search for forbears, place, and Canadian voice in seven young poets, featuring work from John Newlove's *Black Night Window* and Atwood's *The Journals of Susanna Moodie*. Atwood's "Afterword" defines precisely European man's schizophrenic situation in this country; so does Moodie's double vision, in "Thoughts from Underground," and her healing disintegration in "Alternate Thoughts from Underground," where she sees the truth of our present.

5 BOLTON, ROSEMARY. "Writer Atwood Dislikes Honorary Male Ranking." *Winnipeg Free Press*, 24 October, p. 12.

Interviews Atwood in Winnipeg, after her League of Canadian Poets reading at the University of Winnipeg, the week before *Survival* is due to be published: Atwood discusses reviewers' stereotypes of women's writing and women writers as either sentimental or motherly, or else as scary, like wicked witches; being a writer versus being a propagandist for the women's movement; real nationalism versus spouting anti-American cliches; and readers psyching out the author instead of the book.

6 BOWERING, GEORGE. "Get Used to It." *Canadian Literature*, no. 52 (Spring), pp. 91-92.

Appreciates *Power Politics* as beautiful poetry, Atwood's best; in her simultaneously hallucinated and engineered world, you want to know more. Here love is a political struggle; as with Doris Lessing and [Gertrude] Stein, the consciousness matters. People become ikonic, she the Tarot's "hanged (wo)man," he a statue and effigy. Though this love is the old story of a destructive man-woman relationship, that's all there is. This book hurts, as few do nowadays. Reprinted, slightly revised, as part of 1981.9. Excerpted: 1974.37.

7 B[URI], S.G. "It's How You Play the Game." *Aspen Grove*, no. 1 [1972], pp. 34-46.

Dislikes *Power Politics*; a detailed commentary. Though the twofold structure – a mosaic of modes, plus a symphonic three movements – succeeds as blueprint, and the theme gets attention, overall the book fails. Atwood's effects are too tame, her surreal is bizarre but boring, her compulsively-turned phrases and aphorisms pile up. Finds some successful lyrics, epigrams, and passages; "Hesitations outside the door" is the book's best and its only satisfying surreal poem. Others are flashy, pretentious, incoherent, melodramatic, and tear-jerking. "What I dislike most is the poet's airily pretending to allude to something"; and also her surreal persona, which sounds "hypersensitive and bitchy." 42 pages of these 56 should not have been published.

8 CLERY, VAL. "A Plea for the Victims." *Books in Canada* 1, no. 12 (November-December):45-46.

Though *Surfacing*'s style at first reading compels admiration, further readings are disquieting, when one considers its, and Atwood's, almost reverential reviews and interviews – and *Survival*. *The Edible Woman*'s ironic comedy of manners allowed the supporting characters some reality and pathos, but in *Surfacing* the central character's morbid introspection and contempt reduces the secondary characters to caricature. *Survival*'s arbitrary victim themes make *Surfacing* a set-up; many of our young nationalist writers will be victimized by imitating *Surfacing* and *Survival*.

9 CUTHBERT, SCOTT CLARKE. "*Surfacing* Narrative 'Frightening' Work." *Windsor Star*, 23 September, p. 13.

Praises *Surfacing*. Atwood "crystalliz[es] the essence of the poetic soul into narrative form." Despite the limited, neurotic, egocentric

1972

protagonist and her bizarre metamorphosis, "*Surfacing* is an exciting, a frightening, and intensely engrossing, if somewhat disturbing, novel." It is also distinctly Canadian yet universal, not "noxiously 'regional'"; and significant, not imitative.

10 DAVIS, FRANCES. Review of *Surfacing*. *Dalhousie Review* 52, no. 4 (Winter):679-82.

Praises highly Atwood's brilliant writing, masterful imagery, and excellent plotting; unlike Hemingway's followers, *Surfacing* brings even stock fishing scenes to life. A sensitive reader will follow the narrator's changing awareness, the redefinition of American as twentieth-century man, the quest beyond language. But a sloppy reader might misread *Surfacing* as anti-American Canadian identity, or merely the bicultural problem. The final, honestly wordless mysticism disappoints, perhaps because a novel can't go beyond language.

11 DOBBS, KILDARE. "Canadian's Second Novel Even Better than Her First." *Toronto Star*, 12 September, p. 31.

Enthusiastically praises *Surfacing*. What Bell 1970.5 called "'truth-telling dementia'" in *The Edible Woman* is here "madness that blazes a trail to healing insight." *Surfacing*'s fable dramatizes Canada's current obsessions – "nationalism, feminism, death, culture, art, nature, pollution" – it's as if Thoreau had fathered on Sylvia Plath a meditating Indian wood nymph. The resolution may be a Thoreau-like cop-out, but *Surfacing*'s poetic force carries us past intellectual snags, such as the narrator's condescension to Joe, and her unconvincing love. Atwood almost persuades us back to the woods – where her superb storytelling and compelling vision would not help us survive.

12 DOYLE, MIKE. "Made in Canada?" *Poetry* 119, no. 6 (March):360-62.

Praises Atwood in a Canadian round-up review. *The Journals of Susanna Moodie* is very like earlier poems that attempt a feared assimilation and, simultaneously, self-identification. *Power Politics* concentrates intensely on an "I"-"you" relationship; the need for sustenance, and self, results in probing poems, "coolly achieved, fascinating as surgery."

13 FRENCH, WILLIAM. "Exhilarating: An All-Purpose Novel." *Globe and Mail*, 16 September, p. 30.

Acclaims *Surfacing* and Atwood, who as current writer-in-residence at the University of Toronto, poet, critic, House of Anansi director, and novelist, seems a master of literary trades. We soon guess that *Surfacing*'s narrator "may be unreliable" [subheading: "She may be unreliable"; see Barbour 1973.5], and we later learn her past; she represents a type of contemporary woman, cool, unemotional, a casualty of accelerated social change.

Surfacing is about alienation, dehumanizing urban society, the generation gap, and very much about Canadian anti-Americanism, as needed or foolish – is Atwood saying we should start over with the Americans? *Surfacing* is an exhilarating performance, with beautiful writing, vivid imagery, a menacing undercurrent, and an x-ray probing of emotions.

14 FULFORD, ROBERT. "A Clever and Effective Analysis of the Literature of Canada." *Toronto Star*, 4 November, p. 79.

Welcomes *Survival* as a critical book, a literary event, and a new way of reading Anglo-Canadian literature. As a colonized people, Atwood argues, we see ourselves in our literature as victims and losers, as survivors but not winners; we identify with endangered and killed animals. Though *Survival* slights Morley Callaghan and Mordecai Richler, still it is a challenging, searching book, that forces readers to consider their country's books and what shaped them. Reprinted: 1972.15 (below).

15 ____. "Teacher's Guide Turns Out to Be Work of Significance." *Ottawa Citizen*, 4 November, p. 43.

A reprint of 1972.14 (above), with altered title and subtitles.

16 GROSSKURTH, PHYLLIS. "Truth – and a Major Talent." *Globe and Mail*, 28 October, p. 33.

Hails *Survival* as "the most important book that has come out of this country"; *Survival* "seized me, a Canadian, by the shoulders and forced me to look unflinchingly into the mirror." We skeptical Canadians now have a major writer, whose analysis makes our own literature compelling reading. *Survival*'s victim thesis is undeniable; its nature and women chapters point also to Atwood's creative work. As in *Surfacing*, there's an underlying anger, against accepting colonial-victim

1972

roles, against an "American" dehumanization. What we do with *Survival*'s map may involve enthusiastic, determined pioneering.

17 HAAS, MAARA. Review of *Surfacing*. *Canadian Author and Bookman* 48, no. 2 (Winter):23.

Praises highly *Surfacing*'s one-dimensional Woman and "more than exceptional writing," which is poetic, exact, passionless, and dramatically pure, like August Strindberg. This is Canadian fiction's first autopsy; the terrified, withdrawn Woman "bisects and vivisects the anatomy of things, people and Self. A dying animal in a dying environment, she stoically insists on the human/animal right to suffer." Her companions will die from their hatred and weakness; her own immunity to humans means survival. She mystically envisions a child of her kind, then finally considers becoming one of THEM. Throughout she is real and alive for the reader.

18 HORNYANSKY, MICHAEL. "Letters in Canada, 1971: Poetry." *University of Toronto Quarterly* 41, no. 4 (Summer):334-35.

Appreciates *Power Politics* which, as Robert Weaver says, "marks 'a new stage in Miss Atwood's astonishing, cruel talent.'" Here Atwood focuses on an ambivalent, twitchy, Laingian politics of love; and, as in the quoted "you fit into me" epigraph, counterpoints "sharply incongruous worlds on a needle." The reviewer enjoys sharing this sardonic, not "'cruel,'" perspective on love – especially from a woman.

19 JOHNSON, BRIAN. "Margaret Atwood's *Surfacing*: Written with Her Blood." *Gazette* (Montreal), 23 September, p. 50.

A rave review of *Surfacing*: "In this brilliant work, her revolt against the barbarism of a disembodied, insane civilization flowers on a national scale. She guts the Canadian Dream" in this magnificent adventure. As in *Power Politics*, Atwood writes from the wounded prey's point of view, with her own blood, and with an explosive anger that refuses masochism or romantic escapes. The unnamed woman, who is the author and the only mind, goes to a northern Quebec bush island with her three bilious, pathetic, nature-invading city friends. She "seeks immunity from imperialism in a cold-sweat quest for God and nature. . . . The climax is hair-raising." In the end, Atwood rejects the urban intellectual's nationalist mystique of the hinterland – which may blow her chance at the Great Canadian novel.

1972

20 LEVENSON, CHRISTOPHER. Interview. *Manna*, no. 2, pp. 46-54.

Atwood, who "came to Ottawa 4 April to read her poetry at Carleton University," discusses poetry. Early influences or readings include Edgar Allen Poe, Lord Byron, Jay M[a]c[p]herson, James Reaney, P.K. Page, A.M. Klein, Anne Hébert, and Marie-Claire Blaise; later, Al Purdy and Doug Jones. Poetry is always written locally, not internationally; it evokes rather than expresses emotion; it uses the magical element in language, as autistic children do. Sylvia Plath is a formal, not confessional, poet. Atwood reads with her vocal cords, hears poetry "as a voice," and objects to actors who dramatize rather than transmit poetry. She starts with images, and throws out a lot. There aren't "so many" Canadian women poets – not when 54% should be women. Comments also on *The Edible Woman*'s composition, tactics, and ethics.

21 McCUTCHEON, SARAH E. "The Atwood Guide to 'Canlit.'" *Gazette* (Montreal), 16 December, p.35.

Hails *Survival*, which heads Anansi's impressive list of good new Canadian writing, as a very much needed landmark and a lucid, brutally truthful, imaginative, and lively book, from a very qualified poet, novelist, and critic. An explorer creating a map from unknown territory, Atwood asks, and answers, "'What's Canadian about Canadian literature?'" by examining themes and her central survivor/victim concept in various writers. With apt, poetic asides and quotes, Atwood "digs to our very roots to expose the sources of our literature." Our survival-mentality literature, of heroes who never win, unfulfilled love, and citizens in limbo, reflects our own self-envisionings.

22 McDONALD, MARCI. "A New Literary Star Emerges in Canadian Letters." *Toronto Star*, 21 October, p. 77.

An extensive profile of Atwood's celebrity image, publishing successes, Anansi editing, Quebec bush childhood, education, writing *The Edible Woman*'s screenplay with George Kaczender and Tony Richardson, and romantic involvements. Quotes Atwood's friends on Atwood as complex and vulnerable; quotes Atwood on success ("a crock of s – "), the word poetess, craziness, knowing about society and the bush, and being a writer before women's lib.

1972

23 MacSWEEN, R.J. Review of *Surfacing*. *Antigonish Review*, no. 11 (Autumn), pp. 113-14.

Mixes criticism with praise. *Surfacing*'s three accompanying characters are banal and unworthy, "almost cancers on the healthy body of the wilderness." This second novel succeeds, with its fine nature writing and some of its poetic intensity, but, unlike *The Edible Woman*, *Surfacing* lacks humour and even one worthy character.

24 MAGID, NORA. "Canadian Club." *Commonweal* 95, no. 15 (7 January):328.

A round-up review; relishes *The Edible Woman* and its characters and artifacts of Ontario, Toronto, Westmount, and English graduate departments. The cake-lady is delectable; the book a bizarre, original, surreal and real commentary on man as consumer.

25 MANDEL, ELI, ed. Introduction to *Poets of Contemporary Canada 1960-1970*. New Canadian Library Original, edited by Malcolm Ross, no. 7. Toronto: McClelland and Stewart, p. x-xvi.

Appreciates Canadian, gothic, romantic, and psychological elements in Atwood and the nine other modern Canadian poets included here. Atwood's terrifyingly cool language and jagged-edge images are haunting. "Not only time but space takes on mythic form in her work, the contemporary world as well as the historical one becomes psychological symbol, and the war of the divided self provides an ultimate political metaphor." Her paranoid schizophrenic Susanna Moodie, who encounters the Canadian land, embodies contemporary alienation and primitivism.

26 MATHEWS, ROBIN. "Survival and Struggle in Canadian Literature: A Review of Margaret Atwood's *Survival*." *This Magazine Is About Schools* 6, no. 4 (Winter):109-24.

Charges that *Survival* ignores Canadian works of community and struggle to focus on a literature of victims and surrender; argues that *Survival* is part of a Northrop Frye-George Grant-D.G. Jones colonial establishment tradition of supposedly nonevaluative exclusions, class-biased alienation, and a dangerous liberal individual anarchism. Neglecting works of conviction by D.C. Scott and Stephen Leacock, Atwood focusses on works of colonial stagnation by David Godfrey, Dennis Lee, Bill Bissett, and too many of Anansi's chic, experimental, nicely nationalistic writers. Every idea is "oversimplified, naggingly half-true," as with Indians, whose dignity in John Richardson's *Wacousta* Atwood misreads. Personal liberation, which can be a cop-out, needs to be distinguished from community liberation. See Atwood 1973.2. Revision: 1978.62.

27 MORLEY, PATRICIA. "Multiple Surfaces." *Journal of Canadian Fiction* 1, no. 4 (Fall):99-100.
     Praises *Surfacing*, which is adventure thriller, detective story, psychological novel, religious novel – and a step towards the Great Canadian Novel; discusses *Surfacing*'s Americans, who fictionalize the technological man of Jacques Ellul. The narrator, like many Hugh MacLennan characters, is an orphan figure, and female Odysseus, searching for roots; after increasingly surreal, fantastic scenes, she surfaces by choosing love. Atwood's Carleton poetry reading, last April, was enigmatically deadpan, and her comments noncommittal. Reprinted: 1972.28 (below). Excerpted: 1977.21; 1980.14.

28 _____. "A Novel of the Week." *Ottawa Journal*, 16 September, p. 36.
     Reprint, almost verbatim, of 1972.27 (above).

29 _____. "Where Is Here?" *Ottawa Journal*, 16 December, p. 36.
     Survival will be controversial; its ideas command respect; its style is not dull. Nationalism is not only, as Atwood claims, skipped in Canadian schools and university; it's been suspect, a dirty word, until recently. "How does one explain the high proportion of gloom and doom in Canadian literature," the victims, the identification with animals and losers? Canadians should read Atwood's creative, iconoclastic explanation – and refute it if they can. Atwood does underemphasize humour and joy, omitting work like Gabrielle Roy's *Where Nests the Water Hen*, and overemphasizing work like Graeme Gibson's, which fits its thesis. But it's a pioneer effort – and long overdue.

30 NEWMAN, CHRISTINA. "In Search of a Native Tongue." *Maclean's* 85, no. 9 (September):88.
     Hails Atwood as the champion of the new Canadian consciousness; acclaims *Surfacing*. Only Doris Lessing and Margaret Drabble convey so well how women deal with the politics of sex.

1972

Atwood writes from inside her country and her culture, holding up a true mirror that makes our experience real, an answer to Frye's "Where is Here?" Canada has been mentally colonized for so long, that Mordecai Richler once seemed our spokesman – but, as his *Shovelling Trouble* shows, all that's real to him is his own pain, suffered in some other country. Both he and Atwood are archetypes – but she represents the new consciousness, of the Sixties on, searching through our past, seeking our roots. Reprinted: 1988.35.

31 _____. Review of *Survival*. *Maclean's* 85, no. 12 (December):104.

Recommends *Survival* highly, in a Christmas books round-up, as a most crucial book of this nationalistic decade. *Survival* is a discerning thematic guide not only to Canadian literature but to Canadian life; we're all victims and unlovely losers. Atwood's terrific, alive, enraging, funny book should be given to every Cabinet continentalist and smug academic in this colonized country.

32 NODELMAN, PERRY. "Two Novels in One." *Winnipeg Free Press*, 18 November, p. 21.

Praises Atwood's remarkable and excellent *Surfacing* as "a brilliant tour-de-force" of two novels: the first 140 pages are a typical poet's novel, with a totally self-absorbed heroine, pretty phrases, and sensitively-perceived landscapes. "Then the other novel happens. The heroine 'surfaces.' . . . [She] is forced to remember the truth, the reader is forced to reinterpret everything he has been told." As in Atwood's earlier poetry, "memory is both prison and salvation"; relationships are power above all; the Canadian landscape is as destructive as civilization: and all these concerns are "inter-related parts of a deeply Canadian, deeply human whole." *Surfacing*'s satire of aging groovies is charmingly vicious.

33 REYNOLDS, MARILYNN. "A Trip to the Margins of Madness." *Edmonton Journal*, 20 October, p. 78.

Recommends *Surfacing* as a "fascinating, sometimes frightening novel" of our Canadian landscape, our paranoia, our present and future. Atwood's fresh language is our own, not ivory tower. Passing through a tawdry landscape, *Surfacing*'s heroine goes to Northern Quebec to search for her father, and for herself, in her childhood memories. When she surfaces from her isolating bottle, what she finds is chilling; Atwood confidently takes us to the edge of madness. Atwood understands Canada's forests uniquely.

34 STEPHEN, SID. "*The Journals of Susanna Moodie*: A Self-Portrait of Margaret Atwood." *White Pelican* 2, no. 2 (Spring):32-36.

Explicates the three Journals as "a struggle between two very powerful voices," of poet and persona. The Moodie voice dominates Journal I. "The Double Voice" at the end of Journal II shows Moodie evolving into Atwood; their duality, of dark and violent memories versus a pretended genteel civilization, "is central to the Canadian myth." The Atwood voice dominates Journal III, with its practical details, its references to *Procedures for Underground* and Canada's present, and its final pantheism. The book began with Atwood's epigraph invoking Moodie; it ends with the old woman, Moodie, becoming Atwood again.

35 SUTHERLAND, FRASER. "Fast and Loose." *Books in Canada* 1, no. 1 (October):10-11.

Praises *Survival*'s brilliant, challenging analysis, which follows George Grant and Northrop Frye, and its considerable wit, but finds its form rushed and slipshod. Atwood's conclusions are well-founded, on wide reading, even if Anansi books are over- represented. The victim model is ingenious and flexible. The asides range from delightful to frivolous to annoying. Quotations and appendices should have been incorporated in the text, and the introductory Hungover Lecturer phrases cut. Atwood is the Canadian Joyce Carol Oates, and better; *Survival* should have been better.

36 WALKER, SUSAN. Review of *Surfacing. Quill and Quire* 38, no.10 (October):11.

Praises *Surfacing*'s mastery of complex imagery; Atwood's second novel successfully moves from *The Edible Woman*'s grimy social realities to the symbolist landscapes of her poetry. Searching for her father, the protagonist recovers her fragmented self. After a surreal confrontation with the primitive, she surfaces to confront her own real life.

37 WARKENTIN, GERMAINE. Review of *Survival. Quill and Quire* 38, no.9 (September):9.

1972

Acclaims Atwood's essential, necessary, breezy, and intensely personal guide. No book like this has ever been written here; addressing the common reader, not academics or poets, and generalizing from a host of sources, Atwood shows how we have focussed on loss, death, suppressing natural instincts, fears, victims, survival. Though some readings are arguable, many are stimulating insights. The victim positions, from total bondage to an almost-mystical personal liberation, are mischievously applied. Each chapter ends in considering new solutions.

38 WATERS, KATHERINE E. "Margaret Atwood: Love on the Dark Side of the Moon." In *Mother Was Not a Person*. Compiled by Margret Andersen. Montreal: Content Publishing and Black Rose Books, pp. 102-19.

In Atwood's five books of poetry, especially *Power Politics*, and also her two novels, sexual politics is a metaphor for larger political and technological imperialisms. Man versus woman dramatizes Atwood's own opposing aspects: art-life, head-body, predator-victim, history-ecology, barbaric civilization-Edenic centre, fixed ego-roles-fluid "I." The numinous is lost; man is a fallen hero-god, a linear, visual ego; the female perspective is tactile, fluid, creative. Atwood writes love poetry, moving from alienation to partial, potential affirmations; even *Power Politics* finds in nature's tenacious cactus ("Beyond truth") and dormant snowy fields ["They are hostile nations"] strategies for survival, and for becoming human.

39 WIMSATT, MARGARET. Review of *Procedures for Underground*. *Commonweal* 96, no. 1 (10 March):21-22.

Concludes a five-book appreciation of women-poets – not unequal poetesses now – with praise for Atwood's unique world, where you see archeology and geology through your own skull's sockets, where objects come alive with sinister transfusions, where most things are on the other side of a wall. In this unstable and polluted age, we need Atwood's courageous traveler, "helmeted in fear," who remembers archeopteryx.

40 WOODCOCK, GEORGE. "Margaret Atwood." *Literary Half-Yearly* 13, no. 2 (July):233-42.

1972

Acclaims Atwood's poetry, especially *Power Politics*, also *The Journals of Susanna Moodie* and "Progressive insanities of a pioneer," in essay incorporating, almost verbatim, his 1969.17 acclaim for *The Edible Woman* and *The Circle Game. Power Politics* is not ordinary love poetry but, as in "you fit into me," the work of an extraordinary and laconically disciplined visual sensibility, verse clear as Orwell's window pane, truly Imagistic, where perception and metaphor merge and resonate. Atwood is now one of the best established Canadian poets, with "capillary links between her poetry, her fiction, her criticism"; her affinities include Eli Mandel, Jay Macpherson, Phyllis Webb, and the Canadian consciousness of George Bowering, John Newlove, and Al Purdy. "Beyond truth" is a personal poetic, and ethic, of a defensive, cactus-like survival, doing one's best. See 1973.107. Reprinted as part of 1975.52.

41 WRIGHT, JEAN. "Second to None." *Montreal Star*, 16 September, p. C3.

Praises Atwood's strange, powerful, compelling *Surfacing*, with its eccentric and over-sensitive heroine, who can be both heart-breaking and maddening. The atmosphere is menacing, and the plot very like a murder mystery. The style is highly metaphorical, sometimes strikingly original, sometimes overly earnest or coarse. But the final occult rites are hair-raising and surreal; and the final, human resolution is "a hopelessly hopeful 'happy' ending." This second novel is even better than Atwood's triumphant first.

42 YOUNG, CHRISTOPHER. "Rich Banquet of Canadian Books." *Ottawa Citizen*, 2 December, p. 6.

Includes the "much-praised *Survival*" in an article that recommends giving new Canadian books for Christmas.

1973

1 ALTMAN, PETER. "Canadian Writer, 33, Secures Her Reputation with a New Novel." *Minneapolis Star*, 30 April, p. B5.

Praises *Surfacing* as "a bold, cathartically angry, often startling and ultimately moving novel by a remarkable writer." Sensations and images may be the greatest strength of this poet's novel. "It is also militantly nationalistic and militantly the work of a woman who writes

1973

as a woman," without disguise, prettification, or blurring. The story, pushed forward in the search and backward in memory, is compellingly suspenseful. Despite its rarely likeable characters, uncompromising spirit, and hard, unpolished brilliance, *Surfacing* reveals much, and creates profound impressions.

2 ATWOOD, MARGARET. "Mathews and Misrepresentation." *This Magazine* 7, no. 1 (May-June):29-33.

Replies, at the request of *This Magazine*'s editors, to Mathews 1972.26: assesses the range of responses to *Survival*, defending its victim thesis as an accurate description of Canadian literature, and a working hypothesis, not a dogma; charges Mathews with misreading *Survival*'s ideas and evidence, particularly on the historic *Wacousta*, and claiming more Canadian struggle literature than existed; agrees on the need for change, but wants to begin with where we really are, not with wishful or ideological distortions. Reprinted: 1982.11.

3 B[ALFE], E. M[ARI]. Review of *Surfacing. British Columbia Library Quarterly* 36, no. 4 (April):80-81.

Most modern novels stay on the surface; this skillful, gripping work plumbs depths where old gods live, and exemplifies the contemporary hapless search for what is "'real'" and "'natural.'" Sex is trivialized, but the god-possessed heroine may be saved by her ritualistic attempt to give meaning to sex.

4 [BANNON, BARBARA A.] . Review of *Surfacing. Publishers Weekly* 203, no. 5 (29 January):249.

Takes seriously Atwood's icily fascinating, superbly controlled *Surfacing;* it may sound like other alienation novels, but this story of survival, wilderness, and a final purging of the soul forces us to re-examine our lives. "Expect very important review attention for this one."

5 BARBOUR,DOUGLAS. Review of *Surfacing. Canadian Fiction Magazine*, no. 9 (Winter), pp. 74-79.

Acclaims *Surfacing* as one of Canada's best novels ever, and *Survival* as a major study that forces deeper vision. Contrary to William French 1972.13, the heroine's perceptions are mostly clear and true. The mysticism, foreshadowed in the "Procedures for Underground" poem and paralleled by Leonard Cohen's *The Beautiful Losers,* could be called madness, but in context is absolutely real. The ambiguously hopeful end, where she accepts Joe, works. So much is marvelous – the wilderness situations, the disturbing comedy, the sexual power politics, the Americanization as a terrifying spiritual imperialism. Only the present tense in parts 1 and 3 seems a minor flaw. As art *Surfacing* can move us tremendously – and might help us change, to non-victims.

6 BESSAI, DIANE. "Surfaces." *Lakehead University Review* 6, no. 2 (Fall-Winter):255-57.
Mixes praise with reservations; the provocative contemporary themes – victimization, liberation and the alien "Americans" versus nature – are carefully developed, but somehow constrain the work. *Surfacing* is undeniably absorbing, and carefully controlled, with its myths, self-discovery, irony, and its solipsistic presentation that precludes realistic secondary characters. What is disturbing is the final women's liberation life view – the narrator is restored to creativity, but what about the dismissed impregnator, man?

7 BICKERSTAFF, ISSAC [sic]. "Series on a Series: New Canadian Library – Part 2." *Books in Canada* 2, no. 3 (July-September):54.
Though disappointed by the over-praised *Surfacing,* and unimpressed by a tale of Atwood's classmates retracing *The Edible Woman*'s locales, the reviewer delighted in Atwood's irresistible first novel – and now contemplates his own pilgrimage, to the bar of the Park Plaza Hotel.

8 BRESSLER, FAITH. "A Gulp of Air and into the Deeps." *Sun* (Baltimore), 18 March, p. D5.
Praises *Surfacing,* whose powerful language "creates the texture and rhythm of the narrator's emotions, from her cold alienation to her animal fear to her desperate trust." The final savage, ecstatic language sweeps us away. This novel works because we both identify closely with the narrator yet always stand outside her. At the end we know which world, the natural or the Americanized modern, she – and we – will choose.

1973

9 "Briefly Noted." *New Yorker* 49, no. 8 (14 April):154-55.
    Mixes praise and complaints on *Surfacing*. The heroine's inward journey leads to a terrifying nervous breakdown; the Canadian hinterland is strongly evoked; the characters' feelings are vividly and sparely described. But the overdone, too exquisite prose detracts, as does the completely unjustified upbeat end.

10 BROOKS, JEREMY. "Under the Net." *Sunday Times* (London), 27 May, p. 40.
    Gives *Surfacing* the second-best praise in a four-book review. Atwood's novel is really about a submerging, into the narrator's past and "into a concept of 'natural' that verges at times on madness"; the narrator's irretrievably lost "innocence is the true quarry" of her search. "What makes *Surfacing* so utterly absorbing and satisfying is the balance Miss Atwood achieves between the narrator's interior vision and her sharp observation of the 'real' world outside her head."

11 CLARK, J. WILSON. "Two Lines in Canadian Literary History." *Literature and Ideology*, no. 15, pp. 27-36.
    Rejects *Survival* as pro-imperialist, anti-working people, bourgeois literary history; also rejects S.D. Clark's colonialist separatist history of Canadian political protest, and Northrop Frye's reactionary, obscurantist, idealist garrison mentality. Historians and literary historians either conform to Marxist theory or to bourgeois theory. Atwood varies Frye's and Clark's comprador theories by having "'survival'" as the only hope in an "'isolated'" "'garrison.'" Her propaganda about Canadian national "'survival,'" with its "pious rhetoric and passive acceptance of an English Canada which the Americans are taking over," benefits imperialism. Standing on Frye's shoulders, she speculates wildly, and conjures up anti-working-people images. Her four victim positions treat colonialism frivolously, and unmask her "kitsch literary history," that has sinister consequences for Quebec literature. But history shows that imperialism will collapse.

12 C[LEMONS], W[ALTER]. Review of *Surfacing*. *Newsweek* 81, no. 11 (12 March):95-96.
    Finds *Surfacing* acrid, powerful, and bleakly unlikable; finds its heroine uncaring, demented, and given to ice-cube aphorisms. Atwood

devises acute sexual tensions. It's unclear whether she sees her heroine's baleful superiority as a symptom, or endorses it.

13 COCHRAN, CAROLYN. "The Pains of Being Female." *Dallas Morning News*, 27 May, p. G18.

Recommends *Surfacing* highly, despite its partly implausible plot, to outdoors enthusiasts and serious modern readers. Just as *The Edible Woman* showed marriage as exploitative and dehumanizing, so *Surfacing* depicts man as an overly aggressive animal, whose civilization masks his dehumanizing barbarity. *Surfacing* ends with the narrator "ready to endure a bleak future with her callous lover and her unborn child." *Power Politics* "again" satirizes and "attacks" the man-woman relationship as false and exploitative. "Margaret Atwood has been called a connoisseur of pain," specializing in 1970s female pains. "*Power Politics* is a love poem which, while celebrating a man-woman relationship, makes the reader sadly aware of the life flowing out of the body and the light going out in this world."

14 CODY, ELIZABETH. "'This Above All, to Refuse to Be a Victim . . . '" *Chicago Daily News*, 24-25 March, Panorama sec., p. 4.

Praises *Surfacing*. Atwood's characters, the young artist and her three counterculture-cartoon companions, come "in varying states of psychic amputation" to a graveyard North. *Surfacing* is more than "another tale of disaffected youth"; a poet, Atwood creates "her own symbolic country, where physical life means spiritual death, and the narrator's dead parents are seen as figures of grace and vitality." The narrator surfaces from concealment and "a near-drowning into a sudden recognition of her human power and potential." Refusing victimhood, she proves herself a survivor.

15 COLEMAN, MARGARET. Review of *Surfacing*. *Descant*, no. 6 (Spring), pp. 70-73.

Praises Atwood's powerful, complexly suggestive, fully developed novel. The alienated narrator moves through a nature that is both threatened by humanity and dangerously threatening. Searching for her father, and her parents' gifts, she goes beyond logic to redemption, recovering her true memories, power, and lost child. In three days of mystic purgation, she devolves into an elemental, natural state. Her final rejection of victimized passivity could be read as feminist, but is

1973

really an integrated humanity, which is difficult. Nelly redeemed at the end, she and the "'half-formed'" Joe will nonetheless begin.

16 COYNE, PATRICIA S. "Furry Babies and Indiscretions." *National Review* 25, no. 31 (3 August):852-53.

Complains, in a two-book review of *Surfacing* and Pamela Hansford Johnson's *The Holiday Friend*, that Atwood has gone from *The Edible Woman*'s now-passé politicizing of personal problems to supernaturalizing them; "yesterday's garden-variety women's libber today sings songs to the sprouting corn." When the urban, world-weary heroine returns to the wilderness with three unsavory hippies, "[i]nsight pops out of the ground like poplars and everyone sprouts an aura." Atwood has added to nervous breakdown "enough hard-core paganism" for campus sales. Given Atwood's precise, evocative prose and ambitious humanity-in-nature theme, *Surfacing* could have been more than the trendy book it is.

17 DAVEY, FRANK. "Atwood Walking Backwards." *Open Letter*, 2d ser., no. 5 (Summer), pp. 74-84.

Contends that Atwood's poetry is too narrow, her novels contrived *romans à thèse*, and *Survival* a dangerous, canon-fixing distortion. *Surfacing* reworks *The Edible Woman*'s plot, issues, and characters; both narrators are "rigidly controlled," and presented with "no sense of irony," as absolutely trustworthy. But *Surfacing* is powerful, and technically an advance; the therapeutic descent is more convincingly caused, the ending clearer. The writer's manipulation of language becomes a strengthening irony in the poems, particularly with *Power Politics*'s "'castrating bitch'" persona. *Survival* has overemphasized Anansi and Ontario WASP writers; suppressed writers outside its victim thesis and distorted others; practiced Frye's unfortunate, nonevaluative thematic criticism while ignoring distinctive Canadian form; and tried to culture-fix "an untouchable canon of CanLit according to Atwood," here and in Anansi's advertised "Survival II" anthology. See 1976.17 and Mallinson 1978.59. Revised: 1984.18.

18 DAVIDSON, JANE. "The Anguish of Identity." *Financial Post* (Toronto), 24 February, p. C5.

Defends *Surfacing*, against criticism, as certainly a woman's book, probably created in part from nationalistic passion, and honestly against a "victim" posture – what's wrong with any of these? Like Sylvia Fraser, Margaret Laurence, Audrey Thomas, and Alice Munro, Atwood doesn't try to write like a man. In the northern Quebec woods the narrator realizes the truth of her abortion; and of her companions' lost humanness – especially the anti-American and anti-women David; and of the "Americanized" Canadians who rape the land and the mind. Near the end the carefully delineated style slips into a dream-like poetry that portrays the narrator's madness.

19 DAWE, ALAN. Introduction to *The Edible Woman*, by Margaret Atwood. New Canadian Library, no. 93. Toronto: McClelland & Stewart, pp. [2-7].

Written in 1965, before Women's Liberation, Atwood's re-issued first novel is about how anyone, male or female, can stay sane and human in our plastic, over-packaged world. Discusses the hero's choices, as embodied or offered by the other characters; the *Alice in Wonderland* parallels; and Duncan's elusive, perhaps fantasied, nature. Under the surface, Atwood's comic tone conceals rage and terror, female victims and dangerous males. Praises the poet's sustained eating metaphor, and the ambiguously triumphant end.

20 DELANY, PAUL. "Clearing a Canadian Space." *New York Times Book Review*, 4 March, p. 5.

Gives *Surfacing* serious praise; discusses literary and national traditions. In contrast to the desperate, finally resigned heroine of Sylvia Plath's *The Bell Jar*, Atwood's heroine revolts more actively, and moves confidently into freedom at the end. With *Survival* and *Surfacing*, Atwood is now the literary standard-bearer of Canada's resurgent nationalism, eclipsing more cosmopolitan writers like Mordecai Richler, Irving Layton, and Leonard Cohen. *Surfacing* recalls wilderness initiation tales; after her psychic voyage and shamanistic possession, the narrator is ready to bear a child and take an identity. *Surfacing* redefines "American," not as non-European innocence, but as malignant power politics. Excerpted: Riley 1975.40.

21 DeMOTT, BENJAMIN. "Recycling Art." *Saturday Review of the Arts* 1, no. 4 (7 April):85-86.

Acclaims Atwood's wilderness themes and imaginative integrity in a two-book review of *Surfacing* and Edna O'Brien's *Night*. *Surfacing*

1973

recycles, extraordinarily well, North America's weary old frontier myth, as city versus wilderness, the plastic *cinéma vérité* versus the narrator's completely convincing natural work and observations of nature. As in Atwood's poetry, and more than in *The Edible Woman*, the imaginative language links and extends meanings; the metaphors evolve to crises. The overarching sin, of trivializing one's own seriousness, is better shown than some lesser themes, such as America's corruption. The writing is mannered, but always in a real social context; this is a moving and instructive novel, for younger women and for everyone. Excerpted: 1974.37; 1985.11.

22 DICK, KAY. "A Dockland Family." *Scotsman* (Edinburgh), 26 May, Weekend sec., p. 2.

Briefly finds *Surfacing*, in a three-book review, a well-done, realistic, suspenseful, and eerie fable of American consumer materialism and "New Yorkers" in search of a fast-vanishing natural past.

23 FERRISS, DIANNE. "Her Only True Feeling." *New Republic* 168, no. 17 (28 April):27.

Praises *Surfacing* as well-executed and subtle, and debates its feminism. The main problem is alienation; the narrator overcomes the fear of not being really alive that is her one true feeling. The recurrent surfacings are very effectively presented. "In some ways this is a feminist novel," for we see the woman's consciousness raised, as she learns to appreciates her female qualities and animal, reproductive functions. Although she is crazed in the impregnation scene, this animalistic reversion does restore her positive feelings for her body. "Nevertheless this is not essentially in the feminist mode," for it is a sensitive novel of a woman's struggle, not a fictional treatise.

24 FRENCH, WILLIAM. "Icon and Target: Atwood as Thing." *Globe and Mail*, 7 April, p. 28.

Speaking to the Empire Club, Atwood discusses her new status as thing, both worshipped and shot-at; *Survival*, its English Canadian and Quebec receptions; and the proliferation of Canadian nationalisms, from advertising to Women's Lib, from silly to serious.

25 FULFORD, ROBERT. "*Moby Dick*, conté du point de vue de la baleine." *Devoir* (Montréal), 10 March, p. 20.

Survival, a landmark study of English Canadian literature, should be read by anyone interested in the cultural future of English Canada. Atwood's thesis of survival is summed up in this idea: if *Moby Dick* had been written by a Canadian, the story would have been narrated from the whale's point of view. Much of Canadian culture has been imported. Historically, the Canadian artists who have been most active worked in isolation and resigned themselves to living on the fringe of society and world culture; *Survival* gives us hope that the future will be different.

26 GEDDES, GARY. Review of *Survival*. *Malahat Review*, no. 26 (April), pp. 233-34.

Finds, in a three-book review, that "*Survival* is a fascinating set of lecture-notes, stimulating, tentative, punchy, and wrong-headed." Its central premise, of our negativism and preoccupation with failure, is not unique to Canada, but common to modern developed countries and their literatures. *Survival*'s map distorts, by ignoring form (humour, irony, satire), and by omitting too much. "This is not criticism; it is therapy, a tract, a call to arms against the materialist-imperialist mentality, a rejection of [George Grant's] pessimism." *Survival* is superb as sociology and propaganda, but unforgivable, even from the happy evangelists of Anansi, as a textbook.

27 GIBSON, GRAEME. "Margaret Atwood." In *Eleven Canadian Novelists*. Interviewed by Graeme Gibson. Toronto: House of Anansi Press, pp. 5-31.

Atwood discusses being a poet and novelist, a Canadian writer, and a woman writer; social responsibility and social mythology; literary forms; men and women; surviving and victims. "*The Edible Woman* is an anti-comedy," where the fiancé embodies society's restrictions, and the wrong person marries. *Surfacing* is a Henry James kind of ghost story, where the ghost is a split-off fragment of one's self; the marriage is not real; the narrator may be crazy, or right – or both. *Surfacing* is really about "the great Canadian victim complex," where you refuse responsibility and play innocent; women also do this. The ideal would be "a whole human being," neither killer nor victim, but achieving some creative or productive "harmony with the world."

1973

28 GLEICHER, DAVID. "Female Chauvinism." *New Leader* 56, no. 17 (3 September):18-19.

Attacks *Surfacing*'s feminism. Like *The Edible Woman*, *Surfacing* imitates Sylvia Plath's *The Bell Jar*, absconding with its title image, but providing no dramatic basis for the narrator's nervous breakdown. Characters, plot, and lyric power are reduced to a simplistic thesis on woman in capitalist society. David turns into a "pseudohip" male chauvinist pig. That Anna is a one-dimensional, dominated, passive, painted doll shows Atwood's cruel condescension to women who haven't "'made it.'" The narrator's transcendence seems ludicrous. Feminists like Ms. Atwood should stop repeating stereotypes; they're "in danger of being absorbed" by the same society they "'refuse to be a victim of.'" See 1975.19. Excerpted 1975.39.

29 GLOVER, ELAINE. "Recent and Not So Recent Fiction." *Stand* 14, no. 4:69-70.

Admires, in an eight-book review, *Surfacing*'s imagery, themes, and magnificent last chapters. The images, which correlate with the narrator's emotions, are tough, particular, and deeply poetic; most of them critique the human and favor the natural. The city/country theme is effectively worked out in the characters, and in a greedy, hollow, cruel Americanism that colonizes Canada. The narrator as animal-being is completely acceptable, the end tenuously positive.

30 GODFREY, ELLEN. Review of *Surfacing*. *Canadian Forum* 52 (January):34.

Compares the narrow, tightly controlled *The Edible Woman* to *Surfacing*'s depth, passion, and power. Both novels begin with the familiar flat, boring WASP emotions of Upper Canadian fiction; but in *Surfacing* the deadpan is deeper, almost pathological, and the breakout is not a mild psychosomatic transference, but complete release, into a primitive madness. Here, unlike the classic Jewish novel, emotions are an unfamiliar wilderness. The frightened, deadened characters are wonderful caricatures; foolish victims, they dehumanize each other while glibly promoting new game plans.

31 GROSS, KONRAD. Review of *Survival*. *Kritikon Litterarum* (Frankfurt am Main) 2, no. 1:66-67.

1973

Attributes *Survival*'s success to its provocative search for Canadian identity, and enjoys its witty, non-academic style. The Frye-influenced thematic approach is too narrow and rigid. Atwood sees only one central theme in Canadian literature, that of victim. Her victim evidence is wide-ranging, and although victims do abound in Canadian literature, there are other issues and other writers that should be recognized. If viewed as Atwood's personal outlook, and as a provocative challenge, *Survival* is valuable.

32 GROSSKURTH, PHYLLIS. "Survival Kit." *New Statesman* 86 (24 August):254-55.
A capsule history-overview, which documents the emerging Canadian identity, and *Survival*'s impact and controversy: political, intellectual, and economic causes of the new nationalism; House of Anansi and New Press, both founded by Dave Godfrey to encourage Canadian writing; *Survival*'s and Atwood's immense popularity, especially among the young; Margaret Laurence's reservations and Morley Callaghan's irritation; *Survival*'s neglect of Callaghan, Robertson Davies, and Canadian humourous irony. Reprinted: 1988.22.

33 ____. "Victimization or Survival." *Canadian Literature*, no. 55 (Winter), pp. 108-10.
Acclaims *Surfacing*: as in Atwood's poetry, but not in *The Edible Woman*, the narrative style fuses form and content. As in "The trappers," the theme is victimization. The tripartite structure is key to the narrator's growing self-awareness: in the present-tense first part, she has lost her bearings; in the past-tense second part, fears are exposed, protective city "armours" crack, and the narrator withdraws. In the third part, the narrator can live in the present tense, after accepting her father's death; she deliberately gets pregnant, and destroys the film, which is a more affirmative act than Marian's consuming the surrogate self; she learns to search for her mother, and something of how to survive. After immersion in Atwood's work, the reader surfaces, to a startlingly new world. Reprinted: 1985.11. Excerpted: 1974.37

34 GUTTERIDGE, DON. Review of *Survival*. *Canadian Forum* 53 (May):39-41.

1973

Subscribes to the reviewers' consensus on *Survival*'s importance, insights, and limits; but without in-depth criticism, "teaching [*Survival*] could be disastrous." First, Atwood's psychological judgment, that "only Position Four is creative . . . [and] cut[s] out God, the presbyterian (Calvinist/Jansenist) mode of feeling," and Canadians' complex, two-hundred-year-old creative experience of guilt, struggle, and enduring. Second, Atwood misreads ambiguities, as with E.J. Pratt's *Brébeuf* and the reviewer's *Riel*. Third, Atwood implies that a new breed of writers (from Anansi) have exposed our complex experiences as victimization by the U.S. – but Haliburton, whom Atwood omits, said that more truly, long ago.

35 ____. "Surviving the Fittest: Margaret Atwood and the Sparrow's Fall." *Journal of Canadian Studies* 8, no. 3 (August):59-64.

Finds *Survival* "so good" but "so dangerous," powerful but semi-flawed, brilliant but one-sided. Its biased selections and "contrived politico-psychological matrix" focus on Anansi's "'breakthrough'" writers, patronize elder writers, and their readers, and devalue our complex Canadian experience of the "land, Nature, God, Fate, Necessity, guilt, courage, love, struggle, endurance." Teachers need accurate guides to literature's revelatory, myth-making powers. Offers, as illustration, his own analysis of Fred Bodsworth's *The Last of the Curlews* and *The Sparrow's Fall*, a Canadian allegory of creative victims.

36 HALL, VIRGINIA. "A Compelling New Vision of the Evolving Self." *Kansas City Star*, 25 March, p. E3.

Praises *Surfacing*. Incredibly, Atwood has shaped, from conceptual flotsam on nature, God, man, woman, and Americans, "a strong, self-actualizing, risk-taking woman," who searches for her father and her aborted ability to love. The plot has several levels, the most enticing being an undertow of survival. The real force is in the telling. The characters are uniquely and revealingly described. The narrative style veers effectively. Though *Surfacing*'s message may offend the New Woman proponents, "the heroine is that, and more."

37 HAND, JUDSON. "Man Against Nature, Again . . . Only This Time It's a Woman." *Daily News* (New York), 11 March, Leisure sec., p. 21.

Recommends *Surfacing*: though it may be depressing, it shows how today's self-indulgent people treat each other and what raw nature is left. Like Joseph Conrad, and like James Dickey in *Deliverance*, Atwood subjects the main character to mindless nature to reveal him and his society–but Atwood's main character, and atmosphere, are feminine. At the end, is it society or the young woman who is irrational? We don't know whether she will die there in the wilderness, or be captured and returned to the civilization she rejects.

38 HARCOURT, JOAN. "Atwood Country." *Queen's Quarterly* 80, no. 2 (Summer):278-81.

Survival's victim themes intrude, overshadowing *Surfacing's* final third; perhaps this happened when the original title, *Forehead Eye*, was changed. The eerie forehead (psychic) eye is a key to the initial theme of self-discovering and acceptance, which is neglected after the first part. The northern Quebec island is Atwood country, and the underwater vision a recurrent poetic image, as in *Procedures for Underground*. After the dive, *Surfacing* becomes a nightmare, paranoid territory; the narrator fears the Americans, and everyone, as *Survival* themes take over, and she becomes an animal victim. The final refusal of victimhood, and the breakthrough trusting and letting go, which merge the survival and acceptance themes, are hard to credit, after so much disintegration. But Atwood's work must be seen as an expanding whole.

39 HARRINGTON, LYN. Review of *Survival*. *Canadian Author and Bookman* 48, no. 3 (Spring):23-24.

Describes *Survival* as revealing "our depressing national symbolism." Survival, not success or joyous challenge, dominates our literature in Atwood's far-ranging examples. The reader fights "a retreat against her conclusions," with counter examples and parallels from other nations' literatures.

40 HARRISON, RICHARD T. "The Literary Geography of Canada." *Lakehead University Review* 6, no. 2 (Fall-Winter):274-76.

Welcomes *Survival*, in a two-book review of it and William New's *Articulating West*, as a major event; finds Atwood's survival and victim themes accurate, the treatment of settlers particularly good, and the style simple, vivid, and accessible. Though some omissions are

1973

debatable, and the young may now write cliché victimization stories, Atwood does warn of *Survival*'s limits – but this persuasive book overrides its own warnings. Though nationalism may distort, Canadian literature has long been judged by other nations' methods.

41 JACKSON, MARNI. "The Survivor as Hero." *Last Post* 3, no. 1 (January):41-42.

Has at least two different responses to the praiseworthy *Survival*: first, though the plausible survival and victims thesis does fit Canadian literature, an unintended "air of inflexible authority" appears in the Basic Victim Positions. The chapter on women is brilliantly distracting. What holds Atwood's analysis together is "her metaphorical tone of voice" and asides. "*Survival* is original because Atwood has looked for her guidelines *within* our writing rather than importing her criteria." She accepts our collective or failed heroes. For Atwood an accurate self-image, even if dour, is better than none, or a cosmetic one. The reviewer's different and immediate response, however, was to see *Survival* confirming her own high-school craving for Canadian poetry.

42 JOHNSON, DIANE. "Cultural Innocence in Canada." *Washington Post*, 19 March, p. B8.

Critiques *Surfacing*: "a highly romanticized conception of nature is contrasted with the violations devised by civilization, of women by men, of nature by man, and of Canada . . . [by an America that symbolizes] aspects of the Worst." The narrator, a "'modern'" young woman with the usual angers, as about pregnancy and hospital childbirth, has given her baby to her ex-husband, and gone north with a lover and friends. This heroine, who narrates in a rather exhausting present tense, is too puritanically natural to use insect repellant. Why does she have such boring, disgusting people for friends? Role-reversing, she uses the man to get pregnant; one hopes that Dr. Grantley Dick Read's kind shade, as well as the moon, will be pulling for her natural childbirth. In the end, after a frenzied, nature-girl breakdown, she must sensibly return to civilization. If Canadians are as culturally innocent as this book, they have sinister shocks coming.

43 JONAS, GEORGE. "Maggie Is a Thing Apart." *Maclean's* 86, no. 8 (August):11, 14.

Reviews *Survival*'s reviews, from the joyous nationalists, the ecstatic With It group, and those who read and admired its argument, to those Out of It, and who objected to its exclusions, particularly of Robertson Davies. Cites Atwood's Empire Club address, and offers his own opinion, which is that controversy helps insure literary survival.

44 KATTAN, NAIM. "L'oeuvre de Margaret Atwood." *Devoir* (Montréal), 10 March, pp. 16, 18.

Despite Canada's colonial mentality, Atwood's work reaches far beyond the United States. *Survival* affirms the differences between Canadian and American literature. Canadian literature consists mostly of geographical and historical victims, who fear nature and identify with animals. American literature shows man as the hunter of animals. According to *Survival*, there are no heroes in Canadian literature, only a few martyrs at best. *Survival* focuses on the British-tradition Canadian writers. [Annotated from incomplete copy.]

45 KOLTZ, NEWTON. Review of *Surfacing*. *America* 128, no. 23 (16 June):562.

Praises, with reservations, Atwood's strong, well-written, deeply perceptive book of a woman's life. The heroine slips through dreams, fantasies, and changing memories, losing her civilized self to reach her primitive self and be reborn a true woman. But the other characters don't breathe; and trusting primal nature to renew our lives is a trap – as Robinson Crusoe shows, "we need some protection from the heart of darkness."

46 LARKIN, JOAN. "Soul Survivor." *Ms*. 1, no. 11 (May):33-35.

Acclaims *Surfacing* and *Power Politics*; Atwood, as a woman, Canadian, and human, speaks for all our planet's life. *Surfacing*'s alienated, brokenhearted narrator finds in the wilderness a way back to self, feeling, and ritual reconnection with nature. She undergoes not "madness" but a primal, healing Laingian voyage of discovery; her surfacing is a rebirth and reawakening. *Power Politics* also explores victimization, as in "you fit into me." "They are hostile nations" is a plea for shared survival, against war games. Atwood sees language as political; her own is understated, stripped down to essentials. Quotes Atwood on the Women's Movement and *The Edible Woman*, *Power*

1973

Politics, and women's and men's criticism of the latter. Reprinted: 1988.25.

47 LAURENCE, MARGARET. Review of *Surfacing*. *Quarry* 22, no. 2 (Spring):62-64.
Acclaims *Surfacing*'s language, images, themes, and mythic quest, choosing to read the woman's inner journey as breakthrough, not breakdown or breakup. The alienated woman searches for her father, and truth, in a false and irrational world. (The "Americans" who slaughter nature are Canadians, us.) *Surfacing* is a *rite de passage*, a descent to dark regions, where special knowledge is given, before a return to the human world. Contemporary themes, of women's role, urban life, and the wounding of Earth, are interwoven with the central myth – "of humankind's quest for the archetypal parents, for our gods, for our own [mortal] meanings." Reprinted: 1988.26.

48 LEARY, C.J. Review of *Surfacing*. *Best Sellers* 33, no. 3 (1 May):50.
Summarizes this engrossing novel: the narrator is Canadian, and snide about Americans, and lives in a Greenwich Village-like basement apartment. Earlier she had abandoned her husband, baby, and parents; now she goes with her friends to her missing father's cabin. That unsettled problem preys on her mind; as her friends are leaving, she disappears and "wanders about, deciding to revert to the nothingness of all beginnings."

49 LEHMANN-HAUPT, CHRISTOPHER. "Novels with Anxious Moments." *New York Times*, 7 March, p. 41.
Briefly worries, in a two-book review, that *Surfacing*'s narrator might be about to go mad, kill herself, or renounce men and civilization, thus reducing this thoroughly brilliant novel to merely anti-masculine propaganda. But she doesn't; the island ordeal is a test, a rite of passage. In this brooding, ominous tale Atwood peels away her characters' civilized skins, alchemizing everything – the inward-turned, run-on sentences, the protagonist's recurring memories, the preyed-on landscape. The woman who knows the woods reverses what are usually masculine adventures, as with the Deerslayer and James Dickey's Lewis. The final reconciliation is satisfying, if not entirely believable. Reprinted: 1973.50 (below).

50 ____. Review of *Surfacing* and *The Autograph Hound*, by John Lahr. *International Herald Tribune* (Paris), 21 March, p. 12.
Reprint of 1973.49 (above).

51 LOTTMAN, EILEEN. "Nature and Femaleness." *Providence Journal*, 22 April, p. H21.
Praises *Surfacing* highly: though traditionally it's been masculine to use nature as a metaphor of "'the human condition,'" as James Dickey recently did, Atwood's "perfectly conceived and executed novel" shocks the reader into realizing "that nature is the perfect metaphor for woman. . . . If this leads to alienation from the modern world, it may also point the way back. . . ." *Surfacing* takes the reader inside the protagonist's head to experience and understand her overlapping, non-sequential past and present, even as her grasp of reality drifts. Nature is not described, but experienced; the reader slows to savor every nuance, symbol, and level. Women particularly, but also men, will be richly satisfied.

52 McCOMBS, JUDITH. "*Power Politics*: The Book and Its Cover." *Moving Out* 3, no. 2:54-69.
Explicates Atwood's book, and Tarot cover, as an inevitable modern, woman-centered breakthrough in love poetry; as multiple, permuting Victor/Victim games; and above all as a book about the Head's generic, human ability to see and reason, to invent games and alternatives. The Victor/Victim games are not only between the two lovers/beloveds, who each compete for both roles; but also between the more public, imperialist Them/Us, in the center section; and between Human/Nature throughout, but especially in the third section. The *I* is both generic human author and character; the *you* can be read as one or various men, as a generic masculine role, as part of her divided self, as a Muse. *Power Politics* is a critique of love, of power games, and above all of the human *I*, who imposes reason and games, synthesizes and permutes the divisions made by sanity, logic, and intelligence.

53 McLEAN, ROBERT A. "Journeying Back to Self-Knowledge." *Boston Globe*, 25 February, p. B17.
Finds *Surfacing*, in a two-book review, an astonishingly powerful account of a search for identity in remote wilderness. The widely

acclaimed Atwood creates a new heroine of survival, a new "'centerfold.'"

54 MADDOCKS, MELVIN. "Out of the Woods." *Time* 101, no. 12 (19 March):77-78 (pp. 66, 70 in Canadian edition).

Reviews *Surfacing*, terming Atwood "a connoisseur of pain" who specializes in the contemporary female variety. Like a supercasual Dante, she judges her generation of young, pseudosophisticated Canadians. Her anti-heroine regresses into a private wilderness, beyond the defoliating chain saws. This may sound modish, but Atwood is satiric, lyric, and "a mistress of controlled hysteria . . . . [A]s only a really gifted writer can, she turns paranoia into art," forcing the industrializing world to see the hate in the victim's bloody eye.

*55 MAGID, NORA L. "'No Longer Any Rational Points of View.'" *Philadelphia Bulletin*, 18 March.

Describes a "savage, complex, romantic, and peculiar" *Surfacing* that travels many roads at once – "anthropological, satiric, poetic, philosophic, theological, psychological, mystic. . . . [I]t is so idiosyncratic that readers may be mesmerized, overwhelmed, disturbed, or simply exhausted." For the dislocated, desperate narrator, everything – gods, home, words, Yanks – is something else. "Meticulous details are juxtaposed with all the tricks the mind can play and with fluid and colliding nightmares." The characters are both the living and the dead. Is this monologue "'coldblooded'"?

56 MAHON, DEREK. "Message in the Bloodstream." *Listener* 89 (24 May):696.

Appreciates *Surfacing*, in a four-book review, as intellectual, poetic, and a good read. The narrator journeys towards self-discovery, withdrawing from her superficial companions into a consciously primitive communing with nature. Atwood's perceptions are precise and luminous. The diverse experiences come together in new apprehensions for the disassociated narrator; the frank, startling anti-Americanism connects to her final pregnancy with perhaps "'the first true human,'" who must be allowed.

57 MARTIN, PETER. "A Dual Selection: 1, *Surfacing*." *Canadian Reader* 14, no. 1 [1973]:2-3.

Enthuses over *Surfacing*; the deceptive calm builds to an overwhelming, powerful climax, and then a final peace. Outwardly, on the surface, little happens, but underneath, the relentless and terrifying search goes on, in the heroine's mind. An absolutely convincing horror builds, moves outward, becomes a frenzied – and Canadian – rite of purification. This is much more than madness. Some day Atwood will get a Governor General's Award for fiction.

58 MELLORS, JOHN. "Mostly Losers." *London Magazine*, n.s. 13, no. 3 (August-September):150.

Ranks *Surfacing* in between success and flop, in a four-book review. The narrator is a loser; the atmosphere, style, and action sometimes recall Hemingway's Nick Adams stories. But this vivid and impressive book collapses "when the girl sees something nasty in the Atwoodshed," starts looking for primitive gods and noble savagery, and literally goes wild.

59 MITCHELL, BEVERLEY. "Five Fiction Reprints." *Journal of Canadian Fiction* 2, no. 4 (Fall):112-14.

Judges *The Edible Woman*, in a five-novel review, stylistically delightful and mordantly witty; a batty woman with batty friends; finds Dawe's 1973.19 points about women's choices moot. Atwood tries to correct by ridicule; her deliberately and grossly exaggerated satire is in part disturbingly true, but its real weakness is the lack of constructive alternatives. Judges Margaret Laurence's *The Fire-Dwellers*, which sees our essential goodness, a great achievement; in comparison, wants to kick Atwood's glib, self-dramatizing Marian.

60 MOJTABAI, ANN GRACE. Review of *Surfacing*. *Library Journal* 98, no. 3 (1 February):433-34.

Finds *Surfacing* faultless as a journal of self-discovery, and almost terrifyingly true; it hardly matters that this is less than a self-subsistent novel. Falseness and civilization are challenged here.

61 MOODY, MINNIE HITE. "Powerful Novel Pits Primitive vs. Modern." *Columbus Dispatch*, 22 April, p. D7.

Admits *Surfacing*'s strength and many lyric, beautiful moments, but dislikes the characters and the disenchanted raw times in between. Atwood's description of the protagonist is poetically gifted, and the sexual tension is supremely skillful; but "[t]his reviewer frankly doesn't go for the sort of people portrayed." The main girl is "a hypersensitive freak" you want to shake, and the others are indeed with us. Atwood is against pollution, civilization, cities, and, seemingly, Americans, at least the hunters, fishers, and campers.

62 MURRAY, MICHELE. "Margaret Atwood Sets a Woman Against Nature – and Nature Wins." *National Observer*, 7 April, p. 23.

Acclaims Atwood's powerful *Surfacing*, which renews the New World myth of consciousness versus wilderness. The superbly imagined characters and story make the shopworn alienation theme real. Journeying into her past, the narrator fears the destructive Americans, trusts Indian ways, and retreats from humanity into an uncontaminated animal world.

63 NADEL, IRA BRUCE. "What's Canadian About Canadian Literature?" *Event* 2, no. 3 (Spring):81-85.

Survival's direct, unpretentious, anecdotal approach engages Canadian literature as never before. Refining D.G. Jones's duality and Northrop Frye's culture/nature antagonism, Atwood is an involved writer, an explorer mapping the territory, emphasizing the cultural and the national. But her approach is narrow, and her English-American-Canadian comparisons rigid. Canada gets only the survival theme, only failed heroes, or collective ones; Canada is a "'collective victim.'" She blames civilization, not writers, for the inferiority of Canada's literature. *Survival's* engaging style, close readings, helpful bibliographic lists, and excellent resource sections make fascinating reading: but Atwood over-categorizes, and imposes on literature a political radicalism that undermines her useful and long-needed discussion of important Canadian texts.

64 NICHOL, b.p. "What Is CAN LIT? a review." *Open Letter*, 2d ser. 5 (Summer):69-70.

A two-page cartoon, with a figure searching inside maze-like grids. Page 69 names Sheila Watson, Gerry Gil[ber]t, James Reaney, and Margaret Avison. Page 70 has one figure wondering "But what the hell is CAN LIT?" and another saying "it's just a quest- / ion of SURVIVAL!"

1973

65 OLSON, CLARENCE E. "Set the Cruel Victims Free." *St. Louis Post Dispatch*, 11 March, p. C4.

Reviews "two excellent but quirky novels, " *Surfacing* and *The Hawk Is Dying*, by Harry Crews. "Miss Atwood's coolly controlled style is one of psychological submersion. Words and images are shaped and distorted by unseen currents like sealife [sic] drifting past a submarine window." Images float by, from the narrator's past affair, abortion, and the marriage she deserted. The end may be fantasy or breakdown, but she "emerges cauterized if not cured," refusing victimhood. The protagonists of both novels try to avoid artificial, socially-imposed roles, and "look to nature for the meaning of freedom," which begins with self-acceptance.

66 ONLEY, GLORIA. "Margaret Atwood: Surfacing in the Interests of Survival." *West Coast Review* 7, no. 3 (January):51-54.

The poet of exploitative sex roles in *Power Politics* now sees sadomasochistic patterns in Canadian literature. *Survival*'s thematic analysis is almost "a non-symmetrical 'mapping' of Laing's psychology onto Northrop Frye's theory of fictional modes," from ironic to mythic. Atwood's poetic and fictional alienation versus communication parallels Roszak's *Sources* and Michael McClure's "Revolt." *Surfacing*'s schizophrenic narrator comes close to madness, and metamorphoses into a human part of the biosphere; the novel fuses literary forms, from Menippean satire through Canadian animal story. *Survival* is sometimes scathingly witty, and a first step to awareness, if used flexibly. But what if victimization is inherent in our civilized human condition? See 1974.33. Excerpted: 1980.14.

67 PACHE, WALTER. Review of *Survival. Jahrbuch für Amerikastudien* (Heidelberg) 18:285-87.

Approves *Survival* as a useful handbook for overseas readers, and a better introduction than standard works, such as Klinck's *Literary History of Canada* and the *Oxford Companion to Canadian History and Literature*. Modern Canadian literature is virtually unknown in Germany; two recent anthologies of world literature scarcely noticed Canadian writing. Atwood is one of the most promising English-speaking writers in Canada today. Northrop Frye, and especially his poetry reviews, very strongly influence *Survival*. Considering that Canadian literature is too young to employ a normative critique,

1973

Survival succeeds as a comparative history of motives [motifs?] in Canadian literature. *Survival* is also a critical self-portrait of the colonial mentality of a "'client culture.'"

68 PASHLER, MURRAY. Review of *Survival*. *Ontario Naturalist* 13, no. 1 (March):40.

Compares *Survival* to an exciting canoe trip through the rapids: you're challenged and distressed, but above all exhilarated and brought alive. Writers shape our attitudes to our environment. Like a liberating Jungian analysis, the immediately relevant chapter on "Nature the Monster" exposes some of the myths in our heads, and lays bare, with surgeon's hands, some rotten beliefs. Atwood may share Alasdàir Maclean's belief that the wilderness is the source of our human spirit, imagination, and poetry. Atwood shows how identifying with suffering "Animal Victims" can be a self-fulfilling prophecy of doom, unless we change. Perhaps *Survival* should be called "*A Field Guide to the Canadian Psyche*."

69 PASTAN, LINDA. Review of *Power Politics*. *Library Journal* 98, no. 20 (15 November):3380.

Compares Atwood's book to Ai's rougher *Cruelty* and Marge Piercy's polemic *To Be of Use*; praises Atwood's less overtly political distillation of man-woman warfare into sharply defined, icy language. The quoted "you fit into me" is pain masquerading as the coldest fury; but these poems go beyond anger and the personal.

70 PETERSON, KEVIN. "Atwood's *Survival*: Spreading the Good Word." *Calgary Herald*, 19 January, Magazine sec., p. 8.

Though *Survival* is not a great book–it's sketchy and chatty as literary criticism, and equally unsatisfactory as a first introduction, because it cites hundreds of things–its success is refreshing, and it does fill a real need by making Canadian literature more accessible. Probably it won't be remembered in universities in a few decades, because it paves the way for better work to come. Its focus on available paperbacks is most valuable, and its lists are essential. The survival thesis and Canada as a "'collective victim,'" depict Canadian fiction as grim, but Atwood does see some ways out.

71 PICKERSGILL, ALAN. "Survival for Whom?" *Alive*, no. 25 [1973], pp. 12-14.

Critiques *Survival*'s political analysis: though Atwood recognizes that Canadian literature reflects our long victimization by British colonialism and U.S. imperialism, she ignores Canada's class struggle, and our literature's bourgeois base and distortions. The "'Canadianize'" Committee for an Independent Canada followers want little empires of their own. Because Atwood sees collective liberation as a sum of individual liberations, she blames individuals – Canadians generally, Indians and Quebeckers particularly – for not rising up against oppression. *Survival* misreads George Ryga and Roch Carrier, and misrepresents history. We have struggled, and therefore survived.

72 PIERCY, MARGE. "Margaret Atwood: Beyond Victimhood." *American Poetry Review* 2, no. 6 (November-December):41-44.

Assesses quest for self and *Survival*'s themes in two novels and five books of poetry; hopes that this "extraordinarily good writer" will consciously identify her themes as part of the emerging women's culture. The alienated Marian flees a society that would consume her, but ends up with the user Duncan. The desperately alienated *Surfacing* protagonist descends deep into the primitive, wild, holy, and irrational natural psyche to reintegrate and heal. Both protagonists fight alone; how can they really stop being victims without some social act? *Power Politics* is less successful than the immigrant *The Journals of Susanna Moodie* and the mythic *Procedures for Underground*; its power struggles deepen mythologically, but do not break through like *Surfacing*. See Christ 1976.13, 1980.17. Reprinted: 1982.130; 1988.39. Excerpted: 1975.39; 1985.11.

73 PRITCHARD, WILLIAM H. "Poetry Matters." *Hudson Review* 26, no. 3 (Autumn):586-87.

Hesitates, in a round-up review, concerning *Power Politics*'s experimental poems. Atwood's jacket note says writing poems is "'like walking in the dark'"; so is reading these: you move by sound and touch. Love is collision, surreal, as in the quoted ["They travel by air"]. Though many here are fragmentary, and some pretentious, one feels that Atwood's poems, like Eliot's, have to work their way out from a true, germinal "'obscure impulse.'" Excerpted 1975.39.

1973

74 Review of *Power Politics*. *Booklist* 69, no. 21 (1 July):1003.
Briefly describes Atwood's economical, intense style, victor-victim view of the man-woman relationship, finesse, honesty, publication and broadcast credits.

75 Review of *Surfacing*. *Booklist* 69, no. 17 (1 May):833.
Finds a well-designed, introspective, but disturbing novel. The narrator searches for her father and identity; in the end she discards civilization and returns to nature.

76 Review of *Surfacing*. *British Book News*, October, p. 696.
Recapitulates the novel, from Anna's [sic] Quebec childhood through Anna's [sic] intensifying self-awareness. The supporting characters are barely outlined; *Surfacing* depends on the descriptions of nature and of Anna's [sic] near breakdown.

77 Review of *Surfacing*. *Choice* 10, no. 7 (September):970.
Recommends *Surfacing*; here, as in *Moby Dick*, the modern hero/heroine surfaces after confronting the old gods or destructive forces; the final, honest "insanity" permits a sane return to the city. (Atwood equates "modern" with "American," and satirizes "Canadians" who are "American.") *Surfacing* has obvious affinities with *The Journals of Susanna Moodie*, "Progressive insanities of a pioneer," *The Edible Woman*, and the nationalist *Survival*.

78 Review of *Surfacing*. *Kirkus Reviews* 41, no. 1 (1 January):15.
Finds *Surfacing* clearly, cleanly styled, and as intense and delusional as Atwood's talented *The Edible Woman*; but because *Surfacing*'s life-repudiating heroine is so unfeeling, this novel remains "suicide chic," even when distanced from its fashionable lost causes (liberation, ecology, etc.).

79 ROSENTHAL, DAVID H. "And the Shoe Fits, Worse Luck." *Nation* 216, no. 12 (19 March):374-75.
Finds *Surfacing* "a genuine Great American Novel," reconsidering myths we Americans also share, of communion with nature, and of the pioneer philosopher. Modern Canada is shown as a violated primeval landscape; male-female relationships as degraded. But it is hard to accept all the heroine's perceptions, which are colored by her despair,

hysteria, brief insanity, and a nastiness that is hers as well as external. Her fantasy of a divine pregnancy contrasts with her indifference to her real child's fate. But, as recent events with hippie farmers in Vermont suggest, *Surfacing* may be what our Thoreau frontier myths have come to.

80 ROSS, MALCOLM. Review of *Survival. Dalhousie Review* 53, no. 1 (Spring):159-60.

Rejects Atwood's "fine grave-digger's vision of our unique cultural identity" as victims. "No, by heaven – not faceless, stuffy colonial Puritans we, . . . but rather a people of profound and iron stoicism," from our first writers to Anansi's "sophisticated trickeries of word-play." Remember the suffering in other literatures – from the Latins and Don Quixote to Melville, Hemingway, Bellow? *Survival* fails to mention Robertson Davies, Stephen Leacock, F.R. Scott, and Thomas Raddall; and misreads others. Atwood has bent Frye's suggestive but elusive "'garrison mentality' . . . into a stiff, metallic, cup-shaped and capricious formula which is then clamped down hard on the wriggling body of Canadian writing." Much is contained therein, but much more "is left mangled or headless or untouched without."

81 RUDZIK, O.H.T. "Letters in Canada, 1972: Fiction." *University of Toronto Quarterly* 42, no. 4 (Summer):344-45.

Finds *Surfacing*'s rite of passage difficult, and the narrator's intense possession problematic, in part because applying Atwood's polemical program and survival paradigm detracts from the narrator's imaginative status.

82 SCOBIE, STEPHEN. Review of *Survival. Canadian Fiction Magazine*, no. 10 (Spring), pp. 117-20.

Survival is political, and has become an extra-literary, public phenomenon; some fear that the announced *Survival II* anthology will convert Atwood's thesis to Holy Writ. *Surfacing* does not merely illustrate *Survival*; Atwood's ideas are cohesive, but limited. *Survival* reflects her, and Anansi's, tastes, and slights internationally focused writers such as B.P. Nichol and Dorothy Livesay. It is hard to challenge *Survival* without fitting into a logical victim position. *Survival* would be very dangerous to give to unformed students, because it so convincingly channels future responses. But if it opens up discussion of Canadian literature, that will be very admirable.

83 SHRAPNEL, NORMAN. "Journeys in Space and Time." *Guardian* (Manchester), 9 June, p. 26.
      A brief two-book review, which finds *Surfacing* not only a young woman's journey across the landscape, but also a rather deep, subjective, perpendicular search for her past and its well-springs.

84 SONTHOFF, HELEN. "The Long Will to Be in Canada." *Quarry* 22, no. 3 (Summer):75-77.
      Accepts *Survival* as a good starting point, but comes to different conclusions: finds disasters interesting, not gloomy; finds Canadian literature very aware of its precarious balance between threat and hope. The sense of place is very strong in Vancouver, and Emily Carr. Appreciates Canada's "lovely stubborn realism. . . . For me, for the world I've seen, to live with a land and people studying survival is a great hope."

85 STEVENS, PETER. "No, Margaret Atwood, No! Your Narrow Viewpoint Missed Our Smiles." *Windsor Star*, 20 January, p. 11.
      Finds *Survival*, which may become dogma, partial and too limited. Atwood argues that our colonial mentality keeps us victims; emphasizes newer novelists, especially from [Anansi Press], where she is an editor; omits Thomas Haliburton, Steven Leacock, Robertson Davies, and Wallace Stegner; and omits or slights many other twentieth- and nineteenth-century writers. She avoids seeing the humorous and comic side of Birney, Souster, Purdy, and Nowlan. However stimulating the best-selling *Survival* is, however admirable Atwood's interpretations are, *Survival* completely disregards "Canadian humor and satire, our positive political stances (especially in the literature of the 1930s), and our writers' real," considered affirmations.

86 STONE, ELIZABETH. "Loss, Madness, and (but Only Rarely) Recovery." *Crawdaddy*, December, p. 89.
      Appreciates *Surfacing* as the most life-affirming of the three novels by young women reviewed here. The narrator's Canadian identity sides with life, against death-driven Americanism; her "madness" is R.D. Laing's breakthrough, not breakdown.

87 SUDLER, BARBARA. "*Surfacing* Is Imperfect Women's Lib Parallel to *Deliverance*." *Denver Post*, 15 April, Roundup sec., p. 28.

A rave review of *Surfacing*: "This woman's lib parallel of James Dickey's *Deliverance* (not a perfect analogy, but serviceable) is taut, suspenseful, heart-breaking, and hopeful." Atwood is "a very gutsy writer with laser-beam vision that cuts deep into the forest." The narrator, a typical drop-out from modern society, is an alienated, apolitical loser who has left behind a marriage and a child. "There are fascinating nuggets of thought to chew on cudlike" – on children's books, on the amputation of divorce, on heart and headline. "In the final analysis, these Rousseauesque child-creatures are vulnerable because they have bought the [unrealistic] Great American Dream." The heroine must chose between death and imperfect, compromised life.

88 SWAN, SUSAN. "Moodie Reflections." *Books in Canada* 2, no. 2 (April-June):19.

Finds Mia Anderson's CBC LP reading of *The Journals of Susanna Moodie* a good introduction to the quirky Englishwoman who inspired Atwood. Anderson follows Atwood closely, with two voices, divided between the "strident, almost hysterical English prig and the softer, more approachable female" who knows she hasn't learned what the bush could teach. Likes best "The Wereman."

89 THOMPSON, J. LEE. "Can Canada Survive *Survival*? An Article on *Survival: A Thematic Guide to Canadian Literature*." *American Review of Canadian Studies* 3, no. 2 (Autumn):101-7.

Surveys *Survival*'s reviews, pro and con, as of September 1973: reviews correspond to the four victim positions; the negative ones have been more animated, sometimes bitchy. Atwood's introduction anticipated the complaints of sloppiness, oversimplification, distortions, omissions. The attackers invariably acknowledge her imagination, intelligence, and wit – and her making Canadian literature controversial and popular. Certain journals have, so far, been silent – were they waiting for the *University of Toronto Quarterly*'s Olympian judgment? *Survival*'s imaginative appeal and "largely unflattering portrait of the national psyche" provide an antidote to chauvinism and to apathy. Brief bibliography.

1973

90 THOMPSON, KENT. "Three Recent Novels." *Fiddlehead*, no. 97 (Spring), pp. 114-16.

Acclaims *Surfacing* as totally successful, significant, poetic. Language and matter are one, as with the term "American," whose meanings change, ironically, to include Canadians. The heart of Canadian consciousness is pre-historic and pagan; the narrator's personal search is therefore representative. *Surfacing*'s dimensions – nationalism, feminism, art, the Québecois, Atwood's survival theme – will give the serious critics work to do.

91 THORNTON, EUGENIA. "Menace and Survival in North Woods." *Plain Dealer* (Cleveland), 11 March, p. H8.

Recommends without reservation the deeply original, moving, strange, and menacing *Surfacing*. The reviewer, who was delighted with Atwood's first, serio-comic novel, finds in *Surfacing* a second self-searching woman, but "no comedy in this shatteringly effective tour-de-force." The narrator, whose consciousness is rooted in her remote wilderness childhood, is different from her three unconcerned friends. When she strips away the present, everything basic surfaces, frighteningly and powerfully. "Woven into this pattern of destruction and eventual salvation is the sharply colored thread of survival," of the heroine, and of Canada, against second-hand Americanism.

92 Van STEEN, MARCUS. "An Amazing Discovery: Canada's Writers Canadian All the Time." *Citizen* (Ottawa), 27 January, p. 43.

Hails the extraordinary *Survival*: "In straightforward, down-to-earth, common-sense language, Miss Atwood has achieved what all our politicians and constitutional experts have failed miserably in doing – she has outlined a distinctive Canadian point of view on which we can build a separate and united nation." Atwood has apparently stumbled on the central symbol of Canadian identity, survival, in our literature. She attributes our ready acceptance of victim roles to "our ingrained colonial mentality"; she deplores the deluge of imported artifacts and values. Recent Canadian writers have been facing our main problem, of "'where is here?'" Now Canadian readers may be able to accept their answers. Atwood's detailed lists complement the very useful *Read Canadian*, by David Godfrey and others.

93 ____ . "Margaret Atwood: A Canada-First Poet." *Canadian Scene*, no. 878 (6 April), pp. 2-4.

Portrays the award-winning poet and internationally recognized novelist as a dedicated Canadian nationalist who chooses to remain here. Atwood grew up knowing and loving the Canadian wilderness. She became a conscious Canadianist when, as a Harvard Ph.D. student, she realized how young Canadians were encouraged to find their cultural standards abroad. *Surfacing's* people search for their identity, and reject false, imposed values. *Survival* argues that the colonial mentality is French and English Canadians' greatest obstacle. Atwood argues "that the cause of Canadian unity will be won, not in Parliament," but in our classrooms, libraries, homes, and theatres.

94 VENDLER, HELEN. "Do Women Have Distinctive Subjects, Roles, and Styles?" *New York Times Book Review*, 12 August, pp. 6-7.

Has mixed reactions to separatist feminist anthologizing; most women's writing has been too narrow, and limited to their domestic relations. Finds Erica Jong's *Half-Lives* biting and clever; Judith Johnson Sherwin's *Impossible Buildings* uneven; prefers *Power Politics*, a true man-woman death struggle sequence, its poems "all formed perfections." But, contrary to Atwood's preface, these victor/victim patterns are limited to man/woman; the sexual struggle and hatred are believable, but not the love. The reviewer hopes only that the accomplished Atwood will enlarge her scope and vision – and that all three poets will try writing long poems.

95 WALFOORT, MARY. "Secrets in a Lake." *Milwaukee Journal*, 20 May, sec. 5, p. 6.

Describes *Surfacing* favorably. The narrator, an attractive, intelligent commercial artist, finds, while searching for her father on a remote island, snatches of her buried past. Is the baby, or her old life, or her new one, real? She hides from her friends to follow clues to the truth, or go mad. "The nightmarish final pages end" quietly, leaving the reader "much to think about." The poet-novelist author uses present tense and short, comma-linked sentences, which, though difficult, convey the narrator's urgency "and pull the reader into the vortex of a deeply human story."

1973

96 WALKER, CHERYL. "Welcome Eumenides: Contemporary Feminist Poets." *Feminist Art Journal* 2, no. 4 (Winter):6-7.

Cites Trotsky's *Literature and Revolution* in classifying Atwood, Eleanor Ross Taylor, and Carolyn Kizer as not explicitly feminist poets, in contrast to the explicitly feminist Robin Morgan, Adrienne Rich, and Erica Jong; briefly discusses *Power Politics*, whose dust jacket says Atwood doesn't see it "'as a blow struck for the women's movement.'" The book is colored by feminist consciousness, with a non-feminist undertone; Atwood emphasizes the masculine lover over the feminine persona, who is constantly reacting, not acting.

97 WATT, F.W. "Letters in Canada, 1972: Humanities." *University of Toronto Quarterly* 42, no. 4 (Summer):440-41.

Finds *Survival* the most talked-about book on its subject, a part of the recent Atwood cult, and a key to her work–but to Canadian literature? Pratt and Laurence have perhaps religious visions; Atwood's is defensively or belligerently political. Readers who don't think they're exploited colonials may be demonstrating a victim position. "[*Survival*] should be taken as a powerful personal reading of Canadian literature," done with imagination, intelligence, and a generous enthusiasm. Canadian literature will never be the same again.

98 "Way of the Wild." *TLS*, 1 June, p. 604.

Complains that *Surfacing*'s pretentious, poetry-ridden prose interferes with its genuine attempt to analyze difficult relationships, between people, countries, and nature. All the characters are obsessed with America's encroachments on Canadian identity and resources.

99 WEBB, PHYLLIS. "Letters to Margaret Atwood." *Open Letter*, 2d ser., no. 5 (Summer), pp. 71-73.

These eight brief letters or journal entries are a poet's "hollow-eyed celebration" in response to Atwood, *Surfacing*, *Power Politics*, and *Survival*, especially its "Paralyzed Artist" and "Ice Women vs. Earth Mothers" chapters: "It made me feel good. The whole sickness laid bare, making sense, allowing no further excuses." Discusses attacks on Atwood, writer's block, women's sexuality, Apocalypse, animals, sedition, pain.

100 WEEKS, EDWARD. "The Peripatetic Reviewer." *Atlantic* 231, no. 4 (April):127.

A mixed review of *Surfacing*. This poet's novel beautifully conveys the sensibilities of the northern Quebec wilderness. All four characters are fashionably inept and rejected. The heroine's vital work and childhood memories contrast sharply with "the zany photography and amorous dawdling of her companions." But retracing her deadening city life jeopardizes our sympathy and interest in "the character who alone is holding up the tent of the entire narration." There are fine passages and powerful scenes here, but the heroine's final fresh start with Joe is hard to believe. Excerpted: 1975.40.

101 WELCH, SUSAN R. "Meeting the Gods of the Wilds . . . on Their Terms." *Minneapolis Tribune*, 18 March, p. D10.

Finds both *Surfacing* and *Power Politics* morbid, absolutely droll, stunning, and irresistible. "*Surfacing* is an eerie, ominous book that crawls through your mind like a worm," and that may become an archetype. The narrator's purification and rebirth rite recalls R.D. Laing's theory that madness can be sane. The resolution doesn't quite work. *Power Politics* "is lean, lucid and taut with understated agony," and also funny.

102 WHELAN, GLORIA. "Love Reborn on a Hateful Isle." *Detroit Free Press*, 18 March, p. D5.

Praises Atwood's "strange and almost perfect" *Surfacing*, which "pushes beyond man's rational limits" without losing the reader. The nameless heroine (whom the reviewer will name Jean) returns to a northern Quebec island where French and English Canadians hate each other, and everybody hates Americans. Jean's three late-twenties friends are "sullen, alienated, vicious," loveless, and friendless, without values or goals. Jean's Rousseau-like simple, rustic childhood contrasts to her superficial present, and offers salvation. In a chilling climax, she "tries to become a primitive creature at home in nature"; reborn as her parent's child, she is able to love and to bear a child.

103 WIGLE, WIL. "Slow Burn." *Northern Journey* [3 (October)]:13-19.

Includes, in a story of an unloving woman, a scene set at an Atwood poetry reading and party, with a reference to an earlier Atwood reading, in Montreal, where John Glassco paid Atwood "a grand compliment," in telling her she had given him "'a great big erection.'"

104 WIMSATT, MARGARET. "The Lady as Humphrey Bogart." *Commonweal* 98, no. 20 (7 September):483-84.

Acclaims *Surfacing*, whose tough and exceptionally skillful outdoors heroine should not be compared to Sylvia Plath's young lady, but to the "'masculine'" pioneer, Huck Finn, Hemingway in Africa, Humphrey Bogart, the professional guide. Read and reread; it's also a well-plotted detective story. The heroine dives deep, for sanity and salvation; she surfaces with wisdom. Liberationists will read *Surfacing* as a tract, like *Uncle Tom's Cabin*; separationists and nationalists will read it as they please – but should note that its Quebecois are not friendly. A great book, consolidating all the themes of Atwood's earlier creative books. Excerpted: 1975.39.

105 WOLFE, MORRIS. "Atwood's Guide to the Geography of Survival." *Saturday Night* 88, no. 1 (January):32-33.

Acclaims *Survival*, which, like R.D. Laing's *The Politics of the Family*, combines familiar themes in a profoundly liberating way. Building on Northrop Frye's and Douglas Jones's academic criticism, Atwood has created a non-academic, political book. *Survival* avoids forced sociological thinking, but does make many works, including Graeme Gibson's *Communion*, much more interesting. Minor errors occur in this hastily produced major work. Praises the humour and brilliant analysis; if survival dominates modern literature, then the world is being Canadianized.

106 W[OODCOCK], G[EORGE]. "Horizon of Survival." *Canadian Literature*, no. 55 (Winter), pp. 3-6.

An editorial that praises and tries to refute *Survival*: "It is as if Third-Eye were trying to instruct One-Eye on how to guide No-Eye" to our national psyche. Finds brilliant essays, clumsy apparatus, and shrewdly chosen examples; a salutary but depressing vision of failure, survival, and colonial economic domination. *Canadian Literature's* ten years' editorial was called "Getting away with Survival." But many Canadian writers, including Robertson Davies, don't fit Atwood's themes; but so many do fit that, though survival belongs to world literature also, "it is hard not to accept Atwood's horizon of survival as the circle that best defines the bounds of Canadian writing." See 1973.107. Reprinted: 1985.114; reprinted in part 1981.111; 1985.11. Excerpted: 1977.21.

107 WOODCOCK, GEORGE. "Surfacing to Survive: Notes of the Recent Atwood." *ARIEL* (Calgary) 4, no. 3 (July):16-28.

Explains that his 1972.40 conclusion, on Atwood's survival ethic, was written before he knew of its development in *Surfacing* or *Survival*. Finds *Survival*'s victim scheme and polemic mildly exasperating; its failure thesis needs qualification–think of Robertson Davies, and George Orwell–but fits much of Canadian life and literature. *Survival* should be seen as tactical and salutary for Canada–"charts to help us repel a cultural invasion"; and for Atwood, a journey of self-discovery, into her culture's darkness and small, meaningful lights. Compares *Surfacing* with *The Edible Woman* and *Survival*; finds satire, myth, and a final courageous, truly Buddhistic coming into the light of sanity. Acclaims Atwood as her generation's best. See 1973.106. Reprinted, except for circumstantial explanation, as part of 1975.52; reprinted in part: 1981.111; 1985.11.

1974

1 BROWN, ROSELLEN. "Revived Selves." *Parnassus* 2, no. 2 (Spring-Summer):148-52.

Concludes a long review by acclaiming *Power Politics* as extraordinary, shocking, mythic jousts in real fields, a "highly distilled acid nastiness" that moves, with humor, from the personal to the mythic. As in *Procedures for Underground*, the images disintegrate; as in *Surfacing*, the myths are earth-air-water, not fire. As in "You fit into me," Atwood sets up casual expectations, then sneaks round back, like a Zen master wielding a stick. The dynamic, mirroring structure convinces us; the lovers will survive, limping, alone. No man could be offended by Atwood's skillfully wielded knives, for her mirrors are true, and her poems show her naked, impaled, and fiercely alone. Excerpted: 1978.11.

2 CAHILL, F. BURKE. Letter to the Editor. *Canadian Forum* 54 (September):41-42.

Endorses George Galt 1974.13 on the critics' confusion; and offers his own review of *Surfacing*, for the Canadian literature high school course he developed: the heroine rejects a pervasive and horrifying human culture for a primitive creature-hood, but must finally return to the human culture her mate represents.

3 COBRA, DOMINIQUE. Letter to the Editor. *Canadian Forum* 54 (September):41.

Criticizes George Galt 1974.13 for a meretricious critique of *Surfacing* reviews and an inability to see the heroine as a woman, not girl, in a paradigm of female as well as Canadian victimization.

4 DAVEY, FRANK. "Margaret Atwood." In *From There to Here: A Guide to English-Canadian Literature Since 1960*. Our Nature – Our Voices, vol. 2. Erin, Ont.: Press Porcépic, p. 30-36.

Describes Atwood's success, themes, and genres. Atwood "enjoyed a spectacular climb to the summit of Canadian letters," largely dominating 1966-1973. Her poetry is her most accomplished genre; her novels simplify; *Survival* further simplifies. Atwood sees "a shifting and hostile post-modern world" endangered by nature's Heraclitean anarchy and man's alienating, fascistic forms. Her Moodie is very like Atwood; *Power Politics* shows "a mutually sadistic love affair." *Surfacing* and *The Edible Woman* have brilliant dialogue and epigram, but only methodical character and structure; both novels sacrifice character and credibility to thesis. *Survival* has been useful, for the public, less so for educators; its victimization and survival themes are central to her work, not to Canadian literature. *Survival* overemphasizes Anansi writers, and ignores accomplished others. Bibliography. See Mallinson 1978.59.

5 DRIVER, CHRISTOPHER. "Hastings Owl." *Listener* 91 (14 March):342-43.

A two-book review, featuring Lowat Dickson's *Wilderness Man*, and briefly praising *Survival* as a "brisk and brilliant exploration," and describing its animal themes.

6 D[RUMMOND], I[AN]. "Fairy Tales of Canada: II, The Lady of the Lake: Or How the Octopus Got Its Tentacles." *Canadian Forum* 54 (May-June):68-69.

Caricatures Atwood: Once there was a pretty little girl named Margaret living at the bottom of a lake with her moody witch stepmother Susanna in a kingdom ruled by leprechauns. One day Margaret sliced a leprechaun's head off, because he didn't think her little-girl-shaped anemone pie was funny. As an experiment, she slept with another leprechaun, who woke up covered with scales and "soft emerald fur"; she found it fun, but soon boring, and invented The Circle Game, also called Power Politics. The leprechaun went away, and Margaret discovered life had survival and victims, and urged everyone to rise to the top. She had a problem. She ate more and more leprechauns, got bigger and bigger, and changed into a long-sucker-tentacled, thousand-eyed octopus. One day she surfaced, then descended, saying "My lake." See Lee and MacPherson 1974.20 and 23.

7 FRASER, D.M. "Margaret Atwood's *Surfacing*: Some Notes." *3¢ Pulp* 2, no. 7 (1 May):[1-4].

Attacks *Surfacing*: like *Beautiful Losers*, this willfully third-rate book "infuriates to the point of frenzy." This is the Great Canadian Novel for *Maclean's* and *Saturday Night* to "lick up by the shovelful": "Effete City vs. Tough Existential Bush, Conditioned Sanity vs. Primitive Madness, Emerging Woman vs. Oppressive Male, and . . . Rapacious America vs. Victimized Canada"; plus some "Post-Hippie Coitus," "Endangered Scenery," "Hardy Quebecois," and "Graduate School Introspection." But these formulas aren't themes, and don't work. All the characters are one-dimensional clichés, the politics liberal-bourgeois and undigested anti-Americanism, the insights Pop-Psych, the feelings "leftover sentimentalities topped with cheap ironies"; scenes sink like waterlogged condoms. The real outrage is that we are so "obsessed with our (nonexistent) Cultural Identity" that we embrace this pretentious mediocrity. See French 1974.10.

8 FRASER, JOHN D. "From Wilderness to Coterie." *Communist Viewpoint* 6, no. 2 (March-April):31-38.

Rejects *Survival*'s dogmatic simplifications and puerile bourgeois politics, which expose the strategy of some would-be influential Canadian intellectuals. "The argument of *Survival* is a chain of interrelated errors and distortions. . . . First, it identifies 'the nation'–not the two nations– . . . with the 'victim' in Canadian literature." Secondly, it confuses petit bourgeois feelings of dependency with structural exploitation of subordinates and the proletariat. Thirdly, it describes no national dilemma, only "a metaphorical version of the petit bourgeois writer's quest for an audience," and romanticized past. Fourthly, she restricts the writer's vision to petit bourgeois acceptance

1974

of national capitalism. Finally, she simplifies the writer, national literatures, and victims. "Underlying the petit bourgeois writer's self-pity, . . . his choices and pseudo-choices, is a political decision to 'go national' from which the proletariat can draw no satisfaction." Marxism requires a real analysis of Canadian literature, proletariat, and capitalism.

9   FRENCH, WILLIAM. "Atwood Cancels Soviet Tour Because of Solzhenitsyn." *Globe and Mail*, 21 March, p. 13.

Reports on cancellation and on *Surfacing* screenplay. Atwood has cancelled her one-month tour of the Soviet Union, in the first Canadian-Soviet cultural exchange of writers, due to their expulsion of Solzhenitsyn. Meanwhile, she is writing the screenplay for a *Surfacing* film to be produced by Andrew Sugarman and Steven Kesten. Anticipating nationalist criticism, Atwood says there were no acceptable Canadian offers; she wants a film close to the book, without the shift in locale that happened with Margaret Laurence and *Rachel, Rachel*. Her three other film involvements, which came to nothing, were Canadian.

10   ____. "Resurfacing: At Once the Worst and Best of Books." *Globe and Mail*, 25 June, p. 14.

Reports on the critical controversy between George Galt 1974.13 and D.M. Fraser 1974.7 over *Surfacing*; quotes some of Galt's acclaim, disputing his disparagement of newspaper critics; quotes more of Fraser's attack; concludes that controversy, rare in Canada, is healthy, and may attract more readers to *Surfacing*.

11   FULFORD, ROBERT. "Atwood's New Poetry an Exhilarating Trip." *Toronto Star*, 14 September, p. H7.

Finds *You Are Happy* perilous, unnerving, also exhilarating. The title is an Atwoodian accusation. The four sections move in a circular, mythic or fictive, pattern, to a sort of resolution. The first section is bitter; the animals are menacing; the Circe sorceress is "the classic difficult woman"; the last section doesn't exactly celebrate affection, but does come to terms with man/woman relationships. Atwood's poems are terse, reticent, always "charged with menace"; presumably her "tough, cool style" is a mask for passion. Interesting as a novelist, useful as a critic, Atwood is most effective and forceful as a poet.

12 GALT, GEORGE. "George Galt Replies." *Canadian Forum* 54 (September):41.

Defends, in reply to Dominique Cobra 1974.3, his 1974.13 critique and interpretation; *Surfacing*'s heroine is not a cliché of oppression, but a unique human being.

13 _____. "*Surfacing* and the Critics." *Canadian Forum* 54 (May-June):12-14.

Acclaims *Surfacing* and critiques its reviews; though always favorable, and often ecstatic, both Americans and Canadians failed to understand its psychic depths. Approves Canadian resident Paul Delany 1973.20; champions Margaret Laurence 1973.47 as the only true assessment of *Surfacing*'s Quest to the dark regions, its hope, its contemporary issues. Atwood's secondary characters are pathetically real; the Quebec landscape is awesomely alive; the overlooked history theme is key. The narrator is an extraordinary individual, a seer rediscovering a true, primeval religion. *Surfacing* is likely the best fiction "by Atwood's generation in North America or anywhere." See Cahill 1974.2, Cobra 1974.3, French 1974.10, and Galt 1974.12.

14 GLICKSOHN, SUSAN WOOD. "The Martian Point of View." *Extrapolation* 15, no. 2 (May):161-73.

Traces science fiction, fantasy, and horror themes and metaphors in Atwood's early poems and first five books of poetry: the alien Moodie's ghostly, science-fiction metamorphoses, and doubly alienated double vision, in a world perceived as alien; *Procedures for Underground*'s similar artist-shaman; *The Circle Game*'s speaker's metamorphoses into non-human shapes in a non-human world or order; and Mary Shelley's duality of the creator-scientist monster, which shapes the 1966 *Speeches for Doctor Frankenstein* and *Power Politics*. Atwood, who Purdy 1971.14 calls a "'totally subjective Martian,'" uses outer space, extra senses, and time travel, as an artist and as a complex, exploring, "totally human person."

15 HORNE, ALAN J. "A Preliminary Checklist of Writings by and about Margaret Atwood." *Canadian Library Journal* 31, no. 6 (December):576-92.

Provides a chronological listing of primary and secondary work, but does not attempt complete coverage. Newspapers and anthologies

1974

are selectively covered. Lists, under nine primary categories, 18 separately published works; 25 books and anthologies containing Atwood's work; 149 issues of periodicals, each containing one or more of her poems, stories, or other prose (a few issues which contain works from more than one genre are double-listed); 8 audio and audio-visual recordings; and a short list of the 11 boxes of manuscripts in the Thomas Fisher Rare Book Library, University of Toronto. Lists, under two secondary categories, 20 articles and theses; and 113 book reviews, cited by journal, not author or title. Revised: 1977.34; 1979.56; 1980.59; 1981.47.

16 JACOBS, ANN. Review of *You are Happy*. *Dalhousie Review* 54, no. 4 (Winter):790-92.

Celebrates Atwood's transforming magic: she weaves Circe's spells. As Atwood recently said, in a radio interview, poetry is a "'crystallization of words'": so these poems refine and crystallize earlier poems' ideas and images. Is the title a query, plea, or assertion – or all three? This exciting exploration moves from destruction through risks to wholeness; the cover's golden mandala sun wheels through this spiritual centering. Images change, concentrate; ideas play out. Dismembered bodies are charms, and find wholeness. Her islands become our shore, we are transformed, and "even the transformed sing" here.

17 JONES, D[OUGLAS] G[ORDON]. "Cold Eye and Optic Heart: Marshall McLuhan and Some Canadian Poets." *Modern Poetry Studies* 5, no. 2 (Autumn):170-87.

Reads Atwood's poetry of the demonic, alienated, analytic eye and the darker, merging and belonging senses, in *The Circle Game*, *Power Politics*, and elsewhere, as part of a Canadian poets' revolt against cold visual dominance, evident in Anne Hébert, P.K. Page, Margaret Avison, and others.

18 KROETSCH, ROBERT. "Unhiding the Hidden: Recent Canadian Fiction." *Journal of Canadian Fiction* 3, no. 3:43-45.

Speculates, citing Heidegger, on the Canadian writer's need to demythologize a British- or American-defined language and experience: as *Surfacing*'s heroine says, home ground is foreign territory. "The terror resides not in her going insane but in her going sane." Unnamed, she removes the false names adhering to her experience – imitations, camouflage, fakes, language, her sham marriage's ring. Extravagantly uninventing the world, she removes even the notion of being human; "Bare-assed she can become bear-assed" – a seductive, fabulated, female vision of total freedom. Perhaps identity, or ego, is a spent fiction; Atwood, Robertson Davies, and Rudy Wiebe, are uncreating themselves into existence. Reprinted: 1983.78.

19 LAUDER, SCOTT. "We Are Not So Happy." *Canadian Forum* 54 (November-December):17-18.
   Finds it "difficult to be fair," when Atwood is now "the star of Canadian poetry," worshipped and abused as [Leonard] Cohen used to be. In *You Are Happy* "the familiar Atwood persona moves on through the lurking horrors which litter her landscape"; those who resist her vision may find some poems forced or vague or contrived. The final, tentatively positive poems, like "There Is Only One of Everything," are the strongest; the title, which at first seemed accusatory, finally becomes affirmative. Apparently the cynical Circe poems were a passage to happier ground. Atwood's pleasingly ingenious conceits can become unnecessarily clever, particularly in "Songs of the Transformed." Her celebrity status highlights her faults and shadows her strengths.

20 LEE, DENNIS. Letter to the Editor. *Canadian Forum* 54 (September):40.
   Protests I[an] D[rummond]'s wretched, worthless little piece [1974.6], and irresponsible invasion of Atwood's privacy; debates the two principles which I.D.'s feeble fable didn't really raise. First, what is responsible coverage of a celebrity – would an illuminating hatchet job, or a really witty stereotypic octopus-woman satire, be acceptable? Second, how does literary criticism relate an author's own character to his writing? – a complex issue which I.D.'s bungling obscures.

21 McKENNA, ISOBEL. "Women in Canadian Literature." *Canadian Literature*, no. 62 (Autumn), p. 78.
   Concludes a survey of women's roles versus society's limits in English-Canadian novels by discussing how *The Edible Woman*'s Marian, unconsciously and literally fed up with conforming, saves herself by turning against a society that is consuming her individuality.

1974

22 MacLULICH, T.D. "The *Survival* Shoot-Out." *Essays on Canadian Writing*, no. 1 (Winter), pp. 14-20.

Any good western film has a build-up before the shoot-out: CanLit was there, staked out by E.K. Brown, Desmond Pacey, Warren Tallman, Northrop Frye, D.G. Jones, Ronald Sutherland, and W.H. New. Then came *Survival*: "the lady versus the gunslingers." At first some cried *bravo*! and some *foul*! Then the crowd murmured, irritably: *Survival* lacked decorum, and footnotes; its scope and cocky brashness seemed a challenge; it "combined originality with academic poaching," which infuriated critical gamekeepers. It was political: it challenged Canadians to stop being victims; it said colonial politics shaped our literature's themes. Until some gunslinger writes a real thematic or cultural refutation, the lady will be a power in CanLit town.

23 MacPHERSON, JAY. Letter to the Editor. *Canadian Forum* 54 (September):40-41.

Great and recognized creative talent gives to the less-gifted; but it also stimulates an astonishing quantity of envy and hurtful spite: condemns the smart-alecky, pseudonymous, sickening fairy teller [I[an] D[rummond] 1974.6].

24 MACRI, F.M. "Survival Kit: Margaret Atwood and the Canadian Scene." *Modern Poetry Studies* 5, no. 2 (Autumn):187-95.

Claims Atwood's prose, especially *Survival*, makes her five books of poetry look poor: each stacks inversion and paradox, very cleverly, but each adds to the obsessive monotony. *The Journals of Susanna Moodie* is the worst by far, repeating her most recurrent images, of submersion, surfacing, and victimization, in a tone of Calvinist terror, with a bourgeois theme. *Procedures for Underground* reiterates the images and intensifies the schizophrenia and paranoia. *Power Politics'* tone is "confession as aggression." *The Animals in That Country*, which shows animals and man in Canada, is the best; "Backdrop addresses cowboy" is its best. *Survival* succeeds in painting a Canadian tradition, but ideologically; it may confuse students, teachers, and writers into seeing victims all over. Atwood illustrates "a Canadian peculiarity," of many highly successful female authors.

25 MANDEL, ELI. "Criticism as Ghost Story." *Impulse* 3, no. 2 [1974?]:1-6.

Begins with the schematized flower of the Chinese *Mustard Seed Manual of Painting* to understand Atwood's fascinating and puzzling *Survival*, which, like much Canadian criticism and history, is mythic as well as thematic and social. ". . . *Survival* consists almost entirely of metaphors and images. . . . Could it be that *Survival* takes its unusual power precisely from the fact that it is criticism as novel, as [sic] ghost story disguised as politics and criticism?" The gothic tale's fundamental sadomasochistic sexual fantasy, which Atwood calls victor/victim, is *Survival*'s and Canada's mythic, dualistic structure. *Survival*'s ghost story is superb criticism because its sociology rests not in society or history, but in our landscape of language, in what George Steiner called "'the sinews of Western speech.'" Reprinted: 1977.53.

26 MITCHAM, ALLISON. "Woman in the North." *Alive*, no. 39, p. 7.
Praises *Surfacing*'s protagonist as the first woman in modern Canadian fiction to lead a northern quest; and places *Surfacing* in a tradition of French-Canadian novels, where quests head North, not West, and southern influences are attacked. Like Yves Theriault, Grey Owl, and Thoreau, Atwood shows the wilderness and Indian way as the only cure for a sick civilization. In the historic North, women followed and were victimized; now, Atwood's courageous persona survives, and leads her three perverse, troublesome, superficial friends. Her true self is reborn, even though her rebellious attempt at conceiving a "natural" child does get complicated. See also 1975.31. Reprinted 1983.93.

27 MORLEY, PATRICIA. "Survival, Affirmation, and Joy." *Lakehead University Review* 7, no. 1 (Summer):21-30.
Challenges *Survival*: accepts survival as a central Canadian theme, but rejects Atwood's "extremely negative," "gloom and doom" interpretation of survival, and her misreading of Canadian texts. F.P. Grove's "Snow," Ernest Buckler's *The Mountain and the Valley*, and Hugh MacLennan's *Return of the Sphinx* show nature beautiful and loved, not monstrous. Margaret Laurence's *The Stone Angel* shows a life-affirming, very sympathetic old woman. E.J. Pratt makes his victims victors; Seton's animals are heroes, not victims. "Why do Canadians hail so enthusiastically a book which tells us we are losers?" *Survival*'s style is alive. Perhaps Atwood only intended to play devil's advocate? *Survival* is valuable, in sparking debate, but let's not ignore our literature's joy, courage, and affirmation.

1974

28 MUSGRAVE, SUSAN. "Atwood: A Wary Lowering of Defences." *Victoria Times*, 9 November, p. 22.

Appreciates *You Are Happy*'s new voice and new awareness. We are not an ideal audience: we look for our excellent entertainers, especially the poets, to fall off; we have made up a mythical laconic, shrewish "para-Atwood," so that the title *You Are Happy* sounds, to us, like irony or sarcasm. But no: para-Atwood here acknowledges life's necessary vulnerability. The title poem, "You Are Happy," has been cut from a longer original to include the speaker in its "you." *Power Politics* maintained "a constant substratum of mythic allusions (largely to the border ballads). . . . [In *You Are Happy*,] the mythic world has surfaced, inviting us to share in its archetypal maze." Reprinted: 1975.32.

29 "New in Paperback." *New York Times*, 11 August, pp. 20-21.

Briefly summarizes Paul Delany 1973.20 on *Surfacing*.

30 NILSEN, ALLEEN PACE. "The Feminist Influence." *English Journal* 63, no. 4 (April):90.

A round-up discussion of books for young adults and of how the women's movement has influenced publishing; briefly recommends *Surfacing* to mature readers, as a serious and unusually female- rather than male-centered treatment of "'man'" and nature.

31 NORTHEY, MARGOT. "Gothic and Grotesque Elements in Canadian Fiction." Ph.D. dissertation, York University.

Within the category of Modern Gothic fiction, *Surfacing* is an example of Sociological Gothic, rather than Psychological Gothic. See *Dissertation Abstracts International* 36(1976):6676A. Revised for publication 1976.70.

32 ONLEY, GLORIA. "Breaking through Patriarchal Nets to the Peaceable Kingdom: An Ecosystemic Review of Several Ideas, Books, and Events." *West Coast Review* 8, no. 3 (January):43-50.

Sets *Power Politics* in a context of literary, counter-cultural, feminist, theatric, and visual works celebrating a liberated human consciousness and critiquing patriarchal social mythology. *Power Politics* reveals Western romantic love as sex-role engulfment, polarization, and mutual narcissism; as in "The Grave of the Famous Poet," the lovers assume Gothic forms.

33 _____. "Power Politics in Bluebeard's Castle." *Canadian Literature*, no. 60 (Spring), pp. 21-42.

Links Atwood's ironic inversion of courtly love, in *Power Politics* and the two novels, to revelations of Western sadomasochistic social mythology from MacLuhan, [Kate] Millett, Roszak, Chesler. The authentic self may not exist; archetypal presences substitute. Dickens and Bergson underlie *The Edible Woman*'s satire. Depersonalized sex is linked to modern technology, as in George Steiner; the head is disconnected from the body, as in Michael McClure. Like Laing and Szasz, Atwood sees schizophrenia as psychic anarchy, and the "mentally ill" as political prisoners of Western culture. *Surfacing* is a scapegoat animal story, with man returning to nature as the ego dissolves. Though, as in "Polarities," the alienated self is unable to break through, Atwood's creative works are not resigned: they are "iconoclastic keys to getting mentally outside" Steiner's Bluebeard's castle of language. See 1973.66. Reprinted: 1988.37. Excerpted: 1975.40

34 PAGE, SHEILA. "Supermarket Survival: A Critical Analysis of Margaret Atwood's *The Edible Woman*." *Sphinx*, no. 1 (Winter), pp. 9-19.

Follows Dawe 1973.19 in a detailed discussion of *The Edible Woman* as a struggle for survival and liberation in our oppressive consumer society. As Marian moves from passivity to hysteria, Peter becomes a sinister chef/doctor/hunter; Duncan is an amorphous changeling and fellow victim; the other women – the dogmatically Life-Force Ainsley, the domestic Clara, the rejected virgins – are Marian's alternatives. The final cake is a problematic act of liberation.

35 PEARSON, ALAN. "A Skeletal Novella in Plain Diction: A Bestiary under Iron Grey Skies." *Globe and Mail*, 28 September, p. 33.

Reviews images of Atwood and *You Are Happy*; sees "a snaky-haired Medusa" borne "on the whinnying mares of nationalism and women's liberation," and a long-gowned, Brontëan spectral figure, alternately demon-haunted and defiant. Finds an icily deliberate structure, more like a skeletal novella than lyric poetry; a soured love affair; anger; a puzzling "Siren Song" and bestiary; a clever "Tricks with Mirrors"; and a lovely "Late August." Wants celebratory lyric poems, or, at least, subtle thought and rich language, not bleak personal exorcism.

1974

36 PYKE, LANNESLEY. Review of *You Are Happy*. *Quill and Quire* 40, no. 11 (November):22.

Recognizes Atwood's sometimes detached, sometimes warm, but always penetrating voice, and her evolving vision. *You are Happy*'s four sections are highly integrated, from the first section's dead relationships; to the second's primal, victimized animals; to the welcome relief of the third's beautifully wrought Circe-Ulysses relationship; to the final section's surfacing into the actual, celebrated love of man and woman.

37 RILEY, CAROLYN, and HARTE, BARBARA, eds. *Contemporary Literary Criticism*. Vol. 2. Detroit: Gale Research Co., pp. 19-21.

Excerpted from: Van Duyn 1970.38; Bell 1970.5; Bowering 1972.6; Allen 1972.1; Grosskurth 1973.33; DeMott 1973.21.

38 ROGERS, LINDA. "Margaret the Magician." *Canadian Literature*, no. 60 (Spring), pp. 83-85.

Denounces Atwood's icy cover image and loveless books. Reading her culminates, always, in a confrontation with the hypnotizing, icicle-aiming eyes of her back-cover image. She is a magician, puppeteer, female god, witch doctor, extraterrestrial cliché, outsider, an ice-woman refusing to be known. *Power Politics* is a liturgy for romantic love's funeral. Physical love is cold; childbearing is repellent. *The Edible Woman*'s Marian copulates and flees; her refusal to eat is a psychiatric-case rejection of motherhood; dialogue and novel fail. In *Surfacing*, the woman's lover becomes an animal so she can give birth to her own image. Her poems are indelible petroglyphs; her words distort. Her imagery chills. Her characters "dance in an involuntary circle around her ice-woman." There is no humanity, no warmth, not in nature or water, no escape. "She is a knife cutting through onion." The layers are beautiful, symmetric, but unrelated; and the centre, hollow. Excerpted: 1975.40. See Davidson 1979.24.

39 ROSS, GARY. "*The Circle Game*." *Canadian Literature*, no. 60 (Spring), pp. 51-63.

Explicates *Circle* in detail, following a *Survival* remark that landscapes in poetry may map interior states of mind. In *Circle*'s first half, both land and city are seen as threatening wildernesses that preclude and alienate the human; the speaker is fearful, schizophrenic, isolated. After the pivotal title sequence, the speaker moves towards a tentative sharing, and both the exterior wilderness and the interior alienation become less threatening. By the end even death is shared, relative, regenerative. Excerpted 1975.40.

40 SANDLER, LINDA. "Gustafson and Others." *Tamarack Review*, no. 64 (November), pp. 92-93.

Gives mixed praise to *You Are Happy*, in a review featuring Ralph Gustafson's *Fire on Stone*. Atwood's torments seem completely solipsistic, and her anti-romantic war images are clichés; a surrealist pro with dazzling metaphors, she plays professional masochist. The two mythic sections move brilliantly into theatre. As "Tricks with Mirrors" suggests, Atwood's vision is most persuasive when framed, by myth or history, as in *The Journals of Susanna Moodie*.

41 SCHAEFFER, SUSAN FROMBERG. "'It Is Time That Separates Us': Margaret Atwood's *Surfacing*." *Centennial Review* 18, no. 4 (Fall):319-37.

Appreciates *Surfacing* as one mortal's religious and psychological quest for her lost parents and acceptance of human mortality, not as a women's liberation novel. Injured by her mother's death, and perhaps her father's, the narrator directs her hatred against the Americans; and, despite her denials, most strongly against men. Tracing her own guilt, she becomes an animal, insane. She wants to resurrect and to punish her logical father and her powerful, mysterious mother. Diving into the redemptive lake, she finds the truth of her dead father, and of her own aborted child, which was salted out, and covered over with a story of marriage, birth, and desertion. She seduces Joe to resurrect her lost child. After her hallucinatory visions of her parents, and her return to sanity, the end – whether she will live "normally" in the city, or "naturally" in the bush – is unresolved.

42 SELLERS, JILL. "*The Spokeswoman* Review: Margaret Atwood." *Spokeswoman* (Chicago) 4, no. 12 (15 June):6.

Introduces this important Canadian poet and novelist; briefly describes *The Journals of Susanna Moodie* and *Power Politics*; describes the inward journey of *Surfacing*'s heroine. American readers, particularly women, should enter Atwood's explorations and territory, which are ours, too.

1974

43 SPETTIGUE, D.O. Review of *Survival* and *Articulating West*, by W.H. New. *Queen's Quarterly* 81, no. 1 (Spring):122-24.

Disagrees with *Survival*. Can. Lit. has been taught for over a decade. Some of Atwood's victims should "stick a long pin back at her." *Survival* avoids almost all of the Canadian comic tradition. Twentieth-century man is the victim of Americanization everywhere. But perhaps modern man is Canadian, the watcher at the window or TV, ironic, but good-humoured still.

44 SPRIET, P[IERRE]. "La mythologie canadienne dans l'oeuvre de Margaret Atwood." *Annals du Centre de Recherches sur l'Amerique Anglophone* (Talence) 3, no. 2:21-38.

Situates Atwood's work, with its essential myths of identity and survival, at the center of the Canadian culture and soul. Atwood's *Survival*, which follows Northrop Frye and D.G. Jones, defines a new mythology that has a direct relation to the history and geography of English Canada. The new mythology is characteristically English Canadian, as opposed to French Canadian, in its refusal to accept traditional order; it is not related to the ideology of Christianity, but is derived from alienation and progress and is politically significant. Canadian culture differs greatly from American culture in how it views society's relationship with nature and the earth. Atwood's novels and poetry are variations on the theme of survival of the human in nature. In *The Journals of Susanna Moodie*, Atwood recognizes Moodie's writings as being mythical and romantic, about states of opposition in the universe. *The Edible Woman* expands the theme of polarization from that of a strictly Canadian condition to a human, and particularly female, condition. *The Animals in That Country*, *Procedures for Underground*, and *The Circle Game* contain similar structural elements of opposition between human and inhuman and the pattern of futile struggle. *Surfacing* is structured by metaphors of descent and surfacing, exhibiting the antithetic qualities present in much of Atwood's poetry. The postscript to *The Journals of Susanna Moodie* is the key to Atwood's work.

45 STEVENS, PETER. "Canada." In *Literatures of the World in English*. Edited by Bruce King. London and Boston: Routledge & Kegan Paul, pp. 46-47.

1974

Briefly cites *The Journals of Susanna Moodie*'s "Afterword" and "Further Arrivals," and *Survival*'s strangely-metamorphosed non-survival theme, in a discussion of Canadian literature's responses to the land.

46 SWAYZE, WALTER E. "Survey and Survival." *Journal of Canadian Fiction* 3, no. 1 (Winter):112-13.
Compares *Survival* to T.S. Eliot's youthful, influential criticism, which was similarly dogmatic, confident, and partisan. Having noted *Survival*'s shortcomings with Burke, Wordsworth, Emerson, and the "Basic Victim Positions," one has to admit that its treatments of Pratt and Birney's *David*, and the "Appendix on Snow" are illuminating, exciting, and thoroughly brilliant. *Survival* may cause occasional distortions when excited readers forget Atwood's cautions, or forget that Victor-Victim relationships, like objective correlatives, are not the only rewarding approach. Both *Survival* and Elizabeth Waterston's *Survey*, also reviewed here, need tighter editing.

47 YOUNG, SCOTT. "Making Hay." *Globe and Mail*, 12 August, p. 25.
Elaborates on Atwood's remark, at her Bohemian Embassy poetry reading, that she was sorry to be away from her Alliston farm "on a nice day for haying." Atwood must either hay with a scythe and apron, or else own $20,000 of haying machines, or use feminine wiles, or read poetry to pay for haying. But her $100 fee here, which would buy only 200 bales of hay, is too small.

48 ZINNES, HARRIET. "Seven Women Poets." *Carleton Miscellany* 14, no. 2 (Spring-Summer):123-24.
Argues against the appalling despair and anti-man political simplifications of some young women poets, and for a wider, human compassion; briefly remarks on *Power Politics*, censuring its despair and fanciful man-killing, but complimenting its elegance, irony, and surreal eloquence.

1975

1 AMABILE, GEORGE. "Consciousness in Ambush." *CV II* 1, no. 1 (Spring):5-6.

1975

Speculates that Atwood's prose successes, with *Surfacing* and *Survival*, may have driven her poetic consciousness into ambush, and caused *You Are Happy*'s unevenness. The first section's title poem is impressive, but its "Tricks with Mirrors" is merely irritating. The animal section is gimmicky, flat, and like Sylvia Plath's poems; its irony and bitterness backfire. "Circe/Mud" is the best section, though Circe herself seems "the archetypal bitch," filled "with sexual coldness and intellectual savagery," scarcely recognizable as Homer's persona. The last section "proclaims the new woman's independence," but the real problem may be the alienation from her own physical pleasures; the final rich insights remain abstract. See Mallinson 1978.59.

2 ANDERSEN, MARGRET. "Feminism and the Literary Critic." *Atlantis* 1, no. 1 (Fall):3-13.
    Rewrites, in a discussion of feminist criticism from Christine de Pisan to the present, *Survival*'s map paragraph: "What a lost woman needs is a map of the territory, with her own position marked on it. . . ." *Survival*'s analysis of women and children speaks of women, not ladies, and speaks quite freely of a "Baby Ex Machina" and "nonentity mothers." *The Edible Woman* "clearly analyses the lack of a female identity." Women need the feminist critique "to recognize themselves, to find their position on [sic] a territory which used to be exclusively male, to surface, to survive."

3 BRADY, ELIZABETH. "Towards a Happier History: Women and Domination." In *Domination: Essays*. Edited by Alkis Kontos. Toronto: University of Toronto Press, pp. 17-31.
    The concluding section analyzes *The Edible Woman* as a critique of women's roles within the sexist, capitalist consumer society. Atwood examines "woman as underpaid worker divorced from production; as lover/mistress alienated from her emotions; and as mother/wife whose capacity for maternity subverts everything that falls outside her reproductive system." The tentative end is a realistic first step.

4 BURTON, LYDIA, and MORLEY, DAVID. "A Sense of Grievance: Attitudes toward Men in Contemporary Fiction." *Canadian Forum* 55 (September):57-60.
    Discusses the current breakdown of women's core relationships with men, in life and in seven novels by Atwood, C[onstance]

Beresford-Howe, Marian Engel, and Margaret Laurence; categorizes both *Surfacing*'s heroine and *The Edible Woman*'s Marian as women who reject marriages to conventionally inadequate men and long-term relationships with perhaps "'alternative'" men.

5 CHAMBERLIN, J.E. Review of *You Are Happy*. *Hudson Review* 28, no. 1 (Spring):128-30.
Cannot trust *You Are Happy*, in a round-up review, because, as ["Chaos Poem"] shows, Atwood clearly does not care. Finds a limited victim pose, "diary/chop grammar," illegitimate paradoxes, fruitless acts "hearsed and re-hearsed"; cheap "Tricks with Mirrors" that laugh at one's expectations. "Is/Not" is abysmally typical of Atwood's willful obscurity and facile imperatives. Excerpted: 1978.11.

6 CLERY, VAL. "Backwords and Forewords." *Quill and Quire* 41, no. 2 (February):8.
Informs Patrick Conlon that he and his editor have, in letting Atwood control the 1975.8 profile, "signed away [their] independence and integrity merely to add to the already overstuffed Myth Atwood file." Why does he think Atwood was laughing? Her letter of agreement controls interviews. This columnist knows of at least one Toronto writer "who would have welcomed the means to control her poetic profile of their relationship." See Clery 1975.7, Conlon 1975.9, Laurence 1975.22, and Ross 1975.41.

7 ____. "A Simple Plea for Respect." *Quill and Quire* 41, no. 3 (March):2
Briefly defends his 1975.6 and replies to the 1975 letters to the editor from Conlon, Laurence, and Ross. In twenty years experience, he has only twice faced – and refused – such demands, which imply control over much more than facts. "Why should a writer yield up the prerogatives of his/her editor?" Atwood has lately "been declared sacrosanct; the vitriol has been reserved for those whose admiration falls even slightly short of idolatry."

8 CONLON, PATRICK. "Margaret Atwood: Beneath the Surface: Notes on Our Most Private Celebrity." *Toronto Life*, February, pp. 45, 47, 49-51.

1975

Profiles Atwood as the "undisputed but beleaguered Queen of Canadian Letters": her cool, resolutely unfeminine image; her threatening or thrilling themes of survival and women's strength; her control of, and humour in, interviews; love and writing with Graeme Gibson, who is also interviewed; her reactions to Alan Pearson 1974.35 and to Wil Wigle 1973.103; in conclusion, quotes Margaret Laurence on Atwood's and women's strength. See Clery 1975.6-7, Conlon 1975.9, Laurence 1975.22, and Ross 1975.41.

9 ____. "A Simple Plea for Respect." *Quill and Quire* 41, no. 3 (March):2.

Explains, in a letter to the editor concerning Clery 1975.6, Atwood's letter of agreement for Conlon's 1975.8 profile. First, *Toronto Life* editor Alexander Ross rightly asked that Atwood's requested right to 'delete' third party references be changed to 'consult,' and Atwood agreed. Second, Atwood, who has received a great deal of vitriol, was naturally trying to protect herself, and those around her, for her grandmother had been deeply hurt by inaccuracies in an earlier interview. Third, such agreements are not unusual outside Canada; *Playboy* subjects get final cuts. Though the interviewer originally bridled at Atwood's letter, he realized he would have so insisted, in her position; he now hopes his profile will be judged on its own merits, "and not weighed against a piece of paper that was a simple plea for respect."

10 DAVIDSON, CATHY N. "Chopin and Atwood: Woman Drowning, Woman Surfacing." *Kate Chopin Newsletter* 1, no. 3 (Winter):6-10.

On one level, *Surfacing* effectively revises and parallels Kate Chopin's early feminist novel, *The Awakening*, with an "'emancipated,'" aspiring artist protagonist, who focusses on love, marriage, sexuality, and identity; and with informing water scenes and metaphors. Even more intriguing are Atwood's necessary and subtle changes, which show how essentially similar 1899 and 1972 situations reflect a woman's "somewhat changed estate" vis-à-vis a sexist society. The 1972 hero's Pill, vote, freedom to live on her own, to abort, to sleep with a man, do not mean equality, or more options; sexual freedom especially is shown as deeply compromised, still sexist, and perhaps a subtler tyranny now. And, though one hero drowns and the other surfaces, each "'awakening'" goes only to a verge, and is tentative, difficult, and relative.

11 DURAND, RÉGIS. "L'individuel et le politique: Notes sur les romans de Margaret Atwood et Leonard Cohen." *Etudes canadiennes* (Talence), no. 1, pp. 63-72.

Explores the parallel qualities of works by Atwood and Leonard Cohen. Mentions *Favorite Games* and *The Edible Woman* as being autobiographical and having traditional archetypes, but focuses on *Beautiful Losers* and *Surfacing* because they are important turning points for the authors and for the entire body of Canadian fiction. While crisis and neurosis are individual, they are also simultaneously perceived as collective or political, eventually affecting the Canadian identity. Both stories exhibit a wide range of intensity and go beyond conventional literary themes; both are examples of "minor literature," or the literature of a cultural minority that has a foreign quality, like the work of William Burroughs, Severo Sarduy, and Peter Handke.

12 ENGEL, MARIAN. "The Woman as Storyteller." *Communiqué*, no. 8 (May), pp. 6-7, 44-45 (English text); pp. 6-7, 38 (French text).

Characterizes Atwood as a Canadian woman writer, not in the "reigning triumvirate" of Margaret Laurence, Adele Wiseman, and Alice Munro; but a huge talent, cult-figure, uncompromising *Survival* nationalist, and target.

13 FRANKEL, VIVIAN. "Margaret Atwood: A Personal View." *Branching Out* 2, no. 1 (January-February):24, 26.

Interviews Atwood in Montreal; describes her poetry readings at McGill University and Sir George Williams; discusses critics' misconceptions of the Atwood legend, and misreadings of her works. The real Atwood is not hostile to men, nor threatening; she sees men, and women, as individuals, since long before Women's Liberation. She is an economic and cultural nationalist; and a private, impish, resilient yet serene creative individual.

14 FRENCH, WILLIAM. "The Women in Our Literary Life." *Imperial Oil Review* 59, no. 1:6-7.

Describes *Power Politics*, *The Edible Woman*, *Surfacing*, the "highly personal" *Survival*, and Atwood's best-known celebrity status

1975

among Canada's leading women writers; mentions her protest of Alexander Solzhenitsyn's expulsion from the Soviet Union, and her Empire Club address. Reprinted: 1976.26.

15 GREENBERG, JAN. "To Take That Risk, to Offer Life." *St. Louis Post Dispatch*, 12 January, p. B4.

Gives *You Are Happy* mixed praise. In "Chaos Poem" as in *Power Politics*, Atwood probes her relationships as relentlessly as Oedipus. "But beyond the author's personal world of daily tensions and small betrayals, another," mythic world emerges. Violence and acquiescence are juxtaposed, as in "Newsreel." Language is icy and brittle, as in "Chaos Poem," or vibrant and rich, as in "Late August." Overall, the clear, moving poems outweigh the too cerebral and confusing ones; and Atwood "admits the need to experience" both spiritual and earthly love in the final "Book of Ancestors."

16 HULLEY, KATHLEEN. "Margaret Atwood and Leonard Cohen: The Feminine Voice." *Etudes canadiennes* (Talence), no. 1, pp. 73-78.

Argues that *Surfacing* speaks, not in a *langage mineur* like Cohen's *Beautiful Losers*, but in two voices, for two minorities: and both are enemy languages. A Canadian, but speaking American, she is trapped in an oppressor's tongue; a woman writer, she is trapped in the "*Father Tongue*." To reterritorialize a new, organic, feminine space, Atwood's narrator must evade both the traditional and the dissenting enemy territories. But if the Word is patriarchal, feminine recovery can only be in silence or in vision. Her resistance denies both social and archetypal structures; but she does not transform language's roots. The language that makes feminine, colonized minorities human, cripples and oppresses them. Her book circles into the silence of the first, sleeping Garden, the trees "'asking and giving nothing.'"

17 KAMINSKI, MARGARET. "Interview with Margaret Atwood." *Waves* 4, no. 1 (Autumn):8-13.

Atwood comments on *The Edible Woman*'s pre-feminism, central cake-woman image, setting, and Moose Beer and other ads; on making novels and books, not biography; on reviews, including Pearson 1974.35; on male costumes and man-woman relationships in *Power Politics* and life; on mirror images as counterparts or complements;

and on making mythologies in *Surfacing*, ["Circe/Mud Poems"], and *Power Politics*.

18 KINSMAN, CLARE D., ed. *Contemporary Authors*. Vol. 49-52. Detroit: Gale Research Co., pp. 38-39.

A brief biographical sketch, identifying Atwood's politics as "William Morrisite" and religion as "'Pessimistic Panthiest'"; lists her books 1961-1974; mentions an American edition of *Survival* as work in progress. Excerpted from: Maddocks 1970.25; Gibbs 1969.4; Thompson 1968.8; Ondaatje 1967.5.

19 KOLODNY, ANNETTE. "Some Notes on Defining a 'Feminist Literary Criticism.'" *Critical Inquiry* 2, no. 1 (Autumn):75-92 passim.

The Edible Woman's heroine most dramatically exemplifies the "'reflexive perceptions'" that signify amputated self-perceptions in contemporary Canadian and American women writers. Atwood's poetry, and *Surfacing*, use "'inversions'" of stereotypes and iconographies. Critics should not cavalierly dismiss female experience, as Gleicher 1973.28 did with *Surfacing*.

20 LALONDE, MICHÈLE. "En un pays étranger." *Maclean* (Montréal) 15, no. 6 (June):26-27, 46-49, 51-52.

Interview. Atwood discusses the heroines in *The Edible Woman* and *Surfacing* in relation to women's conflicts brought on by society and affirms that *The Edible Woman* is not autobiographical; describes English-Canadians as being both colonizers and colonized and considers the subject from nationalistic, economic and social points of view; fears vulnerability to the United States if Canada should become more than one autonomous entity; explains that she is "not political," but has convictions; and elaborates on the interaction of her nationalistic, political, and feminist views and identities.

21 LASK, THOMAS. "A World Lurking in the Lines." *New York Times*, 2 August, p. 19.

Briefly compliments, in a three-book appreciation of women's consciousness in poetry, *You Are Happy*'s ["Is/Not"] assertion of independence; and briefly compares the splendid animal songs to Roethke's naturalistic yet evocative greenhouse poems.

1975

22 LAURENCE, MARGARET. "A Simple Plea for Respect." *Quill and Quire* 41, no. 3 (March):2.

Protests, in a letter to the editor, Clery 1975.6. Allowing an interviewed person to check the accuracy of facts, dates, spellings, and quotes is quite standard; the writer has often checked her own interviews, simply for accuracy, not to jeopardize a journalist's independence. If Mr. Clery finds our literary society "'inbred'" (the writer does not), he is not helping by dealing in gossip. Atwood, one of our finest writers, deserves better treatment.

23 LEVENSON, CHRISTOPHER. Review of *You Are Happy*. *Queen's Quarterly* 82, no. 2 (Summer):297-98.

Appreciates Atwood's interlocking poetry sequences and books, from *The Journals of Susanna Moodie* on. *You Are Happy*'s first two sections extend *Power Politics*'s ideas, symbols, and personae. The second and third sections show the animal victims and Circe shrewdly hitting back against man's arrogance; as before, man means both mankind in a new country, and the male animal as oppressor. The final section moves from Circe's metamorphoses to the affirmation of a journey of equals. *You Are Happy* intensifies Atwood's themes, with a less strident, more open, movingly and truly human tone.

24 McLAY, CATHERINE. "The Divided Self: Theme and Pattern in Margaret Atwood's *Surfacing*." *Journal of Canadian Fiction* 4, no. 1:82-95.

Like *The Edible Woman*, *Surfacing* explores the modern dilemma that R.D. Laing called *The Divided Self*; *Surfacing*'s heroine seeks a healing of the mind-body split, and a reconciliation with humanity. As in "Journey to the Interior" and *Survival*, the exterior landscape in *Surfacing* is interior also: foreign, maze-like, inaccessible; the heroine dives into the lake and into the subconscious. Language and silence divide the characters; communication fails. As *Survival* suggested, the new-conceived child connects its mother to her own body and to nature–but initially that connection divides her from humanity. Finally, after the visions, she accepts her own and others' human limits, and reaches what Atwood in the Gibson interview 1973.27 called "'some kind of harmony with the world.'" Reprinted: 1978.57; 1983.83.

25 McWATT, MARK A. "A Comparative Study of the Language of the Imagination in Contemporary Commonwealth Literature: Wilson Harris, Raja Rao, Wole Soyinka, Margaret Atwood, and Patrick White." Ph.D. dissertation, Leeds University.

Discusses Atwood's New World poetry of the problems of community and freedom; features Wilson Harris. All five writers use a "'language of the imagination'" that involves multiple perspective, ancient myths, and innovative imagery and diction to construct a vision of freedom and community; all five reject theories of the Absurd. Atwood's sinister Canadian outdoors, Patrick White's demonic Australian outback, and Wilson Harris's overwhelming Guyana jungle, all differ from European territory; these new landscapes impose original perspectives. Like Harris, Atwood's poems often look inward to the creative process.

26 MARSHALL, TOM. "Five Poets from Five Countries." *Ontario Review*, no. 2 (Spring-Summer), pp. 86-88.

Praises and defends *You Are Happy*'s affirmations, in a review of three Canadians, two Americans, two women, and three men. Contrary to the usual bleak and morbid, *Power Politics*-revisited Toronto reviews, *You Are Happy* affirms; Atwood is facing our most difficult facts, and "putting the case for joy so minimally and so well." The first section is warmer than any previous icy (if accurate) analyses; perhaps *Surfacing* and *The Journals of Susanna Moodie* foreshadowed these positive, earthier poems, like "Spring Poem." The predatory animals and the "Circe/Mud Poems" are marvelously imaginative. The final poems show a man and woman moving into a new, joyous relationship. This book is not only a turning point, but also a technical advance on *Power Politics*; these new poems are more autonomous, and more varied in form. Excerpted 1978.11.

27 MATSON, MARSHALL. "Seize the Day and the Axe." *Books in Canada* 4, no. 2 (February):24.

Celebrates *You Are Happy*'s new love poems, which move from the first poem's *Power Politics*-like cinematic violence to a love regained, freed from mythic and cinematic repetition. The first section, where love is lost, takes the only recourse, of finding beauty in pain. The second section's animals express a bodily horror, and prepare for the third section's Circe, who is earth mother, virgin, and dangerous fortuneteller. The last section affirms the present and praises the body; its "climactic image of present love," the man dancing in the kitchen [in "There Is Only One of Everything"], was glimpsed in the 1966 ["A Sybil"]. What is new is the more human sexual conflict; and the varying forms, from aphorism to prose poem to the lingering love of the Keatsian "Late August."

28 MILLER, HUGH. "Surfacing to No Purpose: Margaret Atwood's Apparent Survival." *Antigonish Review*, no. 24 (Winter), pp. 59-61.

Dislikes being puzzled by references to the occult, as with *Surfacing*'s references to Indian gods' powers and to the "'dead thing'" the heroine finds underwater. The latter could be her father, or his gods; but she's nearly insane, with American-baiting paranoia and with guilt over her abortion. If these are her *Survival* conditions, then we have to accept them, but uneasily.

29 MINER, VALERIE. "Atwood in Metamorphosis: An Authentic Canadian Fairy Tale." In *Her Own Woman: Profiles of Ten Canadian Women*. Edited by Myrna Kostash, et al. Toronto: Macmillan, pp. 173-94. Reprint. Halifax, N.S.: Goodread Biographies, 1984.

A spring 1974 collage-profile of the protean Atwood's self-images: the elusive writer, pre-Raphaelite princess, farm woman, hippie, scholar, fox-woman, and "'role model'" for feminists. Recounts anecdotes of Atwood's farming and writing life with Graeme Gibson; her Quebec North Woods childhood; her Maritime family; and her University of Toronto education. Quotes Atwood on becoming a writer; sexual relationships; elements of and reactions to *The Edible Woman*, *Surfacing*, *Power Politics*, et al., and particularly on biography, feminism, and madness. Abridged: 1975.30 (below).

30 ____. "The Many Facets of Margaret Atwood." *Chatelaine* 48, no. 6 (June):33, 66, 68, 71.

Abridged text of 1975.29 (above).

31 MITCHAM, ALLISON. "Northern Utopia." *Canadian Literature*, no. 63 (Winter), pp. 35-39 passim.

Places *Surfacing* in a tradition of contemporary novels from French and English Canada, where an idealized, pure yet terrible North offers the individual an escape from the mechanistic and false

Utopia of southern civilization–of Southern Ontario, of the United States, of Western man. Atwood, like Gabrielle Roy and Henry Kreisel, only fleetingly glimpses the ideal North; her *Surfacing*'s hung heron represents the North's pure innocence, sacrificed to the South's insensitive lust. We should learn from our North, which is far wilder than Thoreau's purifying wilderness, before we destroy it.

32 MUSGRAVE, SUSAN. "Atwood." *Open Letter*, 3d ser., no. 2 (Spring), pp. 103-5.
   Reprint of 1974.28.

33 NORRIS, KEN. "Survival in the Writings of Margaret Atwood." *Cross Country*, no. 1 (Winter), pp. 19-29.
   Celebrates, after early dislike, Atwood's work: had, at first, mixed experience with *The Edible Woman*, and had rejected the Ice Mother anti-romanticism of her poetry; but *Surfacing*'s "total depth of feeling" transforms our consciousness, and pioneers a new Canadian territory. The *Survival* theme is central to Canadian literature, and Atwood's work; she aims for survival–physical, emotional, or psychological–and respect for life. The earlier poetry works through the pioneer's perspective, and shows relationships as struggles. "*Power Politics* cuts to the core of it all"; love is seen as violence; the failed relationship must be survived. *You Are Happy* moves from bleakness to beauty, beyond individual survival to commingled feeling. Its "Chaos Poem" and "Circe/Mud Poems" show the writer getting in the way of the woman; in the last section Atwood succeeds as woman and writer, beautifully.

34 OUGHTON, JOHN. "The Encircled Self Game." *Open Letter*, 3d ser., no. 2 (Spring), pp. 105-6.
   Criticizes Atwood's "glass cage of form" in *You Are Happy*: she sees like a visual artist, but like a modern hunter "stalks and displays words, instead of returning their primal energy like a cave-painter." This book continues, in *Power Politics*'s hostile country, her "obsession with place in space." Her formal, arranging and defending style "takes words as tools, rather than friends and teachers like bp Nichol's *Martyrology* saints." The final poems could be moving toward a more lyric sensibility, like Margaret Avison's. One can't deny the force of many metaphors, and the uncharacteristic sensuality of a few poems, like "Late August," but her style remains narrow and controlled. And,

1975

as Geddes 1970.17 said, her line lengths seem arbitrary; they are not mastered like Avison's.

35 PASTAN, LINDA. Review of *You Are Happy*. *Library Journal* 100, no. 4 (15 February):396.
     Finds a predatory and blessing vision in a fierce and intense book. Atwood blends hot metaphor and cold diction; her style could be called "'a dogma of teeth.'" Finds the transformation and Circe poems, and the duality of vision, particularly interesting.

36 REID, JOANNE. "Margaret Atwood: Our Lady of Letters." *Canadian Review* 2, no. 3 (September-October):35, 37-38.
     Interviews Atwood during a poetry reading tour: finds her forceful yet almost fragile; talks with her about *The Edible Woman*; early career choices; Canadian literature's regionalism; reading poetry; and becoming a poet and a novelist.

37 REID, JOHN L. "Margaret Atwood: Amazing Inner Calm." *South End* (Wayne State University), 30 April, pp. 1, 6.
     Interviews, during Detroit reading[s], an Atwood secure in her own identity as a person and writer, and not a "spokesman" for feminism or for Canadian nationalism.

38 Review of *You Are Happy*. *Choice* 12, no. 4 (June):528.
     Briefly recommends *You Are Happy*. After *Power Politics*'s more diffuse images, *You Are Happy* returns to starker images and grotesque analogy. These more richly textured poems "reveal Atwood's surreal projections and introjections of self" in dislocated personae, mirror metaphors, and Circean fantasies. The detached, amused artist-speaker plays verbal games and questions reality, as in ["Tricks with Mirrors"].

39 RILEY, CAROLYN, ed. *Contemporary Literary Criticism*. Vol. 3. Detroit: Gale Research Co., pp. 19-21.
     Excerpted from: Jonas 1971.11; Wimsatt 1973.104; Gleicher 1973.28; Pritchard 1973.73; Piercy 1973.72.

40 ____, ed. *Contemporary Literary Criticism*. Vol. 4. Detroit: Gale Research Co., pp. 24-28.

Excerpted from: Stevens 1971.18; Delany 1973.20; Weeks 1973.100; Onley 1974.33; [Gary] Ross 1974.39; Rogers 1974.38.

41 ROSS, ALEXANDER. "A Simple Plea for Respect." *Quill and Quire* 41, no. 3 (March):2.

Explains, in a letter to the editor concerning Clery 1975.6, Atwood's letter of agreement for Conlon's 1975.8 interview. Atwood's first two demands, for the right to check facts and quotes, did not bother this *Toronto Life* editor; what he could not accept was her demand for the right to delete third-party references. So he proposed the right to consult on those, and Atwood accepted. Though the editor does not feel that he or Conlon "'signed away our independence and integrity,'" he is glad Clery raised the question, and thinks that next time he'd not do an Atwood profile, because anyone so cautious probably won't reveal much.

42 SAVAGE, DAVID. "Not Survival but Responsibility." *Dalhousie Review* 55, no. 2 (Summer):272-79.

Atwood's *Survival* thesis applies to humans and literature generally: what distinguishes Canadian literature, and life, is the abundance of people responsible for themselves and their neighbors, at home and abroad. As Atwood's fine "Further Arrivals" states, Canadians have, in a vast and monstrous nature, a "'neighbor mentality,'" not Frye's "'garrison mentality.'" Argues for responsibility in ten Canadian authors: our strongly Puritan and Presbyterian heritage inspires Sinclair Ross's and Ernest Buckler's truly Canadian, not paralyzed, artists. Sheila Watson and Margaret Laurence depict unselfish responsibility as well as death. Atwood's young, atomic-era generation understandably emphasizes survival, but much of our literature, and character, emphasize our older heritage.

43 SCOTT, ANDREW. "The Poet as Sorceress." *Essays on Canadian Writing*, no. 3 (Fall), pp. 60-62.

Analyzes *You Are Happy*'s mythopoeic structure and poetic form: its four sections, unusual for Atwood, follow Frye's four-part quest. Throughout, inarticulateness is connected to repression. As in *The Journals of Susanna Moodie*, the land is metaphorically a foreign language. "The theme[s] of language as oracle," and of the poet tending, correcting, and protecting language, are becoming more

1975

important for Atwood. The second section's vengeful animals are glib, didactic, and overextended. The bitingly satiric "Circe/Mud" section, which certainly fits Frye's *sparagmos*, and re-uses *Power Politics*'s armoured male, is the book's highpoint. The last lyrics, which include the brilliant, witty "Is/Not" and the climactically sensual "Late August," seem artificially arranged, to create a less bleak vision that may not be heartfelt. The major improvement in style is the subtle repetition and parallel syntax of many poems; the prose poems here, and *Surfacing*'s poetry, suggest that Atwood may be moving toward new syntheses of form.

44 SORFLEET, JOHN ROBERT. Review of *Survival. Journal of Modern Literature* 4, no. 5:917-19.

Rejects *Survival* as too negative and erroneous. First, the survival theme goes back at least to the *Odyssey*. Second, Atwood totally omits many prominent writers, such as Robertson Davies; almost totally neglects many others, such as Raymond Knister; and misinterprets others, such as Fred Bodsworth. She excludes humour, and protest and dissent literature, which would challenge her thesis. She "equates survival with failure": heroic struggle, which is ethical, better identifies most Canadian literature. Atwood's theory, at best partially accurate, is "even more dangerous than total falsity." But it is useful as a guide to her fiction.

45 STEIN, KAREN F. "Reflections in a Jagged Mirror: Some Metaphors of Madness." *Aphra* 6, no. 2 (Spring):2-11.

Delineates a new genre of women writers' fiction, whose heroines use "'madness'" as Laingian self-exploration and discovery; often these writers use mirrors as recurring symbols of self-image and self. Focusses especially on *Surfacing*, Sylvia Plath's *The Bell Jar*, and Doris Lessing's *The Four-Gated City*. Atwood's active heroine, who rejects the corrupt and ugly surfaces by which the other humans live, returns from her quest with moral knowledge and strength, symbolized by her turning of the mirror. In contrast, Plath's heroine, who threw the mirror away, fails.

46 STEVENSON, ANNE. "Is the Emperor of Ice Cream Wearing Clothes?" *New Review* (London) 2, no. 17 (August):43-46.

Asks, in an eight-poet essay, why is the new, so prolific American poetry so depressing? American women poets follow Sylvia Plath and the women's movement to distort experience. The Canadian Atwood's "aggressive, feminist muse seeks desperately for some link with primitivism" in *The Animals in That Country*. At her best ["They are hostile nations," *Power Politics*], Atwood captures America's ecological pathos. Like Plath, her tone is shrill outrage, and her personality absorbs contemporary guilts – unforgivingly, but honestly – but she lacks Plath's formal techniques. Like Plath and Anne Sexton, she has perfected figurative language for crash effects, as in "The Revenant"; her "poems are not windows, but distorting mirrors."

47 SWAN, SUSAN. "Margaret Atwood: The Woman as a Poet." *Communiqué*, no. 8 (May), pp. 9-11, 45-46 (English text); pp. 9-11, 39 (French text).

Interviews Atwood, who contrasts the popular and critical attitudes to the reality of being a woman poet: the castrating, freak, and suicidal, or the white-cloaked, or the pre-Raphaelite images versus the real image, which "should be somebody sitting in a messy office typing at a typewriter." Atwood cites [I[an] D[rummond] 1974.6], Emily Dickinson, the Brontë sisters, Anne Sexton, Sylvia Plath, Graeme Gibson, Betty Friedan, and Marian Engel; and contrasts male cultural groupings with female isolation, her own parents' assumptions with pre-feminist peer pressure, and male poets' hostility to male or female success, with men's capabilities.

48 van VARSEVELD, GAIL. "Talking with Atwood." *Room of One's Own* 1, no. 2 (Summer):66-70.

Interviews Atwood in Vancouver in March; Atwood comments on the writer's responsibility to create literature, not propaganda; three "gynaecological novel[s]" by Marian Engel, Audrey Thomas, and Jean Haggerty; transforming old myths into female mythology; a Women and Religion conference's *Surfacing* paper; labyrinths; women's versus men's images, publications, and clubs; her own York University class's study of sex discrimination in book reviews.

49 VENDLER, HELEN. "A Quarter of Poetry." *New York Times Book Review*, 6 April, pp. 33-34.

1975

Admires Atwood's poems as neat, silent guided missiles, in a sixteen-poet review from one quarter of the year. Though, as in the Circe series, Atwood sees "life as mostly wounds given and received," and man-woman relations "as spiky and lethal," like *Power Politics*, still *You Are Happy* does attempt a new detachment and humanity. Every page has virtues; Circe's "Siren Song" is beautifully comic. The animal transformations have good lines, but seem more fancy than imagination. Nonetheless, Atwood "always repays rereading." Excerpted: 1978.11.

50 WALKER, CHERYL. "Looking Back, Looking Forward." *Nation* 221, no. 7 (13 September):216-17.
Appreciates *You Are Happy* in a three-poet review; compares the demonic flare of "Eating Fire" to Robert Penn Warren's "Remarks of Soul to Body." Her new archetypal book moves, like *Surfacing*, beyond *Power Politics*'s clipped and ironic diction, into radiance, warmth, wit, and scope. Her Circe is a wise woman and healer; the Circe sequence presents feminist insights freshly, but they're not narrowly-defined women's movement politics. Women poets are "on the *qui vive* now," displacing the old guilt theme; Atwood's "Last year I abstained" shows us how.

51 WOOD, SUSAN. "Poems by Canadian Margaret Atwood Offer Vision of World in Which One Must Be Neither Victim nor Victor." *Houston Chronicle*, 26 January, Zest sec., p. 11. Newsbank 1975, 1:C10.
Praises *You Are Happy*'s expanded vision, which goes beyond the victor/victim roles of *Power Politics*. Atwood is part of the women's movement, and a humanist, with holistic, mortal concerns. In these compressed and daring poems, the speaker and her man journey through amazing metamorphoses towards acceptance and connection.

52 WOODCOCK, GEORGE. "Margaret Atwood: Poet as Novelist." In *The Canadian Novel in the Twentieth Century: Essays from Canadian Literature*. New Canadian Library, no. 115. Toronto: McClelland & Stewart, pp. 312-27.
Reprints as one essay his 1972.40 acclaim for Atwood's poetry, especially *Power Politics*, and *The Edible Woman*, and his 1973.107 considered appreciation of *Survival* and *Surfacing*. Omits only 1973.107 circumstantial explanation. Reprinted: as Part I of 1980.148; 1988.56.

1976

1 AMIEL, BARBARA. "Once More the Poor WASP Heroine, Sufferer in Search of a Reason." *Maclean's* 89, no. 15 (6 September):68.

Complains that, although Atwood in *Lady Oracle* tackles the agonies of her Anglo-Canadian intellectuals with self-deprecating humour and polished style, she can't transcend that "peanut-butter-and-jelly milieu." Though *Lady Oracle* works best as total realism, and is marvelously funny, still, the faces beneath her characters' symbolic masks are no more interesting than are our suffering WASP intellectuals.

2 ATWOOD, MARGARET. "A Reply." *Signs* 2, no. 2 (Winter):340-41.

Comments on Christ 1976.13 and Plaskow 1976.74: a comparison of *Surfacing*'s Canadian versus American reviews suggests that the domination of Canada may supply a "'social quest'" dimension. Novels are not treatises; they tell stories. The writer's primary duty is to the story being made, not to society. Abortion is a structural element in *Surfacing*'s story where, given person X, Y results.

3 [BANNON, BARBARA A.]. Review of *Lady Oracle*. *Publishers Weekly* 210, no. 3 (19 July):129.

Recommends *Lady Oracle* highly, as a very salable, very funny book, and an achingly honest portrayal, by one of Canada's most exciting young talents. "*Literary Guild Alternate, first serial rights to Redbook*" [italics sic].

4 BENITEZ, ROSALYN. "Journey toward Repair of the World: Two Novels on Feminine Phenomena." *Social Work* 21, no. 6 (November):535-36.

Compares the themes of *Surfacing* and Sheila Ballantyne's *Norma Jean the Termite Queen*; these two novels' heroines search, in wilderness isolation or in the over-filled suburban wilderness of social and familial demands, for their own exiled, alienated selves. Their female companions and their families are no help; their men need, but resist offering, emotional support. The old dependent-woman order is gone; the new is not yet here. Yet it is only if the exiled feminine of the Jewish cabala and of Jung's *anima* can be reclaimed and reunited to the exiled masculine, that the alienated world can be repaired. The women's movement is one important step; professional practitioners should offer women our sensitive support.

5 BETTS, DORIS. "An Escape Artist." *Bookletter* (New York) 3, no. 2 (13 September):12.

Gives *Lady Oracle* a mixed review: like many poets who write fiction, Atwood structures her novels like very large poems – not by character development and plot, but by extended simile and expanding metaphors. *Lady Oracle*'s first flashbacks, which include the cruel, funny girlhood memories, are the best part; after Joan loses weight and flies to London the novel seems abruptly though cleverly to mock itself. The poetic structure causes problems in the second half: metaphors elongate; events become coat hangers for interpretations; and almost all the characters except Joan, her mother, and her aunt, become cameos of few traits and heavy thematic values. As in other gifted women's novels, the men are ones "you wouldn't let your beagle sleep with." The end is unresolved, like poems, like life. Though *Lady Oracle*'s unbalanced mix of serious and fluff entertains and puzzles, at least the heroine is a healthier image of the female writer than Sylvia Plath.

6 BISHOP, DOROTHY. "Margaret Atwood: Poetic Prodigy." *Ottawa Journal*, 22 May, p. 40.

Welcomes the stimulating *Selected Poems*, which again attests to Atwood's accelerated talent and true acclaim. "*Selected Poems* at age 36! . . . Leave Atwood aside as critic but take her as poet" in this fine revealing survey. All of *The Journals of Susanna Moodie*, which is her "most constantly stimulating poetry," is reprinted here, and other work is well represented. Her ironic, "'Beyond truth, / tenacity'" poetry lacks warm humor, and may explain *Survival*, which is provoking and silly. *The Journals*'s more seminal opening lines show the "'everything'" she knows is unique.

7 BJERRING, NANCY E. "The Problem of Language in Margaret Atwood's *Surfacing*." *Queen's Quarterly* 83, no. 4 (Winter):597-612.

If "'language'" includes all meaningful human interactions, verbal and non-verbal, then *Surfacing* has four loosely defined language groups. First, there is the dominant, alienating "'American'" "'social chatter'" of Western social man, which cherishes death-dealing powers over nature, art, and other human beings; the most debased and degrading David, the victimized Anna, and the technological brother speak this language. Second, there is the scientific, empirical/objective language of the father, which imposes his rational order on nature. Third, there is silence, the "'language'" of the mother and Joe, who are close to nature and to animals. Finally, there is the wordless, primitive "'meta-language'" of nature, true art, and meaning, which the narrator rediscovers in memory and vision. (French could be *Surfacing*'s fifth language.) Certain poems, particularly "Progressive insanities of a pioneer" and *The Journals of Susanna Moodie*, also express these languages.

8 BOBAK, E.L. Review of *Selected Poems*. *Dalhousie Review* 56, no. 2 (Summer):404-6.

Welcomes *Selected Poems* warmly. Atwood, who is Oxford University Press's best-selling poet, captures contemporary man's secular, urban, inward-looking attitudes. Her central metaphor, the underground, can be traced from *The Circle Game* poems on. *Power Politics* has been seen, narrowly, as women's movement poetry, but its final ironies are applied to her. Atwood's finest work includes "Journal I" and the dream poems of "Journal II," and the final love poems of *You Are Happy*. But the non-human narrators of "Songs of the Transformed" are awkward.

9 BONNELL, KIMBERLY. "Past Secrets." *Chicago Sun Times*, 10 October, Show sec., p. 8.

Enjoys *Lady Oracle*: "Three narratives – past, present and fiction-within-fiction – define the layers and selves of Joan Delacourt Foster in Margaret Atwood's funny, touching, involving, crashingly crazy but nonetheless realistic novel. . . . It is an expansive book, in which reflective moments and gothic passages fasten together countless details and events and in which a deliberately flat style compresses profundities and absurdities. The result is both troubling and immensely enjoyable."

10 BROPHY, BRIGID. "A Contrary Critic Takes a Crack at *Lady Oracle*." *Globe and Mail*, 9 October, p. 33.

Attacks *Lady Oracle* for slapdash writing, empty characters and relationships, and an anecdotal plot that does not justify the heroine's John Stonehouse fake drowning. The blackmailable wealth of the writer heroine, from just one book of poems, "is certainly hard for a European to swallow." Is Canada really so cushy for writers? The romance parody and the haunting are shamefully inept. This is fat, monotonous, narcissistic, talentless writing.

1976

11 CADY, BARBARA. "Too Much Success Causes Her Demise." *Los Angeles Times*, 5 December, Books sec., p. 14.

Compares *Lady Oracle* to Philip Roth's more appealing [*Portnoy's Complaint*]. While Roth thrilled and informed female as well as male readers, *Lady Oracle* is a "'woman's book.'" Though Joan Foster's opening secret plots are interesting enough, her youthful reminiscences will lose male readers. Joan's erotic dreams and sexual flowering are not exciting like Portnoy's were. Why is the slapdash drowning of the conclusion necessary? Despite Atwood's charm and wit, the reviewer "yearn[s] for more of the Gothic romance fragments sprinkled inexplicably throughout the narrative."

12 CARSON, CATHERINE. "Atwood's Latest Is a Continuous Chuckle." *Edmonton Journal*, 25 October, p. 6.

The reviewer "chuckled quietly all the way through" the wildly improbable, extremely funny *Lady Oracle*, which is "great escape literature" with tremendous substance. The mother-daughter love-hate relationship is a classic that daughters of all ages will understand. Atwood skillfully switches from reality to Gothic fantasy. "Atwood's female characterizations are much stronger than her males," who are shadowy. The end is pure Joan – but can Joan really change?

13 CHRIST, CAROL P. "Margaret Atwood: The Surfacing of Women's Spiritual Quest and Vision." *Signs* 2, no. 2 (Winter):316-30.

Defines in *Surfacing* a female spiritual quest and vision, rooted in women's experience. As a women's social quest, which would move from alienation to social integration, *Surfacing* is incompletely empowering, protofeminist, as Piercy 1973.72 maintained; but spiritual quests tell women's fundamental, empowering religious stories. Beginning with passive victimhood, *Surfacing*'s protagonist identifies with the wilderness and Canada, with innocent nature versus American technology. Facing the truth of her abortion and her own guilt, guided by her childhood pictures, she finds redemption. Her own body, sexual and pregnant, incarnates the great cosmic powers of life and death; she becomes a place of life's transformative energy. Her spiritual "'awakening' or 'surfacing'" from a male-defined world, and her movement from passive victimhood to power, are two aspects of the female quest. Her Canadian Indian visions come, in the urbanized West, more readily to women than to men. Women identify more closely with nature and with their own bodies' natural experiences; and women may more readily experience a nonpersonal identification.

Surfacing, and Annis Pratt's 1972 "Women and Nature," confirm the prevalence of women's nature mysticism. *Surfacing* is not anti-killing, nor is it anti-abortion; but these should be done from need, and with worship. Though the identification of woman with her body and with nature has been oppressive, these identifications can be empowering. See Atwood 1976.2, Plaskow 1976.74, and Gray 1977.28. Revised: 1980.17.

14 CLARKSON, STEPHEN. "Marriage Play." *Canadian Forum* 56 (December-January):58.
    Not a review of *Selected Poems*, but an assemblage of lines from various poems, assigned to a "We," "He," and "She," in three scenes called "Beginning," "Middle," and "End."

15 CLAY, CAROLYN. "Going Nuts up North: Margaret Atwood's Canadian Crazies." *Boston Phoenix*, 7 December, Book suppl., pp. 5, 22.
    A review of *Lady Oracle* that reads Atwood's three novels as thematically one, on the fragmented personality: each heroine is in conflict with her body; each seems outwardly normal, if somewhat spaced-out; each mentally pursues a self beyond reason; each finally panics and bolts. The tense, ironic *Surfacing*, which is the best and least elaborate, "is a diary of psychosis." The slight but amusing *The Edible Woman*, which is Atwood's most conventionally feminist novel, and the ornate and outrageously comic *Lady Oracle*, which is the most elaborate, "are [both] burlesques of the same breakdown." Though Americans will attribute these fragmentations to femininity, *Survival* and the "Afterword" to *The Journals of Susanna Moodie* name the Canadian national disease of paranoia, which all three heroines have. When our clean water runs out, "Canada will be there, as helpless as a woman in the stirrups or a dark alley."

16 COLOMBO, JOHN ROBERT. "There Is a Delight in Exposing Little Secrets." *Globe and Mail*, 24 April, p. 39.
    A mixed review of *Selected Poems* that describes Atwood's career as poet, novelist, and critic. Her weakest work, *Survival*, paradoxically made her a spokesperson for cultural nationalism and the women's movement. As a poet, she has gone from conducting children's games to being "a veritable Circe." There is an unselected poem about watching films that is "pure Atwood," undercutting fantasy, but not idealizing reality. As Woodcock said, her work inclines "'to an almost

Buddhist objectivity,'" but not to impersonality, for it exposes the little secrets of our lives. Though her imagery can be clinical and her self-justifications tiresome, her more objective dramatic monologues are superb, as in "Siren Song," the animal "Songs of the Transformed," and *The Journals of Susanna Moodie*.

17 DAVEY, FRANK. "Surviving the Paraphrase." *Canadian Literature*, no. 70 (Autumn), pp. 5-13 passim.

Affirms, in a formalist attack on the dominant, antievaluative thematic criticism of Frye, Jones, Atwood, and Moss, his 1973.17 rejection of *Survival*. Charges that *Survival*, like the others, ignores literary history; is an attempt at "'culture-fixing'"; denigrates by failing to assume, not argue, the existence of a national identity and literature; and makes inferior writers seem more important than superior ones. Lists *Surfacing* with polemic novels. Mentions *Survival*'s suggestion of closed space in Southern Ontario literature, and a closing space in Prairie literature, as worth investigation. Reprinted: 1983.31.

18 DAWE, ALAN. "Atwood Augury." *Vancouver Sun*, 3 September, p. A33.

Candidly recommends *Lady Oracle* "as absorbing entertainment, a somewhat old-fashioned novel complete with a first-person-female narrator, flashbacks, and a plot that is not resolved until the final page." Unlike some modern writers, Atwood handles plots with considerable care; *Lady Oracle* has two plots in that its central character has two lives. The dominant theme "is the fragility of our identities." Atwood suggests that having double lives, as several characters do, can help sensitive people to survive. Atwood's shrewd observations, style, and wit are also virtues.

19 DOUGLAS, CHARLES. "Poetry: Presence and Presentation." *Lakehead University Review* 7, no. 2 / 8, no. 1-2 [1976]:77-80.

Appreciates *You Are Happy*, in a four-poet review; in spite of its frequent bitterness, the book celebrates Atwood's renewed presence and voice. Though it begins with more broken love affairs, like the tedious, eternal evasions of *Power Politics*, the title poem half-states the underlying theme, of evolving an "identity *beyond* numbness." The keystone "Gothic Letter on a Hot Night" looks both ways, from past disillusion to coming transformations. The predatory animals, with their sharp, entertaining irony, are *Survival* victims newly transformed. The book's zenith, the "Circe/Mud Poems," shows her as both enchantress and jilted. But the fourth section is anticlimactic and too tentative, except for one or two poems ["There Is Only One of Everything"] where the convalescent voice communicates real strength and happiness.

20 DUFFY, DENNIS. "Read It for Its Gracefulness, for Its Good Story, for Its Help in Your Fantasy Life." *Globe and Mail*, 4 September, p. 32.

Recommends highly *Lady Oracle*'s realism, humour, irony, story, and its Canadian consciousness, which Atwood's earlier novels and *Survival* have both expressed and shaped. Joan's split personality and her dabbling in the occult reveal features of our collective fantasy life. Atwood's women, animals, hair, blood, death-and-rebirth by drowning are all part of our literary ambience now. *Lady Oracle*'s fame should not rest only on its satire of Toronto literati. Reprinted: 1976.21 (below).

21 ____. Review of *Lady Oracle*. *Canadian Reader* 17, no. 9 (September):2-4.

Reprint of 1976.20 (above).

22 ELMER, CATHLEEN BURNS. "Takeout to Makeout." *Sunday Herald Advertiser* (Boston), 17 October, sec. 5, p. A15.

Enjoys *Lady Oracle* as a "spontaneous, fluent, outrageously inventive" stylistic tour de force; enjoys also its heroine's compelling emotions and shaky chutzpah; but faults its "doctrinaire avoidance of any values beyond" the present.

23 ENGEL, MARIAN. "She Who Laughs Last. . . ." *Tamarack Review*, no. 69 (Summer), pp. 94-96.

Champions Atwood as social comedian, and *Lady Oracle* as much more than a *roman à clef* and an accurate, even kindly, satire of Toronto literati. Atwood's prose, marvelous humour, and social criticism have been underestimated, while critics, misled by her poetry, praised image or device. Her prose skips and taunts under its flat, deadpan surfaces; she brings grey, staid Toronto to life.

24 FEE, MARGERY, and CAWKER, RUTH. *Canadian Fiction: An Annotated Bibliography*. Toronto: Peter Martin Associates, pp. 16-17.

Briefly describes *The Edible Woman* as a prophetically humorous pre-women's liberation novel about consumers and cannibalism; and *Surfacing* as partly an illustration of *Survival*'s thesis, where a rather

1976

cold woman slowly and painfully comes to terms with not being a victim.

25 FLETCHER, PEGGY. Review of *Selected Poems*. *Canadian Author and Bookman* 52, no. 1 (Fall):26.
Finds a strong, disturbing book, which fans will welcome. Atwood's collected poetry gains intensity and strength; her nightmarish atmosphere, disorientation, and despair are not ordinary. Love is seen as damaging, the machine age as devastating. The encroaching fear stops only in *The Journals of Susanna Moodie*.

26 FRENCH, WILLIAM. "The Women in Our Literary Life." *Canadian Author and Bookman* 51, no. 3 (Spring):3, 5.
Reprint of 1975.14.

27 FRYE, NORTHROP. "Conclusion." In *Literary History of Canada: Canadian Literature in English*. Edited by Carl Klinck. Vol. 3. 2d ed. Toronto and Buffalo: University of Toronto Press, p. 324.
Agrees with Mr. [Desmond?] Pacey that Atwood's very influential *Survival* is "a most perceptive essay on an aspect of the Canadian sensibility." Ross 1973.80 points out some limits; *Survival* clearly was not meant to be comprehensive. But it does not simply say that Canadians are losers. What Atwood means by the important Canadian theme of survival is more clear in her extraordinary *Surfacing*; "survival implies living through a series of crises, . . . each one to be met on its own terms." Reprinted: 1982.60.

28 FULFORD, ROBERT. "Atwood's Poems Show Strength and Anger." *Toronto Star*, 24 April, p. H5.
Acclaims *Selected Poems* as a seamless whole, and champions *Power Politics*. Atwood's style conceals a quiet fuse; her mask implies limitless possibilities and anger, which strengthen her poetry. From 1972 on, so much romantic garbage has been written about her, that it's good to see her poetry here as itself, as acute and confident poetry, not as feminist or nationalist abstractions. The reviewer now sees "Speeches for Dr. Frankenstein" as an artist's ambivalence toward creation; and predicts that *Power Politics* will now be seen as honest, not cruel – it's her best book, in any form.

29 F[ULFORD], R[OBERT]. "Derring-do: Bombing the Peace Bridge over Troubled Waters and Other Feats of Strength, Daring, and Desperate Doubt." *Saturday Night* 91, no. 8 (November):46.

Observes a trend in *Lady Oracle*'s satiric depiction of Canadian nationalist intellectuals as fools and clowns, and in Dennis Lee's *Ladoo* poetry, which depicts the same tiresome, greedy, "'performing rebels.'" Lee's nationalist Anansi, which means spider god, is *Lady Oracle*'s Black Widow Press. Why are Atwood and Lee repudiating their own earlier cultural nationalism? Perhaps it's because, as *Lady Oracle* says, the masses have gotten involved; which means it's time for the poets to capture some new trend.

30 _____. "Thrills." *Saturday Night* 91, no. 8 (November):38.

Briefly suggests, while discussing Canadian *romans à clef*, that Doug Fetherling could be *Lady Oracle*'s Royal Porcupine. See 1977.4.

31 GALLOWAY, PRISCILLA. Review of *Lady Oracle*. *Canadian Book Review Annual*:136-37.

Praises highly Atwood's third major novel, which speaks so directly to women's lives that men may find it too uncomfortable. Joan's several identities and creative genres, and her metamorphosis from fat to thin, mingle fantasy and realism. The end, where Joan accepts her identities and prepares to rescue her friends, is prosaic, but so is reality. Tension, structure, reversals are superbly handled. But the *Redbook* condensation seemed glib and superficial.

*32 _____. Review of *Selected Poems*. *Indirections* 2, no. 1 (Fall):54-55.

Atwood's always unexpected, tremendously powerful poetry makes the reader stretch to encompass her vision, to see the familiar as strange, and the external from within. "Atwood is Tiresias, the seer; Cassandra, crier of doom; Moodie outcast from England, outcast even from the forest" where she might have finally learned. Atwood's vision is bleak, and filled with pain. Yet there is occasionally a "manic sense of fun," as in the mud woman of the "Circe/Mud Poems." Young Canadians in grade 12 and 13 enrichment classes, and in every Canadian university, should be studying at least some of Atwood's selected poetry. Her work belongs to our place and time, and also to literature, which is "built upon literature," as Northrop Frye maintains.

33 GAREBIAN, KEITH. "*Oracle*: The Lady Proves Her Virtuosity." *Gazette* (Montreal), 4 September, p. 42.

Discusses *Lady Oracle* as "a skilful anti-Gothic," a comic quest-romance whose harried heroine flees from bizarre experiences that are very probably projections, and from real dangers. Both the costume Gothics' maze, and the Gothic romance's "substitution of terror for love," extend to Joan's life. Though the excess is implicitly Gothic, the "straight Gothic is lightened and perverted into comedy. . . . The special achievement of this book is the resonant satire of anti-Gothic," which is flawed by Atwood's strong refracting sensibility–she doesn't permit the characters of her three novels to develop independently–Joan, like earlier figures, has to feel pressures of survival. Still, *Lady Oracle* has rich ambiguity and virtuoso technique.

34 ____. "*Surfacing*: Apocalyptic Ghost Story." *Mosaic* 9, no. 3 (Spring):1-9.

Finds mixed literary modes; ghosts projected from the heroine's mind; an impassioned, subjective myth; and a flawed world of victims. The heroine is neurotic, visionary, voyeuristic, and alienated from others. Realism and satire threaten to overwhelm the ghost story, as does the political or moral didacticism. The heroine's credibility borders on insanity; her theology is primitive. Her retreat into mythopoeia is not, as Laurence 1973.47 suggested, a breakthrough, but a breakdown. Although these mixed modes can make *Surfacing* seem a coldly calculated *roman à thèse*, still, they do yield mystery, romance, the marvelous, and a "'queer ghoulish'" pathos.

35 GEDDES, GARY. "Now You See It . . . Now You Don't: An Appreciation of Atwood and MacEwen, Two Grand Illusionists." *Books in Canada* 5, no. 7 (July):4-6.

Champions Atwood's magic, poetic craft, citing Atwood's 1973 ["Reaney Collected," reprinted in *Second Words*]. Like MacEwen and Reaney, Atwood is a fantasist, not a realist. Her obvious themes–women's liberation, sexual politics, Canadian identity–have been overpublicized; her craft, discussed in her more specific criticism [not *Survival*], has been neglected. As the Levenson [1972.20] interview suggests, Atwood sees poetry as magic, and as device and artifact, not as self-expression or confession. Because she's not a bleeding-heart romantic, she's been called a cold poet. *Selected Poems* reveals her innovative techniques: surreal images, matter-of-fact tone, disappearing narrator, shifts in points of view and in views espoused. Magic is in craft, sincerity in technique: Atwood takes the risks that make her poems work.

36 GERSON, CAROLE. "Margaret Atwood and Quebec: A Footnote on *Surfacing*." *Studies in Canadian Literature* 1, no. 1 (Winter):115-19.

Places *Surfacing*'s essential Quebec elements in a romantic, gothic, subliminal nineteenth- and twentieth-century tradition of literature by English Canadians about French Canada, which they see as "'us' and 'not us,'" "home and not home." *Surfacing*'s heroine contrasts Quebec's unique, authentic religion, folklore, and family ties, with English Canada's cultural lies and fragmented families. Her ignorance of Quebec's spoken language initiates her distrust of false language and thus her plunge into the non-verbal and irrational; in Quebec she recovers her buried life. But Quebec itself is shown as rapidly learning the American language that has infiltrated Anglophone Canada.

37 GERSTENBERGER, DONNA. "Conceptions Literary and Otherwise: Women Writers and the Modern Imagination." *Novel* 9, no. 2 (Winter):141-50.

Women writers must, like Genly Ai in Ursula LeGuin's *The Left Hand of Darkness*, somehow describe an inconceivably alien culture. *Surfacing* best confronts, without self-pity or self-blame, the problems that our culture's myth and language pose for women. Atwood's narrator finds herself an alien in the alien world that produced her; she rejects its fragmenting, distorting language. Her images of the closed-off head, and of birth and abortion, recall those of Sylvia Plath and Anaïs Nin. The mythic perilous journey cannot, for modern writers, end in transcendence; or, for feminist writers, in acceptance or control of a world that disenfranchises women. What the narrator of *Surfacing*'s mythic quest asks for is not androgyny, but a wholeness that accommodates humanity, and nature.

38 GIBSON, MARY ELLIS. "A Conversation with Margaret Atwood." *Chicago Review* 27, no. 4 (Spring):105-13.

Interviews Atwood after a reading there: Atwood describes the Canadian literary scene before and after *Survival*; compares Canadian with U.S. and West Indies colonialism, literary publications, studies, and audiences; compares Canadian with U.S. attitudes to animals, nature, and development; and describes her own writing habits as a student and now, on farm near Alliston.

39 GOLD, EDITH. Review of *Lady Oracle*. *Miami Herald*, 14 November, p. E7.

1976

Finds *Lady Oracle*'s many-faced, put-upon heroine thoroughly engaging. Her struggle against her oppressive husband and lovers is as poignant and hilarious as her costume-thriller excerpts. "Who can blame her if she thinks like the Bronte-esque governesses in distress that occupy her spare hours?" Though her escape is as ill-planned as her life, we root for Atwood's likeable lady.

40 GRUMBACH, DORIS. "A Double Life." *Saturday Review* 3, no. 25 (18 September):28-30.

Recommends *Lady Oracle* highly. The opening nightmare vision, of an old man's head, recalls Atwood's impressive *Surfacing*. Heroine Joan-Louisa is a schizophrenic duality whose Gothic romance novels entwine with her own fate. Though the humorous contemporary portraits are very real, the core theme is the life-death-resurrection cycle, of the heroine's first self, and also of the characters appearing and disappearing in her life. Joan's wonderfully funny sexual experiences recall Lisa Alther's otherwise dissimilar *Kinflicks*. Feminism is subtly and indirectly presented. This review may have missed some subtleties of this "wholly readable and engrossing novel."

41 HAECK, PHILIPPE. "La force des femmes." *Devoir* (Montréal), 31 December, p. 12.

Prefers *Selected Poems* in a group review including two volumes of poetry in French. Finds three major themes in *Selected Poems*: tensions between tenderness and struggle, male/female relations, and humour and irony toward men. A French translation would help more women writers see that poetry does not need to be cut off from the real world.

42 HAIDER, VICKY CHEN. Review of *Lady Oracle*. *Fiction International*, nos. 6-7, pp. 150-51.

Welcomes *Lady Oracle* as, finally, an honestly, uproarishly funny novel by a woman: Atwood is a compelling master – even though at times an overuser – of the ridiculous. She makes common, over-used childhood memories unique and touching. *Lady Oracle*'s blend of humor, melodrama, and seriousness works.

43 HEWARD, BURT. "A Mixture of Moods Marks Canada's New Literary Queen." *Citizen* (Ottawa), 21 September, sec. 5, p. 69.

Interviews Atwood after *Lady Oracle*'s publication and her daughter Jess's birth, four months ago: Atwood, who is tough and

112

aware, but softer and less forbidding as a mother, comments on unjust media treatment of Margaret Trudeau and other women celebrities; the intellectual influences of her family and friends; and writing *Lady Oracle*, which Dennis Lee helped edit, and which is neither intellectual nor light entertainment.

44 HINZ, EVELYN J. "Hierogamy Versus Wedlock: Types of Marriage Plots and Their Relationship to Genres of Prose Fiction." *PMLA* 91, no. 5 (October):900-913 passim.

Places *Surfacing*, with Emily Bronte's *Wuthering Heights* and other writers' books, in a proposed genre of "mythic narrative," which is neither a novel nor a dislocated romance; defines *Surfacing*'s union as a hierogamy, or sacred marriage, as of primordial earth and sky. Hierogamous lovers are essentially different, not similar; hierogamy symbolizes a breaking of elemental, not class, barriers. It is a ritual, intended to abolish profane time and to evoke chaos, as when *Surfacing*'s narrator goes "'native.'" Hierogamous union occurs in the open, an *axis mundi*, like the wild Northern Quebec island. Hierogamy seeks cosmic regeneration or rebirth, occasionally symbolized in conception; as in *Surfacing*, the latter fates of mother and child are not important.

45 HOSEK, CHAVIVA. "Powerful Images in Two New Collections." *Quill and Quire* 42, no. 9 (July):36.

Acclaims Atwood's *Selected Poems*, which are not private mythology like Gwendolyn MacEwen's *The Fire-Eaters*. Atwood's lucid surfaces conceal extraordinary suggestiveness; as in "This Is a Photograph of Me," many poems give voices to the unseen, the dead, the absent. Atwood focusses on perception, not as privately privileged, but as issues; *The Journals of Susanna Moodie* thus explores the pioneer's alienation and attempt to claim the land imaginatively. "The Circle Game," *Power Politics*, and "Circe/Mud" sequences all see their lovers in a double perspective, of story and of images.

46 HOULE, ALAIN. "Avec Margaret Atwood, écrivain du 'gros bon sens.'" *Devoir* (Montréal), 18 December, p. 18.

Interview. Atwood discusses her identity as a Canadian and a woman; living and working arrangements in her home; her untheoretical views on writing; and women writers in Quebec.

1976

47 HOWITT, JOHN. "Mermaid's Moodie Depicts Hardships of Pioneer Life." *Halifax Chronicle Herald*, 15 December, p. 27.

Finds the Mermaid Theatre company's production of Donna Smyth's *Susanna Moodie*, which is based on the immigrant Moodie's two books and on Atwood's *The Journals of Susanna Moodie*, "sometimes fascinating, sometimes bogged down with redundant symbolism," especially at the end. [The play, as described by the reviewer, seems to follow Atwood's "Afterword" and a number of specific poems from *The Journals of Susanna Moodie*, more closely than it follows Moodie's books.]

48 HUITT, ISABEL. "*The Edible Woman*, by Margaret Atwood." *English Journal* 65, no. 1 (January):60-61.

This is a good novel to teach in high school. Students like *The Edible Woman*, and identify with the issues it raises: feminism, search for identity, caring for others, responsibility, personal integrity, people's choices and values in life. There is sex, but without explicitly sexual scenes. The sustained eating is an excellent example of metaphor.

49 ICONOCRIT. "The Descent from Olympus: Smith, Frye, and Atwood." *Iconomatrix* 1, no. 2 (January):3-15.

Rejects modern, academic literary criticism, which was fathered by Hippolyte Adolphe Taine, and calls for a return to the nineteenth-century criticism that comprehends and appreciates literature, life, and the common reader. Argues that A.J.M. Smith's so-called cosmopolitanism misunderstands T.S. Eliot and poetry; argues that Northrop Frye's mythopoeic patterns and "'garrison mentality'" have become increasingly prescriptive impositions on Canadian literature. Rejects Atwood's *Survival* as "the most noxious because most popular Frygian travesty," filled with victim positions that sound like sado-masochistic pornography, "gross generalizations and inane simplifications"; deplores thematic criticism, which schmatizes literature into patterns.

50 JACKSON, MARNI. "Atwood As a Satirist Is Too Self-Assured." *Toronto Star*, 28 August, p. H7.

Complains that, although *Lady Oracle*'s piquant satire sounds wonderful, Atwood's careless attitude towards her characters shows; is tempted to blame at least half of the problem on "the occupational hazards of being a Canadian success story."

114

51 JUHASZ, SUZANNE. "Seeking Salvation and Unity." *Library Journal*
101, no. 15 (1 September):1796.

Praises *Lady Oracle*'s truly serious, truly funny themes highly:
heroine-hood, role-playing, identity, which are embedded in the several
literary genres, provoke the fun and fantasy. These common themes
"are our deepest concerns"; this comedy is flawless.

52 KATTAN, NAIM. "Margaret Atwood: Le goût de ressembler à tout le
monde." In *Écrivains des Ameriques*. Vol. 2, *Le Canada anglais*.
Collection contantes. Montreal: Éditions Hurtubise HMH, pp. 105-12.

Expands 1970.24 to include discussion of *Survival* and *Surfacing*.
The Edible Woman is a transitional work where Atwood moves from
poetry to the novel, successfully creating living characters. Ambiguity is
used to avoid sentimentality or sermonizing, and irony to show
Marian's detachment in her struggles against conforming to society's
expectations. *Survival*, appearing after a period of growing nationalism,
has inspired much discussion and debate by challenging those who wish
to discount Canadian literature. *Survival* relates a spectrum of
Canadian literary themes, such as nature, animals, family, and women,
to four victim positions. *Survival*'s challenge to the American influence
on Canadian culture is understandable, but Atwood should have also
examined the British influence on Canadian literature by including
authors like Stephen Leacock. *Surfacing* also shows Canada as victim of
the destructive Americans. The narrator is forced to adapt to nature,
and, paradoxically, is victimized by her own inability to feel and find
integrity within herself.

53 KNELMAN, MARTIN. "An Obsession with Trash, the Trash of
Obsession, and Other Reflections on Junk Culture." *Toronto Life*,
December, pp. 217-19, 221.

Discusses the trash imagination in *Lady Oracle*, which should be
filmed, and in two films, Brian De Palma's *Obsession* and John
Schlesinger's *Marathon Man*. Atwood's heroine, named after Joan
Crawford, lives and writes out of her trash movie-*True Confessions*
sensibility. As a child, Joan needed the soppy masochism of Susan
Hayward and June Allyson movies to escape; later, she learns that
"being smart enough to see through trash doesn't free you from its
grip." Atwood is drawn to trash emotionally even as she debunks its
excesses intellectually. The absurdities she burlesques are peculiar to
English Canada's touchy cultural identity and to eclectic 1960s and

1976

1970s Toronto. Why is Joan's negative satiric vision "such a high?" Perhaps because her humor is not all put-down, but forgiving.

54 LEGATE, DAVID M. "A Remedy for Obesity." *Montreal Star*, 18 September, p. E3.

Gives high praise to the first two-thirds of *Lady Oracle*, which showcases Atwood's roving imagination, barbed irony, observant satire, wry humor, arresting metaphors, expressive compassion, and, above all, disciplined composition. Atwood leads her bulbous heroine gently through chrysalis to adolescence to far beyond innocence. "Every mood of the foregoing is beautifully rendered." But the last part becomes convulsive, "an overdose of characters with little or no character" in trumped-up situations. Naturally the reviewer will not disclose whether the heroine's demise, adroitly anticipated in the opening flashback, is real or not.

55 LEHMANN-HAUPT, CHRISTOPHER. "It's All the Rage." *New York Times*, 23 December, p. 21.

Prefers to think Fay Weldon's *Remember Me* and Atwood's *Lady Oracle* are faultily constructed, but maybe a man can't understand contemporary women's sex-linked existential rage. Repressed rage prompts heroine Joan's compulsive eating, fractures her self-awareness, and eventually leads to her faked suicide and flight. Repressed rage may even explain Joan's entertainingly wry self-view and energetic satire. But Joan's fear of her husband finding out what is only her amusing childhood – a fear on which the plot turns – is unrealistic and unconvincing: it's as if only Joan can know her extreme inner rage; we readers can't.

56 LONG, TANYA C. Review of *Selected Poems*. *Canadian Book Review Annual*:162.

Recommends highly Atwood's poems, which explode in the head like nitroglycerine, forcing new perceptions. The irony masks the intensity. Images of reflection, and of the divided self, abound; perception is a key; life is seen as fluid and treacherous; boundaries blur; her view includes the ancestral, totemic, and mythic. Her imagination is apocalyptic, macabre, but not cold. *Selected Poems* generously includes all her best work.

57 McCALLUM, GARY. Review of *Lady Oracle*. *Canadian Review* 3, no. 6 (December):52.

Finds problems: Atwood's characteristic virtues, which bring her glory and gold for all she writes, are general, and shared by other Canadian writers. Specifically, a random virtue is her adept mixing of mundane life with a melodramatic and humourously improbable plot, which permits the reader to identify without getting bored. But despite all *Lady Oracle*'s virtues, and reviewers heaping "hosannahs," this book displays Atwood's characteristic failings: her peripheral characters are not overly convincing, which means no genuine tension; her superior, sensitive, suffering heroine is too uninteresting. "Atwood's distance from her characters . . . [helps make] *Lady Oracle* rather sour and heartless at the core, for all its surface sweetness and mirth."

58 MacGREGOR, ROY. "Mother Oracle." *Canadian*, 25 September, pp. 15-18.

A cover story that profiles Atwood, her celebrity status, and Canadian reactions, at her farm near Alliston, with Graeme Gibson, six weeks after their daughter's birth. Atwood is a private person who must deal with presumptions, threats, and importunate fans. People cannot separate Atwood from her work. Currently her alter ego is Bart Gerrard, who creates *This Magazine*'s satiric "Kultchur Komix," featuring Survivalwoman, or the Flying Kotex. Atwood comments on her witch/Medusa image; on an Irving Layton reaction; on her early writing and education; on *Survival*, Anansi, and the spread of Canadian nationalism; on her own success in the U.S. and Canada, happiness, pessimism, and the just-published *Lady Oracle*. *Surfacing* may become a movie.

59 MacLEAN, CRYSTAL. "Voices of 5 Women." *New Letters* 43, no. 1 (October):131.

Briefly remarks that *You Are Happy* seems compelled to examine destruction's beauty: yet, as in "Digging," there is something tougher than the usual death-wish poetry; there is the will and plea of "First Prayer."

60 McPHERSON, WILLIAM. "New Lives for Old." *Washington Post Book World*, 26 September, p. H1.

Begins with our universal fantasy of beginning again, which is the pervading theme of Atwood's two earlier novels, and of *Lady Oracle*. The protagonist, Joan/Louisa, is a compulsive eater and a compulsive weaver of fantasies, lies, and secrets. She can no more escape the past than Hamlet can evade his death; but both protagonists voice a readiness. Joan and Atwood are artists; and artists, like saints, "try to make the ideal real, the real ideal." Though a review may serve Atwood's novels ill, by laying out their seemingly bizarre skeletons, *Lady Oracle* is very funny, artful, complexly plotted but always clear; and if its end remains tentative, so does life, till the end. Excerpted: 1978.11.

61 "Margaret Atwood: The Historical Role and Destiny of the Creative Non-Victim.'" *New Literature and Ideology*, no. 20 (May), pp. 71-81.

Citing Marx and Engels, denounces *Survival*. Like her clerical obscurantist mentor, Frye, the bourgeois literary star Atwood ignores the Canadian people's life and historical development, telling Canadians to look inside their own heads for the celebrated "'Canadian identity.'" Who dares suggest that such writers are socially useless parasites? *Survival*'s map is the bourgeois writer's creed, which is why the ruling class and state shower writers like her with honours and money. In return, Atwood's "'Canada as a whole is a victim'" excuses "the sell-out Canadian monopoly capitalist class." Her victim positions blame the "'lower classes,'" question anger, and advocate a self-serving transcendental "'creative non-victim.'" Her fascist fantasies collapse with the Canadian people's real life and continued historic struggles, which she calls failures, but which in the end will trash her "'creative non-victim'" doctrine.

62 MATHEWS, CAROL. "Margaret Atwood." *Goddard-Cambridge Magazine*, May, pp. 43-45.

Gets frustrated with Atwood's growing, but still self-limited and unclearly defined, political and feminist consciousness. *The Animals in That Country* shows a strictly personal, isolated anguish; *Procedures for Underground* develops some political consciousness; *Power Politics* extends the female persona's anger at her male lover to the male power system. *Surfacing* defines the power system's exploiters and victims well. Atwood's political consciousness culminates in *You Are Happy*'s "Songs of the Transformed"; she described "Crow Song" "as the lament of a forgotten 1960's Canadian leftist," and "Song of the Worms" as the people's reply. Though her persona's voyage is still a white, middle-class trip, her work does help women to explore, express, and struggle against their own oppression.

63 MILLER, KARL. "Orphans and Oracles: What Clara Knew." *New York Review of Books*, 28 October, pp. 30-32.

Delineates *Lady Oracle*'s place in a literary tradition of real and imaginary orphans, which he defines; and its literary Gothic elements. Acting like an imaginary orphan signals rejection of, and by, the family, who neglect and coerce their outsider. These orphans may be drawn to dual and multiple personalities and escapes. Being an outcast from the family may mean being an outlaw, as in *Jane Eyre* and Jane Austen's *Emma*. Though *Lady Oracle* is not a Gothic novel, "[t]hese confessions of a justified sinner could be entitled [after Horace Walpole] 'The Mysteries of Toronto.'" *Oracle*'s Gothic tradition focusses on female oppression. Its fake drowning, a Gothic act, recalls the British MP John Stonehouse, who faked drowning off Miami, and claimed a new personality. Duality looms in *Lady Oracle*, where a Heathcliff conceals a Linton. Heroine Joan "'oozes tears like an orphan, like an onion'"; she "'only wanted some human consideration,'" as Robert Louis Stevenson said. From the primal second self of Joan's mother-haunted dreams come other selves, as in Samuel Beckett's orphan tramp *Molloy*; and maybe monsters, like Frankenstein's orphan. Joan writes, in a Gothic dream or trance, of a Canadian Dracula villain, who was foreshadowed in parts of Atwood's oracular *Power Politics* and its cover. *Oracle*'s title may come from Sylvia Plath's "Lady Lazarus," which Atwood's "Returning from the dead" recalls. *Surfacing* used mysterious, magic, and orphan elements. In *Oracle* the orphan's cry shifts into satire and sardonic social comedy, like Erica Jong's. A two-book essay, on Paula Fox's *The Widow's Children* also.

64 MORLEY, PATRICIA. "Atwood with Gothic Fantasies." *Ottawa Journal*, 27 August, p. 36.

Recommends highly, to women and men, Atwood's best and very funny gothic novel, *Lady Oracle*. The autobiographical elements – the protagonist Joan's cult-figure status, her much-reviewed hair, certain Canadian literati, are amusing. Joan herself is zany, unstable, likeable, and has more lives than a cat. Where eighteenth-century gothic used external horrors, later gothics have used psychological symbols: "*Lady Oracle* is simultaneously a gothic novel and a parody of the form." As the Gothic novel Joan is writing changes from sheer parody to realism, her real life also becomes increasingly gothic. In a dramatic finale, Charlotte penetrates the maze; in a brilliant reversal, Joan becomes a Redmond. *Lady Oracle*'s funhouse mirror of men and women has humour, common-sense, and wit. Revised: 1976.65 (below).

1976

65 ____. "The Gothic as Social Realism." *Canadian Forum* 56 (December-January):49-50.

Appreciates *Lady Oracle* most highly as a very funny, gothic, grotesque, and realistic Canadian novel of role-playing, survival, and growth. 1960s Toronto is accurately evoked. The characters, who are Robert Louis Stevenson's Jekyll and Hyde, and a few more *personae*, let us recognize our human duplicity. "Atwood's chief contribution to Women's Lib is the startling concept that traditionally accepted female roles are really gothic in design:" the helpless maiden evades dangers, marries the hero, and lives happily ever after. "*Lady Oracle* is extravagant, macabre, and melodramatic" – like much of life, as James Reaney tells us. Expanded from 1976.64 (above).

66 MORRISON, JOHN F. "Novelist Has Identity Crisis." *Sunday Bulletin* (Philadelphia), 10 October, sec. 4, p. 10.

Finds *Lady Oracle* puzzling and disappointing: "most of the time we are lost," like when stumbling through a Canadian forest fog, with only occasional flashes of *Surfacing*'s brilliant, biting prose. The old identity crisis fad isn't made very original. It's never clear why Joan is so desperate about hiding her secrets. If Atwood is saying something about modern woman's plight, OK, but this sure is an odd way to do it.

67 NELSON, ALIX. "Hooked on Fantasy." *Village Voice*, 11 October, p. 38.

Lauds *Lady Oracle*'s more-than-Walter Mitty, hydra-headed, multiple-self, death-defying escape-artist heroine, whose intricate shaggy-dog story ends patly, as all such do; lauds Atwood as Flannery O'Connor's spiritual heir, extracting the demonic from the real with the same sardonic accuracy, measured flow, and skill at making childhood horrors visually and viscerally real.

68 NICHOLS, MARIANNA da VINCI. "Women on Women: The Looking Glass Novel." *Denver Quarterly* 11, no. 3 (Autumn):10-11.

Praises, in a discussion of stronger heroines versus suffering Eves in contemporary novels by women, *Surfacing*'s courageous, epic quest for self, its use of nature as metaphor, and its heroine's struggle for wholeness and connection.

69 NODELMAN, PERRY. "The Art of Flabby Writing." *Winnipeg Free Press*, 4 September, p. 17.

Enjoys Atwood's surprisingly uncontrolled, voluptuously extravagant *Lady Oracle*, but finds its untidiness frustrating, and its ambivalence confusing. Has Atwood used *Lady Oracle* for literary suicide, to escape her reputation? All her earlier books were controlled, crystal clear, and chilling. Now *Lady Oracle* is surprisingly defenceless, "frivolous, sloppy, and silly," like its heroine, who uses her flabbiness defensively. "Life is a terrible thing"–but is that plus or minus, comic or tragic? Is this book an advance, or self-indulgent? The reviewer enjoyed the wit, the "brilliantly comic and very painful" childhood scenes, and the clever gothic parodies, but finds *Lady Oracle* confusing.

70 NORTHEY, MARGOT. "Sociological Gothic: *Wild Geese* and *Surfacing*." In *The Haunted Wilderness: The Gothic and Grotesque in Canadian Fiction*. Toronto and Buffalo: University of Toronto Press, pp. 62-69.

Revision of 1974.31. Like Martha Ostenso's *Wild Geese*, *Surfacing* paradoxically combines gothic and sociological elements; it is a more didactic, analytic, and better written novel. But the narrator's mental instability, distorting vision, and paranoid distrust and anti-Americanism, even at the end, make it hard to credit her sociological comments. Her pent-up emotions create much of *Surfacing*'s gothic atmosphere, where both wilderness and civilization appear menacing and evil. She seems more hopeful at the end, but still tentative.

71 NOVIK, MARY. "Selected Surfacing." *Vancouver Sun*, 4 June, p. A34.

Argues, in a review of *Selected Poems*, that Atwood's poetry is more successful than her prose. *Survival*'s breezy, "hokied-up" culture-mongering has popularized Canadian literature. *The Edible Woman* is impressive social comedy, and a delightful comedy of manners. *Surfacing*, though fascinating, is less successful, because "it poses as a psychological character study" when it is really an allegory, a novel of ideas. Atwood's weak plot resolutions and characterizations don't matter in poetry, where her startling images successfully embody her allegory of ideas. *Selected Poems*'s only flaw is including most of *You Are Happy*, which is her weakest book. Atwood's central theme "is the misuse of power, by which we exploit nature, other people, and our own selves," in our sadistic sexual relationships and in the excessive, corrupt rationalism that will lead us to atomic holocaust or natural calamity. Atwood's misanthropy, like Jonathan Swift's in *Gulliver's*

1976

Travels, has a rare and humanitarian concern for our survival: we should listen.

72 OWEN, I.M. "Queen of the Maze." *Books in Canada* 5, no. 9 (September):3-5.
   Welcomes the distinguished poet as, finally, a real novelist; *Lady Oracle* is well peopled, fully plotted, and richly layered with symbols and allusions. Comments on the wry reference to instant celebrity, which reflects Atwood's becoming "'a Thing'"; identifies the Toronto ravine, which figures in Hugh Hood's prose also. Praises the Costume Gothics as superb Harlequin pastiche, and the female fear passages as finely written realism. But there are still no credible men characters; and no real warmth or love—some "ice-jam," or "inhibition" stops Atwood the writer (but "not the person) from expressing warmth, delight, joy." Still, *Lady Oracle* is an astonishingly funny, entertaining novel. Excerpted: 1977.21.

73 PETERSON, KEVIN. "Novel Has Great Strengths, but Remains Unsatisfying." *Calgary Herald*, 3 September, p. 51.
   Finds *Lady Oracle* curiously promising yet fizzling; Atwood's strengths of wit, language, and feeling, flash and then recede; finds it "hard not to yearn for the angry poetess of old." *Lady Oracle* is not bad, but unsatisfying and curiously incomplete, compared to the earlier novels that we immediately re-read. Most of *Lady Oracle* is a free-form explanation of how Joan got her schizophrenic identities, but Atwood's theme of the common double or triple personality fails to take hold. Joan, who writes "abominable gothic novels" that slowly take over her life, is ordinary, like Atwood's other heroines, who thus "strike a personal chord in every reader." The supporting characters are again absurd. Joan on the Canadian tightrope, and as a child, are the most powerful parts; but other Canadian writers, including Atwood, have done many aspects of *Lady Oracle* better.

74 PLASKOW, JUDITH. "On Carol Christ on Margaret Atwood: Some Theological Reflections." *Signs* 2, no. 2 (Winter):331-39.
   Debates, in response to Christ 1976.13, whether the special identification of women with nature strengthens or subordinates women; whether this supposed woman/nature link, found in Simone de Beauvoir, Doris Lessing, and *Surfacing*, transcends Western patriarchal polarities, or binds women to social stereotypes of child rearing. Atwood scarcely separates immersion in and transcendence of

nature; her woman/nature linking is, at least potentially, oppressive. Her marvelous metaphors blur issues of human decision. She does not differentiate legitimate versus illegitimate abortions. Her heroine decides only to have a baby, and leaves northern Quebec to the "'Americans.'" A woman's quest for self in the cosmos leaves political power to the status quo men. We need feminist theology, and an identification with nature that is the basis for responsible acts. See Atwood 1976.2 and Gray 1977.28.

75 POLLITT, KATHA. Review of *Lady Oracle. New York Times Book Review*, 26 September, pp. 7-8.

Finds faults: *Lady Oracle* lacks realism, and moves too slowly to cover its clumsy contrivances; the zany story, perhaps meant to spice the feminist woe, has too many unanswered questions, and a too massively self-absorbed heroine. Atwood also seems to have two selves: one writes spare, tense poetry and the extraordinary *Surfacing*, where a powerful sense of place makes up for much vagueness about human beings. The other Atwood writes *Lady Oracle* and *The Edible Woman*, which share the limits but lack the mythic and metaphoric force of the truest and most thoughtful Atwood; these two comic novels offer the "stock figures and pat insights of . . . popular feminist-oriented fiction." Excerpted: 1978.11.

76 PORTER-LADOUSSE, GILLIAN. "Some Aspects of the Theme of Metamorphosis in Margaret Atwood's Poetry." *Études canadiennes* (Talence), no. 2, pp. 71-77.

Comments on the Protean aspect and the Circe myth of Atwood's obsessive metamorphosis theme, from *Double Persephone* through *You Are Happy*. Fixed forms imprison man; he escapes only by adopting other, fluid realities. In the Protean aspect man, after the Fall, returns as vegetation or as the geological earth. In the Circe myth, Atwood, like Jean Burgos's *Pour Circe*, sees animal metamorphosis as a means of man's self-revelation. But metamorphosis makes man confront death: grasping the instant of mutation is the only positive solution.

77 PRESCOTT, PETER S. "Pipe Dreams." *Newsweek* 88 (4 October):94-95.

Praises *Lady Oracle* highly: Atwood superbly recreates the contemporary heroine who graduates from victim to guerrilla warrior. Her theme is disguises, chosen and forced. Few writers can combine

1976

wit and humor; fewer still can use both to show human grief and pain. This Canadian poet and novelist seems able to do anything, including parody, metaphor, and narrative. Though the reviewer is a pessimist, he hopes that readers will snatch up the admirable and likeable *Lady Oracle*.

78 PRITCHARD, WILLIAM H. "Despairing at Styles." *Poetry* 127, no. 5 (February):296-97.

   Ridicules, in an eight-poet review, *You Are Happy*'s joyless outlook; finds throughout imagistic horrors, "Bloody limbs a-falling off," nature at her dirtiest: "Get out of that dungpile, Margaret Atwood!" The title poem does not properly imagine a human being. Atwood badtimes the human spirit "too facilely into grunts and icy mutters."

79 Review of *Lady Oracle*. *Booklist* 73, no. 4 (15 October):302.

   Praises a superior, deliciously droll novel, where the gothic, the occult, and realism blend; the wry humor buoys the heavy plot.

80 Review of *Lady Oracle*. *Kirkus Reviews* 44, no. 13 (1 July):746.

   Recommends the most cheerful of Atwood's three novels: "entertainment de luxe (even a *Redbook* appearance). . . . [A] genuine mood-softener as well as raffishly funny." Abridged: 1976.81 (below).

81 Review of *Lady Oracle*. *Kirkus Reviews* 44, no. 14 (15 July):801.

   An abridged text of 1976.80 (above); under "Adult Books Suggested for Young Adult Consideration."

82 Review of *Lady Oracle*. *Playboy* 23, no. 9 (September):24.

   Praises *Lady Oracle*, over Gail Parent's and Alix Shulman's painful girlhood books, as outrageously funny and hilarious, only sometimes too much so.

83 RICH, ADRIENNE. *Of Woman Born: Motherhood as Experience and Institution*. New York: W.W. Norton, pp. 240-42. Reprint. New York: Bantam, 1977; and New York and London: W.W. Norton, 1986, with a new introduction.

   Finds in *Surfacing* a strange, complex version of the Demeter-Kore myth. Though the narrator is not a feminist, her "search for the father leads to reunion with the mother, who is at home in the wilderness, Mistress of the Animals." Subconsciously, the narrator starts accepting her own power as she envisions her mother; she has gone back, by fasting and sacrifice, beyond patriarchy.

84 RICHLER, MORDECAI. Review of *Lady Oracle*. *Book-of-the-Month-Club News*, August, pp. 1-3.

Acclaims *Lady Oracle*, as "a wonderfully unpretentious comic romp" filled with "dotty, outsize characters" and many incidental delights; a fine and rueful coming of age as a girl in 1950s Toronto; an interwoven, running satire of gothic romance; a telling satire of Toronto literati and nationalism – and surely the year's most amusing Canadian novel.

85 ROSS, GARY. "The Divided Self." *Canadian Literature*, no. 71 (Winter), pp. 39-47.

Discusses *The Animals in That Country* as a journey of the schizophrenic, alienated, isolated self in a random and meaningless world of empty rituals, towards a healing reintegration which, as in *The Circle Game*, can happen only in the presence of another. *The Animals in That Country* starts with departure; moves, as in "A night in the Royal Ontario Museum," to confront the horrors of isolation in a man-made, loveless, violent world, then moves towards escape. Beyond the defensive and self-protective schizophrenia, there is responsibility, sharing, and human touch.

86 ROSS, MALCOLM. "Critical Theory: Some Trends." In *Literary History of Canada: Canadian Literature in English*. Edited by Carl F. Klinck. Vol. 3. 2d ed. Toronto and Buffalo: University of Toronto Press, pp. 166-68, 172-73.

Condemns *Survival* in an essay that terms Frye's "'garrison mentality'" "myth without belief' or commitment: Atwood "flattens the mythopoeic mode into a one-dimensional fiction of fear and failure in Canadian writing." She fails to understand the positive, sacrificial "acceptance of suffering from which flows the water and blood of life," and the larger hopes of the Canadian tradition. Unlike D.G. Jones's *Butterfly on Rock*, which transfigures Frye's mythopoeic theory through dynamic commitment, *Survival* offers only "the latest popular myth of Frye's new metropolitan garrison[;] . . . a rhetoric, not a poetic." Reprinted as part of 1986.208.

87 ROWAN, DIANA. "Atwood Prances in *Lady Oracle*." *Christian Science Monitor*, 24 November, p. 27.

1976

Praises Atwood's multiple-self leitmotiv and change in tone. After *The Edible Woman*'s self-deprecating humor, and *Power Politics*'s victimization and fragmentation, *Surfacing*'s inner-directed, pent-up anger was finally unleashed against ghoulish consumerism and sado-masochistic relationships. *Surfacing* ended with Atwood's powerful statement of wholeness. Though *Lady Oracle* appears to backtrack into confused territory, Atwood has a wry new perspective. The heroine of this chaotic novel manages to be both the classic piecemeal lady and the magician. *Lady Oracle* is a stage in Atwood's development, where she claims the right to pause, consider, and even clown.

88 RUBENSTEIN, ROBERTA. "*Surfacing*: Margaret Atwood's Journey to the Interior." *Modern Fiction Studies* 22, no. 3 (Autumn):387-99.

Analyzes Atwood's motifs and archetypal, multi-level journey into the self in *Surfacing* and, briefly, in Atwood's first five books of poetry, *Survival*, and *Lady Oracle*. Explicates *Surfacing*'s use of mythic and literary sources, which include Joseph Conrad, Joseph Campbell's *The Hero of a Thousand Faces*, Dante, Mircea Eliade, Jungian, Christian, Edenic, and earlier myths. The narrator's journey is simultaneously psychological, mythic, and sacred; from spiritual anaesthesia, down through schizophrenia and the undifferentiated, archaic consciousness; up to reality and sanity, with new wisdom gained. The aborted fetus is not a statement against abortion, but a metaphor for civilization's diseases and for an incomplete self. The newly conceived child reaffirms "sacred ties between generations and between man and nature." Atwood's "journey into both the private and collective heart of darkness . . . [creates] a powerful account of modern civilization and its diseases." Excerpted: 1978.11.

89 SANDLER, LINDA. "Atwoodian Parody of the 1950s." *Saturday Night* 91, no. 6 (September):59.

Acclaims Atwood as a brilliant comedian, and *Lady Oracle* as "an exquisite parody of an obsolete generation." Though "growing-up-female-in-the-1950s" is a threadbare literary genre, Atwood's satiric humour and truly "'common woman'" heroine make *Lady Oracle* utterly unlike feminist novels. Her non-elite Joan has absurd cultural assumptions but, usually, sound instincts: from her "Canadian content," tightrope daydreams, to her Harlequin Romances, to her Gulliveresque naive adventures, to the vaguely pre-Raphaelite Automatic Writing poems that make her the media's instant cult figure. Atwood was right to have Joan instinctively perceive the Royal

York Hotel's bogus nineteenth-century fairyland delights as "the hidden recesses of the national brain." Excerpted: 1978.11.

90 ____. "The Exorcisms of Atwood." *Saturday Night* 91, no. 5 (July-August):59-60.

Acclaims *Selected Poems* and Atwood's nature themes: as in "Tricks with Mirrors," her art mirrors us. *The Circle Game* seems a mid-1960s search for the real Canada, but what's underneath is an attempt to enter nature's cycles. In *The Animals in That Country*, her most overtly political book, the machine takes over the human, prefiguring *Power Politics*. *The Journals of Susanna Moodie* powerfully dramatizes Atwood's central theme of becoming an animal, natural. Only *Procedures for Underground* fails to break new ground. *Power Politics*, which transformed Atwood's image to Medusa and Sybil, is not cruel, but militantly ironic, witty, and extraordinarily passionate, because the woman identifies with nature. The enigmatic *You Are Happy* is primarily a pastoral romance; "Songs of the Transformed," with its resentful domestic animals and sorrowful wild ones, may be her most brilliantly conceived poetic series. Excerpted 1978.11.

91 S[CHILLER], W[ILLIAM]. "Interview with Margaret Atwood." *PWP* (*Poetry Windsor Poésie*) 2, no. 3 (Fall):2-15.

Atwood discusses her five books of poetry: fragmentation versus coalescence and resolution; Hegelian thesis-antithesis-synthesis form; hypotheses ("'if A then B'") and style in individual poems; putative influence of Jung, Laing, Frye, or Freud; her poetry's exploration of "'the subterranean'" rather than the implicitly Freudian "'subconscious'" or "'unconscious'"; early readings of English and Canadian poets; early and present writing; Orphic poetry and the limits of language; and reactions from critics, men, and women, especially to *Power Politics* and *You Are Happy*.

92 SCHREIBER, LE ANNE. "Motley with Method." *Time* 108, no. 15 (11 October):97-98.

Praises *Lady Oracle*'s successful motley highly: heroine Joan is a Toronto Alice in Wonderland, with identities, size-changing pills, looking glass, and a latter-day Mad Hatter for a lover. The novel meanders and circles with the heroine's chaotic psyche; jagged shifts from situation comedy to slapstick farce to surreal nightmare keep the reader off balance. Joan engages the reader's sympathy; perhaps every woman has a ballooning romantic hidden inside her. Atwood's

1976

unobtrusive allusions honor older forms – picaresque, gothic romance, *Bildungsroman*, and Victorian saga.

93 SLINGER, HELEN. "Interview with Margaret Atwood." *Maclean's* 89, no. 15 (6 September):4, 6-7.
Interviews Atwood at the Atwood-Gibson farm near Alliston, three weeks after their daughter's birth: Atwood responds to questions on her pregnancy, childbirth, and mothering; on writer's privacy, citing Farley Mowat; on the Canadian tendency to confuse writers, especially women writers, with their fiction; on 1960s versus current Canadian literature and politics; on writing; and on projecting a frightening image.

94 SLOPEN, BEVERLEY. "PW Interviews: Margaret Atwood." *Publishers Weekly* 210, no. 8 (23 August):6-8.
Profiles Atwood at the farm near Alliston, in July, while Atwood is nursing her baby and Graeme Gibson is haying. Though Atwood, "a reigning superstar of Canadian letters," is called Medusa-haired, lofty, and enigmatic, her new *Lady Oracle* is wonderfully funny, humane, and not autobiographical. Its spiritualism will remind Canadians of Prime Minister Mackenzie King's seances during World War II. Atwood comments on her own fear of an untidy life, present happiness, and youthful visits to many churches; on *Lady Oracle*'s Joan as a likeable clown, and on its inset Gothic as combining the threatening "mansion Gothic" with the Barbara Cartland romance.

95 STIMPSON, CATHARINE R. "Don't Bother Me, I'm Dead." *Ms.* 5, no. 4 (October):36, 40.
Envies Atwood's nervy, funny, brilliant psychological realism, wonderfully inventive plots, and skill in three different novel traditions. *Lady Oracle*'s heroine hides the puniest ego behind multiple public identities; gothics are one of her several fantasy escapes, bulemic binges another. "The difficult necessity of a therapeutic encounter with one's past haunts Atwood's fiction." Ghosts – whether visions or only hallucinations, metaphors, unconscious memories – appear. Atwood's stories begin intriguingly and end with flair. *The Edible Woman* is an urban psychological novel; *Surfacing* is a modern religious quest; *Lady Oracle* is a comedy whose conjured-up heroine endures catastrophes, survival, and a probable rebirth.

96 STRUTHERS, J.R. (TIM). "Tale of Multiple Identities Has More Than One Identity of Its Own." *London Free Press*, 2 October, p. 49.

Appreciates *Lady Oracle* highly as an upside-down, deliberately ironic Frygian romance. *Lady Oracle* follows Northrop Frye's romance features of identity, descent, and alienation; the nineteenth-century split heroine; and Robert Graves's *The White Goddess*, for Joan, her aunt, and her mother. But, though Frye's return or ascent is invoked, Joan remains a victim who has not really learned, or regained a real identity. Because the end is deliberately flat and unresolved, *Lady Oracle* parodies the romances Joan writes; but *Lady Oracle* is also a real, modern romance; and, on a third level, a self-parody. Saint Peggy has surprised us by playing our fairy godmother and clown. Like *Don Quixote*, *Lady Oracle* subtly treats fantasy and reality; and incorporates many forms of popular culture into a surprising, entertaining, psychologically penetrating, thoughtful fiction.

97 STUBBS, ROY ST. GEORGE. "Few Sounds of Cheer." *Winnipeg Free Press*, 29 May, New Leisure sec., p. 16.

Greatly admires *Selected Poems*, but finds little comfort in it. The front-ranking Canadian poet Atwood has been much praised "by cliques and claques of critics. . . . Her poetry is good poetry in the modern manner": neat, brittle, clever, with active verbs and concrete nouns, it truly reflects the mixed-up, exhausted, profligate world. But does it have the power of Milton's *Paradise Lost*? "Miss Atwood's earth is not happy, nor her heaven sure." Poets should mirror the times. Atwood does, admirably, but the reviewer wants some affirmation, such as George Santayana provides.

98 SULLIVAN, ROSEMARY. "Surfacing and Deliverance." *Canadian Literature*, no. 67 (Winter), pp. 6-20.

Compares national mythologies in *Surfacing* and James Dickey's *Deliverance*, and uses Mircea Eliade's *Shamanism* to explicate *Surfacing*'s sacred initiation into nature. Both novels explore, through initially entropied characters who return to a wilderness that is also the unknown self and the unconscious, man's relation to nature. *Deliverance*, like Dickey's *Self-Interviews* and poetry, expresses a particularly American romanticism, a nostalgic, machismo cult of sensation and violence that is exhilaratingly amoral and anti-social. *Surfacing* expresses a particularly Canadian moral self-scrutiny, and rejects the hunter's nostalgia. The Canadian sensibility internalizes violence, as Frye has said; and links personal and collective victimization or liberation, as *Survival* and *Surfacing* show. Though Canadians have seen their fiction as lacking American intensities, perhaps it is developing a deeper, moral, personal, and social vision of survival.

99 SWEETAPPLE, ROSEMARY. "Margaret Atwood: Victims and Survivors." *Southern Review* (Adelaide) 9, no. 1 (March):50-69.

Uses *Survival* as the key to *Surfacing*, which, like the witty *The Edible Woman*, recounts "the plight of the would-be liberated woman" in a sexist society: *Surfacing*'s world is devastatingly predatory, and the narrator cannot transcend it. As *Survival* says, in Canada the family entraps. The father is both oppressor and victim; the mother is a Canadian Hecate with a Diana and a Venus trapped inside her. That the narrator's childhood pictures support the male myth of man with God, woman with man, is hard to stomach. The two women do not help each other. The narrator chooses to have a child, despite her wish to be an artist, and rejects Joe's love. Her image of marriage, with David and Anna, is disturbing. An "unreliable narrator," she turns to primitive thinking for a redemptive ritual. Is woman's biology her destiny? Isn't there some other way than "the inhuman bear man and the inhuman ice woman" producing the first human?

100 THOMAS, JANE RESH. "*Lady Oracle*: When Her Secrets Began to Show . . . ." *Minneapolis Tribune*, 26 December, p. D14.

Likes *Lady Oracle*'s Joan, whose blurred identity is the novel's elusive center. Joan, who often sounds like a witty feminist, is a responsible victim, and a touching figure of the self-divided woman's life. Only in the last scene does Joan stop running, face consequences, and try to connect. Sometimes the unrestrained prose gets tangled. Humor and Gothic quotes keep this episodic melodrama from getting tiresome.

101 TREMBLAY, ANNE. "Reluctant Oracle Atwood Still Busy Studying Roles." *Gazette* (Montreal), 25 September, p. 40.

Interviews Atwood, who is in Montreal with Graeme Gibson and their baby Eleanor Jess publicizing *Lady Oracle*: Atwood discusses the satire of her own artistic role and the futility of romance in *Lady Oracle*; Atwood's own secret identities, as cartoonist Bart Gerrard and, in college, as Shakes Beat [sic] Latweed, with Dennis Lee; her first interview, after *The Circle Game*; public images of the female artist and of successful Canadians; and *Survival* as written for the general reader, not for academics.

102 TYLER, ANNE. "The Woman Who Fled from Her Self." *National Observer*, 9 October, p. 25.

Praises *Lady Oracle* highly, and acclaims *Surfacing*. All three of Atwood's novels focus on a young woman working free of entrapment; in Joan's case, the heroine is trying to escape her own evasions, lies, and identities—which will never be possible. Her history is baroque, wretched, accidental, and downright funny. As in *Surfacing*, the escape from normal life is physical, and survival is a problem. The dark *Surfacing* was a poet's novel, and one of the century's best books; the lighter *Lady Oracle* is a novelist's grittily realistic novel.

103 ULLMAN, LESLIE. "All the People in One Person: Flaky or Fundamentally Wise?" *Kansas City Star*, 7 November, p. D11.

Questions *Lady Oracle*: unlike *Surfacing*'s nameless heroine, who "par[ed] herself down to a kind of mythical bone," the thrice-named heroine of *Lady Oracle* is "an accessorized female, flamboyant and full of herself, a lover of sweets and spangles. . . . Joan flounders wittily, sometimes thoughtfully, often tearfully, and not very coherently." She is a beautiful but clumsy clown; perceptive, but jumping to extreme conclusions. Does she lament or celebrate her life's baroque spread? "Is she congenitally flaky or fundamentally wise?" Hardly any one in *Lady Oracle* "seems dangerous or loveable enough" to cause Joan's turmoils, and the plot thickens "into something uncomfortably like one of '‘Louisa's'" mysteries.

104 VINTCENT, BRIAN. "An Edible Woman with More Bite." *Quill and Quire* 42, no. 11 (September):6.

Judges *Lady Oracle* to be not serious, and its dazzling and "terrifically funny" characters to be overblown caricatures, for which Atwood "feels, ultimately, immense disdain"; wants someone "we can admire or hope for," love, or at least sympathize with. The irony is even heavier than in *The Edible Woman*. Joan is "a creep," and the least likeable of Atwood's three novel's versions of one heroine. Joan's memorable, miserable childhood comes from a Canadian fiction type; her permanently enraged mother comes from Alice Munro and Margaret Laurence stories. Her fake drowning comes from the British M.P. [John Stonehouse] case. This amazingly inventive, amusing, "pretty spectacular" novel is only "a diverting fancy."

1976

105 WALLER, G.F. "New Fiction: Myths and Passions, Rivers and Cities." *Ontario Review*, no. 5 (Fall-Winter), pp. 93-97.

Appreciates *Lady Oracle*'s endearingly wry but nevertheless enlightening confusion. "Lightly, but provokingly, Atwood is reminding us of our need for integration and wholeness – and that we are all artists in our quest for them." Appreciates Paul Theroux's *The Family Arsenal* and Cynthia Ozick's *Bloodshed and Three Novellas* more, Marian Engel's *Bear* less, in this four-book review.

106 WOODCOCK, GEORGE. "Playing with Freezing Fire." *Canadian Literature*, no. 70 (Autumn), pp. 84-86.

Acclaims *Selected Poems*, which fulfills the promise of Atwood's first book, and establishes her at 37 as a major Canadian poet. It rightly reprints *The Journals of Susanna Moodie*, "Songs of the Transformed," and "Circe/Mud Poems" entire; and reveals the consistent, unifying shamanism that informs her novels, and *Survival*. "This Is a Photograph of Me" prefigures *Surfacing*; "After the Flood, We," read as a flood of American culture, prefigures *Survival*. Her virtuoso craft and inventive imagination create each poem's circle, or world. A geographical-historical, mythopoeic, and wit poet, and a polymath, Atwood is the mirror and elucidator of our era; *Survival* accurately isolated our proper themes. A seven-poet review.

107 ZONAILO, CAROLYN. "The Wilderness Metaphor: A Study of Four Novels." *Room of One's Own* 2, no. 1:76-78.

Briefly describes *Surfacing* as a novel where a female protagonist gains identity and strength in the wilderness, even though the end is tentative.

1977

1 ADACHI, KEN. "Literary Mistress-of-All-Trades: Atwood Shares $3,000 Book Prize." *Toronto Star*, 18 February, p. F4.

Reports on the 1976 City of Toronto Book Awards prize of $3,000, to be shared by the front-ranking novelist Atwood, for *Lady Oracle*, and Margaret Gibson, for *The Butterfly Ward*; finds it odd that *Lady Oracle* got "mixed reviews – ranging from the ecstatic to the very sneering – in Britain, the United States and Canada"; cites Pollitt [1976.75], who disliked its "clumsy contrivances", and the *Los Angeles*

Times, which "dealt it the ultimate insult; 'definitely a woman's book.'" Never mind, *Lady Oracle* "has been on the best-sellers' list for 25 weeks."

2 ____. "Margaret Atwood's Short Stories Make Powerful Comment on Life." *Toronto Star*, 2 September, p. E6.

Gives mixed praise to *Dancing Girls* as a powerful, painful study of dehumanized urban men and women, from our endlessly fertile, internationally acclaimed, chief literary heroine. These stories illustrate *Survival*'s themes, of stark survival, entrapment, isolation, and helplessness. The characters, who are sometimes sacrificed to the themes, are usually bewildered, dependent, resentful people in rented rooms. In "The Grave of the Famous Poet," "Atwood coolly dissects the fetid corpse of [a sterile] affair." Though "Giving Birth," with its menace and its hallucinatory experience of childbirth, is perhaps the most contrived, Atwood is a superb writer.

3 ALLEN, CAROLYN. "Margaret Atwood: Power of Transformation, Power of Knowledge." *Essays on Canadian Writing*, no. 6 (Spring), pp. 5-17.

Discusses Atwood's transformations of traditional mythology, which are both mythic and radical, in *The Journals of Susanna Moodie*, *Surfacing*, and the "Circe/Mud Poems." Her female protagonists reject, with some self-hatred, conventional roles for women; and learn from their attempted but incomplete transformations. In life Susanna Moodie sees, but only partly becomes, the wilderness; only after her death does she become its mythic spirit. *Surfacing* uses the mythic search for the father in female and broadly-defined feminist terms; the protagonist comes as near to primal transformation as is humanly possible. Circe attempts to transform not herself, but someone else; though, as in the classic myth, she loses to Ulysses, she ends with trust and love.

4 ATWOOD, MARGARET. "Royal Porcupine's Identikit." *Saturday Night* 92, no. 1 (January/February):3.

Claims, in a letter to the editor, that she neither writes nor approves of *romans à clef*; and rushes "to defend the honours of" Doug Fetherling and all "the other gentlemen who have been cast" as the fictive Royal Porcupine in *Lady Oracle*. A reply to 1976.30.

1977

5 BACH, PEGGY. Review of *Lady Oracle*. *Magill's Literary Annual*. Vol. 1. Englewood Cliffs, N.J.: Salem Press, pp. 400-403.

Discusses characters, structure, elements, parallels to Atwood's two earlier novels, and flaws. The masochistic, psychotic author Joan tries to escape the life she made. Like *Surfacing*, *Lady Oracle* incorporates intriguing, unbelievable mystery and occult imagery, obsession and guilt; Joan's fatness parallels *Surfacing*'s heroine's loss of feeling. Like *The Edible Woman*, *Lady Oracle* waves feminist banners; the male characters are selfish chauvinists, and the females are their willing followers. *Lady Oracle*'s novel within a novel may be more compelling than the main story. Atwood's wry humor is flawed by "'cuteness,'" and her writing is flawed by quirky superfluous short sentences at the ends of paragraphs. *Lady Oracle* is unresolved, and elusive, but adhesive.

6 BISHOP, DOROTHY. "Atwood at Her Best . . . and Most Compassionate." *Ottawa Journal*, 1 October, p. 40.

Praises *Dancing Girls*, especially "Training." The reprinted contemporary urban stories are ceaselessly relevant, as a Toronto review said of *Lady Oracle*, and "witty, penetrating, cool, seemingly effortless." "Giving Birth," where Atwood finds words for an event beyond words, "is a tour de force." "Dancing Girls," like "[The] Man from Mars," is an ironic failure of East-West understanding. The compassionate, tender "Training" is the most haunting–the reviewer had never before found compassion or tenderness in Atwood.

7 BOLAND, VIGA. "Something for Everyone and Much for the Writer . . . ." *Canadian Author and Bookman* 52, no. 3 (Spring):36-37.

Gives mixed praise to *Lady Oracle* in a review of four books by Canadian women. Reviewers have raved about this fascinating best-seller, justly; but these characters dazzle with their unusualness, not their reality. Because the narrator-heroine does not deeply love anyone, she can't impart life to her portrayal of other characters. Another disturbing aspect is the ungrammatical comma splices. Still, *Lady Oracle* is funny and creative, half-ridiculous and half-sublime.

8 BOUTELLE, ANN. "The Dorian Gray Phenomenon in Canadian Literature." *Dalhousie Review* 57, no. 2 (Summer):265, 270-72.

Finds, after Harvard lectures by Atwood ("Canadian Monsters") and Northrop Frye 1977.24 on spooky strangenesses in Canadian literature, female versions of Oscar Wilde's Dorian Gray in *The Journals of Susanna Moodie*'s cover collage and "Looking in a Mirror," and in *Surfacing*'s Anna's disintegrating face beneath her makeup. Atwood's controlling image is of surfacing; the atmosphere is nightmarish. "Dorian Gray comes into the picture when Atwood focusses on the face. Skin then becomes a mask" which may begin to disintegrate at any moment.

9 CARVER, PETER. Review of *Dancing Girls and Other Stories*. *Canadian Reader* 18, no. 8 (August):5-6.

Praises Atwood as a mapmaker, recharting the familiar, revealing the bewildered yet resilient survivors of mid-seventies chaos, focussing always on how people cope, with external crises and threats, or with internal loneliness. Atwood exposes our solitary condition with wry humour and compassion. Though *Dancing Girls* has few diverting highs, we are immensely satisfied to share the writer's perceptive understanding, delicate irony, and humanity.

10 CHALLIS, JOHN. Review of *Selected Poems*. *Laomedon Review* 3, no. 1 (March):73.

Disapproves of edited collections, which implicitly focus on the author, not the poems; and, as with *Selected Poems*, muddle the separate books' themes. Atwood is most intense and surprising; in the startling "Songs of the Transformed" the reader gets King Solomon's ring and can read the animals' thoughts. But collectively her themes lose their intensity, her surprises their impact; *Power Politics* suffers acutely. But, though *Selected Poems* is too technically oriented, it has some better points.

11 CUDE, WILFRED. "The Truth Was Not Convincing." *Fiddlehead*, no. 112 (Winter), pp. 133-37.

Acclaims *Lady Oracle*'s moral satire: as with the classics of the comic novel, Cervantes' *Don Quixote* and Twain's *Huckleberry Finn*, rewarding laughter makes us think. *Lady Oracle* and its incurably innocent, romance-addled heroine expose "Canada's own opiate of the masses, the Harlequin Romances, in a manner at once hilarious, penetrating, and profound." Joan's sloppily sentimental historical romances are, as Atwood slyly intimates, terrible lies, not harmless painkilling illusions. Joan chooses to live by the Miss Flegg syndrome; but the mothball ballet scene, read carefully, exposes that embittered spinster's cruelty and fakery. The traditionally comic victim, Joan, evolves into almost a tragic character. Atwood's first distancing of herself, in *Lady Oracle*, from her novels' self-pitying, spiritually impoverished Canadians, lets us appraise her characters and ourselves: Joan, who prefers her gothics' plasticized Redmonds to the infinitely more worthy real men in her life, "is the daughter of a ticky-tack culture hooked on cotton candy." See also 1980.26. Reprinted, slightly revised, 1978.19, which is reprinted 1983.26. Expanded: 1980.25.

12 DAVEY, FRANK. "Atwood's Gorgon Touch." *Studies in Canadian Literature* 2, no. 2 (Summer):146-63.

Finds in Atwood's seven poetry books, from *Double Persephone*'s "'girl with the gorgon touch'" to *You Are Happy*'s final sculptural "Book of Ancestors" man, a central, irresolvable, modernist-rooted aesthetic and ethical opposition between fixed form versus kinetic, subversive process; art versus life; space versus time. All her evasions affirm space and deny time, but time ultimately triumphs. Statements, syntax, juxtapositions, and structures are often spatial. Her artist-woman-transformer – Medusa, "the Power Politician," Susanna Moodie, Circe – turns life and love to stony art. Reprinted: 1978.20; 1983.29; 1988.15. Revised: 1984.18.

13 DAVIDSON, CATHY N. "Canadian Wry: Comic Vision in Atwood's *Lady Oracle* and Laurence's *The Diviners*." *Regionalism and the Female Imagination* 3, no. 2-3 (Fall-Winter):50-55.

Defines "underdog comedy" as implicitly radical, therapeutic, unifying humor that exposes social suppressions, rather than perpetuating them, as "Uncle Tom" jokes do. Consciousness-raising feminist humor laughs at our selves and at society's sexist assumptions. Thus in *Lady Oracle*'s hilarious mothball ballet, we see Miss Flegg as manipulative, even cruel, but also as pathetically desperate for approval, like Joan is. Joan's question, "'who would think of marrying a mothball?'" encapsulates feminist humor; it questions the sexist beauty ethic, the double standard, and the female search for male approval. Similarly, the narrator-protagonists of Margaret Laurence's *A Jest of*

God and *The Diviners* learn to survey their bleak prospects from an essentially comic perspective.

14 DILLIOTT, MAUREEN. "Emerging from the Cold: Margaret Atwood's *You Are Happy.*" *Modern Poetry Studies* 8, no. 1 (Spring):73-90.

Though, as Linda Rogers 1974.38 charged, Atwood's poems can have an icy, jabbing coldness, even *You Are Happy*'s coldness is often powerfully crafted, and its last poems have a new, luminous warmth. The first section introduces problems of perception, as in D.G. Jones 1974.17, of language, and of human relations. Language's destructiveness, and the intense need to speak, is the book's main theme. The second section's angry animals are "Atwood at her most strident." Though the third section often sounds like *Power Politics*, it is an interesting reversal, and admirably links the other sections. The last section is the best; some poems are paired, or connect to earlier ones. The final, sensuous "Late August" and open, giving "Book of Ancestors" are among Atwood's best ever, vulnerable yet tenacious.

15 DUCHENE, ANNE. "Sex and the Older Man." *Observer* (London), 3 July, p. 24.

Briefly describes *Lady Oracle*, in a five-book review, as a relaxed, wry, funny version of the now familiar "feminine dissociation from what happens to women."

16 DUNN, TIMOTHY. "Procedures for Surfacing." *Canadian Review* 4, no. 1 (February):58.

Reviews the Atwood legend and *Selected Poems*. The most-wanted Atwood hides out like an outlaw; pursuers hunt for an oracle, or an iceberg. She is cornered with her newborn, discovered as human. Even scholars pursue the legend, citing her titles – *Surfacing, Survival, Procedures for Underground* – as a diary of flight. *Selected Poems* confirms the poet; her "mythology of flux" captures not herself, but change, boundaries, perception, as in "This Is a Photograph of Me" and the powerful "Tricks with Mirrors." By taking us away from our self-images, historically in *The Journals of Susanna Moodie* and "Circe/Mud Poems," bizarrely in "Songs of the Transformed," Atwood shows us ourselves. Her masterful disguises – even the madonna-like smile on *Selected Poem*'s cover – matter little to her poetry.

1977

17 ENGEL, MARIAN. "Où en est la littérature anglo-canadienne?" *Liberté* (Montréal) 19, nos. 4-5 (July-October):67-72.

Begins a discussion of the rebirth of English Canadian literature by citing the 1976.10 review of *Lady Oracle* by British novelist Brigid Brophy. Although this review was negative, it is significant that England is paying attention to a Canadian novel. The nationalist movement and the discussion provoked by Atwood's pessimistic *Survival* helped to advance Canadian literature. The literary effects of Canadian authors becoming more political and more active in editing and business will not be understood for twenty years. Admires Atwood's strong and divided women characters.

18 ESPLIN, KATHRYN. "Atwood Collection a Must for Addicts." *Gazette* (Montreal), 1 October, p. 44.

Enjoys *Dancing Girls*, whose complicated stories are full of Atwood's "usual wry humor, intense personal vision, and mellow sarcasm." The title story concerns a young girl and the "odd but earthy creatures" in her rooming house. "The Grave of the Famous Poet" crosses "a marvelously droll joke" about an unnamed long-dead English poet with "a rather unique lover's parting. 'Hair Jewellery' is a beautifully executed self-mocking jab at academia and the absurdity of post-adolescent adult life"; "Lives of the Poets" vaguely recalls what Atwood may feel about giving poetry readings. Atwood's hard-to-define stories "vaguely seem to be about several things at once," while being thoroughly enjoyable.

19 FARKAS, EDIE. "It's Thickheadedly Pessimistic." *Last Post* 6, no. 1 (March):40-41.

Objects to the author, WASP mileu, and politics of *Lady Oracle*. Suddenly our "loudest Nationalist," now pushing 40, tells all, about her alternate life style as "just a regular hippie housewife" on a farm near Alliston. *Lady Oracle*'s critique of the urban WASP milieu appeals only to those so limited. This novel's excellent pastiche gothic romance mirrors its content; *Lady Oracle* is Atwood's most tightly written, smooth, flowing prose. Atwood says romance is necessary because people project ideal images, and make everything – politics too – a game, to escape dull reality. Joan's view of the gothic-reading "'workers'" is naively anachronistic, at best. Reducing politics and political theory to a game is the worst abdication.

1977

20 FAST, LAWRENCE. "Tripping the Light Fantastic." *Vancouver Sun*, 16 September, p. L33.

Appreciates these good *Dancing Girls* stories from the established, insightful, and widely hailed Atwood. The main characters, who are mostly women, find life brutish and short, and struggle to be at ease with themselves. "Polarities" and "A Travel Piece" are particularly effective; "Training" is fascinating; "Giving Birth," which reflects Atwood's recent motherhood, is the best, understandably.

21 FERRES, JOHN H., ed. "Canadian Writers." In *Modern Commonwealth Literature*. Compiled and edited by John H. Ferres and Martin Tucker. A Library of Literary Criticism. New York: Fredrick Ungar Publishing Co., pp. 236-39.

Excerpts from Moon 1968.6, 1969.11, Van Duyn 1970.38, Morley 1972.27, Woodcock 1973.106, and Owen 1976.72.

22 FOSTER, JOHN WILSON. "The Poetry of Margaret Atwood." *Canadian Literature*, no. 74 (Autumn), pp. 5-20.

Defines her root formula, from *The Circle Game* through *You Are Happy*, as "the self's inhabitation of spaces and forms and the metamorphoses entailed therein." From this formula her themes derive: "invasion, displacement, evolution and reversion, . . . survival, ingestion . . . and surfacing." To this formula her currently popular minority psychologies – psychic, feminine, and Canadian – connect; the self reflects from others' surface forms of self. Reads *The Journals of Susanna Moodie*, with its clearing and cabin, as archetypal Canadian literary history, confirmed by ancestral writings of Moodie, Catharine Parr Trail, and Anna Jameson. "Nothing is destroyed in Atwood's universe: it simply assumes another space, another form." Her metamorphosing, divided self journeys "between insight and hysteria," resisting sex and birth; between "safe imprisonment and dreadful freedom"; overland and underland and inward. Her animal imagery is heraldic, totemic, as in the Indian "Owl Song"; Circe, like Moodie, is a female wilderness spirit. Reprinted: 1988.17.

23 FRENCH, WILLIAM. "Quintessential Atwood." *Globe and Mail*, 3 September, p. 34.

Complains, perhaps unfairly, of *Dancing Girls*'s uncheerful, oppressively forceful literary world: the sardonic humour, bitter edge, neurotic women, and selfish men. "Atwood must once have been bitten by a rabid male." Even in stories where relationships aren't dying, the mood is dark. Yet, Atwood has deftly explored her war-of-the-sexes territory; and some flawed stories may be early ones, like perhaps "The War in the Bathroom." "Polarities," which doesn't flatter Edmonton, is better; the poignant, compelling "Training" may be the best. "Giving Birth" is a good try, but still reportage; perhaps maternity will mellow Atwood's fictional world view.

24 FRYE, NORTHROP. "Haunted by Lack of Ghosts: Some Patterns in the Imagery of Canadian Poetry." In *The Canadian Imagination: Dimensions of a Literary Culture*. Edited by David Staines. Cambridge, Mass. and London: Harvard University Press, pp. 24, 29-31, 43.

Praises Canadian themes in *Survival*'s inspired title, "Backdrop Addresses Cowboy," *The Journals of Susanna Moodie*, and *Procedures for Underground*. "Margaret Atwood, who has inherited [E.J.] Pratt's instinct for what is imaginatively central in Canadian sensibility," studies our curious schizophrenia of alienation versus optimism in the Moodie poems.

25 FULFORD, ROBERT. "Ever a Camp Counsellor Atwood Directs a Revue." *Toronto Star*, 14 May, p. H5.

Profiles the real Atwood: "Deep in her soul," she is still the camp counsellor who organized skits night circa 1955 at an Ontario summer camp; now, as subtle organizer and determined manipulator, she is "the real if mainly unseen star" of the Writers' Union All-Star Eclectic Typewriter Revue, which sold out Monday night at the St. Laurence Centre. Atwood wrote and directed the Toronto Literary Mafia, a vicious, self-inflicted attack on William French, as Frenchie; Douglas Marshall, as Doug the Thug; and someone called The Godfulford. All three gamely but ineptly tried to memorize, dance, and act their parts. The reviewer received congratulations which he interprets otherwise. Atwood also wrote a witty Jack the Knife, in which Jack McClelland appeared. Atwood's Farley Mowat Dancers, who included Sylvia Fraser, June Callwood, and Marian Engel, stopped the show twice, in snowshoes and then in kilts. A bear exited with Engel [author of *Bear*].

26 ____. "The Images of Atwood." *Malahat Review*, no. 41 (January), pp. 95-98. See Sandler 1977.81.

Our chief literary heroine approaches a public identity via shy affirmations and vehement denials; throwing out an idea, retrieving it, denying it. Though the elusive Atwood has insisted that the media made her a "Thing," the media begin with clues supplied. Atwood's half-shy and half-assertive public manner works perfectly in Canada's small, quickly sated cultural vacuum. She is endlessly re-usable, because endlessly Protean: feminist, nationalist, literary witch, etc.

27 GOTTLIEB, LOIS C., and KEITNER, WENDY. "Demeter's Daughters: The Mother-Daughter Motif in Fiction by Canadian Women." *Atlantis* 3, no. 1 (Fall):140-42.

Follows Adrienne Rich's *Of Woman Born* in praising *Surfacing* as a version of the Demeter-Kore myth: after surfacing from the lake like Kore from the dead, and after salutary madness, the narrator reclaims her mother's legacy, in the childhood picture, and sees her in vision as an "Earth Mother or 'Mistress of the Animals.'"

28 GRAY, FRANCINE du PLESSIX. "Nature as the Nunnery." *New York Times Book Review*, 17 July, pp. 3, 29.

Celebrates *Surfacing* as the surfacing of a tradition of female visionary novels. Atwood, "the star of Canadian letters," has reversed old stereotypes and created a heroine who is visionary, protector, and provider. An archetypal questing "Heroine of the thousand faces, she descends, like Persephone, into the world of the dead; she tests, like Perseus, the extreme limits of human endurance. . . ." Her vision and transformation blur nature/human; her final resolution, to refuse victimhood, is profoundly feminist. Atwood's naturalistic epiphanies transcend the fascinating issues raised by feminist theologians Christ 1976.13 and Plaskow 1976.74. Reprinted, as an introduction: 1979.47; reprinted, altered: 1987.47; reprinted: 1988.20.

29 GREENSTEIN, MICHAEL. "Quebec's Heart of Darkness: Retreat in *The Cashier, The Apprenticeship of Duddy Kravitz,* and *Surfacing.*" *Annales du Centre de Recherches sur l'Amerique Anglophone* (Talence), n.s., no. 1, pp. 71-87.

Discusses, in these three novels by Gabrielle Roy, Mordecai Richler, and Atwood, the three protagonists' complex, transforming retreats to the Quebec wilderness. In all three novels the result is ambiguous, as with *Surfacing*'s heroine, who "does not necessarily

1977

capitulate and return" to the city; "the land may transform a character or it may be transformed by man," as by *Surfacing*'s American technology; "the alienated child searches for parental guidance and fulfillment in the land," and surfaces to an awareness of life's depths and superficialities. Discusses *Surfacing*'s narrator's paranoia: her distrust of people, events, and experiences; and her vigilance and sense of being watched. The camera is for her an insidious, dangerous instrument, because its glossy images replace reality. She finally "learns to trust by adjusting her life to the land around her."

30 GUERRIERI, OSVALDO. "Intervista con Margaret Atwood, la più nota scrittrice canadese: La fionda letteraria." *Tuttolibri* (Turin), no. 95 (17 September), p. 12.

Interviews Atwood in Italy during a conference on European and North American relations. Italian universities produced 47 theses on Canadian authors this year, with Atwood the newest figure to be studied. *The Edible Woman* has been translated into Italian, and *Lady Oracle* and *Dancing Girls* will soon follow. Atwood discusses *Survival* and the relationship between American and Canadian literature, comparing the Canadians to David, the Americans to Goliath, and literature to the slingshot.

31 HILL, DOUGLAS. "Violations." *Canadian Forum* 57 (December-January):35.

Appreciates *Dancing Girls* as challenging, well-crafted, traditional, realistic Atwoodian stories which, taken together, express Canada's 1960s urban intellectual sensibility, better than Atwood's novels do. These are city stories, of uneasy students and academics; the narrative consciousness comes from Rosedale or Parkdale. Atwood's most characteristic voice is flat, spare, and elliptical. Though the humour of "Rape Fantasies" is overdone, the whole book can be seen, metaphorically, as profounder violations of the self. The shallow, irrational men seem offensively feminist-stereotyped – but perhaps Atwood is dead right. "Polarities," "The Grave of the Famous Poet," and "Lives of the Poets," are among the best; "Giving Birth" suggests that what could be a penultimate violation can become an ultimate existential mastery. Excerpted: 1983.129.

32 HOFSESS, JOHN. "Atwoodioni Presents . . . a Collection of Unhappy Middle-Class Women, None of Whom Look Like Monica Vitti." *Books in Canada* 6, no. 9 (November):27-28.

Praises *Dancing Girls*, which has a pervasive Antonioni-in-middle-class-Canada mood, but lacks a unifying theme. The strong characters are neurasthenic, unbeautiful women; the men are patriarchal civilization's burnt-out cases. Almost every story culminates in witty, slapstick tragedy, not despair. Atwood's dark comedy has a self-effacing, deadpan, complex irony, as in "Under Glass." Characters in dying relationships snipe like amateur guerillas. The reviewer enjoyed most the complete, fulfilled "The Man from Mars," "Polarities," and especially "Training"; but even the minor stories are saved by that playful intelligence, making raspberry noises off-stage.

33 ____. "How to Be Your Own Best Survival." *Malahat Review*, no. 41 (January), pp. 102-6. See Sandler 1977.81.

Responds personally to *Survival*, which he read a week after seeing his alcoholic father dying. "There's no cage, the door is open," *Survival* said. Embarrassed by his own drinking and smoking when he met Atwood, the reviewer began to exercise for fitness. As Keats said, "'That which is creative must first create itself.'" At a second meeting, Atwood said *Survival* had no connection with exercise. But the reviewer had read its victim pages spiritually, or creatively, and been so jolted that he'd changed his life for good.

34 HORNE, ALAN J., comp. "A Preliminary Checklist of Writings by and about Margaret Atwood." *Malahat Review*, no. 41 (January), pp. 195-222. See Sandler 1977.81.

Provides a chronological listing of primary and secondary work, but does not attempt complete coverage; expands 1974.15, using the same eleven categories. Newspapers and anthologies are selectively covered. Lists, under nine primary categories, 20 separately published works; 41 books and anthologies containing Atwood's work; 198 issues of periodicals, each containing one or more of her poems, stories, or other prose (a few issues which contain works from more than one genre are double-listed); 8 audio and audio-visual recordings; and a short list of the 11 boxes of manuscripts in the Thomas Fisher Rare Book Library, University of Toronto. Lists, under two secondary categories, 32 articles and theses; and 130 book reviews, cited by

1977

journal, not author or title. See Fairbanks 1979.32. Revised: 1979.56, 1980.59, and 1981.47.

35 HOSEK, CHAVIVA. "Romance and Realism in Canadian Fiction of the 1960s." *Journal of Canadian Fiction*, no. 20, pp. 125-26, 135-39.

Discusses *Surfacing*, along with Leonard Cohen's *Beautiful Losers* and Robertson Davies's *Fifth Business* and *The Manticore*, as the internalized mythic quest of a romantic rather than a realistic novel, and as part of the growing Canadian canon. *Surfacing*'s profoundly alienated narrator returns from visions and attempted transformations to a final acceptance of adult human life. *Surfacing* means both escaping, and losing, the depths. Compared to American fiction, Canadian romance quests are more spiritual and more social, and often enact Frye's millenial Exodus myth; Canadian romances end with some kind of affirmation, something brought back.

36 IRVINE, LORNA MARIE. "Hostility and Reconciliation: The Mother in English Canadian Fiction." Ph.D. dissertation, American University, 41 pp.

Much contemporary English Canadian fiction, by Alice Munro, Marian Engel, Margaret Atwood, Sylvia Fraser, and Margaret Laurence, focusses on "the daughter's ambivalent journey towards autonomy." This journey moves through three stages, from negation to recognition to assimilation. The daughter is caught between an independence that belittles the mother, and a dependent attachment. These female rites of passage elucidate the human condition, and perhaps a Canadian tradition of unifying reconciliation. See *Dissertation Abstracts International* 38:1380-A. Revised for publication: 1978.46 and 1980.63.

37 JEANNOTTE, M. SHARON. "An Emotional Divide." *Sphinx* 2, no. 3 (Winter):81-85.

Defends the very satisfying *Lady Oracle* against critics' and commentators' somewhat clouded reactions to one more Atwood book. Whether the heroine is you–or me, or both of us–is surely a more valid question than whether she is Margaret Atwood. Economy may not be a virtue in prose narrative–nor a fact in reality. If Joan's escapes are not very healthy, they were obviously not meant to be. Having two careers and three lovers is not uncommon–but Joan's fragmented personalities are curious. Joan's self-realization is in part feminist consciousness-raising – which many readers find difficult. The resolution of Joan's identity crisis is stylistically non-dramatic – like life; perhaps her final self-realization, about never becoming a tidy person, is painfully true, for many of us.

38 KEITNER, WENDY. Review of *Lady Oracle* and *Selected Poems*. *Quarry* 26, no. 2 (Spring):49-52.

Gives *Lady Oracle* mixed praise: feminism, realism, adventure, nationalism, terror, the occult, romance, satire, Atwood survives it all. Her third novel's saner, if eccentric, heroine focusses on social realism versus escape, and sums up what contemporary women want – passion plus pragmatism. Though Leda Sprott, the Polish Count, and the Royal Porcupine enliven the barren main plot, things fall off midway. As in *Surfacing*, the heroine flees the city, sheds clothes, and symbolically drowns while seeking contact with a pre-patriarchal Demeter Earth Mother. Acclaims *Selected Poem*'s lucid vision and cogent design, in each poem and the whole. Tone and image are viscerally intense and accurate, as in "you fit into me." Her poetry blocks escapes. Like Plath, Atwood probes the female psyche wrecked by patriarchy, and expresses underground emotions. She takes us back in time to the female unconscious, the animals, the earth.

39 KENNEDY, MAEV. "Second Best." *Irish Times* (Dublin), 2 July, p. 11.

Imagines, in a four-book review, that *Lady Oracle*, which has little "Gothick" and perhaps too much plausible detail, "might irritate many men and women, being built around a variety of particularly female neuroses. The central neurosis of the narrator is her inability to tell the truth about herself, which has broken her marriage. . . . The root of the problem is, of course, in her childhood." *Lady Oracle* is "very cleverly constructed," psychologically sound, and horribly convincing, but a bit like a confession that goes on too long and becomes tedious.

40 KING, BRUCE. "Margaret Atwood's *Surfacing*." *Journal of Commonwealth Literature* 12, no. 1 (August):23-32.

Praises *Surfacing* as a Canadian and "'counter-culture'" classic that both records and critiques an extreme of contemporary romanticism's return to nature. The narrator's dualism, alienation, and distrust of love represent basic themes of western civilization, English and Canadian culture, and women's liberation. *Surfacing* seems consciously intended, like *Survival*, to illustrate the Canadian imagination; the narrator suggests *Survival*'s categories of Futile Hero, Paralyzed Artist, and Absent Venus. The last, best chapters re-create a sacramental nature, better than in "Dream I: The Bush Garden." *Surfacing*'s profound beauty is flawed by the narrator's simplifying and caricaturing lesser characters, as in *The Edible Woman*.

41 LANDSBERG, MICHELE. "Late Motherhood." *Chatelaine* 50, no. 10 (October):44, 46, 119-21.
　　Profiles Atwood as one of several artistically-established, late-birthing Canadian "'supermums.'" Atwood, the cool, intelligent, "reigning queen of Canadian authors," plays peek-a-boo with one-year-old Eleanor Jess at her farmhouse; and discusses her earlier years, her writing, and her present mothering.

42 LEFCOWITZ, BARBARA F. "The Search Motif in Some Contemporary Female Poets: Atwood, Rukeyser, Rich." *University of Michigan Papers in Women's Studies* 2, no. 3:84-89.
　　Discusses two Atwood poems, Muriel Rukeyser's "Ajanta," and Adrienne Rich's "Diving into the Wreck" as female quest poems; concludes with a female quest poem of her own. Considers "Dream: Bluejay or Archeopteryx" as "a prolegomenon to the fully realized quest poem." Its man surfacing is not the revitalizing "dead father-dead god" of Atwood's female quest novel, *Surfacing*, but an inevitable and sinister "death-force"; the poet doesn't enter the underwater mirror that could yield more awesome, primitive masculine images – "to be confronted or absorbed in the self" – the aim is unclear. In "Procedures for Underground" the journey to the macabre underworld is dangerous; the survivor is tempted to return, and becomes a pariah. That journey into the collective and personal past may scarcely be worth taking.

43 LEVINE, JO ANN. "Atwood Isn't Regarded as Wicked Witch South of Border." *Winnipeg Free Press*, 4 February, p. 23.
　　Reprinted from 1977.44 (below), slightly amplified.

44 ____. "Canadian Writer Talks of Her Work and Outlook." *Christian Science Monitor*, 12 January, p. 18.

Interviews Atwood, who arrived with her baby, and whose "creamy young complexion smoothly caged the ice-blue animals in her eyes," at her Fifth Avenue publisher's office: Atwood discusses her tough, wicked-witch image in Canada and *Survival*; her main characters versus desirable roommates; fatness, frizzy hair, and fitting in during the 1950s; *Lady Oracle*'s mother-daughter relationship (Atwood has just read Adrienne Rich's *Of Woman Born*), anti-Gothic, and Canada's Harlequin Romances. Reprinted, slightly amplified: 1977.43 (above).

45 LILIENFELD, JANE. "Circe's Emergence: Transforming Traditional Love in *You Are Happy*." *Worcester* (Mass.) *Review* 5 (Spring):29-37.

Celebrates "Circe/Mud Poems" as women's anger and power imaginatively transforming traditional love to new, equal, compassionate modes; these poems move beyond *Power Politics*'s questioning. Circe's powers come from the earth, not male mythology; men's animality grows from their own limited perceptions. Circe demystifies Odysseus' heroic exploits with laughter. She recognizes his sickle-shaped scars as "moonmarks," binding him not only to war, but also to The Mother. The renewed, fruitful love of Circe's final poem, and of the final, mortal sequence, transforms earlier poems, as words blaze up, "fade into other words," and ricochet. Reprinted: 1988.27.

46 LYONS, BONNIE. Review of *Lady Oracle*. *New Orleans Review* 5, no. 3:283-84.

Lady Oracle has many witty, excellent, and insightful parts, but is finally unsatisfying as a whole. Its Gothic parody and comedy of manners are each uncannily and precisely right; but they are never a unity; and they detract from the most moving "evocation of the heroine's childhood." The mother is painfully accurate. The vision of fatness is the best. What may be most disturbing is *Lady Oracle*'s strange parody, or distortion, of *Surfacing*'s most serious themes. *Surfacing*'s genuine transformation is a satisfying resolution; *Lady Oracle*'s resolution is a comic gesture that is unsatisfying in this basically serious novel. The zany contrivances belittle the real meaning; our feelings for the struggling heroine can't survive absurd coincidence. Excerpted: 1978.11.

1977

47 McCLUNG, M.G. "Margaret Atwood." In *Women in Canadian Literature*. Women in Canadian Life, edited by Jean Cochrane and Pat Kincaid. Toronto: Fitzhenry & Whiteside, pp. 82-89.

Characterizes Canada's most-read, and internationally known, writer, and her books, which incorporate comedy, satire, and Canadian, nature, female/male, oppressor/victim, and survival themes; emphasizes *Survival*.

48 McDOWELL, JUDITH H. Review of *Lady Oracle*. *World Literature Written in English* 16, no. 1 (April):82-86.

Like Harry Houdini, "Joan/Louisa understands the quintessential need for escape," from strangling, stifling childhood and adult attachments. Perceiving "the fundamental truth that reality is most conspicuous by its absence," she therefore lies, continually. Though she tries to vanish without a trace in Italy, the gothic claptrap she writes intrudes into her real life – and her real past life intrudes into her writing. Joan can never begin to break her most significant, revealing relationship, the mother/daughter tie: she is very much like the mother she finally accepts, for one's parents cannot be uprooted from oneself. Under *Lady Oracle*'s hilarity, then, we see a profound truth: there is no exit or escape from self.

49 MacLEOD, REX. "What Happened to the Comers of 1967?" *Toronto Star*, 30 June, p. B5.

Interviews five of the young movers and shakers that the 1967 *Toronto Star* called "The Canadians Taking Charge in the Nation's Second Century": federal cabinet minister Jean Chretien, Atwood, Manitoba farmer Jim McKinney, Vancouver-Toronto painter Claude Breeze, and Halifax schoolteacher Mike Tzagarakis. Quotes Atwood on the forthcoming Quebec referendum: she predicts a 70-30 vote for separation, which may lead to the U.S. marching, and the break-up of Canada.

50 McMULLEN, LORRAINE. "Images of Women in Canadian Literature: Woman as Hero." *Atlantis* 2, no. 2, pt. 2, (Spring):134-35, 141-42.

Discusses the evolving Canadian literary archetype of the woman hero – not an adjunct heroine, earth mother, or femme fatale – in novels by Martha Ostenso, Morley Callaghan, Margaret Laurence,

1977

Ethel Wilson, Constance Beresford-Howe, and in Atwood's *Surfacing*. Like the archetypal male hero, the woman hero ventures on a mythical quest, which may be an internal voyage of self discovery; she may meet a Jungian *animus*, and a woman guide; she descends to an underworld and returns wiser, or freer. *Surfacing*'s journey-quest is multiple; the protagonist finds her own truth and responsibility when she finds her father's body. Like these other women heroes, she rejects conventional success, and seeks freedom and self worth.

51 MANDEL, ELI. "Atwood Gothic." In *Another Time*. Three Solitudes: Contemporary Literary Criticism in Canada, vol. 3. Erin, Ont.: Press Porcépic Ltd., pp. 137-145.
    Reprint of 1977.52 (below).

52 ____. "Atwood Gothic." *Malahat Review*, no. 41 (January), pp. 165-74. See Sandler 1977.81.
    Atwood's oracular and literary qualities – her novels' gothic elements, her obsessively reduplicating images and reflexive stories, and her totemic animal imagery – have been overshadowed by her powerful social-comment metaphors. *The Journals of Susanna Moodie* is more Gothic tale than ghost story. Ellen Moers's "Female Gothic" suggests that birth is the real taboo; Atwood's "Speeches for Dr. Frankenstein" is unmistakably about a botched birth/death. "How much of [*Surfacing*'s] haunting proceeds from an abortion?" *Survival* lists horrendous stillbirths and worse. But to see Atwood's "*allegory* of gothic" [italics sic] is to explain away *Surfacing*'s ghosts and Atwood's disturbing doubleness. "Tricks with Mirrors," "This Is a Photograph of Me," and the unresolved "Gothic Letter on a Hot Night" reveal her reflexive stories and "insane phenomenology" – which are, as in Borges and Robertson Davies, both fraud and magic; and which try to resolve impossible dilemmas. Reprinted: 1977.51 (above); 1988.34.

53 ____. "Criticism as Ghost Story." *Another Time*. Three Solitudes: Contemporary Literary Criticism in Canada, vol. 3. Erin, Ont.: Press Porcépic Ltd., pp. 146-50.
    Reprint of 1974.25.

54 ____. "Modern Canadian Poetry." In *Another Time*. Three Solitudes:
Contemporary Literary Criticism in Canada, vol. 3. Erin, Ont.: Press
Porcépic Ltd., pp. 81-90.
Reprint of 1970.26.

55 MARSHALL, TOM. "Atwood under and above Water." *Malahat
Review*, no. 41 (January), pp. 89-94. See Sandler 1977.81.
Praises the Canadian themes of Atwood's poetry and two novels.
Using the Canadian '"underwater"' motif, ancestors, animals, and gods
of place, "[i]n her emotional pioneering Atwood moves to the center of
our concerns." Her poetic protagonist "is imprisoned in the haunted
house of Canadian exile," in time, and in her own body, as in ["The
Dwarf."] *The Journals of Susanna Moodie* is Atwood's powerful
objective correlative; *Power Politics* is something else, with its "icy
analyses" and "grim sexual warfare." The more sympathetic, earthier
You Are Happy freely affirms love. *The Edible Woman* is a wickedly
funny, kindly ironic comedy, despite its prolonged satire on
consumerism. *Surfacing* is a psychological ghost story of a desperately
alienated woman, and a Canadian version of James Dickey's
Deliverance. *Surfacing* builds extraordinary tension; its evocation of the
wilderness is marvelous. Revised: 1979.69.

56 MELLORS, JOHN. "Writer's Lib." *Listener* 98 (14 July):62-63.
Praises *Lady Oracle* in a five-book review: like Nigel Williams,
Atwood wittily and forcefully upholds the writer's right to write. Praises
Lady Oracle's Erica Jong-like heroine and predicament; its sly wit and
exuberant farce; and its intriguing end and beginning.

57 MILLER, JANE. "A Pack of Truths." *TLS*, 15 July, p. 872.
Enjoys *Lady Oracle*'s "veritable Pauline," Joan: her duplicity,
multiplicities, and staged, [John] Stonehouse drowning; her parody and
paired reflections, reversals, and transformations; and the bleak
realism of her surface life. What finally confounds this clever novel's
"imaginings, is that we believe the narrator and discount her lies."

58 MILLS, JOHN. Review of *Lady Oracle*. *Queen's Quarterly* 84, no. 1
(Spring):102-104.
Praises, in a four-book review, *Lady Oracle*'s unpretentious,
entertaining comedy; its theatrical mask and anti-mask personages; and

its faintly Chichikovian [after the hero of *Dead Souls*] heroine and faintly Gogolian, perfectly integrated crossing of high tragic stabbing with everyday RyKrisp.

59 MOSS, JOHN. "Strange Bedfellows: Atwood and Richler." In *Sex and Violence in the Canadian Novel: The Ancestral Present.* Toronto: McClelland & Stewart, pp. 123-46.

Atwood's *Surfacing*, like Mordecai Richler's *St. Urbain's Horseman*, blends realism, ironic satire, and moral judgments; both novels exploit the tensions between psychological self and sociological identity. Atwood's protagonists, here and elsewhere, strive for self-knowledge. *Surfacing* exploits poetic language; its everywoman descends through barriers of consciousness to a primeval, evolutionary maternity and the always possible visions. Maternity is her mother's gift to her. *Surfacing* must end with conditional sanity and qualified affirmation, for only our "American"' surfaces will sustain life. Atwood's always-authentic poetic images show the immediate perception of a thing, not the thing or the perceiver. For Atwood, camera and mirror images fix perceptual reality to appearance, as words fix conceptual consciousness.

*60 NODELMAN, PERRY. "Condensed Soup–in One Flavor Only." *Winnipeg Free Press*, 1 October, Leisure sec., p. [6?].

Finds *Dancing Girls* intense, witty, and well-characterized, and all its stories good stories, but too depressingly similar to be read together. Most are about alienated women, who remain uninvolved for safety; the one male point of view sounds like a sex-changed heroine. Atwood's attitude to her characters is unvarying: "'a professional tourist,'" she sits still and watches. Reading these is like having a dinner of three courses of condensed soup straight from the can: "too overpowering to be delectable." Atwood always finds the same good answer to the same damn question.

61 ____. "Trusting the Untrustworthy." *Journal of Canadian Fiction*, no. 21, pp. 73-82.

Follows Dawe 1973.19 and Onley 1974.33, rejecting Rogers 1974.38, to assess *The Edible Woman* as a satiric novel of personal growth. At first we perceive the narrator's conscious voice as untrustworthy and satirized; gradually we perceive the wisdom of her unconscious, revealing images. Discusses in detail the *Alice in Wonderland* parallels, and the pervasive imagery of eating, hunting, camouflage, packaging, eggs, and shells.

62 "Notes on Current Books." *Virginia Quarterly Review* 53, no. 2 (Spring):65.

Terms *Lady Oracle* an essentially shallow but delightfully entertaining and witty satire: though women's relation to food may be an Atwood sub-theme, her novel, like her Scarlet Pimpernel, lacks symbolism and significance.

63 NOVAK, BARBARA. Review of *Dancing Girls*. *Quill and Quire* 43, no. 14 (13 October):7.

Praises Atwood's well-made, insightful stories and novels, whose lonely protagonists struggle with their isolation and "'otherness,'" as in "The Man from Mars." Atwood's mood is darker in these stories of transients and tourists; "A Travel Piece" is one of her best. The obtrusive humour of "Rape Fantasies" undermines its pathos. Many stories explore the desperate self-doubt experienced as a love affair dims.

64 O'TOOLE, LAWRENCE. "Atwood Part of Circe's Song and Dance Routine." *Globe and Mail*, 2 April, p. 39.

Interviews Atwood on the Circe masque for dancers and singers, now in rehearsal, which is a three-way collaboration with Atwood's libretto, Ann Ditchburn's choreography, and music composed by Raymond Pannell. Ditchburn has called the Circe masque perhaps "the first feminist opera"; Atwood describes it as a variation on a well-known story, and the usual Odysseus as "sort of like a bulldozer."

65 OWEN, I.M. "Margaret Atwood as Comic Genius." *Saturday Night* 92, no. 9 (November):60-61, 67.

Acclaims *Dancing Girls* as Atwood's best prose, even better than *Lady Oracle*; her comic genius makes us enjoy the most chilling topics. The reviewer laughed aloud five times during "Rape Fantasies" – which will no doubt be rebuked for frivolity by someone from the women's movement who will not see Atwood's final realism. Atwood's comedy, unlike that of [P.G.] Wodehouse, "haunts you ever after, because like all the highest comedy it is about real life in all its sadness." Perhaps her best comedy comes from her loving but disliking man-woman relationships. Her men tend to be "Martians," from alien cultures; like Dickens, she hasn't yet quite managed an opposite-sex point of view. The hallucinatory, projected alter egos of "The War in the Bathroom" and "Giving Birth" are ingeniously varied; Jeannie, who is in part a projection of the recently primaparous Atwood, has a projection of her own.

66 PACKER, MIRIAM. "Beyond the Garrison: Approaching the Wilderness in Margaret Laurence, Alice Munro, and Margaret Atwood." Ph.D. dissertation, University of Montreal.

Follows and critiques *Survival*'s arguments, which modify Northrop Frye's garrison mentality, in a study of personal growth, beyond the psychological garrison and wilderness, in Laurence, Munro, and Atwood's *The Edible Woman*, *Surfacing*, and *Lady Oracle*; emphasizes the concept of women's internalized prisons in *Survival*'s "Ice Women vs. Earth Mothers" chapter.

67 PETERSON, KEVIN. "Writers and Words." *Calgary Herald*, 15 October, p. E10.

A rave review of *Dancing Girls*, whose excellent short stories combine the acid wit of Atwood's poetry with the deep human understanding of her novels. Read together, "Atwood's stories leave indelible impressions of real people" who could be your friends; "The Grave of the Famous Poet," for example, describes a tenuous, totally collapsing relationship that "leaves the reader shaken." The counterpointing "Rape Fantasies" freezes its characters in their stereotypes, then adds contemplative depth. Atwood's peculiar, ethereal air is devastatingly accurate yet somewhat distanced, intensely personal yet strangely unemotional. Atwood watchers may wonder if "Giving Birth" is autobiographical. Also welcomes a forthcoming University of C[algary] conference on the Canadian novel.

68 PRITCHARD, WILLIAM H. "Merely Fiction." *Hudson Review* 30, no. 1 (Spring):149-50.

Prefers, in a round-up review, Renata Adler's swift, sly, satiric *Speedboat* to *Lady Oracle*'s longish account of a heroine growing up. (Snapshots of Atwood suggest that she coincides with her flowing-red-haired heroine.) Though pleasant-sad comic moments occur, Atwood's

1977

humor has a high-school sophomoric slant, particularly concerning the heroine as sex object, and the Royal Porcupine. The sentences skid along towards nowhere interesting. Perhaps the nine-book Atwood writes "all too effortlessly?"

69 PURDY, AL [W.]. "An Unburnished One-Tenth of One Per Cent of an Event." *Malahat Review*, no. 41 (January), pp. 61-64. See Sandler 1977.81.

Rejects contemporary "'image'"-making; tells how his friendship with Atwood began; and praises her books, including the extremely important *Survival*. John Glassco, in *Time*, has foolishly labeled Irving Layton, Atwood, and Purdy as a professional wild man, a professional virgin, and a professional hick. One can't know one-tenth of any other person. Purdy's friendship with Atwood began at Doug Jones's, where Atwood and Purdy doused one another hilariously with beer, because she mistakenly thought he had disparaged academics. Atwood's "'image'" is far from reality; she reacts to insult like a human being, speaks her own mind to interviewers, is warm and alive.

70 READ, JEANI. "Atwood on a Binge in a Costume Rental Store." *Province* (Vancouver), 30 September, p. 27.

Argues that *Dancing Girls* fails by accentuating the faults of Atwood's novels: her poetry is clean, striking, and resonant; but her novels have inadequate plots and characterizations, and a curious maze of irrelevant superficialities that rarely supports their themes and that obscures their uninteresting metaphors. *Dancing Girls* resembles the proverbial onions, all layers, no core. In these fourteen stories Atwood plays with fourteen identities in a "perplexingly dilettante fashion"; she is "neither brave enough to acknowledge" her own perceptions, "nor responsible enough to defer" to her characters' perceptions. Inability is the connecting theme; the characters, who are "all more darned than damned," are passive submitters. Atwood's writing is as "bleak, inert and unsympathetic" as her vision.

71 Review of *Dancing Girls and Other Stories*. *Chatelaine* 50, no. 10 (October):6.

All these stories are worth reading. Atwood is a deeply serious and wildly funny writer; these stories vary in seriousness, but are always humorous. Most deal with couples who don't communicate, which

Atwood conveys brilliantly; but the less expected stories, like ["A Travel Piece"], are also "acutely observed and superbly presented."

72 Review of *Lady Oracle. Choice* 13, no. 12 (February):1592.
Recommends highly the excellently crafted and baroquely elaborated *Lady Oracle*, which blends the satiric wit and vivid terror of Atwood's first two novels. The ambiguously affirmative end, which undercuts the gothic fear, "tests the conventions by which we order reality."

73 RIDLEY, MICHAEL. Review of *Dancing Girls and Other Stories*. *Canadian Book Review Annual*:129-30.
Criticizes Atwood's fiction, which succeeds as popular light fiction, but not as important art. *Dancing Girls*, like the serious but flawed *Surfacing* and the light, popular *Lady Oracle*, shows Atwood failing to live up to her artistic potential. The most interesting stories are "Polarities," "Training," and "Rape Fantasies," which catches the sparkle and drive of lunch-room conversation. "*Dancing Girls* is above all entertaining"; if that's Atwood's goal, she succeeds.

74 ROCARD, MARCIENNE. "Margaret Atwood's *Surfacing*: A Pilgrimage to the Sources." *Caliban* (Toulouse), no. 14, pp. 39-46.
Discusses *Surfacing*'s linked themes and quest motifs, and the question of Anglo-Canadian identity: antiamerican [sic] nationalism; wilderness primitivism; physical and spiritual survival; Canadian victim themes; and the heroine's maddening, Oedipal search for her father. The wildly antiamerican imaginings are based on facts. The Anglo-Canadians who think themselves morally superior to the Americans turn out to be their servile imitators. Atwood's solution is not socialism, but the traditional Canadian journey to the bush, the French-Canadian pilgrimage to the purifying North, away from alienating technological civilization. The therapeutic journey ends as the hero surfaces, refusing to be a victim, preserving her natural wholeness and Canadian integrity.

75 ROGERS, LINDA. "Dirges to Baby." *Sphinx* 2, no. 3 (Winter):78-80.
Rejects *Selected Poems* as "reptilian artifacts, all jewel beautiful and quite hollow." These poems of the super-ego, the severed head, the articulating mask, lack human contact. There is pain and satire, but no

compassion; even the dying animals are bottled in words as cold as formaldehyde. Atwood is a better poet than novelist because poems do not require dialogue. *The Journals of Susanna Moodie*, with its grieving mother, is the most satisfying; Susanna's shade humanizes the detached poet. There may be some humanity in *Power Politics*'s angry virago. Have we made Atwood a cult figure because we see ourselves as survivors in her hopeless landscape?

76 ROSENBERG, JEROME H. "On Reading the Atwood Papers in the Thomas Fisher Library." *Malahat Review*, no. 41 (January), pp. 191-94. See Sandler 1977.81.

Finds the Atwood papers revealing, exciting, and essential for scholars. Going back ten years, we discover the optimistic determination behind Atwood's initial successes. The professional correspondence, which lets us relive her ascendance, is the most exciting. The several rejections of the unpublished novel, "Up in the Air So Blue," show her determination and, in readers' comments, the virtues and faults of her early fiction. Possibly the most significant are the Atwood-Charles Pachter correspondence, on his lithographs of "The Circle Game," and his proposed cover for *The Circle Game*; and the Contact Press correspondence, on making that book, which shows something of Atwood's witty, energetic professional personality. See 1984.81.

77 ROSENGARTEN, HERBERT. "Urbane Comedy." *Canadian Literature*, no. 72 (Spring), pp. 84-87.

Praises *Lady Oracle*'s characters, style, entertaining and skillful compound of domestic comedy, wit, Jungian psychology, social satire, and the occult. Its ugly-duckling narrator hides behind the identities others want (national identity allegorists, take note). Though Joan's cool, ironic sensibility does not totally match her helpless vulnerability, still, this urbane comedy is a relief–after *Surfacing*'s humourless self-righteousness, feminist hostility, and contempt for everyday human life. *Lady Oracle*'s vision is just as serious, but broadened and matured. Joan's search for emotional and psychic integration holds together the deftly developed episodes of the plot. Excerpted: 1978.11.

78 RULE, JANE. "Life, Liberty, and the Pursuit of Normalcy: The Novels of Margaret Atwood." *Malahat Review*, no. 41 (January), pp. 42-49. See Sandler 1977.81.

Assesses themes, characters, genre, narrative technique, and language in Atwood's three novels; praises *Lady Oracle* most highly. Can one be normal, without being a victim of normalcy? *The Edible Woman*'s Marian wants a limiting normalcy; the role-rejecting Duncan is, for Marian, more Peter's substitute than his opposite. The often-discussed cake is a metaphorical trick of resolution, which works because this novel is only farce, not satire. *Surfacing*'s narrator finds normalcy terrifying, and words, lies. Her mistrust of language, and the final metaphorical godhead, make a questionable resolution. *Lady Oracle*'s several-identity narrator explores language and pursues normalcy most thoroughly; *Lady Oracle* is "satire of the first order," with the artist as "prime trickster."

79 SALUTIN, RICK. "A Note on the Marxism of Atwood's *Survival*." *Malahat Review*, no. 41 (January), pp. 57-60. See Sandler 1977.81.

Suggests that *Survival* is, if not Marxist literary criticism, then proto-Marxist, or *pre*-Marxist; distinguishes this from bourgeois criticism, and from fully developed Marxism. First, "*Survival* grounds the cultural phenomenon (Canlit) in a material historical reality." Second, it focusses on the fulcrum – the imperial, colonial economy – because its intent is *practical* change. Third, this survival is highly dialectical; the "Basic Victim Positions" are a dialectically interrelated "series of strategies for survival"; and survival, not victimization, is the central theme. Affirms Atwood 1973.2; *Survival*'s purpose is political; it emerges from and takes part in Canadian society's historical struggle.

80 SANDLER, LINDA. "Interview with Margaret Atwood." *Malahat Review*, no. 41 (January), pp. 7-27. See Sandler 1977.81.

During March and April 1976, at her farm outside Alliston, Atwood discusses Canadian versus U.S. success and media images, referring to Pearson 1974.35, Davey 1973.17, [D[rummond]] 1974.6, and Erica Jong; her own work, including *Double Persephone*, "Speeches for Dr. Frankenstein," *The Journals of Susanna Moodie*, *Power Politics*, *You Are Happy*, *The Edible Woman*, *Surfacing*, *Survival*, and *Lady Oracle*; metamorphosis in her father's entomology and *Grimm's Fairy*

1977

Tales ("the most influential book I ever read"); the gothic maze, Mary Shelley's *Frankenstein*, and the Henry James ghost story; her own writing versus "self-expression" and "'spontaneity'"; the Canadian artist, heroine, and hero; Canadian literature as mirror and satire; writing versus politics; feminism and women writers; Nova Scotian roots; and Anansi editing.

81 ____, ed. *Margaret Atwood: A Symposium. Malahat Review*, no. 41 (January), 228 pp.
    Contains photographs, worksheets, poetry, fiction, and critical work: "An Album of Photographs" of Atwood from 1945 to 1976, by Graeme Gibson and others; "Anima: A Pictographic Sextain for Margaret Atwood," by Robin Skeleton; Atwood's worksheets for three poems ("I made no choice" and "we walk in the cedar grove" from the "Circe/Mud Poems" and "Tricks with Mirrors" from *You Are Happy*); Atwood's poem "Threes" and her story "The Resplendent Quetzal," reprinted in *Dancing Girls*; poems, some concerning Atwood, by Ralph Gustafson, Janis Rapoport, George Woodcock, Al Purdy, Tom Marshall, Linda Sandler, Susan Musgrave, Gwendolyn MacEwen, and George Jonas; fiction by George Bowering; and the following critical work: Sandler 1977.82 and 1977.80, Sullivan 1977.90, Rule 1977.78, Woodcock 1977.99, Salutin 1977.79, Purdy 1977.69, Marshall 1977.55, Fulford 1977.26, Hofsess 1977.33, Skelton 1977.83, Smith 1977.84, Mandel 1977.52, Rosenberg 1977.76, and Horne 1977.34.

82 ____. Preface to *Margaret Atwood: A Symposium. Malahat Review*, no. 41 (January), pp. 5-6. See Sandler 1977.81.
    Celebrates Atwood as "the presiding genius of Canadian letters" and "the thinking person's alternative" to England's symbolic Queen; *Surfacing* and *The Journals of Susanna Moodie* as "instant Canadian classics," and *Survival* as simplistic truth that triggered Canadian consciousness. Canadian readers see her often satiric books as mirrors. *Power Politics* made her a leading Cassandra to North American feminists, and a Medusa to countless knights. *The Edible Woman* and *Surfacing* have been reissued in the Americans' inimitable underworld-format covers. *Lady Oracle*, which will likely establish Atwood internationally, and as a Canadian comedian, is her tribute to Canada's Harlequin Romances.

83 SKELTON, ROBIN. "Timeless Constructions: A Note on the Poetic Style of Margaret Atwood." *Malahat Review*, no. 41 (January), pp. 107-20. See Sandler 1977.81.

Analyzes Atwood's original, mysterious poetic style and its modular construction, with self-contained, parallel, and often reversible or rearrangeable units, in *Double Persephone*'s "Iconic Landscape" and in poems from *The Circle Game, Power Politics, Procedures for Underground*, "Circe/Mud," and *You Are Happy*. Modular poetry suspends time, by focussing on states of being, rather than events. "Siren Song" has three of the four major kinds of parallelisms found in the King James Bible: synonymous, synthetic, and antithetical. Atwood's style is perceptual, symbolic, and ideogrammatic, rather than conceptual, abstract, or rhetorical. In Atwood's reversible poems, "we are uneasily aware that beginnings could be conclusions, and conclusions are not endings." Progress and certainty are not obtainable; like Alice on the chessboard, we are running madly in place without moving, accumulating information without understanding.

84 SMITH, ROWLAND. "Margaret Atwood: The Stoic Comedian." *Malahat Review*, no. 41 (January), pp. 134-44. See Sandler 1977.81.

Approves the stoic humour and wry scorn of Atwood's three novels, which depict the grotesque banalities of middle Canadian life. "Atwood is a master at the mode of the derailed observer." In all three novels, the reader curiously empathizes with the cooly attractive heroines, who are themselves victims of banality, and accomplices seeking it. All three narrators, even the inept Joan, offer domestic, womanly help. *The Edible Woman* is a bleak comedy of predatory, mindless, hellishly commonplace consumers; *Surfacing*, a menacing satire. *Lady Oracle*'s attractive Joan counters stifling conformity with her own clodhopping banality and superbly trite fantasies; but Joan's mocking mask is more grotesque, and covers a prolonged hysteric scream.

85 SOLECKI, SAM. Review of *Lady Oracle*. *University of Toronto Quarterly* 46, no. 4 (Summer):343-44.

Argues that *Lady Oracle* is a slight, flawed comic novel which, like Marian Engel's *The Bear*, has been vastly overpraised this season. *Lady Oracle*'s light comedy restates Atwood's themes and situations in more attractive form. Structurally, it's her best novel. But much of its

1977

humour is stock, and its Toronto and nationalistic satire is weak. *Lady Oracle* fails because its characters aren't interesting: Joan is a shallow girl, and the males are as shadowy as most of Atwood's men, if not all.

86 STEVENS, PETER. "Explorer/Settler/Poet." *University of Windsor Review* 13, no. 1 (Fall-Winter):63-74.
Discusses the search for Canadian consciousness in historic proto-forms as a basis for an indigenous poetry, in four Canadian poets: John Newlove, Margaret Atwood, Al Purdy, and Florence McNeil. *The Journals of Susanna Moodie* uses Moodie's two books as proto-forms of the writer in Canada. Atwood sees Moodie as exemplifying Canada's national sickness of paranoid schizophrenia, as moving from English patriotism to Canadian consciousness, as trying to "become human." Susanna's doubleness is "the double bind of the poet in the new world."

87 STRUTHERS, J.R. (TIM). "An Interview with Margaret Atwood." *Essays on Canadian Writing*, no. 6 (Spring), pp. 18-27.
Responding to questions, Atwood discusses her poetry, including *Double Persephone*, *The Journals of Susanna Moodie* as a Yeatsian anti-mask, and the *Selected Poems*; her early readings, and ambitions to write and paint; the Canadian literary tradition now versus 1950s Toronto; popular and Canadian literary forms; anti-comedy, ghost story, and anti-gothic in her three novels; reviews by Brophy 1976.10, Duffy 1976.20, Pearson 1974.35, and Colombo 1976.16; characterization versus our fantasized gothic roles and scenarios; *Lady Oracle*'s gothic and popular gothic literary tradition, and parallels to its squashed animals and con-create artist; Canadian women versus men writers; and extra-literary reactions to herself.

88 ____. "Margaret Atwood Has Surfaced: The Fist Is Now a Hand." *London* (Ontario) *Free Press*, 22 January, p. 31.
Appreciates *Selected Poems*'s ascent: Atwood's latest poems have a new warmth, humanity, ripeness, and desire. The contrasting harshness of earlier poems is necessary to repudiate tapeworm-like social myths, and to subvert romantic views. Though many of the best poems move from realism to the fabulous or gothic, as in *Power Politics*, ultimately Atwood celebrates the actual over the fantastic. Darkness and descent prevailed, until *Surfacing*'s ascent prepared the

way for *You Are Happy*'s return. *Selected Poem*'s cyclical shape is Frye's pattern of quest-romance, especially in *Procedures for Underground*'s last poems, *The Journals of Susanna Moodie*, and *You Are Happy*.

89 STUBING, JOHN L. Review of *Lady Oracle*. *Best Sellers* 36, no. 11 (February):346.

Recommends, to all who have failed, or succeeded, this well-written, entertaining, poignant, witty, bitterly humorous tale of a vulnerable woman. *Lady Oracle* threads its way between the happy and sad, real and surreal, sublime and ridiculous.

90 SULLIVAN, ROSEMARY. "Breaking the Circle." *Malahat Review*, no. 41 (January), pp. 30-41. See Sandler 1977.81.

Atwood's central "Circle Game" is a psychological, cultural, and mythic symbol of Canada's garrison mentality and of order versus chaos. Though *Survival* fails as cultural history, it defines a collective Canadian myth, of a passive, narcissistic colonial mentality. Though Atwood can be naively dogmatic, her Susanna Moodie is a Canadian archetype, encircled and invaded by the wilderness, retreating into the ordered circle game. *Surfacing* shows man colonizing nature, and thereby polarizing man and nature. The narrator does break with logic, enter ritual stages that correspond to Mircea Eliade's shamanic initiation, and commune with nature. But because Atwood settles for a ghost story, and logical language, the visionary insights aren't integrated into the story; *Surfacing* ends as an ironic, alienated book, with the circle game unbroken. Revised in part: 1987.150. Reprinted: 1988.49.

91 SYMONS, SCOTT. "The Canadian Bestiary: Ongoing Literary Depravity." *West Coast Review* 11, no. 3 (January):3, 10, 15.

Ridicules Atwood, and the other women and literary mandarins who have acclaimed "authorine" Marian Engel's *Bear*. Groups Atwood with Engel, Fraser, and Munro as "the current gaggle of Canadian feminist harridans . . . [of] '"women's glib."'" Claims that it is dangerous to dare to assess "the lady Amazons," especially Atwood.

1977

92 TEXMO, DELL. "The Other Side of the Looking Glass: Image and Identity in Margaret Atwood's *The Edible Woman*." *Atlantis* 2, no. 2, pt. 1 (Spring):65-76.

Discusses the heroine's search for a meaningful and independent identity in a world of false, stereotyped, superficial images of femininity. Marian moves from bondage, through a surrealistic disintegration, to a final liberation, which is symbolized by eating the cake-woman. The eccentric Duncan guides her through the role-playing labyrinth; the other women, and the threatening Peter, are themselves caught up in meaningless and superficial images, and lack true identity.

93 THOMAS, CLARA. "Feminist or Heroine?" *Essays on Canadian Writing*, no. 6 (Spring), pp. 28-31.

Praises *Lady Oracle*, and defines its theme as the self-dramatizing heroinism, not the self-defining feminism, of Ellen Moers's *Literary Women*. In structure, setting, and full characterizations, this is Atwood's most complex novel. Joan herself is appealingly believable, essentially decent, kind, and good-humoured in her quest for happy endings and her ironic, limited self-knowledge. *Lady Oracle* belongs, in Margot Northey's 1976.70 categories, with the "Sportive Grotesque," which is strongly Gothic; but could be put with the "Satiric Grotesque." Partly incorporated into 1978.98.

94 TRUEBLOOD, VALERIE. "Conscience and Spirit." *American Poetry Review* 6, no. 2 (March-April):19-20.

Analyzes *You Are Happy*'s feminism, conscience, and mysticism. *Surfacing* was not about "self-discovery," but about honoring all life. Like Adrienne Rich and other women poets, Atwood links the political and private, love and death, but not litigiously. Her sorrow shows aboveground as feminism and anger, but its root taps a purer, older "disaffection from people," who mishandle the sacred, and a female kinship with a vulnerable nature. Her sorrow is not conventionally anti-modern nor environmentalist. She is not a poet of happiness, like Annie Dillard, but of conscience, which blesses and curses. Some *You Are Happy* poems are baleful, or Plathian dissections. The strongest, and most pervaded by Atwood's resisted, ironic mysticism, is "First Prayer." As in *Surfacing*, Atwood sees words as things, naming as propitiation; she makes us discover a language, and a world, inhabited by spirit. Excerpted: 1980.14.

95 VINCENTI, FIORA. "Quattro domande alla scrittrice Margaret Atwood." *Uomini e Libri* (Milan), no. 66 (November-December), pp. 48-49.

Interviews Atwood shortly after the publication of *La donna da mangiare*, the Italian translation of *The Edible Woman*. Atwood discusses the reception of *The Edible Woman* in the U.S. and England; describes *Lady Oracle* as a semi-comedy and a parody of gothic romance; gives her personal reactions to bilingualism in Canada and how the issue is reflected in *Surfacing* and "Two-Headed Poems"; and finds common elements in the work of young Canadian poets.

96 WILLISON, MARILYN. "The Feminist Front." *West Coast Review of Books* 3, no. 1:52.

Is bewildered by a worthy but flawed *Lady Oracle* that fails to zero in on the main character's activities. Book circles call *Lady Oracle* "this year's *Goodbar* (Judith Rossner's *Looking for Mr. Goodbar*)." Though Joan's, a.k.a. Louisa's, current Costume Gothic, current life, and painful memories are very ably and cannily combined, the switches sometimes interrupt. "It is a slow-moving book that will stay with the reader for a long time." The main character is the sum of her mistakes. Asides, chance descriptions, and phrases are far better than the book as a whole.

97 WOODCOCK, GEORGE. "Possessing the Land: Notes on Canadian Fiction." In *The Canadian Imagination: Dimensions of a Literary Culture*. Edited by David Staines. Cambridge, Mass. and London: Harvard University Press, pp. 80, 91, 92, 95.

Mentions, in tracing the twentieth-century maturing of Canadian fiction, *Survival* on animals as victims, and as fighting for cultural independence; Ethel Wilson's influence on Atwood; and *Surfacing*'s literally improbable but imaginatively authentic events.

98 _____. Preface to *Women in Canadian Literature*, by M.G. McClung. Women in Canadian Life, edited by Jean Cochrane and Pat Kincaid. Toronto: Fitzhenry & Whiteside, pp. 4-5.

1977

Briefly acclaims Atwood, Dorothy Livesay, and Margaret Laurence as classic Canadian writers. One of Canada's best poets, an original novelist, and an astute, imaginative critic, Atwood is perhaps our first real woman of letters.

99 _____. "Transformation Mask for Margaret Atwood." *Malahat Review*, no. 41 (January), pp. 52-56. See Sandler 1977.81.
Partly disagrees with Atwood's overextended and excluding survival thesis, which externalizes intuitions from her two novels and *Power Politics*, but pays tribute to her concern for man's animal victims, in *Survival, Surfacing*, and her 1975 essay on the new Toronto zoo, "Don't Expect the Bear to Dance." Atwood transcends Canadian writers' self-pity with a rigorous pessimism that does not deny compassion or joy (and which is not the reviewer's Buddhist-Epicurean liberating pessimism). *You Are Happy* shows, as in its title poem, light emerging from darkness and pain, which are recognized as inescapable and as signs of life.

100 WORDSWORTH, CHRISTOPHER. "Noble Privates Parts." *Guardian* (Manchester), 23 June, p. 9.
A three-book review that finds *Oracle Lady* [sic] a sustained pleasure of bubbling picaresque and wittily-examined identity trouble. The heroine gets herself into "such a tangle of fairy tales and fibs to escape the consequences of her double life . . . . When nemesis knocks on the door of her hide-out and she crowns the apparition with a Cinzano bottle, it is far too late for her to unravel herself. . . . Miss Atwood's obvious pleasure in her own high spirits makes her doubly irresistible."

101 ZONAILO, CAROLYN. "Male Stereotypes in *The Diviners* and *The Edible Woman*." *Room of One's Own* 3, no. 1:70-72.
Novels by men have stereotyped their female characters; similarly, *The Edible Woman*'s reliable but chauvinistic Peter and imaginative but unreliable Duncan, who parallel the two kinds of men in Margaret Laurence's *The Diviners*, are one-dimensional stereotypes.

1978

1 ALLEN, CAROLYN. "Failures of Word, Uses of Silence: Djuna Barnes, Adrienne Rich, and Margaret Atwood." *Regionalism and the Female Imagination* 4, no. 1 (Spring):1-7.

The woman writer, struggling with primarily male literary conventions, must use both silence and language in her own way. The original, complex, highly charged language of Barnes's *Nightwood* fails to save its characters from oblivion; and Barnes herself fell silent as a writer after *Nightwood*. Rich's very different explorations, in *The Will to Change* and *Diving into the Wreck*, move from a negative to a positive silence, and from frustration to new possibilities for women speaking and for anger. Atwood's *Surfacing* uses silence more radically than Rich does, proposing non-verbal, visionary messages as the only way to sufficient self-knowledge, of how to act, to live, and to use language.

2 AMEY, LARRY. Review of *Up in the Tree*. *Canadian Book Review Annual*:192.

Likes Atwood's unpretentious, good-humoured rhyme and simple, smiley, energetic sketches, but not the stilted doggerel, which doesn't compete with Dennis Lee's children's books.

3 AUTRAND, DOMINIQUE. "Réconciliation avec la nature." *Quinzaine littéraire* (Paris), no. 279 (31 May), p. 8.

Review of *Faire surface*. *Surfacing*, the first of Atwood's novels to be translated into French, takes place in a vast and unpopulated Canada that is transformed into a primitive and magical universe. The narrator is in search of her lost father and is haunted by him and the image of her aborted baby. In her fight against destruction, symbolized by the Americans, the narrator can "see," in the sense that Carlos Casteneda uses the term, how to reconcile nature and society. The use of symbolism and the narrator's lack of sensitivity recall works by John Hawkes. The end is not convincing, but Atwood's voice is original and poetic, creating a uniquely Canadian, romanesque universe.

4 BECKMANN, SUSAN. "Margaret Atwood: Can. Lit. to Kid Lit." *Canadian Children's Literature*, no. 12, pp. 78-81.

Is delighted chiefly by *Up in the Tree*'s very fine illustrations – by the owl, by the powerful cold blues and warm reds, and by the whimsical faces and postures of the animals and children; praises also the appealing, innovative hand-lettering; but cautions against the dangerously-placed chair on a table, and finds the poetry singularly unremarkable.

5 BELKIN, ROSLYN. "The Worth of the Shadow: Margaret Atwood's *Lady Oracle.*" *Thalia* 1, no. 3 (Winter):3-8.

Places *Lady Oracle* in Pirandello's humorist tradition, defined in his *On Humor* and *It Is So, If You Think So*: seeing reality as illusory, life as both ridiculous and grievous, the humorist laughs and commiserates. Joan is a Pirandello *raisonneur*, both feeling, and reflecting on the phantoms, or shadows, of her own and others' feelings; she sees the multiple roles and masks that humans wear. As in Pirandello, wings symbolize hope, and mirrors reflect people's fantasies. Joan learns of life's illusions from Lou, Leda, and the other "'lady oracles.'" One of Pirandello's "restless spirits,'" Joan will survive, pursuing and creating her illusory shadows.

6 BILAN, R.P. "Letters in Canada 1977: Fiction/2." *University of Toronto Quarterly* 47, no. 4 (Summer):329-31.

Prefers *Dancing Girls'* range and poetic language to Audrey Thomas's *Ladies and Escorts*; prefers the sexual politics and power of *Surfacing* and *Power Politics* to those of *Dancing Girls*. These stories vary in quality, seriousness, and importance. A fine one, "The Resplendent Quetzal," has a mellow tone rare for Atwood. Some are only light comedy, like *Lady Oracle*. Some, like "A Training Piece," have an intense but narrow, grotesque vision. The best one, "Polarities," not only diagnoses but also, in Louise's vision and in the stunningly surreal end, transcends the characters' alienation. Excerpted: 1983.129.

7 ____. "Margaret Atwood's *The Journals of Susanna Moodie*." *Canadian Poetry*, no. 2 (Spring-Summer), pp. 1-12.

Explicates the *Journals* as possibly Atwood's best, and certainly, despite her 1973.27 comments, her most tightly organized book of poetry, unified by Moodie's chronological growth and by key images of trees, fire, and the eventually reversed Victorian values of light and darkness. Journal I goes from alienation to partial transformations, as in "The Two Fires," which condense two chapters from the historic Moodie's *Roughing It in the Bush*. Journal II circles back, as Moodie struggles with old fears, recognizing but not accepting the reality of the land her dead children are part of. In Journal III Moodie is finally transformed, choosing the land and the "dark side of light"; in death she joins the land and becomes its spirit.

8 BODY, MARJORIE. Review of *The Circle Game*. *Canadian Book Review Annual*:98-99.

Argues that *The Circle Game* lacks concreteness and life because it is flawed by Atwood's thematic *Survival* approach and by academic techniques. Concludes that if the now-famous Atwood survives, through *Circle*, "it will be as the darling of the Junior Chamber of Commerce, as the sweetheart of Academe."

9 BRAVERMAN, KATE. "Of Nakedness and Rubber Gloves." *Los Angeles Times*, 26 May, p. D5.

Finds *Selected Poems* an accomplished poet's odyssey, with an original voice and utterly precise imagery, but without surprises. Atwood's topography includes the wild, the unknown, the ancient. Her second and third books seem forced. *Power Politics* is uniquely inspired. She opens up – almost to passion. Her powerful, inescapably intelligent writing plays by the rules, consummately, but doesn't transform them: she's memorized the biologist's rubber-glove procedures.

10 BROWN, RUSSELL M. "In Search of Lost Causes: The Canadian Novelist as Mystery Writer." *Mosaic* 11, no. 3 (Spring):1-15.

Compares, in a genre survey of mystery novels and mystery-like novels in Canada, Atwood's *Surfacing* with Robertson Davies's *The Manticore*, as detective-like novels, and both with Canadian-raised Ross Macdonald's Lew Archer detective novels. Atwood's and Davies's protagonists play the role of detective, investigating a father's death or disappearance, seeking a truth that can never be found. Perhaps the mystery story has become our modern myth, particularly for mythopoeic writers. The Surfacer, who discards the detective's hyper-rationality for a clarifying madness, gains, when her sanity returns, the ability to accept a world without "'theology,'" certainty, or assignable guilt and responsibility. Macdonald's Lew Archer, who is also a decoder on a psychic quest, represents rationality, as an alternative to madness.

1978

11 BRYFONSKI, DEDRIA, and MENDELSON, PHYLLIS CARMEL, eds. *Contemporary Literary Criticism*. Vol. 8. Detroit: Gale Research Co., pp. 28-34.

Excerpted from: Brown 1974.1; Chamberlin 1975.5; Vendler 1975.49; Marshall 1975.26; Sandler 1976.90; Sandler 1976.89; McPherson 1976.60; Pollitt 1976.75; Rubenstein 1976.88; Rosengarten 1977.77; Lyons 1977.46.

12 BURNS, D.R. "The Move to the Middle Ground: A Reading of the English Canadian Novel." *Meanjin* 37, no. 2 (July):178-85 passim.

Refers, in a discussion of sober English Canadian fiction's need to establish a middle ground, between lonely character and bleak environment, to *Surfacing*'s atypical, creative jolt; describes *The Edible Woman*'s ironic, thoughtful, modest success in establishing a middle ground and a Canadian presence; features Robert Kroetsch's elemental Out West trilogy.

13 C., D. "Beavers Strand Two Youngsters 'Up in a Tree.'" *Christian Science Monitor*, 15 May, p. 20.

Is delighted by Atwood's story and skillful verse, which catch the essence of childhood's joy and freedom; finds her sprightly, humorous illustrations simple but powerful.

14 CABAU, JACQUES. "Les nouvelles Sagan s'en vont en querre." *Point* (Paris), no. 290 (10 April), pp. 128-29.

Reviews Atwood's *Faire surface*, the French translation of *Surfacing*, and Brigitte Schwaiger's *Marie-toi, ma fille*. Approves of *Surfacing*'s police novel plot with its inquiry and grand immersions that bring the truth to the surface. The novel begins like a Hitchcock story and is reminiscent of James Dickey's *Deliverance*. Religious themes are strong throughout the story. The past invades the present, and the protagonist, like Ophelia, succumbs to the temptation of water.

15 CAMERON, ELSPETH. "Margaret Atwood: A Patchwork Self." *Book Forum* 4, no. 1:35-45.

Atwood's Bart Gerrard self-parodies resist the images projected onto her; *Lady Oracle* and *Dancing Girls* show the artist's "'self'" as reality and fantasy complexly mixed. Being an artist means choosing between a private and public life, as in *Lady Oracle*'s Red Shoes, and

"Lives of the Poets." *Lady Oracle*'s artists and pseudo-artists show that only the falsely dressed-up self can get the attention; life becomes roles tenuously pieced into "'a patchwork self.'" The romantic persona is sent out to love, as in "Hair Jewellery," while the real self stays hidden. In "Polarities" as in Laing, our "'normality'" may be collective madness, the adjusted self false, and madness true. Like Hugh MacLennan's expert surgeon, or like an anthropologist from another world, Atwood examines the human species. Though her cool, scientific tone has been criticized, it powerfully and rationally penetrates to underlying truth: Atwood shows the absurdity of man's unnatural, self-distorting, social masks. Excerpted: 1980.14.

16 CAMPBELL, JOSIE P. "The Woman as Hero in Margaret Atwood's *Surfacing.*" *Mosaic* 11, no. 3 (Spring):17-28.

   Surfacing's "total structure and meaning are informed by the mythic heroic quest of Joseph Campbell's *The Hero with a Thousand Faces*. Despite *Survival*'s Canadian polemics, Atwood's geography is of the universal human consciousness. As only Gray 1977.28 has seen, *Surfacing*'s protagonist is the radical "'Heroine of the thousand faces,'" descending like Persephone, enduring like Perseus. As in Campbell, the archetypal heroic myth is not a formula, but the metaphor of a myth-generating process. Its three components, "*Separation, Initiation,* and *Return,*" structure *Surfacing*'s three parts. The protagonist begins as a reluctant, alienated hero, separated from her past and present. She is initiated into depths of the self in the mythic, illuminating dive. The last part focuses on her preparation for returning to community. The impregnation seems to follow the Demeter-Korê myth, where Korê is "'resurrected'" by the mother, and the male is only functionary. By the end, the protagonist has confronted "heroically the ghosts of her psyche," and conquered them, if only momentarily. Reprinted: 1988.11.

17 CAPONE, GIOVANNA. "Sistemi antinomici in Margaret Atwood." In *Canada il villaggio della terra: Letteratura canadese di lingua inglese.* Saggi di letterature moderne, edited by Giovanna Capone, Liano Petroni, Raffaele Spongano. Sezione di letteratura inglese, angloamericana, e letterature anglofone, vol. 1. Bologna: Pàtron, pp. 177-207.

   Focuses on key, recurring themes in Atwood's poetry through *You Are Happy* and fiction through *Lady Oracle*. Northrop Frye

1978

influences many of Atwood's essays and early poems, especially *Double Persephone*. Atwood's poetry has an anthropologic-mythic-iconic component. All of her poetics reach out to women and construct a path between the inert and the alive. The theme of woman begins in *Double Persephone*'s field of hieroglyphics, and continues with the blurred and submerged woman in "This Is a Photograph of Me." Looking deeply into the woman as Sibyl, Everywoman, and Earth-Mother, as in *The Edible Woman* and "This Is a Photograph of Me," and exploring the recurring symbols of women's transformation, reveals the balance and equality between earth and woman. Place, primarily the doubling structure of city versus wilderness, is a dominant image. Atwood prefers earth and water over fire and air; aquatic images are primary. Secondary images are of surfaces, including mirrors and ice, and death and metamorphosis, often by way of water.

18 CAPPON, PAUL, ed. *In Our Own House: Social Perspectives on Canadian Literature*. Toronto: McClelland & Stewart, pp. 50-51, 67-69.
   Charges that *Survival*'s liberal ideology mystifies reality, by psychologizing American imperialism; Atwood's solutions are middle-class nationalism; her analysis is anti-materialist and non-historical. James Steele 1978.94 shows how Atwood's anti-Americanism, founded on Frye's idealism, cosmopolitanism, and liberalism, leads to utopian individualism. What makes *Survival* so extraordinarily popular? Its timing; its superficial radicalism; and its elitism, which corresponds to Canada's pervasive liberal ideology, and to American (continentalist) empiro-positivism.

19 CUDE, WILFRED. "Bravo Mothball! An Essay on *Lady Oracle*." In *Here and Now*. Edited by John Moss. The Canadian Novel, vol. 1. Toronto: NC Press, pp. 45-50.
   A slightly revised text of 1977.11. See also 1980.26. Reprinted: 1983.26. Expanded: 1980.25.

20 DAVEY, FRANK. "Atwood's Gorgon Touch." In *Brave New Wave*. Edited by Jack David. Windsor, Ont.: Black Moss Press, pp. 171-95.
   Reprint of 1977.12, which is reprinted 1983.29; 1988.15.

21 DAVIDSON, ARNOLD E., and DAVIDSON, CATHY N. "Margaret Atwood's *Lady Oracle*: The Artist as Escapist and Seer." *Studies in Canadian Literature* 3, no. 2 (Summer):166-77.

This essay should be titled "'The Pseudo-Artist as Escapist and Apprentice Seer.'" "Unreal art imitates unrealized life" in *Lady Oracle*, sustaining a cycle of "unconscious self-victimization and ineffectual escape fantasy." Refusing to be responsible, Joan sees herself as victimized and needing escape, like her readers. Joan's lovers and husband fantasize as much as Joan does. Because each man is two-sided, women have to be correspondingly dual, victims or heroines. Joan's fake death epitomizes her fictitious life and her fraudulent, inauthentic fictions. *Lady Oracle* ends with Joan's recognition that she need not be a victim, and will not in future inflict the victimized woman myth on her readers.

22 DAVIDSON, CATHY N. "A Literature of Survivors: On Teaching Canada's Women Writers." *Women's Studies Newsletter* 6, no. 4 (Fall):12-13.

Recommends fiction by Atwood, Margaret Laurence, and other Canadian women writers for women's literature courses. Atwood herself could be a positive role model. *The Edible Woman*, which confronts women's issues, is very appealing and very teachable; *Surfacing*'s mythic quest romance is even more so; *Lady Oracle*, which joins feminism and humor, shows "how sexist standards, particularly the beauty ethic, pervert both men and women."

23 DAVIDSON, JIM. "Interview: Margaret Atwood." *Meanjin* 37, no. 2 (July):189-205.

Atwood discusses *Survival* and its five victim positions; the politics and literature of English Canada, French Canada, and America; English Canada's copyright law; language in *Surfacing* and Indian language; colonialism and literature in Canada and Australia; women writers and feminism; the city and poetry ; and Farley Mowat's *People of the Deer*. Reprinted: 1983.32.

24 ENDRES, ROBIN. "Marxist Literary Criticism and English Canadian Literature." In *In Our Own House: Social Perspectives on Canadian Literature*. Edited by Paul Cappon. Toronto: McClelland & Stewart, pp. 113-22.

1978

Rejects *Survival* and critiques *Surfacing*. The widely taught *Survival*, which is an ahistorical "'thematic'" approach that seems fashionably radical, is "bourgeois individualism," a politics not of collective struggle but of changing one's "'consciousness'" into a creative non-victim. Equally perniciously, Atwood's literary analysis not only over-emphasizes the "negative symbols in Canadian literature," but also fails to see that many of these are realistic, dialectical struggles. Atwood also ignores the reader's often ironic, determined response to failed struggle. On G[yörgy] Lukács's continuum, Margaret Laurence's *The Stone Angel* succeeds as a realistic novel that achieves irony and historicity; and *Surfacing* fails as a modernist novel whose "social milieu is only a backdrop," whose potentiality is therefore abstract, and whose "reification of insanity" demonstrates Lukács's chain reaction. *Surfacing*'s controlling metaphor of Americanization misuses science fiction; both Atwood and her "queen bee narrator," who distorts her friends into cardboard characters, judge these friends guilty of their own alienation. *Surfacing* lacks Laurence's understanding, forgiving humanism.

25 FERNS, JOHN. "Criticism of Canadian Literature in English: Last Twenty Years." *Bulletin of Canadian Studies* 2, no. 1 (April):69-71.
    Sees *Survival*, Northrop Frye's literary criticism, and D.G. Jones *Butterfly on Rock*, as a "'mythopoeic,'" thematic approach that neglects close analysis, avoids evaluations, and "is in danger of being enshrined as the only 'approach'" to Canadian literature. Atwood's style is often cynical and glib, but also vital and witty. The reviewer hopes Atwood will "escape the whale of specious publicity," and become a major author, not a "'Canlit'" pundit. The survival theme Atwood adds to Frye and Jones is indisputably central; but her "'victim positions' are simply silly," abstract, and schematic. At her best Atwood cares about the Canadian tradition; she rightly protests the joyless gloom and self-obsession of so much of our literature, and rightly calls for comparative criticism.

26 FORCHÉ, CAROLYN. "Margaret Atwood: Poems and Poet." *New York Times Book Review*, 21 May, pp. 15, 42.
    Critiques *Selected Poems*: Atwood [in her "Afterword" to *The Journals of Susanna Moodie*] speaks of Canadians as fearful exiles and invaders. Atwood sees the earth as a surface, and the Western impulse

as map-making, as in "The Circle Game." Her laconic language carves bare outlines. *Selected Poems* excludes little. Like her paranoid schizophrenic Moodie, Atwood's own insistent voice disturbingly romanticizes the wilderness and madness. Her poems emerge from a too-narrow dissociation. Though there are impressive forays here, her voice indulges itself; her themes are overamplified and repeated, as in "November." Perhaps the key she's lost is language.

27 GAREBIAN, KEITH. "Mediocre Cliches [sic] from Atwood." *Montreal Star*, 4 March, p. D3.
    Finds more than half of the *Dancing Girls* stories half-hearted, banal magazine filler. A largely mediocre short story writer, Atwood packs many stories with trivial details, as in "The War in the Bathroom" and, worse, "Rape Fantasies." "Giving Birth" is merely clinical, tinged "with female chauvinist irony." "Under Glass" is only a warmed-over death-in-life story. Yet Atwood at her best has "honed precision, striking intelligence, and superior control of symbolism." The title piece carries its satire before ending unconvincingly. "And four other stories ["Training," "The Man from Mars," "Polarities," and "The Resplendent Quetzal"] are generally excellent," with "an immense amount of pain"; "Quetzal" has Atwood's best and worst.

28 GATENBY, GREG. Review of *Two-Headed Poems*. *Quill and Quire* 44, no. 16 (November):10.
    Acclaims *Two-Headed Poems* as Atwood's advance in poetic subject matter and style, and "a major document of Canadian literature." "Footnote to the Amnesty [Report] on Torture" is "the seminal poem" of the book, and perhaps of the year. Atwood has moved beyond her earlier obsession with man/woman hurts, to violence among groups, and to the real work of identifying human responsibility.

29 GEDDES, GARY, and BRUCE, PHYLLIS, eds. "Notes on the Poets: Margaret Atwood." In *15 Canadian Poets plus 5*. Toronto: Oxford University Press, pp. 378-79.
    Updates and reprints, slightly cut, 1970.17. See 1980.144.

30 GODBOUT, JACQUES. "Le divan de Marie, l'île de Margaret." *Actualité* (Montréal) 3, no. 6 (June):74.

Compares *Faire surface*, the French translation of *Surfacing*, to Marie Cardinal's *Les Mots pour le dire*. The heroines in both novels return to places from their childhood. In *Surfacing*, the island, like the spirit of woman, is trampled on, devoured, and threatened by the "Americans." The novel reveals Atwood's understanding of the Québécois who must "faire surface" to avoid becoming miscarriages of history.

31 GORLIER, CLAUDIO. "La commedia gotica di Margaret Atwood." In *Canadiana: Aspetti della storia e della letteratura canadese*. Edited by Luca Codignola. Ricerche, no. 29. Venice: Marsilio, pp. 121-32.

Atwood's unique treatment of author and language as trickster makes *Lady Oracle* her most experimental text. A simple feminist interpretation of Atwood's work bypasses other important themes, including the quest, the relationship between urban and rural cultures, the ambiguous concept of normality, and the dialectic between victim and victimizer. *The Edible Woman* and *Lady Oracle* are comedies by the eighteenth and nineteenth century definition. *Surfacing*, *Lady Oracle*, and *The Edible Woman* are structured like gothic fiction, with elements of mystery and terror, and the presence of monsters. Atwood approaches a post-modern narrative, interchanging gothic, comedy, and farce. The attitude of her narrators recalls "Speeches for Dr. Frankenstein": "'Knowing that the work is mine, how can I love you.'"

32 GOTTLIEB, LOIS C., and KEITNER, WENDY. "Colonialism as Metaphor and Experience in *The Grass Is Singing* and *Surfacing*." In *Awakened Conscience: Studies in Commonwealth Literature*. Edited by C.D. Narasimhaiah. New Delhi: Sterling Publishers, pp. 307-14. Reprinted: Atlantic Highlands, N.J.: Humanities Press, 1978.

Explores sexual colonialism in these two novels by Doris Lessing and Atwood, citing Simone de Beauvoir; traces in *Surfacing* "the painful and erratic emergence of the narrator's feminist consciousness." The more psychological *Surfacing* also implicitly links "woman's personal victimisation by a male-dominated society and the ecological destruction of the land under American economic imperialism. . . . Growing up female in a father-dominated family," in a priest-controlled postwar Quebec, the narrator is socially conditioned to find men superior and women inferior. School, the schoolyard's miniature chauvinists, and older women all reinforce female passivity. The

1978

narrator gradually comes to see "her estrangement from her body, not as individual sickness, but as a function of society's treatment of women." Even women's giving birth is dominated; women are losers in the sexual power struggle. Woman's increasing independence, sanity, and wholeness, threaten men. The narrator undergoes an anguishing rebirth to reject the repressive but comforting feminine assumptions, and achieve responsible, adult status; she surfaces revitalized, pregnant, and autonomous.

33 GRACE, SHERRILL E. Introduction to *The Circle Game*, by Margaret Atwood. Toronto: House of Anansi Press, pp. 9-15.
Analyzes structure and themes, which appear incompletely in *Selected Poems*. *The Circle Game* of 1966-1967 got general praise, and some misreadings, as narrowly autobiographical or "'mythopoeic.'" This first book has Atwood's mature voice, poetic style, preoccupation with doubleness, and themes – "the traps of reality, myth, language," roles, self, and perception. "This Is a Photograph of Me," with its ironic double structure, challenges perception. The opening poems are circle games where the speaker struggles to escape. Defeat and impasse climax in the title poem's wish to break the circle. "Journey to the Interior," "Pre-Amphibian," and others explore possible escapes. In the last three poems, "A Place: Fragments," "The Explorers," and "The Settlers," there is a tentative release, and then a final alternative vision, of happy children in nature. The negations of these last poems are not nihilism.

34 GREALISH, GERARD. Review of *Selected Poems*. *Best Sellers* 38, no. 5 (August):165-66.
Praises Atwood's poetry, which evokes intimacy; *Selected Poems* shows how her voice, craft, and metaphors have developed. Though *The Circle Game* has deliberate metaphors, like the flood-motherhood conceit of "After the Flood, We," its poems are powerful, especially "This Is a Photograph of Me" and the presumptuous but resonant title poem. *The Animals in That Country* and *The Journals of Susanna Moodie* are more contrived and self-indulgent; *Procedures for Underground* is powerful. *Power Politics*, with its admittedly realistic but unlikable monster "he," is well-written women's movement rhetoric. *You Are Happy* most fully realizes Atwood's power;

1978

"Circe/Mud" is magnificent; Circe lives in our time and hers; Circe's last poem is poignant.

35 HAMMOND, KARLA. "A Margaret Atwood Interview with Karla Hammond." *Concerning Poetry* 12, no. 2 (Fall):73-81.
    Atwood discusses her family's maritime, educational, scientific orientation versus 1940s peer pressure for girls; teaching; women writers and feminism; "Backdrop addresses cowboy," "Marrying the Hangman," *Survival*, and *Lady Oracle*; and writing poetry versus writing prose.

36 HEDENSTROM, JOANNE. "Puzzled Patriarchs and Free Women: Patterns in the Canadian Novel." *Atlantis* 4, no. 1 (Fall):2-9.
    Follows *Survival* in defining the feminine and the masculine traditions in English Canadian novels by Alice Munro, Atwood, Marian Engel, Ethel Wilson, Dennis Patrick Sears, George Ryga, Hugh MacLennan, Frederick Philip Grove, and Robert Kroetsch. In novels by women, "escape and metamorphosis is a dominant motif," and a creative force; the novels are hopeful, positive: as in *The Edible Woman*, *Surfacing*, and *Lady Oracle*, women escape confining situations, shed weight, clothes, even humanity, as they grow and surface, triumphantly. "The 'creative non-victim' in Canadian literature is the 'free woman' of English Canadian women novelists; the 'puzzled patriarchs' [of men novelists] are, at best, survivors."

37 HENIGHAN, TOM. "Margaret Atwood's *Two-Headed Poems*: A Ruthless Vision, a Fiercely Clenched Language." *Ottawa Revue*, no. 117 (19-25 October), p. 18.
    Finds Atwood still powerful, unsettling, and painfully honest; still "the dour snake-lady with the stoney [sic] eye and the flickering tongue, . . . who is fascinated by the dark and disturbing particulars of mortal existence." Manichean toward the body, and dubious about the spirit, "Atwood refuses to fake integration or joy." The poetry is still technically excellent, although Atwood "projects her own shadow everywhere," and puritanically neglects the positive energies and eros. The title poem seems less successful, but has memorable moments, and a portrait of Pierre Eliot Trudeau; Atwood's language is too purified for public poetry. The reviewer much prefers the uncannily disturbing "Five Poems for Dolls," "The Man with a Hole in His

1978

Throat," "Marrying the Hangman," and also "Five Poems for Grandmothers," with its honesty, striving, and final success. Atwood's bleak themes affirm Thomas Hardy's and T.S. Eliot's bleak, uncomforted views of life; domestic routine offers the safest harbour; "Solstice Poem" [iv] voices her central wisdom.

38 HENIGHAN, TOM, and HENIGHAN, MARILYN. "Branching out with Margaret Atwood: A Dialogue on *Up in the Tree*." *Ottawa Revue*, no. 90 (13-19 April), p. 2.

"She" and "He" appreciatively discuss, and recommend, *Up in the Tree*, as an unpretentious children's story that involves adult ideas in its practical approach to life's problems, its Beatrix Potter comforts, its reassuring, middle-class end, and its children who become creative non-victims, as defined in *Survival*. He questions whether the red bird is an owl; an Editor's Note explains that the owl, acting as a familiar in the animal spirit world, brings back the magical red bird rescuer. She likes the illustrations of the goggle-eyed, innocent, unisexual children, and of the reassuringly rooted tree.

39 HEWARD, BURT. "Free Advice for Canadian Writer: Get More Serious." *Citizen* (Ottawa), 7 April, p. 49.

Interviews Atwood, who is in Ottawa to publicize *Up in the Tree*, and suggests that she write her novels more seriously; Atwood responds that she did, with *Surfacing*, but "comedy is comedy," with the other two. Reports on Atwood's travels: after Australia, and a current five-week poetry reading tour in the United States, then she and Jess [Atwood's and Gibson's daughter] will accompany Graeme Gibson, who will be the University of Edinburg's first Canadian writer in residence. *Up in the Tree* comes from doggerel verse done seven years ago, during *Surfacing*; Atwood waited to draw and hand-letter it herself; one drawing is flawed. Atwood says Canadian writers are better off now than most U.S. writers.

40 HINZ, EVELYN J. "Contemporary North American Literary Primitivism: *Deliverance* and *Surfacing*." In *Hemispheric Perspectives on the United States: Papers from the New World Conference*. Edited by Joseph S. Tulchin. Contributions in American Studies, no. 36. Westport, Conn.: Greenwood, pp. 150-71.

1978

Compares James Dickey's *Deliverance* and Atwood's *Surfacing* as serious explorations of the major contemporary problem of primitivism. Lewis in *Deliverance*, and the father in *Surfacing*, represent a rational, survival primitivism, which returns to eighteenth-century attitudes to escape a collapsing modern civilization: but their rational primitivism accomplishes nothing, and precipitates the destructive, atavistic transformations of the two protagonists, *Deliverance*'s Ed and *Surfacing*'s narrator. For, as Otto Rank perceived, the irrational life force must revolt against man's attempts to master it. Both novels depict North America's cultural failure, in its loss of religious symbols and ritual; both protagonists search, in psychological journeys, for new religious symbols. As a Jungian analysis shows, both protagonists are logos-oriented, though one explores an American, masculine problem, and the other a Canadian, feminine problem. Revised: 1978.41 (below).

41 ____. "The Masculine/Feminine Psychology of American/Canadian Primitivism: *Deliverance* and *Surfacing*." In *Other Voices, Other Views: An International Collection of Essays from the Bicentennial*. Edited by Robin W. Winks. Contributions in American Studies, no. 34. Westport, Conn.: Greenwood, pp. 75-96.
An enlarged text of 1978.40 (above).

42 HOWES, VICTOR. "The Shapes That Love Takes on." *Christian Science Monitor*, 12 July, p. 18.
Praises *Selected Poems*'s metamorphoses, which are ironic, comic, and ominous. Humans, animals, vegetation are transformed. Love is Protean, happily domestic or unhappily politic. Her striking images live; these luminous poems glow and flicker richly. Atwood is a poet to reread, a transposition of Kafka onto Ovid.

43 HUNT, JACQUIE. "Atwood Good for Children." *Citizen* (Ottawa), 8 April, p. 43.
Praises *Up in the Tree* highly: its rhythmic verse; its true-to-life, light-hearted, reassuring tale of joy, fear, isolation, and final triumphant insouciance; its humorous illustrations, friendly hand-lettering, and fine format. Atwood is also cartoonist Bart Gerrard. Atwood "has so completely entered the child's world" that she captures its simultaneously "momentous and transitory" experiences. The eminently quotable *Up in the Tree* will be asked for night after night.

1978

44 HUTCHEON, LINDA. "Atwood and Laurence: Poet and Novelist." *Studies in Canadian Literature* 3, no. 2 (Summer):255-63.

Compares *The Edible Woman* with Margaret Laurence's *The Stone Angel*. Both are novels of feminine identity, in which the title image structures the narrative and theme. Perhaps because Atwood is a poet, she *shows* rather then tells, trusting the reader to make the thematic connections between images. Atwood's method yields more upon re-reading, and compares to other poet's novels, including Sylvia Plath's *The Bell Jar*.

45 INNESS, LORNA. "Margaret Atwood's Magical Tree House." *Halifax Chronicle Herald*, 1 April, p. 34.

Praises *Up in the Tree*'s appealing story, sprightly verse, and lively illustrations.

46 IRVINE, LORNA. "Hostility and Reconciliation: The Mother in English Canadian Fiction." *American Review of Canadian Studies* 8, no. 1 (Spring):56-64.

Revision of 1977.36. Discusses (as 1977.36 did not) two Atwood novels as examples of the daughter's ambivalent struggle, which threatens the necessary generational transference of power. In *Lady Oracle* the daughter recreates a destructive maternal imago, and uses childhood obesity as a defense against becoming her mother's reflection. In *Surfacing*, the daughter struggles to accept her own femininity and to understand the reversal of the mother-daughter roles; the daughter's anger and guilt initiate the quest for reconciliation. Revised: 1980.63.

47 J[ACOB], J[OHN]. Review of *Selected Poems*. *Booklist* 74, no. 21 (1 July):1658.

Welcomes Atwood's definitive *Selected Poems*: her transformations involve us all. She is concerned with personal growth (strangely revealed in *The Journals of Susanna Moodie*) and more basic, even alchemical changes, as in "Siren Song."

48 JUHASZ, SUZANNE. Review of *Selected Poems*. *Library Journal* 103, no. 12 (15 June):1273.

Welcomes *Selected Poems*, which outline Atwood's developing vision; speculates on her Canadian roots, and her fascination with

1978

geography and language; praises *Power Politics*, "Circe/Mud Poems," and especially *The Journals of Susanna Moodie*.

49 KERTZER, JON. Review of *Dancing Girls and Other Stories*. *Fiddlehead*, no. 117 (Spring), pp. 133-35.

Compares *Dancing Girls* with Elizabeth Brewster's *It's Easy to Fall on the Ice* stories; both authors' heroines have the inability to rejoice of Hagar Shipley in Margaret Laurence's *The Stone Angel*, but lack Hagar's strength. Atwood's characters are more desperately solitary, and their stories are more varied, painful, and shocking, than Brewster's. *Dancing Girls*'s heroines find inner richness, fear, and value; but never joy, happy endings, or love attained. Yet love is the only hope, and "Polarities," then, the key story; its ending's finely balanced doubt offers the book's widest vision.

50 LANDSBERG, MICHELE. "A Gentle Plot with Good Humored [sic] Charm in Red, White, and Blue." *Globe and Mail*, 1 April, p. 36.

Praises *Up in a Tree* [sic] for its understated humor, gentle plot, engaging characters, whimsical drawings, and clear hand lettering. This is not one of those condescending clunkers of children's books that Canadian literary royalty crank out.

51 LAUBER, JOHN. "Alice in Consumer-Land: The Self-Discovery of Marian MacAlpine." In *Here and Now*. Edited by John Moss. The Canadian Novel, vol. 1. Toronto: NC Press, pp. 19-31.

Follows Dawe 1973.19 and R.D. Laing, assessing *The Edible Woman* as a realistic, comic novel of masculine and feminine identity in our artificial, manipulating consumer society. As in *Surfacing*, the heroine's schizophrenic-like withdrawal is healing; though she cannot escape or change her society, she does learn to cope with it. Praises Atwood's surprising wit, brilliant imagery, and revealing comedy. Reprinted: 1983.79.

52 LORENZINI, AMLETO. "Intervista a Margaret Atwood alla Fondazione Cini." *Argomenti Canadesi* (Rome) [1]:150-52.

An interview accompanying translations of selected poems by Atwood and other Canadian poets. Atwood describes the writing styles of bissett, Rosenblatt, Newlove, Bowering, Lee, Ondaatje, and MacEwen; summarizes *Lady Oracle* as a Gothic romance and a parody that explores the frustrated and paranoid feminine psyche of North America, and says her books are not feminist works; discusses bilingualism and the two cultures in *Surfacing* and *Two-Headed Poems*; and says French Canadian writers may not become known in Italy until they have a Italian representative like the interviewer.

53 LYONS, BONNIE. "'Neither Victims nor Executioners' in Margaret Atwood's Fiction." *World Literature Written in English* 17, no. 1 (April):181-87.

Camus's injunction, to be "'neither victims nor executioners,'" is the underlying theme of Atwood's two novels. All her work is about achieving wholeness and integrity in the modern world. Her two novels draw on motifs in her poetry, which show objectification as victimization, aggression, and mechanization. *The Edible Woman*'s central character becomes unable to objectify and consume when her fiance makes an object of her. As *Surfacing*'s characters fail as people, they become mechanical, inhuman, American; the polarization between victim and executioner reaches a climax in the "'objectifying rape'" of the camera. *Surfacing* closely parallels *Survival*'s victim themes; as the narrator struggles against victimization, so must Canada.

54 L[YONS], L[IZBETH] M. Review of *Selected Poems*. *Kliatt Young Adult Paperback Book Guide* 12, no. 6 (September):21.

Selected Poems shows Atwood's constant concerns, and unsteady progress from bleak pessimism to hope. She notes too clearly lovers' keen cruelties. After descending uncertain crags, and chronicling precisely the danger points, she reaches the solid ground of love and humanity, travel-worn but quietly satisfied.

55 McCOMBS, JUDITH. "Atwood's Nature Concepts: An Overview." *Waves* 7, no. 1 (Fall):68-77.

Argues that Atwood's nature concepts, in the poetry and *Surfacing*, are part of an emerging myth of woman allied with nature. Though, as *Survival*'s examples show, the man against nature myth is prevalent in Canadian literature, Atwood's creative work critiques it. "Progressive insanities of a pioneer" exposes man's antagonism to nature as bad for him and for female-imaged nature. "Backdrop addresses cowboy," which critiques American frontier imperialism as

1978

well as the men's nature myth, radically restructures the human/nature myth, as woman allied with nature. The three complications of Atwood's woman/nature myth are: the problem of nature as non-human death-bringer; the attempt to use an Other as a gate into nature – in *Surfacing* the unborn child becomes, finally, the only real gate to nature; and the split human character, or female I and masculine Other. From *Power Politics* and *The Journals of Susanna Moodie* through *Surfacing*, nature changes from death-bringer to life-source; the narrator changes from refusing children and therefore nature, to accepting both; and the myth changes from negative critique to positive alliance. This woman-centered myth is surfacing also in Annie Dillard, Marge Piercy, Susan Griffin, and others, who depict nature as a vulnerable, finite woman.

56 McKENNA, SUSAN PURCELL. "Atwood for Kids." *Montreal Star*, 8 April, p. D3.

Praises highly *Up in the Tree*'s fine story, charming drawings, poetic rhythms, and neat lettering, which appeal especially to two-to-three-year-olds, like the reviewer's own daughter, who chants and giggles in response to Atwood's book.

57 McLAY, CATHARINE. "The Divided Self: Theme and Pattern in *Surfacing*." In *Here and Now*. Edited by John Moss. The Canadian Novel, vol. 1. Toronto: NC Press, pp. 32-44.

Reprint of 1975.24; reprinted: 1983.83.

58 MacLULICH, T.D. "Atwood's Adult Fairy Tale: Levi-Strauss, Bettelheim, and *The Edible Woman*." *Essays on Canadian Writing*, no. 11 (Summer), pp. 111-129.

Argues that *The Edible Woman*'s haunting images and "uneasy appeal" come from its folkloric transformations of motifs from children's story and fairy tale. Using Claude Levi-Strauss's method, MacLulich compares the structural motifs of "The Gingerbread Man" and Atwood's novel: Marian parallels the Gingerbread Man, Duncan the trickster fox, sex parallels eating. Marian's metaphors project a "ruthless dualism" of aggressor and victim. Following Bruno Bettelheim on "Little Red Cap," MacLulich discusses Marian's childish and irrational fear of sexuality and pregnancy, and her rejection of her femininity. The complex end is both fairy tale and realism. Reprinted: 1988.31.

59 MALLINSON, JEAN. "Ideology and Poetry: An Examination of Some Recent Trends in Canadian Criticism." *Studies in Canadian Literature* 3, no. 1 (Winter):93-109.

Critiques doctrinaire readings of poetry by women; argues that Davey 1973.17 projects his own abstract, diagrammatic thinking onto *The Edible Woman* and *Surfacing*; and applies machismo clichés to *Power Politics*, ignoring its cover. His warning of a *Survival* canon applies to his own 1974.4 Davey canon. Amabile 1975.1 is not doctrinaire, but does follow preconceptions of womanliness to misread *You Are Happy* as anti-body and anti-sensual, and Circe as bitchy. *You Are Happy* should be read as subversive and ironic, with its Orphic "Song of the Hen's Head" and witty, iconoclastic "Siren Song." The ruthless, comic "Circe/Mud Poems" subvert the heroic stance, reject destructive mythical paradigms, and contrive escapes. The final "Late August" and "Book of Ancestors" are not abstract but sensuous, not proclamations of self-sufficiency but celebrations of relatedness, risk, and life. See 1984.60 or 1985.70.

60 MANSBRIDGE, FRANCIS. "Search for Self in the Novels of Margaret Atwood." *Journal of Canadian Fiction*, no. 22, pp. 106-17.

The central theme of Atwood's three novels is a young woman struggling to emerge from the false social controls of our modern society to personal fulfillment. Other themes, of the split between mind/body, conscious/instinctual, man/nature, man/woman, and fantasy/reality, are variants; other characters highlight the protagonist. In *The Edible Woman*'s social comedy of the consumer society, the mind is commercialized; cameras control; mirrors and dolls express the split between Marian's conscious and unconscious. *Surfacing*'s protagonist turns from human control of nature to a mystical vision of her fish totem, which returns her to sane reality, her mind/body split healed. In the ingenious but slick *Lady Oracle*, the split is more between fantasy and the unconscious, and conscious reality; schizophrenia, if not paranoia, becomes a condition of modern life. Atwood's novels reflect Canadian society's moods, from fifties conservatism to late sixties questing to our mid-seventies loss of direction.

1978

61 MASKOULIS, JULIA. "Serious Writer: Cooking Up the Novel." *Gazette* (Montreal), 1 April, p. 29.

Interviews Atwood, who is in Montreal to publicize *Up in the Tree*: Atwood comments on success; her own eating versus that of her heroines in *The Edible Woman* and *Lady Oracle*; her own reading, which includes Graham Greene; Quebec and the national unity crisis; and abortion.

62 MATHEWS, ROBIN. "Margaret Atwood: Survivalism." In *Canadian Literature: Surrender or Revolution*. Edited by Gail Dexter. Toronto: Steel Rail Educational Publishing, pp. 119-30.

Revision of 1972.26. Adds: *Survival*, which has now sold over 35,000 copies, attempts to see our literature in relation to colonialism, but gets mired in celebrating a bizarre need to be victim, which leads to idiosyncratic selections. Atwood accepts a liberal individualist anarchism which sees success as money and power; rejects Canadian spiritual and moral success, tenacity and struggle; and therefore misreads our literature. Omits: Indian and *Wacousta* argument. Concludes: "*Survival* must be seen as a book that prepares the consciousness to submerge in fatalistic surrender."

63 MAYS, JOHN BENTLEY. Review of *Two-Headed Poems*. *Globe and Mail*, 16 September, p. 39.

Reviews title sequence only: commends Atwood's earnest courage in confronting Canada's current dilemma of separation; praises the poems' complex resonances, cruel humour, and technical virtuosity; but rejects their political despair and simplifications, which invite defeatism.

64 MELNYK, HELEN. "Oh for a Little Love." *Edmonton Journal*, 4 March, p. F4.

Disapproves of *Dancing Girls's* "unloving, ungiving, disconnected," immature characters. "Atwood has a fine wit [as in "Under Glass"] but one-liners don't make for great literature." "The War in the Bathroom" has a fine narrative, and "Rape Fantasies" is very funny, and realistic. "'Giving Birth,' the collection's richest piece, describes how a woman undergoes the greatest violation of her body but comes through it to an existential mastery." The *Lord of the Flies* [William Golding] "When It Happens" and "A Travel Piece" are the least imaginative. Atwood's males are all like Joe in *Surfacing*–stolid, insensitive, self-absorbed, unable to love, which makes her women eternally frustrated. Her loveless, cynical, always sterile relationships make sterile reading. Mature authors like Margaret Laurence and Alice Munro "can write about both love and hate."

65 MIDDLEBRO', TOM. "Withdrawal: A Fearful Mom Doubting Survival." *Citizen* (Ottawa), 28 October, p. 38.

Values *Two-Headed Poems*: for Atwood, language and love are sources of community and communion "to which the poet must return constantly for dangerous but necessary renewal. . . . *Two-Headed Poems* returns [after three books of more narrow, personal love] to the larger community, but the tone is a pervading melancholy." The title poem, which is the saddest, depicts Canada's loss of pride and its rifts; "Solstice Poem" ominously portrays the fear and callousness that precede violence. "Four Small Elegies" and "Footnote to the Amnesty Report on Torture" reinforce the theme of violence. "Five Poems for Grandmothers" is one of the most moving. *Two-Headed Poems* concludes with personal roles, but has earlier shown that "there is no private refuge." Amidst our present backbiting and evasion we need Atwood's compassionate voice.

66 MINNI, C.D. Review of *Dancing Girls and Other Stories*. *Canadian Author and Bookman* 53, no. 2:31, 33.

Appreciates, in a two-book review, Atwood's deftly characterized, forceful, insightful stories, which have a constant feminist bias of women's viewpoints and mostly exploiting, threatening men, as in "Rape Fantasies." The ironic juxtapositions in "The Resplendent Quetzal" and others are masterful. Some have archaeologically complex layers of meaning, like "Polarities," which may contain the seed of *Surfacing*. The almost schizophrenic "The War in the Bathroom" and "[Giving] Birth" create universal characters. "The Man from Mars" and "Dancing Girls" are the weakest, because their ethnic characters remain curios.

67 MORLEY, PATRICIA. Review of *Dancing Girls and Other Stories*. *World Literature Written in English* 17, no. 1 (April):188-90.

Praises Atwood's modern, female, and universal stories; discusses their Ontario WASP-land present, with its surface tolerance and

1978

lurking prejudice; their *Survival*-style victor/victim relationships between men and woman, particularly in "At the Grave of the Famous Poet"; their *doppelgängers*; their ironic comedy and optimism; and their fantasy and parody of fantasy, as in "Rape Fantasies." Two *doppelgänger* stories, "The War in the Bathroom" and the imaginative, accurate "Giving Birth," "frame a collection which moves thematically from spite to generosity and wonder."

68 NICOLL, SHARON. "Pirouettes and Falls." *Branching Out* 5, no. 1:44-45.
    Finds a few good stories, but too many mediocre and even bad ones, in *Dancing Girls*. The strong, amused, disillusioned romantic narrator in "Hair Jewellery" makes it perhaps the best of all the stories, despite a weak end; the perceptive "The Grave of the Famous Poet" is one of the two best. "The War in the Bathroom" is amusing but slight. "Polarities" and "Under Glass" have energetic protagonists. But too many others are predictable "'idea' pieces," with type characters and situations, and "A Travel [Piece]" is the worst of those. Perhaps Atwood publishes too much.

69 NOVAK, BARBARA. "Quality for Children Thriving, Lucrative." *London* (Ontario) *Free Press*, 27 May, p. B4.
    Appreciates *Up in the Tree* in a two-book review: the reviewer's six-year-old consultant read it all by himself, joyfully, out loud, with plenty of giggles for the story and the illustrations, and only wanted to know why the children didn't jump down from the tree. Atwood's illustrations wisely let the child discover things not in the text, and her hand-lettering sometimes makes the words look like their meanings.

70 OATES, JOYCE CAROL. "A Conversation with Margaret Atwood." *Ontario Review*, no. 9 (Fall-Winter), pp. 5-18.
    Atwood discusses early readings in British and Canadian poetry; cake decorating and *The Edible Woman*'s cake; *Lady Oracle* and Gothic romances as women's secret plots. Contrasts *Surfacing* with James Dickey's *Deliverance*; compares it with Howard O'Hagan's *Tay John*. Discusses dehumanizing in "The Man from Mars"; university teaching versus waitressing; Harvard, its treatment of women students, and Canadian cultural nationalism, which began not with "'Am I really that oppressed?'" but "'Am I really that boring?'" Discusses work habits

186

(procrastination and terror); "Bart Gerrard" cartoons for *This Magazine*; reigning Queen and Medusa images; literary criticism, fame, and backlash in Canada versus America; Writers' Union lobbying on Remainders Issue; the necessity of small presses and Canadian subsidies to literature, and of defining Canadian themes; her current writing.

71 _____. "Margaret Atwood: Poems and Poet." *New York Times Book Review*, 21 May, pp. 15, 43-45.

Atwood discusses sound, form, and meaning in her poetry; her family background; her early reading of Poe and *Grimms' Fairy Tales*, and Harvard readings in Gothic romance, mentioning her [1977] "Canadian Monsters" article; her current writing; her different voices as a poet, fiction writer, and public speaker; compares readers' autobiographical assumptions by country and gender; discusses Canadian nationalism, anti-Americanism, and Canadian responsibility; poetry as lens not neurosis; and creative writing as widespread, not an activity unique to her.

72 OUELLETTE-MICHALSKA, MADELEINE. "Entre les lignes, les deux solitudes." *Châtelaine* (French ed.) 19, no. 8 (August):16.

Compares, in a group review, *Faire surface*, the French translation of *Surfacing*, and Gabrielle Roy's *Bonheur d'occasion*. Both novels address the problems with communication and perceptions between cultures. *Faire surface* depicts a woman's quest for her lost father and her own identity, and a country's search for itself and its heritage.

73 "Paperbacks: New and Noteworthy." *New York Times Book Review*, 15 January, p. 27.

Notes that, though some reviewers hailed *Lady Oracle* as a major feminist novel, our Pollitt 1976.75, like some others, found "'stock'" characters and "'pat'" insights.

74 PETERSON, LESLIE. "Edible Oracle." *Vancouver Sun*, 16 June, p. L38.

Interviews Atwood, who is in Vancouver for a sold-out, record-setting poetry reading at the Vancouver East Cultural Center, lunch with an academic critic, and a second reading at Simon Fraser

1978

University; Atwood compares media reactions to success and conditions for writers in Canada and the United States.

75 PETROWSKI, NATHALIE. "Une heure avec Margaret Atwood." *Devoir* (Montréal), 8 April, p. 38.

Interviewed shortly after the publication of *Up in the Tree*, Atwood discusses Canada's lack of representation, and search for a historical and cultural identity. Writing children's books lets Atwood diversify. As a woman, she does not dismiss feminism, but is more concerned with human dignity.

76 POGUE, ELIZABETH. "Parents Beware of Literary Horror." *Gazette* (Montreal), 30 June, p. 15.

A round-up review that cautions against some revoltingly inappropriate children's books; recommends *Up in the Tree* as excellent for younger children, who will love its lilting rhymes, its delightful two-colour illustrations, its charming androgynous children, friendly owl, and happy end.

77 PORTER-LADOUSSE, GILLIAN. "The Unicorn and the Booby Hatch: An Interview with Margaret Atwood." *Études canadiennes* (Talence), no. 5, pp. 97-111.

Interviews Atwood in Paris, 4 February 1978: Atwood discusses Canadian literature as perceived in Italy and the United States; Canadian identity as colonial, minority, and dominated; feminism as ideology versus her own pre-feminist experience and parallel writing; women, such as Susanna Moodie and George Eliot, in Canadian and English literature; critics' perceptions of women's writing, and of comic versus serious in *Surfacing*, *Lady Oracle*, and *Dancing Girls*; satire, women writers, and utopianism; [James] Thurber's unicorn story; Canada's two, hydra-headed French and English cultures in *Two-Headed Poems*; language and poetry.

78 QUIGLEY, THERESIA. "*Surfacing*: A Critical Study." *Antigonish Review*, no. 34 (Summer), pp. 77-87.

Explicates *Surfacing* as a fascinating exploration of a Freudian repression, and of alienation resulting from abortion. The purely symbolic ending seems strange, if not mad, but may be illuminated by comparison with the Orestes myth. *Surfacing* condemns mechanized, urban civilization, technology, and Americans. Much of its language is obscene, though forceful.

79 RACKOWSKI, CHERYL STOKES. "Women by Women: Five Contemporary English and French Canadian Novelists." Ph.D. dissertation, University of Connecticut, 316 pp.

Atwood, Marie-Claire Blais, Anne Hebert, Margaret Laurence, and Claire Martin all portray dissatisfied protagonists whose selves are divided and cramped by stereotypes of female roles. "The English Canadians such as Joan in Atwood's *Lady Oracle* are usually caught between the needs for security and self-expression. . . . In many English Canadian novels such as Atwood's *Surfacing*, a descent into madness precedes rebirth. . . . [T]he warm earth-mothers such as the protagonist's mother in Atwood's *Surfacing*" are one of four types of older women. See *Dissertation Abstracts International* 39 (1979):6752A.

80 REGAN, NANCY. "A Home of One's Own: Women's Bodies in Recent Women's Fiction." *Journal of Popular Culture* 11, no. 4 (Spring):772-88.

Describes, in a study of women's sexuality in current popular Gothics and serious women's fiction, *Surfacing*'s reversed Gothic elements, and "pre-narcissistic" narrator who, for most of the novel, does not inhabit her body at all. That the secret crime is her own, and that it is the mother who has just died, and the father who is sought, reverse Gothic elements. After hallucinating her aborted child in the dive, the narrator becomes preconscious, mad, and asexual in her subsequent mating. The end shows her frighteningly isolated.

81 RIGNEY, BARBARA HILL. "'After the Failure of Logic': Descent and Return in *Surfacing*." In *Madness and Sexual Politics in the Feminist Novel: Studies in Brontë, Woolf, Lessing, and Atwood.* Madison: University of Wisconsin Press, pp. 91-115.

Celebrates *Surfacing*'s therapeutic quest for identity. Atwood juxtaposes internal male and female principles, of the father's and brother's reason and destruction, and of the mother's alignment with natural life and death. Like R.D. Laing's patients, Atwood's protagonist is split, alienated, psychologically dead. Her schizophrenia is that of *Survival*'s cut-off Canadian artist, and of Canada. Like Marian in *The Edible Woman*, *Surfacing*'s protagonist must overcome what

1978

Christ 1976.13 called her "'female delusion of innocence.'" Her father's logic guides her part of the way. Her mother's legacy, revealed in the protagonist's childhood drawing, shows her how to "*become* her mother, . . . giving birth to herself as well as to new life." Mystically identified with nature, the protagonist descends into temporary, therapeutic madness; she surfaces carrying the new child, sane, whole, and victorious. See 1982.143 and 1987.129.

82 ____. "Self-Created Other: Integration and Survival." In *Madness and Sexual Politics in the Feminist Novel: Studies in Brontë, Woolf, Lessing, and Atwood*. Madison: University of Wisconsin Press, pp. 117-27.

Compares the protagonists of Charlotte Brontë's *Jane Eyre*, Virginia Woolf's *Mrs. Dalloway*, Doris Lessing's *The Four-Gated City*, and Atwood's *Surfacing*, as women achieving some self-realization and self-actualization, despite their male-supremacist societies. Each protagonist follows prototypes of mythic spiritual journeys and of psychoanalysis. Though all withdraw from psychological danger, none is asexual or unloving. Each searches for some helper to heal the divided self. Each comes to recognize a doppelgänger who must then be annihilated or assimilated; the mother is one of *Surfacing*'s many doppelgängers. See 1982.143 and 1987.129.

83 ROBB, CHRISTINA. "Powerful Poems from Canada." *Boston Globe*, 5 May, p. 34. Newsbank 1978, 30:E11.

Finds the well-known Canadian novelist's *Selected Poems* very powerful, and simple, and often strange. Atwood writes of fear, pain, a hidden sharpness which is hidden from, and a great need to find or become a soft, complete person. *Power Politics* and *You Are Happy* oscillate between fear, anger, and finally, love.

84 ROSENBERG, JEROME H. "Woman as Everyman in Atwood's *Surfacing*: Some Observations on the End of the Novel." *Studies in Canadian Literature* 3, no. 1 (Winter):127-32.

Disputes Sullivan 1977.90: Atwood's narrator cannot, and should not, do more at the end of *Surfacing* than come to terms with her human self. Her mythic wilderness journey is, after all, fantasy. As Atwood says, in the 1977.80 Sandler interview, her heroine is released from her obsessive search for the ghosts once she has found them. Like Henry James, Atwood is a realistic writer. Her narrator's vision does not lead to a superhuman knowledge that could alienate her from common humanity, but to a realization of her human complicity and responsibility. Learning how to become human is no evasion. The final, tentative triumph shows the narrator, like all of us, precariously balanced in an imperfect world.

85 ROSS, CATHERINE SHELDRICK. "'A Singing Spirit': Female Rites of Passage in *Klee Wyck*, *Surfacing*, and *The Diviners*." *Atlantis* 4, no. 1 (Fall):87-94.

In Emily Carr's *Klee Wyck*, Atwood's *Surfacing*, and Margaret Laurence's *The Diviners*, a ritual encounter with Indian shamanism releases the central character's womanly and creative energies, and gives her access to powers that white establishment culture and technology deny. In *Surfacing* and *The Diviners*, the aborted or denied child represents establishment sterility; and conception is the sign that the central character has become a woman. Each of these three books uses some of the Indian shamanic and initiation elements described by Mircea Eliade: separation and wilderness retreat; ordeals; secret language; and ritual death and rebirth into spiritual maturity.

86 RUBIO, MARY. "Breaking into the Children's Market." *Quill and Quire* 44, no. 9 (July):36.

Features Atwood's fantasy *Up in the Tree* in a three-book review of children's books by Atwood, Marian Engel, and Matt Cohen, which continue Canada's long tradition of adult writers creating children's books. *Up in the Tree* is unquestionably one of Canada's best picture books for the very young. Its internal rhymes withstand repeated readings. But one small discrepancy occurs between the pictures and text – a big red apple that is ignored in the text by the hungry children.

87 RUMLEY, LARRY. "Canadian Writer Has Made Her Mark as Poet, Novelist, Critic." *Seattle Times*, 18 June, Magazine sec., p. 13.

Interviews Atwood, who is in Seattle to read her poems at the University of Washington: Atwood, who is personable and wryly humorous, recalls her peripatetic education, trying to get "Up in the Air So Blue" and *The Edible Woman* published, her unfinished early novel, her poetry chapbook [*Double Persephone*], her early influences, *Survival*'s reception, and the unmade film of *The Edible Woman*.

1978

88 SCHOEMPERLEN, DIANE. "Fictional Explorations." *Waves* 6, no. 3 (Spring):90-91.

Compares the stories of *Dancing Girls* and of Hugh Hood's *Dark Glasses*; both explore, rather than explain, the human head. What matters is the process of exploration. "The Resplendent Quetzal" contrasts with Hood's bizarre treatment of a woman losing a child. Both authors use sharp, ironic humour; and curiously permuted viewpoints that suggest reality is not so external, and the self not so distinct.

89 SCRIVANI, MARIA. "Poetry, Novels Both Give Her Satisfaction." *Buffalo Evening News*, 27 April, p. 25.

Interview: Atwood comments briefly on novels versus converting people or speaking for womankind; Canadian women writers, and Atwood's York University class project on discrimination; the Canadian literary scene; Joan Didion; prizes and criticism; genres and truth in Atwood's own writing.

90 SLATER, PETER. *Dynamics of Religion: Meaning and Change in Religious Traditions*. San Francisco: Harper & Row, pp. 120-28, 131-33, 147-48.

Interprets *Surfacing* as an individual transformation in a "'post-Christian'" setting. Though becoming a creative non-victim is not a conversion experience, *Surfacing*'s heroine is divided between "bodily me" and "spiritual and social mes. . . ." Her "husband's" reality has shattered her reality. She is a twentieth-century figure, unsure of her roles, cut off from family, relying on her own unreliable judgments. As in *The Autobiography of Malcolm X*, individual transformation means taking responsibility, despite a destructive environment. As in R.D. Laing, the "'normal'" may be insane, the "'deviant'" realistic.

91 SPAFFORD, ROZ. "Margaret Atwood: Coloring with Words." *Plexus* 5, no. 5 (July):13.

Celebrates Atwood's eleven new poems, which she read at San Francisco State. These are Atwood's best work, improving what she does well: tightly written but not boxed in; more fully comprehending both nature and family relationships; and with larger and more affirmative transformations. As in "You Begin," Atwood extends a simple, familiar thing or act to a metaphor that forcefully changes it, and in language so simple and accessible that it is your own and universal. As in "The Woman Who Could Not Live with Her Faulty Heart," Atwood's re-naming gives a larger life to things. "Marrying the Hangman" mostly succeeds, despite some slowness, Atwood's too-long introduction at the reading, and the poem's generalizations on men versus women. "All Bread" and "You Begin" are the reviewer's favorites. Atwood commented on Canadian versus American literature, writing poetry versus prose, and readers' identifying versus her own eccentricity.

92 SPETTIGUE, D.O. Review of *Dancing Girls and Other Stories*. *Queen's Quarterly* 85, no. 3 (Autumn):516-18.

Considers, in a six-book review, Atwood, Alice Munro, and Audrey Thomas to be unbeatable masters of the short story, but finds it hard to be confident about so many women's "confessions of the never-to-be-ended struggle" for selfhood. There's a limiting sameness of place, and of the "literary semi-attached female," who needs men, and needs not to need men. Compares *Dancing Girls* with Thomas's *Ten Green Bottles* and *Ladies and Escorts*: that these tourists and transients don't belong may be both Canadian and universal, but the imaginative is always elsewhere, and the present becomes obsessively prosaic. "Formally it is the narrow spaces of irony these quietly desperate women (and men) inhabit." Atwood's humour surpasses Thomas's; see "Rape Fantasies." Both authors explore ground zero to start over, affirming.

93 STEELE, CHARLES. "A Map of Metaphor: The Poetic Vision of Canadian Criticism." *Book Forum* 4, no. 1:144-50.

Defines Canadian criticism as post-*Survival* and a poetic synthesis of our elusive identity. Critics constantly invoke *Survival*, too frequently as a knee-jerk response to its popularity, or a facile formula. Remember that D.G. Jones's *Butterfly on Rock* and Northrop Frye's mythopoeic structuralizing, in *The Bush Garden* and elsewhere, preceded Atwood's. *Survival's* nature ideas shape Margot Northey's *The Haunted Wilderness* 1976.70. As *Survival's* map shows, poets' metaphors have structured Canadian criticism.

1978

94 STEELE, JAMES. "The Literary Criticism of Margaret Atwood." In *In Our Own House: Social Perspectives on Canadian Literature*. Edited by Paul Cappon. Toronto: McClelland & Stewart, pp. 73-81.

Welcomes sociological literary criticism, but rejects *Survival*'s. Though *Survival*, with 40,000 copies sold, has introduced many to Canadian literature, its hypothesis fails to explain, and is controverted by, much Canadian writing. Ernest Thompson Seton's animals, for example, are noble, stoic, moral heroes, not pathetic victims. England's literature has victims, too. Atwood's victim positions seem to blend Frye's archetypes with Eric Berne's *Games People Play*. Her idea of nationality follows Frye's idealist epistemology and liberal, utopian individualism. *Survival* projects the typically modernist alienation of her well-made but narrow lyric poems [from The Circle Game and The Animals in That Country] onto Canadian literature.

95 STEVENS, PETER. "A Place of Absolute Unformed Beginning." In *The New Land: Studies in a Literary Theme*. Edited by Richard Chadbourne and Hallvard Dahlie. Waterloo, Ont.: Wilfrid Laurier University Press, pp. 133-34.

In a collection of papers presented at the University of Calgary Institute for the Humanities Workshop, 1-5 August 1977, briefly discusses survival, "ancestry, roots, beginnings and the difficulties surrounding these notions" in Atwood's "Migration: C.P.R.," whose [lines 22-23] are this paper's title.

96 SWARTZ, ESTHER. "Northern Aspect: Atwood Discusses Canada." *Buffalo Courier-Express*, 23 April, p. F9.

Interviews Atwood, who read at the University of Buffalo last week to publicize the American *Selected Poems*: Atwood, who is shy, ironic, and devastatingly witty, compares writers, readers, success, and conservativism in Canada and the United States; characterizes her life as a Canadian "'quiet exterior filled with swirling clouds of snow'"; and shares the reviewer's own "'love-hate relationship with Canada.'"

97 TESHER, ELLIE. "Atwood Surfaces as Writer-Parent." *Toronto Star*, 19 May, p. C1.

Profiles Atwood as mother of two-year-old Jess, at Alliston farm: Atwood comments on child-rearing, which is shared with Graeme Gibson; writing habits; marital status; and women's liberation.

98 THOMAS, CLARA. "Heroinism, Feminism, and Humanism: Anna Jameson to Margaret Laurence." *Atlantis* 4, no. 1 (Fall):19-21.
    Incorporates part of 1977.93. Feminist literary criticism helps us understand our women writers: *Lady Oracle* uses Moers's convention of Heroinism with deliberate irony, setting up Heroinism's tensions with feminism. This "implied 'message'" connects strongly with many Canadian women writers, from the nineteenth-century Anna Jameson to the present.

99 WACHTEL, ELEANOR. "Mellow Motherhood." *Vancouver Sun*, 7 April, p. L37.
    Where have the poet's sharp irony and the critic's Canadian victims gone? Now, after Atwood's Mama and baby interviews, her light third novel, and her delightful comic strip about curly hair, we have her charmingly simple *Up in the Tree*, with its very pleasing, expressive illustrations and happy-ending story.

100 _____. Review of *Up in the Tree*. *Room of One's Own* 3, no. 4:75-76.
    Briefly praises Atwood's disarmingly simple, engaging pictures and story, in a two-book review featuring Elisabeth Margaret Hopkins's *The Painted Cougar*.

101 WILLIAMSON, ALAN. "'Fool! Said My Muse to Me. . . .'" *Poetry* 133, no. 1 (November):102-3.
    Analyzes, in a group review, *Selected Poems*'s unromantic myth of contemporary ambivalence towards civilization. Separated from nature, we are monstrous, human; but the wilderness is dangerous and alienating, as in *The Journals of Susanna Moodie*, which best defines Atwood's myth. The "'disadvantaged'"–women, tribes, Canadians–may more easily reach atavistic truths. The real pain lies in being neither tourists nor Indians. (Atwood's myth also illumines relationships, as in *Power Politics*, which is a most suggestive existential study, not a radical feminist diatribe.) Atwood's style is unmetered, but with tense line-breaks; not far from prose, but subtle. Epigram and parable are her great strengths; thinness and preachiness her faults.

102 WOOD, SUSAN. "A Garland of Verse." *Washington Post Book World*, [3 December], p. 6.

1978

Briefly welcomes, in a round-up review, Atwood's fascinating, powerful, original *Selected Poems*. A champion of Canadian survival and literature, but not a doctrinaire chauvinist, Atwood is increasingly popular here; *Selected Poems* contains work all but impossible to find, including *The Journals of Susanna Moodie*. Atwood's core subjects are myth, nature, power, and metamorphosis. Excerpted: 1980.51.

103 _____. Review of *Up in the Tree*. *Pacific Northwest Review of Books* 1, no. 3 (June):27.

Finds *Up in the Tree* pleasant but slight; a nice whimsy for pre-schoolers and beginning readers, but hardly a children's classic, despite the publisher's claims. Atwood's "life in the media" inevitably tempts one to write a gossip-piece on her motherhood instead of reviewing *Up in the Tree*, which was surely published primarily because of Atwood's name and image. The writing is generally bland, with obvious rhymes that at moments flash into delightful absurdity. The drawings have more wit, originality, and a naive, folk-art charm. The owl is quite delightful; the ladder-devouring beavers look porcupinish.

104 WOODCOCK, GEORGE. "The New Books." *Queen's Quarterly* 85, no. 4 (Winter):699-700.

Ranks Margaret Atwood's *Days of the Rebels* much above the other, journalistically limited, volumes of the *Canadian* [sic] *Illustrated Heritage*. As we might expect from her poetry–particularly *The Journals of Susanna Moodie*, novels, and criticism, Atwood sees our early Canadian struggles with sensitive empathy and historic perspective, despite some imperfect passages.

1979

1 AMIEL, BARBARA. "Best, Worst, and Others of 1978." *Maclean's* 92, no. 2 (8 January):46.

Includes *Two-Headed Poems*, and Al Purdy's *Being Alive*, in a list of the year's best fiction, poetry, and non-fiction.

2 _____. "Life after Surviving." *Maclean's* 93, no. 42 (15 October):66-67.

Praises *Life Before Man* highly as Atwood's witty, skillful, and, at last, thoroughly successful novel of soggy identities, limp marriages, and limper affairs among the highly educated. *Life* is a "'haute'" women's novel, on an Iris Murdoch level, focused on the eternal fascinations of love and lust, John and Mary; Lesje's musings on dinosaurs and mankind are like rouge contours, never tiresomely intruding on sex and plot. Women's novels, unlike Tolstoy or Flaubert, focus on love and lust as "the *entire* stuff." The reviewer would like a sequel, soon, with the characters' decisions made and a clean ending. See 1980.3.

3 ____. "Poetry: Capsule Comments on Canada." *Maclean's* 92, no. 3 (15 January):50.

Praises *Two-Headed Poems* highly, as one of five books from five major Canadian poets. Though Atwood's voice and face seem frail, she writes with an unequalled steeliness. The magnificent *Two-Headed Poems* "is a spare, exquisite and merciless look at the many selves of the poet's persona" – and these are universal poems, about each of us. Excerpted: 1980.51.

4 ANTONELLI, MARYLU. "Atwood: Over the Hurdle." *Edmonton Sun*, 28 October, p. S6.

Interviews Atwood in Edmonton: Atwood, who is pleased that she's succeeded in creating a male character, discusses *Life Before Man*'s sensitive, muddled, role-blurred Nate as a realistic man of mid-1970s Toronto, where the late 1960s anti-establishment revolt, Women's Liberation, and mid-1970s prosperity have opened up options for women and men.

5 "Atwood in a Cocktail Gown Is Touting Her New Book." *Gazette* (Montreal), 31 July, p. 44.

Briefly quotes Atwood as promoting *Life Before Man* to help Canadian publishers.

6 [BANNON, BARBARA A.]. Review of *Life Before Man*. *Publishers Weekly* 216, no. 25 (24 December):49.

Is simultaneously fascinated and repelled by *Life Before Man*, with its shifting relationships and emotionless, relentless, pathetic, and dying characters. Atwood's clear, crystalline style has renounced all drama and compassion. "22,500 first printing; Book-of-the-Month Club alternate; national tour."

1979

7 BARBOUR, DOUGLAS. "Canadian Poetry Chronicle: VII." *Dalhousie Review* 59, no. 1 (Spring):173.

Praises *Two-Headed Poems*'s wider range and hard-won, honest affirmations. Though Atwood's familiar but realistic paranoia is still here, these poems recognize human connections, through grandmothers and daughter, and accept the world. The compassionate "'All Bread' truly sings humanity's place in a living world."

8 _____. Review of *Two-Headed Poems*. *Fiddlehead*, no. 121 (Spring), pp. 139-42.

Appreciates Atwood's new, greater affirmations and wider, more humane compassion, despite her ambiguous, gothic landscape and too-true paranoia. Or do we remember only Atwood's bleakest passages? But Susanna Moodie's fullest acceptance came after her death; this persona has made "her awkward peace with nature in *this* life," as in Daybooks II [10]. Atwood's daughter may have opened new spaces. Praises especially the moving, compassionate "Five Poems for Grandmothers" and "Footnote to the Amnesty Report on Torture," and the hard-won affirmations of "All Bread." Reprinted: 1988.3.

9 BILLINGTON, DAVE. "A Novel of Bleak Brilliance." *Edmonton Sun*, 28 October, p. S6.

Praises *Life Before Man* as brilliant, though bleak, and amazingly realistic. *Life* is a careful, acutely observed, serious but scarcely optimistic examination of our contemporary North American middle-class relationships and marriages. Elizabeth is "a carnivorous bitch," Nate a dithering but well-intentioned lawyer, and Lesje "a willowy paleontologist" who believes in love. The characters lack warmth, and seem like specimens, because Atwood makes us stand too far back from them. *Life* captures that "weird old dowager," Toronto, so realistically that readers who don't truly know the city could be alienated.

10 BJÖRKSTEN, INGMAR. "Margaret Atwood: Hör Kanada Tala" [Margaret Atwood: hear Canada speak]. *Svenska Dagbladet* (Stockholm), 28 October, p. 8.

In Swedish. *Survival* examines Canadian literature as a search for identity and a struggle for cultural independence. *Upp till ytan*, the recently released Swedish translation of *Surfacing*, illustrates *Survival*'s themes through a narrator who survives a quest in the wilderness that brings her to terms with her parents, a past abortion, and her divorce. Like Margaret Drabble, Atwood focuses on her own generation's issues; but Atwood's work is more cynical, with a more unusual sense of humor.

11 BOLD, CHRISTINE. Review of *Surfacing. Cencrastus* (Edinburgh), no. 1 (Autumn), p. 40.

American literature looks for Huck Finn's next frontier; *Surfacing*, in contrast, has a wilderness that is the North and Canada, a space that is vertical, and a protagonist who is female. Though the retreat into the past, the vision of death, and the final message, on not being a victim, seem negative, Atwood does precariously balance the whole, the human, and the possibility of new life, and of surfacing from a half-crazed animalistic empathy to rejoin society. *Surfacing*, which is republished by Virago, "is not stridently feminist or nationalist"; Atwood subtly constructs her perilous and perhaps "necessary Myth of the age."

12 BOWERING, GEORGE [Edward Prato]. Review of *Two-Headed Poems*. *West Coast Review* 14, no. 1 (June):43-46.

Features *Two-Headed Poems*, in a two-book review of it and Patrick Lane's *Poems New & Selected*. *Two-Headed Poems* may be Atwood's best, most enduring, and most caring poetry. Atwood is still our entrancing "verse-witch," with her tricks of masks and mirrors; but now there are many endearing farm and family poems, like "Daybooks I and II" and "The Bus to Alliston, Ontario."

> Despite the title, the most important anatomical image in the book is of hands. Hands wear puppets, reach out in a darkened staircase, stroke the air around bodies, fashion clothes and toys for the child, grapple with one another as emissaries of the bicameral mind, and appear over and over, trying to touch a world the eyes can not always see. Hands act to complete the locution of the first poem, and a hand appears as the last word of the last poem, a word to a daughter who will use it to start her meeting with the world. (Paragraph quoted from pages 44-45.)

The title poem disappoints, as all our national allegories do. "Five Poems for Grandmothers" balances the Canadian canon of grandfather poems. "Marrying the Hangman," which is already famous, is probably

1979

the book's most exciting achievement. Despite occasional self-parodies and banalities, *Two-Headed Poems* is mainly "an unusually good book." The Atwood portion of this review is reprinted, slightly revised, as part of 1981.9.

13 BRAENDLIN, BONNIE HOOVER. "Alther, Atwood, Ballantyne, and Gray: Secular Salvation in the Contemporary Feminist Bildungsroman." *Frontiers* 4, no. 1 (Spring):18-22.

Compares *Lady Oracle*, Lisa Alther's *Kinflicks*, Sheila Ballantyne's *Norma Jean the Termite Queen*, and Francine du Plessix Gray's *Lovers and Tyrants* as feminist bildungsromans and, following Christ 1976.13 and Gray 1977.28, as social rather than spiritual quests. The bildungsroman has moved from the picaresque toward the confessional, and the self has become a Proustian creation of recollection and reconstruction. Shifts from first- to third-person narrators and flashback juxtapositions reveal these narrators' fragmented selves and society's conditioning. Like women's spiritual quests, these developmental journeys end with hope, as the newly integrated, reborn woman transcends patriarchy's roles, and chooses inner adaptation, or exiled freedom.

14 BROWN, RUSSELL M. "A Search for America: Some Canadian Literary Responses." *Journal of American Culture* 2, no. 4 (Winter):670, 679-81.

Includes *Surfacing*'s American hunters and encroachments in a discussion of Canadian literary portraits of a strong, menacing, masculine America versus a weak, virtuous, feminine Canada. As in Atwood's first two novels, Canadian nationalism and feminism are parallel pursuits of self-determination. The gothic sadomasochistic fantasy Mandel 1974.25 (1977.53) found in *Survival*'s Canadian victor/victim relationships, and all Atwood's work, is one of threatening male versus endangered woman. The Canadian bifocal vision of the two Americas, and Canadian irony, will recast extreme nationalist rejections of America: the *Surfacing* hunters, ironically, turn out to be Canadian.

15 CARTER, NANCY C. "Demeter and Persephone in Margaret Atwood's Novels: Mother-Daughter Transformations." *Journal of Analytical Psychology* 24, no. 4 (October):326-42.

Reads Atwood's three novels in relation to the archetypal Demeter-Persephone (Kore) myth, which provides enabling insights for men and women now. *The Edible Woman*'s Marian transforms herself, after a kind of fasting that corresponds to *anorexia nervosa*, and a symbolic self-consuming of the cake, from a forlorn Kore into a Kore-Demeter. *Surfacing* follows the myth most directly: its narrator journeys like Persephone into the dark, feminine lake of rebirth and death; she re-visions her "'rape,'" abortion, and long Hades numbing, and deliberately eats the pomegranate when she deliberately makes love; she returns, re-integrated after mythic vision, to mundane struggles. *Lady Oracle* has an ironic, ambiguous relation to the myth; its inept, ill-fated Kore heroine may become truly transformed after seeing a Hecate-like apparition of her mother.

16 CASSELTON, VAL. "Reality Is Atwood's Tool – and It Includes a Utopia." *Vancouver Courier*, 22 July, p. 16.

Profiles an Atwood who is gentle, compassionate, and an earth-mother, yet tough, intense, and ultra-feminist. Atwood, who is reading at a Vancouver benefit for bill bissett, discusses pornography in literature and advertising; censorship, of bissett, *Surfacing* (which was banned in Prince George), Margaret Laurence, and Alice Munro; Amnesty International; and realism, not pessimism, in her work. She also says that the title of *Life Before Man* has five meanings.

17 C[LAPP], S[USANNAH]. Review of *Surfacing*. *TLS*, 23 November, p. 42.

Finds an unusual, remarkable, patiently observed book where a wildness that not everyone will sympathize with is central. Though *Surfacing* is "too peculiar to be simply a feminist tract, it is more persuasive than oddity alone would allow."

18 COLEMAN, S.J. "Margaret Atwood, Lucien Goldmann's Pascal, and the Meaning of 'Canada.'" *University of Toronto Quarterly* 48, no. 3 (Spring):245-62.

Survival assumed that an undifferentiated Canadian national culture exists. Consider, however, Lucien Goldmann's universal theory of world-views, and his linking of social group membership to the individual's choice of world-view. *Surfacing*'s artist persona criticizes both the "'American'" city and false Canadian nationalism. "Her

1979

struggle is not [like Pascal's] with Christianity but with a late romantic revival of an alien animism, which first enlightens, then fails her." Like Pascal's mankind, she must wager on a dubious outcome; *Surfacing* "has expressed Goldmann's tragic world-view brilliantly and completely." Atwood belongs to a social group whose ambiguous position is analogous to Pascal's *noblesse de robe*: the Canadian intellectuals and publicists whose livelihood depends on their speaking of an achieved Canadian nationhood, for an "'American'" mass market they cannot control.

19 CORBEIL, CAROLE. "Surfacing from a Damaging Decade." *Quill and Quire* 45, no. 12 (October):31.

Acclaims *Life Before Man*: its portrait of the confused, tragi-comic 1970s; its playful, subtle metaphor of extinction; and its characterization, including the fully-realized male character, Nate, who lives through women, as women have done through men. Atwood exposes her characters' flaws, but never judges; *Life Before Man* is her most compassionate and encompassing work.

20 CRITTENDEN, YVONNE. "This One's a Real Find." *Sunday Sun* (Toronto), 30 September, p. S15.

Praises *Life Before Man*'s acute perceptions, vivid imagery, and new compassion and understanding. Atwood takes a wry, penetrating look at how modern marriages, relationships, and even humanity may be perishing as the dinosaurs did. *Life*'s pace is leisurely, its turmoil inward. Atwood points out, with Nate, the difficulty of escaping one's earlier commitments; and accurately describes the conflicting emotions of married men and women in affairs. She also "takes a swipe at the muddled thinking of the women's movement" on manstealing versus personal growth.

*21 CURTIS, TONY. "Interview with Margaret Atwood, March 25th, 1979." *Madog* [(Wales?) 3, no. 1 (1979)]:48-56.

Atwood, who has spent the 1978-79 academic year in Scotland, writing *Life Before Man*, discusses her writing habits; form in her poetry and fiction; *Surfacing* as autobiographical only in its setting and perhaps in its wilderness childhood followed by adjustment to the city, which mirrors *The Journals of Susanna Moodie*'s urban to wilderness experience; American as a metaphor of behaviour in *Surfacing*;

language; and British recognition of Canadian and American writers, which Atwood links to national power. "I think the writer is always both the lover of language and its enemy, because any single language will only do so many things for you. . . . [Y]our mother tongue conditions the way you think." English is very noun-centered, with short and mostly solid words. Because Canada is an ex-colony, Britains are less likely to review Canadian than American books.

22 DAHLIE, HALLVARD. Review of *Life Before Man*. *Dalhousie Review* 59, no. 3 (Autumn):561-63.

Does not care for *Life Before Man*'s insignificant, unmotivated characters. Ordinary people "must be created with compassion and sympathy," as they are in Alice Munro's work. *Life Before Man* has clever games, not convincing human relationships. The clumsy, divided structure is a problem; the novel lacks a moral centre. Though Atwood's poetry and short stories are excellent, her novels lack compassion, and this is the weakest of the four.

23 DAVID, JACK. Review of *Two-Headed Poems*. *University of Windsor Review* 14, no. 2 (Spring-Summer):100-103.

Juxtaposes, in a two-book review, similarities between Atwood's *Two-Headed Poems* and Leonard Cohen's *Death of a Lady's Man*; prefers earlier books by each. Both cover images are doubled. The adult is restored by the child in both. Though Atwood's similes are still penetrating, there's no appreciable change here. These two successful poets are only treading water in the 1970s; Cohen's *The Energy of Slaves* concluded his poetic cycle, as *Power Politics* did Atwood's.

24 DAVIDSON, ARNOLD E. "Entering *The Circle Game*: Margaret Atwood's Beginnings as a Poet." *Concerning Poetry* 12, no. 2 (Fall):47-54.

Examines Atwood's first book, which reveals her characteristic style and tone, as a book of games, of the creative intelligence at play. Reads "This Is a Photograph of Me" as a hide-and-seek of landscape, perhaps of submerging domestic socialscape, and psychoscape; and as a riddle of reader-persona-art. Examines the games, personae, irony, and humor, of "After the Flood, We," "A Messenger," the title poem, and others; finds the game of love the prevailing game. Contends, against Rogers 1974.38, that Atwood constructs rather than dissects her spheres, circles, and games; *Circle* is "play of a very high order," from a major poet.

25 DAVIDSON, ARNOLD E., and DAVIDSON, CATHY N. "The Anatomy of Margaret Atwood's *Surfacing*." *ARIEL* (Calgary) 10, no. 3 (July):38-54.

Analyses *Surfacing* as a Frygian archetypal quest and romance, modified by its contemporary context. As Frye explains in *The Anatomy of Criticism*, the romance has three stages. *Surfacing*'s narrator passes through the first, the *agon* or perilous journey, into her past; and the second, the *pathos* or death struggle, in which she separates herself from the Americanized victimizers. The third stage, *anagnorisis* or enlightenment, occurs in her discovery of her father's body, visions, and revelations, but cannot be completed with a public exaltation of the returning hero: because she is a woman, and returning to a contemporary society that would think her mad. *Surfacing*'s hero therefore transcends the mythic pattern; she returns to normality pregnant, and struggling to survive contemporary society's hazards.

26 DAWE, ALAN. "Paradise Missed." *Vancouver Sun*, 21 September, p. L35.

Did not much enjoy *Life Before Man*, and questions the publisher's elaborate signed preview edition. Though *Life* has Atwood's lucid prose, distinctively witty yet distant voice, and an important theme, about how to go on living with the complexity of relationships, its static plot line fails, and the reviewer cannot "feel real sympathy for the characters." Elizabeth's opening "catchy complaint," about not knowing how she or anyone should live, sums up the theme. The characters' longing for some paradise at the end "is forceful and clear. [The reviewer] feel[s] for them," and may be at fault because he "can't quite reach them."

27 DELANY, PAUL. "Grim, Nasty Lives." *Vancouver Province Magazine*, 30 Sept, p. 16.

Is not pleased by *Life Before Man*'s cold, moral dissection of a destructive, disintegrating marriage, where the leading characters are "a wife who does not know how to live, and a husband who does not know how to love. . . . The only relief comes from an off-beat, appealing, and blessedly unmarried" Lesje, but she finally becomes almost "as steely and manipulative" as Elizabeth. The Quebec conflict is hard to take seriously. *Life* may most convincingly show the tensions between the overly moral, ethnically paranoid elders, and their rootless, passive descendents. But the latter are burnt-out, one-dimensional, laconic, toneless, and limp or monstrous; and "the structure is awkwardly schematic." Atwood's recent novels lack a social vision. Still, *Life* is "forceful and accomplished"; and the crisis in marriage, and all relations now, is real enough.

28 DOOLEY, D.J. "In Margaret Atwood's Zoology Lab." In *Moral Vision in the Canadian Novel.* Toronto and Vancouver: Clarke, Irwin & Co., pp. 137-47.

   The Edible Woman, like T.S. Eliot's *The Wasteland*, Aldous Huxley's *Antic Hay*, and Evelyn Waugh's *The Loved One*, sees modern man as spiritually and humanly incomplete; Atwood's similar logic and irony apply zoological and botanical analogies to human characters. Satirizing a materialistic society of consumers, Atwood shows that Marian subconsciously resists conditioning; but never shows us what being fully human would mean. The ironic Marian judges others, but avoids moral reflections on her own acts. Under Duncan's influence, she comes to see meat-eating as cannibalism. At the end, the surrogate cake-lady that Marian offers to both Peter and Duncan does reject conventional, self-suppressing femininity; but Marian's uncertainly regained identity is only that of a consumer, who can affirm little more than "'I had steak for lunch, therefore I exist.'"

29 DUFFY, DENNIS. "Splits without Spleen." *Books in Canada* 8, no. 8 (October):10-11.

   Admires *Life Before Man*'s imagery, precision, and elegance, but wants either a vivid satire, or an amused, Chekhovian compassion. As the depiction of Royal Ontario Museum jobs shows, *Life Before Man* is satire, not realism. Atwood's cool, distanced irony, which makes her first and third novels memorable, makes *Life*'s monstrous and banal characters seem inconsequential. Satire needs more than detached irony; it "demands a vivid sense of the monstrous." Can the reviewer be "trying to make Wagner out of Mozart?" It's personal taste.

30 EL-HASSAN, KARLA. Review of *Survival*. *Zeitschrift für Anglistik und Amerikanistik* (Leipzig) 27, no. 2:185-87.

1979

Dislikes Atwood's subjective and accidental selection of literature in *Survival*. The literary examples are restricted to works that support her thesis. Despite Atwood's acknowledgement that she is not a literary theorist, her treatment of Canadian literature and its historical development is too static, her methods too primitive and simplistic.

31 ENDRES, ELISABETH. "Sehnsucht nach dem Fell." *Deutsche Zeitung* (Stuttgart), 20 April, p. 18.

Der lange Traum, the German translation of *Surfacing*, demonstrates a Canadian concern with nature that is like the German concern. Atwood's story is rich with images of nature and people. Atwood uses the United States as a symbol of evil; German literature would use industry. Although Atwood should have represented the negative forces more strongly, to preclude misinterpreting vagueness as romanticism, this small flaw is not significant in this impressive book.

32 FAIRBANKS, CAROL. "Margaret Atwood: A Bibliography of Criticism." *Bulletin of Bibliography* 36, no. 2 (April-June):85-90, 98.

Provides an alphabetical listing of secondary work, updating Horne 1977.34 and including items published in the United States but not covered by Horne. Lists 290 items: 120 articles and theses; and 170 book reviews, cited by author and journal, not title, and arranged under each Atwood book. All items are listed alphabetically by author.

33 FINDLAY, WILLIAM. "Interview with Margaret Atwood." *Cencrastus* (Edinburgh), no. 1 (Autumn), pp. 2-6.

Responding to political questions in Edinburgh, Atwood discusses politics and the writer; *Survival*; Canadian cultural and political nationalism; Canadian self-deprecating humour; Canadian women writers and feminism; and nationalism in small countries.

34 FISHBURN, KATHERINE. "Perceptual Violence in Margaret Atwood's Novels." *Journal of American Culture* 2, no. 4 (Winter):719-38.

Explains the unusual behavior of Atwood's three heroines with perceptual theories that show "our bodies are the source of our knowledge," as Michael Polanyi argues. Atwood's three heroines, who all distrust their own bodies, see the world through sexually-stereotyped Canadian social mythologies of independence and of adjustment. The self-effacing Marian is almost pathologically unable to see herself independently of others' perceptions; when her body rebels subconsciously, she flees from Peter, but clings to Duncan. *Surfacing*'s narrator, who has become alienated from her body after she let her reason convince her to abort, must metaphorically reject rationalism, and conceive, in order to restore her body's paradigms and to reintegrate her selves. Joan, locked in her fantastic paradigms of romance and of her fat past, learns to circumvent them by writing her own fiction; in the ambiguous end, she begins, in Polanyi's terms, "to attend from her heroines to herself"; i.e., "instead of seeing herself as a heroine, Joan finally sees her heroine as herself."

35 FITZGERALD, JOHN. "Atwood Surviving." *Gazette* (Montreal), 29 September, p. 52.

Interviews Atwood, who is taking care of her daughter Jess, in Toronto: Atwood discusses being a writer versus a media event; Canadian literature before 1965, 1965-75, and commercial pressures now; writing *Life Before Man* five hours a day; fiction versus autobiography; men versus women; and egotistic versus mediumistic writers, like herself, who express other things.

36 FLETCHER, PEGGY. "Dialogues and Other Voices." *Canadian Author and Bookman* 54, no. 2 (January):36-37.

Praises, in a four-book review, *Two-Headed Poems*'s powerful images, evolving voices, rituals of the ordinary, and profound but not self-conscious reminders of our mortality.

37 FORD, CATHERINE. "A Novel to Devour before Savoring Its Many Subtleties." *Calgary Herald*, 20 October, p. B20.

Acclaims *Life Before Man*: Atwood's characterizations are so real that it seems she must have lived them. She is a writer of the first magnitude. The guiding epigraph from [Björn Kurtén's] *The Age of the Dinosaurs* echoes throughout the book, as in the revealing scene where Lesje shows Nate and his children through the dinosaur gallery. The necessary sex is handled with perspective and finesse.

38 FRENCH, WILLIAM. "Margaret Atwood, Dinosaurs, and Real People: Confusion Amid Tangled Emotions." *Globe and Mail*, 29 September, p. E10.

Dislikes *Life Before Man*, its puzzling and off-putting dinosaur metaphor, its depressing and immature characters, its hackneyed theme. If man is insignificant, then so is this novel, and its readers. The husband is the most sympathetic character. Elizabeth's background is too melodramatic. The three viewpoints illuminate, but also diffuse intensities; the complicated dates distract. Though Atwood is an expert at showing people tearing at each other's emotions, she has yet to reach her potential as a novelist.

39 FRIESEN, PATRICK. "Dualities, Duets." *CV II* 4, no. 3 (Fall):23-24.
Describes "the fundamental siamese [sic] relationship" of mother and child in *Two-Headed Poems*. "The mother is two-headed," with her adult head and her child's head; and with her adult desire for wholeness and for separation. The child and adult war within the mother. Atwood uses fairy-tale numbers, colours, and rhythms. The mother-child relationship is portrayed memorably and accurately.

40 FRISE, MARIA. "Scheinbar glatte Oberfläche." *Frankfurter Allgemeine*, 2 July, p. 22.
The poet Margaret Atwood has, in her essays [*Survival*], made a great contribution to the previously neglected voice of Canadian literature. *Der lange Traum*, the German translation of *Surfacing*, has the poet's rare intensity and imagery. The artistically constructed story uses everyday jargon in dialogs; nature is minutely detailed. American feminists have misunderstood this novel; not every woman who finds her identity joins the feminist community. But Atwood does seem convinced that women have a richer character than men, and may be more likely to find the lost paradise.

41 FULFORD, ROBERT. "*Life Before Man* Possibly the Best of All Atwood's Books." *Canadian Reader* 20, no. 9:1-2.
Acclaims *Life Before Man*: its absorbing characters; its highly readable style; and its meticulously realistic depiction of 1970s relationships among the educated middle class. Elizabeth and Lesje are sensitively drawn; the passive Nate is a triumph as Atwood's first successful male viewpoint. Finds Atwood's eye unerring, her ear nearly flawless, and "her own cool unsentimental tone constantly engaging."

42 GALLOWAY, PRISCILLA. Review of *Life Before Man. Canadian Book Review Annual*:108-9.

Admires Atwood's absorbing, skillful, meticulously characterized, chillingly precise novel, but wants the grand vision of a great novel, and characters to take "into one's heart." Time's grandeur is only suggested; the Toronto present is minutely detailed. Elizabeth comes closest to being a grand character. "In a stereotyped novel, Nate's role would be played by a woman."

43 GATENBY, GREG. "Poetry Chronicle." *Tamarack Review*, no. 77-78 (Summer), pp. 89-91.

Praises *Two-Headed Poems* highly, as Atwood's finest and most mature book, and as an analysis of the Canadian condition, in poems such as "The Woman Who Could Not Live with Her Faulty Heart" as well as in the forthright and accomplished, if unsubtle, title sequence. Though "Footnote to the Amnesty Report on Torture" owes much to Auden's "Musée des Beaux Arts," it is one of Atwood's best poems ever, and a warning exhortation to Canadians.

44 GERVAIS, MARTY. "Fans, Questions, Hotels: Atwood on Tour." *Windsor Star*, 3 November, p. 34.

Interviews Atwood during the day of 1 November, promoting *Life Before Man*: a morning CBE radio interview with Elizabeth Kishk, a CBE-TV taping with Warner Troyer, for "On the Record," a booksigning at South Shore Books, dinner, and a poetry reading at the Windsor Art Gallery. Atwood comments on *Life*'s sales, mixed reviews, realism rather than pessimism, and male character; and recalls playing a headless horseman on Halloween, and a hot dog in another year.

45 GIBBONS, REGINALD. "Hayden, Peck, and Atwood." *Ontario Review*, no. 10 (Spring-Summer), pp. 92-94.

Critiques *Two-Headed Poems* in a three-book review of it, Robert Hayden's *American Journal*, and John Peck's *The Broken Blockhouse Wall*. Atwood's method is to cast about for images as possibilities, not inevitabilities. This can be richly imaginative, as in "Burned Space," or merely groping, as in "The Bus to Alliston, Ontario." The title sequence lacks "the sort of authority that good poems require," and is flawed by poetic invention, lax structure and rhythm, and often indistinguishable speakers. Lists the eleven

1979

admirably good poems, plus perhaps one sequence, that Atwood should have published, in a smaller volume.

46 GIBSON, GRAEME. "Travels of a Family Man." *Chatelaine* 52, no. 3 (March):36, 38, 132-33, 135-37.

Focuses on how his and Atwood's 20-month-old daughter, Eleanor Jess, sees the world, in a nine-week tour that includes an Ontario artists exhibit in Paris and the Adelaide Poetry Festival, with stops in Tehran, Kabul, India, and Fiji. Provides anecdotes of Jess's responses and interactions, family routines, purdah in Afghanistan, and sexual stereotyping in Australia.

47 GRAY, FRANCINE du PLESSIX. Introduction to *Surfacing*, by Margaret Atwood. Virago Modern Classic, no. 8. London: Virago, pp. 1-6.

A reprint of 1977.28 that omits the "Nature as the Nunnery" title.

48 GRÖNDAHL, CARL HENRIK. "Kanadisk litteratur er bare femten år gammell" [Canadian literature only fifteen years old]. *Aftenposten* (Oslo), 1 March, p. 7.

In Norwegian. Interviewed in Oslo, Atwood discusses the publishing industry's reluctance to publish Canadian authors; the success of *Survival*; the early publishing companies organized by writers in Canada; and the state of literature in Quebec.

49 GUBAR, SUSAN. "Mother, Maiden, and the Marriage of Death: Women Writers and an Ancient Myth." *Women's Studies* 6, no. 3:301-15 passim.

Interprets *Surfacing*, and works by eight other women writers from Mary Shelley to Adrienne Rich, as re-inventions of the Demeter-Persephone myth that re-define and celebrate female consciousness. Atwood's motherless heroine may give birth to a mythic child, and does re-birth a new, integrated self. She "is not alone" in feeling alienated from her culture's language and false, degrading images. Her dive "down into the sea [sic] to encounter her dead father . . . liberates [her] from belief in his power."

50 HAMMOND, KARLA. "An Interview with Margaret Atwood." *American Poetry Review* 8, no. 5 (September-October):27-29.

Atwood discusses her early career choices, scientific background, recent travels, and readings of Canadian women poets, Adrienne Rich, and others; Canadian nationalistic consciousness, from the mid-sixties on; winter and water as Canadian elements in her poetry; maps, geography, and lenses versus mirrors; language as an immersion; Canadian, American, and sexist reviews; language and nature in women's poetry; some of her own poems, including "Arctic syndrome: dream fox" and "Dream 2: Brian the Still-Hunter"; visionary, Indian-influenced language in *Surfacing*; Biblical myths of nature and women; Christianity and pantheism; women's powers in *Grimm's Fairy Tales*, political oppression and poetry; and identification with nature as potentially empowering. A cover story.

51 HARRISON, JAMES. "The 20,000,000 Solitudes of *Surfacing*." *Dalhousie Review* 59, no. 1 (Spring):74-81.

Surfacing's images, symbols, and motifs recur and interact, as in the conception scene, which pulls together a plethora of dichotomies. Are Atwood's themes of male/female, Canadian/American, and man/nature exploitation, metaphors for one another? Fragmentation, not polarization or domination, is *Surfacing*'s underlying nightmare. Even the pervasive head/body dichotomy is a kind of dismemberment. Images of segregation and imprisonment overlap; language may be the greatest trap. When the narrator becomes whole, she cannot distinguish her self; in Western culture, this means insanity. She surfaces into separateness and identity, alone. Language divides, but also unites. *Surfacing*'s end is hopeful, not pessimistic.

52 HEWARD, BURT. "Canadian Author Riding Crest of Success." *Citizen* (Ottawa), 11 October, p. 77.

Interviews Atwood in Ottawa; discusses *Life Before Man*'s sales, Beryl Fox's forthcoming *Surfacing* film, and Margot Kidder's forthcoming *Lady Oracle* film; quotes the 1979.75 and 1979.2 praises of *Life Before Man* in *Maclean's*. Atwood indicates that the suicides of two Canadian writers, and murder of one, helped start her on *Life Before Man*.

53 ____. "Mid-Life Love on Dinosaurs' Path." *Citizen* (Ottawa), 29 September, p. 35.

Celebrates *Life Before Man*: "Canada's literary queen has written her most mature, best controlled novel." A serene detachment, like Lesje's girlhood prehistoric daydreams, underpins this portrayal of "life after love, life in limbo," and undecided mid-life crises. The pivotal "Elizabeth is an emotional Doris Lessing type with black abysses opening below her"; Chris, a potent gamekeeper, has been Elizabeth's savage child and masculine lightning rod. Many marriages collapse; many men are gentle, flawed, "befuddled sinners with consciences," like Nate. Analysis of this wonderful novel could go on and on; readers who want what really matters "in our troubled times will find *Life Before Man* a revolving pleasure."

54 HINZ, EVELYN J., and TEUNISSEN, JOHN J. "*Surfacing*: Margaret Atwood's 'Nymph Complaining.'" *Contemporary Literature* 20, no. 2 (Spring):221-36.

Argues that *Surfacing*, like Andrew Marvell's "A Nymph Complaining for the Death of Her Fawn," manifests the Grieving Mother (*Mater Dolorosa*) archetype. Though *Surfacing*'s nationalism and feminism seem extremely contemporary, its real impact and significance are archetypal, ahistorical, nonpolitical. Atwood invokes the icon of a young woman betrayed by a lover and projecting her grief upon the fawn he has left her in two stages, with ironic etymology and wordplay. The narrator's childhood drawings depict a male God as a satyr and consort of a "Lady of the Beasts," who appears in primitive North American and in European art. As Marvell's pastoral makes clear, *Surfacing*'s wanton killers are demanded by the Great Mother archetype, regardless of anti-Americanism. Both Marvell and Atwood use grief for a brother as a projection. Though Atwood may have read Marvell's pastoral – her narrator alludes to Captain Marvel's thunderbolt sweatshirt – archetypes can be transmitted directly.

55 "Honorés à Concordia." *Devoir* (Montréal), 4 December, p. 19.

Briefly announces Atwood's honorary doctorate from the University of Concordia for her contribution to literature. Mentions that she has received several awards and that her works have been translated into 8 languages.

56 HORNE, ALAN J. "Margaret Atwood: An Annotated Bibliography (Prose)." *The Annotated Bibliography of Canada's Major Authors*.

Edited by Robert Lecker and Jack David. Vol. 1. Downsview, Ont.: ECW Press, pp. 13-46.

Provides an overview of Canadian critics' responses to Atwood, *The Edible Woman*, *Surfacing*, *Survival*, *Lady Oracle*, and *Dancing Girls*; a chronological primary listing of 115 items of prose and graphic work, 1954-early 1979; and an annotated bibliography of 139 items of secondary work, mostly Canadian, in English, 1969-late 1979, arranged chronologically by category, with the book reviews arranged chronologically under each Atwood book. Notes that some recent items may have been missed; provides an index of secondary authors. Lists under primary six books 1969-78, with editions and translations; one television drama; manuscripts, listed as one item, which include 15 boxes; and 107 contributions to periodicals, books, and anthologies, 1954-early 1979, which include 25 short stories, 67 articles and book reviews, 11 items of graphic work, and four selected anthology contributions. Annotates, under secondary, one book, the 1977.81 *Malahat Review*, edited by Linda Sandler; 51 articles and sections of books, [1972]-early 1979; 6 theses and dissertations; and 16 interviews; lists 10 awards and honours; annotates 65 selected book reviews, 1969-1978. See Fairbanks 1979.32 and Horne 1980.59. Abridged and updated as part of 1981.47.

57 HORNYANSKY, MICHAEL. "Letters in Canada, 1978: Poetry." *University of Toronto Quarterly* 48, no. 4 (Summer):341-42.

Salutes *Two-Headed Poems* with some warmth: praises Atwood's old savage tone, as in "Marrying the Hangman," as well as her new accents, locale, astringent sympathy, and domestic desolation. "Either way, Atwood does not make exhilarating reading, but one might develop a habit for a very dry strong wine, of gravelly aftertaste and purgative effect."

58 HUTCHEON, LINDA. "'Snow Storm of Paper': The Act of Reading in Self-Reflexive Canadian Verse." *Dalhousie Review* 59, no. 1 (Spring):114-18.

Like other modern, self-reflexive Canadian poetry, Michael Ondaatje's *The Collected Works of Billy the Kid* and Atwood's *The Journals of Susanna Moodie* use black and white photography as a somewhat sinister metaphor of visual perception and poetic creation. Frank Davey 1977.12 saw Atwood's stasis/kinesis duality; Atwood's

1979

Journals, like Ondaatje's *Works*, contrast the stasis of photography and poetry to kinetic and temporal flow.

59 IRVINE, LORNA. "The Red and Silver Heroes Have Collapsed." *Concerning Poetry* 12, no. 2 (Fall):59-68.

Analyzes how Atwood's poetic language demythicizes threatening sexual stereotypes. Terrible "father/gods" lurk under the surface of *The Circle Game*, *The Animals in That Country*, *Procedures for Underground*, *Power Politics*, and *You Are Happy*; the poet journeys among disguised masculine heroes and villains. Plunging into her unconscious, she is terrified and angry as these masculine images disintegrate, and the boundaries of self are lost. Regeneration begins in loss and in acknowledging her own passive complicity. *Power Politics* ends with the death-bearing man in control; *You Are Happy*'s final "Book of Ancestors" restates the journey from past gods to present freedom.

60 JACKSON, RICHARD. Review of *Selected Poems*. *South Carolina Review* 12, no. 1 (Fall):65-66.

Appreciates, in a four-book review, the four poets' post-Romantic strategies for dealing with "the fictionality of origins." *The Circle Game* deploys spatial metaphors to connect "outside and inside, surface and depth, . . . origin and present," moving toward an identity of word and thing, history and origin. In "Progressive insanities of a pioneer," "'an ordered absence'" develops as the world resists the word. *The Journals of Susanna Moodie* dramatizes the tension between word and world; from *Journals* on, the poems confront the absence of the self. In "Tricks with Mirrors" the self and its image enter an unsolvable play of surfaces leading to depth. In "Procedures for Underground" the orphic communicates between the two possibilities of surface and depth. These two possibilities "produce a double consciousness containing two complementary voices, the natural and the mythic," as in "Rat Song" and the Circe poems.

61 JONES, ANNE G. "Margaret Atwood: Songs of the Transformer, Songs of the Transformed." *Hollins Critic* 16, no. 3 (June):1-15.

Describes paradoxes in Atwood's poetry and prose. Atwood is fascinated with form – literary, natural, and human. Form gives life but may entrap or destroy; but formlessness is death, as in "Polarities."

Growth or decay means transformation in nature; humans and writers also transform. Nature and human consciousness join in the mystical "Giving Birth," *Surfacing*, and *The Journals of Susanna Moodie*. Words have powers, to heal or harm; language is therefore ethical, as in *Two-Headed Poems*. Atwood does not advocate relinquishing power. *Lady Oracle's* humor may be a defense against the city; its dangers may be harmless. The transformation of "Apple Jelly" takes us to *Survival's* position four, of creative non-victim.

62 KAPPLER, MARY ELLEN, and ZIZIS, MIKE. "An Interview with Margaret Atwood." *Intrinsic*, nos. 7-8 (Spring), pp. 92-95.

Atwood comments, before leaving for Scotland, on *Survival* and *The Journals of Susanna Moodie*; and describes her limited energy for teaching plus writing, for writing poetry plus novels, and for parenting her two-and-one-half-year-old plus writing plus reading.

63 KAREDA, URJO. "Men, Dinosaurs, and Margaret Atwood." *Saturday Night* 94, no. 9 (November):37, 39.

Appreciates Atwood's sustaining dinosaur image, evolutionary perspective, shifting viewpoints, uncannily intuitive detail, vigorous wit, and ironic resonance, but finds *Life Before Man* her saddest and coolest fiction. Atwood deftly explores her characters' genetic inheritance, adaptations, selections of mates, and methods of survival. *Life Before Man* is filled with the painful urgency of our efforts to define our lives, and to adapt to an environment which is at best neutral. The answer may be pollution control or social crusades, or ethnicity–or even Auntie Muriel, who is *Life's* most splendid and forthright character.

64 KEITNER, WENDY. Review of *Two-Headed Poems*. *Quarry* 28, no. 4 (Autumn):77-81.

Praises *Two-Headed Poems's* new, maternal affirmations: Atwood's recent motherhood has restructured her vision, as in "Giving Birth." Her persona has gone beyond the bleak struggles of victor-victim games, to celebrate, tentatively, a domestic family refuge and blood ties. Her feminism now charts the mother-daughter bond, as in the compelling "Five Poems for Grandmothers." Atwood's new political poems are more compassionate, and use domestic detail. The title sequence deals with Quebec separatism, anti-Americanism, and bilingualism. *Two-Headed Poems* is, finally, about language itself.

1979

65 KUCHERAWY, DENNIS. "*Life Before Man* Wins Over Critics of Atwood's Novels." *London* (Ontario) *Free Press*, 22 November, p. C8.

Interviews Atwood, who is promoting *Life Before Man*. Atwood comments on *Life's* realism, eternal triangle, and characters; and argues that man's emotional evolution must catch up with the technical level, "or he'll self-destruct."

66 LIVESAY, DOROTHY. "A Balance between Darkness and Noon." *Branching Out* 6, no. 2:40-42.

Welcomes *Two-Headed Poems's* political engagement and Atwood's new balance, warmth, and colour. Though Atwood has always avoided the trap of merely private agonies, her earlier work was often bitterly ironic – a grey landscape, with cartoons of people. Praises especially the tender "Five Poems for Grandmothers," the political poems, the historical documentary of "Four Small Elegies," and the title sequence, which deals with "'the bilingual question,'" Canada, the U.S., and Quebec. "Atwood is a woman at home in the universe, yet sitting in her kitchen with man, with child, with ancestors."

67 McCORMICK, MARION. "Dry Bones." *Gazette* (Montreal), 29 September, p. 53.

Finds Atwood's characters growing older in *Life Before Man*, but still feverishly erratic, and therefore hard to believe in. Elizabeth's and Nate's marriage "just blew open, as ramshackle structures will. . . . Considering the company [Lesje] keeps," her ideas that man is not central, and human survival perhaps not desirable, "are not surprising." Nate and Lesje, and Elizabeth and Chris, "are more like collisions than love affairs, accidental and motiveless." Perhaps the short episodes, and disruptive flashbacks, are partly to blame. The enigmatic title may mean that this is "a story of a lower form of life – Toronto Man, circa 1978," incompletely evolved."

68 MacGREGOR, ROY. "Atwood's World." *Maclean's* 92, no. 42 (15 October):64-66.

Cover story: profiles Atwood, at the Alliston farm and in Rosemont and Toronto, in September 1979, as a serious writer and an intensely private individual. Describes the writing cabin at the farm and *Life Before Man's* publishing success; mentions the Atwood-Gibson failed screenplay of Margaret Laurence's *The Diviners* and the forthcoming Beryl Fox film of *Surfacing*; describes domestic life, friendships, and Atwood's dislike of public attention. Quotes Atwood on publicity, media images of women writers and of herself, and Afghanistan's concealing chador. Kafka would have approved *Life Before Man*, as two fists "'hammering on the skull.'" See 1980.139.

69 MARSHALL, TOM. "Atwood under and above Water." In *Harsh and Lovely Land: The Major Canadian Poets and the Making of a Canadian Tradition*. Vancouver: University of British Columbia Press, pp. 154-61.

   Revision of 1977.55. Elaborates Canadian themes in poetry; praises *You Are Happy* as perhaps a sequel to *Power Politics*, and as moving towards the wordless Canadian flux of life. Though *The Edible Woman* is feminist, it satirizes Canadian women's as well as men's absurdities. Acclaims *Surfacing*'s protagonist, power, images, and its simultaneously Canadian and universal themes of quest and journey. Though *Lady Oracle*'s female picaresque is in places very enjoyable and insightful, and a parody, it lacks seriousness; its narrator has a "fuzzy personality," supposedly both shrewd and confused. Excerpted: 1983.129.

70 MASSIE, ALAN [sic]. "'Surfacing with the Flower of Canada's Renaissance." *Glasgow Herald*, 7 April, p. 9.

   Interviews Atwood, whose *Surfacing* is being reissued by Virago, in Edinburgh: Atwood discusses the Canadian literary "renaissance"; Quebec; *Surfacing* as a ghost story; Canadian, feminine, Scotsman, etc. versus American, English, masculine, etc.; and feminism and Gothicism in her novels. The novel Atwood most admires is [George Eliot's] *Middlemarch*, but the one she is most passionately attached to is [Emily Brontë's] *Wuthering Heights*.

71 MATSON, MARSHALL. "Yoked by Violence." *Books in Canada* 8, no. 1 (January):12-13.

   Finds political and personal disappointments in *Two-Headed Poems*: in the title sequence; in the male versus female two-mindedness of the right and left hands; in the Ontario landowners' struggle with weeds; in the exquisite four elegies; in the muddy spring and recurring winter. These are sadder poems than those of *You Are Happy*. Wit still flashes, sometimes too quickly, as in "Marrying the Hangman," with its *non sequitur* criticism of men. Many biological images blend disgust and relish; blood and bleeding are used too frequently, but sometimes with grace. Excerpted: 1980.51.

72 MITTLEMAN, LESLIE B. Review of *Selected Poems*. *Magill's Literary Annual*. Edited by Frank N. Magill. Vol. 2. Englewood Cliffs, N.J.: Salem Press, pp. 661-65.

Commends Atwood's growing poetic mastery. A visionary like Theodore Roethke, Atwood sees a reality divided between primitive essences and civilized man's brutality. She distrusts human motives; cameras defile; mirrors distort. In psychosexual relationships she fears the man's trickery and coercion. Like D.H. Lawrence, Atwood polarizes rational man and intuitive woman. *You Are Happy* offers some tentative hope and passion; we want her greater happiness, warmed with hope, not steeled to cold.

73 MOISAN, CLÉMENT. "Poésie de la libération." In *Poésie des frontières: Étude comparée des poésies canadienne et québécoise*. Collections constantes, no. 38. LaSalle, Quebec: Editions HMH, pp. 169-71, 195-218.

A comparison of themes, imagery, and style in Atwood's *The Circle Game*, *The Animals in That Country*, and *The Journals of Susanna Moodie* and Michèle Lalonde's *Geôles*, *Fiancée*, and other work. See English translation: 1983.94.

*74 MORLEY, PAT[RICIA]. "From a Dubious Past, a Bleak Future." *Ottawa Journal*, 6 October, p. 41.

Considers *Life Before Man* to be Atwood's bleakest novel, with its honest pessimism and rarer, blacker humour. The characters have "'normal'" 1970s urban attitudes about casually changing lovers. Atwood's bleak view, which comes through the whole novel, often coincides with her characters' despair.

75 NEWMAN, PETER C. "Atwood Is the Disturbing Truth-Teller Who Has Given Canada Its Sense of Place." *Maclean's* 92, no. 42 (15 October):3.

Praises *Life Before Man* as an important book, though perhaps not the great Canadian novel; and Atwood as a powerful, Canadian-rooted writer who understands her characters, love, and loneliness.

"Atwood is one of those rare writers with the agitating voice of a born truth-teller."

76 NODELMAN, PERRY. "New Novel Atwood's Best." *Winnipeg Free Press*, 27 October, Insert, p. 18.

Finds *Life Before Man* "'thoroughly engrossing and frighteningly believable – the best of Margaret Atwood's novels, and one of the best novels ever written by a Canadian'"; but rejects Atwood's fake public personalities, and her successful Winnipeg reading from *Life*. Atwood drew laughs by making the character sound witty, perceptive, and snide – just like Atwood. But the character in the book "turned out to be quiet, unwitty, and almost pathologically" passive. All three characters, and their points of view, and relationships, are "subtly perceived, carefully drawn," and so convincing that trusting the writer's ability was exhilarating. The reviewer was so involved in their lives that he does not care what the book means, about dinosaurs or the seventies. Atwood's publishers can quote his praise, which he means; and he hopes they'll stop sending her on tour.

77 NOVAK, BARBARA. "Atwood's Love-Triangle Theme Avoids Pitfall of Banality." *London* (Ontario) *Free Press*, 27 October, p. B4.

Praises *Life Before Man*. Its tightly controlled structure illuminates the characters in turn; much "unfolds like a ballet, with solos," varied pas-de-deux, and trios. All the main characters are "manipulated by their own past." Unfortunately, the other characters are incompletely developed; and William "suffers unduly from having been raised in London. . . . *Life Before Man* is essentially a novel of manners. Atwood depicts, with stunning insights and sharp-edged humor, the helplessness of the educated, analytical, professionally competent set to take responsibility for their own lives."

78 _____. "Atwood's Political Poetic Vision Extends to Raw Anger." *London* (Ontario) *Free Press*, 20 January, p. B3.

Appreciates *Two-Headed Poems*. The title sequence poems, with their separation-dreaming, two-headed Siamese twins, "are angry outcries against the nature of our political situation." Their mood varies – bitter despair, sarcasm, irony, raw anger. We "have created our own reality," these frankly disturbing poems repeat. "Marrying the Hangman" is Kafkaesque, horrifying, yet true Canadian history.

1979

Atwood's mature vision now extends much further into the world; she has made peace with herself, with her private and public heads. "You Begin" beautifully balances, with Atwood's trademark "warmth and self-conscious irony," the mother's knowledge against the child's new awareness.

79 NUDELL, ROSLYN. "A Frail Exterior Hides the Toughness in Atwood." *Winnipeg Free Press*, 17 October, p. 35.

Interviews Atwood, who is in Winnipeg to promote *Life Before Man*: Atwood comments on some interviewers who have been hostile or inaccurate; and on success and being recognized – once, when she was asked, while bird-watching, if she were Margaret Atwood, she said, "'Not today.'" The interviewer finds *Life Before Man* unsettling and not happy; Atwood finds it realistic.

80 PETERSEN, FRAN HOPENWASSER. "Portraet: Interview med Margaret Atwood of Fran Hopenwasser Petersen" [Portrait: interview with Margaret Atwood by Fran Hopenwasser Petersen]. *Chancen* (Copenhagen) 1, no. 3 (November):12-15.

In Danish. Interviewed in Alliston, Ontario, Atwood discusses significant influences and her non-autobiographical writing; women and knowledge; Alice Walker versus American feminists with narrow views; the function of literature for women and society; *Surfacing*; *Lady Oracle*'s treatment of mothers, politics, and the female medium; and eating behaviors in *The Edible Woman* and *Lady Oracle*.

81 PREUSS, EVELYN. "Eine Entdeckung: Dichterin aus Kanada." *Hamburger Abendblatt*, 11 May, p. 14.

Interviews Atwood in Hamburg after the publication of *Der lange Traum*, the German translation of *Surfacing*. Atwood says the story's characters are fictional, but the landscape is from her childhood in Nova Scotia [sic]; and discusses her first poems and becoming a writer.

82 RAEITHEL, GERT. "Sensibilität und Antiamerikanismus." *Merkur* (Stuttgart) 33, no. 8 (August):818-22.

Der lange Traum, the recent German translation of *Surfacing*, has received universal praise. Atwood, who looks the part of the sensitive female poet, has traveled to Munich with her husband, a robust Canadian farmer and writer. Many Americans have recently made

Canada their home, including Joyce Carol Oates, who is "tired of America'"; Atwood communicates a kindred "America-phobia" in *Surfacing*. The interviewer objects to Atwood, who is a sophisticated poet, defending the wave of anti-Americanism in Canada, and suggests a similarity between Canadian anti-Americanism and German anti-Semiticism.

83 REDMON, ANNE. "Birth and Rebirth." *Books and Bookmen* 24, no. 8 (May):47.

Features *Surfacing* in a two-book review, praising Atwood's "extraordinary union with the wilderness," but rejecting the exorbitant claims in Francine du Plessix Gray's 1979.47 introduction. *Surfacing* is not a spiritual classic, but a Jungian, psychic journey through unconscious depths towards wholeness. The protagonist goes from a weak sense of self, through guilt and redemption or rebirth, to refusing victimhood; but there's nothing that is really transcendent or outside the self.

84 Review of *Life Before Man*. *Kirkus Reviews* 47, no. 23 (1 December):1385-86.

Features Atwood's monumentally depressing but thoroughly gifted *Life Before Man*. Atwood writes "'poet's novels'" with controlling, spooking metaphors – here, of the extinction of our era. Finds desperate, unsubtle acts; bleak air; and an entropic confinement, like a tar pit. The numbed, struggling characters go through rituals that are as spare as poems.

85 ROSENBERG, JEROME. "'For of Such Is the Kingdom . . . ': Margaret Atwood's *Two-Headed Poems*." *Essays on Canadian Writing*, no. 16 (Fall-Winter), pp. 130-39.

Welcomes Atwood's new tone of compassion and love, and her familiar yet new belief in some unity emerging from our self-motivated divisions; explicates the Julian Jaynes right hemisphere versus left hemisphere theories, from *The Origin of Consciousness in the Breakdown of the Bicameral Mind*, which underlie the title sequence, the pivotal "The Right Hand Fights the Left," and "Daybooks I, 6, 'After Jaynes'"; explicates also the French and English Canadian allusions of the title sequence. "The Bus to Alliston, Ontario" becomes a microcosm of humanity, voyaging through dangers. The sacramental

1979

"All Bread" reworks Holy Communion. In "A Red Shirt," "The Puppet of the Wolf," and "You Begin," the innocent child transcends adult fears, and connects us to life's bittersweet joys. Reprinted, slightly altered, in 1984.81, pp. 83-91.

86 ROSS, CATHERINE SHELDRICK. "Calling Back the Ghost of the Old-Time Heroine: Duncan, Montgomery, Atwood, Laurence, and Munro." *Studies in Canadian Literature* 4, no. 1 (Winter):43-58.

Lady Oracle, Sara Jeanette Duncan's *The Imperialist*, Lucy Maud Montgomery's *Anne of Green Gables*, Margaret Laurence's "Jericho's Brick Battlements," and Alice Munro's *Lives of Girls and Women* all contrast their new, realistic heroines with the old-fashioned romance heroine, and parody romance conventions to create a realistic effect. Like Montgomery's Anne, Atwood's red-haired Joan tries unsuccessfully to shape her life to fictional patterns, chooses Camelot and Elaine the Lady of Shalott as her romance image, and writes her mirror-doubles into plots that stylize her own life. But Joan, unlike Anne, returns to her old romance patterns, and still sees herself as an old-time heroine in *Lady Oracle*'s multiple, farcical, Gothic, and realistic end.

87 SCHACHTSIEK-FREITAG, NORBERT. "Eine Frau sucht sich." *Frankfurter Rundschau*, 2 June, Zeit und Bild sec., p. 2.

Der lange Traum, the recent German translation of *Surfacing*, will help diversify the German literature market by introducing a truly important author. Atwood uses the familiar literary return to a "native place" unconventionally, to explore female personalization and conflict between civilization and nature. Atwood is not a "female John Updike." Her lyric narrative prose uses metaphors derived from nature and magic. The novel combines existential ideas from the 1970s, a dialectic of progress and regression in history, and an examination of the repressive relationships between men and women.

88 SCHWARZKOPF, MARGARETE von. "Wie in einem Hühnerstall auf der Prärie." *Welt* (Hamburg), 26 June, p. 27.

Interview: Atwood discusses her involvement in Canadian literature; collecting ideas for her books; her first two novels; the hybrid Canadian identity; and the triumph of becoming a mother at age 37.

89 SILLERS, PAT. "Power Impinging: Hearing Atwood's Vision." *Studies in Canadian Literature* 4, no. 1 (Winter):59-70.

Analyzes how *Selected Poems* uses rhetoric to achieve power. From "This Is a Photograph of Me" on, Atwood involves, lures, and implicates the reader, jolting us out of stock responses and received ideas; eventually we see the pattern of "Photograph." Perception, pictures, visions, eyes, views preoccupy her poems. Two presences – watcher and watched – dominate. Even backgrounds speak. "Circe/Mud Poems" offers us a witch's choice of speakers – Circe or Mud? Atwood's laconic, almost ascetic "language is so 'cleaned of geographies' that the associative aura surrounding words emanates from the [reader]"; her lines are poetry imitating speech – or speech transformed to poetry. Contrary to Skelton 1977.83, Atwood's poems are rhetorical, not 'modular,'" not reversible.

90 SNOW, DUART. Canadian Writer Sees Fresh Hope in Bleak Society." *Ottawa Journal*, 13 October, p. C29.

Interviews Atwood, who is in Ottawa to promote *Life Before Man*, on her politics: like Nate in *Life*, Atwood collected signatures on Yonge Street to protest RCMP wrongdoing, for the Canadian Civil Liberties Union; she is a contributing editor and, as Bart Gerrard, cartoonist, for *This Magazine*; she considers herself "'a political writer in that the fabric of life is political and I include it'"; she sees contemporary politics as the source of *Life*'s bleak despair and its characters' aimless lives. "Society is rudderless . . . . [In *Life*] people are hanging on by their fingernails. . . . [but there is] modified hope'" at the end. Beryl Fox's film of *Surfacing* is forthcoming, and Margot Kidder has the film option for *Lady Oracle*; Atwood, who has written screenplays, insists that she avoids doing so.

91 SOLECKI, SAM. "Circles of Despair." *Canadian Forum* 59 (November):28-29.

Paradoxically admires Atwood's art in *Life Before Man* – particularly her lyricism and sardonic wit – yet feels that her total pessimism "is ultimately irrelevant to most of our lives." Male-female relationships in her first three novels were uncertain and difficult, but not completely hopeless. It is inevitable that we respond to Atwood's realistic contemporary Toronto novels not only as art but also as commentaries on ourselves. But joy is absent and all relationships fail in *Life Before Man*; only the "slightly demonic Aunt Muriel" seems to get any satisfaction from life or death. Feminism, nationalism, and political activism are cited to be discredited – even though Atwood is a leading nationalist and feminist. This book finds life not worth living; most of us find that an untenable extreme. See Salutin 1980.119.

92 SOMERVILLE-LARGE, GILLIAN. "Resurfaced." *Irish Times* (Dublin), 1 September, p. 11.

Recommends the reissued Virago *Surfacing*, in a four-book review, as a remarkable "book to be reread; one of the best things to come out of Canada since ginger ale." *Surfacing* recounts an intense mystical experience; though its mother nature and feminist principles are so familiar, its clear narrative and vigourously poetic descriptions produce a fierce, exhilarating, individual revelation.

93 STEVENS, PETER. "Atwood's Double Vision is 20/20, Almost All the Time." *Windsor Star*, 6 January, p. 17.

Appreciates *Two-Headed Poem*'s carefully wrought, three-part reflecting structure, and the good acceptances of the final section, but finds the central title poems muddied and finally unsatisfactory. The two outer sections reflect and parallel each other, as with the two heart poems, and the beginning and ending image of the hand. The first section's poems become increasingly bleaker and blacker. Though the title poems look both ways, Janus-like, and "resonate with all kinds of dualities," the poet has left them deliberately and unnecessarily puzzling. But the last section makes amends: the poet moves to a guarded acceptance; "[m]oments of goodness, clarity and joy keep surfacing, as in ["Apple Jelly"]; and destructions are richly transformed in the life-giving ["All Bread"].

94 ____. "Dinosaurs in the Waste Land." *Windsor Star*, 20 October, p. 59.

Finds *Life Before Man* bleak, pointless, and cynical: it dissects lives of "aimless drifting and manipulation," with some good confrontations, but without resolution; and it insists that human ties are meaningless selfishness. Its "haphazard selection of days" chronicles the destructiveness unleashed by Chris's suicide. "The characters do a clumsy gavotte of personal relationships." Though *Life* mordantly emphasizes the bad effects of previous generations, it "totally ignores" what is happening to the daughters. It has no compassion for the characters; nor are they comic. If the characters are meant to be seen as dinosaurs who can't adapt, that's limited, and unclear.

95 STEWART, GRACE. *A New Mythos: The Novel of the Artist as Heroine 1877-1977*. Monographs in Women's Studies, edited by Sherri Clarkson. St. Alban's, Vt. and Montreal: Eden Press Women's Publications, pp. 93-97, 157-61, 170-74.

Describes mother/daughter/artist relationships and journeys to the interior in *Lady Oracle* and *Surfacing*. Joan longs for and renounces her rejecting mother. *Surfacing's* heroine sacrifices her art to embrace her mother's role and a mythic motherhood; her journey, to the mythic and unconscious, ends in her gaining only minimal knowledge. Joan's comic, fantasy journey raises questions about myth-making and self-deception; she becomes paranoid from being a precarious artist/woman on society's tightrope.

96 SULLIVAN, ROSEMARY. "Atwood's New Directions." *Tamarack Review*, no. 76 (Winter), pp. 108-9.

Welcomes *Two-Headed Poems*, with some reservations. Atwood's latest book has her best gifts: her fiercely original, iconographic imagination and extraordinary images, her strong wit and Trickster's bag of ironic deflation. The tired, middle-aged poems are balanced by the new mother ones. But some poems seem factitious, predictable, contrived, or flatly prosaic. Yet others do have a new, freeing psychic rhythm. The mother-to-child love poems are the most exciting; perhaps this theme will open a new visionary dimension.

97 TUFTE, LEIF. "Sjelenød og sivilisasjonskrise" [Angst and civilization's crisis]. *Aftenposten* (Oslo), 8 February, p. 26.

In Norwegian. *Surfacing*, translated as *Gjenkjennelsen* by Inger Elisabeth Hansen, is a good choice for the first Atwood novel to be translated into Norwegian. *Surfacing's* female protagonist and her companions, the archetypal western youth of the 1960s and 1970s, and their journey through the Canadian wilderness, demonstrate Atwood's rare understanding of interpersonal interactions and emotional nuance. The narrator's profound confrontation with her subconscious, and with mystical nature elements, allows her to discover reality. Atwood's generation will identify with the adventure story and the finely woven characters.

1979

98 TWIGG, ALAN. "Margaret Atwood." *Vancouver Free Press*, 9-15 November, p. 10-12.

Briefly finds the seeds of *Survival* and the controversial *Life Before Man* in Atwood's earlier poetry, her obsession with a lopsided inner duality in *Two-Headed Poems*, and the same tension made social in [the "Afterword" to] *The Journals of Susanna Moodie*. Interviews Atwood: see 1981.99, for a slightly altered reprint, which omits two questions and answers. First, asked about whether the possible nuclear holocaust affects how people behave, Atwood responds: "'I'm worried about slow death. About oil spills or how people cutting down all the trees in the Amazon basin will cause us to run out of oxygen. These are things which are just as dangerous in the long run.'" Later, asked about her analytic intelligence, Atwood responds that she has that, but "'my strength is probably dredging up precise images. Blind-sider images that you're not expecting.'"

99 _____. "Margaret Atwood Hypes bill bissett: Vankouvr Keeps Going Thru Weird Phazes." *Vancouver Free Press*, 20-29 July, p. 24.

Announces Atwood's reading at the 21 July "Friends of [bissett's] Blewointment Press" benefit, and her cancellation of an adjacent reading; complains of bissett's worn-out media image; and praises bissett's *Sailor* highly, as excellent and truly revolutionary poetry.

100 WATLING, DOUG. "Atwood's Fourth Novel." *Books Now* (Halifax, N.S.) 2, no. 38 (9 November):1.

Is unenthusiastic: *Life Before Man* doesn't elicit smiles; its humour is ironic, edgy, acrid. It is about relationships. The clinical style suits the three main characters, but occasionally becomes more animated. "Elizabeth, Lesje, and Nate are all sympathetic, but unable to cope in some ineffable way. . . . Atwood's writing and presentation . . . are expert and engrossing. As in much other modern fiction, though, the reader wonders whether a spiritless response is a measure of Atwood's failure or of her success." If even grim visions should be revelatory, *Life* offers little.

101 WEIR, LORRAINE. "'Fauna of Mirrors': The Poetry of Hébert and Atwood." *ARIEL* (Calgary) 10, no. 3 (July):99-113.

Jorge Luis Borges's parable, "Fauna of Mirrors," tells of creatures enslaved in a mirror world, who will revolt against humans. Compares

Anne Hébert's masterpiece, *Le tombeau des rois* sequence of a woman trapped in a death-filled kingdom of mirrors, and Atwood's mirror, reflection, and Narcissistic lover poems, from *The Circle Game* through *Two-Headed Poems*. "Two codes of eyes, two concepts of language, structure not only the Susanna Moodie poems but Atwood's work as a whole." Mirrors and cameras are part of the human eye code. Contrasts Atwood's bitter, conscious irony, direct physical pain, individual will, and possible liberation to women's lack of power in Hébert. Suggests that Atwood may have been influenced by Hébert.

102 WISEMAN, ADELE. "Readers Can Rejoice: Atwood's in Form." *Toronto Star*, 29 September, p. F7.

Celebrates Atwood's engrossing, ingenious, mischievous *Life Before Man*. The Royal Ontario Museum locale is brilliantly significant. The dated chapters encapsulate each character's isolated dramas. Haunting and comic parallels are suggested between dinosaurs, man, and characters. An erudite poet says the title comes from Levi-Strauss: "'Found humanism does not begin with oneself, but puts the world before life, life before man, and respect for others before self-interest.'" Life is a moral search for how to live. Even Elizabeth finally accepts her common humanity with her abominated dying aunt. There are no heroic transformations here; but the book ends with the enormous temerity of hope, for Nate, Lesje, and Elizabeth.

103 WOOD, GAYLE. "On Margaret Atwood's *Selected Poems*." *American Poetry Review* 8, no. 5 (September-October):30-32.

Celebrates Atwood's evolution from *The Circle Game*'s vague, passive hostility and pain, to the welcome, exploding surliness of "Song of the Transformed," and the joy of "There Is Only One of Everything." "The Circle Game" fails to identify herself or the source of pain. The animal "Songs" are all brilliant, shocking, foul, delectable; the sophisticated "Rat Song" sustains us, as do Atwood's three sardonic novels. Anger evolves in *Power Politics*, and is identified. Later [in the "Circe/Mud Poems"], Atwood understands "her own part in the romantic malaise," and the self matures. "The Double Voice" strikes out against passivity, but many of *The Journals of Susanna Moodie*'s poems drone on around one cleverness, as does "Resurrection." Excerpted: 1980.51.

1979

104 WOODCOCK, GEORGE. *The Canadians*. Cambridge, Mass.: Harvard University Press, p. 271.

Briefly characterizes Atwood the writer as most prolific, yet always tight, ironic, and aloof; Atwood the person as a Protean and paradoxical celebrity, feminist, and nationalist. She follows in all "a politics of the creative person," revealing to us the human condition in our time.

1980

1 ADAMS, PHOEBE-LOU. Review of *Life Before Man*. *Atlantic Monthly* 245, no. 4 (April):123.

Praises the yearning main characters, the almost scientific style, the stunning images, the clever plot, and the sly irony of *Life Before Man*.

2 ADAMSON, ARTHUR. "Identity through Metaphor: An Approach to the Question of Regionalism in Canadian Literature." *Studies in Canadian Literature* 5, no. 1 (Spring):83-99 passim.

Includes *Surfacing* in a Frygian discussion of civilization, nature, identity, and regionalism: Atwood uses "'American'" as a metaphor of man's mechanized, sterile civilization; the rational, civilized father comes to see nature as not merely chaotic, but also spiritually creative; and the heroine turns away from a life-denying, civilized man to a primordial buffalo man.

3 "An Atlantis Interview with Margaret Atwood." *Atlantis* 5, no. 2 (Spring):202-11.

Atwood explains *Life Before Man*'s realistic political analysis, her primary commitment as a writer, and her support of feminism as part of human and biological rights. *Life*'s Canadian reviews have been two-thirds good, but, as usual, one-third bad. The way that Amiel's widely read *Maclean's* 1979.2 review called *Life* a woman's novel slights its political analysis, and would include most mainstream novels as woman's novels. The Women's Movement changed the audience for *The Edible Woman*, which anticipated some of its trends, and made Atwood's choice to be a writer seem right, not weird. Her 1971 York University study group found women writers' concerns, which men also wrote about, but no woman's style. *Life* is realistic, as the next two novels will be, without the fantasy or gothic of the first three. As Flannery O'Connor's *Mystery and Manners* says, a correct but dead novel is useless because it fails to critique our real, imperfect world. Atwood wants to be free to depict real, human, flawed women, not role models. The media have used and discarded both feminism and nationalism; Canada is now conservative, hanging on in hard times. You can deduce what's wrong with society in *Life* by seeing what its characters do and what's missing: Elizabeth, a strong but very alone woman, sees politics as a boys' game; Nate, like Germany before Hitler, has lost faith in politics; Lesje rejects politics for paleontology. Marge Piercy's new *Vida* depicts a violent, very American politics.

4 AUFFERMANN, VERENA. "Eine Leiche und drei Tote." *Rhein-Neckar Zeitung* (Büchen), 30 September, p. 23.

Finds *Unmöglichkeit der Nähe*, the German translation of *Life Before Man*, only partly successful and often bordering on kitsch. Nate is an insecure man because of the strong women around him. All the characters are denied happiness, and experience true feelings only by accident. The reader, who is not moved by this passionless suffering, prefers the detective story quality and literary skill of *Surfacing*.

5 BALZ, DOUGLAS. "*Life Before Man*: Creating a Biology of Hope." *Miami Herald*, 3 February, p. E7. Newsbank 1979-1980, 50:F3-4.

Enjoys *Life Before Man*, which is not strident feminism, but "a poet's book of life." Atwood's multiple sympathies with her characters do not prevent her from offering chapters that resemble biological specimens. Despite the Toronto setting, "the sensibility seems distinctly American. Call it late 20th-Century functional depression." The characters adapt to survive. As the universe recombines its molecules, so Atwood recombines old plot elements, to create a new, reborn world.

6 BELOV, S[ERGEI]. "Eti knigi prishli iz kanadi: obretenie golosa" [These books came from Canada: new found voices]. *Inostrannaia Litertura* (Moscow), no. 3 (March), pp. 254-56.

In Russian. In a review of three Canadian books published in the 1970s, approves of *Lady Oracle* as a study of life's contradictions and the relationship between art and society. The narrative is presented in layers: domestic novel, satiric story, and drama of ideas. Atwood successfully combines psychology with the grotesque and farce with tragedy. While Joan is hiding in Italy, she faces the dissolution of her imaginary values and false grandeur. Atwood does not offer answers, but the end of the book implies the necessity of conquering apathy and indifference.

7 BILAN, R.P. "Letters in Canada, 1979: Fiction." *University of Toronto Quarterly* 49, no. 4 (Summer):329-31.

Gives mixed complaints and praise to *Life Before Man*, its implied diagnosis of our contemporary malaise, and its characterizations. The incompletely socialized Lesje is a familiar Atwood woman; her amusing, exuberant fantasies are the book's best parts. Atwood is always good at describing "'civilized'" brutality, as with Elizabeth. The ineffectual, entangled Nate is Atwood's most successful male character. *Life*'s successes are often local; as a whole it is flat and monotonous. Atwood's emotional range has always been limited, to intense negatives and detachment. *Life*'s bleakness seems extreme and forced. Its final positives are admirably ambivalent, but a bit too willed.

8 BITKER, MARJORIE. "Half Honey, Half Vitriol." *Milwaukee Journal*, 17 February, sec. 5, p. 5. Newsbank 1979-1980, 50:G1.

Praises the timely, original, compelling *Life Before Man*, which reveals its characters, and how they resemble us. Atwood's allegory of modern Western insecurities has been written with an "ink that is half honey, half vitriol."

9 BJÖRKSTEN, INGMAR. "Utan rötter ingen identitet" [Without roots, no identity]. *Artes* (Stockholm), no. 6, pp. 12-16.

In Swedish. An analysis of Atwood's prose work. *Survival*'s illuminating thematic study of Canadian literature exposes, partly through its subjectivity, a specifically Canadian literary color. Atwood's psychological prose, like that of George Eliot, the Brontës, and Margaret Drabble, fits well into the Anglo-Saxon tradition, but is unique in its satirical edge and bizarre humor. *The Edible Woman* shows how Atwood uses women characters as critical observers in an unremarkable plot. The structurally impressive *Surfacing* is narrated by a woman character who, through recollections, reveals a wise, experienced voice. *Lady Oracle*'s woman writer works to develop a new perspective on her life and learns how to live within social conventions.

Dancing Girls similarly shows glimpses of contemporary lives from various perspectives. In the same fashion, *Life Before Man* is a "generational odyssey."

10 BRADSHAW, LEAH. "Portraits in Women's Literature." *Queen's Quarterly* 87, no. 3 (Autumn):458-64.

Atwood's 1976 York University address described stereotypes of women in literature and as writers. What is conventional for women must be sorted out from what is natural; *Two-Headed Poems* seems to focus on this sorting process. Many of its poems, like the grandmother ones, depict women's traditionally warm, private space as disturbingly transient, and women's lives as dispensable; and yet affirm women's life-sustaining biological, reproductive continuity. Red is shown as a color native to women. *Two-Headed Poems* is not about women's oppression by men; but about looking inward for new models, as in "Solstice Poem," which counsels women to be courageous.

11 BROOKS, VALERIE. "Novel Peopled by Walking Neuroses." *Los Angeles Times Book Review*, 17 February, p. 4. Newsbank 1979-1980, 50:F2.

Rejects *Life Before Man*'s bleak vision; its dreary, failing, spiritless characters; and its claustrophobic void. These characters don't breathe, though Lesje is somewhat endearing. Unlike Sylvia Plath, Joan Didion, and John Cheever, Atwood sees only victor/victim relationships, and writes pretentiously.

12 BROWN, ROSELLEN. "Anatomy of Melancholia." *Saturday Review* 7, no. 3 (2 February):33-35.

Praises *Life Before Man* highly, as Atwood's finest novel. Like "Midwinter, Presolstice," *Life* makes potent connections with a poet's economy. The powerful but suffering Elizabeth "challenges the reader to decide whether characters need to be liked or only (only?) understood." That Elizabeth, the mild Nate, and the affecting Lesje sound alike, and that their situations slowly accrete, are not flaws: the book's voice is very nearly objective, like a satisfyingly exhaustive scientific treatise on primate love/hate behavior. Atwood has uncompromisingly and imaginatively "given us real lives that are far more true than what we want." Excerpted: 1980.51.

1980

13 BROWN, RUSSELL M. "Atwood's Sacred Wells." *Essays on Canadian Writing*, no. 17 (Spring), pp. 5-43.

Explicates the sacred depths beneath Atwood's recurrent, clustered, numinous images, in *Dancing Girls, The Circle Game, The Animals in That Country, Procedures for Underground*, and the first four novels. Dislocated, alienated tourists pervade Atwood's work; her Susanna Moodie embodies these failures to claim a territory and, therefore, an identity. The home ground is lost, as in *Surfacing* and "Roominghouse, winter." Totems and totem-like objects, as in "Some Objects of Wood and Stone," give glimpses of a persisting numinous world which Atwood, like Joseph Campbell, links to the unconscious. The once-sacred well of "The Resplendent Quetzal" is an omphalos, a portal to the mysterious, sacred world beneath our surface world. As Rubenstein 1976.88 points out, Atwood's quest for depths is "'an archetypal journey into the self.'" Atwood sees our history as after a fall and a deluge; we live in a world overwhelmed by mass culture and its products, including advertising and escape literature. This mass culture is not simply American—Atwood's Mexicans, Canadians, and artists collaborate. The *Surfacing* notebooks record the child's recapitulation of the fall, as her primal religious vision is layered over with secular, commercial images. Atwood's mirrors may be pools, as in "Tricks with Mirrors"; her photographs may have worlds behind them; language itself may be a surface layering, as in the metafictive, visionary "Giving Birth." Atwood is a mystic (*Survival*'s position five) who wants to draw us through the world's surfaces to its essential depths. Abridged: 1988.8.

14 BRYFONSKI, DEDRIA, ed. *Contemporary Literary Criticism*. Vol. 13. Detroit: Gale Research Co., pp. 41-47.

Excerpted from: Morley 1972.27; Onley 1973.66; Trueblood 1977.94; Cameron 1978.15.

15 CADOGAN, MARY. "Marital Conflicts." *Books and Bookmen* 25, no. 7 (April):44-45.

Briefly praises *Life Before Man*, in a four-book review, as vigorous, resonant, and starkly and beautifully symbolic.

16 CALARCO, M.J. Review of *To See Our World*. *Nature Canada* 9, no. 4 (October-December):39.

Mentions that Atwood introduces Catherine M. Young's collection of occasionally very beautiful, but mostly disappointing, nature photographs, which too often fall short of their foreword, their complementary Thoreau quotes, and their publisher's blurb.

17 CHRIST, CAROL P. "Refusing to Be Victim: Margaret Atwood." In *Diving Deep and Surfacing: Women Writers on Spiritual Quest*. Boston: Beacon Press, pp. 41-53. 2d ed. 1986.
Revision and updating of 1976.13.

18 CLAY, CAROLYN. "Tyrannosaurus in Toronto: Margaret Atwood and Her New Novel." *Boston Phoenix*, 18 March, sec. 3, pp. 9, 16-17.
Interviews Atwood, who was in town last week to promote *Life Before Man*. In *Life*, which scientifically dissects "marriage and *other* dinosaurs," Atwood focuses not on the predictable marital-triangle emotions but "on manipulation, civility, and despair"; and sometimes reverses the expected sexual dynamics, with the strong, calculating Elizabeth. Atwood, who is tiny but who "seems utterly in control," unlike her earlier heroines, recounts her own capsule history with remarkable detachment. Atwood critiques reader's autobiographical perceptions of women's writing, and some reviewers' fallacious expectations of female niceness and male strength, regarding Elizabeth and Nate. Atwood explains that the scientist Lesje, though as vague and vacillating as Nate, does by the end start to see "'human beings as we instead of they.'"

19 COBURN, RANDY SUE. "Atwood: Life before Man, Life on the Road." *Washington* (D.C.) *Star*, 11 March, pp. D1, 3. Newsbank 1979-1980, 68:D2-3.
Interviews Atwood in Washington D.C., at the end of *Life Before Man* promotional tour. Atwood comments on Canadian writers, feminists, and success; on the meanings of *Life Before Man*'s title, on Nate's mother as not satirical but "the novel's moral key–a character who lives in a state of despair but acts nevertheless," and on "nevertheless" as *Life*'s most important word; on her current life in Alliston; and on adapting *Lady Oracle* as a screenplay for actress Margot Kidder.

1980

20 COLE, DIANE J. "A Gifted Canadian Novelist Returns to Form (a Triangle)." *Sun* (Baltimore), 24 February, p. D7.

Praises *Life Before Man*'s powerful tale, controlled voice, and unique, recognizable characters. Elizabeth, Nate, and Lesje are fragmented and isolated; specimens who survive, breed, and learn to adapt, a little. Though the older women characters sometimes approach caricature, even they become sympathetic and real.

21 COLE, SUSAN G. "Margaret Atwood: In Vertebrates Veritas." *Broadside* (Toronto) 1, no. 5 [1980?]:14.

Questions why Atwood uses her considerable gifts on *Life Before Man*, which "seems to be nothing more than a romantic triangle of singularly unattractive persons?" Atwood's craft, toughness, poetic economy, and uncannily exact answers are all still there. At moments she does go beyond her individual characters' quirks, to say something about human relationships. In a way Elizabeth and Nate represent the 70s Me decade. In the ironic Lifeboat scene, only Lesje has a life outside herself – and only she is unable to prove her social usefulness. Atwood understands commitment to values beyond personal satisfaction; women have to take her warning seriously. But *Life* is still a slim volume and a narrowed perspective.

22 COOKE, JUDY. "Green Island." *New Statesman* 99 (9 May):715.

Praises *Life Before Man*, in a four-book review, as a bleak, ironic story of three people struggling against despair in the contemporary, post-Updike wasteland. Lesje is restored by love and a somewhat complacent pregnancy; Elizabeth's recovery is "a candid, sometimes moving account of survival."

23 COUGHLIN, ELLEN. "Margaret Atwood." *Books and Arts* 1, no. 12 (7 March):5-6.

Interviews Atwood during *Life Before Man* promotion: Atwood discusses in detail Canadian publishing; her own literary career, background, and current life on farm; feminism; Cinderella happy endings versus Marilyn French's *The Women's Room*; writing poetry versus writing novels; *Life Before Man*'s epigrammatic prose; and *Survival* versus Canadian academics. Cover story.

24 CRACE, JIM. "Dusk Jackets." *Quarto*, April, p. 17.

Complains, in a review of four of Virago's so-called "'Modern Classics,'" that *The Edible Woman* is a listless, "sprawling soft-headed sermon"; but appreciates *Life Before Man* as "an excellent and involving novel," "ill-humoured fun," and "a perceptive and hard-hearted display of misanthropy." "The [first] novel makes a fairly strident if undemanding start but soon loses its first wind and the stitch sets in. . . . One has no quarrel with the plot or the politics of *The Edible Woman*, but the debate is low- level, the comic set-pieces mirthless, the metaphors sloppy," and the prose lethargic. The accomplished *Life Before Man*'s stiff opening sections, in contrast, give "way to prose and characterisation" that may lack energy or warmth, but not elegance or style. *Life*'s everyday, bored, incestuous city folk are all sad, venomous, joyless discards. "[T]his is a *post*-feminist novel" where parents and husbands "get an equally measured kick in the teeth from Margaret Atwood."

25 CUDE, WILFRED. "The Female Quixote as Junkie." In *A Due Sense of Differences: An Evaluative Approach to Canadian Literature*. Lanham, Md.: University Press of America, pp. 133-53.

An expansion of 1977.11: discusses *Lady Oracle* in more detail; the close resemblances between the addicted, irresponsible Joan and her mother; the Fat Lady as a profound symbol of our mediocre materialism; and compares Joan to Arabella of the once-popular *The Female Quixote*, by Charlotte Lennox, and to Catherine Moreland of *Northanger Abbey*, by Jane Austen.

26 ____. "Learning Something from All This." In *A Due Sense of Differences: An Evaluative Approach to Canadian Literature*. Lanham, Md.: University Press of America, pp. 154-71.

Acclaims Atwood's didactic satire: as with *Don Quixote*, Northanger Abbey, and *Huckleberry Finn*, *Lady Oracle*'s rich laughter makes us think. Our girl Joan remains blind to the menace of her ingrained disorder; she is something of a witch, and her mother is her familiar and spectral link with evil powers. The unsolvable mystery, of who sent Joan the menacing animal messages, is our clue to the real mystery, of how Joan's mother died. The answer is not in Joan's Gothic melodrama fantasies, but in her own never-confronted guilt: we readers know that "'Joan dunit.'" Though Joan presents herself as a victim of her almost pathologically insensitive mother, the adolescent Joan literally drives her mother to drink. *Lady Oracle*'s real lesson concerns the violence of "the escapist imagination gone berserk." (Joan's dynamite would have inevitably exploded in the cold.) Joan has mislaid her humanity and her soul. We must learn to see Joan clearly, and to see our own fat, materialistic, rationalizing selves in her. Reprinted: 1980.28. See also 1978.19.

27 _____. "Negative Criticism." In *A Due Sense of Differences: An Evaluative Approach to Canadian Literature*. Lanham, Md.: University Press of America, pp. 203-6.

Argues that Brophy's 1976.10 review of *Lady Oracle* is incensed, limited, confused, and petty. Brophy failed to catch certain Canadian references, as well as Atwood's satire and its meaning. Joan's multiple selves are only undifferentiated on the surface; behind them are the frightening, negative twins of her nightmares and fantasies. The spectre of Joan's mother, the Fat Lady, and the Dark Lady are Joan's "unholy Gothic trinity," emanating from her "one benighted soul."

28 _____. "Nobody Dunit: The Loose End as Structural Element in *Lady Oracle*." *Journal of Canadian Studies* 15, no. 1 (Spring):30-44.

Reprint of 1980.26. See also 1978.19.

29 DAVEY, FRANK. "*Lady Oracle*'s Secret: Atwood's Comic Novels." *Studies in Canadian Literature* 5, no. 2 (Fall):209-21.

Argues that, contrary to the misleading "'anti-comedy'" of Atwood's 1973.27 and 1977.87 interviews, her three novels rework a comic structure of alienation, desperation, escape, and reintegration, which is a twentieth-century equivalent to Shakespearean comedy, with the unconscious as a green world of exile. Her three very similar narrators are deluded, extremely passive, and lacking in passion and human relationships. *The Edible Woman*, *Surfacing*, and *Lady Oracle* have the optimistic structure of psychoanalytic therapy: conscious neurosis, reductive catharsis, then tentative reconstruction. *Lady Oracle*'s most tentative end is the most convincing; Joan keeps her regressive projection and transference fantasies. Reprinted: 1983.30. Revised: 1984.18.

1980

30 ____. "Margaret Atwood." In *Profiles in Canadian Literature*. Edited by Jeffrey M. Heath. Vol. 2. Toronto and Charlottetown: Dundurn Press, pp. 57-64.

Atwood's poetry and fiction focus on tense relationships of mankind and nature, man and woman, where woman and nature are victimized by technological man, unless we read past the main characters. Her usual voice is that of a frightened, alienated, bitter woman. Her poetry rests on a dialectic of static order versus natural temporal process (see 1977.12). The women narrators of *Dancing Girls* suppress all personal feelings. Atwood's first three novels are basically optimistic, with a comic structure; her poetry is basically tragic. Recent writings expand her range: *Life Before Man* portrays static, trapped, tragic relationships; *Two-Headed Poems* and "[The Festival of] Missed Crass" story embrace a comic, redemptive vision. Includes a *Profiles*-format chronology, comments by and on Atwood, and bibliography.

31 DAVIDSON, ARNOLD E. "The Different Voices in Margaret Atwood's *The Journals of Susanna Moodie*." *CEA Critic* 43, no. 1 (November):14-20.

Atwood is attracted to the inherent duplicity or duality of journals, and to Moodie's particularly Canadian "other voice." These are journals of the self's exterior and interior voyages, of landscape as psychoscape. Journal I draws on the historic Moodie's *Roughing It in the Bush* to chronicle the changing self; the less subtle, more settled Journal II draws on Moodie's *Life in the Clearings*. Journal III traces a third cycle of perception, search for self, and illumination, resolving earlier dualities as Moodie becomes the mythic spirit of the land.

32 DeCONCINI, BARBARA. "Remembering: A Hermeneutic of Narrative Time." Ph.D. dissertation, Emory University, 419 pp.

Discusses *Surfacing*, and Saul Bellow's *Henderson the Rain King*, as fictions which confirm the fundamental human significance of remembering. See *Dissertation Abstracts International* 41:3092A.

33 DELANY, PAUL. "Letters: Atwood and the Reviewers." *Saturday Night* 95, no. 6 (July-August):11

Protests Fulford 1980.42, which naively suggests that Canadian reviewers should follow the *New York Times Book Review* acclaim, from Marilyn French 1980.41, for *Life Before Man*. Delany, whose

1980

1979.27 was cited as misguided, did review *Surfacing* very favourably for the *New York Times Book Review*, 1973.20. Perhaps Canadian reviewers, who surely all read Atwood's earlier fiction, found *Life Before Man* disappointing. Atwood's talent is really endangered not by media criticism but by "the cult of personality that has come to surround her in recent years." Is Fulford's idea of unacknowledged envy among Canadian critics a warning – or a threat?

34 DIOT, ROLANDE. "'Image du corps et stade du miroir': Un aspect de l'humour de Margaret Atwood dans *Lady Oracle*." *Études canadiennes* (Talence), no. 9, pp. 51-61.

The obsessions, phobias, fantasies, and neurotic compulsions that Atwood's poetry sublimates are expressed in a cathartic, comic voice in *Lady Oracle*. The novel's black humour develops through attacks on the bastions of social and sexual order, and through the "self-debunking" and auto-caricature of three subjects: I, the narrator; me, the woman; and me, the woman/writer. Point of view, narrative structures, and language techniques playfully reflect various styles of parody. Atwood mixes dream-like and mock stream of consciousness sequences, and in the end successfully braids together the two parallel texts of serious novel and trashy gothic. *Lady Oracle* carnivalizes, through a highly orchestrated, dance-like text, the absurdity of existence.

35 EDGINGTON, K[AY]. "Victims, Survivors, and Modern Literature." *Women: A Journal of Liberation* (Baltimore) 7, no. 1:44-46.

A six-book discussion of positive role models versus female victims in women writers that focuses on survival and the divided self, survival and time, survival and choice; and briefly describes *Surfacing*'s protagonist's divided self and healing insanity, her fixed, fraudulent past, and her choice of survival, not victimization.

36 FLAHERTY, ROGER. "More Than Victims: Atwood's Characters." *Chicago Sun-Times*, 10 February, sec. 3, p. 13. Newsbank 1979-1980, 50:F5.

Appreciates *Life Before Man*'s characterizations: Elizabeth, Nate, and Lesje are all struggling survivors, who must accept their limited powers and choices, as Chris, the suicide, could not. Although at times one senses a predetermined, gothic doom, as in Joyce Carol Oates's novels, Atwood's characters are more than victims; they choose, and change.

37 FOOTE, TIMOTHY. "Human Rex: Atwood on the Extinction of Man." *Esquire* 93, no. 2 (February):87-88.

Praises *Life Before Man*. Canada has now gone from wilderness to modern weltschmertz survival. Atwood writes with savage humor, compressed emotion, and polished irony. The feminist survivor and "Memorable Monster," Elizabeth, finally stirs both pity and admiration. The lapsed liberal and "Eternal Husband," Nate, is what feminism seems to encourage, then find unsatisfying. Lesje seems to have the last word on man's survival.

38 FORREST, AL. "Letters: Atwood and the Reviewers." *Saturday Night* 95, no. 6 (July-August):11.

Corroborates and extends Fulford 1980.42. As Fulford and Atwood observe, there is "a subconscious tendency to tear down anyone whose success appears to be soaring too quickly, no matter who" he or she may be, or in what country. As the example of Francoise Sagan's celebrated first novel and unfairly panned second novel demonstrates, this tendency is not only Canadian but, unfortunately, human.

39 FREEDMAN, ADELE. "Happy Heroine and 'Freak' of CanLit." *Globe and Mail*, 25 October, p. E1.

Interviews Atwood, who is happy, famous, and successful–then why is *Life Before Man* depressing? Atwood discusses Marilyn French's *The Women's Room*, different generations' experiences of Women's Liberation; art as realism, not self-expression; human rights and writers' concerns. "'No one knows yet what being a man or a woman really means,'" Atwood claims.

40 ____. "$6,000 a Copy for Atwood/Pachter Book." *Globe and Mail*, 16 August, p. E3.

Promotes the Atwood/Pachter *The Journals of Susanna Moodie* as a most ambitious artist's book, in the European tradition of art for connoisseurs; and interviews Charles Pachter in Toronto about his long friendship with Atwood, and his artist's books that were triggered by her poetry. Master printers Manuel and Abel Bello-Sanchez regard

1980

The Journals of Susanna Moodie as a major step in printmaking; master binder Marion Mertens will produce the boxes.

41 FRENCH, MARILYN. "Spouses and Lovers." *New York Times Book Review*, 3 February, pp. 1, 26.

Acclaims *Life Before Man*, as superb and complete in its characters and theme, and as the best of Atwood's four novels, all of which "search for a better way to be," more than for identity. Elizabeth is powerful yet pitiable; cruel, but suffering, and surviving, which is a triumph. Nate is brilliantly depicted as a liberal, "'liberated'" man. "All of the characters are deracinated." Only Nate's mother sees beyond the self, and understands that she must change the world; the main characters only glimpse her vision. *Life Before Man* suggests that we are living before man–before the human has evolved. "[W]e may become extinct . . . ; we may be only a beginning." Excerpted: 1980.51.

42 FULFORD, ROBERT. "Do Canadians Fear Excellence? Consider the Case of Atwood." *Saturday Night* 95, no. 4 (May):12.

Critiques the negative Canadian reviews of *Life Before Man*, and affirms its international acclaim. Although Atwood's fourth novel has been widely acclaimed in the United States and England, there's been a note of rejection, or grudging praise, in Canada. Where is the Canadian appreciation of this brilliant, unique novel? What other Canadian novelist has Atwood's precision, contemporary insight, ingenious metaphors, skillful male and female characterizations, or her "transcendently comic melancholy" and gleeful discoveries? The reviewer does not suggest that Canadians review with spite or jealousy–but he does suggest that, as Atwood has said, Canadians may feel threatened by another Canadian's international success. See Delany 1980.33, Forrest 1980.38, and Pratt 1980.103.

43 GLENDINNING, VICTORIA. "Survival of the Fittest." *Washington Post Book World*, 27 January, p. 4.

Appreciates *Life Before Man* as a good, "utterly realized" novel, but wants more. The evolution that produced the three main characters is traced through their mothers, aunts, and grandmothers. *Life Before Man* is precise, perceptive, very skillful, and never boring; it is completely ordered and controlled–like a school report. This provokes a slight unease, for great art has something irrational, some anarchy, which *Life* lacks. Excerpted: 1980.51.

44 GOLDSTEIN, ERIC D. "Turning Inward." *New Leader* 63, no. 11 (16 June):20-21.

Praises *Life Before Man*'s controlled, complex, open-ended characterization: the intense Elizabeth is the most fully realized; Lesje's and Nate's "self-absorption is too compassionately drawn." Ironically, the only social misfit is Chris, who acts directly on what he feels. There is nothing gratuitous or trendy about the characters' unhappiness, given their world.

45 GRACE, SHERRILL E. "Moodie and Atwood: Notes on a Literary Reincarnation." In *The Canadian Novel: A Critical Anthology.* Edited by John Moss. Vol. 2, *Beginnings.* Rev. ed. Toronto: NC Press, pp. 73-79.

Explores, following Carol Shield's *Susanna Moodie: Voice and Vision,* the literary relationship between Atwood's mythic *The Journals of Susanna Moodie* and the historic Moodie's *Roughing It in the Bush* and *Life in the Clearings.* Atwood develops the historic Moodie's divided allegiance, hatred, and fear into her *Journal*'s Canadian 'paranoid schizophrenia,'" doubleness, and violent dualities. For both Shields and Atwood, Moodie's men are absent, weak, or bad; but enforced pioneer independence is not the same as twentieth-century feminism. In "Death of a Young Son by Drowning," "Visit to Toronto, with Companions," and other *Journals* poems, Atwood develops Moodie's material and captures her other, counterpointing voice. Atwood's unpublished play, "Grace Marks," probably comes from *Life in the Clearings.*

46 ____. "'Time Present and Time Past': *Life Before Man.*" *Essays on Canadian Writing,* no. 20 (Winter), pp. 165-70.

Considers characterization, epigraphs, structure, and time in Atwood's disturbing, intriguing first novel of "social and domestic Realism." The three main characters are frustratingly alike in their very ordinary, colourless, repressed, and passive lives in grey middle-class Toronto; the three discarded lovers are more dramatic. But Atwood evokes our interest gradually in the main three; and especially in Elizabeth, with her occasionally first-person voice, her opening thematic statement about how to live, and "the gradual tunnelling-out (to adapt Virginia Woolf's phrase) of Elizabeth's" traumatic childhood. Narrative time is manipulated; thematic time is used ironically, as contrast and analogy to the present. The Björn Kurtén epigraph implies that the novel's dated, labelled scenarios are file cards, or field notes, on a species nearly fossilized. The Abram Tertz epigraph is ironically unbelievable and, in Tertz's story, unbelieved. As T.S. Eliot said, "'If all time is eternally present / all time is unredeemable,'" but Atwood's narrative may be an act of faith.

47 GRACE, SHERRILL [E]. *Violent Duality: A Study of Margaret Atwood*. Montreal: Véhicule Press, 156 pp.

Assesses the pervasive duality of theme and form in Atwood's work, from the early poetry sequences, chapbooks, and *Double Persephone*, through seven books of poetry, *Survival, Dancing Girls*, and four novels; discusses development, imagery, collages and covers, genre, structure, viewpoint, influences – treating Jay Macpherson and James Reaney as the most formative – Canadian elements, language, and metaphor. Argues that Atwood's double vision is rooted in the old subjective/objective dualities – we both see, and, in seeing, create our world and our art – and in Atwood's concept of the self as no fixed ego, but a place where things happen, which is changed by things happening in it – as, literally, in *Surfacing*'s visions and in "Giving Birth." Finds Atwood's dualities valid, fluid, and a source of dynamic aesthetic tension; *Survival* struggles for affirmations.

Explicates *The Circle Game*'s imagery and structure; treats *The Journals of Susanna Moodie* as Atwood's major poetry, a Canadian archetype and Gravesian Triple Goddess myth, and a portrait of our national schizophrenia. Treats *You Are Happy*, with its delightful Circe de-mythologizing, and its final, tender but incomplete affirmations, as a plateau in Atwood's development. Discusses *The Edible Woman*'s witty, urbane anti-comedy and consumer society satire; *Surfacing*'s ghost story, narrative voice, visions, language, imagery, psychological quest and attempted multi-level quests; and *Lady Oracle*'s anti-gothic, fairy-tale, and gothic romance elements, self-reflexive parody, satire, irony, and multiplicity. Suggests that the more reflective and mellow *Two-Headed Poems*, and the more realistic *Life Before Man*, may begin a new stage in Atwood's development; see Grace 1980.46, 1981.40, and

1983.54. Provides a chronology and selected bibliography. Excerpted: 1983.129.

48 GRAY, PAUL. "Marital Blahs." *Time* 115, no. 8 (25 February):89, 93.

Praises *Life Before Man*: Atwood risks banality, with marriage triangles and commonplace characters, but wins. Her self-regarding, suffering characters perform a comic, mannered burlesque. Atwood neither mocks nor exalts their pain; and she gives them small insights into their absurdities. "It is hard not to like Elizabeth and her antagonists," even though they mostly qualify "for a good throttling."

49 GRIFFITH, MARGARET. "Verbal Terrain in the Novels of Margaret Atwood." *Critique* (Atlanta) 21, no. 3:85-93.

Reads three novels and "Journey to the Interior" as Atwood's journey to self-knowledge, where she maps an ultimately verbal terrain, one linguistically confused, and littered with false categories and forms. In *The Edible Woman* Atwood maps a consumers' land where language is another alienating product; she measures her characters by their use or abuse of language. That the final cake-woman may not translate into words "is perhaps Atwood's final word." *Surfacing*'s failed artist journeys, literally and figuratively, through a land of transformation, where the strange pictographs deliver her from civilization's linguistic abstractions to her "'multilingual'" self. In *Lady Oracle* language becomes the artist Joan's transformation cloak, and her straitjacket. All three protagonists may share Joan's artist's terror of fixed form, of [Keats's] "'cold pastoral.'"

50 GRUMBACH, DORIS. "Men without Women, Women without Men: New Novels from Margaret Atwood, Vance Bourjaily, and Johanna Kaplan." *Books and Arts* 1, no. 12 (7 March):7-8.

Finds *Life Before Man*, in a three-book review, "subtle, beautifully written and shaped, but, oddly enough, not always interesting. . . . Elizabeth is absent from her domestic life, motionless, and typical of Atwood's women" in the first scene, where unneeded details of her habiliment unbalance the sentence and lose the reader. Well-placed flashbacks reveal her terrible childhood; but, in the novel's most chilling scene, where Elizabeth and her sister glimpse their mother, after a children's Christmas show, Atwood's overstuffed first sentence again diminishes the scene's undeniable force. Elizabeth's exhaustion wearies the novel; the reviewer admires Atwood's skill and themes, but wishes for greater intensity.

51 GUNTON, SHARON R., and HARRIS, LAURIE LANZEN, eds. *Contemporary Literary Criticism*. Vol 15. Detroit: Gale Research Co., pp. 36-40.

Excerpted from: Wood 1978.102; Matson 1979.71; Amiel 1979.3; Wood 1979.103; Stone 1980.129; Glendinning 1980.43; Brown 1980.12; French 1980.41.

52 HALL, JOAN JOFFE. Review of *Life Before Man*. *Houston Post*, 17 February. Newsbank 1979-1980, 50:F13.

Praises *Life Before Man*'s clear, *Surfacing*-like poetry, and clinically analyzed characters. Lesje "is a typical Canadian fictional character, doomed by withdrawal." Nate is Atwood's first thoroughly believable, but not admirable, male. Elizabeth is both an admirable survivor and a chilling manipulator; she thaws a little, when she takes her dying aunt's hand, and at the end, when she longs for peace and paradise.

53 HALLDÉN, RUTH. "Margaret Atwoods nya roman: Identitetssökande" [Margaret Atwood's new novel: seeker of identity]. *Dagens Nyheter* (Stockholm), 4 February, p. 4.

In Swedish. *Upp till ytan* (*Surfacing*), which has been competently translated by Vanja Lantz, is a strange and upsetting story about alienation and a woman who rejects civilization. *Surfacing*'s originality is not in the seductively banal themes, but in the intelligent and lyrical presentation of the motive [motif?]. The protagonist's stark, flooding memories force her to face the inadequacies and compromises of her life. Her search for her father symbolizes the search for her lost identity. The reader witnesses her reunion with nature firsthand; the coldness and wetness oozes out of the book from a world of stinking fish, rotting seaweed, and crawling insects. Atwood's primitivism works with this otherwise worn-out theme of man's difficulties in civilization.

54 HANCOCK, GEOFF. "This Little Peggy Went to Market: Atwood on Being an International Literary Success." *Books in Canada* 9, no. 6 (June-July):30-31.

Interviews Atwood in Toronto, after *Life Before Man* promotional tour: Atwood contrasts U.S. and Canadian marketing of *Life Before Man*; commercial and literary success; and Canadian versus U.S. and English reviews.

55 HARRIS, LIS. "The Other Side of the Glass." *New Yorker* 56, no. 20 (7 July):98-100.

Finds Atwood's stubborn, semi-eccentric characters always oddly miscast for their roles, and her cities not nice. *Life Before Man*'s triangle is unconvincingly joined. "In most novels [Nate] would be a woman." The pivotal events "inspire little emotion in the reader." *Surfacing* was more successful, probably because Atwood writes best about nature and about human wildness, outside conventions. *Life Before Man* suggests, unconvincingly, that we are at a loss because our corrupt culture has separated us from nature.

56 HAYMAN, RONALD. "Margaret Atwood in Interview." *Books and Bookmen* 25, no. 7 (April):40-41.

Quotes Atwood in detail on *Life Before Man* and *Surfacing*: *Life Before Man*'s scientists, realism, its Canadian foreground and background, and its middle ground of Quebec, Nate, and Nate's mother; writing habits; style and genre in her four novels; the Canadian audience; feminism; and *Surfacing* as a ghost story like Henry James's "The Jolly Corner" and *The Turn of the Screw*.

57 HERBERT, MICHAEL. "A Canadian Mistresspiece." *Literary Review* (Edinburgh), no. 15 (2-15 May), p. 13.

Appreciates highly Atwood's liberating *Life Before Man*: her archetypal Canadian *Survival* themes are made totally personal, without banality or melodrama, in the three main stories. Predictable relationships are wilily developed; all the minor characters "are splendidly distinct, individual, quirky. . . . The two females [Elizabeth and Lesje] are especially well developed, although Nate more than holds his own in the middle." A playful, largely verbal, [James] Joycean "humour bubbles up here and there to break the bleak surface." If the unified narratives are too similar, that would be a small debit for the "tender, funny, absorbing, moving, idiosyncratic, truthful, heartening" *Life Before Man*.

1980

58 HORNE, ALAN [J]. Review of *Life Before Man*. *CM* 8, no. 3
    (Summer):144.
       Recommends the brilliant, internationally acclaimed *Life Before
    Man*, whose Canadian detractors find success somehow unacceptable;
    Life is middle-class domestic realism, and more than its soap-opera
    storyline; it is certainly depressing, but because society continues to
    evolve, there is hope.

59 HORNE, ALAN J. "Margaret Atwood: An Annotated Bibliography
    (Poetry)." In *The Annotated Bibliography of Canada's Major Authors*.
    Edited by Robert Lecker and Jack David. Vol. 2. Downsview, Ont.:
    ECW Press, pp. 13-53.
       Provides an overview of Canadian responses to Atwood, *The
    Circle Game*, *The Animals in That Country*, *The Journals of Susanna
    Moodie*, *Procedures for Underground*, *Power Politics*, and *You Are
    Happy*; a chronological primary listing of 344 items of poetry, audio
    recordings, and graphic work, 1954-early 1979; and an annotated
    bibliography of 128 items of secondary work, mostly Canadian, in
    English, 1962-late 1979, arranged chronologically under each Atwood
    book. Explains that although some items have been missed, the
    coverage of newspapers and anthologies is deliberately selective;
    provides an index of secondary authors. Lists under primary fifteen
    books, 1961-1978, which include limited editions; three broadsides and
    one libretto; manuscripts, listed as one item, which include 15 boxes;
    296 poems in periodicals and books; selected contributions of one or
    more poems to 11 anthologies; 6 audio and audio-visual recordings;
    and 11 items of published graphic work. Annotates, under secondary,
    two books, 1977.81 and 1980.47; 33 articles and sections of books, 1970-
    1979; 7 theses and dissertations; and 18 interviews; lists 10 awards and
    honours; annotates 68 book reviews, 1962-1979. See 1979.56. Abridged
    and updated as part of 1981.47.

60 HOWARD, PHILIP. Review of *Life Before Man*. *Times* (London), 13
    March, p. 14.
       Celebrates *Life Before Man*: "Atwood is a wordchild with the gift
    of tongues, puns, echoes, and symbols. . . . [She is] both witty and
    humorous about her unhappy vertebrates," and sharp-eyed. Though
    triply handicapped, as a feminist, Canadian, and poet, "Atwood
    manages to be a true novelist," who opens our eyes to our own

thoughts and behaviour, regardless of sex or nationality. "*Life Before Man* takes a beady look at the bleak anthropology of middle-class, middle-aged, Homo *moyen* [italics sic] Sapiens Canadiensis, and the middling muddle he (and particularly she) gets into over life (and particularly sex)." Elizabeth, Nate, and Lesje "have all been down the yellow brick road once or twice," and discovered there is no Oz. As in Jane Austen, and perhaps generally, the women are the more interesting characters. Quotes Atwood, who is on a publicity visit for *Life*, on being a feminist, Canadian, and poet.

61 ____. "Survival of the Fittest." *Times* (London), 5 April, p. 9.
    A review of *The Edible Woman* and Grace Paley's *The Little Disturbances of Man* that compliments Paley and Atwood for most perceptively "open[ing] up the feminist truths, without becoming intense, or shrill, or bad tempered about them." Both write comically, movingly, and beautifully, with idiosyncratic styles. Atwood writes of her heroine's choices, and "discovers the oddness" of daily life. Both Paley and Atwood are sharp, witty, and clever; the reviewer, though male, finds it a delight and honour to be their contemporary.

62 HURLEY, MICHAEL. "Dance of Death in Toronto the Good." *Journal of Canadian Studies* 15, no. 1 (Spring):122-23.
    Celebrates the imagery, Toronto realism, and Southern Ontario gothic metamorphoses of *Life Before Man*. The incestuous, claustrophobic, garrison-legacy Royal Ontario Museum focuses Atwood's themes perfectly. The dinosaurs, [*Survival's*] "dead animal-victim par excellence," describe Toronto's fossilized hearts and walking dead. Auntie Muriel is the Victorian "Wicked Witch" in "the Canadian family-as-trap." Like Joyce's Dubliners, Atwood's emotionally and spiritually paralyzed Torontonians pursue their constricted fantasies. As in any respectable Southern Ontario novel, there's a gothic eeriness: the dead haunt the living; there are doppelgangers, parallels, monsters. Characters fragment, float, disappear, as in the seminal "'Cosmic Disasters'" scene. Innocence festers into gothic nightmares; "'Paradise'" has dwindled to posters; "life during man is a wasteland," and insects will be the life after man.

63 IRVINE, LORNA. "A Psychological Journey: Mothers and Daughters in English-Canadian Fiction." In *The Lost Tradition: Mothers and*

1980

Daughters in Literature. Edited by Cathy N. Davidson and E.M. Broner. New York: Frederick Ungar Publishing Co., pp. 242-52.

Revision of 1977.36 and 1978.46; briefly discusses *Lady Oracle* and, very briefly, *Surfacing*. The Canadian literary tradition, which emerged alongside the 1960s and 1970s women's movements, treats women's quests seriously and emphasizes the maternal past. The negation-recognition-reconciliation stages of psychological journeys in English Canadian novels by women suggest that the radical anger of recent feminist writers is a necessary phase. In *Lady Oracle*, Joan's smouldering resentment and malevolent maternal image lead, finally, to Joan's articulating her love for her mother, and longing for a not-quite-completed reconciliation. In *Surfacing* also, the daughter's salvation lies in discovering her love and in valuing her own femininity.

64 JELINEK, ESTELLE. "A Novel About Humans as Evolutionary Garbage." *Oakland Tribune*, 30 November. Newsbank 1980-1981, 39:E2.

Finds a depressing, disturbing cynicism in *Life Before Man*. The deceptively feminist-sounding title refers to anthropological time, which "is a silent character" here. Humans are shown as deficient, destructive survivors. Lesje evolves from innocence to distrust and manipulation; Elizabeth evolves from ruthlessness to isolation. Atwood scorns human life, feminism, and left political causes. She never lets us like or admire any character. But her imagination does sustain our respect and interest.

65 JOHNSTON, ANN. "Tales to Keep the Nightlights Burning." *Maclean's* 93, no. 50 (15 December):52.

Finds, in a round-up review, that *Anna's Pet*, by Atwood and Joyce Barkhouse, is a sturdy, simple, funny book, without emotional depth or suspense. But "those who buy it for Atwood's name" will be disappointed, as with *Up in [the] Tree*. Praises Ann Blades's illustrations highly.

66 JOHNSTON, GORDON. "'The Ruthless Story and the Future Tense' in Margaret Atwood's 'Circe/Mud Poems.'" *Studies in Canadian Literature* 5, no. 1 (Spring):167-76.

Analyzes this sequence's mythological versus historical time (or classical versus Canadian worlds, which may explain critics' neglect).

The ordered, formal structure follows Homer, with four-poem groups, and contains chaotically varying poetic forms, and Atwood's characteristic "free similes." Title, speaker, and Ulysses are double: as prophet Circe has language's transforming powers; as Mud she distrusts words. There is a private or autobiographical level of significance; a banal level of a man and woman on a farm; and a double allegorical level, of man-woman relations (Circe), and of human dominance over earth (Mud). Atwood plays with levels of time and meaning; her central issue is mythopoeic determinism, the ruthless story. Is Circe, who knows only Ulysses' story, a willing victim?

67 JONES, FRANK. "Woman of the Moment." *Edmonton Journal*, 22 March, p. L1.
   Describes an Atwood-Marge Piercy reading [in Toronto]. Describes Atwood as getting limousines on her tours now; and *Life Before Man*, which is getting rave U.S. notices and a lot of money, as "a dreary story" of men who are wimps or boobies, "and women who are misled or terrifically competent"; describes the audience as "the new sister-archy," writing feminist books for glowing feminist reviews, or handbooks for children of divorcing parents, and "breeding a new journalism of violence keyed to rape and abortion. Theirs is the new orthodoxy that none, least of all men, dare challenge. Atwood . . . is so marvelously right as a hero of the new order." Describes Piercy as "an attractive woman"; her rape poem and Atwood's torture poems are "strong meat." Atwood comments on U.S. versus Canadian reviews, her family, men's reactions, the women's movement, and becoming a Canadian woman writer. See Kostash 1980.72.

68 KEMP, PETER. "Messy Pasts." *Listener* 103 (13 March):350-51.
   Features and praises highly *Life Before Man*'s psychology in a four-book review: Atwood's novel skillfully illumines the way early pressures form personalities, and the links between human and animal behaviour. The pervasive animal imagery shows Lesje as a "'herbivore'" and Elizabeth as an "'armadillo'"; Nate is like a fleet-hoofed runner. Atwood does full justice to her characters' feral energies, pair-bondings, and territorial imperatives. Praises *Life*'s fascinating and detailed personalities, beautiful construction, ironic felicities, and wide, rich range.

1980

69 KING, BRUCE. "More than Novelists." *CRNLE Reviews Journal*, no. 2, pp. 3-5.

Praises *Life Before Man* highly, in a two-book review, as Atwood's best novel, and an extremely full social and evolutionary novel. *Life* has Atwood's familiar power plays, fantasies, divided personalities, love, sex, social roles, and identity. The predictable *Survival* theme seems human, not Canadian only. Atwood shows how "past, family, class and money shape . . . the main characters' sense of reality." Elizabeth is "an excellent portrait of someone who has willed her way from poverty and a broken background" to an appearance of being establishment. "Lesje is one of the best presentations" of second-generation immigrant tensions outside American Jewish fiction. Nate is well drawn. The end lacks resolution; and, as in *Surfacing*, the final weak hope seems arbitrary.

70 KING, FRANCIS. "Cheesed Off." *Spectator* 244 (15 March):20-21.

As with Alison Lurie, is impressed by *Life Before Man*'s mordant intelligence, always vivid style, and formidable insights into human self-destruction. The remarkable Elizabeth is "at once pitiable and odious," deeply cicatrised and furiously egotistic. Lesje is the perfect simple lamb; Nate an ineffectual blunderer; and the children are victimized. Atwood's technique is totally secure, and her wit electric. Some of the 25 acknowledgments sound "Firbankian"; the paleontology researcher is superfluous.

71 KLINE, BETSY. "Man's Emoting May Be Cause for Extinction." *Kansas City Star*, 10 February, pp. E5, 15. Newsbank 1979-1980, 50:F8.

Praises the unusual *Life Before Man*, whose characters are meticulously, mercilessly scrutinized, like slides under a microscope, as they struggle for emotional survival. Elizabeth is a cunning survivor who lives with her ghosts and guilt; her mothering is territorial; only her aunt's death softens her. Nate is more sympathetic and loving, but fatally indecisive and inept, and uneasy with his mother's liberalism. Lesje is a timid, awkward daydreamer; she and Nate are vulnerable herbivores, and Elizabeth a prime carnivore.

72 KOSTASH, MYRNA. "Margaret Atwood No Flash in the Pan." *Edmonton Journal*, 5 April, p. I4.

Defends Atwood, women's literature, and women against Frank Jones's [1980.67] "snide and bitchy" insults. Atwood has been an important and responsible poet, novelist, teacher, and speaker for fifteen years now. Of what "'new order'" is she a hero? "He seems shocked that [Atwood's and Marge Piercy's] work is full of images of the violence that has been done to women and of hostility towards the aggression in men which seeks in women its target." Women writers voice our pain and bitterness: "If not they, then who?" Jones's "paranoia and obtuseness" trivialize "the literature of protest of half of humanity"; where his "conspiracy of litcrit" can be found is in the boys'-club literary establishment. And, though many of us were disappointed by *Life Before Man*, despite its rave American reviews, *Life Before Man* is not "'little.'"

73 LALIBERTÉ, YVES. "Margaret Atwood: Vers plus de contradictions." *Devoir* (Montréal), 22 November, Book sec., p. 14.
A group review of *The Edible Woman*, and the French Canadian publications *Lady Oracle* and *Faire surface (Surfacing)*, that finds *Lady Oracle* less amusing than the superficial *Edible Woman*, and much less captivating than the mythic *Surfacing*. *Lady Oracle* does succeed, however, in analyzing the individual behind the image of the humiliated woman. The three novels, whether based on banality or a clever plot of discovery, put the reader in a world obsessed with varied omnipresent symbols ranging from subtle to violent.

74 LASK, THOMAS. "Publishing: Another Aspect of a Mystery Writer." *New York Times*, 8 February, p. C27.
A literary news article whose second part is an interview of Atwood in New York. Atwood comments on readers' reactions to *Life Before Man* and its Canadian sales, her writing schedule, Canadian publishing, and Canadian versus U.S. attitudes.

75 LEHMANN-HAUPT, CHRISTOPHER. Review of *Life Before Man*. *Books of the Times* 3, no. 2:71-73.
Reprint of 1980.76 (below).

76 _____. Review of *Life Before Man*. *New York Times*, 10 January, p. C21.
Appreciates *Life Before Man* as a gentle tragicomedy, about growing up to resemble your least-liked adult, and as Atwood's best

novel so far. The title refers to Lesje before pregnancy. If you saw the plot objectively, *Life* would be a black farce, with little happening. Because you discover the plot in episodic leaps, through the three prismatic viewpoints, *Life* becomes a gentle tragicomedy, as in Lesje's aborted, grapefruit-knife suicide. But is the reviewer being sentimental? Do the dinosaurs, title, and epigraphs mean that these characters will soon be extinct fossils? But Atwood's characterization and humor make him hope and believe in their survival. Reprinted: 1980.75 (above).

77 LILIENFELD, JANE. "Silence and Scorn in a Lyric of Intimacy: The Progress of Margaret Atwood's Poetry." *Women's Studies* 7, nos. 1-2:185-94.

Traces a progression, from refusal of anger to anger to wit to transformation, in five books of poetry. "The Director of Protocol," saying No, is the denying, silencing patriarchal voice that women have ingested. The voice of "A Sibyl," an alienated freak of women's poetry, is blocked off but not completely denied; the speaker is divided between her sibyl and the menacing patriarchal man. In "Interview with a Tourist," she speaks two languages, of patriarchal culture and of her underground. *Power Politics* uses direct anger and wit to ridicule the mock heroic. In *You Are Happy*, the radiant, heroic seer Circe moves from ridicule to compassion; its final "Book of Ancestors" moves from patriarchal sacrifice to open, transforming human love.

78 LINDMAN-STAFFORD, KERSTIN. "Plagsam individualism" [Painful individuality]. *Hufvudstadsbladet* (Helsinki), 4 May, p. 4.

In Finnish. Surveys Atwood's *The Edible Woman*, *Life Before Man*, and *Upp till ytan*, the Swedish translation of *Surfacing*, in a group review that includes *Puffball* by Fay Weldon and *Problems* by John Updike. Atwood's style is dry, and tends to de-emphasize emotional intensity. Although Nate is convincing in his marital struggles in *Life Before Man*, he is the prototype of an Atwood character: an honorable individual who continues to be confused and who lacks direction and insight into himself and his life.

79 LYNDON, NEIL. "Love Among the Dinosaurs." *Sunday Times* (London), 23 March, p. 42.

Features and critiques *Life Before Man* in a two-book review. For Atwood, humans are mischievous, spiteful apes, and civilization's securities are illusory. All her characters "are Canadian, whatever that means." All are portrayed as aliens, with pointless, ill-paying, or silly jobs; they playfully destroy each other, for want of better activity. At times Atwood's inventiveness and symbols are too much. The narrative machinery is awkward, and the mysteries mostly uninteresting. "However, the emblems of primeval life which inform this domestic story match very well the laborious and clumsy efforts of the characters to outmanoeuvre each other and pierce each other's armour."

80 McCALL, CHERYL. "Canadian Author Margaret Atwood Writes *Life Before Man* and Ponders Life after Success." *People* 13, no. 20 (19 May):69-70.

Profiles Atwood's success, writing, background, and family life on Alliston farm; mentions *Surfacing* film, screen rights to *Life Before Man*, and Atwood's current screenplay for *Lady Oracle*.

81 MacLEAN, SUSAN. "*Lady Oracle*: The Art of Reality and the Reality of Art." *Journal of Canadian Fiction*, nos. 28-29, pp. 179-97.

Finding *Lady Oracle* entertaining but difficult, argues that its comic surface themes conceal the reflexiveness and duplication Eli Mandel 1977.52 has called "'oracular qualities.'" On the surface, *Lady Oracle* satirizes conventional, Gothic-patterned female roles, Canadian literati, and fashionable radical politics. Joan's multiple personality may be seen psychologically, as extreme self-alienation, and a conscious-unconscious fantasy split; and also theatrically, as roles played out. Confusion comes from *Lady Oracle*'s being both a satire and a first-person narrative – and from a deceptive narrator. Duplication, duplicities, doubleness, and projected characters complicate this dizzying mirror world – does life imitate art?

82 McMULLEN, LORRAINE. "The Divided Self." *Atlantis* 5, no. 2 (Spring):53-67.

Traces, in Canadian women's novels, the woman writer's tradition of using two contrasting women characters, one conventional and one unconventional, who represent not projected others but conflicting attitudes within the writer's self. Focuses on Frances Brooke's *The History of Emily Montague*, Sara Jeannette Duncan's

1980

Cousin Cinderella, Atwood's *The Edible Woman*, and Audrey Thomas's *Mrs. Blood*. Both Atwood's conventional Marian and her unconventional Ainsley have problems coping with woman's role; both reverse themselves under stress. Cites Atwood's statements on the conflict between being a woman and being a writer.

83 McNALLY, PAUL. Review of *Life Before Man*. *Queen's Quarterly* 87, no. 2 (Summer):343-45.
    Approves the poignant, wise *Life Before Man*, as an urbane novel of manners that consolidates the considerable talents for social observation and characterization that Atwood's first three novels and her critical book had used somewhat recklessly. *Life*'s three perspectives, one of them male, prove fair-minded. The plot "is the agonizingly gradual emergence of life" in these three regressing, fantasizing characters; the varied symbols and motifs of extinction show how they have chosen to die. Elizabeth is a prototypical emancipated woman, haunted by her two unholy childhoods; and a curiously sympathetic manipulative bitch. Nate's and Quebec's separations are equally anticlimactic and complicated. "But the human capacity to evolve is nevertheless declared": the characters finally take risks, change, and cope.

84 MADDOCKS, MELVIN. "In Defense of the Dinosaur." *Christian Science Monitor*, 14 April, p. 23.
    Refers to the musings of *Life Before Man*'s paleontologist Lesje, and to the mini-dinosaur precursor in Norma Faber's poem, "Theory of Flight," in a column on Dr. Walter Alvarez's recent finding that extraterrestrial iridium, not the dinosaurs' stupidity, caused their extinction.

85 MARSHALL, JOYCE. Review of *Life Before Man*. *Branching Out* 7, no. 1:48-49.
    The Atwood mystique makes it hard to see her books as books; but *Life* simply takes "a cool penetrating look" at particular contemporary people, and their circumstances, in delightfully wry, lucid, funny prose. Neither Atwood's principal male nor female characters are treated with special charity. All three main characters "have highly singular pasts." The reviewer does not feel that Atwood has generalized or, as someone stated, "declared the human male extinct"; ultimately, we mischievous human apes are all we have.

86 MARTEL, REGINALD. "Margaret Atwood: Les talents de la voisine." *Presse* (Montréal), 16 August, p. B3.

Finds *Lady Oracle* extraordinarily rich, but the French translation detestable. The Québécois believe that English Canadian literature is a narrow appendix of American literature. *Lady Oracle* mordantly exposes Atwood's ideas on literary art and genres. *Lady Oracle* can be read as a magnificent eulogy to the lie, or as a reflection of life as a grand ennui enlightened by multiple incarnations.

87 MASSIE, ALLAN. "Marriages End, Novels Begin." *Scotsman* (Edinburgh), 8 March, Weekend sec., p. 3.

Commends highly *Life Before Man*'s contemporary realism and classical virtues, which are neither meretricious nor derivative. The three principal characters are thoroughly realised, imaginatively true, and justly "weighed in the balance and found wanting, and yet acceptable." Elizabeth is "a sort of civilised vampire," Nate "a liberal victim," and Lesje a regressive dreamer. Atwood has the essential Victorian virtue of giving her characters a home, heritage, and biography. Story, dialogue, and characters all suggest further depths and extensions. A three-book review featuring Atwood.

88 MATTHEWS, JOHN. "Canada: Introductory." In *Commonwealth Literature in the Curriculum: A Teaching Guide*. Edited by K.L. Goodwin. St. Lucia: South Pacific Association for Commonwealth Literature and Language Studies, pp. 79-85.

Features Atwood, praising *The Journals of Susanna Moodie* and *Surfacing* highly, as exemplifying settlers' attitudes to the Canadian land, and Canadian traditions. Survival and nature in Canada differ from the U.S. transcendentalism, and from the Wordsworthian return to nature.

89 MAZZARELLA, MERETE. "Om kulturens obehag och naturens demoni" [Culture's unpleasantness and nature's demonism]. *Hufvudstadsbladet* (Helsinki), 27 February, p. 3.

In Finnish. Praises *Upp till ytan* (*Surfacing*), finding it an uncommon *bildungsroman*. Powerful, and almost visionary, the laconically and precisely told story follows a woman's journey to self-knowledge . The heroine, who has become detached from her emotions, returns to the place of her childhood, an environment close to nature. In the wilderness, she relives her past during her search for social, metaphysical, and possibly religious knowledge. The reader experiences her memories, as well as her metamorphosis.

90 MIDDLETON, HARRY. "Woman's Search for Self and a Steady, Reliable Past." *Louisville Courier-Journal*, 17 February. Newsbank 1979-1980, 50:F6-7.

Celebrates the intense, honest, unsentimental *Life Before Man*, which shows the small rips and explosions that underlie everyday details and that define us and our world. Not exactly a feminist, Atwood writes about Canada and women, but focuses on what being a human means and costs. Elizabeth is an overpowering, feral monster, but also a survivor who sees life's evil clearly; we pity and admire her strength. Nate is timid, eviscerated, uncomfortable, and, like all Atwood's men, out-manned by women and by his own softness and decency–qualities which are usually called female. Lesje is gracious and guileless; she manages to be vulnerable and to survive. Atwood gives us "life in flux, life still evolving, still capable of choice and chance," where man is ending–or beginning.

91 MILLER, ALICIA METCALF. "Margaret Atwood Falters in Elaborate Soap Opera." *Plain Dealer* (Cleveland), 24 February, p. C22. Newsbank 1979-1980, 50:F10-11.

Finds *Life Before Man* overembellished, melodramatic, and chilling; some flickers of insight and hope; a troubling, flawed, and disturbing book. We are meant to see Elizabeth's somehow monstrous coldness as a response to her bizarrely cruel childhood. The dreamy, charming Lesje is a drifter who wins only Nate, who isn't much. Yet there are flickering insights into contemporary self-preoccupations; there is Nate's more alive, do-gooder mother; and the three main characters do glimpse something larger at the end.

92 MINER, VALERIE. "Complex Canadian Novel of Three Painful Lives." *San Francisco Sunday Examiner and Chronicle*, 16 March, This World sec., p. 38.

Praises *Life Before Man*'s psychological acuity, political irony, and poetry. As in Margaret Drabble's *The Ice Age*, the separate sections create multiple perspectives and emphasize the characters' isolation. *Survival*'s chapter titles–"The Reluctant Immigrant," "Ice Women vs.

Earth Mothers," and "Futile Heroes, Unconvincing Martyrs and Other Bad Ends" – capsulize *Life*'s indelibly Canadian themes. "Elizabeth, Nate and Lesje all proceed through the darkness with intelligent and humorous resignation, aware that mere survival has been a challenge since life before man."

93 MITCHELL, LEILA G. "The External World in the Novels of Margaret Atwood." *Journal of Canadian Studies* 15, no. 1 (Spring):45-55.

Appreciates Atwood's skillful use of external reality. Clothing and physical appearance define character: in the symbolic *The Edible Woman*, clothes become almost animate; in the political *Surfacing*, clothes stereotype, and convey didactic themes. Clothing in *Lady Oracle* not only defines character, but reveals Joan's inner and gothic visions. Interior places also define the self, particularly in the first novel. Atwood's omnipresent settings lend specifics and verisimilitude to her unreliable narrators' tales. Her Toronto and Quebec wilderness settings create or convey mood, atmosphere, themes, and states of mind. In the most successful novel, *Lady Oracle*, the shifting settings reflect Joan's disintegration, trigger her female memories and associations, and structure the theme of fiction versus reality.

94 MORRISON, BLAKE. "Love among the Fossils." *Observer* (London), 16 March, p. 39.

Describes *Life Before Man*, in a four-book review. Lesje's Sleeping Beauty discovery of love would have been triumphant in D.H. Lawrence; in Atwood it's ambivalent, for love is painful, messy, and complicated. *Life Before Man* is strongly Canadian, not only in the contemporary details, but principally in "the ecology-conscious central metaphor, with its typically Canadian nostalgia for an uncorrupted, pre-human" nature. Atwood's sharp insights prevent the heavy symbols from overwhelming the middle-class material.

95 MORSE, SUSAN. "Complex Emotion Made Simple." *Detroit Free Press*, 23 March, p. B6.

Praises *Life Before Man*'s terse, rich sentences, uncannily acute insights into fleeting thoughts and complex emotions, and the integrity and spareness of its plot. After a violent act disrupts the lives of Elizabeth, Nate, and Lesje, "their time-honored rationalizations, deceptions, and accommodations no longer work," and each must adapt, slowly and painfully. Atwood's distinct style, which can "coldly fix a sensation," is exemplified in the startling comparison of copulating with William to sleeping with a "'fairly active slab of Philadelphia cream cheese . . . '"

96 NEWMAN, RICHARD. "'Bristling' in Margaret Atwood's Style: This TV Show Makes the 'Commonplace Vibrate.'" *London* (Ontario) *Free Press TV Times*, 5 December, pp. 40-41.

Describes the Atwood-Peter Pearson collaboration that created the incredibly well-performed, vibrant *Snowbird* for CBC TV's For the Record. Pearson met an "over-80-year-old former Ontario school inspector" who summered in Canadian parks and wintered in California and Florida, got the story approved, and gave the outline to researcher Carlin Moulton. Atwood, who is Pearson's childhood friend and Alliston neighbor, agreed to do the screenplay. "'The show is more than 90 per cent Atwood's,'" says Pearson, who will work with her on "Heaven on Earth," based on Kenneth Bagnall's book.

97 "Notes on Current Books." *Virginia Quarterly Review* 56, no. 3 (Summer):108-9.

Briefly praises *Life Before Man* as Atwood's best work, and more artistry than feminist ideology; "her highly polished portraits of the two ladies . . . address our primal sympathies."

98 OUELLETTE-MICHALSKA, MADELEINE. "Dépoussierer la vie." *Châtelaine* (French ed.) 21, no. 12 (December):32.

Briefly discusses, in a group review, the French publication of *Lady Oracle*. The most original voices in English Canada and Quebec come from women writers. Atwood's Canadians, portrayed as spouse, skimpy intellectual, and functionary parvenu, are triple minorities striving for liberation.

99 ____. "Margaret Atwood: De l'ignorance des puissants." *Devoir* (Montréal), 28 June, pp. 13-14.

Interviews Atwood at Helene Holden's house shortly after the publication of *Life Before Man*. Atwood discusses the current referendum in Quebec; anti-Americanism versus anti-imperialism; the change in her position since *Survival*; Canada as a garrison society or colony; the struggles for power and the end of feminism; her acceptance by Americans in spite of her criticism of them; and humor as a way to counter fatality.

100 PERRY, RICHARD A. Review of *To See Our World*. *Quill and Quire* 46, no. 1 (January):28.

Rejects this commercially inflated production of Catherine M. Young's middling, calendar photographs and Atwood's brief, vapid introduction.

101 PERSKY, STAN. "*Life Before Man*." *Canadian Dimension* 14, no. 6 (May):47-48.

A two-book review of *Life Before Man* versus Richard Rohmer's *Balls!* that reluctantly finds the methodically jabbing, "bionic vision" Atwood still the number one CanLit champion. *Life*'s people are the Torontonians you've met at parties; they're not lovable, or interesting, or sexy, except for the one delicious cream cheese moment. Unlike Margaret Drabble's *The Ice Age*, politics provides no rescuing analysis, just more alienation. *Life*'s "sole redeeming feature" is Atwood's spare, unsentimental, competent prose; but Rohmer has bigger faults.

102 POLLITT, KATHA. "Margaret Atwood Finally Surfaces as a Major Novelist." *Ms.* 8, no. 9 (March):27, 29.

Acclaims *Life Before Man*, over the poetic and mythicized modern classic, *Surfacing*, and the two humorous novels with their stock figures. Poets are rarely equally good at fiction: but in *Life Before Man* Atwood gives us three complex, subtle, rounded characters; a shifting viewpoint that achieves a 19th-century largeness of sympathy; and a melancholy, powerful, adult tragedy—not of oppressive sex roles, but of the human condition.

103 PRATT, COLIN. "Letters: Atwood and the Reviewers." *Saturday Night* 95, no. 6 (July-August):11.

Protests Fulford 1980.42. Canadians do not fear excellence: the writer, who reads widely, "found *Life Before Man* hard to read, disjointed, rambling," and puzzling. The average—not the artsy—reader wants what *Life* lacks: a plot line you can follow, and a character "you can sympathize or at least identify with."

1980

104 PRESCOTT, PETER S. "Three Human Flies Caught in a Web."
Newsweek 95, no. 7 (18 February):108.

Appreciates *Life Before Man* as Atwood's web. Her work refines
the Canadian traditions of survival and failure she identified. *Life*
shows that becoming one's own woman is lonely and not always
satisfactory. "With chilly compassion and an even colder wit, Atwood
exposes the interior lives of her specimens: three flies writhing in a
web, or perhaps trying to free their wings from amber." As her insect
imagery hums, "we get to know her victims well:" the rather admirable
Elizabeth, who unwittingly imitates her malevolent aunt to gain
control; the curator Lesje; and the immature Nate, who is, like all
Atwood's men, ineffective. "Their anteriority [in the title] is precisely
man's condition."

105 PRITCHARD, WILLIAM H. "Fictional Fixes." *Hudson Review* 33, no.
2 (Summer):259-61.

Finds faults, and some talent, in *Life Before Man*; a group review.
Life's title and prehistory are puzzling. Atwood is "a better poet in her
novels than in her poems," as the vigorous satire of the creamcheese
and jumping beans paragraph shows. The rather nasty Elizabeth is the
most interesting character; Nate is sadder and more appealing. Atwood
artfully alternates the sardonic and the pathetic; well, maybe life is like
that; but the restive reviewer yearns for some change. He is troubled
that these "'educated,'" self-preoccupied people are so dismally
controlled by this very talented writer's hopeless, inflexible vision.

106 QUIGLY, ISABEL. "Bicycle Made for Two." *Financial Times*
(London), 22 March, p. 12.

Praises *Life Before Man* highly, in a three-book review: though
Life sounds like [Margaret] Drabble country, these ordinary,
recognisable, middling people and their situations are seen with an
extraordinary imagination, "[w]itty, lightfooted, realistic yet with
shooting insights" into personality and love. Nate, bicycling between
home and mistress, is wryly half-comic, but there is also "a great flow
of feeling, a sense of the tidal nature of love, need, familiarity: nothing
ordinary about it. Margaret Atwood is a poet and so something of a
seer."

107 REDMOND, JOHN. "Shrapnel of Exploding Marriages." *Glasgow Herald*, 5 April, p. 9.

Praises *Life Before Man*, in a six-book review, as "a complex, evocative, associative novel" whose subtlety is "functional – as in evolution. . . . How do we – as a species and as individuals – get to be what we are?" Who wouldn't yearn for the unlikely China of the "impossibly innocent Maoist paintings," as Elizabeth does?

108 REEVES, JOHN. "John Reeves' Literary Portraits." *Canadian Fiction Magazine*, nos. 34-35, pp. [71-72].

Photographs and briefly describes Canadian literary figures; photograph of Atwood, page 71; description of her "astonishingly opalescent skin," that the camera loves, page 72.

109 Review of *Life Before Man*. *Booklist* 76, no. 12 (15 February):813.

Finds *Life Before Man* a credible, hard-hitting novel about the consequences of a married woman's liberation. The museum is a metaphoric mirror of the characters' desiccated lives. The powerfully developed, "mid-life changeling" Elizabeth subjects the tentative others to her new self. Atwood's concise language "artfully captures states of mind," and her very subtle point of view may applaud or mock the changes that have freed some women emotionally.

110 Review of *Life Before Man*. *Choice* 17, no. 3 (May):383.

"*Life Before Man* is a powerful, introspective view of contemporary marriage and the changing roles of the sexes" that incorporates the themes of Atwood's three earlier novels, and transcends the nationalism of her survival and identity book of thematic criticism. Atwood's prehistorically rooted novel makes us "confront a harrowing present that anticipates an ecologically" doomed future; generally recommended.

111 RHETTS, JOANN. "People, Imagery Usurp Corners of Your Mind." *Charlotte Observer*, 24 February, p. F6.

Finds *Life Before Man* chilling, like Canada, and beautiful. Atwood meticulously, heartlessly dissects a triangle of two women and one man. You want warmth and heart – yet Atwood's laser craft imprints her characters and images in you. Both Elizabeth and Lesje are dark-haired, self-sufficient, and almost raped. Only Lesje is fertile.

1980

Atwood fishes through the ice to see what keeps the fish hearts – especially those of the Amazonian mother fish fertilized by the then-superfluous daddy fish – alive in winter. "Her interest is cool, and her question is Lesje's:" does she care if the human race survives or not?

112 ROCARD, MARCIENNE. "La femme object-de-consommation dans *The Edible Woman* de Margaret Atwood." *Caliban* (Toulouse), no. 17, pp. 111-20.

    The Edible Woman poses, less systematically than *Surfacing*, the problems of woman's alienation and her struggle for physical and moral survival. Woman is fixed as object by man, who is the absolute subject. All the women characters are presented as objects [to be] consumed by others, or, like Marian, in the process of being consumed. *The Edible Woman* shows the consequences of postulated phallicism in professional, public, and matrimonial situations in a society where woman has become cheap merchandise. Atwood revolts against the mythic image of women and the Freudian heritage of feminine passivity.

113 ROSE, DAN A. "Feminist Writer's Passionate Vision of Love and Loss." *Providence Journal*, 9 March. Newsbank 1979-1980, 68:D9.

    Praises *Life Before Man*'s dense, confident characterization; and its passionate, charged, transforming vision of life, which leavens the characters' melodramatic miseries. But Atwood should not cheapen her power with simple-minded sex politics, as in the two buffoonish pseudo-rapes.

114 ROSS, CATHERINE SHELDRICK. "'Banished to This Other Place': Atwood's *Lady Oracle*." *English Studies in Canada* 6, no. 4 (Winter):460-74.

    Like Atwood's poetry, her farcical, *tour de force* parody of romance, *Lady Oracle*, shows us two separate worlds, of shifting, metamorphosizing life and of ritualized art. This shore has "caterpillars, pain, and change"; the Other Shore has "winged butterflies, happy endings, and art" – and shadowy death. Joan's movie heroines must choose between art and love, like Tennyson's Lady of Shalott; Joan splits herself to have both. As in Atwood's first two novels, an Alice-like heroine descends, seeking a treasure that is her own identity. The chief irony is that Joan both wants romance, and knows better. The realistically unresolved end, which parallels Joan's fantasy-confused meeting with Arthur, has "all the elements of the Nurse Story" romance.

115 ____. "Nancy Drew as Shaman: Atwood's *Surfacing*." *Canadian Literature*, no. 84 (Spring), pp. 7-17.
    Discusses *Surfacing*'s quest for a healing ritual. *Surfacing* is also a detective story and a ghost story, and ironically invokes *True Romances*, fairy tales, and grail legends. Because the narrator is an artist figure, her quest represents Canada's quest. The ritual of Christianity fails her. The ritual of Americanization kills, and brings the evil grail of the abortion. The third ritual, of Indian shamanism, succeeds. Atwood uses Mircea Eliade's shamanic dismemberment, identification of man with animals, multi-level universe, soul-boat, secret language, and journey to the underworld. Like Joseph Campbell's *The Hero with a Thousand Faces*, the hero must return to society; and confront, as Canada must, the advancing American technology.

116 RUBENSTEIN, ROBERTA. "Lively Artifacts in a Museum." *Chicago Tribune*, 3 February, sec. 7, p. 1.
    Appreciates Atwood's unique literary territory, and *Life Before Man*'s splendidly mixed irony, humor, and realism. Elizabeth is both vulnerable and callous; her Auntie Muriel is comic, wicked, and unforgettable. Lesje is the most intriguing member of the peculiar sexual triangle. Atwood's convincing, if not likable, characters survive in an uneven, unpredictable contemporary emotional landscape of strong women, weak men, and unclear assumptions. The verve is not in the plot, but in the interwoven telling, deadly accurate satire, and masterful understatement, which move flawlessly between wit and pathos.

117 RUMLEY, LARRY. "Toronto Is the Setting for This Novel of Subdued Optimism." *Seattle Times*, 6 April, Magazine sec., p. 13.
    Interviews Atwood in Seattle, and reviews *Life Before Man*: Atwood insists on her optimism and *Life*'s optimistically-modified realism; the reviewer is impressed most with *Life*'s subtle psychological insight. "We recognize these people – perhaps ourselves in varying

degrees–as quite normal people trying to cope with realistic situations."

118 SAGE, LORNA. "The Glacier in the Cupboard." *TLS*, 14 March, p. 289.

Finds *Life Before Man* both "spacious and narrow," and links that to Atwood's being Canadian, feminist, and a poet. Her characters imitate life; "the more plausible (representative) her people are, the more cardboard and crazy they become." Their implausibilities–such as Lesje's and Elizabeth's museum jobs–"turn out to have depth." The non-human images are a witty conceit. Are the men equal here? The title implies a feminist "Before Man–and After," but *Life* is not the feminist Utopia Atwood needs to "'make it solid.'"

119 SALUTIN, RICK. "The Culture Vulture: Chomsky, Atwood, and a Political Analysis of the Maple Leafs." *This Magazine* 14, no. 2 (March):31-32.

Suggests, in the Atwood portion of this article, that reviewers have misread *Life Before Man*, by finding it depressing and non-political, as in the attentive Solecki 1979.91 review. Atwood's triangle does create the tension of good soap operas, and its politics do seem peripheral, compared to *Surfacing* and *Lady Oracle*. But *Life*'s characters' bleak prospects of fulfillment are realistic for this group, in this society. Sly references to other social contexts–the Parti Québécois, protests against the War Measures Act, and the final New China exhibit–suggest that the character's existing social horizon is the problem. The only character who moves from suffering to relative satisfaction gets involved in a women's half-way house. *Life* goes beyond the sentimental "'independence'" of recent women's fiction; it "is resolutely political" and implicitly, persistently hopeful. The title suggests that human beings have not yet evolved into what they might become: consider Marx's statement that "'we are living in the prehistory of Mankind'"; and *Life*'s original title, which was *Notes from the Mesozoic*," which was a middle period in the evolution of life–that's optimism.

120 SCHAPIRO, NANCY. "Thin-Shelled Lives." *St. Louis Post-Dispatch*, 20 January, p. C4. Newsbank 1979-1980, 50:F9.

Appreciates *Life Before Man*, whose major themes and metaphors begin in its two epigraphs from Kurten and Terz. Atwood presents her three uprooted, alienated, past-damaged characters as if they were exhibits in a museum. All three are vulnerable, thin-shelled, like the last of the dinosaurs' eggs. Atwood brings us news of our "post-feminist, post-monogamous, post-traditional society. We are in danger of extinction, she warns"; and yet, as long as there are survivors, children, caring, and memory, there is hope.

121 SCOTT, GAIL. "Ontario Gothic." [Title in English.] *Spirale* (Montréal), no. 10 (June), pp. 1, 4.

In French. Atwood takes few risks in the regressive, cynical, but well written *Life Before Man*. The convincing characters live their lives like museum pieces, trapped in the bleakly portrayed Ontario city. Elizabeth is austere; Nate's sympathies for the future of Quebec make him more human; Lesje is only comfortable among the museum artifacts. The title, *Life Before Man*, refers to the deadly effect of patriarchy on English Canadian society.

122 SHAPCOTT, TOM. "Margaret Atwood's *Surfacing*." *Commonwealth Literature in The Curriculum: A Teaching Guide*. Edited by K.L. Goodwin. St. Lucia: South Pacific Association for Commonwealth Literature and Language Studies, pp. 86-96.

Praises Atwood's superb *Surfacing* highly, for its aphorisms, discoveries, and final responsibility. Its powerful feminist rejection of women's social conditioning is also a statement of Canadian social conditioning, under the masculine American eagle. Suggests a comparison of Canadian and Australian identity, and of rites of passage in *Surfacing* and in Les Murray's *The Boys Who Stole the Funeral*.

123 SLOPEN, BEVERLEY. "Sisterhood Celebrated in Poetry and Politics . . . the Ghost of Quotations Past . . . and Women against Virginity." *Quill and Quire* 46, no. 4 (April):26.

Prints, in the first section of this article, a feminist friend's report of the recent Atwood and Marge Piercy Writers in Dialogue reading at the Ontario Institute for Studies in Education; contrasts Piercy's American, intellectual polemic to Atwood's Canadian, otherworldly

1980

poetry; mentions Piercy's *Vida* and *The Moon Is Always Female*, and Atwood's Amnesty International and motherhood poems.

124 SMITH, MARY AINSLIE. "Feeding the Cubs." *Books in Canada* 9, no. 10 (December):18.

Briefly praises *Anna's Pet*, by Atwood and Jo[yce] Barkhouse, in a round-up review of children's books, many by established "literary lionesses."

125 SNITOW, ANN BARR. "The Front Line: Notes on Sex in Novels by Women, 1969-1979." *Signs* 5, no. 4 (Summer):702-18 passim.

A general discussion that briefly includes *Surfacing*, with its sexism and its matriarchal goddess cult conception, as a germinal and visionary book – atavistic and yet promising human evolution. *Surfacing* "sacrifices sexual pleasure to motherhood as the more profound experience and source of sexual identity."

126 SPRIET, PIERRE. "L'homme de *Lady Oracle*." *Études canadiennes* (Talence), no. 9, pp. 63-73.

Countering the literary tradition of stories structured around men, *Lady Oracle*'s male characters exist only in relation to women. Man is deemed the omniscient narrator, playing the passive and restrictive role of mirror, simultaneously reflecting and telling the heroine what she must be. *Lady Oracle* meticulously describes a woman who looks for her identity by attaching herself to a series of men, each one as contradictory as the fragments of her self. Atwood's feminism is uniquely intellectual, an axiologic system that accepts weakness and finds strength in awareness and knowledge. *Lady Oracle* is not a call for hope or despair for women, but rather a tale of irony. Man is imprisoned in his personage, never given the power to laugh at himself, and thus lacks the freedom of knowledge possible for women.

127 ____. "Margaret Atwood et la condition de l'écrivain au Canada: Réflexions d'un témoin privilégié." In *Séminaires 1979*. Edited by Jean Beranger, Jean Cazemajou, and Pierre Spriet. Annales du Centre de Recherches sur l'Amérique Anglophone, n.s., no. 5. Talence: Centre de Recherches sur l'Amérique Anglophone, [Université de Bordeaux III], pp. 131-40.

Provides excerpts from and comments on Atwood's talk on the Canadian literary revolution, at the Center for Canadian Studies, University of Bordeaux III, on 20 February 1979. Atwood outlined three stages in the progress of Canadian literature: the "desert" before 1960, caused by the colonial mentality of the culture; the "explosion" between 1960 and 1970, when she was developing as an author and the small publishing houses were getting established; and the "present," which is still precarious, but basically better for writers, now that Canadians are reading Canadian novels and poetry. Emphasizes that Atwood focused on English-Canadian and Quebec attitudes and national identity, rather than socio-economic structures.

128 STEWART, IAN. "Recent Fiction." *Illustrated London News* 268 (June):103.
   Briefly describes *Life Before Man*, in a four-book review: the author's remorseless probing shows us her characters' disturbing self-discoveries; there are "many arresting perceptions of the fragility of human life."

129 STONE, LAURIE. "Dinosaur Dance." *Village Voice*, 7 January, p. 32.
   Dislikes *Life Before Man*'s pitiless theme, stereotyped characters, and too-clever literary games; but finds it sometimes moving and powerful. Though the knowledge of human extinction is almost unbearably nauseating, these characters obsess about it, and Atwood keeps satirizing small-scale extinctions and failures. Her narrator parodies, and speaks for, the dissimulating characters. *Life Before Man* is like a theme-heavy, too-precious poem where nothing happens. Still, there are insights and fine ironies, and the meditations on extinction and survival deepen, page by page; and her danse macabre of dinosaurs can be powerful. Excerpted: 1980.51; 1985.11.

130 STROMBERG, KYRA. "Verlassenheit breitet sich aus . . . ."
   Suddeutsche Zeitung (Munich), 8 October, Buch und Zeit sec., p. 9.
   Describes *Die Unmöglichkeit der Nähe* (*Life Before Man*) as a story of a love triangle that exists within daily struggles. The primitive world and the involvement of a pregnancy are two themes that closely parallel *Surfacing*. Atwood uses objective observation and humor without being indulgent. *Life*'s title is freely, but fittingly, translated as

"the impossibility of closeness." The translator, Werner Waldhoff, has maintained Atwood's fearless and vigorous language.

131 STUEWE, PAUL. "On the Racks." *Books in Canada* 9, no. 10 (December):28.
Features and briefly waxes ecstatic over Atwood's brilliant, fascinating, impeccable, sensitive *Life Before Man* – it's a shame that many reviewers haven't caught up to Atwood's exhilaratingly open new fiction.

132 STUMPF, EDNA. "With Remarkable Clarity, a Writer Sees How We Live." *Philadelphia Inquirer*, 3 February, p. L10. Newsbank 1979-1980, 50:F12.
Praises *Life Before Man*: Atwood sees people "with a crucial hallucinatory sharpness" – the sad and powerful Elizabeth, the beginner Lesje, the reluctantly shifting Nate; none is expendable. Of course there is no life before, or after man; the best women novelists – Atwood, Margaret Drabble, and Anne Tyler – write of life during man, showing us the pain and pleasure of our lives.

133 TANNER, STEPHEN L. "Those Tedious Extremist Victories." *Chronicles of Culture* 4, no. 4 (July-August):13-14.
Condemns the modern tradition of *Life Before Man* as "cynical and pessimistic in a way that makes it irrelevant for most readers." The plot is a hexagon. "Nothing works out well for anybody. . . . The dominant influence in each case is feminine. . . . Elizabeth seems to represent the liberated woman. . . . Nate is the liberated man, the uxorious man" that feminism creates and then finds disappointing. Sexual intercourse is never performed for genuine, responsible, procreating love. There are no satisfactory man-woman relationships. Feminism, activism, and nationalism are brought up to be discredited – even though Atwood is a leading nationalist and feminist. Perhaps *Life* shows the empty victory of extreme feminism.

134 TAYLOR, MICHAEL. Review of *Life Before Man. Fiddlehead*, no. 124 (Winter), pp. 111-12.
Has difficulty getting interested in the three main characters, partly because of "Atwood's deliberately laconic style, where ironic, undercutting after-thoughts . . . sap the strength of the sentences and

the characters"; finds the significance of the prehistoric landscapes elusive, for *Life* is "squarely about the large failures and small successes" of men/women relationships. "Although the book is not hostage to a single female character, the two women, Elizabeth and Lesje, absorb more than two thirds of our interest and combine to suck Nate's vestigial life-blood as he hovers unhappily between his two establishments." Atwood's first three novels are "dominated by their women narrators," who are beleaguered by predatory men and mothers and awful friends; but Atwood "is less tactful than Alice Munro in manipulating our sympathies for these harassed women."

135 TIMLECK, FRANCES. Review of *Life Before Man*. *Quarry* 29, no. 1 (Winter):90-92.

Rejects *Life Before Man* as spoiled, because the critical rod has been spared too long for "Canadian literature's favourite child." Finds the characters dull – Elizabeth is a melodramatic monster, Lesje dense, Nate irredeemably dim; the plot pre-dinosaur; the journal entries simplistic; the present tense shallow; the pace "all-too laconic" and indifferent. The pernicious, unsinkable Auntie Muriel is Atwood's metaphor of heartless Toronto the good – but "where there should be a heart [in Atwood's four novels] there is only some clever variation on Auntie Muriel."

136 TOTH, SUSAN ALLEN. "Skilled Authors Fail to Keep Reader's Attention." *Minneapolis Tribune*, 6 April. Newsbank 1979-1980, 68:D6-7.

Weary of contemporary novels, the reviewer praises the compelling backgrounds of *Life Before Man* and of Shirley Hazzard's *The Transit of Venus* over their foregrounds of human miseries; is particularly drawn to Lesje's prehistoric fantasies and her memories of her Lithuanian grandmother. Praises *Life Before Man* over Atwood's earlier novels. Its three characters are explored in detail, without blame, as they try to love. Atwood shows us as doomed, self-defeating, and selfish. Elizabeth's clear, cutting mind is meant to redeem her, but the reviewer prefers Lesje's dinosaurs.

137 TULLY, JACQI. "Atwood Draws Reader into Three Chaotic Lives." *Arizona Daily Star* (Tucson), 11 May. Newsbank 1979-1980, 68:D4.

1980

Praises *Life Before Man* as "the chilly, engrossing tale of three people struggling to clarify the profound chaos of their lives. It is a strange, oddly compelling book" of increasingly interesting characters and acute alienation. Though *Life* reaches no major conclusions, it illuminates our often unpredictable, jarring lives.

138 TYLER, ANNE. "Pale People, but Rich, Cosmic Dreams." *Detroit News*, 17 February, p. C2.

Gives mixed praise to *Life Before Man*, whose strongest passages are in its characters' [Elizabeth's and Lesje's] unpopulated, eerily silent dream worlds. Like the unforgettable *Surfacing*, *Life* "finds animals purer than humans, jungle more comprehensible than civilization." Atwood may be above all a poet, but her ordinary, sometimes shallow characters "seem too slight to bear the weight of their dream lives." Elizabeth's dismissal of her lover is the event that sets the spreading-ripple plot in motion. Because "there's no one here we can truly like, . . . it's difficult to sink into the story. . . . *Life Before Man* does nothing to lessen [Atwood's] reputation, but this time the miracles" are in the cosmic periphery, not in the story.

139 WATTS, JANET. "Pain on Ice." *Observer* (London), 23 March, p. 56.

Interviews Atwood in March in London, finding her impeccably reasonable, uncompromising, unassuming, and disconcerting. Quotes Atwood on biographical criticism; art; the Kafka "'fist hammering on the skull'" talisman that belongs to [Graeme] Gibson (see 1979.68); *Life Before Man*'s bleakness and pain as realistic; Auntie Muriel as *Life*'s only character based on a real person; and glee in writing well, even about pain.

140 WEIGEL, JOHN A. "Anxiety Is Common in Battle of Sexes, Life." *Atlanta Journal*, 2 March. Newsbank 1979-1980, 68:D5.

Gives *Life Before Man* scholarly praise: like the Greek dramatists, Atwood comforts us by projecting life's evils, irresolution, and entropy; and reminds us that intelligent, well-intentioned women and men are still worried and baffled by reality. We may still be in prehistory, awakening from the nightmares of recent history and the menacing future. Elizabeth, who is the strongest of the three fully revealed characters, gallantly imitates the civilized roles as she "struggles to survive her intelligence." Nate is decent, but indifferent, and helpless. Lesje has the best lines, when she wonders if her pregnancy has blown it: perhaps Atwood shows us here that courage means not mourning our mistakes.

141 WEIR, LORRAINE. "Echo Poems." *Canadian Literature*, no. 86 (Autumn), pp. 118-19.

Praises *Two-Headed Poems* as a significant development in Atwood's style and themes. The political Canadian-American title poems present a rationale for the others. Echoing Simone de Beauvoir, Atwood stresses woman as "always Other," operating within a frame that is not hers, creating her own oral history, becoming "perforce bilingual and bicultural." "Marrying the Hangman" evokes the two kinds of history, official versus oral. In "Daybooks I and II," banal tasks contrast with a growth in understanding. In the echo poems, a woman's fears, of her duplicitous heart or of the emptiness of words, evolve into wry acceptance of assertion of the claims words make. "And the metaphor of twins, doubling, duplicity, finally becomes the metonymy of woman's experience . . . and of her kinship with the land."

142 [WHITEN, CLIFTON.] "*PCR* Interview with Margaret Atwood." *Poetry Canada Review* 1, no. 4 (Spring):8, 10.

Cover story: Atwood discusses writing poetry and prose, present tense and comma splices, *Life Before Man*, Canadian attitudes to writers, prizes, and human creativity; finds some questions naive or erroneous.

143 WIEHE, JANET. "Victimization and Survival." *Library Journal* 105, no. 2 (15 January):223.

Recommends *Life Before Man*; as the title suggests, paleontology informs this accomplished story of entangled contemporary relationships. Characters are revealed "through rich juxtaposition of cultures, roles, and events." Victimization and survival are strikingly explored.

144 WIELAND, JAMES. "'Where the Raw of Feelings Exist' [sic]: Moving Images in Recent Canadian Poetry." *CRNLE Reviews Journal*, no. 1 (May), pp. 3-6, 9.

Appreciates *Two-Headed Poems*, in a review of three single collections and Geddes and Bruce's [1978.29] anthology: Atwood's reality, like Patrick Lane's, Michael Ondaatje's, and others discussed here, is "human-kind at bedrock." Like her earlier *You Are Happy*, *Two-Headed Poems* places us in the "contemporary ice age" she sees; but now more than before she catches the moment's complexities and "tak[es] her characters to the edge of being. And sometimes in the struggle there is a kind of subdued joy." The title sequence mirrors political tensions in word manipulations. "Solstice Poem" is bedrock familial reality, a winter world of little hope. Self and state, present and history, merge, as in "Four Small Elegies" and "The Bus to Alliston, Ontario"; Atwood sees infinite ambiguity, but no certainties.

145 WIMSATT, MARGARET. Review of *Life Before Man*. *America* 142, no. 25 (28 June):545-46.
Recognizes the Toronto settings of this middle-class, middle-American novel; complains of Atwood's usual useless men and harpy-victim women, and the super-constructed, "irritating little triads" of Day, Date, and Speaker; yet does not willingly close the book, because Atwood the poet "invests each scene with strong life."

146 WOLCOTT, JAMES. "Some Fun!" *New York Review of Books* 27, no. 5 (3 April):34-35.
Rejects, in a two-book review, *Life Before Man*'s existential sulk: there's no joy; politics are futile; sex is mostly rape, and cream cheese; mankind is lumbering like the dinosaurs into extinction, or is merely a molecule in time. *Life* is like a Bergmanesque movie; its "'nevertheless'" echoes Beckett's "'*I can't go on, I'll go on*'"–what fun! The reviewer admired *Surfacing* and especially *Lady Oracle*, but can't stomach Atwood's brittle contempt for *Life*'s stunted characters.

147 WOO, ELAINE. "Margaret Atwood's *Life Before Man* and as a Writer."[sic] *Los Angeles Herald Examiner*, 3 March, pp. B1, 5. Newsbank 1979-1980, C14, D1.
Interviews Atwood, with agent Phoebe Larmore, in Beverly Hills: Atwood cites Simone de Beauvoir on the difficulties of an open marriage relationship; tells the story of her home economics opera [*Synthesia*] on synthetics, starring Sir William Woolly, whose tragic flaw was that "'he shrank from washing'"; and discusses writing, her scientific training in observing particular forms, her current works in progress, human imperfection, and life's lack of resolution, until death.

148 WOODCOCK, GEORGE. "Margaret Atwood: Poet as Novelist." In *The World of Canadian Writing: Critiques and Recollections*. Vancouver: Douglas & McIntyre; Seattle: University of Washington Press, pp. 149-73.

Part I reprints 1975.52; Part II reviews Atwood's four subsequent books. Atwood is a major novelist and poet, but only a minor short story writer in Canada. Many of the *Dancing Girls* stories could be better handled in Atwood's laconic verse, or in her novels, or as memoirs. *Lady Oracle*, with its recognizable Toronto literati, accurately satirizes both bohemian and philistine Canadian bourgeois life; its sustained, uninhibited comedy raises Atwood's themes of the divided personality and of abrasive man-woman relationships to a higher level, and removes any doubt of her abilities as a novelist. *You Are Happy* balances the mythological against the actual, the Circean transformations against the scarred present and its poetry of endurance. *Two-Headed Poems*, written after four years of literary success, personal happiness, and the birth of a loved young daughter, is closer to the actualities of daily life. The concrete, suggestive country "Daybooks I and II," and the final lines to the poet's daughter, go beyond tenacity to a higher recognition of human, universal realities. Part II is revised: 1983.147.

149 _____. "Victor – or Victim." *Canadian Literature*, no. 86 (Autumn), pp. 136-38.

Is disturbed by the flamboyant marketing of the deliberately modest *Life Before Man*; applies to *Life* Oscar Wilde's critique of Henry James: "'James writes fiction as if it were a painful duty, and wastes upon mean motives and imperceptible "points of view" his neat literary style, his felicitous phrases, his swift and caustic satire.'" Discusses *Life*'s dutiful ascetism, its diminished fantasy elements, and its characters' confused, territorially compelled, passionless, sentimental, and nearly instinctual thoughts. *Life* has all the virtues Wilde attributed to James; but it is "essentially anti-novelistic" for it rejects, with a quiet rigour like Camus's, the novel's traditional assumption that men's and women's lives have values worth cherishing.

150 WORDSWORTH, CHRISTOPHER. "A Man's a Man." *Guardian* (Manchester), 30 March, p. 21.

Deals with *Life Before Man* most briefly, in a four-book review: finds a poet's telling, quelling phrases; an odd museum setting; and

1980

precisely impaled, dissected characters. Prefers Taba Ubaldo Ribeira's *Sergeant Getulo*.

1981

1 ABLEY, MARK. "Bitter Wisdom of Moral Concern: Atwood, Purdy, and Layton Offer Tough Poetry for Hard Times." *Maclean's* 94, no. 13 (30 March):52-53.

    Features *True Stories*, which is centered on the "Notes Towards a Poem That Can Never Be Written" sequence, in a review of five Canadian poets (Phyllis Webb and Patrick Lane are also included). Atwood does not flinch from present-day torture or past evils; perhaps the bitterest wisdom is in ["Trainride, Vienna-Bonn"]. Finds brilliant fluency, cool sardonic intelligence, and an abrasiveness subdued by tenderness. "Because it is blooded by political commitment, *True Stories* may not be" immediately appealing, but it's among Atwood's best. Excerpted: 1983.129.

2 ADACHI, KEN. "Atwood on Bodily Harm: 'It Isn't Autobiographical.'" *Toronto Star*, 27 September, p. F17.

    Interviews Atwood in Toronto, and praises the just-published *Bodily Harm* highly. Atwood discusses reviews, journalists, and Amnesty International; and *Bodily Harm*'s Rennie, pornographic film, sources, and breast cancer, citing the Australian poet, Jennifer Rankin, who died of breast cancer, Susan Sontag, and Ann Landers. The powerful, polished, enigmatic *Bodily Harm* is Atwood's best novel yet; it has her familiar themes and humour, but the evil that used to be off-stage has pounced. *Bodily Harm* is the prose version of the harrowing "Notes Towards a Poem That Can Never Be Written" poems.

3 BAER, ELIZABETH. "'The Pilgrimage Inward': The Quest Motif in the Fiction of Margaret Atwood, Doris Lessing, and Jean Rhys." Ph.D. dissertation, Indiana University, 177 pp.

    Explores the female quest in contemporary women's literature, focusing on *Surfacing*, Doris Lessing's *The Summer Before the Dark*, and Jean Rhys's *Wide Sargasso Sea*. Influenced by their childhood reading, all three writers create a fairly realistic surface text and a counteracting subtext of dream or imagery. These dual texts fuse the novel's realism with the fairy tale's romance, and integrate the rational with the irrational, which is the quester's goal. Female quests create new paradigms that differ from male quests. See 1988.2; *Dissertation Abstracts International* 42 (1982):3606A.

4 BAGNALL, JANET. "Atwood: A Spotlight on Reality." *Gazette* (Montreal), 9 October, p. 33.

Interviews Atwood, who is in Montreal to promote *Bodily Harm*. Atwood comments on its bleakness versus realism; its attractive male characters, including Dr. Minnow; male interviewers; and the unselfconscious creative process.

5 BARTON, JOHN. "Victims, Saints, and Angels." *From an Island* (Victoria, B.C.) 13, no. 1 (Spring):81-84.

Acclaims Atwood's Zolaesque authenticity in a review of *True Stories* and *Wilson's Bowl*, by Phyllis Webb: Atwood prevails on us to look beyond our comforts, and to bear witness. All these poems of social and ecological disaster, political corruption, repression, dissent, love, and poetry show that the undeniable facts behind issues "do not add up to what we imagine the true story to be." Because Atwood challenges herself and us, "*True Stories* is moving and often terrifying," as in "Torture," where she makes us consider our complicity, and question our innocence and passivity. "Christmas Carols" and other poems "are iron fists beating down the walls of the West's complaisance about human rights"; Atwood's anger and commitment are rooted in her passionate, familial love poems; her best work may be yet to come. "Notes Towards a Poem That Can Never Be Written" is unequalled in the astute *True Stories*.

6 BASTIAN, D.G. "Life since Atwood." *Vic Report* 10, no. 1 (Fall):8, 10-12.

Interviews Atwood in Toronto, before *Bodily Harm*, which Atwood "'started on May 23, 1980,'" and finished spring 1981, appears: Atwood discusses images of writers, the Canadian poetry scene of her high school and college years; realism and humour in *Life Before Man*; and creativity versus professionalism in simple and technologically complex societies. Atwood describes herself as a silent Victoria College student, but active all-round, in drama, *Acta Victoriana*, the Bob Revue, and the Debating Club.

7 BECKMAN, SUSAN. "Language as Cultural Identity in Achebe, Ihimaera, Laurence, and Atwood." *World Literature Written in English* 20, no. 1 (Spring):117-34.

Begins with *Surfacing*'s "'A language is everything you do'"; ends by discussing the postmodern *Surfacing*, where "the imperialism of American technology," rather than of British Empire or Commonwealth, alienates from language and ancestors. As in Margaret Laurence and Witi Ihimaera, an orphaning metaphor is used; but Atwood's protagonist has cut herself off from the future as well as the past, with her abortion. Searching for her father and the gods of the land, she must relearn the language of nature he had taught her. Returning totally to a state of nature, she hears its other language, and the animal gods, and gains strength to fight the Americans. Nameless, she is an archetypal Canadian, keeping alive a potential for Canadian life.

8 BELOV, SERGEI. "Kanada" [Canada]. *Sovremennaia Khudezhestvennaia Literatura za Rubezhom* (Moscow), no. 150 (November-December), pp. 42-44.

In Russian. Highly praised in the United States, *Life Before Man* is structured like a complex geometric form made up of a series of fragments. The narrative fragments unfold to reveal the internal and external condition of each character and their confusing relationships. The discontinuity emphasizes their dismal and hopeless lives. The tone may result from a poet's prose, or may be the typical lack of optimism of much Western literature. Atwood is one of Canadian literature's central figures.

9 BOWERING, GEORGE. "Margaret Atwood's Hands." *Studies in Canadian Literature* 6, no. 1:39-52.

Reprints, with slight revisions, the Atwood portion of his 1970.6 review of *The Journals of Susanna Moodie*, his 1972.6 review of *Power Politics*, and the Atwood portion of the pseudonymous 1979.12 review of *Two-Headed Poems*; discusses persona and autobiography, mask and motherhood. "Despite the title of the book, its most important anatomical image is of hands. Hands wear puppets, reach out over a darkened staircase, stroke the air around bodies, fashion clothes and toys for a child, grapple with one another as emissaries of the bicameral mind, and appear over and over, trying to touch a world the eyes can not always see. Hands act to complete the locution of the first poem: . . . [quote from poem] and a hand appears as the last word of the last poem, a word to a daughter who will use it to begin her meeting with the world." (Paragraph quoted from pages 48-49.)

10 BROEGE, VALERIE. "Margaret Atwood's Americans and Canadians." *Essays on Canadian Writing*, no. 22 (Summer), pp. 111-35.

Traces Atwood's perceptive and typically Canadian ambivalence to Americans versus Canadians through her interviews and books. Her childhood reading of American comic books shapes her "Comic Books vs. History," which contrasts exciting American fantasy with mundane Canadian reality. Her disillusioning experience of America's urban blight and crime shapes "Hair Jewellery" and "Dancing Girls." "At the tourist centre in Boston" questions Canada's exported self-image. Atwood sees Americans as frighteningly ignorant of Canada, and the world, and contrasts their expansiveness to Canadian self-effacement, in the novels and in "Two-Headed Poems." Atwood uses American science fiction films and westerns as paradigms of the Canadian-American relationships in *The Edible Woman*, *Surfacing*, and "Backdrop addresses cowboy," which criticizes America's vigilante syndrome and frontier myth. Americans are despoilers and exploiters in "Polarities" and *Surfacing*; *Survival* contrasts American and Canadian attitudes to animals. *Surfacing*, like other Canadian works, reflects Canadian fears of an American invasion and a CIA takeover; *Surfacing* and *Lady Oracle* depict Canadian collusion and assimilation of American culture. *Lady Oracle* satirizes only misguided, too-narrow Canadian nationalism. Atwood's hopes are "'inter-nationalist,'" as in "They are hostile nations."

11 BROWN, GEORGIA A. "Recent Fiction." *Yale Review* 70, no. 2 (Winter):275-77.

Dislikes, in a round-up review, *Life Before Man*'s relentless depiction of meanness, and its cynicism about human life. The persistent metaphor of prehistory is an intelligent conceit, not a vision. The title could be *Life After Man*; its men are outmatched, bullied, or caricatured. *Life* needs satiric wit, a clear moral standard, and a persuasive irony; but its brief, conventionally pretty end is an "ironic tour de force."

1981

12 BROWN, LINDSAY. "Atwood's Back, Bleaker than Ever." *Gazette* (Montreal), 3 October, p. 28.

Complains that *Bodily Harm* is "the dead opposite of escape [reading] – it's capture and incarceration in 300-odd pages of the grimmest, bleakest imaginings imaginable." Finds cold-blooded sexual entanglement, and chilling comments on sex between men and women, and Atwood's sly humour lessened. *Bodily Harm* does put Rennie's personal problems in sharp political perspective, but Atwood doesn't invite the reader or characters to enjoy anything.

13 BRUNI, VALERIO. "La crisi della comunicazione in *Surfacing* di Margaret Atwood." In *Canada: Metafora per la letteratura; saggi sul romanzo canadese del '900*. Edited by Alfredo Rizzardi. Saggi e ricerche de lingue e letterature straniere, vol. 7. Abano Terme: Piovan Editore, pp. 106-16.

As Mansbridge 1978.60 saw, *Surfacing* focuses on the protagonist's search for identity. This internal search for the self coincides with the character's attempt to regain the ability to communicate with the external world. The breakdown of language, and the resulting damage to the character's integrity of body and mind, can be compared to the theme of the loss of communication in modern civilization, seen in T.S. Eliot and the early twentieth-century writers who followed the late French symbolists. *Surfacing* illustrates the need to accept a simple language that can function for everyday communication, and will not interfere, or deform reality.

14 BRYDON, DIANA. "Landscape and Authenticity: The Development of National Literatures in Canada and Australia." *Dalhousie Review* 61, no. 2:278-90 passim.

Briefly discusses *Survival* and *Surfacing*, and cites *The Journals of Susanna Moodie*, in a comparative analysis. That Australians identify with *Survival* shows its theme to be universal, not uniquely Canadian. Both *Surfacing* and Patrick White's *Voss* are spiritual quests; both imply "that the rational, masculine and European intelligence must die before an indigenous imagination may take shape."

15 CEDERSTROM, LORELEI. "The Regeneration of Time in Atwood's *Surfacing*." *Atlantis* 6, no. 2 (Spring):24-37.

Celebrates *Surfacing*'s movement out of the time and history of masculine consciousness, into the regenerative, archetypal myths of the feminine unconscious; cites *The Journals of Susanna Moodie*, Jung, and Eliade. In the beginning the protagonist is alienated from nature and from her unconscious, cut off from her past pain, her dreams, real art, and religion. The killed heron, who recalls the archetypal cross, the Tarot's Hanged Man, and Othin (Wotan), provides the shock that loosens her ego's hold; she then begins to seek the earth gods in rituals, to remember, and to envision. *Surfacing* recalls the myth of Inanna (Ishtar), who descended to the underworld in search of a dead child, met her shadow, and death; only after Inanna returned to earth could fertility and desire resume. The narrator achieves a cosmic consciousness in her impregnation, ritual rebirth, and visions. By the end conscious and unconscious interpenetrate; she can dream of her parents, and return to the human world, an Eve capable of love and at ease with nature.

16 CHERNIN, KIM. *The Obsession: Reflections on the Tyranny of Slenderness*. New York: Harper and Row, pp. 66-75, 80-81.

Argues that *The Edible Woman*'s anorexic Marian is alienated from her body, her emotions, the natural life cycle, and woman's natural powers. Marian's anorexic alienation expresses her – and our – uneasiness about the meaningless and inauthentic identity our culture offers women. When Marian eats the cake fetish, she ritually reclaims her own legitimate hunger. Atwood's fat, rebellious Lady Oracle is Marian's sister, for the obese and the anorexic woman share the same uneasiness and alienations. So, too, do Margaret Laurence's Stacey and Tess, in *The Fire Dwellers*.

Briefly comments on the archetypal matriarch glimpsed in a Lady Oracle self-description.

17 CLARK, JOAN. "Atwood: Plunging a 'Sweet Canadian' into Caribbean Politics." *Calgary Herald*, 3 October, p. E22.

Admires *Bodily Harm*, its believable though not particularly likable characters, its intrigue, satiric wit, sheer virtuosity, and skill. Atwood's prose "pummels the reader forward to experience what she has to say," about sex, surfaces, political corruption, wholeness, and humanity. The metaphor of hands partly bridges the terrible gap of man's inhumanity. Something does get born at the end, in the reader and in Rennie.

18 COCCHI, RAFFAELE. "*The Edible Woman* ovvero 'L'uomo da Mangiare.'" In *Canada: Metafora per la letteratura; saggi romanzo canadese del '900*. Edited by Alfredo Rizzardi. Saggi e ricerche di lingue e letterature straniere, vol 7. Abano Terme: Piovan Editore, pp. 90-105.

The Edible Woman is constructed triadically, with three narrative parts, three male-female relationships, and three escapes by the protagonist. Dyadic elements, used to show conflicts between appearance and reality, mind and body, and man and woman, are evident in the images of clothes, cosmetics, and mirrors. Woman as mother, man as father or son, and other paternal images disappear by the end, symbolizing sterility and death. All three unhealthy relationships, Clara/Joe, Ainsley/Len, and Marian/Peter/Duncan, emphasize sterility, death, and de-masculinization. The eating of cake at the end of the novel represents both fertility/reproduction and sterility/death. All three relationships overturn the traditional male/female roles and the Christian myth of love. *The Edible Woman* reveals the regressive process in relationships between men and women, while offering no resolutions or suggestions for achieving love or a more humane society.

19 COLLINS, AILEEN. "Atwood: Victory for the Victims." *Gazette* (Montreal), 28 February, p. 55.

Appreciates *True Stories*'s broader scope, affirmations, and tentative hope. All Atwood's work obsessively explores themes of psychological victimization and survival, as in the limited *Survival*. In *True Stories* voyages into truth and poetry are the central motif, as in the title poem and "Spelling," with its poet as "'burning witch.'" The poet's responsibility is to bear witness to the world's terrible truths. There are love poems here, and sardonic comments on love. Atwood's spare, cold language and controlled tone are illuminated and relieved by her striking imagery.

20 CRITTENDEN, YVONNE. "Memorable Atwood." *Sunday Star* (Toronto), 11 October, p. S23.

Praises *Bodily Harm* as another incisively perceptive and memorable Atwood book. The heroine, Rennie, is a mildly ambitious journalist and neutral observer who has fled from her small-town Ontario upbringing, and who now flees, after cancer surgery, a sinister break-in, and the breakdown of her love affair, from Toronto to a strange island. Her narrow escape from the island's revolutionary violence "gives Rennie the perspective she needs to face her uncertain future."

21 CZARNECKI, MARK. "Redeemed by the Laying on of Hands." *Maclean's* 94, no. 40 (5 October):43-44.

Mainly praises *Bodily Harm*: the emotionally damaged, cancer-jolted Rennie, on spiritual quest for healing, is sucked into an ugly Caribbean revolution and an awareness of shared responsibility for injustices. The imagery is as visceral as Atwood's poetry. Hands–lost, inhuman, or redeeming–are key. *Bodily Harm*'s case against men is "hard to rebut"; they do cause bodily harm, they are "pawns to biological determinism." Though Atwood is self-indulgent and intrusive, "the climax is passionate and convincing"; Rennie miraculously survives and returns home, healed.

22 DAVEY, FRANK. "Life after Man." *Canadian Forum* 61 (December-January):29-30.

Compares *Bodily Harm* to Atwood's earlier novels, finding again a healing pattern of Shakespearean "'green world'" comedy and a Virgilian descent to the underworld, and another self-preoccupied female Toronto intellectual. The everyday world again masks barbarism; the human body is again a metaphor of surface and depth. The central irony is that Rennie's cancer heals her spiritually. Her vision of archetypal violence is "based on undeniable sadism. Atwood here suggests that 'the man with the rope' lurks within us all." *Bodily Harm* is more satisfying than earlier novels, because civilization's veneer conceals more than mere bourgeois unhappiness; and because the ending is future tense, perhaps a fantasy of return; we know only that Rennie has had a new vision of her life. One wishes, however, that Atwood's patterns and elements were not so predictable. Excerpted: 1983.129. Revised: 1984.18.

1981

23 DAVIDSON, ARNOLD E., and DAVIDSON, CATHY N., eds. *The Art of Margaret Atwood: Essays in Criticism*. Toronto: Anansi, 304 pp.

Contains: Introduction 1981.24, Djwa 1981.28, McCombs 1981.66, Grace 1981.40, Weir 1981.108, Wagner 1981.104, Irvine 1981.52, Thompson 1981.95, McLay 1981.69, Pratt 1981.83, Thomas 1981.94, Lecker 1981.64, Davidson and Davidson 1981.25, Woodcock 1981.111, Horne 1981.47.

24 _____. Introduction to *The Art of Margaret Atwood: Essays in Criticism*. See Davidson and Davidson 1981.23, pp. 9-14.

Introduces the book's thirteen essays on literary traditions, style, imagery, themes, forms, plot, quest, and genre in Atwood's poetry through *Two-Headed Poems*, *Dancing Girls*, four novels, and criticism; and the checklist on writings by and about Atwood. As poet, short story writer, novelist, and critic, Atwood is at least four authors; her work has many facets, continuing change, and a sense of free play.

25 DAVIDSON, CATHY N., AND DAVIDSON, ARNOLD E. "Prospects and Retrospects in *Life Before Man*." In *The Art of Margaret Atwood: Essays in Criticism*. See Davidson and Davidson 1981.23, pp. 205-21.

Appreciates *Life Before Man*'s portrayal of Joseph Campbell's bleak, secularized, fragmented age. Temples have become museums; reason and civilization have become a "'civility'" of repressed, hypocritical distortions. As in William Faulkner's *As I Lay Dying*, a dead main character (Chris) has power among the living, and the reader must synthesize a greater whole from seemingly discontinuous sections. The museum tropes suggest that *Life* exhibits specimens and reconstructs reality. Chris and Nate are opposites of natural, physical action versus civilized evasion and fantasy; it is Nate who survives and perpetuates his genes. The pregnant Lesje, and the remembering Elizabeth, each embody time past and future. Elizabeth is a survivor and fighter, a helpless victim and able victimizer; her epiphany at her aunt's grave returns her to the quotidian. Unlike the first three novels, *Life*'s ending is closed, but lacks traditional affirmations. Yet, despite Campbell's corrupt secularization, there is hope, for Chris, Elizabeth, Nate, and Lesje are artificers, who order and create; and the museum not only re-collects the dead and doomed, but also implies a future.

26 DAWE, ALAN. "Tough, True Stories." *Vancouver Sun*, 13 February, p. L39.

Appreciates *True Stories*'s remarkable, tough, gloomy voice, which finds small mercies in poetry and, more ambiguously, in love. When the subject is "man's inhumanity to women," or grimmer tortures for men and women, the tone becomes even fiercer. Though reading these 40 poems is, in Anthony Powell's phrase, "'lowering to the spirit,'" what makes them bearable and even memorable is Atwood's powerful imagery.

27 DJWA, SANDRA. "A Developing Tradition." *Essays on Canadian Writing*, no. 21 (Spring), pp. 49-51.

Traces a nationalist, modernist, Darwinian Romantic tradition in Canadian poetry and in Earle Birney's poems; discusses Atwood's "Progressive insanities of a pioneer" as influenced by Birney's *David* and "Bushed," and as a psychological version of Frye's "'garrison mentality.'" The Atwood portion, and other portions, are developed and incorporated in 1981.28 (below).

28 ____. "The Where of Here: Margaret Atwood and a Canadian Tradition." In *The Art of Margaret Atwood: Essays in Criticism*. See Davidson and Davidson 1981.23, pp. 15-34.

Atwood's poetry inherits from late fifties and early sixties recognition of a Canadian poetic canon, nationalism, feminism, and archetypal criticism; specifically from poets E.J. Pratt, Earle Birney, F.R. Scott, A.M. Klein, Jay Macpherson, and Margaret Avison, and critics Milton Wilson and Northrop Frye. *Double Persephone*'s authoritative female archetypes owe much to Macpherson's *The Boatman*. From *The Circle Game* through *Power Politics*, Atwood's poetry reworks primal fertility myths and explores contemporary woman's position through male and female archetypes. Atwood's mythic descent or journey is linked to sexual, aesthetic, and national identity; and to Canadian identity as landscape, as in Frye's "'Where is here?" Many poems in *The Circle Game* evoke Atwood's Canadian poetic ancestors. Explicates "A Descent through the Carpet" as an evolutionary descent which evokes F.R. Scott's "Lakeshore" and Pratt's undersea Darwinian "Silences." Explicates "Progressive insanities of a pioneer" as evoking Birney's *David* and "Bushed," which were shaped by Pratt's Darwinian Romanticism; "Progressive insanities" also evokes

1981

Macpherson's *The Boatman* and Frye's irrational, threatening "'whale'" of nature. Incorporates and develops the Atwood portion, and other portions, of 1981.27 (above).

29 DORWARD, ENID. Review of *Anna's Pet*, by Margaret Atwood and Joyce Barkhouse. *CM* 9, no. 2:120-21.

Recommends highly this lovely, simple, sturdy book, and Ann Blades's simple, bold illustrations.

30 EWELL, BARBARA C. "The Language of Alienation in Margaret Atwood's *Surfacing.*" *Centennial Review* 25, no. 2 (Spring):185-202.

Surfacing examines how the language of post-Cartesian rationalism and modern technological, patriarchal society alienates the female quester from wholeness, truth, nature, and communication. Language categorizes arbitrarily, to control and to project evil: the brother's "'bad'" leeches, David's "'Americans,'" the art teacher's "'accident'" that justified abortion. When the narrator uses society's language to falsify her past pain, she loses her present feelings. Anna and especially David are also self-alienated, betrayed by a debased language into victimizer and victim roles. The narrator seeks a new dialect, beyond her father's inadequate rationalism. The map and pictures she finds are visual, and therefore simultaneous and contextual, unlike language. After the dive, she moves away from language, which "'divides us,'" into broken syntax and a visionary unity. At the end she returns, wary of language's alienating power, as we should be.

31 FITZGERALD, JUDITH. Review of *Bodily Harm*. *Quill and Quire* 47, no. 10 (October):34.

A rave review: *Bodily Harm* is not merely a gripping, horrific adventure thriller; it "possesses the unrelenting sub-surface terror of [Malcolm Lowry's] *Under the Volcano*, the irony and condemnation of innocence and *laissez-faire*" of [Graham Greene's] *The Quiet American*, and Atwood's unflinching belief in her characters. This overwhelming novel, that goes for the hands . . . and arrives at the throat," extends our understanding of violence and fairness. Excerpted 1983.129.

32 FREDSON, MICHAEL. Review of *Two-Headed Poems*. *Seattle Times*, 25 October. Newsbank 1981-1982, 25:D6.

Praises Atwood's unique vision and terse language; the convincing love that scores the whole book; and the moving feminine strength, endurance, and joy.

34 FRENCH, WILLIAM. "Sardonic Humor and the Malignancy of Modern Life: Margaret Atwood's Most Satisfying Novel Yet." *Globe and Mail*, 3 October, p. E17.

Praises *Bodily Harm* as Atwood's most skillful novel, intricately structured, sardonically humorous, satiric, and ironic; and Rennie as Atwood's most believable and memorable character. *Bodily Harm* focuses on the cancerous malignancy of contemporary life, on corruptions of the body and of the body politic. Menace pervades. The political intrigue is skillfully handled, but Rennie's innocence is sometimes implausible. Rennie does return to Toronto; and "we're left with the optimistic feeling" that she will now deal with the brutal corruption she has witnessed. But *Bodily Harm*'s overriding pessimism conveys "that as long as men run the world, things won't change much."

35 GELLERT, JAMES. "Rousseau for Young Readers." *Canadian Children's Literature*, no. 21, pp. 65-68.

Praises *Anna's Pet* highly and seriously. The internationally established Atwood, with her beautiful *Up in the Tree*, and the Canadian children's author Joyce Barkhouse, are a formidable writing team, and sensitively complemented by the Canadian children's award-winning illustrator Ann Blades. This delightful, beautiful story transcends its simple realism to evoke universal concerns. Its didacticism is never overt; as Anna learns to share in the natural world and its metamorphoses, the moral evolves naturally.

36 GERVAIS, MARTY. "In New Novel Atwood Has Taken Stand." *Windsor Star*, 3 October, p. E14.

Praises *Bodily Harm*, which tackles harsh, disturbing questions of politics, feminism, and sexuality. Atwood's now-sharper portrayal of relationships bothers you long after you finish reading. Her motif of feminism provides barbed, satiric, often hilarious moments, especially with Jocasta, the liberated woman who is left wanting. Rennie's relationship with Paul becomes a therapeutic recovery of feeling. Unlike *Life Before Man*, the central character here does improve, and learn, beyond feminism. Atwood seems to comment didactically on modern life, showing its preciousness, and the destructive, demoralizing onslaughts on it.

37 _____. "Unfunny Valentine of Atwood's World." *Windsor Star*, 14 February, p. E7.

Finds *True Stories* a significant, intense "portrait of contemporary relationships." Released on Valentine's Day, with "a warped, raw and bleeding heart" cover, *True Stories* painstakingly unmasks "a little of our authentic selves," which isn't encouraging, or easy to take, but it's real. The opening ["True Stories"] introduces her theme of avoiding the truth; "Christmas Carols" shatters myths of motherhood and ends in bitterness. The bleak prose poem, "True Romances," which is Atwood's best realism, "captures the gossipy snivelling chatter of women telling their stories," of course with irony and parody. As in *Life Before Man*, which most Canadian critics hammered, Atwood gives us commonplace soap opera, which is true, tragically so, from her point of view.

*38 GORDON, CHRISTINE MACK. Review of *Two-Headed Poems*. *Minnesota Daily*, 7 April.

Is inspired by Atwood's compelling, complexly human vision, that "challenges us to recognize our world in new ways and to commit ourselves" to enhancing life, not destruction. Atwood has done most to bring "'Canadian consciousness'" to the United States; her vision "embodies political awareness, an intense sense of place," and acute human insights. The "Two-Headed Poems" sequence captures the French-English Canadian dilemma. The woman's vividly physical faulty heart, in two poems, precludes romantic readings. As in "Five Poems for Grandmothers" and *Surfacing*, we must recognize and move beyond our guilt, act for justice, believe in "our own spiritual and political power, to make our charms of paper in the face of death." "The Red Shirt," which reveals the power of women's re-creating work and history, most beautifully captures this human possibility.

*39 _____. "Woman from the North Country." *Minnesota Daily*, 5 May, p. 8.

Interviews Atwood in Minneapolis [8 April]: Atwood discusses her current collaboration on a television script about the English orphans transported to Canada ["Heaven on Earth"]; her first, unpublished novel ["Up in the Air So Blue"]; Canadian writers; and realism versus happy endings in fairy tales, Harlequins, and her own books; defines her politics as a nineteenth-century Red Tory belief in social responsibility, not the nineteenth-century liberalism that has become modern conservatism; and finds a recent New York group's rejection of right-wing women's support against pornography "very silly" and "wrong, wrong politics."

40 GRACE, SHERRILL E. "Margaret Atwood and the Poetics of Duplicity." In *The Art of Margaret Atwood: Essays in Criticism*. See Davidson and Davidson 1981.23, pp. 55-68.

Analyzes Atwood's duplicity, from early poems through *Two-Headed Poems*. Duplicity is both the doubleness of most organic forms, including the eye's retina, and the deceit of language's irony; it should not be confused with polarized oppositions, as of victor/victim. Atwood sees us not as self-enclosed egos but as duplicitously co-extensive with environment. *The Journals of Susanna Moodie*, her best work, best conveys her vision of duplicity, in Canadian myth and in Moodie's double vision. Atwood's poems are persistently double, with aural/visual effects. Her mirrors both reduce and create the self. Eyes are usually mistrusted, as in the Moodie epigraph; occasionally insightful, as in "Book of Ancestors." Her double structures may shift from metaphor to metonymy, as in "'you fit into me.'" "The Double Nun," an early poem, asserts doubleness; "This Is a Photograph of Me" "fully mirrors its theme," with a double structure of "surface/depth, outside/inside," reader's eye/I. Double voices occur in "Corpse Song" and, sometimes unclearly, in "Two-Headed Poems." The latter, which contains many topical Canadian allusions, portrays Canadian duplicity less successfully than the Moodie *Journals* did. "Two-Headed Poems's" treatment of language is more successful than its double voices are. Develops Grace 1980.47.

41 GRAHAM, BARBARA J. Review of *True Stories*. *CM* 9, no. 3:192.

Acclaims the exciting, excellent, thought-provoking *True Stories*, for any Canadian poetry collection, praising its honest tenderness and pain, and its searing, tragic commentary on human existence. Atwood's highly sensual images contrast travellers' romanticizings with harsh tropical realities. She tries to express the inexpressible, of love, joy, woman's pain, and unspeakable cruelty. She believes our unpredictable "life must be lived in the present."

1981

42 GUY, DAVID A. Atwood entry in *Contemporary Authors*. Edited by Ann Evory. Vol. 3. New rev. ser. Detroit: Gale Research Co., pp. 39-40.

A brief biographical sketch; lists Atwood's books 1961-1981; lists work in progress, including *Lady Oracle* screenplay and two television scripts, "Snowbirds" [sic] and "Heaven on Earth." Briefly quotes high praise of Atwood's poetry from Marge Piercy, Dick Allen, Rosellen Brown, George Bowering, Helen Vendler, and Tom Marshall; acclaim for *Surfacing* from Benjamin DeMott and Paul Delany; critical debate on *Lady Oracle* from Katha Pollitt and Bonnie Lyons versus Linda Sandler and William McPherson; and high praise for *Life Before Man* from Roberta Rubenstein and Marilyn French; quotes Atwood on writing poetry (1978.71).

43 HARPUR, TOM. "Atwood: On Sexuality, Morality and Success." *Vancouver Sun*, 16 October, p. L39.

An abridged version of 1981.44 (below), that omits questions and answers on aggression versus altruism and on facing mortality, and shortens several other passages.

44 ____. "Atwood's Priority: How Do We Stop War?" *Toronto Star*, 5 October, p. D1, 3.

Interviewed in her Toronto home, Atwood discusses monetary success versus real achievement; *Bodily Harm* and Amnesty International; the optimism of writing to communicate with an audience; the need to investigate aggression and altruism, before we blow ourselves up; religion, the Bible, and demagogic killings; conservative religion's attacks on Margaret Laurence rather than on Mafia pornography; facing mortality; ethical choice, as in Bulgaria and Denmark, where Jews were saved during World War II; and promiscuity versus love, whether in or out of marriage, heterosexual or homosexual. Abridged: 1981.43 (above).

45 HELWIG, DAVID. "Atwood: New Power Growing From Old Roots." *Toronto Star*, 14 February, p. G10.

Praises *True Stories* very highly. Atwood's poetry has two peaks, *The Journals of Susanna Moodie*'s dream-history, and *You Are Happy*'s new emotional range. *True Stories* has a new sensuality in the tropical poems, and some very touching love poems. Public and private realities still collide, but more explicitly and painfully, as in the "Notes Towards a Poem That Can Never Be Written" section. The perceiving self is fuller and richer; the world "is better known, more beautiful, and infinitely more dangerous." There are stronger rhythms, more sensual sound; less indirection and clever irony; more appetite, anger, and a new power.

46 HOLLIDAY, BARBARA. "It Took Time for Canada to Accept Its Daughter." *Detroit Free Press*, 25 October, p. B5.

Interviews Atwood at a *Bodily Harm* booksigning, South Shore bookstore, Windsor: Atwood recounts and comments on a Canadian publisher's reactions to her first, unpublished novel; Canadian reviews of *Bodily Harm* and *Life Before Man*; the U.S. hunting and fishing promotion of *Surfacing*; flattering, ideal, Harlequin Romance characters versus realism; the novelist as Vergil and the reader as Dante; her Governor General's Award for *The Circle Game*, and Charles Pachter's now-costly folio edition of *The Circle Game*.

47 HORNE, ALAN J. "Margaret Atwood: A Checklist of Writings by and about Margaret Atwood." In *The Art of Margaret Atwood: Essays in Criticism*. See Davidson and Davidson 1981.23, pp. 243-85.

Provides a chronological listing of selected primary and Anglophone secondary work, abridging and updating 1979.56 and 1980.59. Lists, under four primary categories, 18 books of poetry and six of prose, with editions and translations; one television drama; 152 poems in periodicals but not in Atwood's books; 12 selected anthologies containing Atwood's poems; six audio and audio-visual recordings; nine short stories [not in the 1977 *Dancing Girls*]; 65 articles and book reviews; and four selected anthologies containing Atwood's short stories. Lists under secondary, with some brief annotations, two books (1977.81 and 1980.47); 77 articles [1970]-1979, seven theses, and 17 interviews; lists 67 selected reviews of poetry and 72 selected reviews of prose books, 1962-1980, arranged chronologically under titles of each Atwood book.

48 HOSEK, CHAVIVA. "The Real Story." *Canadian Forum* 61 (June-July):38-39.

Assesses *True Stories*'s themes and voice: Atwood shows that the true story is political violence or organic death, decay, and eating. A number of love poems show a tenderness and vulnerability rare in her earlier poetry. *True Stories* takes apart *Power Politics*'s dynamic synthesis of love and power, political and personal. Here "the public world is the realm of torture" and corruption; the poet's private world "becomes a source of guilt. . . . Much of the authority in [all] Atwood's poetry comes from that flat voice, unwilling to betray feeling, and the sense of barely expressed disgust conveyed in her sensory images." Some poems treat poetry self-consciously; others show how poetry bears witness, or is ordinary, or is "the ultimate source of identity and power," as in the ancestral "'burning witch'" of "Spelling."

49 HOUGHTON, GREGORY. "Margaret Atwood: Some Observations and Textual Considerations." *World Literature Written in English* 20, no. 1 (Spring):85-92.

Articulates de-construction in *Dancing Girls*: as a person and writer, Atwood resists being named, and constructs in order to deconstruct. The flawed utopias envisioned in "Polarities" and "Dancing Girls" show how our attempts to construct meaning inevitably fabricate and oppress. When, as in "Giving Birth," Atwood articulates this tension, language is often the battleground, as Foucault says. Secondly, biographical criticism offers illusory meaning, which Atwood denies. Biographical criticism of women artists is ideologically reductive, even when feminists try to do it positively. At least Atwood's self-conscious play, in "Giving Birth," stays one step ahead of the biographical complaints. Thirdly, Atwood's unwillingness to name places in *Dancing Girls* reveals the characters' alienation from their problematic country, Canada. "Giving Birth's" deceptive narrative "reveals the forces against which de-construction must struggle."

50 HUGHES, KATE. "Atwood's Peek at Politics." *Gazette* (Montreal), 9 October, p. 11.

Praises the highly complex, polished, witty, perceptive but shocking *Bodily Harm*, that shows us "'sweet Canadians'. . . . the real politics: powerplays of torture, rape, starvation, clitoridectomy, pornography." Rennie, "a typical ignorer of these 'true stories,'" at the end "decides she is now a 'subversive' and a 'reporter' of the truth."

51 HUTCHEON, LINDA. "Reading Atwood's *Life Before Man*: Structural Form through Psychic Verisimilitude." *Comparison*, no. 12 (Spring), pp. 41-58.

In *Life Before Man*'s study of the imagination, fantasy functions primarily to establish the three main psychic realities, and a structural unity. The central love triangle unites the three point of view characters, who each have significant other ties. Elizabeth's intricate, revealing verbal associations are both psychic realism and links between sections; her "'dying star'" sky imagery for Chris connects to the Planetarium's "'black hole'" and her "'night with no stars'" with the panty salesman. Lesje's regressive, escapist fantasies most clearly show Atwood's thematic concern with imagination. Nate's adolescent, or Freudian, wishfulfilling fantasies link him to Lesje's fantasies of Conan Doyle's *The Lost World*. In *Life*, Atwood's postmodernist focus on aesthetic creation takes its paradigm from pregnancy and child-bearing; "the novelist's act is that of every*woman*." See 1983.66.

52 IRVINE, LORNA. "One Woman Leads to Another." In *The Art of Margaret Atwood: Essays in Criticism*. See Davidson and Davidson 1981.23, pp. 95-106.

Analyzes images and themes in Atwood's seven books of poetry to show that *Two-Headed Poems* celebrates, for the first time, a female world, where the matriarchal generations connect, and the child becomes real and welcome. Now, though political tensions still exist, the body and its creativity become positive, not Frankensteinian; landscape, season, and home become real and generative. *The Circle Game* and *The Animals in That Country* show children and birth as frightening; adults as solipsistic, rootless, empty; seasons and landscape as dead. In *The Journals of Susanna Moodie*, children are linked to loss and death. *Procedures for Underground*'s apocalyptic imagery continues in *Power Politics*, where landscape and body are barren, spring unregenerative, and abortion preferable to birth. The *You Are Happy* poems are transitional, moving towards a somewhat positive generation.

53 ____. "Surfacing, Surviving, Surpassing: Canada's Women Writers." *Journal of Popular Culture* 15, no. 3 (Winter):70-79 passim.

Discusses Canadian women writers, and Canada's feminine and feminist elements, in contrast to the predominantly masculine

American literary tradition. Mentions the sexual rhetoric of Atwood's first novel, and the female ancestry of her "Five Poems for Grandmothers." Atwood frequently masks cultural conflicts as sexual ones; *Power Politics*'s overtly female versus male struggle also represents Canada versus the United States. *Surfacing*'s epic female narrator represents creative Canadian values of nature, generativity, and continuance, in her self-imagery and in the pregnancy she imagines at the end.

54 JACOBSEN, JOSEPHINE. "A Poet of Power without Pretension." *Sun* (Baltimore), 19 April, p. D5. Newsbank 1980-1981, 82:E1.

Discusses "the kudzu-like growth of [American] poetry"; then praises highly *Two-Headed Poems*'s keen intelligence, truth-telling, and passionate concerns, which create, despite the paucity of joys, an extraordinary exhilaration. Everything is two-headed, split, dualistic: nationalities, love, ego. Praises especially the poems for dolls and on making apple jelly.

55 JAMES, WILLIAM C. "Atwood's *Surfacing*." *Canadian Literature*, no. 91 (Winter), pp. 174-81.

Sides with Laurence's 1973.47 and Woodcock's 1975.52 view of *Surfacing*'s affirmative "'breakthrough,'" self-realization and hope, contrary to Sullivan 1977.90 and other Canadian critics. The narrator begins logically, with binary oppositions, in her quest for her father. But dualistic thinking can be transcended; *Surfacing*'s tripartite structure suggests an affirmative resolution of its oppositions. The narrator's "temporary descent into madness" may be following her father into insanity, or compensating for living in her head, or bringing together her "'headline'" and "'heartline.'" She returns to sanity when she perceives her parents, and her own footprints, which recall the Winnebago initiation ritual's "'footprints of light.'" Tillich and others affirm that apprehension of the divine comes from realizing the limits of the finite. The narrator's final heroic stance is both realistic and affirmative – what Atwood 1973.27 called a creative "'harmony with the world'"; the final ironic distancing is Canadian, and not complete alienation.

56 JEANNOTTE, M. SHARON. "Tension Between the Mundane and the Cosmic." *Sphinx* 3, no. 4:74-82.

Appreciates *Life Before Man*'s power, symmetry, main and subordinate characterization, perfect phrasing, and its ironic tension between mundane and cosmic events. Atwood uses several techniques to transform the soap-opera "plot into a timeless statement on human isolation": the split narrative and three points of view show the characters as ions lost in time, lost from, and misunderstanding, each other. Their isolation comes to seem an inevitable part of the human condition. Elizabeth, the most powerful character, is both a manipulative bitch and a tragic heroine; only her lovers and Auntie Muriel elicit more than "'imitations'" from her. The fantasies that dominate the narrative show the characters in their tiny moments of time: Lesje's prehistoric refuge, Nate's shining illusions, Elizabeth's primal fantasies of "time before life itself," the void, the vacuum. "The denouement is an uneasy assertion of temporal reality" over cosmic, but the characters may still be isolated. Atwood seems to suggest that accepting the human reality without fantasies will require a quiet heroism.

57 JONES, JOSEPH, and JONES, JOHANNA. *Canadian Fiction*. Twayne World Author Series, no. 630. Boston: Twayne Publishers, G.K. Hall & Co., pp. 122-23.

Briefly discusses Atwood's three novels, which emphasize the treatment of women. *The Edible Woman* sees women as social victims. Quotes Rubenstein 1976.88 on *Surfacing*'s complex symbolic rebirth, but wonders if such metaphorical intricacy fits with the condemnation of machinery. Does *Lady Oracle* comically recognize this? Is the comic, pathetic Joan an anti-heroine?

58 JUHASZ, SUZANNE. Review of *Two-Headed Poems*. *Library Journal* 106, no. 5 (1 March):561.

Praises Atwood's often-visionary sense of place, colloquial rhythms, ambitious political poems, and resonant poems of seasonal and domestic farm life.

59 ____. "Subjective Formalism; or, the Lady and the Text, a Demonstration." *CLA Journal* 24, no. 4 (June):465-80.

Uses A.R. Ammons's "Plunder" and Atwood's "More and more" to demonstrate the interplay between subjective and objective reading processes as reader meets text. Identifies with the theme and

1981

experience in Atwood's speech by the lover to the beloved; also discusses form, and colloquial and figurative language.

60 KAREDA, URJO. "Atwood on Automatic." *Saturday Night* 96, no. 10 (November):70, 72.

Rejects Atwood's *Bodily Harm*: "We feel ourselves caught in the machinery of her anger while she hectors us with ever more appalling instances of physical, psychic, and political violence." Most of the novel's sexual-political issues are picked-over and behind the times now; her outrage advances "too predictably, as if her anger were on automatic." And, instead of a "sympathetic central character through whom we could interpret" the horrors, Atwood gives us Rennie, who is another "zonked heroine" of English-language women's fiction. Though Atwood provides surrogates, Rennie is the only character developed enough to connect with. The men are particularly shadowy; the political plot is heavy and yet half-hearted. The climax, of Rennie as healer, is unbelievable, despite Atwood's cadences.

61 KATES, JOANNE. "*Bodily Harm*: Terminal Trendiness." *Broadside* (Toronto) 3, no. 3 (December-January):12.

Appreciates *Bodily Harm*'s surfaces and levels, complex epiphanies, painfully accurate realism, and "moving and wonderful" metaphors, but finds its failed revolution superficial. Under Atwood's "rather puerile thriller is the story of Rennie Wilford's awakening – to herself and to the world." This hero/anti-hero's initial trendy cynicism, which covers over her Griswold values, masks her profound hopelessness about any better world. Cancer, which "is Atwood's best metaphor," forces Rennie to see beneath her surfaces and illusions, to see "that no Daniel can rescue her from life, or death." Atwood's portrait of sexual relationships is painful, cannibalistic, pessimistic, and true. By the end, having been forced "to discover her hope and her power, [Rennie] flies home, knowing she will report the truth as she sees it," immediately. Rennie's surprise-ending involvement is nice, but the reviewer wants Atwood to do what her most sympathetic character, Dr. Minnow, says, "'to imagine things being different.'"

62 KNIGHT, STEVEN. Review of *Two-Headed Poems*. *Best Sellers* 41, no. 2 (May):67-68.

Writing as a woman and as a Canadian, Atwood reaffirms her political commitment. "Four Small Elegies" and "Footnote to the Amnesty Report on Torture" explore how violent cultures beget violence or complicity. The title poems, of a linguistically divided but head-joined Canada, are preoccupied with what Adrienne Rich has called the "Dream of a Common Language," but Atwood seems pessimistic about its coming true in Canada. Atwood's young daughter, Jessica, inspires several fine poems.

63 KUBELKA, SUSANNA. "Drei Personen und kein Glück Ein Loblied auf die Depressionen." *Presse* (Vienna), 10-11 January, Neue Buch sec., p. 6.

Reviews *Die Unmöglichkeit der Nähe*, the German translation of *Life Before Man*. The novel revolves around three common people and their senseless and exhausting interpersonal relations, which have no future. Lesje becomes mentally ill, Elizabeth hates her husband and starts to drink, and the reader learns about North American eating habits. Nate is portrayed realistically, especially in the love scene with Lesje. Literature would be better off if male writers could do this well with their female characters. Although the book lacks content, it is technically excellent.

64 LECKER, ROBERT. "Janus through the Looking Glass: Atwood's First Three Novels." In *The Art of Margaret Atwood: Essays in Criticism*. See Davidson and Davidson 1981.23, pp. 177-203.

Follows *Lady Oracle*'s duplicity and Mandel 1977.52, to argue that in all three novels the heroines' affirmations remain ambivalent, and the ritual patterns powerless, in a duplicitous, fragmented, secular culture. *The Edible Woman* is ambiguous throughout; its plot is metaphorically circular; its ostensible dichotomies, of eating/non-eating, consuming/non-consuming, predator/prey, tend to cancel each other out. Like other comedies of manners, *The Edible Woman* deals with a duplicitous, debased world. *Surfacing*'s heroine is divided between nature and culture. *Lady Oracle*, and the other two novels, parody "'search for identity'" conventions. Atwood's descents, from Gothic romance literature, end in duplicity. Contrary to Rubenstein 1976.88 and others, *Surfacing*'s heroine's rebirth and self-discovery remain ambivalent, and the mythic return must be seen as sham in a secular culture. *Lady Oracle* is narrated by the reporter, not by Joan

Foster; like the other two novels, it disrupts, parodies, and corrupts Frye's prototypical romance structure. Excerpted: 1985.11.

65 LIPSCOMB, ELIZABETH JOHNSTON. Review of *Life Before Man*. *Magill's Literary Annual*. Edited by Frank N. Magill. Vol. 2. Englewood Cliffs, N.J.: Salem Press, pp. 512-16.

Praises *Life Before Man* as "a devastating portrait of a hollow society" where people suffer alone, and as Atwood's most mature fiction. *Life*'s dark, bleak views may not give pleasure, but its haunting images raise it above social criticism, to universal significance. Atwood's feminist perspective has expanded; now her males are as trapped and powerless as her females. The intimidating but vulnerable Elizabeth, the caring but unassertive Nate, and the child-like dreamer Lesje, are presented with considerable insight. Their imagery for themselves–Elizabeth's hourglass and dwindling candle, Nate's eroding bones and tin man, Lesje's lungfish and molecules–brilliantly conveys their dissatisfaction, isolation, and intrinsic hopelessness.

66 McCOMBS, JUDITH. "Atwood's Haunted Sequences: *The Circle Game*, *The Journals of Susanna Moodie*, and *Power Politics*." In *The Art of Margaret Atwood: Essays in Criticism*. See Davidson and Davidson 1981.23, pp. 35-54.

Finds a Gothic spirit of terror, "emanating from the major elements" of British Gothic literature, and an Ellen Moers female Gothic hero-victim, in three poetry books. Like Ann Radcliffe's persecuted victim-courageous heroine, Atwood's *I* is trapped, but the chamber of horrors is inside her skull; and menaced by an inhuman universe, icy wastes, or a haunted wilderness. She is tempted by a male hero-villain, "who offers an exciting but threatening escape from the boredom and constraints of ordinary female life. . . ." As in Mary Shelley's *Frankenstein* "the creator-villain [is linked] to his monster-creature, so Atwood's creating *I* is author-victim to her lover-Other." As in traditional Gothic, terror feeds on divided and doubled realities. Analyzes the interior Gothic and encircling horrors of *The Circle Game*. In the most Gothic sequence, *The Journals of Susanna Moodie*, "the wilderness is not personified," but "nonetheless tempts the hero as the Gothic Heathcliff" or demon-lover would, by offering her "an escape from the proper menfolks' rule" and a savage kingdom. In the three journals, Moodie first witnesses terrors; then inwardly celebrates

Gothic horrors; then, in death, crosses over, like a hero or witch, to her wild kingdom. In *Power Politics*'s divided, mirrored Gothic, "a male who is both wretch and victim, monster and villain, stalks a female who is both distorter and creator, adventurer and victim." These divided realities begin with Atwood's Tarot cover design. The three sections correspond roughly to stages in Shelley's *Frankenstein*. Reprinted: 1986.152. Excerpted: 1985.11.

67 MACFARLANE, DAVID. "A Terrible Beauty." *Books in Canada* 10, no. 3 (March):10.

Acclaims the magnificently cohesive, powerful *True Stories*. The "St. Joan of Canadian letters . . . . deserves even more attention than she [gets]. . . . Reading Atwood has always been like following a guide's brilliant flashlight through an eerie but not entirely unfamiliar cellar." Now, in the daylight of *True Stories*, love, family and daily life "jive in a *danse macabre* with the incomprehensible" chaos of poverty, imprisonment, and torture. Many poems reflect Atwood's Amnesty International involvement, and her ten years of Southern Caribbean travel. "Even the most gruesome poems – "Torture," "A Women's Issue," and "Spelling" – possess a grim, sardonic awareness of the cruel and absurd co-existence of love and hate. . . . If there is not much that is pretty here, there is a great deal that is beautiful." Atwood's powerful language can be magical, as in "Spelling"; her compassion is level-headed, her humour subtle. Excerpted: 1983.129.

68 McGOOGAN, KENNETH. "Lunch with Margaret Atwood Feast for Mind, Eyes." *Calgary Herald*, 30 October, p. D7.

Interviews Atwood on *Bodily Harm* during a Calgary book-tour lunch. *Bodily Harm*, which has had mixed reviews, is Atwood's best and most political novel. Atwood discusses its politics, beginnings, four-time lines, realism versus pessimism, and Rennie's delivering the machine gun she thinks is dope, which Atwood finds plausible, given Rennie's drunken promise and rural Ontario upbringing. The interviewer enjoys Atwood's intellectual thrust and parry, presence, irony, and nice laughter.

69 McLAY, CATHERINE. "The Dark Voyage: *The Edible Woman* as Romance." In *The Art of Margaret Atwood: Essays in Criticism*. See Davidson and Davidson 1981.23, pp. 123-38.

1981

Interprets Atwood's first novel as a disguised Frygian romance and mythic descent. Under the very realistic surface of this anti-comedy, the romantic hero/heroine Marian descends into a surreal and nightmare underworld, where she is transformed through regression and alienation. Structure and shifted viewpoint suggest her enchantment and disintegration; her suitor, Peter, becomes a dangerous hunter; she becomes a victim and sacrifice. The withdrawn, dehumanized Duncan is her guide to the underworld. The substitute cake-woman is a riddle her suitor fails to solve. The end shows Marian released from enchantment, reintegrated, actively alive, and joyfully consuming.

70 MALLINSON, ANNA JEAN. "Versions and Subversions: Formal Strategies in the Poetry of Contemporary Canadian Women." Ph.D. dissertation, Simon Fraser University.

Investigates how contemporary Canadian women poets adapt and transform genre and formal strategies, by refashioning traditional fictions, and by discovering new or neglected fictions. Separate chapters focus on how women poets use fictions of muse and vocation; of classical mythology; of North American Indian lore; of the domestic; and of women's body. Women's new authority can enlarge and enrich poetic tradition. See *Dissertation Abstracts International* 42:4454A. See 1984.60 or 1985.70.

71 MANSBRIDGE, FRANCIS. "Narcissism in the Modern Canadian Novel." *Studies in Canadian Literature* 6, no. 2:232-44 passim.

The recurrent Narcissus myth in Canadian novels expresses both destructive self-love, and union with nature; and is linked to contemporary alienation, a way out of the Frygian garrison mentality, portraits of the artist, drowning, and other suicides. Discusses especially the union with nature in *Surfacing* and the narcissistic figures in Robert Kroetsch's *Badlands*. In *Surfacing*, the narrator's dive almost re-enacts the Narcissus myth; but she searches for her father, not directly for herself, and sees her Jungian "'shadow,'" not her reflection. The father's plunge may be purely narcissistic. "'Man's insistence on humanizing [the stuffed moose, the murdered heron, the flooded lake] results in narcissism"; the narrator's striving to be more open to the world "would in other ages be heroic."

72 MIGLIOR, GIORGIO. "Articolazione sintattica in tre poems [sic] di Margaret Atwood." In *Canada: L'immaginazione letteraria*. Edited by Alfredo Rizzardi. Abano Terme: Piovan Editore, pp. 109-17.

Discusses Atwood's poetry, focusing on "Against Still Life," "They Travel by Air," and "The Circle Game." The power of Atwood's poetry comes from its "spatial" quality–the geographic dimension set up within the language. Human landscapes are created by arranging memories as if they were objects and by comparing external things to internal visions. The complex "Against Still Life" is significant on three levels: philosophical, narrative, and figurative. The dimensional quality is formed by highlighting objects in contrast to human life. "The animals in that country," with its fundamental Canadian literary theme, is less sophisticated. European readers may find it difficult to understand the discontent and self-flogging of much Canadian literature.

73 MONTAGNES, ANNE. "Atwood Moves to Epic Substance, as a Maturing Culture Moves on from the Lyric." *Globe and Mail*, 14 February, p. E15.

Praises *True Stories*. Atwood seems to say a polluted urban river can't make conventional romantic poems, but "when was any of Atwood's writing conventional, lyric or romantic?" What's changed since the mangled words washed ashore in *The Animals in That Country*? One answer is that these poems are called stories. The tide has taken the writer outside herself, to contemplate the world's atrocities, with valid tears. The "Notes Towards a Poem That Can Never Be Written" section bears witness, not to Atwood's own life or creative processes, but to atrocious tortures and deaths: "can poems come from such horrors? Well, this is a different kind of poetry, verging toward epic substance," like a culture maturing beyond the lyric.

74 MORLEY, PATRICIA. "Atwood's New Poems Significant." *Citizen* (Ottawa), 14 February, p. 31.

Finds *True Stories* uneven, with some failures, but integrity and strength in the best poems, like "Vultures" and "Variations on the Word *Love*." The book's ironic title parodies the writer and true-confession magazines. There are "poems about torture in (apparently) Third World countries run by sadistic fascists," and poems about our own psychic tortures. The sub-text is veiled menace, slightly surreal. Though Atwood tries to broaden the traditionally private lyric with her theme of torture, which connects to her second theme, of private love, the poems remain mostly personal.

75 ____. "Margaret Atwood." In *Encyclopedia of World Literature in the Twentieth Century*. Edited by Leonard S. Klein. Vol. 1. Rev. ed. New York: Frederick Ungar Publishing Co., pp. 133-34.
 Describes Atwood as a complex and internationally known writer, a sensitive poet, and a talented humorist; briefly discusses *Survival*, and the gothic sensibility in four novels. *Surfacing*, which became "almost a cult novel" in women's studies, takes the gothic seriously. *Survival*, which rode a crest of nationalism, is influenced by Atwood's own themes, but lacks her ironic humor, and "greatly underestimates" Canadian literature's affirmations. *Lady Oracle*, which surpasses *The Edible Woman*'s comic gothic, parodies the macabre and gothic. In *Life Before Man*, which sees human life bleakly and harshly, the gothic becomes an analogue for duplicity and the necessity of growth.

76 MOSS, JOHN. *A Reader's Guide to the Canadian Novel*. Toronto: McClelland & Stewart, pp. 1-6.
 Gives reluctant praise to the ubiquitous Atwood, whose four precise, witty, commanding novels still, despite their increasingly dated 1960s sensibility, satisfy the literate public, and critics outside Canada. *The Edible Woman* is striking because it fuses confessional and satiric modes, but it fails to examine the root causes of the plastic world. The formidable, brilliant *Surfacing* is one of our best novels, and has a "perfect command of images and words as poetic determinants of reality"; Atwood's wit safely distances us from the narrator's madness. *Lady Oracle* is both shallow and deep, a fascinating gothic comedy whose passive protagonist satirically embodies our times. *Life Before Man* has an uncontrolled compound narrative voice, conventional characters, and trivial relationships. Perhaps critics outside Canada have lower expectations.

77 MÜLLER, MARIANNE. Review of *Strömung*. *Zeitschrift für Anglistik und Amerikanistik* (Leipzig) 29, no. 4:381-83.

Describes *Strömung*, the East German translation of *Surfacing*, as the Canadian perspective on the problems inherent in the late stages of capitalistic society. Like the heroine of Marilyn French's *The Women's Room*, the main character is emancipated, but remains dissatisfied. Like James Dickey's *Deliverance*, the story reflects the crisis relationship between a developed capitalistic society and the natural environment. The protagonist's new attitude at the end of the novel is a call for cooperative behavior in a society that is hostile to humanity.

78 NAIDEN, JAMES. Review of *Two-Headed Poems*. *Minneapolis Tribune*, 5 April, p. G11.
     A favorable review of *Two-Headed Poems*. Atwood's Canadian history themes are not provincial or monotonously regionalist. The poems are mostly of daily existence and an examined life. "Her language has a serenity"; her implosive imagery builds up and then sets free "an aggregate detachment" that is not distance or "'objectivity'" but an acceptance. "A Red Shirt" is one of the reviewer's favorites. While some poems seem excessively vernacular, Atwood's "poetic concerns are universal."

79 NEW, WILLIAM H. "After Wilderness: Recent English Canadian Literature." *Américas* 33, no. 1:26-32 passim.
     Refers to three of Atwood's novels and her poetry in a general discussion: behind her feminist quests lie inherited Loyalist and Ontario attitudes to nature, and nineteenth-century women's difficulties with a male, Protestant, wilderness-fearing culture. "Journey to the Interior" speaks of survival with irony and despair; *Surfacing*'s "'Americans'" turn out to be Canadians.

80 P[ARISI], J[OSEPH]. Review of *Two-Headed Poems*. *Booklist* 77, no. 14 (15 March):1006.
     Finds personal and patriotic divisions, basic matters of love and loss, and some obscurity and dullness; still, Atwood's second best is mostly better than others' best.

81 PEARSON, CAROL, and POPE, KATHERINE. *The Female Hero in American and British Literature*. New York and London: R.R. Bowker Company, pp. 68, 72-78, 127-28, 205-11, 238-39.

Uses Atwood's first three novels as examples of mythic patterns of female heroism. The fantasy and gothic *Lady Oracle* clearly illustrates the three stages of the "heroic journey to self-fulfillment"–the exit from the garden of dependency, the awakening to experience, and the reconciliation with the mother. "In each stage, the protagonist is faced with a powerful figure to interpret, a dragon to slay, and a treasure to win." At the end Joan, after reconciling with her mother, demystifying the patriarch, and conquering self-hatred, is reborn to her true self, and begins her "first honest relationship," with the reporter. In *The Edible Woman*, Marian's loss of appetite is "her call to the quest," and the cake is a substitute sacrifice that frees her from Peter, who is consuming her identity. The *Surfacing* hero is a casualty of internalized patriarchal ideas who can, after accepting her father's mortality, "reclaim the female power to give birth–to the repressed woman within, and to a truly human child." Her mother rescues her, by means of the childhood drawing of a maternal deity figure. By the end the hero is reconciled with both parents, but especially the mother, and integrates the best of their roles; but, like other female heroes, she is at risk in an uncomprehending world.

82 PRATT, ANNIS. "Novels of Rebirth and Transformation." In *Archetypal Patterns in Women's Fiction*, with Barbara White, Andrea Loewenstein, and Mary Wyer. Bloomington: Indiana University Press, pp. 135-66. Reprint. Brighton, Sussex: Harvester Press, 1982.

An altered presentation of 1981.83 (below), with a five-phase rebirth journey, and a section on the "Collective Vision" in Doris Lessing's *The Four-Gated City*.

83 ____. "*Surfacing* and the Rebirth Journey." In *The Art of Margaret Atwood: Essays in Criticism*. See Davidson and Davidson 1981.23, pp. 139-57.

Follows Gray 1977.28, Christ 1976.13, and Jung, to define in British and American women's fiction, and in *Surfacing*, an empowering, transforming archetypal rebirth journey. In Jung's masculine rebirth journey, where the myths of the hero's unconscious are shared by his society, the transformed quester can more easily rejoin society. Women's unconscious reflects a lost, non-western culture, which society may reject as deviant or crazy; hence the irresolutions of much women's fiction. The rebirth journey of women's fiction has seven phases: "Splitting Off from the World of the Ego"; "Green World Guide or Token" (*Surfacing*'s lake); "Confrontation with Parental Figures"; "Green World Lover" (Joe); "Shadow" (the violent brother); "Final Descent to the Nadir"; and "Ascent and Re-Entry into Society as Known." Discusses Demeter/Kore archetypes; the "Androgynous Elixir" in Virginia Woolf's *To the Lighthouse*; the encoded, "Hieroglyphic Elixir" in Anaïs Nin's *Seduction of the Minotaur*; and the "Elixir of Maternity" in *Surfacing*. The scrapbooks Atwood's hero finds are not stereotyped but androgynous "feminine" and "masculine" archetypes; the conception is self-actualizing and empowering; the "'lost child surfacing'" is both the aborted fetus and the hero's own lost childhood. Atwood's "wholly transformed" hero is unique in her determination to return to society. These reclaimed archetypes may radically transform the reader as well as the hero, and thus lead to social change. Presented, in altered form, in 1981.82 (above).

84 Review of *Two-Headed Poems*. *Choice* 18, nos. 11-12 (July-August):1542.

Is taken "precariously" through what is familiar and what is dangerously unknown. At first these poems are duplicitous; halfway through, they "give over entirely to death." The reader finds in these barren poems no hint of language, mind, or emotions working.

85 Review of *Two-Headed Poems*. *Kirkus Reviews* 49, no. 2 (15 January):133.

Acclaims *Two-Headed Poems* as generic–it's too good to be acclaimed as merely women's writing. Atwood's poems are both general history and intimately personal, direct, and scrupulously honest. Though flaws of poetic form occur, her best work, such as "Marrying the Hangman," with its subtle politics of gender and power, should be taken very seriously indeed.

86 ROSOWSKI, SUSAN J. "Margaret Atwood's *Lady Oracle*: Social Mythology and the Gothic Novel." *Research Studies* 49, no. 2 (June):87-98.

Reads *Lady Oracle* as a reversed Gothic, where the horror is located not outside but within our social mythology. Atwood's three novels discover an increasingly supernatural and Gothic social mythology, as Northey 1976.70 perceived in *Surfacing*. *Lady Oracle*'s narrator moves through temporal, cultural myths – advertising ideals, social rituals, the fantasy roles of Costume Gothics and films – that are inadequate for human reality, but impervious to it. As human complexities and morality are sacrificed to the fictive fantasy, demonic selves or ghosts result. As in Henry James, these ghosts are fragmentary, split-off selves; in *Lady Oracle* they become monsters who threaten to destroy the self that created them; birth-death struggles of the self result. The narrator lacks a core of personal identity to counter others' mythologies; as the book ends, she is assuming yet another fantasy role, in a thinly veiled Costume Gothic myth. Revised: 1988.43.

87 SCHIEFER, NANCY A. "Gloom and Peril but Little to Sustain the Reader." *London* (Ontario) *Free Press*, 10 October, p. B10.

Is dissatisfied with *Bodily Harm*, which dazzles and confounds, but only partly succeeds. It's hard to say why. The gloomy atmosphere tends to be stifling; Atwood contends that men demand control; the island events strain our credulity. But the flashbacks to Rennie's childhood Griswold are "worthy of Alice Munro"; contemporary Toronto is authentically detailed; and the appealing Rennie is the most original and convincing woman in Atwood's novels. Still, despite the potentially redemptive conclusion, *Bodily Harm* unfortunately recalls Graham Greene revisited, and "Flannery O'Connor's acid advice" about drawing large pictures for the blind; it's a moral manifesto, not a work of art.

88 SMITH, DELLA. Review of *Life Before Man*. *Maenad* 1, no. 3 (Spring):85-87.

Praises *Life Before Man*'s recognizable, realistic story of contemporary love relationships, whose trapped characters ultimately struggle more for survival than for happiness; and defends Elizabeth, who has been much maligned by reviewers. She is overpowering, but seeks love, and has had to survive past terrors and become strong; her "'Clean up your own mess'" is positive, not tyrannical. Nate is a drifter and ineffectual husband whose "lack of passion drives Elizabeth up the wall." Elizabeth's poignant reaction, at the China exhibit, "represents the sad, paradoxical feelings of many modern women." We have to survive; Atwood shows how far we are from our goal of creating a meaningful, victimless life that does not depend on man.

89 STANLEY, DON. "She Should've Stayed Home." *Province* (Vancouver), 11 October, Magazine sec., p. 8.

Reviews *Bodily Harm*: "strong title, clever writing, weak plot, possible mid-life-crisis, Jill-Clayburgh-type flick about Toronto freelance journalist who contracts cancer, loses lover, experiences adventure in exotic Caribbean." The heroine, who once reported significant events, has gotten as superficial as her present articles. The Caribbean coup is deliberately confused and fragmentary, perhaps to parallel the unresolved opening. We're supposed to think Rennie is transformed by holding her cellmate's hand, but some may doubt it.

90 [STUTTAFORD, GENEVIEVE]. Review of *Two-Headed Poems*. *Publishers Weekly* 219, no. 1 (2 January):50.

The prolific, accomplished Atwood has done more than anyone to make Canadian literature visible; and, although a leading feminist, she has been reshaping our basic ideas about men and women. Her genius in *Two-Headed Poems* knits together daybooks poems and a poem on torture. Marrying the Hangman" is *Two-Headed Poems*'s masterpiece.

91 SUTTON, JOAN. "Margaret Atwood: No Will-of-the-Wisp, This Lady!" *Sunday Sun* (Toronto), 29 November, p. G18.

Profiles Atwood in Washington D.C., after her university residence there and a Canadian book tour for *Bodily Harm*. Atwood is neither a hippie nor a fragile masterpiece, but a strong, responsible, creative person, who does not dwell on criticism or praise, such as the *New York Times Book Review*'s front-page rave for *Life Before Man* [1980.41]. Atwood discusses U.S. versus Canadian book tours, cancer, femininity, love, relationships, mothering, political responsibility, and *Bodily Harm*'s flawed men and women. The "poignant, profoundly moving" *Bodily Harm* is dedicated "to a close friend who died of cancer at the age of 38 [Jennifer Rankin]. To a suggestion of being anti-male, Atwood responds, "'It's true, I don't like Superman. I prefer Clark Kent myself, maybe even Batman.'"

92 SWARD, ROBERT. Review of *True Stories*. *Quill and Quire* 47, no. 4 (April):37.

Praises highly *True Stories*'s humour, wit, passion, lyricism, precision, and unwavering moral perspective. During Atwood's recent

1981

Harbourfront reading, she remarked that most reviews have given a false impression that all of *True Stories* is about torture; only one section, "Notes Towards a Poem That Can Never Be Written," is; and all its specific details really happened. *True Stories's* central theme "is love, the misuse of power, lies and perversions of love," as in the funny, scathingly true "Variations on the Word Love."

93 THOMAS, AUDREY. "Topic of Cancer." *Books in Canada* 10, no. 8 (October):9, 11-12.
     Assesses *Bodily Harm*, vouching from experience for the realism of its third-world, homemade but dangerous, revolution. The lifestyles journalist Rennie develops Annette of "A Travel Piece," the travel writer who looks, trying not to see or know. "Dr. Minnow is the only truly good man in the book," but Daniel is a close second; there aren't any good women, except maybe Elva. Three things bothered the reviewer: the flip but wearing, radio-show conversations; the unbelievably-presented Paul, who is almost a Harlequin Presents hero; and Rennie's implausible willingness to pick up the parcel. *Bodily Harm* is a strong book about violence and despair: Rennie's final compassion and touching are beautifully done – "hands – and the laying on of hands" could be an essay; the metaphors and images are brilliant. At the end, Rennie is flying home, sadder but wiser, and ready to report – but who will hear her, even if she does?

94 THOMAS, CLARA. "*Lady Oracle*: The Narrative of a Fool-Heroine." In *The Art of Margaret Atwood: Essays in Criticism*. See Davidson and Davidson 1981.23, pp. 159-75.
     Proposes a new Ellen Moers category, of the Fool-Heroine, a truly comic clown who learns individual and social responsibility; and analyzes *Lady Oracle*'s five-part structure. Because comedy is a process towards balance, Joan is irrepressibly, but not irreversibly, in process. Part I establishes the vulnerable, kind, fantasizing Joan and her many mysteries. (Joan's hair troubles and orphanhood recall [L.M. Montgomery's] Anne of Green Gables.) Part II tells, with self-pity and self-mockery, the story of Fat Joan the clown. Part III, which mixes Costume Gothic and reality, establishes Joan as a self-deluded and unreliable narrator. The surreal, kaleidoscopic Part IV shows Joan as an attention-craving Fool-Heroine, not the passive victim she claims she is. Part V brings the still irrepressibly adventuring Joan to an

acceptance of her responsibilities. Women students identify with Joan, and laugh with her; men students seem slightly defensive and offended. Canadian critics have missed *Lady Oracle*'s subtle balance of comedy.

95 THOMPSON, LEE BRISCOE. "Minuets and Madness: Margaret Atwood's *Dancing Girls*." In *The Art of Margaret Atwood: Essays in Criticism*. See Davidson and Davidson 1981.23, pp. 107-22.

Argues that the many voices of Atwood's prose and poetry come from one unified consciousness, contrary to the misleading 1978.71 Oates interview, and to critics complaining of coldly mythic poetry versus warm but shallow comic novels. These virtuoso stories have Atwood's bemused fictive narrator, mundane minuets, and mythic poetic madness. Her aliens confront other aliens, waging small battles for tenuous control. "The Grave of the Famous Poet" has her "first person *very* singular female" narrator; and her "surface minuet and subliminal massacre," with a Canadian observance of the proprieties, between men and women. The zany "Rape Fantasies" shows language's limits, and men as victims, too. "Giving Birth," which has been seen as a maternal mellowing, has a "surreal postpartum illusion." "Polarities," a madness story, competes with dance for metaphorical control of the book; Louise's reasonable Blakean vision of wholeness is treated as insanity by her "'sane'" friends.

96 TIMSON, JUDITH. "Books." *Chatelaine* 54, no. 10 (October):4.

A brief, favorable review of *Bodily Harm*. As with *Life Before Man*, the tone is relentlessly disheartening, but the plot is less aimless; Atwood effectively communicates fear and danger. Rennie is her witness, a victim and survivor.

97 _____. "The Magnificent Atwood." *Chatelaine* 54, no. 1 (January):42-43, 56, 60, 64-65, [67], 70.

Profiles Atwood, who is *Chatelaine*'s cover Woman of the Year: a mysteriously private woman; a famous and controversial writer, nationalist, and critic, who has become a media "Thing"; a "'feminine feminist'" who has now limited interviews (but whose next novel, about a trendy magazine writer, may get revenge); a split Peggy/Margaret; a good, warm friend who is praised at length by artist Charles Pachter, collaborator Peter Pearson, and writer Marian Engel; a responsible member of the writing and feminist communities; and a serious, uncompromising writer who sees herself as a realistic optimist. Discusses Atwood's family background, *Life Before Man*'s American praise from Marilyn French 1980.41 and Canadian detraction from William French 1979.38, Atwood's relationship with Graeme Gibson, and her mothering; quotes from *True Stories* and other poems.

98 TWIGG, ALAN. "Making Words – Not Money." *Province* (Vancouver), 8 March, Magazine sec., p. 4.

Though it's tempting to seek "the enigmatic Mona-Lisa-of-*Macleans*" and the *Chatelaine* cover girl in Atwood's poetry, *True Stories*'s opening [title] poem warns us not to. But ask for *True Stories* plural instead, and you get Atwood's splendidly vindicated belief in poetry as the place where language should be renewed. *True Stories* includes dizzying incantations, intimate postcards, the sardonically titled "True Romances," and "Notes Towards a Poem That Can Never Be Written," which is the heart of the book, recounting man's brutality to man and especially to woman with Atwood's powerful, unsentimental intensity. Examining inanely romanticized love or sanctified childbearing, Atwood never relaxes, or flinches.

99 ____. "What to Write." In *For Openers: Conversations with 24 Canadian Writers*. Madiera Park, B.C.: Harbour Publishing, pp. 219-30.

Interview: Atwood discusses *Life Before Man*; contemporary society, politics, and publishing; Canadian reviews; and *Survival*. *Life*'s original title was *Notes on the Mezaoic* [sic]. *Life*'s actual title has three main meanings: for Lesje, prehistory; for Elizabeth, her own life over a relationship with a man; and, for Nate's political idealism, life "is not yet fully human." *Life* depicts human predatory behaviour, contemporary marriage, fear, and isolation. Happy endings may be false cheer; suffering and death are real. Canadian reviews are one-third bad, one-third good, one-third either, on any Atwood book. "'Women's novels'" includes most novels. Atwood recommends *This Magazine*, and Salutin 1977.79, over *Survival*'s purist Marxist critics. Canada is increasingly foreign-owned, and chain bookstores threaten creative writing. A reprint, slightly altered, of the interview portion of 1979.98.

100 VANHEE-NELSON, LOUISE. Review of *Sur l'arbre perchés*. *In Review* (Toronto) 15, no. 1 (February):28.

Finds *Up in the Tree* humorous and suspenseful, but the end is unrealistic. The author's illustrations are excellent; kids will love the book.

101 V[OGEL], M[AGDALENA]. Review of *Die Unmöglichkeit der N* ̈*ache*. *Neue Zürcher Zeitung*, 14-15 February, p. 39.

Commends *Die Unmöglichkeit der N* ̈*ache*, the translation of *Life Before Man*, though it is a sober novel that does not move toward an event; except for the separation of couples, nothing happens. Atwood concentrates on the internal, primarily the effect of the subconscious on the consciousness. The museum, where the paths of the characters meet, is a dramatically well chosen setting. The superior, yet vulnerable, Elizabeth is the only character allowed to be a narrator. Atwood succeeds in connecting fantasy with literary art.

102 WACHTEL, ELEANOR. "'Tattoo Artist' Calls It as She Sees It." *Vancouver Sun*, 9 October, p. L36.

Admires the truthful, witty, if detached, *Bodily Harm*. Since Atwood became a literary superstar in 1972, Canadian reviewers have raced to find her work overrated, and too bleak, as with the internationally lauded *Life Before Man*. Now *True Stories* and *Bodily Harm* are even more focussed on Amnesty International horrors, not didactically, but truthfully. "Atwood's wry wit is a delight, however acerbic. . . . The story unfolds with cinematic distance, like Joan Didion's *The Book of Common Prayer*." When Rennie returns to Canada, she will bear true witness – a heroic, upbeat, almost conventional conclusion. Though *Bodily Harm*'s single viewpoint is more engaging than *Life Before Man*, you take this book to your head, not your heart.

103 WADE-STADLER, NANCY. Review of *Anna's Pet*, by Atwood and Joyce Barkhouse. *In Review* (Toronto) 15, no. 1 (February):28.

Recommends *Anna's Pet* as a cheerful and unaffected portrayal of a child's affinity with nature; praises Ann Blades's warm, engaging watercolours.

104 WAGNER, LINDA W. "The Making of *Selected Poems*, the Process of Surfacing." In *The Art of Margaret Atwood: Essays in Criticism*. See Davidson and Davidson 1981.23, pp. 81-94.

Atwood's poetic persona is a questioning, often bitter woman, who resists passion, but who progresses, by *You Are Happy*, to accepting the non-verbal knowledge of touch and emotion, and the other as well as the self. The much-cut first book's personae only lament, without making contact; the title poem, like W.D. Snodgrass's "Heart Needle," juxtaposes children, love, war, games. The second book's anthropomorphic and varied personae may have prepared for Atwood's Moodie, who becomes a perfect mask for self-exploration. The fourth book's central, pioneer persona speaks as a Persephone in the title poem. *Selected Poems*'s cuts change the fifth book's comic power struggles, strengthening the woman, but losing passionate poems like "He is last seen." The sixth book's central persona, Circe, is a "fully realized female – maker, lover, poet, prophet"; her verbal magic bests male force. Excerpted 1983.129.

105 WAINWRIGHT, J.A. Review of *Bodily Harm*. *Dalhousie Review* 61, no. 3 (Autumn):581-83.

Rejects Atwood's bleak, uncompromising, limited vision, and the predictable, dogmatic *Bodily Harm*. "Atwood employs a sledgehammer approach to relationships between the sexes that shatters the sympathetic reader's concern for Rennie and for women everywhere caught by male power and dominance." Can one judge harshly anyone who's just been operated on for cancer? Rennie is ambiguous; she never escapes Griswold, or depending on men, or her "'lifestyles'" mentality that constantly misjudges political realities. Her final caring for Lora "is too little and too late." Though Atwood may be one of Canada's finest writers, and internationally acclaimed, *Bodily Harm* is an "immense failure." Atwood's is a closed "world in which men fuck women over" and women suffer. Everyone here is a victim, including the reader.

106 WAYNE, JOYCE. "The Atwood Generation: Notes on Surfacing from the Underground." *Quill and Quire* 47, no. 2 (February):4, 6, 8.

Quotes Atwood, Graeme Gibson, James Polk, and other Canadian writers and publishers, in a survey of the early 1970s Canadian literary renaissance, when Anansi and other new presses launched young, experimental, nationalist writers, versus the 1980s problems of rising costs, shrinking market, indifferent media, and chain book stores; Atwood on cover.

107 WEINGANT, LISELOTTE. "Das Bild des Mannes im Frauenroman der Siebziger Jahre." Ph.D. dissertation, University of Illinois at Urbana-Champaign, pp. 131-69.

A comparative analysis of the patriarchal trinity of "the son-man, the father-man, and the disturbing spirit" in novels by six contemporary North American and European women writers. The male protagonists in Atwood and the Austrian Schwaiger force women into an "inner isolation. Patriarchy in their novels is intact; women do not develop a collective consciousness." Only Reinig, of the German Democratic Republic, and [Doris] Lessing design a possible new man. See *Dissertation Abstracts International* 42 (1982):3992A. (Abstract in English.)

108 WEIR, LORRAINE. "Meridians of Perception: A Reading of *The Journals of Susanna Moodie*." In *The Art of Margaret Atwood: Essays in Criticism*. See Davidson and Davidson 1981.23, pp. 69-79.

Explicates resonances between the eight collages of *The Journals of Susanna Moodie*, their poems, and other Atwood poems, including "Progressive insanities of a pioneer," "Tricks with Mirrors," "The Circle Game," and several from *Procedures for Underground*. Collage and photograph function "as mimetic subtext," as "paradigms of the perceptual stances," and as "icons of the grammar of visual perception which structures Atwood's work." The first, front-cover collage contrasts photograph with nature, and "signifies the equivalence of eye with self, and the triumph" of natural code over mimetic representation. "Collages two and four present two opposed but parallel images of Mrs. Moodie, transformations of external internal landscape." The divided seventh collage is analogous to "mirror poems of reflexive structure like 'This Is a Photograph of Me.'" Moodie envisions a cosmological "'union'" like the final dance of *Procedures for Underground*.

109 WIGOD, REBECCA. "Image and Margaret Atwood." *Times-Colonist* (Victoria, B.C.), 3 November, p. 17.

Interviews the interview-wary Atwood, who is in Victoria to promote *Bodily Harm*. Atwood comments on Canadian resistance to *Life Before Man*'s realism; media images versus privacy, referring to [Timson 1981.97]; and *Bodily Harm*'s Rennie as "more than an amalgam of the journalists who have grilled her."

1981

110 WILSON, JEAN. "Screams Should Be Heard and Not Seen: Poems by Webb and Atwood." *Broadside* (Toronto) 2, no. 7 (May):14.

Welcomes *True Stories* and appreciates *Wilson's Bowl*, by Phyllis Webb, which are important, physically attractive, very different but overlapping books. Atwood focuses on life's harsh or concrete realities, with incisive images; she "insists that we see the facts clearly" in "Notes Towards a Poem That Can Never Be Written." "Not all of *True Stories* bears witness to the unbearable"; there are wry love poems, the bittersweet "True Romances," the vivid "'natural' world" of "Landcrab I," and the ironic defense of the poet as observer in "Small Poems for the Winter Solstice." Atwood's [watercolour] cover is "eye-catching."

111 WOODCOCK, GEORGE. "Bashful but Bold: Notes on Margaret Atwood as Critic." In *The Art of Margaret Atwood: Essays in Criticism*. See Davidson and Davidson 1981.23, pp. 223-41.

Appreciates Atwood's miscellaneous criticism, from the early book reviews through the 1977 "Canadian Monsters" essay, suggesting a miscellany volume; reprints much of 1973.106 and 1973.107 on *Survival*, slightly updated. Atwood's poetic imagination illuminates her own creative work even while she accurately discusses others' work. Her anti-autobiographical and anti-political stances defend the writer's imagination, but are simplistic. Her essays on Reaney's *Alphabet*, his *Collected Poems*, Canadian monsters, and Gwendolyn MacEwen's muse, generalize boldly and convincingly. Contrasts *Surfacing's* collective allegory and self-mockery with *Survival's* personal emotion; suggests that Atwood, as a mutable, good, important critic at a crucial time, be taken "seriously, but not too seriously." Reprinted in part: 1985.11.

112 ____. "Love and Horror." *Saturday Night* 96, no. 5 (May):55-56.

Acclaims the intensely moral *True Stories*, as perhaps Atwood's best verse, honed down, accurate, yet visually luminous. Like the rational Pascal, Atwood speaks of the death of reason. As in *Two-Headed Poems*, and "Landcrab I and II," thoughts metamorphose into sensations, and things are curiously "liberated into thought." The unreasoning barbarity of the "Notes Towards a Poem That Can Never Be Written" section is like a verse abstract from Amnesty International reports. Perhaps most appalling of all is the way cruelty can change to kindness, as in ["Trainride: Vienna-Bonn"], and we face the fear of what we might do. Though such poems cannot portray the rational, they are intensely moral, no less so in savaging romantic ideas of love, motherhood, etc. *True Stories* is not all negative: human love "is a longing over distances, ... [and] a necessary contradiction to a world of violence." And the book's last image is of renewal. Reprinted as part of 1983.147. Excerpted:1983.129.

113 ____. *Taking It to the Letter*. Dunvegan, Ont.: Quadrant Editions, pp. 25, 27-28, 35-36, 38, 43, 47, 51-52, 61-62, 65-66, 82-83, 91-92, 101-102, 152.

Includes 14 letters from Woodcock to Atwood, dated 1971-1976 and 1980, concerning Atwood's two *Canadian Literature* articles on James Reaney's *Alphabet* and on his poetry; Woodcock 1972.40, 1973.107, 1976.106, and 1980.148 on Atwood; American publishers and *Survival*; Herbert Read's *The Green Child*; Atwood's work on nineteenth-century utopias and Nature Goddesses; the *Northern Journey* problem (1973.103); the Canadian Civil Liberties Association; a demand for J.R. Narayan's release; and Woodcock's own non-fiction, verse plays, and poetry, including an Anansi book of poems. See also Woodcock's letters written to others on Atwood criticism, the *Northern Journey* problem, etc.

114 YOUNG, VERNON. "Writers of Mid-Passage: Davison, Atwood, Ammons." *Washington Post Book World*, 3 May, p. 8.

Features Peter Davison's mournful, thoughtful *Barn Fever*; praises Atwood's fierce, indignant, sorrowful *Two-Headed Poems*; complains of A.R. Ammons's mannerisms in *A Coast of Trees*. Atwood's poetry is tempered anger, a brave and haunted witness to the world we have made, of endemic violence, fatuity, and lovelessness. Though the many daughter poems glow with intense affection, Atwood does not allow herself further consolations. And, unlike Adrienne Rich, Atwood sees that "evil has no gender."

115 ZWEIG, PAUL. "Two Poets." *New York Times Book Review*, 11 October, p. 32.

Complains, in a two-book review, of Atwood's terrible, intimidating *Two-Headed Poems*. Her lines growl, bark, attack, or creak with menace. Why is her world so unfriendly? Though there are several fine poems here, her stridency is wearying.

1982

1 ABBEY, MARILYN R. "Margaret Atwood: Wit, Humor and Politics." *Chicago Sun-Times*, 14 March, sec. 5, pp. 23, 25. Newsbank 1981-1982, 80:C4.

Praises *Bodily Harm*'s humor, acerbic wit, comedy, pathos, and astute and more universal political insights. Rennie is intelligently cynical, powerless, a somewhat sensible and somewhat kooky Atwood heroine. Atwood does show "the knottiness of human relationships": Jake, who pretends S-M, would not harm Rennie bodily, but subdues her; Daniel, who is decent and honorable, mutilates her breast, but to save her. The end is ambiguous, about rescue, deaths, and the reporting that Rennie intends but may lack the courage to do, if she gets out.

2 ABRAMS, ALAN. "Atwood's Latest: A Steal at $60." *Windsor Star*, 6 February, p. C13.

"While in Windsor recently, Atwood talked" about her own Salamander Press, which has just published her $60 *Notes Towards a Poem That Can Never Be Written*, and which will publish "Murder in the Dark" and "Cuts"; her friend and art-book printer Charlie Pachter at Cranbrook Academy of Arts; and Joseph Brodsky's disruptive behavior and Susan Sontag's allied tactics at the October 1981 Amnesty International Festival in Toronto. Atwood's favorite author is "'God.'" But she thinks "somebody has done a really bad proofreading job on His book."

3 ADACHI, KEN. "Atwood Makes the Reader See Things to Admire." *Toronto Star*, 4 December, p. F12.

Praises Atwood's "engaging and persuasive" *Second Words*. Despite her introduction's disclaimers, Atwood is a major writer whose forceful personality unifies these occasional pieces; and "there are so many good words, so much intelligence, that the garden-variety reviewer seethes with envy." "Nationalism, Limbo and the Canadian Club" accurately depicts the late 1950s dearth of Canadian literature courses. Atwood's style is "clean but sly," warm irony with cold anger behind it. Atwood makes the reader "examine the nuances and subtleties in writers he thought he had already known," and wittily and knowledgeably guides the ignorant traveller.

4 ____. "Canada's Poetry: Spiky, Tough, Vital." *Toronto Star*, 14 November, p. G11.

Celebrates Atwood's sinewy introduction and knowledgeable, quirky, eclectic selections for *The New Oxford Book of Canadian Verse in English*. Atwood is the ideal editor here: a gifted poet, astute critic, and good guide who holds high A.J.M. Smith's torch. She chooses poems on their intrinsic merit, not their tendencies; though, as she rightly notes, Canadian poetry's dominant motifs set cold, stony nature against the human. The reviewer prefers modern to early Canadian poetry, and praises Al Purdy's powerful poems of Canadian place.

5 ADAMS, PHOEBE-LOU. "Short Reviews." *Atlantic Monthly* 249, no. 4 (April):110.

Praises *Bodily Harm*'s superior writing, wit, characters, and terrifying suspense; it seems to be concerned with responsibility–personal, national, or international.

6 AGER, SUSAN. "The Happy Wonderer." *San Jose Mercury*, 29 March. Newsbank 1981-1982, 91:D13-14.

Interviews Atwood in San Francisco Nob Hotel: quotes Atwood on her own happy life, success, writing, and her "fairly direct pipeline to what others call the unconscious'"; Canadian literature; Toronto Bohemian Embassy poetry readings; and El Salvador's killings of journalists, versus the Caribbean of *Bodily Harm*.

7 ____. "Waiting for Zero, Surreal Rings True." *San Jose Mercury*, 4 April. Newsbank 1981-1982, 91:D7.

Finds *Bodily Harm* shocking, incredible, yet entirely possible. Though no character in the Caribbean is lovable, and though we can't empathize with the stuporous Rennie until the end, we finally understand, in the last, stunning, powerful pages. "*Bodily Harm* is too bewildering and too bloody to be a good bedtime read." Take it to a bright cafe, where you can look up to your own calm "Real Life" now and then.

8 ALMÉRAS, DIANE. "Un vaste jeu de monopoly." *Relations* (Montréal) 42, no. 481 (June):171-72.

Appreciates *La vie avant l'homme*, the French-Canadian translation of *Life Before Man*, as an autopsy of marriage that evaluates the wall put up between the sexes and unveils the misery that lies under the surface structure. Atwood's approach is like a scientific study of relationships that effectively displays feminine and masculine sensibilities. The result is a lucid and honest book.

9 ASHENMACHER, BOB. "Looking out from the Inside." *News-Tribune and Herald* (Duluth, Minn.), 11 April, p. 8, 18, 20, 22.

Interviews Atwood, who will soon give workshops, a discussion, and a reading in Duluth, by phone from her home: Atwood responds to questions on her childhood; on being a poet and novelist, a Canadian writer, and a "'women's writer'"; on autobiographical versus imagined experience in *Surfacing*; and on Americans and responsibility for the environment. Quotes from "Progressive insanities of a pioneer" and ["You Begin"] show Atwood's perceptions of history and her deeply felt love.

10 ATHERTON, STANLEY S. "Tropical Traumas: Images of the Caribbean in Recent Canadian Fiction." *Canadian Literature*, no. 95 (Winter), pp. 8-14.

Discusses the dislocated protagonists and harsh, often nightmare realities of Caribbean-set fiction by Atwood, Diane Giguère, Juan Butler, Harold Horwood, and Timothy Findley. The travel writer protagonist of Atwood's "A Travel Piece" substitutes clichéd fantasies for the violence and pollution her readers do not want to know about. The freelance journalist of *Bodily Harm* fails to understand her alien experience on a troubled, violent island because her Griswold Canadian decency has not prepared her to cope with such realities. "Instead of acting, Rennie fantasizes about her release" when her cell-mate is brutally beaten. When Rennie does hold her suffering cell-mate, the compassionate gesture "is too little and too late."

11 ATWOOD, MARGARET. "Mathews and Misrepresentation." In *Second Words: Selected Critical Prose*. Toronto: Anansi, pp. 129-50.

Reprint of 1973.2.

12 ATWOOD, MARGARETS. "Margaret Atwood, One Suspects, May Be a Front for a Committee. . . ." *Globe and Mail*, 20 November, p. L2.

A tongue-in-cheek review of *Second Words*. Conflicting media sightings support the conclusion that Atwood does not really exist: how could the cookie-baking comedienne of Greta Warmodota's Griswold profile be the threatening succubus of Alan Peevish and Frank Slug? "'Atwood is to literature what urban sprawl is to town planning.'" *Second Words*'s occasional pieces appeared originally not only in *The Globe and Mail*, but also in inferior places, like *The New York Times*, despite the Atwoods's alleged nationalism. These too-favourable reviews are soft in the underbelly; we newspaper readers want blood. As a critic, Atwood is not a pro: "Postmodernism seems to have wafted right by her," and questionable frivolities occur, like comparing men to dung beetles, which goes too far. "What emerges from a swift perusal of this book is that Atwood is to words as a pig is to mud." We can't argue with "some of her positions – on the human-being status of women, not to mention men, on Canadian autonomy, on torture and repression – platitudinous though they" are. We think the Atwoods should go back to poetry and fiction. See Hurst 1982.85. Reprinted: 1988.1.

13 AUGUSTINE, JANE. "Margaret Atwood." In *Critical Survey of Poetry: English Language Series*. Edited by Frank N. Magill. Vol. 1. Englewood Cliffs, N.J.: Salem Press, pp. 63-69.

Atwood's images and themes, in six books of poetry, are shaped by a stark, cold Canadian landscape where the human mind and heart can do little. *The Circle Game* expresses alienated man-woman roles, prehistoric terrors, and historic journeys. *The Animals in That Country* connects the psyche to the deep sea and earth; fear of sex prevails over pleasure, as in "Speeches for Dr. Frankenstein." *The Journals of Susanna Moodie* has a softer persona. *Power Politics*'s lovers are adversaries; *You Are Happy* shows a final break, mythic dehumanizations, a departing Odysseus, and a subtle hope at the end. *Two-Headed Poems* has a new, positive daily life, unwintry mother love, and the togetherness of "All Bread." Includes a short biography.

14 BANN, STEPHEN. "Female Relationships." *London Review of Books* 4, no. 12 (1-14 July):18.

Appreciates, in a seven-book review, the picaresque *Lady Oracle*, and describes female companionship in *Bodily Harm*. Both of these splendidly-crafted novels use what Roland Barthes called the "'zig-zag' or 'saw-toothed' structure," alternating between two narrative levels. Appreciates *Lady Oracle*'s untiring invention, picaresque heroine, parodies of the Gothic, richly comic female roles, and improbable yet possible male types, of which the Royal Porcupine is the choicest specimen. How is *Lady Oracle* feminist? In going beyond stereotypes to show Joan as all-inclusive – succeeding in two literary careers – yet fragmented. *Bodily Harm* is "a quest for sympathetic identity." Rennie's mere journalism cannot carry out Joan's self-analysis. As the epigraph from John Berger's *Ways of Seeing* emphasizes, women are acted on by men. Only with the beaten, unanswering Lora does Rennie escape the rituals of manipulation. The end focuses on female companionship.

15 [BANNON, BARBARA A.]. Review of *Bodily Harm*. *Publishers Weekly* 221, no. 8 (19 February):60.

Finds *Bodily Harm* too bleak and heavy-handed. Rennie is too passive, vulnerable, and naive. Even Atwood's sincere skill can't make believable such a dingy, perverted world, and so much depression and despair.

16 ____. Review of *Dancing Girls and Other Stories*. *Publishers Weekly* 222, no. 3 (16 July):62.

Praises the "exquisite language and wry, quirky perspective" of *Dancing Girls and Other Stories*, citing "The Man from Mars" and "The Resplendant Quetzal." Atwood's always slightly out-of-step characters are seldom too peculiar to identify with; she casts an unsentimental light on the intricate, wordless, and ridiculous in close relationships.

17 BARBOUR, DOUGLAS. "Canadian Poetry Chronicle XI, Part 2." *West Coast Review* 17, no. 2 (October):40.

Celebrates *True Stories*, in a round-up review, as excruciatingly pure, deeply human and compassionately political, incredibly powerful, and one of Atwood's best poetry books. In these attacks on humanity's inhumanity, her wit is darker and more savage, but still precise and acute. Even the most terrifying poems "on torture in 'Notes Towards a Poem That Can Never Be Written,' are exhilarating in their energy, their brilliant craft." Against the suffering she will not evade is the fragile but tough recognition of love's possibilities.

18 BARTLETT, DONALD R. "'Fact' and Form in *Surfacing*." *University of Windsor Review* 17, no. 1 (Fall-Winter):21-28.

Describes the symbolism of "'fact'" – the story and theme – and form in *Surfacing*. The narrator's quest for wholeness moves through dementia to awareness and archetypal reintegration. The three-part form corresponds to stages of her psychological growth. Many of the symbols are ambiguous. The aesthetic structuring blends subgenres, mythic patterns, theme, image, and character. The tentative end is aesthetically correct.

19 BEMROSE, JOHN. "Both Rhyme and Reason." *Maclean's* 95, no. 48 (29 November):64, 66.

Praises Atwood's evenhanded selections for *The New Oxford Book of Canadian Verse in English*. Some will question her following A.J.M. Smith's hefty inclusions of less-impressive 19th-century poems. Her fresh, intelligent, comprehensive choices of mid-20th-century poetry reflect that era's startling depth, versatility, and Canadian articulations. The selection of younger poets ranges from astute to puzzling.

20 BITKER, MARJORIE. "Poems, Stories: An Atwood Feast." *Milwaukee Journal*, 17 October, Entertainment sec., p. 9. Newsbank 1982-1983, 32:B7.

A rave review of Atwood's acutely perceptive, memorable *Dancing Girls and Other Stories* and *True Stories*. *True Stories* reveals, often in everyday words, Atwood's characteristic depth of feeling and acute vision, as in "Spelling." Her poems have the effect of poetry as Emily Dickinson defined it. The equally impressive short stories "present situations tragic, comic, ironic, diverting – all memorable"; describes "Lives of the Poets," "Training," and "Giving Birth."

21 BLAISE, CLARK. "Tale of Two Colonies." *Canadian Literature*, no. 95 (Winter), pp. 110-12.

Is attracted more to *Bodily Harm*'s Toronto lifestyles Rennie than to her political rebirth and return, or to the political, Caribbean coup plot, which follows Naipaul, Greene, Conrad, and others. The island writing is mean and dispirited. The feminist plot catches Rennie's "struggling Southern Ontario Decent" Griswold background and "the beat of the new, 'trés nouveau-wavé' Toronto." Rennie is trendy Queen Street West; Lora is Queen Street East. The counterpointed feminist and political plots are joined, but forcedly, in the much-quoted scene of the courtyard beatings. "Atwood's special, chilly gift" shows the two sexes as alien to each other. Rennie and her lifestyle writings ring true; she's as strangely sophisticated and innocent as Toronto itself, the "'Miss Teen City'" of Canada.

22 BOARDMAN, KATHRYN G. "Romance, Revolution Figure in Novel Set on Exotic Island." *St. Paul Pioneer Press*, 21 March. Newsbank 1981-1982, 80:C6.

Describes *Bodily Harm* as satisfactory: Rennie goes to the unimportant islands to shake her troubles, finds herself in the middle of political struggles, becomes Lora's reluctant friend, has "a satisfactory vacation-time affair with [the very male] Paul," and is imprisoned with Lora, who gets beaten. "Rennie is finally rescued by authorities from civilization and put on her plane for Toronto. The reader knows" that these events have restored Rennie's self-confidence.

23 "Books: Briefly Noted." *New Yorker* 58, no. 8 (12 April):153.

Though in summary *Bodily Harm* sounds like a grab bag of unpleasant contemporary things, Atwood controls her plot; this surprisingly plausible story will probably touch readers ten years from now.

24 "Books: Briefly Noted." *New Yorker* 58, no. 33 (4 October):146.

Dismisses *Dancing Girls* as dated work, inferior to *Bodily Harm*; notes that almost all these stories of small-minded, miscommunicating men and women date from the 1970s, not in the 1980s of the dust-jacket blurb.

25 BRANDEIS, ROBERT C. Review of *Second Words*. *Canadian Book Review Annual*:223-24.

Finds *Second Words* a useful survey. Its 50 reviews, essays, and lectures are divided into three chronological sections, corresponding to periods of Atwood's life, which chart her "critical, cultural, and political development," and provide an interesting perspective on her poetry and fiction. Her response to Robin Mathews on *Survival* 1973.2 is included.

26 B[ROSNAHAN], J[OHN]. Review of *Bodily Harm*. *Booklist* 78, no. 10 (15 January):618.

Finds a psychological odyssey of troubles, handled with "a chilling, almost savage introspection," through flashbacks that bare the character's emotions and carry Atwood's distinct imprint.

27 BROWN, ROSELLEN. "Critical Condition." *New York* 15, no. 12 (22 March):56.

Recounts *Bodily Harm*'s story; appreciates its realism, politics, and ethics; but wants more complexity and understanding in Rennie's character. Rennie has become a pointless, trendy journalist to blot out her deadeningly proper childhood; now, threatened by a rapist and numbed by cancer, she escapes to an unfashionable Caribbean island. The political depravity she confronts there "puts her self-absorbed despair – or her narcissism – in large perspective." Robert Stone's *A Flag for Sunrise* seems, in contrast, dreary fatalism. The failed rebellion is authoritatively handled; Jocasta and Jake are both "mordant and very funny"; Atwood's sentences are like unpredictable melodies. But sometimes Rennie's limits drag the story down.

28 BROYARD, ANATOLE. "And Toronto, Too." *New York Times*, 6 March, p. 21.

Praises Atwood's terrific, casual, knock-out *Bodily Harm*. The invulnerable, ironic Rennie needs a partial mastectomy to humanize her. Rennie's attitudes satirize men. Jake is more disturbed by Rennie's sudden interest in his motives than by the mastectomy. In the Caribbean, "Rennie begins to realize that we all live in a 'third world' now," and to grope for a legitimate message.

29 ____. Review of *Dancing Girls and Other Stories*. *New York Times*, 15 September, p. C23.

Do men and women still love? Anxiety is more pressing than desire or love in these stories. When the man [in "Polarities"] desires an attractive, efficient woman only after she disintegrates, it's as if our age prefers "honest" pathology to boring surface graces. Another couple's anxieties fight like dogs, while their helpless owners watch. Yet these stories have hope, if not cheer, for they shows how we unhappy humans always go on, with yet another symptom, another desperate poem. Reprinted: 1982.30 (below).

1982

30 _____. "Stories Embrace New Idea of Love." *San Jose Mercury*, 26 September. Newsbank 1982-1983, 32:B5.
   Reprint of 1982.29 (above).

31 BRYDON, DIANA. "Caribbean Revolution and Literary Convention." *Canadian Literature*, no. 95 (Winter), pp. 181-85.
   Compares the politics of colonialism, tourism, and language in *Bodily Harm* and Austin Clarke's *The Prime Minister*. Both are outsiders writing about outsiders; both explore the politics of language via simple adventure plots. Rennie's instant journalism blocks thought with illusions; she slowly learns to write, and think, again. Atwood believes that suppression aims to silence the voice and the words – in Canada, through the "market and social pressures on Rennie," and in the Caribbean, through political oppression. *Bodily Harm* combines "images of the journalist who reacts but never acts with . . . the tourist who sightsees but cannot see"; the museum, tourist site, and jail are one. Both novels show tourists as "the new imperialists," happily exploiting and consuming; both link the violences of sex and of tourism. Atwood's epigraph, from John Berger's *Ways of Seeing*, can apply to colony and metropolis, in place of woman and man. Both novels "parody the imperialist novel of an education through a confrontation with the colonial 'heart of darkness.'" Atwood believes that the novel must guard the community's moral and ethical sense; *Bodily Harm* bears witness.

32 _____. Review of *Bodily Harm*. *Westerly* 27, no. 1 (March):98-100.
   Finds *Bodily Harm* serious and interesting, but not great, because it does not take the risks *True Stories* did. The fragmented narrative "forces the reader to share Rennie's alienation and to make sense of her disrupted world." The Caribbean island provides perspective on North American, and especially self-righteous Canadian, life. When Lora's beating finally forces Rennie out of self-absorption, Rennie pulls Lora back from the underworld in a scene that recalls Inuit birth ceremonies. Rennie is then free to return to Canada – but she still has cancer, which signifies her mortality and her human malignancy. Her sex makes her a victim, as the Berger epigraph says. Though Rennie's identification of men as frightening, which implies women as frightened, jars, Rennie is both victor and victim, a tourist who must become a citizen. Atwood "specializes in unsympathetic central

characters . . . [who force readers] beyond identification into speculation and self-criticism."

33 BUCHANAN, CONSTANCE. "Not Merely Adam's Rib." *Washington Times* (Washington, D.C.), 12 October, Magazine sec., C15.

Finds most of *Dancing Girls and Other Stories*'s depiction of women disappointing and its characters annoyingly passive; gives *True Stories* brief, mixed praise. Virginia Woolf counseled women writers, in *A Room of One's Own*, to portray women as "obscured by history and male abstraction," but also as vessels of flashing, coursing spirits. "When It Happens" shows Atwood's great potential for this. But in most of these stories woman is no more than a vessel, a rib from Adam, shaped, caressed, banged up, "or discarded by man." Half are monochromatic stories of emotionally stalemated lovers, like "The Grave of the Famous Poet." Why don't these men and women change their lives? The third-person stories, like "The Man from Mars," permit humor, and objective characterization.

True Stories's lyric poetry better suits Atwood's isolated moments; nature is sharply observed, as in "Landcrab I." These poems' only fault is a tendency, as in the T.S. Eliot-like "Spelling," to over-imitate male language and abstractions.

34 CARRINGTON, ILDIKÓ de PAPP. "'I'm Stuck': The Secret Sharers in *The Edible Woman*." *Essays on Canadian Writing*, no. 23 (Spring), pp. 68-87.

Follows Grace 1980.47 on Duncan as *doppelgänger* to explicate *The Edible Woman*'s fictive doubles and Conradian allusions. Duncan and Clara are each other's doubles, both stuck, dependent, and childish; as intellectually sterile male scholar and unconsciously fertile female body, they suggest not only Marian's choices, but Atwood's as well. The many allusions to Joseph Conrad's "The Secret Sharer" show Duncan as Marian's strange, grey-gowned, reflecting, and disappearing double self. With Atwood as with Conrad, the fictive doubles are the writer's split-off selves; both works may conceal a secret third identity, of writer. Revised as part of 1987.22.

35 CHANTEAU, CARA. Review of *Dancing Girls and Other Stories*. *Books and Bookmen*, no. 325 (October), p. 39.

1982

Praises these very compelling stories that reveal, with humour, the existential and fantastic strangeness beneath the everyday, as in "The Man from Mars" and "Polarities." Sometimes Atwood seems, acutely, a women's writer; perhaps best at the rising hysteria of a dislocated inside/outside. The often pervasive sense of the autobiographical is accompanied by an equal recognition from the reader.

36 CHAREST, ALINE. "Les dinosaures et l'homme." *FFQ petite press* (Montréal) 2, no. 1 (February):14.

Briefly describes *La vie avant l'homme* (*Life Before Man*) as a story about the complex relationship between three people. The characters are pared down to expose their true nature. Marian Viron's translation is excellent.

37 COHEN, GEORGE. "Atwood an Accomplished 'Eavesdropper' in Her Stories." *Chicago Tribune*, 19 September, sec. 7, p. 3. Newsbank 1982-1983, 23:B12.

Praises *Dancing Girls and Other Stories* highly, and describes ten of its stories. There's so much rich, highly evocative writing, as in the descriptive opening of "The Man from Mars," that it's hard to know where to start a review. Atwood has an extraordinary ability to relate feelings, as in the retrospective conclusion of "Betty." Twelve of the protagonists are women, six nameless. Atwood captures the myriad, painful complexities of our intimate human relationships, as in "Lives of the Poets," as if she had eavesdropped.

38 COLLINS, ANNE. "The Guns of Autumn: Cancer in the Caribbean, Fascism in Wartime Austria, and Excrement in Academe." *Books in Canada* 11, no. 8 (October):27-28.

Appreciates *Bodily Harm* in a three-book review of last fall's big-gun books, from Atwood, Timothy Findley, and Robertson Davies. As always, the reviewer needs a second reading to sort out Atwood's "easy wisecracks and humour" from her violent images and incredible poet's metaphors. The first reading was oppressive; the second, captivating. Atwood slides her disconnected hero into a Graham Greene plot "to crack Rennie out of the sweet Canadian bubble, where good people can be good because there are few other demands on them, to connect her" to the world and herself. In jail, Rennie finally reaches out her once useless hands to comfort Lora, in a powerful scene that sums up the metaphors of disconnection and the empty, unfeeling hands.

39 COOKE, JUDY. "Crystal Gazing." *New Statesman* 103 (11 June):31.

A three-book review that acclaims V.S. Pritchett's *Collected Stories* and has mixed reactions to *Bodily Harm*: Atwood's well-written, carefully plotted nightmare of suffering builds, through pained irony, "a convincing, even moving portrait which loses its authenticity" when Rennie becomes politically implicated – "she would have booked a flight home when she found the machine gun in the packing case."

40 COOMER, JOE. "The Creak of Doom: Relationships Die in a Tone of Refined Melancholy." *Dallas Times Herald*, 21 November, p. M5.

Identifies with Atwood's understanding of men and women in the very good *Dancing Girls*; finds women's anger and some love in *True Stories*. Like the woman of Adrienne Rich's poem, "Living in Sin," Atwood's doomed-relationship characters are "on the verge of falling off or jumping on." There are no happy people; the tone is a passive, persistent melancholy, as in "When It Happens," "A Travel Piece," and "Lives of the Poets." Though all Atwood's characters could be one, that one is yourself – and not your good side, if you're male – so you don't mind the lack of range.

The co-issued *True Stories* has Atwood's most blatant anger; its poems on women's suffering and torture overshadow those on love, mushrooms, and poetry. The women who do love passionately usually note it in their lover's absence.

41 CÔTÉ-LÉVESQUE, CORINNE. "Un triangle amoureux 'made in Toronto.'" *Actualité* (Montréal) 7, no. 4 (April):120.

La vie avant l'homme, the French-Canadian translation of *Life Before Man*, continues the literary process invented by André Maurois in *Climats*. The love triangle created by the characters illustrates the pettiness and frustrations of everyday life. Atwood's cynicism and disillusioned tone show that she no longer pretends to have found the final word.

42 COTNOIR, LOUISE. "Rien de confortable." *Spirale* (Montréal), no. 23 (March), p. 11.

1982

Reservedly reviews *La vie avant l'homme*, the French-Canadian translation of *Life Before Man*. Atwood's acid humor speaks to the force of inertia and the futility of the human species. A suicide is the only actual event in the novel. The book is made up of family backgrounds, conflicts, social-cultural situations, and the history of each character's dreams. In the end, the story offers no comfort or reassurance.

43 CURTIS, TONY. "True Stories and Other Fictions: Margaret Atwood." *Book News from Wales*, Autumn, pp. 3-4.

Praises highly *True Stories* and *Bodily Harm*, and congratulates the Welsh Arts Council for bringing Atwood back to Wales. In the reviewer's 1979.21 interview Atwood linked literary recognition to national power. *True Stories* develops, with razor edges, the concerns of earlier poems and of her seminal *Surfacing*. As in ["Postcard,"] the individual life enlarges to let the world's true, grim stories break through; "we in these islands may well find the [poems's relentless] tone according to the world's realities as we have experienced them in 1982." *Bodily Harm* controls and mediates this raw anger with the novelist's wit; its protagonist, a woman recovering from cancer, "is forced to move out of herself, to engage the political cancer of the islands." Her soul healed, she "comes fully back to life" aware of the true human world.

44 DEWAR, ELAINE. "Thoroughly Modern Orphans." *City Women* (Toronto), Spring, pp. 23-26, 28, 30, 32.

Discusses feminine exile to the edge of the male world, and "dissatisfaction with the new female mythology," in the writer's own life, *Bodily Harm*, Mavis Gallant's *Home Truths*, and three other Canadian women's books of fiction. Atwood's independent, objective, very modern journalist, Rennie, lives a stylishly disconnected life; she journeys from passive to active, and returns home a changed, subversive reporter. Gallant's revolution of independence, objectivity, and experience, ends, for Atwood, in women carving a new path to sterility and a living death. These five writers show us "as orphans without roots, as women without men, without fathers, at odds with our mothers." Are these fears true?

1982

45 DIXON, MICHAEL. Review of *Bodily Harm*. *Fiddlehead*, no. 132 (April), pp. 87-89.

Rejects Atwood's formulaic fiction of power, victims, and survival, and the polemic *Bodily Harm*. Cancer serves first to catalyze the plot, then as a bridging metaphor of malignant politics. Addicted to surfaces and self-absorbed, Rennie, in her "imperception" simplifies the other characters, except for the "American," Lora Lucas. The verb tenses indicate that "we and Rennie are fixed in that cell and all escape is illusory." Rennie's gesture to Lora does not recognize their common humanity, "only their identity as women-victimized-by-men." That "all men are perverted thugs" is *Bodily Harm*'s great truth. Rennie either submits to power, or uses the power of art to serve "class-hatred based on sexual stereotypes," becoming, ironically, a carrier of malignancy.

46 DJWA, SANDRA. "Letters in Canada, 1981: Poetry." *University of Toronto Quarterly* 51, no. 4 (Summer):345-47.

Appreciates *True Stories*'s witty moralism, in a round-up review, and suggests links to Robert Graves and Jay Macpherson. Atwood's paradoxically lying and multiple true story might reply to Graves's "'There is one story and one story only,'" in his "To Juan at the Winter Solstice." As in "Landcrab I and II," Atwood's multiple perspectives force "the satiric recognition that the true story is not quite what we presume." *True Stories*, with its atrocity poems centred inside a love story, argues that "all humans are land crabs of sorts, equally capable of atrocity or love." Atwood often writes from the perspective of the woman victim, as in "A Women's Issue." Readers often identify, perhaps because of her accessible voice, which modifies Jay Macpherson's, with its modern ambivalence and distinct irony.

47 DUDEK, LOUIS. Review of *The New Oxford Book of Canadian Verse in English*. *Globe and Mail*, 11 December, p. E14.

Faults Atwood's selections and introductory claims. Contrary to the latter, her selections purge and constrict those of A.J.M. Smith; 60 per cent of this book is new material, from the 1960s poetry explosion, which makes for a lively, youth culture anthology. Atwood cannot follow Smith, because she is neither a modernist nor an aesthetic critic. Worse still, her choices are often based on ideological and moral obsessions, such as the bleeding-heart syndrome for Indians and wilderness. As we know from *Survival*, her interest in poetry is

1982

thematic, not aesthetic; feminism is a theme, like nationalism; and, contrary to Atwood's introduction, some poets are included because they are female. Other minor invidiousnesses include the preferential display of Atwood's own poems. Yet there are diamonds to be mined here.

48 DYMENT, MARGARET. Review of *Bodily Harm*. *Quarry* 31, no. 2 (Spring):73-76.

Praises *Bodily Harm*'s marvelous irony, entertaining humour, serious and informed concerns, and really excellent end–but wants a sympathetic and memorable character. Something is missing–we do not accept Rennie's depression and despair as we would in real life. Why does Rennie stay on in St. Antoine–only so Atwood can show us Canadian involvement in torture and terrorism? Rennie dies when you put the book down. The men are unconvincing. Jocasta and Lora are much livelier–we care for Lora especially–why can't we see things through Lora's eyes? "Never mind": read *Bodily Harm*, and the end will be worth it.

49 EDEL, LEON. "Well Versed." *Saturday Night* 97, no. 12 (December):61-62.

Appreciates Atwood's selections, in *The New Oxford Book of Canadian Verse in English*, of the new, "neo-modern" poetry, from poets born in the late 1930s: Atwood herself, John Newlove, John Thompson, David Donnell, Dennis Lee, Fred Wah, and bill bissett. Their work is less lonely, more comfortable, exuberantly cosmopolitan, and, as Atwood says, "'spiky, tough, flexible, various.'" Newlove, Thompson, and Donnell sing of love without romanticizing. Michael Ondaatje, born 1943, has an extraordinary, visually evocative talent. Atwood deals with geological life before man, and life with man; her concretions metamorphose, as do John Newlove's profound aboriginal poems. These new poets go beyond empathy into true Canadian identity.

50 ELDRIDGE, MARIAN. "Richness and Hilarity." *Canberra Times*, 4 September, p. 14.

Enjoys and admires *Lady Oracle* as a "complex, beautifully articulated, highly satisfying piece of literature that speaks for our times." We all (men, too) must play multiple roles for others. "There are no real villains in *Lady Oracle*, just imperfect people latching onto others for self-preservation." Costume romance villains, masks and allusions, "resolved and unresolved plots," are all subtly worked in. Joan's Aunt Lou, father, mother, and Con-create lover "all have the ring of truth." But–a minor point–wouldn't Joan's husband wonder more about her income and time?

51 EMERSON, SALLY. "Recent Fiction." *Illustrated London News* 270 (August):59.

Features *Bodily Harm* and praises it highly, in a three-book review, as a sharp, funny, profound thriller. Horror waits for Rennie in the intruder's rope; cancer threatens her life; as the Caribbean island erupts into violence, "the slight discomfort of being a woman alone in a foreign place becomes absolute terror." *Bodily Harm* is not slick or conventional; "even the horror is touched with wit." By the end Rennie is a different person, "ready to 'pay attention'" to as much life as she has left.

52 EPSTEIN, DANIEL MARK. "Atwood's Stories: 'Urgency, Economy.'" *Sun* (Baltimore), 26 September, p. D4. Newsbank 1982-1983, 23:B13.

Praises *Dancing Girls* highly; finds one gem in *True Stories*. Atwood's fiction has progressed from *Surfacing*'s overwritten, self-absorbed lyricist to *Bodily Harm*'s compelling story-teller to *Dancing Girls*'s new urgency and economy. Eight of its 14 are love stories, many of unrequited love, like "Polarities," "Hair Jewel[le]ry," and "Lives of the Poets"; perhaps the best is "The Man from Mars." Many stories come from an isolated narrator looking through glass; "A Travel Piece," which goes "from irony to discomfort to horror" as the glass shatters, is the book's most powerful story, and as good as Stephen Crane's best. *True Stories* goes from seaside meditations to poems to an absent, vague lover to the "Notes Towards a Poem That Can Never Be Written" section, whose catalogue of atrocities is strangled by the "self-absorbed, rambling line" of Atwood's early novels. There is one gem in the last section, a love poem, "Variations on the Word *Sleep*."

53 EPSTEIN, JULIA. "The Language of Love and Survival." *Washington Post Book World*, 19 September, pp. 3, 8.

Acclaims *Dancing Girls*: Atwood wrests an immutable power from language; readers experience viscerally her images, events, objects, words. Like *Bodily Harm, Dancing Girls* explores the body's frightful otherness, in "Giving Birth" and in other stories. These alienated, irritated couples compete to be victims. Atwood's mesmerizing speed comes in part from her frequently rapid-fire, comma-splice sentence structures. Language is the real subject here, "words as talisman and icon,. . . . language as quagmire and bloodsucker." Yet in these tales of survival and failed speech, Atwood, like the poet [in "Lives of the Poets"], flies.

54 FERTILE, CANDACE. "Hard To Say Who Will Enjoy This Book of Atwood Reviews." *Edmonton Journal*, 31 December, p. C3.

Dislikes *Second Words*. In the introduction, Atwood treats her criticism as secondary, and homework, which is slightly whining. Her refusal to review books she doesn't like is generous. Her [1973.2] counterattack on Robin Mathews shows her lack of humor, but elsewhere, as in "Witches," there are some good lines. Her style is informal. Her longer essays tend to repeat. Though Atwood's work for Canadian literature and feminism is commendable, and was pioneering, she inconsistently comments on Jay Macpherson's clothes in reviewing her poetry. These reviews are not academically useful, because incomplete; but one wonders, with three *Acta Victoriana* reviews, what she left out.

55 FLOWER, DEAN. "Fiction Chronicle." *Hudson Review* 35, no. 2 (Summer):287-89.

Praises highly, in a round-up review, *Bodily Harm*'s characterization, interwoven narrative, and unsparing, ironic vision, which avoids any feminist cant. Atwood handles feminism "by disappearing into her fiction." The tough-talking journalist, Rennie, must have a Hemingway antecedent. Atwood's interwoven vignettes extend one character through another: Rennie's unexpressed anger at her father comes out through Lora's battered childhood. The paired stories gain depth: the more depressed Rennie becomes, the jauntier and funnier the maverick Jocasta becomes. As in Robert Stone's *A Flag for Sunrise*, "the unconscious North American assumption of personal safety" is beaten down. Rennie's Canadian innocence could be American. Atwood's impressive, formidable severities will endure.

1982

56 FORSTER, MARGARET. "Survivors." *Books and Bookmen*, no. 322 (July), p. 17.

Praises *Bodily Harm*, in a three-book review, as a cancer novel; and praises Rennie as a marvelous, self-questioning, honest, resilient survivor. Unlike other recent cancer novels, *Bodily Harm* avoids the maudlin, and focuses on the real issue of how cancer affects the psyche. Rennie, who sensibly goes to the Caribbean to heal herself with new experiences, is curious, eager, and courageous. She knows cancer colours her reactions; she sees cancer as an insult and a warning, and re-values life. *Bodily Harm* is suspenseful, funny, satirical, and feminist.

57 FREIBERT, LUCY M. "The Artist as Picaro: The Revelation of Margaret Atwood's *Lady Oracle*." *Canadian Literature*, no. 92 (Spring), pp. 23-33.

Acclaims Atwood's picaresque *Lady Oracle*: Joan is a picaro, a Protean rogue, adventuring among rogues, learning from various masters, and drawing the reader into her episodic, first-person narrative. Atwood varies the picaresque with *Kunstlerroman* insights, and by ending mid-episode. Like Moll Flanders, Joan is "a disarmingly honest narrator of a patently dishonest life," lulling the reader's trust. A fat, unwanted child, Joan suffers and learns, dancing her vengeance, exploiting her mother. A Protean trickster and escape artist, she acts many roles. She learns manipulation from the devious, dual figures who are her successive masters. The end shows her thriving on psychic danger, like a true picaro, and effecting a new, Protean escape. Atwood suggests that women should reject society's false roles – or continue being picaros.

58 FRENCH, WILLIAM. "Atwood Sets the Tone for Lively Writers' Meeting." *Globe and Mail*, 17 May, p. 15.

Quotes Atwood's witty ad libs, as national chairman of the three-day annual meeting of the Writers' Union of Canada at the University of Guelph. Atwood, who had invited Communications Minister Francis Fox, presented a poster to him that said "'We love Francis Fox because . . . ,'" with the rest blank, for him to fill out. Copyright payments, library compensation, insurance, Canada Council reading tours, membership, and belonging to the Book and Periodical Development Council were discussed.

1982

59 ____. "Radio to Mark Bloomsday with 30-Hour Reading." *Globe and Mail*, 8 June, p. 17.

Reports, in a literary news article, Atwood's winning the fifth, 1982 Welsh Arts Council's International Writer's Prize for the body of her work. The award carries a [£]1,000 prize, translation of one of her books into Welsh, and an invitation to Welsh readings, seminars, and conferences on her work.

60 FRYE, NORTHROP. "'Conclusion' to *Literary History of Canada*, Second Edition." In *Divisions on a Ground: Essays on Canadian Culture*. Edited by James Polk. Toronto: Anansi, p. 79-80.
Reprint of 1976.27.

61 FULLBROOK, KATE. Review of *Bodily Harm*. *British Book News*, November, p. 705.

Commends Atwood's accomplished, morally serious, gripping *Bodily Harm*. Rennie, a journalist who has abandoned ideals for trends, has her life tipped off course by cancer. In the Caribbean to escape and to write a travel piece, she ends up in prison, and learns that there's no way out of duty, commitment, living. This fine, perhaps brilliant, novel deserves to be read.

62 GERVAIS, MARTY. "'The Dream of Reason Breeds Nightmares.'" *Windsor Star*, 16 January, p. B10.

Interviews Atwood on religion: Atwood discusses her agnostic upbringing and early experiences with churches; self-righteousness and fundamentalism versus truly Christian social activism, mentioning Blake's nightmare-breeding sleep of reason; the Bible, mythology, and literature, citing Christian symbols in *Life Before Man*, *Surfacing*, and Margaret Laurence; and Timothy Leary's LSD experiments.

63 ____. "Poetry . . . Then and Now." *Windsor Star*, 6 November, p. C9.

Contrasts what Atwood's introduction to the *New Oxford Book of Canadian Verse* discusses as the 1960s "'renaissance'" in Canadian poetry to the more sophisticated, slicker, but perhaps less important 1980s Canadian poetry scene; praises the good balance of Atwood's selections, which mainly follow A.J.M. Smith's rules; and briefly praises Patrick Lane's amazing *Old Mother* poems of the prairie and China.

64 _____. "Writing: An Act of Love." *Windsor Star*, 27 November, p. C9.
     Finds *Second Words* "a useful, illuminating and invaluable compendium of pieces" that sometimes go beyond the masks of Atwood's poetry and fiction, and at other times support her creative works. *Second Words* accurately describes the creative process and how it led her into "a world of isms: nationalism, sexism, feminism." But even when Atwood confines herself to issues, she can be wry and enjoyable.

65 GILBERT, HARRIETT. "Lunacies." *New Statesman* 104 (12 November):33.
     Praises *Dancing Girls*, in a four-book review; a Laingian reversal of sanity and madness flashes stroboscopically beneath the surface of these witty, urbane social comedies. Atwood's left hand plays with humour and technique; her right, with alienation – why do we construct social frameworks inimical to our psyches? Atwood's characters are mostly women, who did little of the constructing. Yet we do give more "'reality'" to our constructs; and "'madness,'" as in "Giving Birth," is a way to accommodate that lie.

66 GILES, BARBARA. "Margaret Atwood at Latrobe University." *Luna*, no. 15, pp. 12-13.
     Interviews Atwood at Latrobe University: Atwood comments on Canadian versus U.S. women in literature, feminism, French Canada, poetry, Jane Austen, and being a novelist. Committed, intelligent, and honest, "Atwood does women proud."

67 GIOIA, DANA. "Eight Poets." *Poetry* 140, no. 2 (May):110-11.
     Finds *Two-Headed Poems* ineffective. Though Atwood has the images and ideas of a major poet, her language does not heighten one's awareness, and her rhythms do not gather force. One notices her curiously flat, neutral language most in "Marrying the Hangman." Genuinely arresting rhythms, as in "Foretelling the Future," are rare. Excerpted: 1983.129; 1985.11.

68 GLENDINNING, VICTORIA. "Affairs of the Head." *Sunday Times* (London), 28 November, p. 43.
     Finds the *Dancing Girls* stories remarkable, "fierce parables about the horror of city life and the power politics of relationships. The

fierceness filters insidiously through the leisurely realism of her domestic interiors, clothes, meals, weather." The most affecting story, "When It Happens," justifies this method; perhaps everyone, not just the reviewer, shares Mrs. Burridge's imaginings, not only as projected future, but as race-memory. Atwood's scenarios do not try to reassure. "Disillusion, betrayal, and the ends of affairs" occasion many of these stories, whose "characters huddle in human zoos. . . . The inadequate can only love the more grossly inadequate" in "Polarities" and "Training." Language deceives but gives visions in the title story.

69 GOLDSTEIN, ENID. "Atwood's *Harm* – Heartless or 'With It?'" *San Francisco Chronicle*, 18 April, Review sec., p. 3.

This title covers two reviews, by Goldstein and by Holt 1982.78. Goldstein complains that *Bodily Harm*, despite its philosophic probing, seductive suspense, and humor, takes us only "from surfaces to deeper surfaces." The odor of ladies' fiction is never totally dispelled. The characters are simplified and closed, not resonant. *Bodily Harm* emanates from the intellect, not the heart. Rennie never really breaks through to confront the truth; even the end may not be worth what precedes it.

70 GOULD, ALLAN M. "*Chatelaine*'s Celebrity I.D.: Margaret Atwood." *Chatelaine* 55 (May):44.

Records Atwood's pithy statements on her habits; favorite foods, cities, music, books, radio, and films; superstitions; religious and philosophical beliefs; worst difficulties and best childhood memories; ethics of fairness; politics of Amnesty International and abortion; women and sexism; and on pigeonholing people and Canadian mingymindedness.

71 GUCKENGERGER, KATHERINE. "Atwood Loses Ground with *Bodily Harm*." *Cincinnati Enquirer*, 11 April. Newsbank 1981-1982, 80:C7.

Finds *Bodily Harm* displeasingly anti-men and disappointingly commercial. Though the writing is still high-caliber, and the leading lady interesting, the male characters are mean, invasive, and ciphers. Though the Griswold house is believable, the Caribbean island and black insurgents are not. Worse, Atwood mixes Rennie's vulnerability to death and to men. In the end, flying back to Canada, and "disengaged from her creepy male friends," Rennie may be able to handle mortality.

72 HAESEKER, FRED. "Atwood Spurns Film Version of Her Novel." *Calgary Herald*, 13 September, p. F5.

Quotes Atwood, at Saturday's Harbourfront Centre reading, on the *Surfacing* film, and on the two screenplays of the unfilmed *The Edible Woman*. Atwood's father would have been bothered not by the *Surfacing* film's confusion of her novel with Philip Roth's *The Breast*, but by the inept canoeing and incorrect mushrooms. Under Tony Richardson, *The Edible Woman* screenplay came out English social comedy; under a Hungarian director, it came out very Hungarian, and paranoid.

73 HALL, JOAN JOFFE. "Heroine from the North." *Houston Post*, 28 March. Newsbank 1981-1982, 80:C8.

Appreciates *Bodily Harm* as Atwood's best novel since *Surfacing*, and the one most like *Surfacing*, with its disconnected heroine and quest for wholeness. But *Surfacing*'s heroine sees the U.S. as a disease; Rennie learns that the "'sweet Canadians'" are stupidly fattening the local corruption. There are no good guys in the Caribbean, except perhaps Dr. Minnow. One hopes that Rennie, if she survives, will write about more than fashion. Although at times Atwood may be using politics, "Rennie's fears are at once female and middle class; the political is personal." Justice is not far from "'decency.'"

74 HALLIGAN, MARION. "A Novel to Compel Respect." *Canberra Times*, 18 September, p. 14.

Respects *Bodily Harm*'s honesty, but enjoyed *Lady Oracle* more. In the rich, high comedy of *Lady Oracle*, life was easy to take; but *Bodily Harm* is spare, more difficult, rather uncomfortable. Its honest, worried heroine "brings out the bleakness of the world she inhabits." We take our bodies for granted till something happens, like Rennie's breast cancer. Atwood plaits together past and present, different stories and different tenses, with subtle charm. Rennie finally rejects men altogether, as frightening, in the island jail. *Bodily Harm* ends with her "not particularly noble or joyful survival" of men's malice.

1982

75 HARLAUB, GENO. "Dinosaurier sind Wir Alle." *Deutsches Allgemeines Sonntagsblatt* (Hamburg), 10 October, p. 29.

Favorably reviews *Die Unmöglichkeit der Näche* and *Verletzungen*, the German translations of *Life Before Man* and *Bodily Harm*. Atwood's novels are far removed from Europe and its ancient culture; her poetic language and fresh metaphors are effective without relying on the cliches and veiled allusions still employed by European literature. Atwood's characters seem well adjusted on the outside, but are troubled in their intimate lives. The women in *Life Before Man* struggle to enjoy being alone and to maintain their integrity. Rennie, in *Bodily Harm*, resembles an Amazon, a one-breasted woman who wins the battle against the men. Atwood convinces because she is truly creative and does not rely on feminist theories to bolster her writing.

76 HOFSESS, JOHN. "Living Dangerously: The Art of Margaret Atwood." *Monday Magazine* (Victoria, B.C.) 8, no. 7 (12-18 February):14-15.

Recommends *Bodily Harm* highly, as Canada's "most important and rewarding" novel in recent years; values Atwood's commitment to writing as a moral vocation and to human rights; and quotes extensively from her 1980 Killam lecture ["An End to Audience?"], soon forthcoming in *Second Words*. Steering between academic elitism and trendy journalism, Atwood writes seriously for a wide audience; she works to change the world, participating in the recent Amnesty International conference on *The Writer and Human Rights*, which is also a forthcoming book. *Bodily Harm*'s Rennie, a writer turned trendy lifestyles journalist, finally, after harrowing crises, becomes morally and politically aware, and flies home to report. What Rennie reports might be like Susan Sontag's *Illness as Metaphor*, or Oakland Ross's El Salvador series in the *Globe and Mail* (which Atwood commended to the reviewer); or perhaps like Jacobo Timerman's extraordinarily courageous *Prisoner without a Name*. Atwood calls us all to consider and strive toward our possible excellence.

77 HOLLIDAY, BARBARA. "Man's Inhumanity Etches Her Poetry." *Detroit Free Press*, 4 April, p. B5.

Refers, in an appreciative review of Carolyn Forché's *The Country Between Us* and its realistic, urgent, horrifying El Salvador poems, to the Atwood-Forché friendship. Though some of *Bodily*

Harm's strongest writing shows unspeakable prison conditions, "Forché is not Atwood's uncertain heroine."

78 HOLT, PATRICIA. "Atwood's *Harm* – Heartless or 'With It?'" *San Francisco Chronicle*, 18 April, Review sec., pp. 3, 13.

This title covers two reviews, by Goldstein 1982.69 and by Holt. Holt praises the superb *Bodily Harm*: Rennie may be "Atwood's most complicated yet accessible character," and this is her most remarkable novel. *Bodily Harm* is less a story than the development of Rennie's character; the mastectomy, which cuts into her own surfaces, changes her Brillo-pad toughness. Caught in a revolution's upheaval, she thinks back, and is forced to go deeper into her mind and emotions, and "turn herself inside out. . . . the Rennie who emerges is no simple I-had-my-catharsis-and-am-better-for-it person."

79 H[OOPER], W[ILLIAM] B[RADLEY]. Review of *Dancing Girls and Other Stories*. *Booklist* 79, no. 2 (15 September):90.

Approves Atwood's respect for the short-fiction form, solid plots, and steady pace; and recommends equally all these high-quality, attractive stories.

80 HOPKINS, ADAM. "The Survivor." *Guardian* (Manchester), 23 October, p. 9.

Interviews Atwood, who is presently in Wales to receive the Welsh Arts Council's International Writer's Prize, and who is greatly gifted, serious, piercingly funny, a freely playing and extremely clever intellect. Atwood discusses realistic and autobiographical elements in *Bodily Harm, Surfacing, Life Before Man, The Edible Woman, Lady Oracle*, and *Survival*; her *Snow White* film trauma, woodsy family background, education, past marriage, and present commitment; her own and others' attitudes to feminism; and men's violence to women and, more so, to other men.

81 HOWE, LINDA. "Narratives of Survival." *Literary Review* (Madison, N.J.) 26, no. 1 (Fall):177-84.

Discusses *Bodily Harm*, Sheila Ballantyne's *Imaginary Crimes*, Sara McAulay's *Choice*, and Marge Piercy's *Braided Lives*, as narratives of survival; approves most Atwood's critique of uncommitted independence. In contrast to the usually masculine *bildungsroman*, the survival narrative is feminine; its heroine struggles for independence, and against more threatening obstacles. Rennie is a liberated, successful survivor – but selfish and naive. Atwood makes our common metaphors real even as she implicitly critiques them; Rennie's spiritual journey takes her to the depths of jail, where she learns commitment, and her vulnerability to real bodily harm and death. That she escapes and survives is enough; we don't have to see how she lives later.

82 HOY, HELEN. "Letters in Canada, 1981: Fiction 2." *University of Toronto Quarterly* 51, no. 4 (Summer):328-29.

Questions, in a round-up review, whether we gain or lose by Atwood's broadening her repertoire to include serious human suffering in *Bodily Harm*. What emerges from the novel's "assaults on middle-class self-absorption" is valid but banal. The psychologically-rescued Rennie goes from radical chic to subversive attentiveness. *Bodily Harm* has Atwood's usual verbal dexterity, skillful imagery, and merciless irony for our fashionable urban phrases and gestures.

83 HUGHES, JUDY. "Backwards around the World to Wales." *Western Mail* (Cardiff), 18 October, p. 6.

Interviews Atwood, who is in Wales for a lecture tour, [£]1,000 prize, and a weekend conference that has been sold out for weeks. Atwood, whose great-great-grandmother, Mrs. Davies, came from Wales, is tired, this being the last stop in an eight-week world tour with her family. Her daughter Jess re-creates a scene from "Spelling" as she reads and crayons. Is *Survival's* claim that you must know your country's literature to know yourself and to survive "a message for Wales?" The intricately patterned *Surfacing* ends with words that "will strike chords with women and with Welsh people," on refusing victimhood and the old, lying games.

84 HULBERT, ANN. "Femininity and Its Discontents." *New Republic* 187, nos. 12-13 (20 & 27 September):40-42.

Argues, in a three-book review, that contemporary women's stories are still troubled by Virginia Woolf's Angel in the House, more than by the problem of women writing about their own bodies and passion. Most of the stories in *Dancing Girls and Other Stories* are as diffuse and flat as their female characters. Atwood's women drift, superficially, while men distract them, and an unvanquished Angel of the House hovers over them, adding to their passive doom. As in "Giving Birth," Atwood's women can recount bodily experience, but find no solid self or fixed identity there.

85 HURST, LYNDA. "Peggy Is Getting Boring." *Toronto Star*, 5 December, p. D1.

Complains of Atwood's complaints about the press in 1982.12. Atwood is a good and bestselling writer, and the reigning empress of Canadian literature – and an over-exposed sacred cow. How many times has she complained of unfair journalists, when most of her coverage is tributes – and most Canadian writers are lucky if *Quill & Quire* gives them a mention. Atwood's cute Varsity-style parody review counter-attacks the press. This reviewer is weary of all the Atwood coverage; Atwood should stop granting interviews indiscriminately, take the praise, and ignore the criticism.

86 HUTCHEON, LINDA. "Romanciers ontariens des années soixante-dix." *Protée* (Chicoutimi, Québec) 10, no. 2 (Summer):16-17.

Cites, in an overview of contemporary Ontario fiction, major themes in Atwood's first five novels. *The Edible Woman* presents diverse identities in a comical book; *Surfacing* reveals the internal feminine psyche; *Lady Oracle* pokes fun at the critics and at Atwood's media image. Feminine fecundity becomes the paradigm of the act of creation in *Life Before Man*, and *Bodily Harm* tackles the problems of women and all humankind.

87 HYNES, JOHN LEO. "Propp and His Progeny: An Evaluation of Story Grammars and a Reappraisal of the Value of Propp's Theories for Literary Analysis and Reading Research." Ph.D. dissertation, State University of New York at Albany. pp. 76-86.

Includes, in Chapter IV, a sentence-by-sentence analysis of "Lives of the Poets." See *Dissertation Abstracts International* 43 (1983):2580A.

88 "In Search of the Real Canadian." *Age* (Melbourne), 25 September, p. 2.

Reports on Atwood's thought-provoking *Survival* talk in Melbourne. The backwoods-raised Atwood, who does not look like a fur trapper, sounds like an awesomely learned academic. Her *Survival*

1982

theory of Canadian literature "should cause literary brows to furrow thoughtfully in Brisbane."

89 JACKSON, MARNI. "The Writer as a Global Politician." *Maclean's* 95, no. 49 (6 December):64-65.
    Praises *Second Words*, which demonstrates Atwood's commitment as a writer. For the past twenty years, Atwood has stubbornly asserted her identity as a writer, a woman, and a Canadian. Often she has simply stated the obvious – when it needed stating. While her novelist's eye catches the particular, her peripheral vision has seen deserving writers and ideas ready for development. Her quarrels, as with Al Purdy's poetry, are more energetic than her praise, or her dull academic essays. "Atwood has been a passionate literary citizen," from the dismal early 1960s on. The weakest piece, "Writing the Male Character," merely reacts to criticism of her *Life Before Man* and *Bodily Harm* – or is it another of her difficult truths?

90 KALIN, DIANE. "Luminous Glimpses into the Lives of Women." *Philadelphia Inquirer*, 10 October, p. R5. Newsbank 1982-1983, 32:B6.
    Praises *Dancing Girls*: Atwood paradoxically combines depth psychology and the irrational with good sense; she offsets characters "ripe for melodrama" with delicate wit; her stories "fluster bourgeois normalcy." These well-matched, luminous stories depict chronological and spiritual stages in women's lives. The young protagonists of "[The] Man from Mars" and "Betty" learn from the mysterious, wholesome, and destructive adult world. The mid-life artists, writers, and students lose courage before the world's expectations, as in "[A] Travel Piece" and "Lives of the Poets." The senescent protagonist of "When It Happens" imagines war in her mundane kitchen.

91 KAPLAN, JUSTIN. "Civilized Human Beings and Others." *Harvard Magazine* 84, no. 6 (July-August):6-7.
    Praises *Bodily Harm*, in a four-book review, as a novel about how we adapt to loss. Rennie "learns that 'bodily harm' has meanings beyond her own deep and superficial scarring and that even in the most secular and abandoned of worlds," some grace can be found – "'she is lucky, suddenly, finally . . . .'" The novel shuttles beautifully between her past and present, "for Atwood is a born storyteller with a formidable literary intelligence."

340

92 KEMP, PETER. "A Case of Curing." *TLS*, 11 June, p. 643.

Admires *Bodily Harm*'s mordant satire and mature, accurate view of life; and finds its "tough wit and precise poetry" exhilarating. Atwood's novels specialize in trial by ordeal: Rennie moves from voguish journalism and post-operative shock to the healthy massive involvement of a journalist prepared to fight for the exploited; she is driven "out of terrified self-pity into horrified compassion." Atwood excels at making the ordinary seem weird. Like many Atwood characters, Rennie is two-ply, concealing anxieties under a confident exterior. The cancer vocabulary applies, with grisly irony, to political corruption and violence.

93 KETCHAM, DIANA. "Bodily Harm and Other Perils." *Oakland Tribune*, 28 March. Newsbank 1981-1982, 80:C2-3.

Interviews Atwood, during her visit to San Francisco the week before, on *Bodily Harm* as a political novel: Atwood discusses the realism of all its violence—the housebreaker who left a rope behind came from a newspaper; its cathartic rather than depressing effect; the writer's responsibility not to endanger real people; her own quiet rural life, childhood, and current script for a TV documentary on Canada's stigmatized "Home Children"; and readers confusing authors with their characters. Like Robert Stone, Paul Theroux, and Joan Didion, Atwood could be accused of exploiting Third World political tragedies to symbolize North American angst. *Bodily Harm* is relentlessly moralistic; in its astonishing end, the heroine risks her own life to save a woman she dislikes.

94 KILGORE, KATHRYN. "More Mickey Mouse, Amigos." *VLS* (Village Voice Literary Supplement), no. 5 (March), pp. 14-15.

Rejects the North American late-imperial guilt syndrome, in a three-book comparative review of *Bodily Harm*, Albert Haley's *Exotic*, and Paul Theroux's *The Mosquito Coast*. As in Paul Stone's *A Flag for Sunrise*, weak characters witness projected Central American or Caribbean violence. Facing violence, Rennie languishes and daydreams; unfortunately she will soon get rescued from prison. The reader is outraged—"Why bother to create a character so intensely unsympathetic?"—and finds *Bodily Harm* a diseased, carelessly written novel. These three authors, who "are too deep in the trough of American guilt," distort small revolutionary countries into metaphors for their own disturbed emotions. Their set-up, stereotyping characters witness only "their own slightly surreal delusions. . . . The societies they see are only mirrors which reflect our fear of chaos, violence, and madness."

95 KLEMESRUD, JUDY. "Canada's High Priestess of Angst." *New York Times*, 28 March, p. 66.
   Interviews Atwood in New York: Atwood discusses success in Canada versus the United States; women's suffering and triumphing, generations of feminism, and *Bodily Harm*; and her own happiness with writer Graeme Gibson. Reprinted: 1982.97. Reprinted, cut, 1982.96 and 98.

96 ____. "Her Women Suffer, Survive." *Post-Intelligencer* (Seattle), 11 April, p. E7.
   Reprints 1982.95 (above), with several minor cuts, and without one of two paragraphs on her happiness with Graeme Gibson, and without the last two and one-half paragraphs on Canada versus the United States. See 1982.98.

97 ____. "Margaret Atwood: High Priestess of Angst." *New York Times Biographical Service* 13, no. 3 (March):283-84.
   Reprint of 1982.95. Reprinted, cut, 1982.96 and 98.

98 ____. "Novelizing the New Feminism." *Los Angeles Herald Examiner*, 29 March, pp. B2, 5. Newsbank 1981-1982, 80:C9-10.
   Reprints 1982.95, with several minor cuts, and without the last two and one-half paragraphs on Canada versus the United States. See 1982.96.

99 KLINE, BETSY. "Life Is Easy as Long as They Don't Get Involved." *Kansas City Star*, 21 November, p. I8.
   Reviews Atwood's fine *Dancing Girls* and brilliant, merciless *True Stories*. In "A Travel Piece, as in *Bodily Harm*, in "The Grave of the Famous Poet," and "Under Glass," Atwood's men and women deny involvement, perpetuate the misunderstandings of their relationships, and coexist as aliens.
   True Stories, which was written with *Bodily Harm*, glows white hot as the poet attacks indifference, evil, banalities, and delusions.

Anger flares in "A Women's Issue" and "Christmas Carols." *True Stories'* every word punctures complacency.

100 ____. "A Torture That Can't Be Escaped: Harsh Realities Jolt Journalist in *Bodily Harm*." *Kansas City Star*, 4 April, p. L8. Newsbank 1981-1982, 91:D9-10.

Does not find *Bodily Harm* pleasant. Atwood unrelentingly depicts the mental and physical violence that first stuns Rennie and later, under harrowing threats of torture and death, shocks her into life and commitment. Though Rennie learns about involvement from the slovenly, foul mouthed Lora, Rennie is ill-equipped for her forced awakening. This harsh, brooding novel will rivet some readers and repulse others. Atwood achieves her aim: to "toy with our nerve endings."

101 KOLTZ, NEWTON. "Wisdom and Limits." *Commonweal* 109, no. 16 (24 September):506-7.

A comparative appreciation of *Bodily Harm* and Paul Theroux's *The Mosquito Coast* as classic misanthropic novels that drop their characters into punishing situations. In the Canadian version, the horror results from underextending yourself; in the American, from overruling your limits. Atwood's *Survival* understands the Canadian national personality; its feminine myth shows the self-protective Survivor convinced that she (or he) is impermeable, virgin, exempt. Rennie is less modern than "'sweet'—naive, innocent, passive, and ultimately helpless." She is tested, "for several terrifying weeks," in a nasty native jail; luckily, she comes out unharmed, and perhaps wiser and more compassionate.

102 KURTZMAN, SALLY. "Atwood's Brilliance Shines in Collection." *Denver Post*, 31 October, p. R8. Newsbank 1982-1983, 40:B13.

Praises *Dancing Girls and Other Stories'*s truly impressive, delicately detailed, subtle, low-key, sweet stories. "There's no violence, ambition or death, just people involved with people who have unusual occurrences in their lives." Most of the stories focus on women and relationships. The collection is filled with Bettys, "working through life in slow motion, trying to make some sense of the Freds of this world." These stories are the "'bouquet of nice clean words'" that the poet of *True Stories* wanted to present.

1982

103 LANE, PATRICK. "Atwood's Anthology a Massive Work." *Edmonton Journal*, 26 December, p. E7.

Appreciates, despite occasional errors, Atwood's lucid, touching introduction and the "catholic sweep of excellence" revealed in her selections from two centuries of Canadian poetry in the authoritative *New Oxford Book of Canadian Verse in English*. Dennis Lee, who recommended post-1960s poets, should also be thanked. The reviewer is personally pleased that Atwood, who is "Central Canada's chosen one," is the editor, though he too would have welcomed the job. Unlike A.J.M. Smith, Atwood raises the inappropriate issue of sexual distinctions. Though her *Survival* thesis and "psycho-sexualism" run through her selections, she does, generally, chose objectively, outside her own style, as John Newlove did not in his *Canadian Poetry*. The prairie is inadequately represented, and some "suspiciously mediocre" poets, including the "monomaniacal critic" Frank Davey, appear. Our Canadian poetry excels that in *The New Oxford Book of American Verse*. One can only admire Atwood's hardworking, audacious mastery of yet another genre, the anthology.

104 L[EITENBERGER], I[LSE]. "Schuldig, weil nutzlos." *Presse* (Vienna) 10 November, p. 5.

Praises *Verletzungen*, the German translation of *Bodily Harm*. Atwood is the most significant living author in Canada. She brings a new tone to modern women's literature. The story is about a woman who comes to realize that her uselessness during serious events makes her an accessory to the crime. Atwood shows that she is as accomplished in the adventure genre as any male writer.

105 LEONARD, JOHN. "The Heroine: A Contraption of Attitudes." *New York Times Book Review*, 21 March, pp. 3, 20-21.

Finds *Bodily Harm* deliberately unpleasant. As with Joan Didion, Margaret Drabble, and others, an intelligent, deracinated heroine flees a menacing, Jerzy Kosinski Gothic world. Atwood's Rennie, a lifestyles journalist, cohabits with Jake, who is Jewish for no particular reason. St. Antoine is psychologically and politically cancerous, deathstyles. (Do Latin American writers "resent our blue-eyed exploitation of their continent" as the libidinal and the symbolic?) We aren't meant to sympathize with Rennie, who is "a contraption of attitudes," until the unlikely last-paragraph epiphany. The sermon is eloquent, gnarled, and ugly; the triumph is Rennie's pledge to loyal Lora. Though one can't "*like* such a novel," one must admire its uncompromising author.

106 LIPINSKI, ANN MARIE. "Meet Canada's Other Margaret: A Favorite Target in Her Own Land." *Chicago Tribune*, 16 May, sec. 12, pp. 1, 3.

Interviews Atwood, who is in Chicago to promote *Bodily Harm*. After warning a bookstore browser that only Margaret Trudeau found *Bodily Harm* "'a total laugh riot,'" Atwood, who is chair of the Canadian writers' union, recounts stories of Canadian attacks on herself and other Canadian writers and actors who succeed; her favorite attack on herself is the column that said such "'a sweet young thing'" couldn't possibly be doing her own haying, which she and Graeme Gibson were doing. Atwood argues that her work is not gloomy but realistic, citing Jonathan Schell's *The Fate of the Earth* nuclear-threat stories, Charles Dickens's and Thomas Hardy's plots, and, on the idea that women writers should provide warmth instead of dealing with the world, Alice Munro.

107 McCOMBS, JUDITH. "Crossing Over: Atwood's Wilderness *Journals* and *Surfacing*." In *Essays on the Literature of Mountaineering*. Edited by Armand E. Singer. Morgantown: West Virginia University Press, pp. 106-17.

Reads both *The Journals of Susanna Moodie* and *Surfacing* as transformed wendigo myth and woman/nature myth. The wendigo is a creature who, in Amerindian myth filtered through white culture-bearers, crosses over from the human to the natural universe; see Atwood's 1977 "Canadian Monsters." *The Journals of Susanna Moodie* "radically transforms the wendigo tale from a myth of men against a monstrous nature into a myth of woman allied with the deadly wilderness powers against rational, civilizing man." *Surfacing*'s narrator, "crossing over into nature and becoming it with her own natural body, womb and child," is part of a woman/nature myth that "transforms the novel's other myths, of Nature the Monster and Other, of man against nature, of wendigo [the vanished father] and shaman, of Christian creation, of classic and Jungian quests." Moodie, who sees pregnancy as horrible, and whose children are death-linked, crosses over into nature only in death; *Surfacing*'s birth-affirming narrator crosses over in life.

1982

108 MacDONALD, JOHN W. "Last, First, and Second Words." *Reviewing Librarian* 7 (December):38.

Acclaims *Second Words*: "no contemporary writer in Canada today writes better non-fiction prose." The three chronological periods show Atwood's maturing prose style, paradox, wit, mastery of reviewing, and her early and middle literary taxonomies. Her [1973.2] counterblast to Robin Mathews's [1972.26] "perverse distortion" of *Survival* is splendid, but the interesting Canadian humour essay is sometimes lumpish. "Where Atwood flames out 'like shining from shook foil' is in her analysis of two issues–the difficulty of being a woman writer and the problems facing contemporary Canadian culture." "On Being a Woman Writer," "The Curse of Eve," and the unsurpassed "Writing the Male Character" are all wise and witty masterpieces. "An End to Audience?" should be obligatory reading in every Canadian high school; "Canadian-American Relations" is equally important and brilliant.

109 MacKINNON, JANICE. "Atwood: Where 'Nobody Is Playing.'" *Houston Chronicle*, 18 April, Zest sec., p. 21.

Appreciates *Bodily Harm* as a rite of passage and an allegorical examination of modern evil. Protagonist Rennie Wilford, an innocent who lives on the surface, journeys into experience; after cancer makes her vulnerable, she flees to a third-rate island where violence erupts. "In the apocalyptic denouement, Rennie is agonizingly born out of her chrysalis into massive involvement with real life and the knowledge that she is not exempt from responsibility." Atwood renders excellently "the island and its ugly politics" where, as one incumbent says, "'Nobody is playing.'" Rennie finally "enters the world of experience irrevocably changed" in both outlook and determination.

110 MANDEL, ANN. Review of *True Stories* and *Wilson's Bowl*, by Phyllis Webb. *Fiddlehead*, no. 131 (January), pp. 63-70.

Features *True Stories* and welcomes *Wilson's Bowl*, assessing their struggle for mortal, political, fragmentary truth. Like Alain Resnais' film *Mon Oncle d'Amerique*, *True Stories* opens with a valentine-shaped heart, the sea, crabs, and questions of origin; but Atwood's [watercolour] cover heart "is also a vagina and glows with light, like a sun, like a nuclear explosion." For both Atwood and Webb, knowledge is not simple, or absolute; in their elemental, seasonal books, the "earth and its new growth" remind of death; "both poets struggle with the inadequacy of language," and reject society's received truths. For Atwood as for Michel Foucault, truth, relationships, and sex are political; Atwood shows the vagina as repeatedly attacked, in true stories. Her political poems are powerful because they are not abstract: torture is physical, bodies are torn. Both Atwood and Webb move from the personal centre to humanity and back; Atwood sees the physical world as finally indifferent, not tragic; her "poems move, as we all do, towards a dark solstice." As before, Atwood's romantic technique and Gothic devices create anti-romantic results; love is real, messy, human, not romantic. Like Webb, Atwood offers "what fragmentary gifts are possible in a multiple and unperfectable world." The Atwood portions are reprinted: 1988.33.

111 MELLORS, JOHN. "Sweet Canadians." *London Magazine*, n.s. 22, no. 3 (June):61-65.

Values *Bodily Harm*, despite the problems of its complexities, and the three novels before it, as guides to Canadian life. Atwood's protagonists are what the enigmatic Dr. Minnow calls "'Sweet Canadians'"—youngish, intelligent, sexually active, vulnerable Canadian women. Atwood's novels have wit, humour, powerful narratives, and authenticity—not an insensitive feminism. *Bodily Harm* depicts the boredom and self-righteousness of small-town Ontario. *Lady Oracle* best develops Atwood's absurd comedy; *Life Before Man* allows flashes of humour. *Bodily Harm* may end with hope and Rennie's release—or, more likely, with disaster; its compelling story shows that women's independence, like that of ex-colonies, is still tainted by past subjugation.

112 MILAZZO, LEE. "Atwood Scores with Short Fiction Collection." *Dallas Morning News*, 7 November, G4.

Praises the faultlessly organized, always memorable stories of *Dancing Girls and Other Stories*: a paragraph, phrase, even a word illuminates a whole story; and smooth surfaces mask frightening complexities. Atwood uses her style to examine significant themes, of violence, of the real in the surreal, of the tragic inability of men and women to communicate, as in "The Man from Mars" and "Polarities," which questions sanity. "Giving Birth" has a beautifully controlled surrealism.

1982

113 MILLER, ALICIA METCALF. "A Stark Novel of a Woman Confronting Life's Reality." *Plain Dealer* (Cleveland), 2 May, p. C20.

Finds *Bodily Harm* powerful and rigorously stark rather than endearing; intensely readable and often extraordinarily moving; and, despite some flaws of characterization, Atwood's best novel yet. "*Bodily Harm* is a severe, uncompromising novel about a woman who sees connections everywhere but studiously avoids the feelings that would make them real." She covers with smart-talking irony, but finally must face her illusions; she leaves St. Antoine with a changed vision.

114 MONKMAN, LESLIE. "The Poetry of Margaret Atwood: An Introduction." *Poetry Wales* 18, no. 1:83-92.

Appreciates Atwood's first eight books of poetry: *The Circle Game*'s fragmentations, games, and journeys; *The Animals in That Country*'s vision of Canada and quest for spiritual principles; *The Journals of Susanna Moodie*'s much-quoted "Afterword"; *Procedures for Underground*'s primitivism; *Power Politics*'s epigrammatic tension; *You Are Happy*'s qualified optimism; *Two-Headed Poems*'s more public voice; and *True Stories*'s scepticism; commends Skelton's 1977.83 most insightful analysis of Atwood's modular style. Atwood is clearly "the most important Canadian poet of her generation."

115 MOOREHEAD, CAROLINE. Review of *Life Before Man*. *Times* (London), 4 February, p. 11.

Mostly praises the reissued *Life Before Man*. Atwood is occasionally lyric in this long, fragmented saga of modern life. Never tacky, though sometimes humourless, she is highly intelligent, with a fine ear and quick wit; and "very good indeed" on the accommodations, memories, tortures, and guilts in people's lives.

116 MORLEY, PATRICIA. "Atwood Chooses Conservatively but Wisely in Poetry Anthology." *Citizen* (Ottawa), 4 December, p. 38.

Approves Atwood's sound selections and conservative, readable, solid introduction to *The New Oxford Book of Canadian Verse in English*. The dustjacket, with David Milne's *Wicker Chair*, is delightful. Atwood here acknowledges the major influence of A.J.M. Smith – not Northrop Frye. "Women poets are represented more by quality than by quantity. Atwood frankly acknowledges their relative scarcity." The introduction avoids Smith's far-fetched Canadian-international contrast, and *Survival*'s bizarre motifs and language. Despite omissions and debatable points, this book is a considerable achievement, and a testament to Canada's mature poetic tradition.

117 ____. "Atwood's Non-Fiction Truly Secondary." *Citizen* (Ottawa), 11 December, p. 38.

Second Words may disappoint Atwood's many admirers: though her criticism is good journalism, and often witty, it alone would never make her famous. Her brief introduction makes an untenable criticism of the literary critic as parasite, and suggests that she herself writes criticism for duty, not creative pleasure. The three parts, which correspond to Atwood's life, are a good working structure, and make the book a partial autobiography, with a nod to intellectual history. Feminists will enjoy pieces such as "The Curse of Eve," and many on individual women. Atwood's critical prose is strong and often dogmatic; her language wisely stays midway between *Survival*'s jargon and academic rhetoric. Abridged: 1983.99.

118 MORT, MARY-ELLEN. Review of *Bodily Harm*. *Library Journal* 107, no. 4 (15 February):471.

Praises *Bodily Harm*. Fleeing crises, Rennie becomes the lone witness to violence. Atwood continues to dissect Canadian-North American mores convincingly. Her hallmark wit and acute observation offset her somber themes.

119 ____. Review of *Dancing Girls and Other Stories*. *Library Journal* 107, no. 16 (15 September):1767.

"A minor collection from a major novelist and poet." These stories, published in 1977 in Canada, are better read individually; together, their tone and characters become repetitious. "A Travel Piece" prefigures *Bodily Harm*.

120 NICHOLLS, SUSAN, ed. "She's Little, but This Author-Poet Walks Tall." *Canberra Times*, 29 September, p. 30.

Interviews Atwood at her Canberra hotel and reports on her *Canberra Times* literary luncheon. Atwood describes the writer's status in Canada, her own fiction-writing habits and the family life that keeps her normal, the 1978 Australian Arts Council writers' wine tour, and fronting for Amnesty International and other political causes.

1982

121 O'BRIEN, KATE CRUISE. "Pilgrims' Ways." *Listener* 108 (22 July):24.

Finds *Bodily Harm* disturbing, and its Renata "the least satisfactory" of the pilgrim-traveller protagonists in four books reviewed. Atwood writes best about politics. "Unfortunately politics merely play a part in Renata's journey towards recovery, a journey which frightened and disturbed me in its obsessive direction. For Renata is a victim of men"; and the frighteningly poor island people are victims of the same sexual violence.

122 O'FAOLAIN, JULIA. "Desperate Remedies." *Observer* (London), 13 June, p. 31.

Wonders, in a four-book review, why the reviewer did not enjoy more the intelligent, witty *Bodily Harm*. Perhaps it's the clever but obtrusive and overused tropes; "almost anything can stand for something else," as when Rennie's blouse becomes an empty container. The mastectomy prefigures worse bodily harm. Reification runs rampant. Rennie starts with wise-cracking self-pity; when she finally escapes, she has been politicised, and plans some serious reporting. But the neat end suggests that the revolutionary country is only a device to bring Rennie to a moment of truth. *Bodily Harm* is imaginative and thoughtful, but perhaps too controlled. Excerpted: 1983.129.

123 OSTRIKER, ALICIA. "The Thieves of Language: Women Poets and Revisionist Mythmaking." *Signs* 8, no. 1:72, 78.

Discusses "Circe/Mud" as revisionist mythmaking, and Circe as angry but quite powerless. Reprinted: 1985.80; reprinted as pages 212 and 222 of 1986.185, within a chapter that revises this article.

124 OUELLETTE-MICHALSKA, MADELEINE. Review of *La vie avant l'homme*. *Châtelaine* (French ed.) 23, no. 5 (May):18.

Finds, in a short review of the French-Canadian translation of *Life Before Man*, a tender, lucid story and an excellent portrait of couples in North American society. *La vie avant l'homme* successfully shows how easily we can become frozen in our past, and questions our ability to influence or create our own future.

125 P[ARISI], J[OSEPH]. Review of *True Stories*. *Booklist* 79, no. 7 (1 December):478-79.

Acclaims *True Stories*'s tough, tender poems, which often "seem seared upon the page." In Atwood's "unusual love poems, a hard, biting urgency infuses the sensuality. . . . In her 'True Romances,' love usually means desperate need. . . . But the most compelling–*shocking* is a better word–poems here protest the horrifying cruelties presently practiced worldwide. . . ." Atwood's unflinching depiction of inhumanities and torture, especially of women, is necessarily gruesome. "Hers is not fashionably rhetorical commitment . . . but an almost unbearably painful response to brutality, raised to the level of anguished art."

126 PATTERSON, JAYNE. "The Taming of Externals: A Linguistic Study of Character Transformation in Margaret Atwood's *The Edible Woman*." *Studies in Canadian Literature* 7, no. 2:151-67.

Examines Marian's character transformation through a linguistic analysis of the paired shopping, food preparation, and eating scenes. Thus, in the first supermarket scene, Marian's powerlessness is shown in the self-reflexive, distancing verbs, in the absence of verbs of choice, in the food lexemes layered over with consumer-society modifiers, in the paranoid it/they syntax. When Marian becomes a creative non-victim, an artist making and eating her own cake, the syntax is focussed and ordered, the verbs active and energetic, the words stripped down to essentials.

127 PAUL, BARBARA. "Author Confronts Male Power Plays." *Pittsburgh Press*, 11 April, Family Magazine sec., pp. 4-5.

Praises *Bodily Harm*: this beautiful, powerful, courageous book says things many won't want to hear. Primarily, it shows how women won't admit the truth of the male power drive that harms weaker males and women, who are physically vulnerable. Rennie finds the same power assertions that she could rationalize away in Canada, enlarged on the island: her lover uses her, the police enjoy intimidating women. Finally Rennie admits that "'men are frightening.'" But when she barely escapes alive, she's again made to feel she's lucky, like with the mastectomy. Atwood is saying it's time for women to stop excusing men's violence and destruction.

1982

128 PELLETIER, MARIO. "Margaret Atwood: Par delà les solitudes." *Devoir* (Montréal) 9 January, pp. 13, 24.

Surveys a range of Atwood's work, including *Lady Oracle*, *Surfacing*, *Bodily Harm*, *Two-Headed Poems*, and *True Stories*, shortly after Atwood's visit to Montreal for the release of the French translation of *Life Before Man*. Victimization, nationalism, and feminism are key themes in all Atwood's writing; *Survival* is brilliant criticism. Compares Atwood's poetry to work by writers like Marie Claire Blais and Poe. Perhaps Anne Hebert influenced Atwood's work.

129 PENNER, JONATHAN. "Plots and Counterplots." *Washington Post Book World*, 14 March, pp. 1-2.

Enjoys the constantly diverting *Bodily Harm*, which "fairly breathes narrative grace and skill," despite its flaws. One watches with nervous awe as Atwood juggles subplots and confounds disbelief by catching them all. The best Canadian scenes deal with Rennie's journalism, like the list of what has class or not: "Atwood knows the ridiculous as a terrier knows a rat." There are flaws: "One is narrative design run riot." One doesn't understand until the end all the first-person and third-person points of view. And the genre novel-of-adventure plot squeezes out the literary novel's characterization. The writing is brilliant. Excerpted: 1983.129.

130 PIERCY, MARGE. "Margaret Atwood: Beyond Victimhood." In *Parti-Colored Blocks for a Quilt*. Poets on Poetry. Ann Arbor: University of Michigan Press, pp. 281-99.

Reprint of 1973.72. Reprinted: 1988.39.

131 POUSNER, HOWARD. "This Novelist Prefers the Allure of Reality." *Atlanta Constitution*, 21 April, pp. B1, 7.

A telephone interview: Atwood, whose *Bodily Harm* got kudos from the *New York Times* [Broyard 1982.28], talks about success versus writing; feminism, realism, and optimism in her work; and her childhood and present life.

132 PRESCOTT, PETER S. "Tropical Education." *Newsweek* 99, no. 13 (29 March):71-72.

Prefers Atwood's earlier, energetic novels, to *Bodily Harm*. Rennie, like other Atwood protagonists, has problems with physical and emotional survival, and inadequate men. Rennie's education is efficient enough; the seedy island and its spooky politics, and the acerbic, humorous monologues on woman's lot, from the two secondary characters, are all first-rate. But *Bodily Harm* still seems flaccid, perhaps because the delaying flashback narrative leaves the reader waiting for something to happen in the island narrative.

133 PRITCHARD, ALLAN. "West of the Great Divide: A View of the Literature of British Columbia." *Canadian Literature*, no. 94 (Autumn), pp. 96-112 passim.

Reverses the central propositions of Atwood's highly stimulating and admirable *Survival* thesis to define the regional characteristics of British Columbia literature, including documentary accounts. British Columbia writings show a continuing harmony between man and an Edenic nature, rather than survival against a hostile nature. Here spring with its growth is the central season; Indians are helpful; exploration and immigration lead not to defeat and exile but to joy, a new home, and heartfelt possession of the land. Jack Hodgins's fiction, with its celebrations and heroes, particularly contradicts the survival thesis.

134 RAMSEY, NANCY. Review of *Bodily Harm*. *San Francisco Review of Books* 7, no. 2 (Summer):21.

Dislikes Atwood's detached voice, and the shallow, neurotic, unchanging characters of her earlier novels, like *Life Before Man*; finds *Bodily Harm* her most readable novel, because revolution and cancer do, in a sense, save Rennie from the stagnant fate of Atwood's other characters. The urgent Caribbean sections move more quickly than the frustratingly stagnant Canadian sections. Prefers, in this two-book review, the engaged voice and likeable characters of Anne Tyler's *Dinner at the Homesick Restaurant*. Excerpted: 1983.129.

135 RAPHAEL, ISABEL. Review of *Bodily Harm* and *The Groundling*, by Meredith Daneman. *Times* (London), 10 June, p. 10.

Both Atwood's and Daneman's heroines are bright, beautiful, and too busy escaping the constraints of their provincial colonial societies to see that they're still emotionally immature. Atwood's Rennie adeptly sidesteps reality, until violence and brutality move in. "Atwood has a rare ability to get under one's skin [without preaching;]

1982

Rennie's life in Canada reads like a tract for our times, instantly recognizable and deadly accurate." But the tropical parts are less sure, and the island lacks a menacing build-up for its horrifying climax. Briefly reviews two other books after praising Atwood and Daneman.

136 REICHART, MANUELA. "Eine Frau mit Grundsätzen." *Zeit* (Hamburg), 8 October, Zeit zur Buchmesse sec., p. 11.

Approves *Verletzungen*, the German translation of *Bodily Harm*. Rennie's journey to the Caribbean takes her through internal and external chaos, political corruption, and violence. *Bodily Harm* entertains without being trite, and confronts separation and hopelessness without becoming sentimental. This laconic novel is a pleasant deviation from popular female rite-of-passage literature.

*137 REID, MALCOLM. "Atwood at the Temporel." *Vancouver Sun*, 15 March, p. A6.

Reports on Atwood's reading at Quebec's Cafe chez Temporel, from the just-released French translation of *Life Before Man* and, in English, from her poetry. Atwood, who drew an overflow audience, mostly of women, exudes goodness and warmth. She commented, in the question period, on the British imperialism depicted in ["Four Small Elegies"]; and, in the radio interviews that followed, on Quebec nationalism and English Canadians.

138 Review of *Bodily Harm*. *Book Choice*, no. 18 (June), p. 25.

Praises *Bodily Harm* as another skilled, poetic masterpiece from one of the best Canadian writers. Atwood reveals "the threatening undertones of relationships" with tight, witty dialogue. Her observations have a poet's precision and reverberations. Atwood very skillfully mixes suspense and self-revelation; Rennie just barely survives. *Bodily Harm* is more like Joan Didion and Diane Johnston than Graham Greene, whom the publisher's blurb invokes.

139 Review of *Bodily Harm*. *Kirkus Reviews* 50, no. 2 (15 January):76-77.

Finds *Bodily Harm* powerful but bleak, didactic, and obvious. The banal scenario, with its operetta revolution, does support Atwood's dark philosophy—of sex as aggression, if not violence, and of our universal vulnerability to bodily harm—but *Life Before Man* did so more artfully and far less didactically. The final, appallingly immediate

1982

degradations echo back on the overly-long and empty narrative corridor.

140 Review of *Dancing Girls and Other Stories*. *Kirkus Reviews* 50, no. 14 (15 July):806-7.

Finds Atwood's themes–"a little terror, a lot of ennui, and women's hunger" for what they most detest–less effective in *Dancing Girls and Other Stories* than in her poems and novels. The romantic couples are often casualties, in brilliant tableaux of disappointment and frustration. The story form doesn't suit Atwood's unsparing and discomforting talent.

141 Review of *Survival*. *Wilson Quarterly* 6, no. 3 (Summer):74.

Briefly describes Atwood's idiosyncratic *Survival*, as one of two books of literary criticism in a total of twelve recommended background books.

142 RIGHTON, BARBARA, ed. "People." *Maclean's* 95, no. 40 (4 October):36.

Atwood, who is in Australia on a lecture tour this week, sent a life-size "Peggy doll" to the annual fund-raising Writers' Development Trust banquet in Toronto. Seated with Mordecai Richler, Farley Mowat, and Marie-Claire Blais, "the Peggy doll was programmed to say, from a tape concealed in her purse, 'Oh, you're a novelist, too.' (Pause). 'Oh, I wouldn't really have time to do that right now. I'm writing my own novel.'"

143 RIGNEY, BARBARA HILL. *Lilith's Daughters: Women and Religion in Contemporary Fiction*. Madison: University of Wisconsin Press, pp. 23-30, 52-57, 86-90.

Argues that, contrary to Christ's [1976.13 and/or 1980.17] spiritual and Rigney's former [1978.81 and 1978.82] psychoanalytic interpretations, the nameless protagonist of *Surfacing* survives by renouncing her identification with Christ the innocent victim, and with other possible myths, as, Atwood's irony insists, she must do in order to confront her real, sane, existential self. "Her [Atwood's] purpose is not to condone the mystical, but to explore the psychological." The protagonist's reversed re-enactment of the Demeter-Kore myth that Rich [1976.83] defined "is as delusive as her search for the Indian gods or for Christ. . . . The 'other language' is, of course, gibberish;" her attempts to transform herself and to conceive are madness and fantasies, not cures. The destructive mother fantasies of *Lady Oracle* corroborate that, for Atwood, sanity means moving "behind mythology, including the myth of the Great Mother." As in *Surfacing,* insanity is "a dangerous romance, the ultimate myth, the denial of humanity." Atwood's vision of nature is unsentimental and non-pastoral; the *Surfacing* protagonist archetypally "searches out her private garden in the Canadian wilderness, finds" strength there, and returns to the city, sanity, and human existence. Atwood does not advocate a primal return to nature, or female biology; rather, she sees both the metaphoric garden and nature not as answers or ends but as "agents in the human confrontation with existence." See 1987.129.

144 ROBINSON, JILL. "Atwood's Brave Heroine Plunges into a Revolution." *Chicago Tribune,* 28 March, sec. 7, p. 3. Newsbank 1981-1982, 80:C5.

Celebrates *Bodily Harm* as a major, heroic novel of the battles between men and women, and of humanity's instinct to turn away. The climax will have you bolt upright, "eyes eating words like Pac-Man." It's not romance, but "the lost romance of redemption that Rennie finds when she thinks she's running away." Power, which mostly men have had, generates frightening brutality, but also human heroism. Rennie transcends herself and becomes "a heroine to stand beside Sidney Carton [of Charles Dickens's *A Tale of Two Cities*], . . . beautiful in her decency" when she helps Lora. This brave novel recreates "the triumph of the human soul."

145 ROLENS, LINDA. "Women Too Alone to Realize Their Aloneness." *Los Angeles Times Book Review,* 17 October, p. 3. Newsbank 1982-1983, 32:B4.

A rave review of *Dancing Girls*: Atwood's painful, subtle stories go deeper than mere external drama. Most of the characters are women too alone to realize it; many are not attractive. They yearn for love but insist on being hurt; they are best at loss, which somehow comforts them. These dark stories become extraordinary because Atwood trusts her characters to survive, with strengths they do not understand. The collection's heroines move from vulnerability to humor, coping, and tenderness. This is a poet's prose, with startlingly accurate images. *Dancing Girls* makes you feel, as Hemingway said, that "'it all happened to you.'" Excerpted: 1983.129.

146 ROMINE, DANNYE. "Author's Characters Hunt for More Than Identity." *Charlotte Observer*, 28 March, p. F10.

Interviews Atwood, who will soon read at a university there: Atwood discusses individual choice versus external circumstances, as in altruism and suicide; being open or closed; her realistic male characters; self-knowledge; and creativity not as a neurosis but as a human desire to make.

147 SAGE, LORNA. "Dark Doings in Old Wessex." *Observer* (London), 21 November, p. 34.

Senses, in a three-book review, a reluctant growing up into an apocalyptic world in Emma Tennant's *Queen of Stones* and in Atwood's ironic, inevitably disillusioned *Dancing Girls*. "Atwood modulates from realistically–'sensitively'–observed detail, into the 'hard' language of survival almost imperceptibly." "When It Happens" is perhaps the most memorable of these stories.

148 SCHEN, MOLLY. "*Bodily Harm*: Women's Rage vs. Desire." *Providence Journal*, 28 March, p. H16.

"Margaret Atwood has written yet another women's book, touching the bone of emotion with the shivering flash of a surgeon's knife. Her writing is so precise, so agonizingly sharp, that the reader must often turn pages with clenched teeth or a grimace of self-recognition." *Bodily Harm* is her most severe, most complex, and toughest book. The brutality and sex are not gratuitous. "This is not *Lesbian Nation*," but an attempt at modern real-life feminism: women desire and fear men; and psychological and physical harm are equally nightmare-causing, she suggests.

149 SCHIEFER, NANCY A. "Especially for Fans of Atwood." *London* (Ontario) *Free Press*, 24 December, p. E9.

Finds Atwood's *Second Words* astonishing, delightful, lively, and irritating, a provocative pastiche that simultaneously rivets our attention and exasperates us. "She is the ultimate novelist-at-large, attentive, heedful, compassionate, alert to the sorry shams and broken promises of modern life," but her carping is faintly irritating. Her

1982

unfair and snide anti-Americanism undermines the reader's sympathy. Still, her views are deeply sincere and continually fascinating, on politics, literature, and mothering.

150 SCHOSTACK, RENATE. "Frauenleiden, cool serviert." *Frankfurter Allgemeine*, 5 October, p. L7.

Surfacing and Life Before Man put Margaret Atwood on the same international level as Joyce Carol Oates and Margaret Drabble. *Verletzungen (Bodily Harm)* deserves our respect for successfully combining in a work of serious literature the female themes of emancipation, cancer, and the female body, with the typically male topics of drug smugglers and CIA agents. The suspenseful story weaves several plots, using discrete symbolism and faultless language, but in the end falls short by trying to convey too much, making the novel difficult to enjoy. The reader is not touched by the heroine's bodily harm or her fears, and questions much of the plot.

151 SEE, CAROLYN. "Games Men Play–and the Real Losers." *Los Angeles Times*, 22 March, sec. 5, p. 6.

Celebrates *Bodily Harm*: the reviewer would like to buy 4,000 copies, for all her friends, enemies, and students; multiple copies for "divorce lawyers, mechanics, certain male physicians," and 1,000 for the secretaries of state and defense. But real men don't read lady novelists. "*Bodily Harm* starts deceptively–just another woman's novel." A "'girl reporter,'" grown older, a mastectomy, an intruder, and then a tropical island with a blue-eyed, maybe dangerous, hero. Stuck in daydreams and memories, maybe dying, how can Rennie "be expected to pay attention" to political reruns? After lies, violence, prison, and murders, Rennie "finally gets out of herself enough to notice what's really happening"–the tortured and the torturers. "*Bodily Harm* asks us to imagine the reality behind" news snippets, and who's responsible for it.

152 SEYMOUR, MIRANDA. "Recent Fiction." *Spectator* 249 (10 July):27.

Finds *Bodily Harm* absorbing, felicitously worded, and acutely perceived, but, despite its blurb, not quite in Graham Greene's class. Atwood pinpoints the dreary seediness of the Caribbean island, and graphically describes Rennie's frightening, very unsanitary internment, which ends when she agrees to go home and report nothing. The brief encounter with violent bodily harm has made Rennie realize her luck in being alive. *Bodily Harm* is a long way from Atwood's best; the reviewer hopes Atwood will return to the Canadian settings, where she excels. A four-book review that features Carlos Fuentes.

153 SEYMOUR-SMITH, MARTIN. "Women Often with Men." *Financial Times* (London), 19 June, p. 12.

Praises, in a five-book review, *Bodily Harm* as the most substantial novel of Canada's leading woman poet. Using Graham Greene's admirable intrigue and espionage as a framework, Atwood creates a metaphorical thriller or allegory of "how the feminine becomes enmeshed in masculine ways." *Bodily Harm* seeks to understand, not blame; it implicitly acknowledges the co-existence of masculine and feminine within the individual.

154 SHRAPNEL, NORMAN. "With Ingredient X." *Guardian* (Manchester), 10 June, Books sec., p. 8.

Features, in a four-book review, *Bodily Harm* and the paperback *Lady Oracle*: Atwood has the unanalysable X factor that gives life to real novels, and the authentic voice, grounded in wit; she doesn't need the blurb-writer's Graham Greene labelling. Praises *Bodily Harm*'s strong theme and atmosphere, poet's wording, and style; enjoys *Lady Oracle*'s entertaining ebullience and shadowed hilarity–how funny can childhood miseries be? *Lady Oracle*'s heroine, like a former Postmaster-General, fakes her own death.

155 SIEGEL, EVE. Review of *True Stories*. *San Francisco Review of Books* 6, no. 10 (January):21.

Celebrates *True Stories*, which moves from the personal to the political, avoiding polemicism with control, detachment, and craft: consider how the innocent hands of "Small Poems for the Winter Solstice" progress to the tortured woman's fingers in the second section, "Notes Towards a Poem That Can Never Be Written," where they suggest "the voice of revolution." Truth is kaleidoscopic and relative; dynamic tension is always there. As in "Last Poem," Atwood asserts "the importance of self, whether alone," imprisoned, or sharing with a beloved. Though her primal, bold imagery recalls Sylvia Plath, Atwood goes beyond critics' stereotyping of strong women poets: as in "Spelling," Atwood defines a new model of the assertive, feminist-perspective poet "who can step away from the wholly personal to a more powerful, universal language." Excerpted: 1983.129.

156 SMITH, DAVE. "Atwood: Watcher in the Backwoods." *Los Angeles Times*, 22 April, sec. 5, pp. 9, 30. Newsbank 1981-1982, 91:D11-12.
    Interviews Atwood in Los Angeles on *Bodily Harm* promotion tour; compares her to Mary McCarthy, and praises her writing. Atwood describes her happy if isolated childhood, and calls herself a feminist, but not a feminist writer.

157 SOMERVILLE-LARGE, GILLIAN. "Wives, Sons, and Lovers." *Irish Times* (Dublin), 4 December, p. 13.
    A five-book review that finds *Dancing Girls*, by the brooding "Ice Madam" Atwood, stunning. The "awful gloom" of the Canadian environment appears to mould Atwood's talent for showing progressive disillusionment. Her irony is memorable; her "conclusions are invariably depressing, at times positively sick, like a reflective Roald Dahl. But it is always exhilarating to share her fierce misery."

158 STAINES, DAVID. "To Be or Just to See? The Fears of Rennie Wilford." *Dallas Morning News*, 25 April, p. G4.
    Praises highly *Bodily Harm*'s honesty, masterful art, and passionate indictment of Canadian and personal passivity. Radical chic journalist Rennie Wilford, who sees herself as a tourist and voyeur, becomes an unwitting participant in a Caribbean island's political intrigues that climax, terrifyingly and fantastically, in the island's prison. In this non-Canadian setting Atwood indicts her country's smug non-involvement; "her own passionate commitment to Canada is audible in Dr. Minnow's admission: [that] 'The love of your own country . . . [tempts you] to change things.'" *Bodily Harm* "is also an impassioned and pained plea" to all who stand back passively and, like the disturbing Rennie Wilford, refuse personal responsibility. "The ray of hope in this [Matthew] Arnoldian universe is the possibility of love, the tangled and complex commitment Rennie wants and fears."

159 STOKES, GEOFFREY. "Brief Encounters: Short Fiction." *VLS* (Village Voice Literary Supplement), no. 12 (November), p. 6.
    Has mixed reactions to *Dancing Girls*. Atwood's mainly professional, always intelligent women dance with "middling grace and

maximum self-awareness"; her details are telling, her language accomplished, her smiles wry and rueful. Though there's nothing wrong with all this, the reviewer would sometimes, perhaps aberrantly, like to shake these women, and see the end of these perfectly crafted, smoothly rolling stories.

160 STROMBERG, KYRA. "Es ist alles da unter der Oberfläche." *Suddeutsche Zeitung* (Munich), 10 November, Literatur sec., p. 4.

Verletzungen, the translation of *Bodily Harm*, should establish Atwood as an important and readable writer in Germany. From *The Edible Woman* on, Atwood's major topic has been female protest against "the American life." The counter-world present in *Surfacing* and *Life Before Man* looms more threateningly in *Bodily Harm*, and eventually explodes into violence. Atwood's third world setting recalls *July's People*, by Nadine Gordimer, and indicates the increasingly central insights of peripheral European literature. The translation is well done.

161 STRUTHERS, BETSY. Review of *The New Oxford Book of Canadian Verse in English*. *Canadian Book Review Annual*:190-91.

Protests Atwood's *Survival*-distorted, thematic selections. Unfortunately, Atwood's *Survival* thesis "(CanLit expressing only concern with the land, alienation, struggle to overcome geography, male/female power politics, etc.) and her current concern with third world politics have distorted her choice of poems." She includes every Canadian "Bushed" poem written; she excludes all Tom Wayman's best, work poems. Though this Procrustean editing makes her anthology handy for school teachers (and an indispensable companion to *Survival*), "it fails to do justice" to most of the writers chosen.

162 [STUTTAFORD, GENEVIEVE]. Review of *True Stories*. *Publishers Weekly* 222, no. 9 (27 August):354.

Finds that *True Stories* "teeters between love and despair," yearning for a redeeming love, but bemoaning an absent partner. Atwood's "sense of futility" foils romantic hopes. The ironic title refers to "the fables we invent to give our lives a feeling of continuity." Praises the beautifully lyric "High Summer" and the semisurreal, light but horrifying "True Romances"; finds the "explicitly feminist poems" of sexual exploitation and rape less successful.

1982

163 TAYLOR, ROBERT. "An Exciting Feminist Allegory." *Boston Globe*, 17 March, p. 61.

Gives high praises to *Bodily Harm*: its feminist allegory, atmosphere of suspense, exciting and sturdy plot, "intricate ironic pattern of alternative scenes," admirably modeled characters, and tone of humor mingled with malevolence. Atwood captures "the trendy, magpie sensibility" of her fashionable journalist, and balances it with darker implications. The seedy island is a travesty of Prospero's [in Shakespeare's *Tempest*]. Rennie, the innocent tourist and former provincial, hesitates to come "to terms with herself, which means coming to terms with death and violence and injustice." But *Bodily Harm* never preaches; its quest goes from dependence to independence, and the reader senses palpably a woman's psyche.

164 _____. "'Superstar of Canadian Letters': Margaret Atwood's Tally: 5 Novels, 7 Poetry Books." *Boston Globe*, 7 April, pp. 61-62.

Interviews Atwood, whose serious yet surprisingly comic *Bodily Harm* seems fated for best sellerdom. Atwood talks about lifestyle reporters, who seem to agree that *Bodily Harm* captures their argot; her graduate student days in Victorian Literature at Radcliffe; her birth family (a solitary burrower bee has been named after her entomologist father), bush childhood, early career choice of home economics, and her present life.

165 TESHER, ELLIE, and PERUN, HALYNA. "Our Achievers Fifteen Years Later." *Toronto Star*, 1 July, p. A14.

Briefly interviews Atwood, and a number of Canadian achievers in other fields, on their own careers and on Canada today; quotes Atwood on Canada surviving the economic slump, and being "'a civilized country with regard for our fellow human beings,'" in contrast to distressed and repressive countries.

166 TILLINGHAST, RICHARD. "Scattered Nebulae." *Sewanee Review* 90, no. 2 (Spring):297-98.

Rejects, in a group review, *Two-Headed Poems*: though Atwood has a large "eco-political" readership, these are numbingly bland, prosaic lines, and trendy simplifications of psychology and politics.

167 TREMBLAY, RÉGIS. "Margaret Atwood, mot à mot, syllabe à syllabe." *Soleil* (Québec), 16 January, p. E6.

Focuses, in a report on a recent lecture by Atwood, on the fact that she spoke in French, forgiving her few minor pronunciation mistakes. Describes Atwood as a woman, a Canadian, president of the Canadian Writers Union, and an Amnesty International activist. Her work is concerned with sexual duality and the problems of language.

168 TYLER, ANNE. "The Complexities of Ordinary Life." *New York Times Book Review*, 19 September, pp. 3, 26.

Praises highly *Dancing Girls*'s poetic precision, vivid characters, sly comedy, and revealing polarities. A poet's ear shapes Atwood's beautiful novels, and these arresting, vital, memorable stories. The elephant-mouse pursuit of "The Man from Mars" has stayed with the reviewer for years; "Hair Jewellery's" rueful, youthful despair is closely akin. The pervasive, brutal northern cold of "Polarities" is almost itself a character. "Betty" and "Giving Birth," with its two pregnant women in one body, are also stories of polarized people. A few stories of demanding men and wronged women are too narrow and bitter.

169 ____. "Island of Menace: Where Decay Is King, a Victim Stumbles." *Detroit News*, 4 April, p. M2.

Finds *Bodily Harm* sometimes difficult, or downright unpleasant, but also intelligent, provocative, and, at the end, uplifting. Menace pervades, from the John Berger epigraph on. Fleeing cancer's decay, Rennie ironically goes "where decay is king," in a tropical setting as hopeless and blighted as that of Joan Didion's *A Book of Common Prayer*. The political tension eventually focuses the novel; its prison scenes are powerful, convincing, almost unbearable. But the fragmented storytelling is disjointed and non-linear; you need a second reading to see that Rennie's first-person flashbacks are told in prison. Another problem is Rennie's often-forced victimhood. Still, as in *Surfacing*, Atwood is an uncommonly deft and perceptive writer.

170 VERDERESE, CAROL. Review of *Bodily Harm*. *Saturday Review* 9, no. 3 (March):62.

Praises *Bodily Harm*'s sophisticated allegory, very cohesive plot, and undidactic political theme; finds it Atwood's richest and most fully realized book. Despite the slow start, there's nothing unneeded here.

1982

Rennie's realization that the authorities are the brutalizers leads her "to an ironic discovery of the source of her own power."

171 WATERMAN, CARY. "A Fine, Compassionate Tale by Margaret Atwood." *Minneapolis Tribune*, 16 May. Newsbank 1981-1982, 91:D8.

Praises *Bodily Harm*'s terrific, compassionate story and fascinating contemporary women characters. *Bodily Harm* raises issues of personal and political victimization, of our lives, of women inviting victimization. The mistreated Lora is Rennie's counterpart; Lora, brutalized for her steadfast love, "gives Rennie the chance to grow beyond herself." One recognizes the astounding similarities between woman's body and the island men fight to dominate. One recalls Susan Sontag's *Illness as Metaphor*. In the end we find Rennie, who has gained health and consciousness, and come to terms with mortality, comforting Lora; we hope for both of them. Atwood has skillfully and compassionately shown us "our own personal and political fears, . . . [and handed] us a life line to climb up."

172 WEIR, LORRAINE. "True Dilemmas." *Canadian Literature*, no. 95 (Winter), pp. 112-13.

Two-Headed Poems balances poems of torture with affirmations. *True Stories* is different: like the opening of Bunuel's "Un chien andalou," Atwood's equally violent truths ("the razor across the eyeball") abjure "both silence and myth as guises of story-telling" which fail to bear witness. These poems "seek to go beyond words, . . . in order to render the force of pain. . . . "Notes [Towards] a Poem That Can Never Be Written" dares the reader . . . to employ aesthetic categories in the face of moral injunction." Compared to *The Journals of Susanna Moodie*'s perfect structuring, *True Stories*'s painful confrontations are less aesthetic and more daring.

173 WHELAN, GLORIA. "Prisoners of a Trivial World." *Detroit Free Press*, 4 April, p. B5.

Praises the poet's diction, tough wit, shrewd observation, and superb women characters of *Bodily Harm*. Jocasta is unforgettable, and Lora a gutsy heroine. Rennie may be too gullible; and, as in earlier work, the men are weaker, self-centered power players. Rennie, who has avoided commitment and opted for surfaces, finds her world invaded, by cancer and by an intruder. She flees to a Caribbean island, where she tries but fails to escape misery and violence, and finds herself a helpless "'political'" prisoner. As Wallace Stevens said, nobility lies not in what people look like, but in what and how they endure.

174 WHITAKER, MURIEL. "For Young Readers." *Canadian Literature*, no. 92 (Spring), pp. 95-97.

Finds, in a round-up review, that *Anna's Pet* is less entertaining than A.A. Milne's Tigger. "Anna seems extraordinarily naive," and her adventures "less than breathtaking." One wonders why it took two authors, Atwood and Joyce Barkhouse, to produce this simple, obviously didactic tale. Illustrator Ann Blades has responded simplistically, even carelessly, to their prosaic text.

175 WHITEMAN, BRUCE. "Some Books of Canadian Poetry in 1981." *Journal of Canadian Studies* 17, no. 2 (Summer):152-53.

Disagrees, in a round-up review, with *True Stories*, where "the existence of torture and execution" threaten "the entire mechanics of day-to-day life." Poems of graphic torture may be self-defeating. Though cruelty and inhumanity are true, and not ignorable, "yet the ability to continue one's life, to write gentle poems, is surely not to be gained from an immersion in those details"–though Atwood would find that statement superficial. These poems–many of them fine poems–focus "relentlessly on the decaying postlapsarian jungle that man has made of the garden." But the world is more complex than that, and not always vicious, multiple, and untrue.

176 WILSON, SHARON R. "The Fragmented Self in *Lady Oracle*." *Commonwealth Novel in English* 1, no. 1 (January):50-85.

Discusses Joan as a pathologically narcissistic and fragmented self, using psychoanalytic theory by Christopher Lasch and Otto Kernberg, and exploring literary aspects. An unreliable narrator who sees herself and others as fragmented, Joan is also, like Survivalwoman, a self-parody of Atwood. *Lady Oracle* both dramatizes and parodies the woman writer's dilemma. *Lady Oracle*'s fragmentation and narrative split typify a genre of modern self-conscious, self-reflexive fiction by Joyce, Woolf, Beckett, Sartre, and Camus. Joan's overeating and her relationship to her mother seem to be, in Heinz Kohut's terms, a failure of the "self-object mirroring function." As Lasch and Susan Sontag point out, photography can be used for "narcissistic 'self-surveillance,'" as Joan does. Her fears and fantasies of multiple heads, monsters, double and unreal selves, are common to narcissistic patients. As Susie Orbach points out, a woman's fat may resist inadequate mothering and society. In the end, Joan faces only herself, and her self-knowledge.

177 WINEAPPLE, BRENDA. "Margaret Atwood's Poetry: Against Still Life." *Dalhousie Review* 62, no. 2 (Summer):212-22.

Citing Adrienne Rich and Tillie Olsen, praises *Selected Poems* as the struggle of a woman's voice to reformulate power; but, as in Atwood's novels, articulating alienation and disparaging stereotypes may be insightful, yet remain trapped. Though the speaker of "Against Still Life" fails, the image releases energy, and makes us re-experience the world; as *Survival* shows, we need maps. In Moodie's divided and dismembered sensibility we learn to see ourselves. Atwood explores our divisions to evoke life's precious transiency, as in "Two-Headed Poems." Her horrifyingly suppressed, ironic, detached voice charts the territory we inhabit; she risks flatness, but opens spaces.

178 WOODCOCK, GEORGE. "Recent Canadian Novels: Major Publishers." *Queen's Quarterly* 89, no. 4 (Winter):744-48.

Praises *Bodily Harm* highly, in a seven-book review, finding it Atwood's most impressive novel, except for *Surfacing*. Perhaps the harsh but very moving *True Stories*, whose Caribbean island and Amnesty International poems correspond very closely to *Bodily Harm*, has transferred some poetic intensity. The reader experiences a strangely combined agony, in the subject, and delight, in the artistry. *Bodily Harm* balances Rennie's events and people to show us that neither she nor we can escape human misery. Atwood reveals, with exemplary sobriety, "not the drama, but the banality, the negative innocence that is the most appalling characteristic" of real evil. Reprints most of 1982.179 (below).

179 _____. "Though Every Prospect Pleases." *Ontario Review*, no. 16 (Spring-Summer), pp. 106-8.

Praises *Bodily Harm*, as in 1982.178 (above), but without ranking it among Atwood's novels. Many reviewers have felt uncomfortable with *Bodily Harm*'s "peculiar intensity and harshness"; like *Survival*, it is about survival; but Atwood's novels have always been as much about social and political issues as about individual predicaments.

1983

1 ABLEY, MARK. "Quiet Desperation." *Books in Canada* 12, no. 10 (December):18-19.

> *Bluebeard's Egg* shows, despite occasional lapses and the unanalyzed "The Sin Eater," Atwood's "offhand mastery" of short stories. The first and last stories, of the narrator's parents, have a radiant, gentle, amused love and admiration one doesn't associate with Atwood. Even the title story, of blindness, betrayal, and egotism, has tenderness – is Atwood mellowing in middle age? The central characters often hypocritically fail their own concepts, as in "Loulou" and "The Sunrise." Like Mavis Gallant, Atwood sees "through our evasions and our cherished weaknesses" to the real experiences our slogans hide; and she is not exempt from our quiet desperation.

2 ADAMS, JAMES. "Atwood Highest on Canada's Literary Totem." *Edmonton Journal*, 26 February, p. C1.

> Interviews Canada's terse-eyed, internationally praised, and most dominant writer in Edmonton. Atwood comments on writing poetry and prose; Canadian resentment of success and American disinterest in Canada; and civil rights, anti-nuclear, and pornography protests.

3 ADCOCK, FLEUR. "Scenes of Torture." *TLS*, 18 March, p. 278.

> Praises *True Stories*, but less than Atwood's novels, in a three-poet review featuring Atwood. Her poems seem to scout out terrain that her novels later develop more thoroughly and powerfully; *True Stories*'s first section describes a *Bodily Harm* setting. The central "Notes Towards a Poem That Can Never Be Written" is occasionally strident, or incoherent, but its best poems successfully implicate the reader in helpless guilt. As in her novels, truth and fiction interact; no one is safe. Good as Atwood's poems are, "they are not now her major achievement."

4 APPELBAUM, JUDITH. "Paperbacks: New and Noteworthy." *New York Times Book Review*, 17 July, p. 27.

1983

Cites Marilyn French's 1980.41 praise of the densely interwoven, splendid *Life Before Man*.

5 APPENZELL, ANTHONY. "Tenuous Past, Open Future." *Canadian Literature*, no. 97 (Summer), pp. 108-9.
Values Atwood's faithful selections and sensible introduction to *The New Oxford Book of Canadian Verse in English*. A fine poet, astute critic, and sensitive scholar, Atwood is an excellent editor; her selection stands well beside A.J.M. Smith's classic anthologies. As Atwood says, ours is a young, still-forming poetic tradition; her *New Oxford Book*, which includes no French, is therefore much longer than Smith's – 121 poets against his 71 English poets. That Atwood excludes 20 poets Smith included is due more to "a general shift in taste" than to her own preferences. Atwood naturally builds around "'old chestnuts,'" but often selects unfamiliar poems, especially from living poets, which reveal "new, yet faithful" aspects. 70 are new choices, with post-1960s work. The anthology reaches out to younger, 1980s poets, whose future is as open as that of Canadian poetry.

6 "Atwood's Ironic Eye Turns on Poets, Poetry." *Toronto Star*, 30 October, p. C8.
The characters of *Bluebeard's Egg* "register defeat and bafflement"; marriages survive, as in the title story, by inertia; but Atwood's observant, ironic eye makes these stories succeed. Her handling of speech is flawless. "Loulou" may most sharply dramatize her characters' losses; and it is a delicious satire of the literary world. To Atwood's people, world events seem distant, but domestic events may impose unpredictable burdens. Her characters are often "mean-minded, even brutal." Only "Unearthing Suite" affirms life.

7 BEAULIEU, MICHEL. "Litterature: Le Canada existe-t'il?" *Nuit blanche* (Québec), no. 11 (December-January), pp. 42-44.
Interview: Atwood discusses the politics, culture, and writers of Québec and Canada; writing strategies in *Murder in the Dark* and *Surfacing*; content and subject matter in her first five novels; and the reception of the French translations of her work.

8 BENNETT, DONNA. "Criticism in English 5: The Sixties to the Eighties." In *The Oxford Companion to Canadian Literature*. Edited by

William Toye. Toronto; Oxford; New York: Oxford University Press, pp. 160-62.

Assesses *Survival* as "'thematic'" criticism influenced by Northrop Frye's controlling archetypes and myths. *Survival*'s "brevity and casual style. . . made it the most influential work of Canadian criticism in the last decade." Underlying its evaluative nationalism is Frye's garrison thesis; under the unsurprising idea that Canadians victimize themselves is a witty guide to Canadian literature's images and themes. Though *Survival*'s ideas became popular, critics polarized, and most academic critics rejected it. As Mandel 1977.52 and 1977.53 first saw, in *Survival* "the important images, archetypes, and genres in Canadian literature are tied to concepts of monsters, ghosts, and the Gothic"; see Atwood's 1977 "Canadian Monsters" reprinted in *Second Words*. Her mystery and horror genres lead to "at least a redemptive hope." See Sullivan 1983.134.

9 BENNETT, ELIZABETH. "Margaret Atwood." *Houston Post*, 13 November. Newsbank 1983-1984, 49:C7-8.

Interviews Atwood at the University of Houston, after her several readings there; Atwood comments on her royalties, *Survival*, women and Canadian readers, feminism, Canadian reviews of successful writers; and on her travels and "'boringly normal,'" happy home life with Graeme Gibson and their daughter Jess.

10 BLACK, BARBARA. "Atwood's Collection Ranges from Desolate to Hilarious." *Gazette* (Montreal), 29 October, p. I1.

Praises Atwood's careful, telling, ironic, deeply concerned *Bluebeard's Egg* stories—except for the tawdry "Uglypuss." The theme of our nuclear-threatened future, embodied in the title story's folk tale of a fragile egg in a forbidden room, runs through these stories, especially "The Salt Garden." The several autobiographical reminiscences "glow with wisdom and humor." The witty, daring, very original title story is one of the best.

11 ____. "A Literary Survey of the Recent Past." *Gazette* (Montreal), 15 January, p. C6.

Praises Atwood's vivid, sensible, witty *Second Words*. Atwood has steadily clarified her approach to women in literature, the Canadian sensibility, writers, and human rights. Her wide-ranging,

1983

knowledgeable reviews focus often on poets, women, or Canadians. Perhaps being a poet made her sensitive to being a Canadian. Her tribute to James Reaney's *Alphabet* defines the Canadian urge to synthesize – "a wonderfully attractive thesis for a country with a cultural inferiority complex, as attractive as" *Survival*'s thesis. In the mid-seventies, Atwood defends her views against detractors; but the last piece ["Writing the Male Character"] does not make her own male characters more endearing. Her recent activism matches her views of literature; her writing has taken her far.

12 BLAKELY, BARBARA. "The Pronunciation of Flesh: A Feminist Reading of Margaret Atwood's Poetry." In *Margaret Atwood: Language, Text and System*. See Grace and Weir 1983.56, pp.33-51.

Analyzes Atwood's circle game of oppression and transformation in eight books of poetry, from *The Circle Game* through *True Stories*, using Maurice Merleau-Ponty's phenomenological paradigm as a basis for a feminist reading. In the circle game, man's oppression of woman, through eye, body, and word, provides a paradigm for other oppressions. Atwood delineates the game's dominating masculine eye and vulnerable woman's eye; the masculine imperialism of touch and reification of flesh versus woman's and nature's vulnerable boundaries; the violence of masculine speech and the violation of woman's speech. Transformation of the circle game and players occurs in three movements: first, the field shifts to a place beyond and beneath; second, vulnerability becomes transformation, as in Susanna Moodie's totemic metamorphosis and transcendence, or in synaesthetic ecstasy; third, woman identifies with women's bloodlines, image, naming, and history to transform the circle game and celebrate earth's gifts.

13 BÖHME, WOLFGANG. "Nichts von Gott." *Zeitwende* (Karlsruhe) 54, no. 3 (July):185-86.

Although readers may at first anticipate an introspective story about a cancer patient, *Verletzungen*, the German translation of *Bodily Harm*, is an absorbing and exotic adventure story. In the end, while Rennie is experiencing the brutality of prison, she comes to understand that her usual standards no longer apply, and that the breaking point is always near.

14 BRANS, JO. "Using What You're Given: An Interview with Margaret Atwood." *Southwest Review* 68, no. 4 (Autumn):301-15.

Interviews Atwood at Southern Methodist University, during their eighth annual Literary Festival. Atwood discusses feminism; pregnancy in *Surfacing, Life Before Man*, and "Giving Birth"; love poems; regional and national versus "'international'" writing in William Faulkner, [Herman] Melville, and Canada; writing about men; wimpiness in Nate and Lasha [sic] of *Life Before Man*; her own writing habits, upbringing, and rebirth symbolism; *Bodily Harm*'s final affirmation; and politics and freedom versus political labels. Reprinted, slightly revised, with a new preface: 1988.5.

15 BROOKNER, ANITA. "Enthusiasts." *London Review of Books* 5, no. 2 (3-16 February):16-17.

Praises *Dancing Girls*, in a five-book review; Atwood studies odd, inexplicable situations. She knows, as in "The Man from Mars" and the beautiful, acute "Hair Jewellery," how to write about women's emotions; she is courageous and extremely funny, not mournful. Focussing on the enigmatic, eternal masculine, she preserves dignity in defeat, and survives.

16 [BROWN, RUSSELL]. "Margaret Atwood." In *An Anthology of Canadian Literature in English*. Edited by Donna Bennett and Russell Brown. Vol. 2. Toronto: Oxford University Press, pp. 454-56.

Provides a brief biography, and outlines the two main periods in Atwood's work. From *The Circle Game* through *Dancing Girls*, Atwood uses a starkly unemotional style that can startle readers into new perceptions, as in "'You fit into me.'" Frequently her individuals are alienated women and Canadians who distrust the everyday, surface world; only by making a journey to the psychic, mythic depths can they become whole. The popular *Survival*, which builds on Frye's "'garrison'" thesis, has been criticized as one-sided, but did reveal a Canadian tradition to many; it also illuminates Atwood's own work. From *Two-Headed Poems* on through *Murder in the Dark*, Atwood uses a greater range of style and subject, and more fully drawn characters; she becomes "by turns more lyrical, more personal, and more [internationally] political."

1983

17 BURKE, ANNE. "Atwood as Critic Waxes Polemical." *Calgary Herald*, 9 April, p. J4.

Describes *Second Words*. Atwood's anecdotal introduction groups the selections into three periods. *Second Words* records an artist's coming of age; it is "reminiscent, reflective, defensive, often autobiographical and intimate in tone." Atwood's topics range widely, and include writing, education, male and female, Canadian and American. Canadian literature fans will value her pieces on little magazines and presses. Atwood is a centralist and a polemical critic concerned with Canadian identity, women's rights, pornography, and the neutron bomb. Her insightful reviews are mainly of Canadians and women. "Her anger suggests ways to change a society she does not feel part of."

18 ____. "Atwood Winnows Canadian Poetry." *Calgary Herald*, 12 March, p. G4.

Finds *The New Oxford Book of Canadian Verse in English* heartening but not daring, harmonious but not explosively transforming. Atwood is indebted to A.J.M. Smith, whose cosmopolitan bias shapes her mythic approach. She offers a "post-modernist view of the 19th century" poets prefiguring 20th century poets, and winnows early modernists, as Smith winnowed the Maple Leaf School of Confederation poets. She seems critically comfortable only from 1960 on. Much avant-garde poetry, and almost all long poems, are excluded; most of the poetry included has appeared in book-form.

19 CAMERON, ELSPETH. "In Darkest Atwood." *Saturday Night* 98, no. 3 (March):70, 72.

Appreciates *Murder in the Dark*'s form, aesthetics, structure, and unifying resonances. The title piece, which uses the parlour game as a metaphor of the writer, links fiction to the dark arts. Plot becomes conspiracy, or burial place. "Iconography" reveals Atwood's "disdain for neat plans" or claustrophobic interiors; she strives instead for "an arrangement like that in nature: one in which function defines space, line, and colour with ruthless economy," as in ["Strawberries"]. The four loosely-grouped categories move from early autobiography to the ironic similarities of Mexico; to experimental aesthetics and writerly problems, as in "The Page"; to the final Atwoodian "pieces that let the darkness through." Recurrent words and images unite these four sections poetically. Though the anti-Atwoods will attack these plotless themes and variations, others will hear her subtle, penetrating, eerie resonances. Reprinted: 1988.10.

20 CARMEAN, KAREN. "Margaret Atwood." In *Critical Survey of Long Fiction: English Language Series*. Edited by Frank N. Magill. Vol. 1. Englewood Cliffs, N.J.: Salem Press, pp. 94-102.

Atwood's fiction expresses her views of Canadian survival and territorial identity. Her alienated, ambivalent heroines are emotional refugees; their journeys, which are metaphors of inner explorations, end tenuously, with estrangement, survival, and some hope. *Surfacing's* *bildungsroman* of self-recovery acquires mythic overtones, and exposes romantic literary conventions; its unnamed, alienated, victimized heroine learns self-discovery from nature, and becomes a powerful survivor. The stark *Life Before Man*, which peels away its characters' protective deceptions, ends with some hope; its characters' emotions are reflected in Quebec's political separatism. Cancer is *Bodily Harm's* controlling metaphor; its protagonist, Rennie, moves from superficial expertise to self-discovery and spiritual growth; in the end, comforting Lora, Rennie embodies the best of Griswold, whether or not she survives to report the truth. Includes a short biography.

21 CARRINGTON, ILDIKÓ de PAPP. "Another Symbolic Descent." *Essays on Canadian Writing*, no. 26 (Summer), pp. 45-63.

Explicates *Bodily Harm's* didactic theme, structure, viewpoints, controlling metaphors of hands and faces, and ambiguous end. *Bodily Harm* "urges compassion for human suffering" and demands that human evil be denounced; but first, suffering and evil must be perceived as real. Like Annette in "A Travel Piece," Rennie is plunged through surfaces and illusions to reality. The intricate six-part structure conceals the cell setting until the climactic sixth part. Lora's first-person flashbacks are chronological. Rennie's flashbacks, which are associational and chronological, shift between her first-person memories and her third-person dramatizations, to imply significance and contrasts. Jocasta's narrative provides minor comic and satiric relief. As in the four earlier novels, the protagonist journeys and descends to a dark, death-associated place to confront a truth of herself; as before, recurring images "evolve into thematic metaphors."

1983

Here hands give or refuse touch; faces and facelessness recur. Rennie learns to stop being a voyeur, to use her hands, to recognize the beaten face as Lora's. Love and language "create human identity" as Rennie cradles Lora, in a maternal *pietà*; but Lora's rebirth is ambiguous. Atwood re-educates Rennie through sometimes flat expository lessons, from Lora, Paul, and Dr. Minnow; and dramatically, by exposing her to suffering, as with the mother and baby. The ambiguous end, of future tense or fantasy ascent, partly avoids sacrificing credibility to message. Revised as part of 1987.22.

22 CLARK, MEERA T. "Margaret Atwood's *Surfacing*: Language, Logic, and the Art of Fiction." *Modern Language Studies* 13, no. 3 (Summer):3-15.

Surfacing's narrative technique, which constantly exposes so-called facts as fictions, embodies Atwood's views on language. The narrator's apparently detached, factual collage of impressions and memories must be read like mythical images, which lie about facts to reach essential truths. Diving, she finds the powers of the gods and of the unconscious. Abandoning the rational, she tries to abandon language. When her sanity and selfish ego break down, she sees visions and, like Lear in the storm, strips away facades. No longer "'sane,'" her visionary language recreates primal reality. Atwood's attitude toward language parallels that of Ludwig Wittgenstein, and of modern structuralism and semiotics. *Surfacing's* exultation of nature, madness, and the visionary belong to Romanticism.

23 CLUETT, ROBERT. "Surface Structures: The Syntactic Profile of *Surfacing*." In *Margaret Atwood: Language, Text and System*. See Grace and Weir 1983.56, pp. 67-90.

Presents *Surfacing's* computerized syntactic profile, in graphs and text, in comparison with five novels by Morley Callaghan, Robertson Davies, Margaret Laurence, and Leonard Cohen, from the York Computer Inventory of Prose Style. *Surfacing's* syntactic profile – "its short clauses, its utter eschewing of modifying words, its pronominality, its clause-end additions (participials and appositives), its nearly total avoidance of subject-minus zeugmatic additioning" – deviate greatly from Atwood's other novels, and from all other twentieth-century fiction. Subordinate clauses are used "in a disproportionately right-branching way." Locative left-branching clauses are frequent, which fits with the theme of "'Where is he?'" [sic] and "'*Where* am I?'" rather than *whodunit. Surfacing*'s linguistic retrenchment is a retreat from "ornate 'civilized' values," corresponding to the heroine's wilderness retreat from civilization.

24 COLE, WILLIAM. "Classy Titles." *Saturday Review* 9, no. 11 (November-December):46.

Reviews *The New Oxford Book of Canadian Verse in English* positively, referring to Irving Layton, Alden Nowlan, and Earle Birney as his favorites. Except for Robert W. Service, Leonard Cohen, Malcolm Lowry, and Atwood, most of these poets are unfamiliar to American readers.

25 CRAIG, TERRENCE. "A Three-Piece Suite." *CRNLE Reviews Journal*, no. 2, pp. 23-27.

Considers *Dancing Girls* [*and Other Stories*] and two books by Greg Hollinshead and Leon Rooke as post-modern short stories. Post-modernism is a vague but increasingly accepted term involving surrealist confusions, chaos, and absurdities. Atwood's stories are the most objectively real, least surreal, and most depressing, with their dry tone, bleak plots, struggling female protagonists, and dissected relationships. Atwood negates illusions. "What she does provide is an almost unbearable reality." Though few would enjoy these stories, few would fail to admire their craftsmanship or "'stripped-down'" realism. The 1973 "Grave of the Famous Poet" juxtaposes romantic conventions to decisive realization. "The Sin Eater," which is the only one of these mostly 1971-1977 stories that moves towards post-modernism, is an excellent examination of guilt and madness, with an unreliable, perhaps insane, narrator.

26 CUDE, WILFRED. "Bravo Mothball! An Essay on *Lady Oracle*." In *The Canadian Novel: A Critical Anthology*. Edited by John Moss. Vol. 1, *Here and Now*. Toronto: NC Press, pp. 45-50.

Reprint of 1978.19, which is a slightly revised text of 1977.11; see also the expanded text of 1980.25.

27 DAFOE, CHRISTOPHER. "Atwood's Stories Compel Belief." *Winnipeg Free Press*, 5 November, p. 49.

1983

Praises Atwood's compassionate perception and convincingly real, often personal *Bluebeard's Egg* stories, whether they are autobiography or imagination. "Significant Moments in the Life of My Mother" is a "beautifully realized character study" of "a woman real enough to step off the page." Atwood underpaints her vivid surfaces so that "pentimento" effects shine through. She shrewdly captures not only contemporary life and the recent "Age of Aquarius," but also the postwar 1940s. Her comedy makes serious points; she sees human absurdity with compassion.

28 ____. "Baby Boots, Bronzed in Oxford." *Winnipeg Free Press*, 8 January, p. 66.

Approves Atwood's sound, comprehensive, and generously inclusive selections for *The New Oxford Book of Canadian Verse in English*. Though the Canadian literary tradition is not long, Atwood's selections show that Canadians need not blush for their poetry. The earliest poems are literary curiosities; the real collection begins with the nineteenth century. Atwood's choices are generally fair and apt, and entirely so with the established poets. Younger poets – James Reaney and others – are represented admirably. Atwood's own poems are "not unduly self-effacing." Though there are bound to be a few left out, James McIntyre, the famous "'Cheese Poet,'" should have been included.

29 DAVEY, FRANK. "Atwood's Gorgon Touch." In *Surviving the Paraphrase: Eleven Essays on Canadian Literature*. Winnipeg: Turnstone Press, pp. 87-111.

Reprint of 1977.12, which is reprinted 1978.20 and 1988.15. (1983 reprint omits on page 106 a 1977.12 quote from "Memory": imprint of you / glowing against me, / burnt-out match in a dark room.")

30 ____. "Lady Oracle's Secret; Atwood's Comic Novels." In *Surviving the Paraphrase: Eleven Essays on Canadian Literature*. Winnipeg: Turnstone Press, pp. 151-66.

Reprint of 1980.29.

31 ____. "Surviving the Paraphrase." In *Surviving the Paraphrase: Eleven Essays on Canadian Literature*. Winnipeg: Turnstone Press, pp. 1-12.

Reprint of 1976.17.

32 DAVIDSON, JIM. Interview. In *Sideways from the Page: The Meanjin Interviews*. Melbourne: Fontana/Collins, pp. 85-108.
   Reprint of 1978.23.

33 DAVIES, DIANE. Review of *True Stories*. *Poetry Wales* 18, no. 4:104-7.
   The ironically-titled *True Stories* not only reveals too-true stories of injustice and atrocity; it also attempts to define the place of poetry in a world that challenges it, as in "Small Poems for the Winter Solstice." The ironically-named "Notes Towards a Poem That Can Never Be Written" builds a last-resort case for poetry as inevitable when freedom is destroyed. Fortunately, these black, disturbing aspects do not ruin Atwood's style or vision; "Trainride: Vienna-Bonn" transcends the documentary and becomes more personal. Appreciates Atwood's startling images, syntactical range, and satiric "True Romances."

34 DAVIS, DICK. "Violence in the Garden." *Listener* 109 (5 May):24.
   Rejects *True Stories*'s gruesome horrors, in an eight-poet review that features Derek Mahon and finds Adrienne Rich annoying. Atwood lacks lyric sensibility, offers "a fair pastiche" of the later Sylvia Plath, and has a penchant for nauseating horror stories "(largely the bestial indignities suffered by women)." "But when [Atwood] moves away from horror," one sees more easily that her writing is simply inept, self-indulgent, and subtle as a bludgeon.

35 DEMPSTER, BARRY. Review of *The New Oxford Book of Canadian Verse in English* and *Canadian Poetry*, edited by Jack David and Robert Lecker. *Poetry Canada Review* 4, no. 3 (Spring):3.
   Welcomes both collections, with metaphors. *Oxford* offers an Eaton's catalogue or smorgasbord; *Canadian*, a sit-down dinner of fewer poets whose work is better chosen. *Oxford* could be subtitled "The Abridged Encyclopedia of Canadian Poetry"; *Canadian*, "The Encyclopedia of Some Major Canadian Poets . . . 'refusing to be abridged.'" Both choose their pioneers almost flawlessly; *Oxford* includes many of the worthy younger poets, but omits some. That both omit the French is a fault. But what both have is very good, "the Canadian poet as world class." Like a Canadian airplane tour and a train ride, the two complement one another.

1983

36 DONALDSON, ANNE. "A Cool Canadian with Incisive Pen." *Glasgow Herald*, 19 September, p. 6.

Interviews Atwood, who will read from *Bodily Harm* in Glasgow tonight, and spend the winter in Norfolk with her daughter and Scots-born Graeme Gibson, who was writer-in-residence last year at Edinburgh University. Atwood comments on pulp fiction, Canadian writing, and discovering the structures in her own work.

37 DRAINE, BETSY. "An Interview with Margaret Atwood." In *Interviews with Contemporary Writers: Second Series, 1972-1982*. Edited by L.S. Dembo. Madison: University of Wisconsin Press, pp. 366-81.

An April 1981 University of Wisconsin question-and-answer session, whose first half comes from students' questions, and second half from Draine's follow-up questions. Atwood discusses her formal and extracurricular education, and her student and current writing habits; argues against autobiographical criticism, which is used against women – what counts in your own writing "is what is real to you, not what has 'happened' to you"; argues against the ghettoization of writing into female or male, by Sir Anthony Quiller-Couch, women, or anyone, citing a class project that found different styles by period but not by sex, and different reactions by critics to women's versus men's work; recounts her publishing experiences with the rejected early poetry and novel ["Up in the Air So Blue"], *The Edible Woman*, and *Surfacing*; comments on anti-genres and Menippean satire in her five novels; and discusses *Life Before Man*'s evolution, three balanced points of view, main-line realism, Elizabeth and her Auntie Muriel, and the three main characters' final movements outwards from self.

38 DUCHÊNE, ANNE. "Scouting." *TLS*, 7 January, p. 23.

Praises most those few *Dancing Girls* stories that go beyond Atwood's usually disconsolate, lonely characters craving and clawing for love; the best, "When It Happens," details in light water-colours what is now everyone's "secret scenario of horror and apocalypse." Atwood's always-expert search for sore places can become predictable. But "Training" and "Dancing Girls," which is a muted study of racism and isolation, prove Atwood a very brave scout, ready to go beyond the Upper St. Lawrence-Updike area.

39 EDWARDS, CATERINA. "Atwood at Her Best." *Edmonton Journal*, 9 April, p. D8.

Welcomes the witty, allusive, often satirical *Murder in the Dark*, which avoids the faults of Atwood's novels. The meditations on writing are powerful; but often surpassed, as in "Liking Men," by the adroitly explored male/female relationships. Perhaps Atwood has found her form at last.

40 FEE, MARGERY. Review of *Second Words* and *Murder in the Dark*, and of *Margaret Atwood: Language, Text and System*, edited by Sherrill E. Grace and Lorraine Weir. *Malahat Review*, no. 65 (July), pp. 134-37.

Finds nothing second-rate in the witty, thoughtful, polemical *Second Words*; enjoys Atwood's masterful shifts, "from comic-book heroine to beleaguered writer to mild-mannered reviewer and critic"; from oratory's opinion and attack, to criticism's balance and reason, to the complex and apparently universal voice of fiction and poetry. *Murder in the Dark*, which varies Atwood's favourite themes, has several excellent pieces, including "Instructions for the Third Eye"; its first section is the best. The less satisfactory "Simmering," "Women's Novels," and "Happy Endings," are amusing, but best saved for readings. Finds Grace and Weir's *Language* 1983.56 solid and varied; its moral consensus is that Atwood shows us how to break out of oppressive circle games. But Atwood's "An End to Audience?" makes it clear that moral critiques without political and economic contexts are not enough.

41 FINN, GERALDINE. "Feminism and Fiction: In Praise of *Praxis*, beyond *Bodily Harm*." *Socialist Studies*:51-78.

Wants contemporary women's fiction to be truly revolutionary, like Fay Weldon's *Praxis*, with a vision of alternatives, a retrospective historical perspective, and a collective heroine; critiques *Bodily Harm* as pre-revolutionary. Though Atwood's work is more "'representative'" of our lives as contemporary women than Weldon's is, Atwood does bind us to present despair. Her heroines, who pursue idiosyncratic individual solutions, are not collective heroes. From a socialist-feminist perspective, both *Survival* and *Bodily Harm* show a limited political awareness. *Bodily Harm* goes further than Atwood's earlier novels in attributing "all political atrocities as well as women's 'personal' mutilations to men *as men*," as in *True Stories*; and in Rennie's revolutionary turn to sisterhood and to anticipated subversive reporting. But the final words, which "refer Rennie's salvation to 'luck,'" are counterproductive, and show her stuck between *Survival*'s basic victim positions two and three.

42 FITZGERALD, JUDITH. "The Art of Pitching Poetry." *Globe and Mail*, 28 May, p. F1.

Briefly quotes Atwood, who enjoys reading her poetry, but needs a microphone for a big hall, and recommends B complex and C vitamins to writers on tour.

43 FLOWER, DEAN. "Fiction Chronicle." *Hudson Review* 36, no. 2 (Summer):364-66.

Complains that, except for "Hair Jewellery," the *Dancing Girls* stories are unoriginal, monotonous, and predictable. At least four are driven forcibly by sexual politics; the nameless people and Plathian rhetoric of "Under Glass" need more human context, not pointless anger. Atwood seems to think that one interior dialogue, generalized rhetoric, and minimal references to reality, make a short story. The exception, "Hair Jewellery," has a less narrow, more adult and remembering, narrator, and Atwood's ironic humor. "Without the humor, we get nothing but Ms. Found in a Bottle."

44 FRENCH, WILLIAM. "Atwood's Snappy Snippets Pack a Wallop." *Globe and Mail*, 15 March, p. 17.

The accomplished and provocative *Murder in the Dark* is not a major work, but not merely opportunistic or minor. "The stories bristle with concealed fish hooks and exposed, vulnerable eyes." Atwood's sardonic humor makes us smile despite her major themes of loss, menace, and "bitterness about men's power and their abuse of it," as in the two most provocative pieces, "Simmering" and "Liking Men." The general despair ends with some hope, in "Instructions for the Third Eye." The title story has the critic as detective; this critic-detective finds Atwood guilty of making us swallow unpalatable truths – and that's no crime.

45 ____. "The Fruits of Rare Insight." *Globe and Mail*, 22 October, p. E14.

Compares the *Bluebeard's Egg* stories to yoghurt, deceptively smooth, but concealing puckery or bitter or occasionally mellow fruit. Avoiding risks, Atwood does here what she does best – mapping male-female relationships of victims and survivors. She does not deal with love, or with politics beyond sexual politics. The four apparently autobiographical stories may offer insights into her becoming a writer; "Hurricane Hazel" is the best of these; "Betty" is almost as good. Many of the urban Toronto stories feature divorced or separated partners, sometimes in ludicrous situations, as in "The Salt Garden." "The Sunrise," artist, Yvonne, who paints men's erect penises, typifies Atwood's wit; "Loulou" most specifically shows a woman exploited by men; the title story, with its folk tale level, is perhaps the best.

46 _____. "'I'm an Expert on Anorexia.'" *Globe and Mail*, 3 November, p. E1.

Thinks about anorexia and eating in *The Edible Woman*, *Lady Oracle*, and three *Bluebeard's Egg* stories, while lunching with Atwood. Atwood comments on the letters she gets from anorexics, on nineteenth-century women's undiagnosed anorexia, and on the body's resistance to dieting.

47 FRIEDMANN, PEGGY. "Margaret Atwood's Collections are Treasures of Word Power." *Florida Times-Union* (Jacksonville), 13 February. Newsbank 1982-1983, 65:B1.

Welcomes Atwood's two virtuoso books, *Dancing Girls* and *True Stories*, which explore her novels' major themes. *True Stories*'s central, elegantly crafted, yet passionate love poems deal with communication difficulties between men and women; so do the stories where "'lovers'" try to manipulate, consume, and control, as in "Polarities," "Under Glass," and "The Resplendent Quetzal." Atwood's major themes – of self-definition, survival, and victimization-objectification – are primary concerns of feminism; "Torture," "A Woman's Issue," and "Christmas Carols" acknowledge this perspective. "Spelling," one of the strongest, is not only a "'purely magical poem'" for her child; it is also about women who could not have daughters, or give birth; it "proclaims a woman's right to self-definition."

48 GERSON, CAROLE. "First Thoughts." *Canadian Literature*, no. 99 (Winter), pp. 176-77.

1983

Appreciates the versatile, wry, far-ranging *Second Words*, which charts the emergence of Atwood the critic, from student book-reviewer to committed social activist. Her essential concerns – "individual and national identity, sexual and power politics," language, perceptions, North American materialism – have been more or less constant. In 1973 she spoke of the writer's connection to society; more recently, she has used her international popularity to speak, at Amnesty International's world meeting and elsewhere, of the writer's moral and ethical responsibilities to bear witness. General Atwood fans and literary historians will enjoy the lectures and early work; CanLit students and teachers will be tempted to apply Atwood's critical insights to her own poetry and fiction.

49 GERVAIS, MARTY. "Atwood Can Still Keep Us on Edge." *Windsor Star*, 29 October, p. C12.

Appreciates *Bluebeard's Egg*'s style, tone, and well-rooted message; and tries to describe the "funny edge that seems to exist at the beginning of each novel, short story or poem [by Atwood,] . . . an anxiety or uncertainty as you sink into her writing," plus a willing belief. The patchwork images, usually gleaned from a character, weave a world of detail. Atwood's didacticism and barely humorous to barely serious tone tie together this bizarre assortment of women-centred stories. Dialogue and event are minimal. Both "Significant Moments in the Life of My Mother" and "Hurricane Hazel" look at the consequences underlying stereotypes; both leave a warm and comfortable feeling.

50 ____. "Spreading the Satire around." *Windsor Star*, 30 April, p. C10.

Welcomes *Murder in the Dark*, which, like all Atwood's work, disturbs and moves readers. She shows us the world around us, as in the role-reversal "Simmering," and the biting feminist satire of "Liking Men." Because we do miss obvious nuances of our lives, we're faced with the social injustices Atwood reveals. "Happy Endings" is the most impressive of these powerful satires; its companion piece, "Women's Novels," makes it clear that we can't go on turning away from reality.

51 GLASTONBURY, MARION. "Images of Land and Sea." *Times Educational Supplement* (London), 29 April, p. 32.

Appreciates *True Stories*'s imagery, unity, truth, and rage in a two-book review. Atwood's lyrics combine "dreams with analysis, private visions with public reckoning." Her sea-shore images yield "endless symbols of transition and contrast"—survival, dissolution, the actual, the imaginary; she discovers the drowned histories of things. Desire and "domestic intimacy are sharpened by awareness of surrounding violence: war, famine, torture, the subjugation of women, dictatorships. . . ." Our daily news of random, banal carnage mocks the justice and logic of traditional tragedy. Yet words do "bear witness to unspeakable facts." The despairingly-titled "Notes Towards a Poem That Can Never Be Written" sequence "voices eloquent and undefeated rage."

52 GLENDINNING, VICTORIA. "Feminist from the Great North Woods." *Sunday Times* (London), 18 September, p. 42.

Interviews Atwood, whose five novels are in Virago paperbacks. Atwood talks about her isolated, fragmented childhood in the Canadian north woods, which made social groups, artifacts, and habits seem strange to her; *Life Before Man* as her "'homage to George Eliot, it's about Middle-everything'"; living in England and Edinburgh; British class distinctions; her feminism, which is not anti-men; and her present life.

53 GODARD, BARBARA. "My (m)Other, My Self: Strategies for Subversion in Atwood and Hébert." *Essays on Canadian Writing*, no. 26 (Summer), pp. 13-44.

Explores women's quest for selfhood themes and the metaphor of refraction in *Lady Oracle* and Anne Hébert's *Kamouraska*, citing Simone de Beauvoir, Lucy Irigaray, and others. Both novels play with and expand patriarchal mirror and polar oppositions: subject/object, author/character, and male/female, which are seen as multiple, fluid aspects. Both narrators fragment and multiply their personalities. Joan's fictive plots merge and metamorphose; her characters are her projections, as she is Atwood's. Though, like *Kamouraska*, *Lady Oracle* refracts women's quests, and fairy tales that may be patriarchal or debased Demeter-Kore myth, and belongs to Ellen Moers's female Gothic tradition, *Oracle* is parody that cannot be taken at face value. Both novels are subversive, but not revolutionary.

1983

54 GRACE, SHERRILL E. "Articulating the 'Space Between': Atwood's Untold Stories and Fresh Beginnings." In *Margaret Atwood: Language, Text and System*. See Grace and Weir 1983.56, pp. 1-16.

Argues that Atwood's system, seen in the 1970s context represented by Dennis Lee and Leslie Armour, does articulate a typically Canadian, synthetic, non-Cartesian third way that Armour calls the "'space between'" American liberalism and Marxian collectivism. Earlier critics have mostly emphasized only Atwood's Canadian nationalism, or feminism; or have misunderstood what Salutin 1977.79 correctly sees as *Survival*'s "'pre-Marxist dialectic'"; or have misperceived Atwood's violent dualities (see 1980.47) as static polarities. A structuralist analysis of duality, nature, self, and language in Atwood's work reveals that her system—the set of codes that structure her work—is not static, but a dynamic, dialectic process. Atwood offers dichotomies of artist and society, language and world (as in "Two-Headed Poems"), culture and nature, self and other, that are interdependent relationships and processes, "functioning dialectically and modelled upon natural life processes." Contrary to Davey 1977.12 and Sullivan 1977.90, "Atwood's art pushes through stasis towards process," and breaks imprisoning circles. See 1986.164.

55 G[RACE], S[HERRILL] E., and W[EIR], L[ORRAINE]. Introduction to *Margaret Atwood: Language, Text and System*. See Grace and Weir 1983.56, pp. ix-x.

Introduces the nine essays of *Margaret Atwood: Language, Text, and System*, which investigate focal points of Atwood's literary system, text, and language, and broader contexts of her work, but not the author's biography.

56 GRACE, SHERRILL E., and WEIR, LORRAINE, eds. *Margaret Atwood: Language, Text and System*. Vancouver: University of British Columbia Press, 160 pp.

Contains Introduction 1983.55, Grace 1983.54, Hutcheon 1983.66, Blakely 1983.12, Mandel 1983.84, Cluett 1983.23, Guédon 1983.58, Stratford 1983.130, Woodcock 1983.147, Weir 1983.142. See 1983.40 and 1983.146.

57 GROENING, LAURA. *"The Journals of Susanna Moodie*: A Twentieth-Century Look at a Nineteenth-Century Life." *Studies in Canadian Literature* 8, no. 2:166-80.

Defends the nineteenth-century Mrs. Moodie against Atwood's twentieth-century distortions. *The Journals of Susanna Moodie*, in its poems and "Afterword," sees Moodie as an alienated paranoid schizophrenic, and totally obscures the authentic meaning of Mrs. Moodie's *Roughing It in the Bush* and *Life in the Clearings*. Atwood uses Moodie to symbolize the rational half of Atwood's own duality, and Canada to symbolize the other half, of unfenced, animal nature. Where Mrs. Moodie described real cholera and near shipwreck, Atwood depicts an alienated sensibility. Atwood's "Two Fires" "beautifully captures. . . the split between rational understanding and irrational nature"; but the real Mrs. Moodie rescued what was most needed from fire, and warned the community against wood shingles. Atwood's solipsistic Moodie "views all reality as metaphor"; her "Afterword" assumes a twentieth-century post-[George] Grant attitude to progress. But Mrs. Moodie had nineteenth-century attitudes towards nature and technology; she was fascinated by people, not obsessed or intolerant, and a genuine Canadian patriot.

58 GUÉDON, MARIE-FRANÇOISE. *"Surfacing*: Amerindian Themes and Shamanism." In *Margaret Atwood: Language, Text and System*. See Grace and Weir 1983.56, pp. 91-111.

Surfacing's Indian elements appear momentarily as "signs recalling the unbroken world of the previous inhabitants," and do not follow, or create, any specific Amerindian cosmology. The antlered figure or horned water god, who corresponds more to Great Lakes rock drawings than to any work yet found in the Ontario-Quebec border area, suggests May-may-gway-shi and Misshipeshu. In *Surfacing* as in North American Indian cultures, ghosts, pregnant women, and the unborn child commune with the spirits; and power involves transformations and new ways of seeing. The vision quest corresponds to certain North Algonkian traits, but follows the European division of natural and supernatural. The Christ-like lynched heron is not Objibwa-Cree-Ottawa. The traditional shaman is physiologically and psychologically transformed in an intact spirit world; *Surfacing*'s heroine, in contrast, returns to herself and a fragmented Euro-Canadian culture, or non-culture. Excerpted: 1985.11.

59 GUPTA, LINDA ROBERTA. "Fathers and Daughters in Women's Novels." Ph.D. dissertation, American University, 154 pp.

Studies father-daughter relationships in European *märchen* and in nine nineteenth- and twentieth-century novels by women, including *Surfacing*. Women writers see the maturing heroine's conflict with the father as inevitable; the implicit feminist argument sees father-daughter conflict as a metaphor of women's struggles in patriarchal society. See *Dissertation Abstracts International* 44:1783A.

60 HARMON, GARY L. Review of *Dancing Girls and Other Stories*. In *Magill's Literary Annual*. Edited by Frank N. Magill. Vol. 1. Englewood Cliffs, N.J.: Salem Press, pp. 169-73.

Appreciates Atwood's stories, which probe themes from her five novels, of love, metamorphosis, power, survival, and the continuum of human, animal, and nature. Language often betrays; relationships rarely survive. "The Man from Mars" is one of many stories where female protagonists survive unsatisfactory relationships with men. "Betty" shows, in its narrator, the possibility of escaping such pathological passivity. "Under Glass" demonstrates the continuum between human and nature. The urban design student of "Dancing Girls" feels compassion, and needs to learn about nature. Atwood's vivid images dramatize her protagonists' inner lives. "Beneath the ironic surface of her portraits of representative women . . . there is unappeasable anger and a call to change."

61 HILL, DOUGLAS. "Tales of Human Bondage." *Maclean's* 96, no. 46 (14 November):78.

The *Bluebeard's Egg* stories "take a claw hammer to relationships . . . [not destructively] but in the hope of defining" them; Atwood excels at recording feelings. Though her powerful language still "draw[s] blood from those who substitute roles for selves," on the whole *Bluebeard's Egg* "judges the world less harshly than *Dancing Girls*." Atwood's characters seem more confident and human; the quasi-autobiographical elements are gentler. The best stories, like "The Salt Garden," integrate moral perspective with plot; the title story, with its folk tale wizard's egg, is similarly resonant. The final story illuminates the paradox of Atwood's father's grim vision and joy in life.

62 HOFSESS, JOHN. "The Hand That Holds the Pen." *Books in Canada* 12, no. 2 (February):12-13.

Acclaims Atwood's moral and political courage in *Second Words*, and praises *The New Oxford Book of Canadian Verse in English*. For the past decade, the most important writers – those writing to change what is largely a man's world of injustice and nuclear absurdities – have been women. Even in the *New Oxford*, which is inevitably heavily weighted with male poets, only Dennis Lee and Pier Giorgio Di Cicco seem able to create socially aware poetry. Fourteen of *Second Words*'s articles complement Atwood's anthology choices, which update A.J.M. Smith's classic anthology, and give short shrift to poetic bores. Although *Second Words* will not have *Survival*'s impact, it is an invaluable guide to Atwood's themes, principles, and development. Most reviews are generous appreciations. The public speeches, like the delightful tongue-in-cheek "Writing the Male Character," are more amusing and provocative; these most clearly display, as in the Amnesty International speech, Atwood's fairness, compassion for mankind, and "determination to stand up and be counted."

63 HOMANS, MARGARET. "'Her Very Own Howl.': The Ambiguities of Representation in Recent Women's Fiction." *Signs* 9, no. 2 (Winter):186-205 passim.

Argues, using terms from Elaine Marks and Mary Jacobus, that the two kinds of feminist literary criticism, the French theoretical separatism that sees language as excluding women, and the American pragmatic, liberal appropriation that sees language as controllable by women, should be conjoined, to overcome the circular reasoning and internal contradictions of each; considers the issue of women's relation to language in six novels. Like Toni Morrison's *Sula* and Alice Walker's *Meridian*, Atwood's *Surfacing* and *Life Before Man* dichotomize "language into alternatives of appropriation and separatism." All three authors differentiate between their linguistic exile as minorities and as women; the latter is masked as women's choice. Briefly compares Atwood's Lesje to the heroine of Margaret Drabble's *The Realms of Gold*, and the alternative vision of Elizabeth's mad sister to a situation in Marilyn French's *The Bleeding Heart*.

64 HOSEK, CHAVIVA. Review of *Bodily Harm*. *World Literature Written in English* 22, no. 2 (Autumn):287-90.

1983

Praises Atwood's satire, but not the flat voice of her moral exhortations. Atwood has long been "attuned to what is currently deemed political," and very good at parodying and satirizing currently marketable art and upper middle-class popular culture. Rennie, terrified by cancer, is less cold than most of Atwood's female narrators. The parodic set pieces of the decadent eighties, like Jocasta, are the best. Griswold seems hurriedly sketched; Atwood should stay out of Alice Munro country. Is David exemplary of exploiting? Lora is Rennie's "demonic double"; we are meant to see the released Rennie as transformed. Rennie's flat voice is fine for Atwood's satire, but its contempt "spills over into its exhortation" – perhaps onto the audience?

65 HOY, HELEN. *Modern English-Canadian Prose: A Guide to Information Sources*. Detroit: Gale Research Co., pp. 60-75.
Provides a chronological listing of primary work, and an alphabetical listing of secondary work. Lists, under primary, 20 monographs in fiction, nonfiction prose, and poetry; 12 short stories; and 21 articles. Lists, under secondary, bibliographies by Fairbanks 1979.32 and Horne 1974.15, 1977.34, and 1979.56; 107 works of criticism, including interviews, alphabetized by author; and a number of book reviews, cited alphabetically by journal only, not author or title, for the first four novels, *Dancing Girls*, and *Survival*.

66 HUTCHEON, LINDA. "From Poetic to Narrative Structures: The Novels of Margaret Atwood." In *Margaret Atwood: Language, Text and System*. See Grace and Weir 1983.56, pp. 17-31.
Contrasts *The Edible Woman* and *Life Before Man* to show Atwood's progression from static poetic structures to more kinetic narrative structures; and reassesses what has been seen as Atwood's static "'circle game'" aesthetic as both formally dynamic and thematically moral. *The Edible Woman* is a "'circle game'" whose narrative themes are structured metonymically around the two poles of hunger and love, which reflect Atwood's aesthetic "paradox of process/product, writing/written." *Surfacing* moves from verbal metaphor to narrative symbol. The first novel discusses creativity overtly; the second and third use artist figures; the fourth, *Life*, moves away from self-reflexiveness to show creative imagination as a theme in life, not art. *Life's* temporal strategies replace *The Edible Woman's* static image patterns and thematic configurations. Fantasy in *Life*

appears as the regressions, escapes, wish-fulfillment, associations, and creative imagination that Freud discussed. Lesje and Nate are victims of each other's complementary fantasies. Lesje's morally responsible, "truly creative act" of pregnancy becomes the paradigm of the novelist's creation. Develops 1981.51.

67 INNESS, LORNA. "To Australian Readers, Atwood Is Best-Known Canadian Author." *Halifax Chronicle Herald*, 29 October, p. 19.
Briefly quotes Barry Oakley, the Australian novelist and playwright who won the 1982 Canada-Australia literary award, that Atwood and the questionably Canadian Brian Moore are the only Canadian writers read widely in Australia.

68 JACKSON, MARNI. "Distortions That Tell the Truth." *Maclean's* 96, no. 12 (21 March):59.
"Like a fictional finger bowl, *Murder in the Dark*" lacks protein, but, taken with Atwood's other work, provokes refreshing reflections. Like a children's game, these offhand stories and parables become quite serious. Most involve tricks. Many suggest that memory, like fiction, can distort to tell the truth. "Raw Materials" and the sinister, haunting, mysterious title piece are both more technical and more intimate than Atwood's longer works.

69 JALOWICA, DANIEL. Review of *Bluebeard's Egg*. *Quill and Quire* 49, no. 12 (December):26.
Finds two perspectives in the *Bluebeard's Egg* stories: one, where narrator and subject are emotionally close, produces the sensitive, preternaturally cognitive childhood recollections of "Unearthing Suite" and "Betty." In the second, where distance is restored, Atwood examines characters who, as in *Bodily Harm*, qualify as walking wounded; they are spiritual cripples, "complacent victims or emotional predators" dwelling in a malignant fog, like the coldly manipulative Joel of "Uglypuss." Atwood's prose is powerful and extraordinarily mellifluous. Her odd sense of humour provides a respite from the occasional macabre impersonality.

70 JAMKHANDI, SUDHAKAR R. "An Interview with Margaret Atwood." *Commonwealth Novel in English* 2, no. 1 (January):1-6.

1983

Atwood discusses her 1950s Canadian poetry influences; 1960s and current Canadian publishing; autobiography and realism in her own novels—the real settings, the pastiche and improvised characters, and the fictitious but plausible plots; and writing versus propaganda, as with women and Commonwealth writers being told what to write.

71 JOHNSTON, GEORGE. "Diction in Poetry." *Canadian Literature*, no. 97 (Summer), pp. 39-44.

A discussion of poetic diction in four poems, by Atwood, Raymond Souster, Robert Finch, and Michael Ondaatje; appreciates the very modern "'bad movie'" diction of ["'You take my hand,'"] which is used with dazzling skill.

72 JONES, D.G. "Canadian Poetry, Roots and New Directions." *Credences*, n.s. 2, nos. 2-3 (Fall-Winter):254-75 passim.

Locates Atwood's poetic strategy, satiric vision, and basic imagery in an English-Canadian poetic tradition that goes back to the Halifax Oliver Goldsmith's "The Rising Village"; briefly compares Atwood's and Dennis Lee's satire and anti-Americanism. Her seemingly modern poetry ironically isolates Canada's metonymical figures of community and order. She rewrites nineteenth-century Canadian heroes satirically, as in "Progressive insanities of a pioneer." Atwood's complex Susanna Moodie knows her own imperialism, failures, and partial successes; when Moodie is buried under pavement, the rising village becomes the grave of older poems' central feminine presence and intimate space. Only recently does Atwood affirm the local, domestic space, as in "Book of Ancestors."

73 KEITH, W.J. "Atwood as (Infuriating) Critic." *Canadian Forum* 62 (February):26-28.

Finds "*Survival* infuriating and [*Second Words*] scarcely less so," with its allusion to sneering academics. Objects to *Survival*'s thematic criticism; frequent thematic distortions and occasional inaccuracies; omission of important positive writers; slang and jokes for shaky arguments; and "irresistibly funny," indistinguishable "'basic victim positions.'" These faults, not an absence of footnotes, are why the reviewer warns his students against *Survival*.

Second Words's "What's So Funny?" uses, like *Survival*, inadequate evidence to reach its generalizations. The 32 reviews are among its best work; Atwood here shows "a wide range of appreciation for Canadian poetry"; and her bias towards the Gothic suggests links to her own fiction. "Her articles and lectures tend to raise [the reviewer's] hackles again. . . . all too often she gives the impression that she covertly despises her audience." She is careless with facts. The reviewer "never encountered anything resembling the total hostility or indifference to Canadian literature that she claims to remember." She often tells stories of inept critics and academics, but never once mentions the serious, positive attention that academic critics, many of them male, have given her work.

74 ____. "Editors and Texts: Reflections of Some Recent Anthologies of Canadian Poetry." *Canadian Poetry*, no. 12 (Spring-Summer), pp. 77-86.

Commends Atwood's admirable editing and clear, firm, witty, sensible introduction to *The New Oxford Book of Canadian Verse in English*; critiques Jack David and Robert Lecker's careless editing of *Canadian Poetry, Volume One and Volume Two*. Atwood rightly says nothing of Wilfred Campbell's disastrous 1912 *Oxford Book of Canadian Verse*, and justly praises, and follows, A.J.M. Smith's genius. Atwood had someone else (William Toye) choose her own work – as Campbell and Smith should have done. She chooses, for the cultivated general reader, Canada's best, best-known, and representative verse, but can print only modest selections from each poet; yet she manages to include both Earle Birney's "David" and John Newlove's "The Pride," both essential, both omitted by David and Lecker. One misses most A.M. Klein's Jewish poems, and D.C. Scott's seminal "The Height of Land." Atwood has been particularly scrupulous with the earlier work; and, though a few errors occur, she has edited much more carefully than David and Lecker. Both anthologies are biased towards the avant-garde and experimental.

75 KINGSTONE, JAMES. Review of *Second Words*. *CM* 11, no. 3 (May):118-19.

Exposes some weaknesses and brings to light a few chief strengths of *Second Words*. This may be a publisher's book that risks capitalizing on Atwood's status; but it may also, and more validly, encourage "scholar-worms and literary critics" to assess her creative work. Given the deflective main concerns, many casually articulated ideas, and much loose, bland criticism, one is glad Atwood did not make criticism her career. The essays and speeches are generally better than the short reviews: "On Being a Woman Writer" deals convincingly with the "infuriating discrepancies that a woman writer must confront"; and "Northrop Frye Observed" reveals a vital inspiration.

76 KLEIN, CARROLL. Review of *Bodily Harm*. *Room of One's Own* 8, no. 3:86-89.

Praises Atwood's elegant, witty, highly serious novel of compassion and sexual politics. Rennie, who has been both seduced by and contemptuous of her trend-making lifestyles journalism, must journey into a heart of darkness to learn compassion and love. She is alone, abandoned, threatened, her body damaged by cancer. She sees feminism as passé. On the island, the diffident, accepting Paul reawakens Rennie's sexuality and self-esteem; and Lora, "a sort of tacky alter ego," shows Rennie what selflessness and love are, in jail. Rennie is changed forever when she understands the connection between herself and Lora. Atwood confronts us "with wisdom, and with metaphors of women's lives" which we all can heed.

77 KOKOTAILO, PHILIP. "Form in Atwood's *Surfacing*: Toward a Synthesis of Critical Opinion." *Studies in Canadian Literature* 8, no. 2:155-65.

Argues that *Surfacing* fuses the modern and the post-modern novel, as defined by Davey 1974.4. The thesis reading, by McLay 1975.24, Grace 1980.47, Moss 1977.59, and most critics, sees *Surfacing* as a rite of passage where the narrator ends with a newly integrated self. A few critics, Mandel 1977.52, Sullivan 1977.90, and Lecker 1981.64, see *Surfacing* antithetically, as unresolved. Thesis and antithesis here make a paradox: *Surfacing* as a modern novel is a search for unity, yet lacks a coherent structure. The narrator's collaged, non-linear, non-logical, fragmented memories and madness are post-modern; she deconstructs modernistic orders and false selves to reach "an order stripped away from reality." The controversial end is a beginning.

78 KROETSCH, ROBERT. "Unhiding the Hidden: Recent Canadian Fiction." In *An Anthology of Canadian Literature in English*. Edited by

1983

Donna Bennett and Russell Brown. Vol. 2. Toronto: Oxford University Press, pp. 246-50.
    Reprint of 1974.18.

79 LAUBER, JOHN. "Alice in Consumer-Land: The Self-Discovery of Marian MacAlpine." In *The Canadian Novel: A Critical Anthology*. Edited by John Moss. Vol. 1, *Here and Now*. Toronto: NC Press, pp. 19-31.
    Reprint of 1978.51.

80 LeCLAIRE, JACQUES. "*Life Before Man*, critique d'un mode de vie: Les problèmes nés du féminisme et le désenchantement de la liberté." *Études canadiennes* (Talence), no. 15, pp. 129-36.
    Life Before Man raises questions about freedom and identity that have not been resolved by the conquests of feminism. The story proposes a new, more personal ethic in approaching current difficulties in society. Many avenues opened up by the growing equality between men and women lead to problems for the characters in *Life Before Man*. Nate faces the challenges of inventing a new way to live and recovering his identity. Nate and Elizabeth attempt liaisons and divorce within the constraints of financial problems, children, and gossiping colleagues. All the relationships in the book fail as a result of egoism. The protagonists seem bored when they are not picking each other apart. *Life Before Man* puts mankind in a modern Sisyphean situation, with Toronto as anywhere, or the place we find ourselves.

81 LIPSCOMB, ELIZABETH JOHNSTON. "*Bodily Harm*." In *Magill's Literary Annual*. Edited by Frank N. Magill. Vol. 1. Englewood Cliffs, N.J.: Salem Press, pp. 65-69.
    Finds *Bodily Harm* powerful but bleak, melodramatic, and difficult. Atwood suggests that everyone is a victim of bodily harm, though shared compassion offers some hope. The end escape is deliberately ambiguous; what matters is Rennie's compassion for Lora. The image patterns – especially of hands, touching and withholding, and of cancer – are skillfully crafted; and the Canadian scenes ring true. Dislikes the improbable, TV thriller Caribbean, cold Rennie, and stereotyped minor characters; unfortunately, the power and subtlety require rereadings.

1983

82 LORSCH, SUSAN E. "Androgyny and the Idea of the Double: Margaret Atwood's *The Edible Woman.*" *Dalhousie Review* 63, no. 3 (Autumn):464-74.

Reads Atwood's first novel as Marian's *Surfacing*-like descent into madness; argues that Duncan is Marian's *Doppelgänger*, her irrational, shadow self. Duncan's existence is continually questionable; he represents Marian's subconscious self, rebelling against society's self-denying roles for women. Duncan's example teaches Marian to assert herself; as her male double, he shows that the ego is androgynous. The end celebrates Marian's newly-realized, independent identity.

83 McLAY, CATHERINE. "The Divided Self: Theme and Pattern in *Surfacing.*" In *The Canadian Novel: A Critical Anthology.* Edited by John Moss. Vol. 1, *Here and Now.* Toronto: NC Press, pp. 32-44.

Reprint of 1978.57, which reprints 1975.24.

84 MANDEL, ELI. "Atwood's Poetic Politics." See Grace and Weir, 1983.56, pp. 53-66.

Expands much of 1977.52 to include *Two-Headed Poems*; questions critics' perceptions of Atwood's themes and transformations; and considers Atwood's oracular and Gothic elements, obsessive reduplicating images, and "totemic or transforming images of journey and spirit . . . [as] techniques of demystification." Are Atwood's concerns nationalist, as Sullivan 1977.90 argues? or "'minority psychologies,'" as Foster 1977.22 claims? Those concerns, and Atwood's magic or shamanism, lead to her politics of poetry. R.D. Laing's *The Politics of Experience* can gloss Atwood's inner, invisible world. Atwood's magic and shamanism, which as Woodcock 1976.106 and Sullivan 1977.90 point out have North American sources, also function "'to thicken the plot,'" to demystify experience – and as political commentary? Can *Survival* be based on shamanism? or is it mere failed allegory, as "Two-Headed Poems" may be? Other questions are raised by the Amnesty poem and by the very moving "Five Poems for Grandmothers." Excerpted: 1985.11.

85 MANGUEL, ALBERTO. "Small Wonders." *Books in Canada* 12, no. 5 (May):19-20.

Acclaims Atwood's memorable, very personal, "amused and wise" *Murder in the Dark*; and proposes a new literary genre, nuggets, to which these brilliant pieces belong. Nuggets, defined as small, quotable, pointed, illustrative, humourous literary pieces, would include Nathaniel Hawthorne's *Notebooks*, Jorge Luis Borges's "*The Maker* (mistranslated as *Dreamtigers*)," Julio Cortazar's *Chronopios and Famas*, and others. As in "Strawberries" and "Raw Materials," Atwood's snapshots capture memories, sensations, and fleeting thoughts. "The Page" focusses on the writer's craft; "Liking Men" shows "Atwood at her comic best"; the reviewer likes most the classic anthology piece, "Murder in the Dark."

86 MARR, ANDREW. "Journeys beyond Pessimism." *Scotsman* (Edinburgh), 8 January, Weekend sec., p. 5.
Praises *Dancing Girls* highly: these dozen short stories "each contain enough fine characterisation and good writing to sustain a novel." *Dancing Girls* is not joyless or cynical; and, though it deals sometimes "with madness, it is outstandingly sane and sensible." Life, Atwood suggests, has difficulties, but the individual can carry on, with self-awareness, strength, and humour. "Training" charts a young boy's journey to self-confidence. Each finely made, lyric story has its painful pith; the book has variety, style, and on every page "some new felicity of language" that surprises and delights.

87 MATYAS, CATHY. "See." *Brick*, no. 19 (Fall), pp. 22-23.
Praises *Murder in the Dark* as a serious, politically responsible, and visionary work. Atwood lives up to her "social and political responsibility as a popular writer": people listen to her. From the poignant "Bread" to "Happy Endings," *Murder* reveals Atwood's sharp eye and sharper wit; in many ways, it is a less traditional, more imaginative *Second Words*. "Instructions for the Third Eye" shows us how to see, with vision as well as sight, realities we would rather not see, that are our world.

88 MEIGS, MARY. "Atwood's Perfect Pitch." *Broadside* (Toronto) 4, no. 7 (May):8.
Appreciates Atwood's self-made feminism and unflinching vision in *Second Words* and *Murder in the Dark*. Atwood's critical vision increasingly reflects her "Instructions for the Third Eye," the eye that

1983

sees pain clearly, as her 1973 review of Adrienne Rich's *Diving into the Wreck* says. Writers must describe the "'Monster'" with undefeatist, unflinching gaze. As a "self-made feminist," Atwood won't be co-opted by a later movement; but, like Rich, she is now deeply involved politically. The three reviews of Rich show Atwood's widening concerns, in contrast to her 1971 objective musings on Al Purdy's sexual anatomizing of women. Atwood believes in the artist as a "'lens for focussing the world'": *Murder* does so, with "'simple-seeming visionary states that explode in one's mind,'" and yet with real, persisting hope.

89 MELLORS, JOHN. "Dream Girls." *Listener* 109 (6 January):24.
    Features and briefly praises, in a seven-book review, Atwood's *Dancing Girls*, whose "stories are as haunting as her novels." Atwood's expertly handled characters are most often women under stress; despair pervades these stories of hopeless, exhausted men and women.

90 MEZEI, KATHY. Review of *Murder in the Dark*. *West Coast Review* 18, no. 2 (October):51-52.
    Is disturbed by Atwood's clever but fearful *Murder in the Dark*, in a two-book review. Atwood's short pieces recall Quebec feminist work, by Nicole Brossard and others, but are less conscious of *texte-corps*, the text and body relationship. Atwood's underlying motifs are of the writer's imagination and of fear. "The smell of fear is rampant throughout," creating a pervasive and unpleasant negativism, as in the sinister twists of "Making Poison," "Murder in the Dark," and "The Page." This fear – "of war, death, unimaginable horrors, the darkness" is understandable, given Atwood's Amnesty International involvement, but unhealthy, as Atwood herself recognizes in "Instructions for the Third Eye." Her ironic tone "leaves the reader in the dark."

91 MINTIS, MARION. Review of *The New Oxford Book of Canadian Verse in English*. *CM* 11, no. 2 (March):75.
    A short review that finds Atwood's collection excellent. Atwood's selections are comprehensive and vital, and her introduction is fascinating.

92 MIROLLA, MICHAEL. "Poetry Anthology: Sense of a Nation." *Gazette* (Montreal), 11 June, p. I2.

Approves *The New Oxford Book of Canadian Verse in English*. Such anthologies show us English Canada's changing perspectives on the landscape, and the national poetic sensibility. The earliest poems, like Robert Hayman's on Newfoundland, are interesting historically and ironically. Atwood uses the space wisely, representing a wide range; "she can be forgiven quirks such as allotting herself seven poems" and J. Michael Yates only one.

93 MITCHAM, ALLISON. "Margaret Atwood: Woman in the North." In *The Northern Imagination: A Study of Northern Canadian Literature*. Moonbeam, Ont.: Penumbra Press, pp. 95-99.

Reprint of 1974.26, slightly altered. References to the Atwood persona's marriage and childbirth have been cut, along with a paragraph on comparable French Canadian novels; and a [Frederick Philip] Grove point has been condensed.

94 MOISAN, CLÉMENT. *A Poetry of Frontiers: Comparative Studies in Quebec/Canadian Literature*. [Translated by George Lang and Linda Weber.] Victoria and Toronto: Press Porcépic, pp. 43, 121-37.

Compares theme, imagery, and style in *The Circle Game*, *The Animals in That Country*, and *The Journals of Susanna Moodie* with that of Michèle Lalonde's *Geôles*, "La mère patrie," *Fiancée*, and other work. Atwood searches for "identity in *le pays*," as in *Survival*, which the similarly victimized Quebecois quickly adopted. Both Atwood and Lalonde develop their themes in four stages: an unconscious dream journey of warm complicity with nature; a transition to consciousness of isolation from mankind; a search for solutions to alienation; and for "integration of their identities . . . [as] part of *pays*, Quebec and Canada." Their imagery is also surprisingly alike; both use prisons, rooms, circles that "must be opened up"; strange and unconscious wanderings; recurrent water imagery that evokes the past, abandonment, and hopes of conquering the land; images of exploration and inquiry that break out of the circle; images that fuse man and nature; and "*le regard*, objects gazed at, and reflective surfaces." Because both attempt "to plunge poetry into an abyss . . . [both] make a cult of structure": Atwood's style is clean, hard-edged, intellectual; Lalonde's logical and musical. Both grapple with oppression, across borders. Translation of 1979.73.

1983

95 MONEY, JANET. Review of *Murder in the Dark*. *Canadian Book Review Annual*:263.

The strikingly new, unconventional *Murder in the Dark* follows its own "Instructions for the Third Eye" to cast a third and truthful glance at Atwood's favorite themes. The first two sections cover autobiographical musings and a foreign search for reality that ends in fear. The uneven but clever third section's most striking sketch, "Murder in the Dark," forces us to see the writing process with a third eye's view. The fourth section, on male-female relationships, combines "dry feminist wit" with some obscure musing.

96 MONK, PATRICIA. "'I Am Created in You': The Rhetoric of the Dual Consciousness in the Poetry of Margaret Atwood." In *The Commonwealth in Canada*. Proceedings of the Second Triennial Conference of CACLALS, University of Winnipeg, 1-4 October 1981. Edited by Uma Parameswaran. Part 2. Calcutta, India: Writers Workshop, pp. 254-63.

The rhetoric of Atwood's eight books of poetry portrays a double consciousness, or schizophrenia; her syntactical and grammatical structures produce an intense inner drama. Most of her poems, including all of *Power Politics*, are dramatic monologues, whether direct personal address, or oblique, or imperative. Parataxis often reinforces her dramatic structure, most completely in "Two-Headed Poems," where the alleged and deliberately confused speakers babble continuously. A reconstructed historical persona, as in *The Journals of Susanna Moodie*, is a further dramatic technique. Atwood's almost constantly dramatic poems jolt both sophisticated and naive readers, by reducing the distance between poem and reader, and engaging the reader directly in their drama.

97 MOORE, M.L. Review of *Dancing Girls and Other Stories* and *Bodily Harm*. *Epoch* 32, no. 2 (Winter-Spring):169-73.

Considers the Canadian *Survival* themes in *Dancing Girls* and the writer-tourist in *Bodily Harm*. The befuddled, struggling, reluctant, amputated refugees and tourists of *Dancing Girls* elaborate *Survival*'s themes and are specifically Canadian. In "Polarities," perhaps the most powerful story, Atwood suggests that we desire only what cannot touch or love us. "The frustrated courtship of the foreign," as in "The Man from Mars," is a metaphor for all heterosexual relationships, which tend to be distant and chilly in *Dancing Girls*. *Bodily Harm*'s Rennie, prefigured in "A Travel Piece," is the literary journeyer re-mythologized as estranged sightseer. Mortality has edged Rennie into non-participation; she "is a weak-hearted pilgrim who will return unheroically home" to write stories of the Caribbean inferno. Atwood ambivalently disapproves and mocks the writer-tourist, but in *Survival* protects the writer's immunity and neutrality.

98 MORLEY, PATRICIA. "Atwood's Poetry Ranges from Intriguing to Boring." *Citizen* (Ottawa), 19 March, p. 47.

Though some of *Murder in the Dark* is unsuccessful, its best pieces are evocative and witty, intensely poetic and surreally comic. "Everlasting" is poetry in prose. The more typical miniature stories, like "Horror Stories" and "The Victory Burlesk," shows us as the vampires of our own imaginations, or "squeezed together in the vice of time." Atwood is better at horror than at love or joy, which she suspects of sentimentality. Feminism and black humor join in the witty "Simmering," "Liking Men," and "Women's Novels," which parodies popular fiction.

99 _____. Review of *Second Words*. *Quill and Quire* 49, no. 2 (February):34.

Reprints 1982.117, abridged and slightly altered, omitting the comments on feminist pieces.

100 MORT, MARY-ELLEN. Review of *Second Words*. *Library Journal* 108, no. 3 (1 February):208.

These fifty pieces, the best of which compare with the trenchant, influential *Survival*, show Atwood's development from apolitical writer to human rights advocate. American readers will find the witty pieces on Canadian-American relations, Canadian humor, and "Writing the Male Character" most accessible. The book reviews briefly assess American novels, and at more length, Canadian poetry and novels.

101 NORRIE, HELEN. "Atwood's Critical Writing Draws National Portrait." *Winnipeg Free Press*, 30 July, p. 43.

Praises the versatile, witty, opinionated, impressive *Second Words*, which offers a valuable autobiographical record. *Second Words*'s diverse topics cover twenty years, divided into three periods of

1983

Atwood's life; it "is more a fascinating glimpse into the making of a writer than a coherent body of critical essays," though there are unifying themes, such as poet's metaphors. Atwood's irrepressible wit surfaces often, as in "Reaney Collected" and "Canadian-American Relations." The serious reviews are all lively, though not all are still relevant. Atwood shows us our country and literature in a way we might not have otherwise seen.

102 "Notes on Current Books." *Virginia Quarterly Review* 59, no. 2 (Spring):57.
Prefers Atwood's rich, symphonic novels to her metaphoric and subtle but slight *Dancing Girls* stories, which are like "a string quartet with a player or two mysteriously muted."

103 PENNYCOOK, BRUCE W. "*Speeches for Dr. Frankenstein*: An Orchestral Approach to Music Synthesis." *Canadian University Music Review*, no. 4, pp. 196-203.
Describes how the composer/scientist created *Speeches*, a computer-generated tape accompaniment for soprano voice that is based on stanzas I, IV, VII, and X of Atwood's poem: "preparation for the act, the creation, reflection on the deed, and separation of the creator from the monster." The composer sees "Speeches for Dr. Frankenstein" as a complex, unique narrative on man's timeless conflict of creator versus created. Because *Speeches* was commissioned as a fifteen-minute work, not all ten stanzas could be used. *Speeches*'s dramatic song follows conventional rhythm and Atwood's images. Details the computer's capacities and the writer's musical techniques.

104 POWE, B.W. "How to Act': An Essay on Margaret Atwood." *Antigonish Review*, no. 52 (Winter), pp. 127-37.
Objects to Atwood's celebrity image and popular, sophisticated self-help, "Nausea-Romance" novels. In *The Edible Woman, Surfacing, Lady Oracle, Life Before Man,* and *Bodily Harm,* the always damaged, passive, victim-thesis characters never achieve real being, only a constant becoming. Atwood is such a good writer, with impressive symbolism, imagery, and wit, that insisting on her ideas may seem malicious carping. Her popularity may depend on the now-trivialized 1960s enthusiasms of media and academic professionals. Her own answer, to "'what happens *after* Survival?'" has been the make-over re-

creation of her air-brushed *Chatelaine* cover and "Celebrity I.D." [1981.97 and 1982.70]. Her main characters are almost interchangeable. Her urban novels don't show the real, new Toronto. Still, Atwood may yet break through her celebrity shackles and become the serious writer she could be. Reprinted, slightly altered: 1984.75.

105 PRAESENT, ANGELA. "Kastenfrau in Schwierigkeiten." *Spiegel* (Hamburg), 21 March, p. 210, 212-13.

Commends *Verletzungen*, the German translation of *Bodily Harm*. Atwood's work joins Ingeborg Bachmann's *Three Paths to the Lake* in portraying heroines that are part of the new international caste of independent women. Those who have complained that nothing happens in Atwood's novels will find this adventure story quite different. The literary value of the novel's pop-psychology is questionable, but one must admire Atwood's ear for current issues. Those who notice the dedication "To Jennifer Rankin . . ." may see the story as an answer to Susan Sontag's "Illness as Metaphor."

106 PYBUS, RODNEY. "North American and British Poetry." *Stand* 25, no. 1 (Winter):69-70.

Praises, in a round-up review, the poems of *True Stories*'s first section over its "Notes Towards a Poem That Can Never Be Written" group. The best of the first group finely balance the colloquial, laconic tone against intense feeling, with subtly "'literary'" tactics. The two "Landcrab" poems move from the vividly evoked creature to metaphor and back to an awareness of self and world. "Small Poems for a Winter Solstice" both expresses love and loss, and also eyes sceptically "the waywardness of feelings." But some poems in the more ambitious second group, whose motives the reviewer respects, exist too much on the surface of their language. "Trainride: Vienna-Bonn" seems a bit too neat. Though "Torture" and "A Women's Issue" are truly horrendous, and scrupulous, the trite culmination of the latter's catalogue subverts its anger and tension.

107 RASPORICH, BEVERLY. Review of *Bluebeard's Egg. Canadian Book Review Annual*:243-44.

Finds *Bluebeard's Egg*'s dramatization of woman's place and relationships brilliant, as in "Uglypuss"; finds its childhood stories particularly forgettable. Atwood's liberal social conscience concerns

1983

can be wonderfully concise, as in the sushi bar scene of "The Sunrise," where the female sexual adventurer remains the potential female victim of men's violence. The neurotic apocalyptic fantasies of "The Salt Garden," and the Third World dangers and naive Westerners of "Scarlet Ibis," are too predictable. The coolly ironic "Loulou" engages on several levels, of personal identity, the post-modern artist and language, the domestic Earth-Mother Loulou relating to a male world, and the writer and writing. "Significant Moments" and "Hurricane Hazel" seem weak imitations of the early Alice Munro.

108 REANEY, JAMES STEWART. "One More Success for Atwood." *London* (Ontario) *Free Press*, 29 January, p. E10.
　　Rejoices in *The New Oxford Book of Canadian Verse in English*. Atwood's introduction gives kind words to macho Irving Layton. Her selections do well by our earlier poets, older contemporaries, newer ones, and London-area poets, too. If Atwood's love-and-politics choices of her own work can be gruesome, as in "Notes Towards a Poem That Can Never Be Written," that's her tough persona; other poems, such as "Marrying the Hangman," are curiously optimistic. There's great fun throughout the book: Robert Service's "The Cremation of Sam McGee" shows a nation "coming to terms with its doggerel"–proof of Canadian "'identity,'" at last.

109 RELKE, DIANA. M.A. "Double Voice, Single Vision: A Feminist Reading of Margaret Atwood's *The Journals of Susanna Moodie*." *Atlantis* 9, no. 1 (Fall):35-48.
　　Contends that the "Afterword," now omitted in Atwood's *Selected Poems*, had encouraged superficial readings; discerns, beneath the *Journals'* surface, a "near mirror image" story of the woman poet under patriarchy. Atwood subverts the "received" male language with white silences and lines such as "words, my disintegrated children," that become female aphorisms when read out of syntax. The confined and self-imaging Moodie becomes an emblem of women's split selves; the feared landscape becomes her "self," not "other"; "The Double Voice" articulates her female experience. The last Journal dramatizes male versus female cosmologics, as in "Resurrection's" base-line versus drop-line columns; the final Atwood-Moodie is a resurrected literary foremother, and also a Demeter/Persephone, as Atwood's cover, opened flat, suggests.

110 Review of *Dancing Girls and Other Stories*. *Birmingham News*, 9 January. Newsbank 1982-1983, 58:B11.

Praises Atwood's top-notch stories. Her language is poetically compact but not obscure, especially in "Giving Birth," and also in "[The] Grave of the Famous Poet," and "Polarities."

111 Review of *Second Words*. *Choice* 20, no. 8 (April):1133.

Recommends *Second Words* as a starting point for Atwood scholars, and a comprehensive survey, for the student or general reader, of the cultural and political ideas underlying Atwood's fiction and poetry. The pieces are divided chronologically. Atwood characterizes the first period as developmental, and the second, which includes her 1973.2 response to Robin Mathews, as one of being attacked. The third period shows Atwood transcending parochial concerns, and becoming more involved with human rights.

112 Review of *Second Words*. *Kirkus Reviews* 51, no. 23 (1 December):1231.

Finds *Second Words* a bulky but lightweight assemblage, of little general interest. Though Atwood's semi-disavowal of criticism has charm, few entries here are substantial. Early work sounds like book reports; later opinions do sharpen, but are repetitive, and depend heavily on pigeon-holing contrasts between Canadian and American or English categories. Only the essays on H. Rider Haggard, Al Purdy, and problems of the contemporary novel, are full-fledged criticism.

113 RIGNEY, BARBARA. Review of *Bodily Harm*. *Women's Studies Review* 5, nos. 2-3 (Spring):10-11.

Approves *Bodily Harm*. Rennie seems innocent, victimized, "'exempt'": Atwood's point is that we, and women especially, are all guilty of aiding our victimization, and "malignancy is the human condition." Atwood argues for facing mortality and making a commitment to life. Rennie becomes involved, as a lover and as her cell-mate's comforter; she decides to become a subversive reporter. Though the Caribbean sojourn may be a little farfetched, and Rennie too passive at first, still *Bodily Harm* succeeds in showing women our potential power to change the world.

1983

114 ROBSON, RUTHANN, and FARLEY, BLANCHE. "An Interview with Margaret Atwood." *Kalliope* 5, no. 1:41-45.

Interviews Atwood at the Women Writers Conference at the University of Kentucky; Atwood discusses her prose versus poetry–short fiction is not her best form; Canadian versus U.S. publishers; *Survival*'s reception, key patterns, and animal victims; and describes ["Writing the Male Character"] in her forthcoming *Second Words*.

115 ROSENTHAL, M.L. "A Common Sadness." *New York Times Book Review*, 13 March, pp. 6, 19.

Prefers, in a three-book review, Mona Van Duyn's ebullient *Letters from a Father*, and William Stafford's moving *A Glass Face in the Rain*, to Atwood's uneven, oracular, aggressive, yet sometimes nakedly emotional, *True Stories*, with its unsatisfactory title sequence. "Small Poems for the Winter Solstice" is the book's major effort, about an Anne Sexton-like "feverish, distrustful love affair" and the "poet's life priorities." "Three Romances" goes from a male killer to horror and violence. Atwood's perspectives seem "willfully confused–confessional, polemical, coldly witchlike and hectoring all at once." Admires "Torture," "Earth," and "Variations on the Word *Sleep*," which "exaltedly redeems the book's longer flounderings."

116 RUSSELL, JUDITH. "Vintage Atwood." *Whig-Standard Magazine* (Kingston, Ont.), 8 January, p. 19.

Recommends highly Atwood's sure, objective, precise, funny, serious *Second Words*. Even the early reviews, of Margaret Avison, Eli Mandel, and other Canadian poets, display a sophisticated critical grasp. The English, American, and Canadian approaches to a hamburger in ["Eleven Years of *Alphabet*"] offer "a brilliant rule of thumb for the CanLit student." Atwood can break up an audience, and insist, mid-guffaw, on her point. She returns to her basic concerns as "poet, novelist, critic, survivor." Casual readers, if any, will find an overview of this country's twenty-year literary explosion; serious ones will find an absorbing, multi-faceted study of our literature.

117 RUSSO, MICHAEL. "Atwood Tales Eavesdrop on the Souls of Women." *Times-Picayune* (New Orleans), 9 January, sec. 3, p. 8. Newsbank 1982-1983, 58:B12.

Praises highly *Dancing Girls*'s intimate, poetic, unromanticized realism. Reading these stories is "like eavesdropping on the souls of very eloquent women." Atwood taps a reservoir of poetry and language. We readily identify the realism of the poet's unromantic life in the slightly ironic "Lives of the Poets." "Giving Birth," with its authorial narrator, offers the most affecting "glimpse into a woman's soul"; the unromanticized birth is ultimately a metaphor of birth "within the poet's soul," and of the pain caused by the inadequacy of language.

118 SAGARIS, LAKE. Review of *New Oxford Book of Canadian Verse*. *Resources for Feminist Research* 12, no. 2 (July):14-16.

Appreciates Atwood's introduction and "excellent selection of highly readable Canadian poems," which show, eloquently, how far our still internationally neglected Canadian poets have come. Atwood's introduction "slips the older poets into their own timeslots for us." Canada's overwhelming landscape is the book's most present creation; "'[p]eople-poems'" are under-represented. Most striking is the sizeable number of political struggle poems. Women poets are well represented, and women's images are varied and contradictory.

119 SCHIEFER, NANCY A. "Oddly Satisfying." *London* (Ontario) *Free Press*, 30 April, p. F9.

Finds *Murder in the Dark* curious, oddly satisfying while you read it, but afterwards puzzling; finds Atwood's cover illustration unattractive; finds her concerns "serious and unflinching, despite" the frivolous format. "Simmering" is a hilarious snippet. If you like Atwood you'll want this book, to complete your collection.

120 ___. "This Collection Showcases Atwood's Gifts." *London* (Ontario) *Free Press*, 4 November, p. A15.

Finds *Bluebeard's Egg* a "pure delight," from the Heather Cooper cover illustration through the eerily sardonic end piece, "Unearthing Suite"; and finds Atwood "a far better story teller than" novelist – controlled, brilliant, spare, "defining with authority the razor-thin line" between real and illusory. When the best, title story ends, we don't want to leave Sally. The skillful "Hurricane Hazel," "Uglypuss," and others capture subtleties of male-female relationships.

1983

121 SCHWARZKOPF, MARGARETE von. "Überlebenstraining im Fegefeuer." *Welt* (Hamburg), 30 April, Geistige Welt, p. 5.

Enthusiastically reviews *Die Unmöglichkeit der Nähe* (*Life Before Man*) and *Verletzungen* (*Bodily Harm*): the new novels confirm the overwhelmingly positive reviews of *Surfacing*, and hold Atwood's work in the forefront of English Canadian literature. *Life Before Man* masterfully portrays a love triangle of people who cannot express feelings. *Bodily Harm* is about survival, one of Canada's most significant issues. Atwood covers great distances in short sentences and has a documentary sense of people and situations. She cannot hide the fact that she is a poet.

122 SIMON, SHERRY. "Le nationlisme culturel des autres." *Spirale* (Montréal), no. 33 (April), p. 6.

Declares, in a review of *Second Words* and *The New Oxford Book of Canadian Verse in English*, that the grand silence of Canadian literature is over, and that Margaret Atwood is the symbol of the battle for a Canadian identity. *Second Words* is a service to national and feminist problems, but the *New Oxford* will last the longest, with its rich selection of Canadian poetry.

123 SINGH, SUNAINA. "The New Woman in Margaret Atwood's *Surfacing*." *Indian Journal of American Studies* 13, no. 2 (July):189-92.

Atwood, like other modern women writers, deals with woman's place in male-dominated society. In "The Curse of Eve" and in *Surfacing*, she is concerned to allow women their human imperfections. *Surfacing*'s nameless, disturbed protagonist is a victim struggling for a new identity. Rebelling against victimhood, she overcomes her hatred of men when she decides to return to the menacing city; she has understood her place in the modern situation, and will "struggle and survive with dignity."

124 SKENAZY, PAUL. "Revelations of a Gray North and Dark South." *In These Times* 7, no. 9 (26 January-1 February):19.

Appreciates Atwood's political change from *Dancing Girls and Other Stories* to *Bodily Harm* and *True Stories*. The stories reek of ordinary, isolated lives; her characters live within their "'terrible and deforming niceness,'" terrified of what may happen and of nothing happening. When their control slips, we move "to the sensual, violent or deranged." *Bodily Harm* has even more decay and subterranean chaos than Atwood's earlier work. It also has news clichés and upper-middle-class fashion, an unnecessarily fragmented story, and a Third World that is "too much a heart of darkness. But Atwood escapes facile literary imperialism by developing" analogies and political meanings. Rennie turns from a tourist into a subversive reporter. *True Stories* "confronts the privilege of poets to ignore public suffering" for private feeling; "Notes Towards a Poem That Can Never Be Written" are gems of horror. *True Stories* breaks down old concepts of how poems connect to our poor, real world.

125 SOLECKI, SAM. "Criticism and the Anxiety of Identity." *Queen's Quarterly* 90, no. 4 (Winter):1029-33.

A three-book review which finds *Second Words* a minor book by a major writer. Its mostly admiring reviews range from the precocious undergraduate perceptions to the last decade's reviews of predominantly women writers. As with Adrienne Rich's *Poems, Selected and New*, Atwood communicates the writer's vision and texture of style; as with Purdy and Rich, she defines the outstanding poems. The longer pieces are thin, except for those on John Newlove, James Reaney's *Collected Poems*, and Northrop Frye. The speeches lack originality; even Atwood's strong style can't hide their careless, polemic overstatements, as in "The Curse of Eve." Though most widely praised, Atwood finds no good word for her academic critics or the media. She tries to dismiss mythopoeic poetry, but undeniably it exists, and has been shaped by Frye.

126 "The State of Canadian Poetry." *Credences*, n.s. 2, nos. 2-3 (Fall-Winter):229-36.

In a panel discussion of eleven poets, mostly Canadians, held 16 October 1980, Atwood discusses the currently shrinking Canadian audience for poetry; compares the less active contemporary young poets to her own generation's perhaps unnatural 1960s explosion of poetry; and argues that, without audience, the writing and the form will be lost.

127 STEELE, JUDY McCONNELL. "Advice from Margaret Atwood: Face the Peril." *Idaho Statesman* (Boise), 23 April. Newsbank 1982-1983, 92:C6-7.

1983

Reports on Atwood's Thursday reading and Friday question-and-answer period at the 1982-83 Boise State University Writers and Artists Series. Atwood read "Murder in the Dark" and ["The Page"]; she advises writers "to enter the page, 'Read a lot and write a lot.'" Being published makes good writers feel better, she said, but fame stops people from telling you things.

128 STEWART, ROBERT. "Atwood Plays Hide and Seek with Reader." *Gazette* (Montreal), 16 April, p. I2.

Ridicules *Murder in the Dark* and Cameron 1983.19, then finds some humor and power. Though Atwood may have cut-and-pasted this extremely slim, grant-supported book out of discards and obscure publications, CanLit professor Cameron, who can see things "imperceptible to the unschooled eye," has found breakthrough literary form in cut-and-paste, structure in snippets, and cohesion in repetitions. Once again we get Atwood's obsessions with woman-man power struggles, gruesome deaths, spooky places, repulsive food, mud, and games. As in the title piece, Atwood plays a "game of obfuscation" with the reader. Though writing about writing, as in ["The Page"], can be pretentious or inane literary navel gazing, Atwood does redeem her stuff with humor, as in "Simmering" and "Women's Novels," and with powerful prose.

129 STINE, JEAN C., ed. *Contemporary Literary Criticism*. Vol. 25. Detroit: Gale Research Co., pp. 61-70.

Briefly describes Atwood as an outstanding poet, and a spokesperson for Canada and feminism, who often combines a search for identity with a journey into wilderness. Though her work is widely acclaimed, many critics find her characterizations, especially of males, shallow, and her material predictable; nevertheless she uniquely presents the extraordinary in the ordinary. Excerpted from Hill 1977.31; Bilan 1978.6; Marshall 1979.69; Grace 1980.47; Macfarlane 1981.67; Abley 1981.1; Woodcock 1981.112; Fitzgerald 1981.31; Wagner 1981.104; Davey 1981.22; Siegel 1982.155; Penner 1982.129; Gioia 1982.67; O'Faolain 1982.122; Ramsey 1982.134; and Rolens 1982.145.

130 STRATFORD, PHILIP. "The Uses of Ambiguity: Margaret Atwood and Hubert Aquin." In *Margaret Atwood: Language, Text and System*. See Grace and Weir 1983.56, pp. 113-24.

Compares and contrasts Hubert Aquin's *Prochain Episode* with Atwood's *Surfacing*. Each is a major novelist and an outspoken nationalist who "grew up in the bourgeois mainstream." Aquin's search for self is modelled on the espionage thriller; Atwood's, perhaps, on the juvenile mystery. Both novels are confessional, and both heroes are dualistic and deeply alienated. Aquin's despairing, "'lyric'" hero is chronically voluble, and his story is reflexive, circular, and inconclusive. Atwood's deeply disturbed, dramatically-conceived hero is repressed, and her story progresses linearly, from confusion to resolution. Each writer confirms, as well as deviates from, his French tradition of abstractions, or her English tradition of documentary realism. Atwood's nationalism is didactic; Aquin dramatizes mental process, not moral progress. Reprinted: 1986.239.

131 STUEWE, PAUL. "Beyond Survival." *Books in Canada* 12, no. 2 (February):7-10.

Argues against Frye's ubiquitous and dangerous thematic criticism, which transposes Canadian literature "onto both sub- and meta-literary planes," and makes off-and-on value judgments. *Survival* and D.G. Jones's *Butterfly on Rock* are the two most important of the Frye-influenced critical studies; the widely taught and effusively recommended *Survival* is sloppily casual, with grandiose, irresponsible, poorly grounded assertions.

132 SULLIVAN, ROSEMARY. "Atwood, Margaret." In *The Oxford Companion to Canadian Literature*. Edited by William Toye. Toronto; Oxford; New York: Oxford University Press, pp. 30-33.

Provides a brief biography and characterizes Atwood's creative themes. Influenced by Northrop Frye, Atwood sees the mythological substructure of culture very clearly, as in the ritual exclusions of *The Circle Game*. "The rational mind must be integrated with the dark side of the psyche" that humanist order has repressed, as in *The Journals of Susanna Moodie*. *Power Politics* exposes the implicit sadism of romantic love; the three later books of poetry examine relationships, modern politics, and the mother-child world. Atwood is a peculiarly Canadian staunch moralist who "challenges us to become human." *Surfacing*, which challenges Western ways of seeing nature, and attempts to recover a primitive mysticism, and *Bodily Harm*, are the best of Atwood's five novels. Her short fiction may be her best prose;

see "Polarities" and the most compassionate "The Grave of the Famous Poet." *Murder in the Dark*'s witty experimental pieces on writing are a new direction. See 1983.134.

133 ____. "Northrop Frye: Canadian Mythographer." *Journal of Commonwealth Literature* 18, no. 1:1-13.
    Explains how Frye's archetypal criticism has influenced Canadian writers, especially Atwood. Frye's understanding of "the mythological substructure of popular culture" informs Atwood's uncanny articulations of the conventions underlying social relationships. In *The Circle Game*, her circle game defines a garrison mentality of ritual exclusions, and unleashes an anarchic counter-impulse. She uses Frye's mythic displacement most successfully in *Surfacing*, whose controlling metaphors are of Frye's wilderness as bush garden, and of mythic, cyclical rebirth. The "'wolf eyes'" of *The Journals of Susanna Moodie* follow Frye's idea of an imaginative mythology that humanizes the wilderness. *Survival*, with its survival thesis, victim psyche, and negative literary archetypes, best illustrates Frye's theory of Canadian identity. But, though *Survival* is compelling as belief, it lacks true analysis. See 1983.134 (below).

134 ____. "*Survival: A Thematic Guide to Canadian Literature*." In *The Oxford Companion to Canadian Literature*. Edited by William Toye. Toronto; Oxford; New York: Oxford University Press, pp. 777-78.
    Survival's thesis – that each culture has a central symbol – derives from a Northrop Frye theory; for Atwood, Canada's central image is of a collective victim struggling for survival against a hostile nature and colonialism. There is polemic anger in *Survival*'s assertions of the Canadian will to lose, but change begins with diagnosis. The intelligent, witty, audacious *Survival* simplifies to goad, and may have helped "more than any other work" to galvanize Canadian writing in the 1970s.

135 SUTHERLAND, FRASER. "Sylvia Bayer and the Search for Rubber." *Canadian Poetry*, no. 13 (Fall-Winter), pp. 86-91.
    Professes to discover a seminal influence on *Lady Oracle*, yet of course no plagiarism, in the first Canadian rubber fetish novel, *Fetish Girl*, by the unjustly neglected Sylvia Bayer [pseudonym of John Glassco], whose post-Freudian post-Structuralist "search for latex delves deep into the phylogenetic layers of the human psyche."

136 THOMPSON, LEE. Review of *Second Words*. *World Literature Written In English* 22, no. 2 (Autumn):290-92.

Appreciates Atwood's lively, insightful, unpretentious essays, which annotate her poetry and fiction. *Second Words*'s three parts, which correspond to three periods of her life, indicate her creative and political growth: from poetry, Canadian subjects, and detachment or discomfort with political involvement; to fiction, international foci, and a large involvement in politics. Though Atwood claims to write criticism out of duty, her style is appealingly direct, and gracefully between ivory tower and cracker barrel. Some snideness and sloppiness occur; some repetitions and contradictions are exposed by the juxtaposition of essays. The book reviews are reasonable, perceptive, and generously encouraging, without gushing.

137 VINCENT, SYBIL KORFF. "The Mirror and the Cameo: Margaret Atwood's Comic/Gothic Novel, *Lady Oracle*." In *The Female Gothic*. Edited by Juliann E. Fleenor. Montreal and London: Eden Press, pp. 153-63.

Finds in *Lady Oracle* a new sub-genre, the comic/Gothic, which more accurately depicts the psychology of modern woman than the traditional Gothic does. Though *Lady Oracle* anatomizes the Gothic and Female Gothic, it is not a true Gothic, because it does not arouse terror, or provide relief. Comedy reassures us, as Freud noted; Joan's female-to-female humor releases anxieties about being female, and eases anger and pain. With *Lady Oracle*'s Female Gothic-within-a-Gothic form, readers and narrator prefer the fantasy, which is controllable. Joan's overeating expresses her defiance and her sexual ambivalence; her truly separate identity, of a Costume Gothic writer, gratifies Joan's superego. The suspiciously reassuring conclusion shows Joan adopting a new disguise, of the militant female.

138 V[OGEL], M[AGDALENA]. "Schmerzhafte Häutung." *Neue Zürcher Zeitung*, 21 January, p. 37.

Verletzungen (*Bodily Harm*) uses narrative vocabulary and psychological analysis more radically than Atwood's previous novels, while staying within the usual theme of a woman protagonist breaking away from her empty life and relationships. The German title can mean emotional as well as bodily harm. Although the web of events can become confusing and unbelievable, upsetting the balance between

1983

human perplexity and artistic distance, Rennie's experiences and her final will to live seem painfully real. Waldhoff's translation is tastefully done.

139 VUONG-RIDDICK, THUONG. "Un aspect méconnu de Margaret Atwood." *Devoir* (Montréal), 27 August, p. 16.

Praises the essays in *Second Words*, and particularly Atwood's recognition of the important Quebec writer, Marie-Claire Blais. Admires the novelty of *Murder in the Dark* and its mix of genres. One should see and hear Atwood reading her texts, and be glad that such a gifted, moral voice is gaining influence in the Anglophone society.

140 WACHTEL, ELEANOR. "Atwood as Personal Storyteller." *Vancouver Sun*, 19 November, p. D12.

Is pleased by *Bluebeard's Egg*'s quirky, wary, marvelously clever stories. Though Atwood has spoken against reading women's work as autobiography, the four personal stories resonate with her own peripatetic childhood; in the fondly admiring "Significant Moments in the Life of My Mother" and "Unearthing Suite" she "invites [our] recognition, snares essences in details." In the more familiar sexual politics stories, women and men fear communication, as in "Loulou," "Spring Song of the Frogs," and the title story. But being ignorant and silent is problematic in the intense, apocalyptic world. Yet faint hopes exist; nature offers an eternal connection, and men aren't complete brutes.

141 WALKER, SUSAN. Review of *Canadian Poetry*, Vols. 1 and 2, edited by Jack David and Robert Lecker, and *The New Oxford Book of Canadian Verse in English*. *Quill & Quire* 49, no. 3 (March):66.

Faults Atwood's selections, and finds David and Lecker's survey-consensus choice of poets safer and more useful. Atwood has had to skim over the early period and modernists, and "has had to make some highly personal choices"; many of those chosen are not familiar or not likely to become classic. In fact, Atwood's own poems, chosen by William Toye, seem the most talented. Her *Survival* themes have shaped her selections. Though one can't argue with her inclusions, it's interesting to note who's omitted.

142 WEIR, LORRAINE. "Atwood in a Landscape." In *Margaret Atwood: Language, Text and System*. See Grace and Weir 1983.56, pp. 143-53.

Reflects "on the manifold question of landscape, language, text, body" in Atwood. As Derrida indicates, the humanist cosmos "divides man from 'his' world"; in Atwood's "'border country,' the deception becomes obvious." In "Progressive insanities of a pioneer," self is valorized against the ecosphere. ". . . [I]n proleptic form in *Surfacing* and fully in *Two-Headed Poems*," Atwood balances a "post-Heideggerian understanding of earth/world" strife against an apprehension of art's earth-dwelling and of the unitary cosmology's earth-affirming. Julian Jaynes's simple theory of the bicameral, pre-conscious mind underlies the struggle of left and right in *Two-Headed Poems* and its title sequence; these poems move through blood and world-decay to proclaim the unitary cosmology. *Two-Headed Poems* also celebrates Heidegger's "'dwelling'" and Robin Morgan's "'matriheritage'" of shamanic women.

143 WILLIAMS, PENNY. "Elegant Gems from Atwood." *Calgary Herald*, 30 October, p. F9.

Respects, admires, ponders, and enjoys *Bluebeard's Egg*, but does not get involved, because of Atwood's distance. These well-engraved, lapidary gems of stories range from childhood memories to the "precise snapshots of urban male/female relationships" Atwood does so well. The female characters are stronger than those of her first collection, but still seem "curiously indifferent to their lives" and their men. The bracketed "Significant Moments" and "Unearthing Suite" reevaluate "her" mother's life and record the parents' vital, pleased curiosity. Atwood's wonderful, arresting perceptions are usually asides, as on the placement of the feet in "Loulou." In the most provocative and elegantly constructed title story, Sally wonders what will hatch from the wizard's egg – will real emotions one day hatch from Atwood's perfectly incised eggs?

144 WILLIAMSON, MICHAEL. Review of *The New Oxford Book of Canadian Verse in English*. *Library Journal* 108, no. 19 (1 November):2087.

Praises Atwood's excellent anthology, which effectively supersedes A.J.M. Smith's landmark work: her selections are generous, adding 65 new poets; her choices are mostly perspicacious. Her succinct introduction provides the rationale of selection, a historical survey, and "cogent insight into why English Canadian poetry is 'spiky, tough, flexible, various, and vital.' Readers interested in a fair sampling of English Canadian poetry will find no better anthology."

145 WILSON, JEAN. "Bronzed Baby Boots." *Broadside* (Toronto) 4, no. 7 (May):13.
Recommends *The New Oxford Book of Canadian Verse in English* as a standard reference book for anyone interested in Canadian literature; accepts its probably inevitable limit of English language only; discusses its other imbalance, of only 29 women out of 120 poets. You may want to argue with Atwood's introductory explanation, or read only the women here; but if you want to understand the context they wrote in and share, read the whole book.

146 WINEAPPLE, BRENDA. Review of *Murder in the Dark* and *Margaret Atwood: Language, Text and System*, edited by Sherrill E. Grace and Lorraine Weir. *Dalhousie Review* 63, no. 2 (Summer):360-62.
Appreciates Atwood's clearly focussed, whimsical, ironic *Murder in the Dark*, which "is dedicated to making us see with both our empirical and our imaginary eyes." In the autobiographical pieces "Atwood not only conjures the past, but the way memory fondles an image, a texture, a line. . . . Past, present, and future meet" in her landscapes. Imagination and the *mot juste* are moral act and choice, as in "Bread." "Women's Novels" and "Happy Endings" cleverly expose formulaic plots. "Murder in the Dark" characteristically distrusts language.
Grace and Weir's 1983.56 *Language* helps locate the contexts or systems of Atwood's work, but imputes too much unity to her strong ambivalences.

147 WOODCOCK, GEORGE. "Metamorphosis and Survival: Notes on the Recent Poetry of Margaret Atwood." In *Margaret Atwood: Language, Text and System*. See Grace and Weir 1983.56, pp. 125-42.
Appreciates the stronger affirmations and the powerful Ovidian theme of metamorphosis in *You Are Happy, Two-Headed Poems*, and *True Stories*, in an essay that revises Part II of 1980.148 and reprints his 1981.112 acclaim for *True Stories*, slightly revised. Atwood's earlier survival ethic, of "'Beyond truth, / tenacity,'" did not preclude the metamorphosis evident in Mrs. Moodie's strange revenant survival, and

in the extraordinary Penelope-Odysseus poem, "'At first I was given centuries.'" Appreciates *You Are Happy*'s haunting Imagism, realistic farm life, and Keatsian "Late August"; the mythic animals, appallingly transformed by the earth-mother Circe, display our worst human traits. *Two-Headed Poems*, written after four years of literary success, personal happiness, and the birth of a loved young daughter, is Atwood's most tender and affirming book: here myths become the protean folk tales of daily life; the Hesiod-like "Daybooks I and II" show farm life realistically and emotionally; there are darker political poems, but also the epiphany of mankind's community in "The Bus to Alliston, Ontario," and man's primordial hand in "You Begin." Atwood has a visual, Orwellian, deeply moral, wise, and visionary poetic excellence. Revised: 1987.176. Excerpted: 1985.11.

1984

1 ABLEY, MARK. "Hating the Beautiful Trees." *TLS*, 27 April, p. 460.
    Traces the historic development of Canadian poetry; and finds *The New Oxford Book of Canadian Verse in English*, with Atwood's trenchant introduction, the best guide available, for readers outside Canada, to Canadian poetry. Canadian poetry began miserably, and nineteenth-century Canadian poetry was mediocre, despite Atwood's rhetorical argument for it. Wilfred Campbell's embarrassing, self-serving first *Oxford Book of Canadian Verse* was followed by A.J.M. Smith's accomplished, modernist 1960 *Oxford Book*. Now, after the extraordinary poetry proliferation of the 1960s and 1970s, a new anthology is needed. Canadian poets writing in English, who now come from many nations, seek an authentic voice, and form. Atwood's selections should have drawn on N. Brian Davis's discoveries of lower-class poets. Some of her younger poets are doubtful, and some Toronto writers are over-represented. Commends Al Purdy, John Newlove, and Anne Szumigalski especially; these, along with Phyllis Webb, Margaret Avison, Michael Ondaatje, and Atwood, are Canada's finest, and comparable to those of any English-speaking country.

2 ADACHI, KEN. "Old Hands Differ in Sensibility." *Toronto Star*, 19 May, p. M6.
    Has mixed reactions to Atwood's unsentimental insights, in a two-book review of *Interlunar* and Leonard Cohen's *Book of Mercy*.

1984

Like *True Stories, Interlunar* "delivers real and salutary shocks" with an ironic, pessimistic emotional nakedness "that demands an answering openness of the reader." Though she is often brutal and cold, the irony doesn't weaken the emotion; her metaphors, especially in "Snake Poems," "are often striking, if sometimes wilful." Though Atwood lacks virtuosity, repeats, and dwells on the negative, she is never silly or slight. Her "strangulated vatic posture" precludes fun or sex. The pathos of "Bedside" dissolves in a bold, apocalyptic image that becomes the reader's own. Her bleak vision is softened by her humanity.

3 BAKER, JANET. "Atwood's Surface Glitter." *Atlantic Provinces Book Review* 11, no. 1 (February-March):4.

Is disappointed by *Bluebeard's Egg*: except for "Betty" and "Loulou," these disgruntled, tedious main characters merge. Though occasionally stories are shocked into meaning, as in "Uglypuss," the general mood is an oppressive, sour futility and alienation. "It is as if characters from her earlier novels – Duncan of *The Edible Woman*, Anna of *Surfacing* – have aged but not matured"; the ennui and domestic unhappiness become monotonous. The surface glitter of her style disguises her lack of vital subjects. Though much here is contrived, flaccid, or childishly petty, the surreal title story and "Unearthing Suite" show what Atwood is capable of.

4 BEMROSE, JOHN. "Embracing the Dark." *Globe and Mail*, 7 July, p. E16.

Welcomes *Interlunar*'s new intimacy and sorrow, which embrace "the alien dark," and are rooted in Atwood's motherhood and grief for friends. What is lost in cutting imagery is more than gained in deeply moving threnody. The brilliant "Snake Poems" still evoke the natural world with Atwood's familiar ironic, astringent wizardry; and the provocatively challenging but somehow sexless paradigms of brutal men and chilled, sensitive women are still vintage Atwood. But, especially in the most personal poems, "the sorrowful surrender to those darknesses we cannot change" has created a promising new depth and humanity.

5 BILLINGS, ROBERT. Review of *Interlunar* and of *The Little Flowers of Madame de Montespan*, by Jane Urquhart. *Poetry Toronto*, no. 105 (September), pp. 17-22.

Appreciates these excellent books, that are not merely anecdotal, but critiques of the ideal and the stereotyped; Atwood especially insists on "being at home in the actual" earth. *Interlunar*, which shows Atwood's powers at their peak, is more personal and less feminist-and human-rights-oriented than her recent poetry books have been. Though its landscape is distinctly Canadian (Ontario), place is not confined, but "is the thing out of which vision and meditation come," as in ["A Painting of One Location on the Plain"]. *Interlunar's* key poems are the mythic ones, especially those on Orpheus, Euridice, and Persephone; "Harvest," which may satirize white and corn goddess myths; and the "Snake Poems"—the snake being *Interlunar's* only, and earthbound, god.

6 Biography. *Current Biography Yearbook*:17-20.

Describes Atwood's status, childhood, education, early publication, and present life; and describes the themes of her books of poetry, criticism, and novels, with quotes from some of the critics and reviewers.

7 BJERRING, NANCY EVELYN. "The Whole of the Same Universe: Science and Transcendence in *Fifth Business* and *Surfacing*." Ph.D. dissertation, University of Western Ontario.

Examines, following Theodore Roszak, Dennis Lee, and Northrop Frye, the clash between scientific and transcendent world-views in two displaced romances, *Surfacing* and Robertson Davies's *Fifth Business*: "each protagonist undertakes a journey of self-discovery," finds archetypal patterns in experience, and learns to see the marvelous as an aspect of reality. See *Dissertation Abstracts International* 45:1403A.

*8 BORN, HEIDI von. "Två kanadensiska poeter" [Two Canadian poets]. *Dagens Nyheter* (Stockholm), 1 July, p. 12.

In Swedish. A short general article that describes Atwood as one of Europe's most popular Canadian authors and an inspiration to younger female writers. Atwood reaches her audience with vitality, humor, and elegance. Although Atwood started as a poet, her prose work is more popular. Atwood considers literature to be a geography of the senses; through her writing, she attempts to change our way of seeing the world.

1984

9 BRYDON, DIANA. "'The Thematic Ancestor': Joseph Conrad, Patrick White, and Margaret Atwood." *World Literature Written in English* 24, no. 2 (Autumn):386-97.

Argues, from commonwealth and post-structuralist critical theories, that *Surfacing* and Patrick White's female-narrated *A Fringe of Leaves* subversively rewrite Conrad's complexly Eurocentric *Heart of Darkness*. Both Atwood and White push beyond "the coercion of 'sane' speaking, . . . [and] seek to give a voice to [what Robert Kroetsch calls] Conrad's silent female centre . . . . [Both] write women in, demythologizing the false idealism that denied women power." Both Atwood and White politically parallel the marginalization of female and of colonial experience; but American feminists like Christ 1980.17 misread *Surfacing*'s point that political alliances must take precedence over gender. By eliminating Conrad's mediating narrator, Atwood and White let the real wilderness voices override the single, privileged voice; name, subject, and Western ideas of personality dissolve. The run-on sentences of *Surfacing*'s narrator reinforce a continuous flow; like Kurtz she is a voice we hear but never see. Both Atwood and White create potentially revolutionary shifts to a female, diffused focus, and to multiple, inclusive languages.

10 CARRINGTON, ILDIKÓ de PAPP. "Dark Designs." *Women's Review of Books* 1, no. 7 (April):12-13.

Links *Murder in the Dark* to Atwood's previous work: the autobiographical sketches and travel notes of the first two sections illumine *Surfacing*'s aborted baby and "The Resplendent Quetzal"; the third and fourth sections deal adroitly with Atwood's major essay and *Bodily Harm* themes of fiction, moral responsibility, and men and women. The title piece and Atwood's cover collage offer clues to a complex metaphor of fiction, author, and a narrative that is also literary criticism. The science-fiction "Simmering" both parodies Freud and reminds us of women's holy nurturing. "Raw Materials," "Bread," and *Bodily Harm* force us to recognize human suffering and the basic politics of "who eats what." "Happy Endings," like *Lady Oracle*, satirizes romance plots. The fourth section is ambivalent and contradictory about relationships between men and women in "Worship," "Iconography," and "Liking Men." Loving one man, in *agape*, not *eros*, seems to be the answer, as in "Hand."

11 CASTRO, JAN [GARDEN]. "Interview with Margaret Atwood–April 20, 1983, St. Louis." *River Styx*, no. 15, pp. 6-21.

Atwood discusses her early readings, education, and art work; the realism of her Susanna Moodie, *The Edible Woman*'s mummy, the physical third eye [see "Instructions for the Third Eye"], *Bodily Harm*'s islands and revolution, *Surfacing*'s Indian rock paintings, and "Notes [Towards] a Poem That Can Never Be Written"; *Surfacing*'s composition, publication, narrator, brother, ending, dominance/subservience paradigms, and antecedent "Under Glass"; double endings and meta-fiction; her Anansi editing and the Writer's Union of Canada; Canadian, American, and women writers; and truth as composite, inevitably filtered eye-witnessings, not absolute. Reprinted, with corrections and additions, 1988.13.

12 COOKE, KAIREEN. Review of *Murder in the Dark*. *Scrivener* 5, no. 1 (Winter):37.

Is offended by these "bitter commentaries on the violence and hopelessness of our lives. Crude and horrible images appear in almost all of the pieces," of deer carcasses, human embryos, and a morbid "Making Poison." Perhaps most offensive is Atwood's refusal to accept men as feeling human beings, as in the bitter "Women's Novels" and "Boyfriends," and the cynical "Liking Men." Her third eye sees at the expense of the other two.

13 CRACE, JIM. "Off-Cuts." *TLS*, 23 March, p. 311.

Rejects *Murder in the Dark* as overpriced and indulgent, samples and off-cuts from the swarf bin. Has Atwood's Canadian and feminist standing encouraged publication of this unpolished work? Though there are effective passages, as in "Bread" and "Raw Materials," all the sharper pieces need narrative elaboration. No piece lacks faults, of style, superfluous paragraphs, odd changes, or mystifying ends. At the worst, Atwood's tough-softness becomes a vinegary 1960s psychobabble; and her sentence structure becomes tangled and tuneless, especially in "The Boys' Own Annual, 1911."

14 CRAIG, DAVID. "Middle-Class Tragedy." *Critical Quarterly* 26, no. 3 (Autumn):3-19 passim.

Argues, using *Life Before Man* and Joseph Heller's *Something Happened* as secondary examples, that the key English-speaking novels of the 1970s, Doris Lessing's *The Summer Before the Dark* and David Storey's *Pasmore*, depict the 1970's slump in morale of the professional middle class, and their long-standing, alienated anxiety. Atwood's museum anthropologist, Elizabeth, foresees her own future meanness. Both Lesje and her lover [Nate] began with vocations; but Lesje now sees her work as escapist, fraudulent, and unreal, and [Nate] has lost his belief in the value of making toys and practicing law, even legal aid.

15 CRAIG, PATRICIA. "Paperbacks in Brief." *TLS*, 21 September, p. 1066.

Enjoys Atwood's energetic, knowing, agreeably quirky *Dancing Girls*, with its crises and reconstitutions; finds "The Man from Mars" its funniest story.

16 CURTIS, TONY. Review of *The New Oxford Book of Canadian Verse in English*. *Poetry Wales* 20, no. 1:99-104.

Finds Atwood's anthology rewarding and impressive as it reflects the 1960's renaissance of Canadian literary nationalism. Like Welsh and American poetry, Canadian poetry responds strongly to the land. Early poets romanticised the land and noble savages; later poets like Al Purdy and Dale Zieroth, quoted here, grow into the land's realities. Praises and quotes from Bill Bissett's witty piece on national identity, Leonard Cohen's on lovers, and Atwood's Susanna Moodie, who shows that "Canadians have earned the right to raise a voice." The major Canadian singer-songwriter, Joni Mitchell, should have been included.

17 CZARNECKI, MARK. "Without Fear or Compromise." *Maclean's* 97, no. 22 (28 May):60.

Finds cryptic darkness, a final tentative hope, and abundant images of transition in *Interlunar*, which means between old and new moon. "'I was once the snake woman'" refers to Atwood's earlier harsh sexual politics. The "Snake Poems," with their vivid, humorous images, "are vintage Atwood," and a new perspective on snakes as "poetic and spiritual renewal." In the "Interlunar" section, Atwood as mystic priestess celebrates each object's "'quiet shining,'" and attacks mankind's injustice and abstract love. Atwood speaks as "daughter, mother, healer, poet, and Martian." Though these parables can be overbearing, extreme, and dense, they "bristle with conviction" and confront "the wisdom of the ages" fearlessly and uncompromisingly.

1984

18 DAVEY, FRANK. *Margaret Atwood: A Feminist Poetics*. New Canadian Criticism Series. Vancouver: Talonbooks, 178 pp.

Argues that, from *Double Persephone* on, dichotomies of female versus male space, life/art, actuality/mythology, and biology/technology, pervade Atwood's ten books of poetry, five novels, short fictions, and *Survival*. Mankind denies the female, temporal space that ultimately, as in *The Journals of Susanna Moodie*, prevails. From *Two-Headed Poems* on, Atwood's work becomes increasingly politically violent, and blames men, as in "Liking Men." For Atwood, traditional poetry is male, quantifying, inaccurate; female poetry is non-linguistic, real, as in the paradoxical "Notes Towards a Poem That Can Never Be Written." All Atwood's female artist-figures have the "male 'gorgon touch'" that transforms flesh to stone.

The Edible Woman, Surfacing, Lady Oracle, and *Bodily Harm* are structured as female, Shakespearean comedies, of alienation from nature, descent to a "primitive but healing reality," and some return to wholeness. Archetypal critics McLay 1981.69, Pratt 1981.83, and Rigney 1978.81 misunderstand the first two novels' Freudian catharsis and their limiting, patriarchal comic or romance patterns. *Life Before Man*'s static narrative structure echoes its characters' stilled lives. In Atwood's metaphoric rather than literal male/female dichotomy, Chris is *Life*'s most vigorously female force, and the controlling Elizabeth is its most "'male.'"

There is an Atwood vocabulary of "Technological Skin, Mirrors, The Gothic, Refugees and Tourists, Underground Mazes, Metamorphosis, [and] Signposts/Totems." In the iconic stories of *Dancing Girls* and *Bluebeard's Egg*, "symbolism dwarfs plot" and preoccupies the characters. The highly influential but problematic *Survival* does illumine the non-communicating lovers, paranoid fears of nature, and self-imposed victimhoods of Atwood's own work; but it defies her injunctions against naming and classifying. Though Atwood's distorting female/male dichotomy, "profound mistrust of men," and didactic tone are problems in her "intriguing and engaging" work, the recent playful, metafictive structures of "Happy Endings" and the post-atomic, post-Adamic harmonies of "The Festival of Missed Crass" hint at new qualities.

Provides biographical information and selected bibliography. Revises 1973.17, 1977.12, 1980.29, and 1981.22.

1984

19 DAYMOND, DOUGLAS. Review of *The New Oxford Book of Canadian Verse in English*. *World Literature Written in English* 24, no. 2 (Autumn):337-40.

Finds Atwood's anthology balanced, impressive, and a fitting successor to A.J.M. Smith's two benchmark volumes. Atwood's choices reveal both the inevitable editorial predispositions, and the reassessment in taste since Smith's work. Her changes, which are fresh and individualistic, confirm and impressively extend the tradition Smith defined. Atwood's introduction enlivens its period summaries with wit and acute observations. Her selections confirm her sense of the local, narrative, and anecdotal, as well as of Smith's "'cosmopolitan'" tradition. Selections from the "'classic'" 1940s and 1950s, the "'cultural renaissance'" of the 1960s, and the younger poets, are judicious and far-ranging.

20 DEMPSTER, BARRY. "Ol' Debbil Moon." *Books in Canada* 13, no. 8 (October):26-27.

Describes Atwood, in a two-book review featuring *Interlunar*, as "a poet of cold blue shadows" who is now in interlunar transition. In the somewhat prosaic "Snake Poems," which recall earlier suites of dolls and animals, the real and legendary collide in Atwood's unbreaking circles. "[S]erpent images of shedding and peeling" follow the threatening snake poems; Atwood waits by her father's deathbed, or for a nuclear holocaust, or for belief. In "The Healer" and "The Saints," powerlessness replaces her icy anger. As in earlier poems for her daughter, she "can almost see in the dark. . . . [S]omething has changed, her soul is flickering. . . . Atwood's heart is visible: a firefly," or a flashlight beckoning.

21 DEVESON, RICHARD. "Lashing Out." *New Statesman* 107 (9 March):25.

Briefly describes *Murder in the Dark*, in a four-book review, as difficult: the autobiographical moments need to be part of a larger whole; the essayistic items "veer off in irony" and puzzling ends; yet the poem-like pieces, which are intrinsically difficult, do capture something tantalizingly real, as in "Hand."

22 D[ONAVIN], D[ENISE] P. Review of *Second Words*. *Booklist* 80, no. 11 (1 February):784.

Despite the title, these choice samples of Atwood's critical writing are of primary importance. They reveal her seriousness about reviewing and literary criticism, her loyalty to poets and Canadian as well as better-known writers, and her "growing politicization as a woman, writer, and Canadian."

23 EICHMANN-LEUTENEGGER, BEATRICE. "Abenteuer einer romantischen Lügnerin." *Neue Zürcher Zeitung*, 19 October, p. 41.

Provides a mixed review of *Lady Orakel*. With its many plots, the novel resembles the kind of light reading that the main character produces in her romance novels. Atwood skillfully uses humor and irony to move the story beyond the surface romance to a higher level. The writing lacks economy and the ending lacks substance. The translation has flaws.

24 EPSTEIN, JULIA. "Margaret Atwood's Canadian Culture." *Washington Post Book World*, 4 March, pp. 3-4.

Appreciates *Second Words*: Atwood's central concerns – her belief in language as incantation, and in the writer as a witness who "gives voice to the powerless"; her early Canadian literary nationalism and current Amnesty International involvement – begin with literature and politics separated, but these become intertwined. The book reviews are fiercely subjective gems. The longer essays cover writing, audience, the supernatural, Canadian humor, and Australian culture. And, as in the witty, reverent "Northrop Frye Observed," down-home "warmth and humor permeate all" of *Second Words*.

25 FISHMAN, CHARLES. "Naming Names: Three Recent Novels by Women Writers." *Names* 32, no. 1 (March):33-44.

Discusses how names are used in *Life Before Man*, Alice Walker's *Meridian*, and Toni Morrison's *Tar Baby*: levels and boundaries; class and status; mis-naming and other barriers; real and imaginary power; and roots of identity. Refers, under mis-naming, to Lesje's "'William Wasp.'" Under power, refers to Elizabeth's cursing Auntie Muriel; and discusses Lesje as "a kind of secular witch" who labels rocks and dinosaurs in a secret language, and who senses power in Nate's "'the children,'" ruminates on "'the Mesozoic'" label, and wants to be a "'Mrs. Schoenhof.'" Under identity, discusses Lesje's foreign first name, lost family name, and two lost languages; Lesje

1984

therefore longs to escape to Lesjeland, and "partly heal[s] these wounds of naming" by becoming an expert museum cataloguer and namer.

26 FIZZ, ROBYN. "Margaret Atwood's Poison Pen." *Sojourner* (Cambridge, Mass.), January, p. 8.

Describes how Atwood's November MIT *Murder in the Dark* reading and discussion mix venom and humor; and how, as in *Bodily Harm*, she examines power and our avoidance of its cruelty. Atwood's deadpan delivery of "Simmering," "Women's Novels," and "Happy Endings," which satirize sexual politics, got rounds of laughter. Atwood spoke on becoming a Canadian writer; her present writing habits and politics; and on victimization, of those who are violently persecuted, of those who like many women are disenfranchised, and of those who define themselves solely as victims.

27 FOGEL, STANLEY. "Canada: Atwood and Davies." In *A Tale of Two Countries: Contemporary Fiction in English Canada and the United States*. Toronto: ECW Press, pp. 96-126.

Discusses *Survival* and five novels. Although Atwood in the Gibson interview [1973.27] eschews political purposes, and usually avoids diatribes in her novels, *Survival* does examine Canada's survival self-image most poignantly; and Atwood's *oeuvre* does yield the greatest insight into the Canadian artist's situation. Technique is secondary in her novels; language remains solid, not experimental; her iterative imagery is poetically skillful. The anorectic heroines of her first three novels quest for a stable identity and triumph over victimization as they refuse food, language, and cultural detritus, be it patriarchal or imported. *The Edible Woman*'s epigraph begins its surgeon's or mortician's imagery as well as its food imagery. The *Surfacing* heroine, who contracts a purgative insanity, at the end espouses an unnamed, unvictimized, uncreated self, one not American nor patriarchal. *Lady Oracle*'s protracted concern with language increases its complexity. The potboiler *Bodily Harm* and the lifeless *Life Before Man* have been over-praised. Atwood's novels, like Robertson Davies's, are ontological, modern, and more British than American.

28 FULLBROOK, KATE. Review of *Murder in the Dark*. *British Book News*, July, p. 429.

Finds *Murder in the Dark* exhilarating and sharply pleasing to the mind. Though at first this slim volume looks like a publisher's ploy, or scrapings from an author's bin, these vignettes have Atwood's magic insights and brilliant illuminations. All four sections make the ordinary assume extraordinary knowledge, as in "Strawberries." Dodging and twisting clichés, and "taking them to their logical extremes," are Atwood fortes; her intensity attacks dead conventional meanings even as she sees how devious language is.

29 GEMINDER, KATHLEEN ELAINE. "Callisto: The Recurrence and Variations of Her Myth from Ovid to Atwood." Ph.D. dissertation, University of Manitoba.

A feminist, Jungian tracing of the Callisto myth that treats *Surfacing* and [D.H. Lawrence's] *Lady Chatterly's Lover* as two novels whose Callisto figures achieve their initiation. The perhaps prototypical Callisto myth has two aspects: the patriarchal rape of female sexuality; and Callisto's initiation-like transformation and apotheosis. See *Dissertation Abstracts International* 45:1388A. See 1988.54.

30 GINGELL, SUSAN. "The Animals in Atwood's Country." *Literary Criterion* 19, nos. 3-4:125-37.

As *Survival* points out, Canadian writers habitually project their anxieties onto animal victims; interpreted thus, the faceless, doomed animals of "The Animals in That Country" chillingly depict "a lack of Canadian identity" and a threatened Canadian consciousness. "The trappers" symbolically identifies a violent duality of the hunter becoming the hunted; so does "Dream 2: Brian the Still-Hunter," "Rat Song," "Song of the Worms," and "Arctic syndrome: dream fox," which also suggests the artist tracking art. The "'Nature as Monster'" images of "A Descent through the Carpet" connect to E.J. Pratt's evolutionary "Silences." Later poems link human evolution to loss, especially of language, as in "Fishing for Eel Totems." That people can learn from animals is evident in *The Journals of Susanna Moodie* and "Landcrab I." Atwood's animals are sometimes linked to terror, more often to love; but sexual love is predominantly negative, for the trapped or hounded female. "Vultures" discovers their positive as well as their negative qualities. Analyzes poetic style of "Arctic syndrome: dream fox," "Landcrab I," and "Vultures." Reprinted: 1985.38.

1984

31 GOETSCH, PAUL. "Ökologische Aspekte der Werke von Margaret Atwood." In *Zur Literatur und Kultur Kanadas: Eine Erlanger Ringvorlesung.* Edited by Dieter Meindl. Erlanger Studien, edited by Detlef Bernd Leistner and Dietmar Peschel, vol 54. Erlangen: Palm & Enke, pp. 109-28.

Discusses ecological themes and metaphors, and the related theme of violent duality, throughout Atwood's work. The novels and poetry critique various bad relationships. *Life Before Man*, which characterizes the twentieth century's most depressing couples, alludes to the destruction of the conditions needed for life on earth. *Surfacing* examines Canadian versus U.S. and English Canadian versus French-Canadian relationships. Many poems and the story "Polarities" compare the rape of nature to the domination of woman by man. Another ecological viewpoint, that accepts the biological role of women, appears in the pregnancies of the protagonist in *Surfacing*, Lesje in *Life Before Man*, and Ainsley in *The Edible Woman.* According to Atwood, nature is the primary source of energy, and the degradation of the environment is reflected in human and societal deterioration. The recurrent themes of survival and violent duality in nature suggest some hope that the wilderness will regenerate itself. Atwood understands that the balance between spiritual powers, nature, and the individual must not be disrupted.

32 GRACE, SHERRILL E. "Courting Bluebeard with Bartók, Atwood, and Fowles: Modern Treatment of the Bluebeard Theme." *Journal of Modern Literature* 11, no. 2 (July):245-62.

Analyzes the Bluebeard theme in Bela Bartók's opera, *Duke Bluebeard's Castle*, John Fowles's *The Collector*, and Atwood's *Lady Oracle* and "Hesitations outside the door." The Bluebeard story may be seen as a power struggle, as between Fowles's Few and Many; as a male-female struggle, of Jungian anima and animus; and as a paradigm of creativity, with Bluebeard as the artist and language as the castle. The earliest versions of Bluebeard are cautionary tales. The later fairy tales, Charles Perrault's "Barbe Bleue" and the Grimms's "Fitcher's Bird," and Maurice Maeterlinck's play, *Ariane et Barbe Bleue*, all share what Vladimir Propp would call the same structure of Bluebeard's prohibition or test, the wife's transgression, and a happy transformation or reversal. Bartók's darker opera, which influenced both Fowles and Atwood, differs in focussing on the male psyche, conflating the prohibition and transgression, and ending negatively, without a reversal. *The Collector*'s Miranda represents the elite Few, kinesis, and nature; its Bluebeard/Caliban/Clegg represents the Many, stasis, the denier and destroyer of nature. *Lady Oracle*'s labyrinthine parody is serious: it shows how we destroy other aspects of the feminine self to become a reflected anima, and then, unconsciously rebelling, reduce all men to Bluebeards. Explicitly in *Lady Oracle* and implicitly in "Hesitations," "we are Bluebeard, wife, and castle, repeating the story of our destruction," the hostile dualities that reduce "our relationships with ourselves," others, and nature, to closed castles. As Fowles and Atwood warn us, "we must not only open doors, but destroy the castle."

33 ____. "Quest for the Peaceable Kingdom: Urban/Rural Codes in Roy, Laurence, and Atwood." In *Women Writers and the City: Essays in Feminist Literary Criticism*. Edited by Susan Merrill Squier. Knoxville: University of Tennessee Press, pp. 193-209.

Most Canadian writers have a non-urban, rural perspective, and, as Frye suggests, see civilization as dehumanizing; most male writers stereotype the city as female. The Canadian women writers Gabrielle Roy, Margaret Laurence, and Margaret Atwood see the city as male, patriarchal, technological, and dehumanizing. Atwood's poetics and vision rest on her system of urban/rural polarities; in novels, poetry, and especially in *The Journals of Susanna Moodie*, Atwood identifies with the land against a destructive male civilization. As in Roy and Laurence, this identification of woman with nature claims a potential, rather than entering a patriarchal trap. Reproduces the *Journals*' last collage.

34 GRACE, SHERRILL [E]. "Stories 'Beneath the Page': Atwood's New Fiction." *CRNLE Reviews Journal*, no. 1 (May), pp. 68-71.

Appreciates *Murder in the Dark*'s surreal collage, and enjoys some of *Bluebeard's Egg*'s finely crafted but less exciting stories of ordinary women and wives, like "Betty" and "Loulou." Bluebeard's castle and prohibitions unify the stories' finely detailed and pervasively claustrophobic interiors. In the autobiographical "Unearthing Suite," Atwood plays Bluebeard, seeking her mother's secret. *Murder*'s "Instructions for the Third Eye" shows us how to see fully and responsibly, as *Survival* advocated; its seven-part metonymic structure is a collage that shows us how to read the entire book's collage. The four increasingly disturbing and surreal sections move from the terse "Autobiography" to the ironic "Raw Materials" collage, to the sinister parodies and surreal fictions of "Bread" and "The Page," to the nightmare imaginings of ["Liking Men"] and the "Sadean 'belle captive'" of "Iconography." As in earlier work, Atwood shocks us into seeing; *Murder's* finer and more sustained surreal collages recall Magritte, Remedios Varo, fairy tales, and Max Ernst.

35 GUPTA, SHYAM RATNA. "High-Priestess of New Feminism." *Hindustan Times* (New Delhi) 27 May, p. 8.

Praises the enchanting, eerie, ordinary yet supra-real world of *Dancing Girls and Other Stories* and *Lady Oracle*. Atwood "is the high priestess of today's New Feminism": passionate, rational, and observant, she differentiates masculine from feminine, and tells the feminist movement to "'Know Thyself.'" Her language has a haunting word-music. Her highly intelligent, pessimistic work has a streak of sado-masochism.

36 HAYNE, BEVERLY. "First Lady of the Frontier." *Sunday Times Magazine* (London), 19 February, p. 49.

Interviews Canada's most exported novelist, whose *Murder in the Dark* and paperback *Dancing Girls* are soon forthcoming. Atwood, who is writing her next novel in Norfolk, recounts getting the $2,500 Governor General's Award for *The Circle Game* when she was a broke student. More recently, Atwood discovered "that three-quarters of the poets at a poetry society meeting admitted to having muses," which inspired "Instructions for the Third Eye." *Murder in the Dark* is full of literary games and jokes, like the satirical parable "Simmering." "Liking Man" praises civilised manhood.

37 HELLER, ARNO. "Literarischer Öko-Feminismus: Margaret Atwood's *Surfacing*." *Arbeiten aus Anglistik und Amerikanistik* (Graz, Austria) 9, no. 1:39-50.

To read *Surfacing* as a strictly feminist text, ignoring its crucial contradictions to modern feminism, is misleading and limiting. The psychological, mythic, and Canadian interpretations are also incomplete. Cites Rigney's 1978.81 comprehensive perspective of *Surfacing*. Examining the various levels of meaning together creates an "eco-feminist" perspective that equates the victimization of nature in Western civilization with the victimization of women. The text is a supra-national, "green" manifesto that illustrates the self-destructive tendencies of modern society and offers some hope for solving the problems.

38 HILL, HEATHER. "*Look Ma* Tells You More about Tories." *Gazette* (Montreal), 8 September, p. F10.

Reviews *Bluebeard's Egg* and five other paperbacks. The somewhat softened "High Priestess of CanLit seems intent on persuading the reader that with adulthood, innocence dies, love languishes." Some tales evoke a sun-dappled childhood and, tenderly, Atwood's mother; the rest exhibit "contemporary urban angst" as their characters search for love that eludes them.

39 HOEPPNER, A. KENNETH. "The Political Implications of Literature: Contemporary Theoretical Perspectives and Their Applications to Some Novels by Atwood, Kroetsch, and Wiebe." Ph.D. dissertation, University of Calgary.

Considers the political implications of three literary theories and of three novels, reading *Surfacing* from a Frygian mythopoeic structuralist approach, Rudy Wiebe's *The Scorched-Wood People* from a mimeticist-historical perspective, and Robert Kroetsch's *What the Crow Said* from Derridean deconstructionist assumptions. See *Dissertation Abstracts International* 45:3347-48A.

40 HOY, HELEN. "Letters in Canada, 1983: Fiction." *University of Toronto Quarterly* 53, no. 4 (Summer):323-24.

Briefly finds the affectionate *Unearthing Suite* the most satisfying of the Writers' Union's three expensive fund-raiser editions from Grand Union Press. Enjoys *Murder in the Dark*'s odd, delightful, skillful, unpredictable miscellany, especially the funny ones – the wry "Women's Novels," the parodic "Happy Endings," and the satiric ["Simmering"]. Other pieces cryptically explore perception, identity, and writing, or examine human horrors and sexual politics.

Bluebeard's Egg, one of the year's two notable short-story collections, mostly tells of modern anxieties, especially about the opposite sex. The title story retells the Bluebeard legend to clarify a modern woman's uncertainty about her husband. At times larger problems intrude, as in "The Salt Garden." Atwood's male protagonists are not yet wholeheartedly created. The warm autobiographical stories, which have an Alice Munro self-mockery of adolescence, "are strengthened by the love with which they are told."

41 HULCOOP, JOHN F. "Dark Mother." *Canadian Literature*, no. 103 (Winter), pp. 88-89.

Portrays Atwood, in a review of *Interlunar*, as a dark lady and a poet casting a cold eye, like T.S. Eliot, on mortality. "Eyes blazing" from back-cover photographs, she "stares into the heart of this world's darkness," seeing through tears that magnify and distort the world's facts, like Hieronymous Bosch's surreal paintings. Some of the "Snake Poems" are as fine as Emily Dickinson's and D.H. Lawrence's – but, like all Atwood's poetry, they are also "a grand Boschean guignol" of Canadian Gothic scenes, as in "Three Denizen Songs," the feminist ["Orpheus II," "A Harvest,"] and others. Atwood's vision is not happy or easy. Seeing is more excruciating because man (of both sexes) is tragically mortal, as in "A Blazed Trail," which is the reviewer's favourite. [The title poem] seeks to encourage us, but this reviewer, who is older, is not consoled.

42 HULSE, MICHAEL. "Loaves and Fictions." *PN Review*, no. 42, p. 60.

Finds *Murder in the Dark* uneven. "Bread," "The Page," and "Happy Endings" are most intelligent and imaginative. The five ways of looking at "Bread" – realistic, moral-economic, political, Grimm, and fictive – "are a critique of loaf (or life)." But most of the other texts, including the ham-fisted title piece and the two tendentious feminist tracts, are much less powerful. Atwood's mysticism, as in "Instructions for the Third Eye," is always hard to swallow; her permuted "Happy Endings" is much more convincing.

43 IRIE, KEVIN. Review of *Murder in the Dark*. *Quarry* 33, no. 1 (Winter):86-87.

Enjoys, in a two-book review, Atwood's wry, witty, anecdotal, whimsical *Murder in the Dark*. Her humour teaches and warns us, as in "Simmering," "Happy Endings," and "Him." The [Sylvia] Plath-like anger of "Strawberries" "zap[s] the reader into self-recognition. . . . *Murder in the Dark* is filled with such little shocks, or pleasures, a joy to [read]."

*44 JAIDEV. "Functions and Uses of Woman." *Newstime*, Magazine sec., 21 October.

Approves Atwood's political feminism, in the paperback *Bodily Harm*, where, as in the first two novels and in "Hair Jewellery," Atwood "is always, and rightly, concerned with the '(ab)usability' of woman for man." Rennie learns that the fulfillment called love is only "using and being used." *Bodily Harm* lacks Atwood's earlier, spell-like intensity, but its international range more than compensates. *Bodily Harm* shows that in Canada as in the Caribbean, women are powerless, and therefore abused. "The issue of women's abuse is extended to encompass the whole weak population of the world." One wishes Rennie success in her future subversions; her telling of her life's truths in *Bodily Harm* is already subversive of male interests and illusions. Comforting the beaten Lora, identifying with her and licking her face clean, Rennie discovers her own, unexpected identity and role, in a magnificent, brutally realistic, deeply ritualistic scene.

45 JOHNSTON, SUE ANN. "The Daughter as Escape Artist." *Atlantis* 9, no. 2 (Spring):10-22.

Discusses Atwood's *Lady Oracle*, Margaret Drabble's *Jerusalem the Golden*, and Anne Tyler's *Earthly Possessions*, as novels where "the heroines' escape from the mother becomes a search for her that is also a search for the self." In all three novels, the true mothers withhold the love that surrogate mothers provide. Joan's schizophrenic split, between unconscious fantasy and conscious reality, results from her conflicting desires, to escape and yet, as her dreams and automatic writing show, to be at one with her mother. Joan feels the same impulse to escape husband and lovers. The end is irresolute; Joan has confronted her ambivalence only in her unconscious, and may, as Grace 1980.47 points out, be spinning a new fantasy plot.

46 JONES, DOROTHY. "'Waiting for the Rescue': A Discussion of Margaret Atwood's *Bodily Harm*." *Kunapipi* (Aarhus, Denmark) 6, no. 3:86-100.

Explicates the religious and symbolic referents of Rennie's development and journey. Although *Bodily Harm*'s moral vision is secular, Rennie journeys from the old dispensation of life under law into a new dispensation of life under grace. Her journey is a pilgrimage, and a night-sea crossing of the heroic quest. Her journey begins in Griswold, which suggests Dante's dark wood, and which has a blighted, loveless moral vision under the old dispensation. In trendy Toronto, which suggests [John Bunyan's] Vanity Fair, good and evil dwindle to good and bad taste. Jake, like the Old Testament Jacob, is a trickster; Daniel, whose Old Testament name means "'the Lord is Judge,'" also belongs to the old dispensation. Dr. Minnow may be a sort of Christ figure, calling Rennie to write the truth. Paul belongs to the New World. Lora knows far more about male power than Rennie does: as on *Power Politics*'s cover, woman is captive not only to one man, but to society's power structures. Rennie's compassion to Lora assures her own salvation; and she envisions a new, politically committed life. The novel ends on tentative hope, with Lora alive and Rennie escaped by a luck equivalent to divine grace.

47 KINGSTONE, JAMES. Review of *Bluebeard's Egg. CM* 12, no. 5 (September):190.

Is impressed by Atwood's modest, splendid, subtle, original, and varied *Bluebeard's Egg*. The two opening stories, "Significant Moments in the Life of My Mother" and "Hurricane Hazel," console the reader with their narrator's measured voice and accessible, comforting landscape. "Loulou" explores a wider world, of an earthy potter's creative sensibility versus that of the poets she boards. The very different "Uglypuss" is unsettling, vaguely grisly, and provocative as it penetrates a cold, calculating world. The reviewer enjoys most the more poetic, and more subtly characterized, fairy tale "Bluebeard's Egg."

48 KIRTZ, MARY KRYWOKULSKY. "Mapping the Territory: Figurative Modes of Didacticism in the Novels of Margaret Atwood." Ph.D. dissertation, Case Western Reserve University, 225 pp.

Examines Atwood's novels as primarily didactic, but also mimetic, and shows how Atwood figuratively, through image patterns, settings, and characters, represents a system of ideas. Discusses Atwood's assertion of the social function of literature; examines specific constructs, especially "patterns of imagery, beginning quotations, and open endings," to establish themes; and explores her didactic use of the Gothic and allegorical in setting and character. See *Dissertation Abstracts International* 45 (1985):2531A; and 1987.76.

49 KNAPP, MONA. Review of *Second Words*. *World Literature Today* 58, no. 4 (Autumn):602-3.

Welcomes this weighty collection of Atwood's scattered lectures and writings, and her illuminating introduction and prefaces, as an indispensable companion to her novels. In the first section, which focuses on Canadian writers, Atwood argues for Canadian partisanship to counteract British and American "'cultural imperialism.'" The second section includes an excellent [1973.2] defense of *Survival*, which sparked reappraisal of "'Canlit,'" reviews of Adrienne Rich, and the insightful, funny "On Being a Woman [Writer]" and "The Curse of Eve." The third and most thought-provoking section has the best piece, "An End to Audience?" These interrelated essays document Atwood's gradual politicizing, from particular to general oppressions.

50 LANGER, BERYL DONALDSON. "Women and Literary Production: Canada and Australia." *Australian-Canadian Studies* 2 (January):70-83.

Cites Atwood as Canada's most eminent woman writer in a comparison of the prominence of women fiction writers in English Canada versus their marginality in Australia, 1970-79. Australia has no woman writer parallel to Atwood, or to Margaret Laurence; Christina Stead worked as an expatriate, outside the Australian national tradition. Though books of men's fiction outnumber women's three to one in both countries, in Canada the women's books published are 88.2 percent contemporary, but in Australia, only 62.7 percent are. Canadian women writers generally publish more books each; and, unlike in Australia, their legitimation in critical books and articles is proportionate to their presence, with Atwood receiving 86 studies in 8 years, Laurence 54. The partly true myth of Australian national identity, as masculine mateship and the noble bush worker, marginalizes women. The confusion about Canadian identity, the central mosaic image, and the rejection of rampant American individualism for British or French civilization, leave openings for women and include the feminine. And, most explicitly in Atwood, the intersecting 1960s and 1970s Canadian nationalism and feminism become metaphors for each other. Reprinted: 1987.82.

51 LAUTER, ESTELLA. "Margaret Atwood: Remythologizing Circe." In *Women as Mythmakers: Poetry and Visual Art by Twentieth-Century*

1984

Women. Bloomington: Indiana University Press, pp. 62-78; [also 192-94, 215-17].

Defines, in "Remythologizing Circe" chapter, Atwood's *re*mythologizing of Homer's *Odyssey* – not a *de*mythologizing, not Katherine Anne Porter's lightly retouched Circe, but a radical re-envisioning of the quest myth, from Circe's perspective. Atwood's Circe is an independent yet vulnerable woman, a witch/healer, a seer, a Venus partly liberated from *Survival*'s "Rapunzel Syndrome." Atwood improvises on Homer's structure. The image of Circe opening like a cut-off hand is grotesque; the final poem's envisioned second island is too open, yet powerful, a story for us to finish. The Circe poems give a mythic status to *You Are Happy*'s final sequence of the transcendent lovers. The Circe poems are not a female rebirth journey (Pratt 1981.82), not a journey, not a sham ritual, but, as in *Two-Headed Poems*, a radical rearranging of the quest myth.

Like other women poets, Atwood voices an unromantic kinship with nature ("Songs of the Transformed") and the earth ("Daybooks II").

52 LAWRENCE, JANICE. "The Thoughts of a Writer That Endure." *Washington Times* (Washington, D.C.), 11 September, Magazine sec., pp. M3, 12.

Recommends Atwood's balanced, intelligent, witty *Second Words*. "Her integrity shines through her work and she avoids stridency, even when discussing" Canadian nationalism, *Survival*, and feminism. Atwood introduces us to our northern neighbor's literature and culture, especially to Canadian poets. "Writing the Male Character" and "The Curse of Eve" call for an end to sexual stereotyping; don't miss "Canadian-American Relations" and "'Down Hairy Under'" ["Diary Down Under"].

53 LECKIE, BARBARA. Review of *Bluebeard's Egg*. *Rubicon*, no. 3 (Summer), pp. 199-201.

Appreciates these stories' "appearance/reality dialectic," subtle yet challenging politics, balance, compassionate insight, wit, and precision. The family stories that frame the collection show parents who have learned to live and affirm, despite complexities and death. The core stories, of the narrator's generation, "represent despair, fear, anxiety, ignorance and impotence in a world which seems to be spinning slowly out of control." Two anecdotes, of the sinking boat in "Scarlet Ibis" and of the girl dragged by a moving streetcar in "The Salt Garden," show the real, private yet political need to confront problems, not submit. Atwood's didacticism and politics are subtle, resonant, not preachy; her egg of story-telling remains unblemished.

54 L[EITENBERGER], I[LSE]. "Ungetrübtes Vergnügen mit Margaret Atwood." *Presse* (Vienna), 22-23 September, Spectrum sec., p. 6.

Finds *Lady Orakel* and its Anglo-Saxon sense of humor enthralling; comic literature at its best. Atwood's secure and witty writing maintains tension throughout the novel, only to reveal that the heroine is fleeing from nothing but the misery of a fat, red-haired childhood. The ability to amuse is not a strength of the young German female authors.

55 LOOSE, PATRICE K. "Critic Casts New Light on Reading." *Minneapolis Star and Tribune*, 8 April, p. G15.

Recommends *Second Words*: that Atwood reads generously and closely, and writes honestly and clearly, may make us better readers. The feminist novelist, formidable poet, and pioneering *Survival* scholar is also a remarkably versatile, perceptive critic here. Her good earlier reviews make us want those books. Though "On Being a Woman Writer" has staled a little, the reviews of Adrienne Rich's *Poems* and Kate Millett's *Flying* are still fresh. "Canadian Monsters" is surprising and fascinating. The last section, which includes "Writing the Male Character," is the best.

56 McCOMBS, JUDITH. "Researching Atwood Scholarship: Canadian Sources." *Newsletter of the Margaret Atwood Society*, no. 1, pp. 1, 3.

Recommends the excellent and extensive Canadian criticism on Atwood to U.S. researchers, citing Alan J. Horne 1979.56 and 1980.59 and Atwood's *Survival* as indispensable; and also citing Linda Sandler 1977.81, Sherrill Grace 1980.47, Arnold E. Davidson and Cathy N. Davidson 1981.23, and Sherrill [E.] Grace and Lorraine Weir 1983.56. Primary and secondary Atwood work may be obtained from Longhouse Bookstore in Toronto.

1984

57 McDONALD, LARRY. "Psychologism and the Philosophy of Progress: The Recent Fiction of MacLennan, Davies, and Atwood." *Studies in Canadian Literature* 9, no. 2:121-43.

Rejects the liberal psychologism of Hugh MacLennan, Robertson Davies, and Atwood. These three authors, in their last ten novels, address social and collective problems only in terms of healing individual psyches; consequently, in the end, they urge individual adaptation to the intolerable status quo, and, unlike George Grant, advocate the liberal ideology their books often appear to attack. Though Atwood, unlike the neo-Freudian MacLennan and the Jungian Davies, has not publicly declared her psychologism, we recall her associations with Frye, with James Reaney's mythopoeic *Alphabet*, and with archetypal criticism, all of which lead to Jung. All three novelists reduce social unrest to psychological symptoms. All the left nationalists in *Surfacing* and *Lady Oracle* are laughable psychological misfits and narcissistic fools who trivialize ideas. *Surfacing* attacks reason and glorifies primitivism. Unlike Grant, none of these novelists offers a reciprocal analysis of material and social history. *Bodily Harm* reduces political reality to a muddled conflict of states of consciousness; its protagonist promises to write articles that will "be as 'committed' as an Amnesty International report – apolitical and scrupulously silent" about the social causes of torture and repression. See errata, 1986.153.

58 McFADDEN, DAVID. "The Life of a Writer-in-Residence in a Nuclear Age." *Quill and Quire* 50, no. 2 (January):24.

Praises *Bluebeard's Egg*, in a parenthetical aside to his article on a writer's life after TV's nuclear *The Day After*, as Atwood's "richest and most rewarding book" and "a big breakthrough for [her] both artistically and in terms of basic human understanding."

59 McL[ELLAN], L[EIGH]. "Salamander Press." *Fine Print* 10, no. 3 (July):97-98.

Appreciates Atwood's forceful poetry in a review of two Salamander Press limited editions, hand-printed at The Nightshade Press. Approves Glenn Goluska's red-and-black, initial-impaling design for the violent images of the September 1981 *Notes Towards a Poem That Can Never Be Written*, but not the high price for "undistinguished machinemade papers"; appreciates Atwood's snake lore and "usual no-holds-barred style" in the November 1983 *Snake Poems*, and the appropriate snaky typeface, accordion fold, and crushed dark green Japanese cover paper. Provides colophon for both.

60 MALLINSON, JEAN. *Margaret Atwood*. Toronto: ECW Press, 65 pp.

Appreciatively analyzes the development of Atwood's poetic form and themes, from the early, uncollected poems through *True Stories*. Traces poetic influences, especially of James Reaney's Gothic on the early verse, Jay Macpherson on *Double Persephone*, T.S. Eliot's *The Wasteland* on *The Circle Game*, and Sylvia Plath. Atwood writes analytic, reflective lyrics, in modernist rather than imagist free verse. Rebuts the misreadings of Davey 1977.12 and Skelton 1977.83; recommends Mandel 1977.51, McCombs 1981.66, Djwa 1981.28, Onley 1974.33, Irvine 1981.52, and Bowering 1981.9 on Atwood's Canadian, Gothic, feminist, and feminine elements. Appreciates the postcatastrophic time, implied narrative, and disappearing speaker of "This Is a Color Photo"; the female Gothic of "Speeches for Dr. Frankenstein"; the flawless mask lyrics of *The Journals of Susanna Moodie*; the family poems of *Procedures for Underground*; and the exuberantly inventive, Metaphysical, story-telling *Power Politics*. *You Are Happy* moves from *Power Politics* leftovers, through the high-spirited animal songs and the Homeric "Circe/Mud" mask lyrics, to the immanence and realistic affirmations of "There Is Only One of Everything" and "Late August." Those final poems begin the more real, less Gothic, sometimes shared epiphanies of daily life, family, and love that continue in *Two-Headed Poems* and *True Stories*; see, for example, "Apple Jelly" [Daybooks II] and "Variations on the Word Sleep." Provides biography and selected bibliography. Reprinted: 1985.70.

61 MANION, EILEEN. "Neither Rain nor Sleet Deters Atwood Fans." *Gazette* (Montreal), 24 November, p. I1.

Reports on Atwood's overflow audience, despite a cold, rainy night and a transit strike, at the McGill University Literary Imagination reading; and quotes Atwood on: Canadian cultural self-consciousness; Canadian and Quebecois literature; U.S. versus Canadian politics; the women's movement, jobs, and censorship; men's versus women's power fantasies in pornography and romance; and the consumer society in *The Edible Woman* versus the factual Third World coup in *Bodily Harm*.

1984

62 ____. Review of *Bluebeard's Egg* and *Murder in the Dark*. *Literary Criterion* 20, no. 1:259-63.

Recommends the compassionate yet ironic *Bluebeard's Egg*, and finds the more experimental *Murder in the Dark* disturbing. Atwood gives us semi-divorced, semi-committed, ambivalent, indeterminate relationships, where men evade responsibility, as in "Spring Song of the Frogs," and women struggle, deny, drift, or rebel, as in the title story, "Scarlet Ibis," "The Salt Garden," and "Uglypuss." How can Sally, in the title story, gain power over Bluebeard, if she casts her husband as the egg, and the egg is independent of her? The lighter "Loulou" defines relationships and art, as does the more poignant "The Sunrise," with its obsessive, vulnerable artist, Yvonne. In the four childhood and adolescent stories, the narrator struggles to define herself in a modern world where Bluebeard's chambers are thrown open. *Murder in the Dark* has equally disturbing metaphors of writing, as in its title piece, and nastiness and power in the "'sexual politics'" of "Liking Men" and "Iconography." Atwood's understanding of human destructiveness, as in "Bread," "Making Poison," and "Instructions for the Third Eye," doesn't "promote optimism or complacency about our fate." Reprinted: 1985.71.

63 MARTENS, CATHRINE. "Mother-Figures in *Surfacing* and *Lady Oracle*: An Interview with Margaret Atwood." *American Studies in Scandinavia* 16, no. 1:45-54.

Interviews Atwood after her February [1979?] University of Oslo lecture: Atwood explains myth and form in *Lady Oracle*; comments briefly on *Surfacing*'s search for both parents; and contrasts Canadian to American ideas of self, women, and women writers. Atwood sees *Lady Oracle* as "a search for 'the real mother,'" like finding the Great Mother at the end of the labyrinth; and as "a parody of the Gothic Romance" that originated in [Charlotte Brontë's] *Jane Eyre*. The Gothic Romance has two men, one seeming good but really evil, and one the reverse; and two women, one the orphan heroine, and the other a mad or evil woman, who competes with and may try to kill the heroine. *Lady Oracle* also comes from an Ann Landers column that linked a daughter's fatness to her mother's relationship with her. *Lady Oracle* has the mother monster, and two good surrogate mothers, Aunt Lou and the Spiritualist fraud; the Brownie leader is also a good mother. As often happens in mother-monster books by women, the father is eclipsed, not there. *Lady Oracle* is told by the heroine to the man she hits with a bottle. Superimposing mythic stereotypes, Joan sees herself as an orphan, and her husband as a killer.

Though Canadian readers do confuse writers with their characters, Canadian women writers do outsell the men; our British tradition includes women novelists; and Canadian women have been less suppressed and less Freudianized than in the States. Because Canada is a small country, "we see things from the maid's point of view"; in *The Seventh Seal*, we'd be the practical, sceptical servant, and America the romanticizing master.

64 MILROY, SARAH. "Pachter's Homage." *Canadian Forum* 64 (November):33-34.

Praises highly Charles Pachter's silkscreen 120-copy edition of Atwood's *The Journals of Susanna Moodie*, first displayed in fall 1984 at the Art Gallery of Ontario; praises also his early, promising edition of Atwood's *The Circle Game*. Pachter's sensitive and vigorous prints honor his longtime friend-and-collaborator's poetic themes of the alienated Canadian pioneer, which parallel her Canadian fiction. Pachter also draws from the historic Moodie's work to add, usually appropriately, some light touches and humour.

65 MINER, VALERIE. "Margaret Atwood and the Roots of Defensiveness." *Christian Science Monitor*, 7 September, p. B4.

Finds *Second Words* "written in a distant voice, by a critic passionately concerned about the world, but somehow immune to it"; the reviewer yearns for community and "a compassionate synthesis" instead. Atwood apparently found her voice on the edge, but will her role of moral ringmaster lead to self-parody? She is spare, intelligent, and ironic, but sometimes starkly defensive. The first section will interest Canadians and those who know Canadian literature. The second section describes the *Survival*-era pyrotechnics and Atwood's own reunion with Canada. She keeps her distance from issues; she calls the writer and reader "'he,'" and rigidly resists feminism, though she ardently promotes women's achievements. Is her defensiveness a paranoia that community would undermine her self-image?

66 MIROLLA, MICHAEL. "*Interlunar* Sparkles with Clarity, Insight." *Gazette* (Montreal), 13 October, p. I2.

1984

Praises *Interlunar*'s clarity, transcendence of the personal and the provincial, and the totemism that gives her poetry its haunting mystery. Atwood connects our animate selves to the inanimate world, and everyday life to ritual; her work therefore often seems pessimistic and brutal, with little hope. Although in almost every poem some metaphor or image "strikes out at the reader," these poems do grapple with the mute unanswering world. Atwood digs to the sometimes unpretty or unknowable "roots of that silence," as we must, "to break the webs that" frustrate us.

67 MITCHELL, ADRIAN. "Hotch-Potch and Hop-Scotch." *CRNLE Reviews Journal*, no. 1 (May), pp. 1-3.

Why publish *Second Words*? Apparently, to document Atwood's views. She admires scrapbook, patchwork quilt, diary, asides, and hotch-potch presentations that "achieve coherence through discontinuity"; her inclination to seek pattern and myth where none apparently are emerges in her early review of [James Reaney's] *Alphabet*. Her piece on Frye is really a defence against his having influenced her. *Second Words* does show something of Atwood's world, wit, and sensitivity; and lets us trace changes and characteristic images, conceits, and puns used as structures. There's enough to delight the chronic reader, or original audiences, but not enough on Atwood's creative processes or Canadian perceptions.

68 MORLEY, PATRICIA. "Atwood's Poetic Vision Still Clear." *Citizen* (Ottawa), 19 May, p. [43].

Welcomes *Interlunar* and describes its Absurdist, existential themes. Atwood's vision is still clear, hard, and chilling, with beautiful or ominous images made stronger by their subtle metaphysical or psychological analogies. "Snake Poems" depict "the human condition without the leap of faith." The three "Interlunar" sections develop a Theatre of the Absurd or existential vision, like Sartre or Camus, first with threatening images of pain, loss, and death. The next group has feminist poems of anger or sadness; some, like "A Massacre Before It Is Heard About," are coldly beautiful. The last section returns to the meaningless human condition, as in "A Painting of One Location on the Plain."

69 MURRAY, HEATHER MURIEL. "Language and Land in English-Canadian Prose Fiction." Ph.D. dissertation, York University.

Though Canadian criticism often uses dichotomies, as of nature/culture, "the terrain of English-Canadian fiction" is better viewed as a "continuum of land values," from city to a mid-point pseudo-wilderness (cottage or rural) to wilderness. "Onto this continuum of land values is mapped a spectrum of linguistic values"; the city may be the place of art, or cliché, and so on. Examines, in texts from Atwood and ten other English Canadian writers, 1830-1980, the thematic and stylistic development of these ideas. See *Dissertation Abstracts International* 45:3133A. See 1985.75 and 1986.175.

70 "New Books." *Queen's Quarterly* 91, no. 2 (Summer):491.

Atwood's rich tribute to Canada's creative spirit will become the standard anthology. Her up-to-date *New Oxford Book of Canadian Verse in English* represents both sexes fairly, and gives strong coverage to the 1950s, 1960s, and 1970's. Her intelligent and free-wheeling introduction calls Canadian poetry unique, "'spiky, tough, flexible, various, and vital.'" Her selections justify that claim.

71 NORRIS, KEN. "The Iconography of the Imagination: *Alphabet*." In *The Little Magazine in Canada 1925-80: Its Role in the Development of Modernism and Post-Modernism in Canadian Poetry*. Toronto: ECW Press, pp. 82-96 passim.

Quotes, in a discussion of Northrop Frye's criticism, the mythopoeic poets, and James Reaney's *Alphabet*, Atwood on Reaney's originality; and [from her 1971 "Eleven Years of Alphabet," reprinted in *Second Words*] on *Alphabet*'s programme and its Canadian form. Mentions *Alphabet*'s Atwood poems and its Eli Mandel 1962.1 review of her *Double Persephone* chapbook.

72 OSBORNE, FRANCINE. "Margaret Atwood: Un livre d'atmosphère plutôt que d'action." *Presse* (Montréal), 14 January, p. C4.

Marquée au corps, the French-Canadian translation of *Bodily Harm*, is built on the creation of atmosphere rather than action. The story gives a dim view of Canada's exterior politics with the third world. Indicates page numbers of specific mistakes in the translation.

1984

73 OSTRIKER, ALICIA. "'What Are Patterns For?': Anger and Polarization in Women's Poetry." *Feminist Studies* 10, no. 3 (Fall):485-503.

Compares *Power Politics*, Diane Wakoski's *The George Washington Poems*, and Anne Sexton's "The Jesus Papers," as radical, experimental, powerful but ultimately entrapped critiques of gender-polarized patterns, offering an intensification of women's anger, not catharsis. In *Power Politics* dominance-victimization patterns reverse, male-female and female-male – but still are patterns; the slideshow structure defies time and resolution. In all three, the sexes are locked in inescapable power struggles; the poet's authority is a dominance weapon; and the heavily surreal modes make polarizations seem arbitrary, questionable, ridiculous. Revised: 1986.185.

74 [PARKS, JOY.] *"Interlunar* Transcends Atwood's Horizons." *Herizons* 2, no. 6 (October):45.

Praises the tough, demanding *Interlunar* as perhaps the best work of the prolific, internationally recognized Atwood. *Interlunar* "probes deep, tearing at the scabs of complacency," destroying our defenses, and opening our psyches. The "Snake Poems" transcend Biblical and Freudian concepts to show the snake as an innocent scapegoat of human evil. Atwood's skill is in her terse, essential, powerful language, that readers must meet head on.

75 PHILIPS, DEBORAH. "How to Spot a Killer." *City Limits* (London), 2-8 March, p. 17.

Interviews Atwood, who is writing a novel in Norfolk, England. Atwood discusses autobiography versus personae; popular romance and traditional Gothic novels; men's power and women's fears in "Women's Novels" and "Liking Men"; and male violence versus [Ronald] Reagan's posturing. Atwood views the Greenham Common women favorably, but rejects the "Woman" with a capital W that assumes all women are identical: "'Some women are horrible. I reserve their right to be horrible.'"

76 POWE, B.W. "'How to Act': An Essay on Margaret Atwood." In *A Climate Charged.* Oakville, Ont.; New York; London: Mosaic Press, pp. 143-54.

Reprint, slightly altered, of 1983.104. Mentions, in a brief addendum, that *Second Words*, *Murder in the Dark*, and other work show Atwood still at a pivotal point.

77 "Prince Myshkin, Gigi, and Dr. Johnston." *New York Times Book Review*, 2 December, p. 42.

Asks Atwood, and other prominent persons, what character from a novel or from non-fiction they would most want to be, and why. Atwood responds: "*To be* rather than *to have written*? Fiction? Not many women characters in fiction have a very good time." Elizabeth Bennet, in [Jane Austen's] *Pride and Prejudice*, manages, within limits. "Professor Challenger, in Arthur Conan Doyle's *The Lost World*? He gets travel, pterodactyls," and temper tantrums, and acts like a pig to women. "Nonfiction? Lady Hester Stanhope. Or Anna Jameson, who" went into the nineteenth-century north woods with her parasol.

78 REDEKOP, MAGDALENE. "Charms and Riddles." *Canadian Forum* 63 (January):30-31.

Appreciates *Bluebeard's Egg* highly. Skating on thin ice, like Yvonne in "The Sunrise," Atwood's people inhabit "'the freedom of the present tense, this sliding edge,'" as they look for something worth seeing. Atwood's story-telling voice is eerily alienating; her stories are haunted by ghosts "not yet dead"; her ironic inversions correct Betty's optimism and Sally's illusions, and make us "sense the darkness in the corners." Atwood alternates between surface and depth: "The more demonic and threatening the background, the flatter the characters." While the egg in the title gothic story can never be put together again, the final "Unearthing Suite" affirms what is worth seeing: there we are curiously most included in the father's marvel that we are excluded from seeing directly; for, like the ghostly narrator, "we are unable to re-enter the paradisal world of our first parents." The mother, who sees the dropping as a sign of grace, restores the charm to the parents' riddle. Reprinted: 1988.41.

79 REICHART, MANUELA. "Kritik in Kürze." *Zeit* (Hamburg), 26 October, p. 71.

Admires *Lady Orakel*, especially the heroine who fakes her own death and invents a new identity for herself because "'the truth was not convincing.'" Atwood has created an intriguing story of a passionate and clever liar. But the curiosity aroused by trying to discover what is a lie and what is truth soon vanishes, and the trivial ending disappoints.

80 ROLENS, LINDA. "The Joy of Margaret Atwood as a Critic and Essayist." *Los Angeles Times Book Review*, 25 March, p. 7.

Enjoys Atwood's accomplished *Second Words*. Her considered, critical appreciations enlighten, rather than entertain, and make you want to read the books she reviews. She reads Anne Sexton's letters for their life, not death, and Marge Piercy's *Woman on the Edge of Time* as a Utopia. Atwood's Canadian perspective shapes her sense of American fiction. She handles women in novels with humor and a cold eye – and, in "The Curse of Eve," with a devastating and hilarious list of female prototypes. The only strident anger here is about being Canadian. Atwood moves effortlessly "through the mine field of feminism on being a woman writer."

81 ROSENBERG, JEROME. *Margaret Atwood*. Twayne World Author Series, Canadian Literature, edited by Robert Lecker, no. 740. Boston: Twayne Publishers, G.K. Hall & Co., 184 pp.

Appreciates Atwood's affirmations and her double vision of our human balance between the circle games of order and the dark truths of chaos, time, and death, in nine books of poetry, five novels, and *Dancing Girls*. Traces her literary career from juvenilia, *Double Persephone*, the manuscript "My Poetic Principles on Oct. 29 1962," and the production of *The Circle Game*, to her present canonized but attacked celebrity status. Details Frank Davey's, Robin Mathews's, and Atwood's positions on the controversial, timely *Survival*; discusses her synthetic world view, feminism, nationalism, and concern for a third alternative to killers and victims, in *Second Words* and elsewhere.

Explicates "The Circle Game's" Prufrockian fears, garrison mentality rituals, and final releasing cry for breaking all the circles that dehumanize us. Explains *The Animals in That Country* as an ecological critique of America's rampant commercialism and Faustian technology, and of the Americanization of Canada. Finds Atwood's poetic transmutations of the historic Susanna Moodie's two books a major and compelling achievement, but cold. Finds a more political or more "compassionate, humane, and affirmative" voice in Atwood's later poetry: finds the controversial *Power Politics* clever and political, but limited and intensely pessimistic; welcomes *You Are Happy's* progression from numbed alienation through the grotesquely one-dimensional "Circe/Mud" affair to a final freer, ambiguous joy. Praises *Two-Headed Poems*'s enlarged love, warmth, and compassion; and explicates the political allusions and the Julian Jaynes theories, from *The Origin of Consciousness in the Breakdown of the Bicameral Mind*, underlying its title sequence and its pivotal "The Right Hand Fights the Left." *True Stories* also ends with affirmations, even in a world of sewers and torture.

Assesses pessimism versus affirmations in five novels: *The Edible Woman* ends realistically, with no escape from the circle. *Surfacing*, which may be Atwood's masterwork, is not only a woman's, but a universal, Conradian journey, through multi-layered stories to a final triumphant, though necessarily partial, knowledge of one's humanity. Discusses *Lady Oracle*'s mother/daughter conflict, multiple genres, identities, and fantasies; and *Dancing Girls*'s themes of the divided self, modern fears and destruction, and "Giving Birth's" creative affirmation. *Life Before Man*'s banal melodrama depicts our spiritually empty lives. *Bodily Harm*'s political realism ends with a spiritual transformation, but in a brutally pessimistic imprisonment.

Provides chronology and briefly annotated selected bibliography. Reprints, slightly altered, 1979.85.

82 ROSENBERG, KAREN. "On Becoming a Writer." *In These Times* 8, no. 31 (8-21 August):18.

Appreciates *Second Words* as a portrait of the writer. Atwood's reviews almost let one hear the intensity and concentration with which she reads. A former student of Northrop Frye, she is drawn to writers who create myths. She poses the dilemma of oppression and identity wisely; see *Survival*'s basic victim positions. Initially, Atwood was uncomfortable with the women's movement; she still, and rightly, resents critics who demand role models, or "the feminist equivalent of social realism." Her understanding of oppression began at Harvard. She has moved from being profoundly apolitical to seeing literature as a moral and ethical guardian, in "An End to Audience?" which may be the strongest essay here.

83 RUSSELL, BRANDON. "Eavesdropping." *Times Educational Supplement* (London), 17 August, p. 21.

1984

Features, in a four-book review, the eminent poet's *Dancing Girls*. Successful short stories eavesdrop, and shock. In Atwood's fresh, chilly, shadowy stories, ordinary people sense, suddenly and disastrously, the separate identities of others. Images and sacrifice – usually of women to men – blood, infidelities, and birth, are plentiful. Atwood, who has Dorothy Parker's cynicism, but does not manipulate her wit, adeptly shapes irrecoverable disintegrations of private worlds in "Training" and "The Man from Mars."

84 SKELTON, ROBIN. "Recent Canadian Poetry." *Poetry* 144, no. 5 (August): 297-99, 307.

A round-up review that begins by praising Atwood's poetry and ends in praising *The New Oxford Book of Canadian Verse in English* as the major Canadian anthology. Atwood's sharp images, clear narrative, and haunted imagination are revealed in ["Some Objects of Wood and Stone: ii)] Pebbles"; her *Murder in the Dark* is entirely brilliant; *The New Oxford* has a good introduction, and not one bad poem, however chosen.

85 SMITH, JEAN. "A Question of Violence." *Scotsman* (Edinburgh), 9 January, p. 6.

Interviews Atwood, whose *Bodily Harm* and *Surfacing* are still surprisingly unknown here, despite her spending a year in Scotland and this winter in Norfolk. Atwood comments on stereotypes of feminists, overt versus mental violence in her novels, and becoming a Canadian writer and poet.

86 SÖDERLIND, SYLVIA. "Identity and Metamorphosis in Canadian Fiction Since the Sixties." In *A Sense of Place: Essays in Post-Colonial Literatures*. Edited by Britta Olinder. Göteborg, Sweden: The English Department, Gothenburg University, pp. 78-84.

Discusses *Surfacing* as one of four Canadian novels whose thematic progression represents anglophone Canada's late 1960s-1970s progression from a postcolonial search for identity/difference to the complex, magic possibilities of metamorphosis. In *Surfacing*, which is "on the surface," the orphaned heroine searches for identity in a regressive metamorphosis that ends in her becoming a place, which is "an almost complete loss of identity." Atwood's equation of identity and language makes the individual quest collective and cultural. Metaphor involves clear perceptions of identity/difference; Atwood's metaphoric "metamorphosis remains on the surface."

87 STERNHELL, CAROL. "Copulating with William: Margaret Atwood's Modest Virtues." *Village Voice*, 20 March, p. 39.

Finds *Second Words* partly admirable, partly unremarkable and repetitive: "reading Margaret Atwood is a bit like copulating with William [of *Life Before Man*]; I admire her craft, and her poet's ear for language, without being swept off my feet." Though Atwood is politically engaged, her novel characters seem hermetic and indifferent to others. *Second Words*'s book reviews are "of the most ephemeral sort, always accomplished and intelligent but never remarkable." The longer pieces, like "The Curse of Eve," "An End to Audience?" and "Canadian-American Relations," are witty and original. Atwood's dominant theme "is the relationship of colonizer and colonized"; her most powerful essays examine Canadian identity.

88 STIEG, ELIZABETH. Review of *Interlunar*. *Canadian Book Review Annual*:212.

Praises Atwood's powerful poetry of our unconscious, instinctual side, and her magic incantations that create what is described. *Interlunar*'s darkness symbolizes not only fear and death, but also, like the snake, regeneration, and the descent before renewal. "Snake Poems" initiate the recurrent theme of "transformation and rebirth," which the feared and attacked snake symbolizes. "*Interlunar* leads its reader through the darkness of savagery and death, the life of instinct and intuition, in the belief that" these forces are more powerful than the purely intellectual or rational. Atwood shows us the darkness we fear, powerfully and with "a strange and wonderful beauty."

89 STROBL, INGRID. "Heldinnen und Lügen." *Emma* (Cologne), October, p. 46.

Lady Orakel is an entangled comedy that succeeds at pulling the reader's leg. The protagonist constantly lies to the reader, while simultaneously revealing lies that are part of her own multiple lives. The novel is a dream-like, artistic maze that cleverly discloses bits and pieces of the truth over time. *Lady Orakel* is a tragedy disguised as a comedy.

1984

90 STROMBERG, KYRA. "Die Flucht aus der Identität: Gedichte von Margaret Atwood und ihr Roman *Lady Orakel*." *Süddeutsche Zeitung* (Munich), 7 November, p. 48.

Recommends the German translations of *True Stories* and *Lady Oracle*. *Wahre Geschichten* (*True Stories*) is the first book of Atwood's poetry to be translated into German. For Atwood, poetry is the heart of language. These sceptical love poems contain her strongest insights, that penetrate everyday situations with serious intensity. *Lady Orakel* is a comical and profound story of a woman trying to escape her identity. The escape-artist heroine moves amusingly between her different personifications. Waldhoff's translation of *Lady Orakel* reads well, but he falters with the genitive case.

91 STUEWE, PAUL. "Thematic Criticism in Practise." In *Clearing the Ground: English-Canadian Literature after Survival*. Toronto: Proper Tales Press, pp. 15-19.

Rejects *Survival*'s misuse of thematic criticism, and approves D[ouglas] G[ordon] Jones's well-supported, ethical *Butterfly on Rock*, in a discussion of five Canadian thematic critics whose work has been negatively influenced by Northrop Frye's remarks. Finds *Survival*'s goals limited, its assumptions of national identity grandiose but dubious, and its sweeping assertions ill-supported; "one would dismiss it out of hand" if *Survival* weren't already widely taught and effusively recommended.

92 [STUTTAFORD, GENEVIEVE]. "PW Forecasts." *Publishers Weekly* 225, no. 1 (6 January):81.

Though Atwood's wide-ranging *Second Words* lacks the intensity and intelligence of Adrienne Rich's criticism, *Second Words* does provide coherent, accessible, even-handed opinions, on creating female characters, on the writer's role in society, and on Canadian literary identity. As Atwood says, her criticism is secondary to her creative work.

93 TAYLOR, ROBERT. "The View from Canada through Atwood Eyes." *Boston Globe*, 15 February, p. 71.

Approves Atwood's fine *Second Words* and nonexclusive concern for Canadian nationalism and women's rights. Some essays deal with writers familiar here, like Marge Piercy and E.L. Doctorow; many with those, like John Newlove and Marie-Claire Blais, unfamiliar to shamefully ethnocentric Americans. Except for a reply to a critic, the longer essays engage Atwood's imagination more than the short reviews do. The essays on Canadian humor and Canadian monsters are illuminating; the scholarly H. Rider Haggard essay is solid but lacks Atwood's strong and brilliantly individual voice, which developed around 1970.

94 THIEME, JOHN. "Beyond History: Margaret Atwood's *Surfacing* and Robert Kroetsch's *Badlands*." In *Re-visions of Canadian Literature*. Papers Presented at a Seminar in Canadian Literature held at the University of Leeds, April 1984. Edited by Shirley Chew. Leeds: Institute of Bibliography and Textual Criticism, University of Leeds, pp. 71-87.

Compares Atwood's 1972 *Surfacing* and Robert Kroetsch's strikingly similar yet complexly different 1975 *Badlands*. As *Survival* explains, Canadian animal stories identify with the animal victims; *Surfacing's* isolated female quester and senselessly slaughtered Canadian heron invert both the normal quest story and the imperialistic American hunting story. Both *Surfacing* and *Badlands* use animals to represent an integrated, prehistoric Canada; both are based on a series of partly shared binary oppositions; both investigate a possible prehistoric monism; both explore gender roles as products of nurture, not nature; both end with women's returns to origins. But where *Surfacing's* female quester moves back beyond binary oppositions that include male/female to a distinctively female prehistory, *Badlands's* male and female questers journey back to a prehistory that can't be classified male or female. Both novels try to avoid perpetuating history's victor/victim dualities.

95 TREGEBOV, RHEA. Review of *Interlunar*. *Quill and Quire* 50, no. 9 (September):82.

Though Atwood may have acquired fresh power by turning outward to political subjects in *True Stories*, *Interlunar* returns to more conventional subjects, "the isolated inner world, the pain of mortality and loss." Though there is rich language here, Atwood still makes spare rhetoric and syntax work, as in "Lesson on Snakes." Perhaps "because of the darkness the book confronts," Atwood's very authoritative voice

1984

is shored up with allusions; but in "Letter from Persephone," perhaps the strongest poem, the classical reference is extraneous.

96 TROWELL, IAN. "Cool Atwood, Playful Layton and the Poetry of Love." *London* (Ontario) *Free Press*, 23 November, p. A15.

Finds Atwood's poetry, in a three-book review, "calculating, clinical and fundamentally cold," like Alex Colville's paintings. Her humor, "humility, passion and compassion, seem . . . to rise from permafrost. Appropriately Canadian"; and Atwood is peerless at it. Though "her freeze-dried followers" among our intelligensia will like *Interlunar*, most people want warmth. Then, too, shouldn't poetry make sense, as random snatches from ["Giselle in Daytime"] and "Keep" do not? The reviewer finds [Leonard] Cohen's love poem, "Now of Sleeping," beautiful.

97 VanSPANCKEREN, KATHRYN, ed. *Newsletter of the Margaret Atwood Society*, no. 1, [4] pp.

Contains Judith McCombs 1984.56 on obtaining primary and secondary Atwood material from Canada; a brief description of the Atwood Session, Reading, and the Society's second annual meeting at the 1984 Modern Language Association Convention; news of current and forthcoming books, articles, conference papers, and sessions on Atwood; and Atwood's current reading and travel schedule.

98 WAELTI-WALTERS, JENNIFER. "Double-Read: On Margaret Atwood's *Bodily Harm*." *Room of One's Own* 8, no. 4:116-22.

Rejects the "overt misogyny" of *Bodily Harm*, which reinforces "stereotyping and oppression of women." The paperback blurb writer and the critics have praised *Bodily Harm*'s comedy, compassion and love. French 1981.34 did partly see its "'overriding pessimism'" about men running the world. This reviewer found no compassion, or love, or comedy. "*Bodily Harm* is dominated by its women characters and they are all portrayed as defective." Rennie is viewed as a "faulty love object/sex machine." Jocasta is a "potential lesbian"; Lora a boring, "aging hippie" – all the women are victims, brutalized because of their sex, as the epigraph from John Berger's *Ways of Seeing* suggests. The men use their hands to harm; "the women's hands are cut off." Women's books are much more apt to be misread than men's, because readers are trained in male-dominated approaches.

99 WEIR, LORRAINE. "Third Eye." *Canadian Literature*, no. 103 (Winter), pp. 86-87.

Appreciates Atwood's recurrent themes of sexual politics, violence, and the duplicity of language in the deeply Borgesian *Murder in the Dark*. Like [Jorge Luis] Borges's writings, these ambiguously subtitled "short fictions and prose poems" refuse genre distinctions, are complete despite their brevity, and suddenly reveal "the triviality of plot," custom, and cliché, and the fantastic in the ordinary, as in "Before the War," with its tales of a lost golden age. Atwood's resolutely plain language refuses to become "'art.'" Belief in "the cherished norms of Realist fiction and bourgeois heterosexuality" produces victimage in "Happy Endings." Power produces fear in "Iconography." "Liking Men" and "Him" argue for faith and forgiveness; Atwood's visionary eye, like her "probing, mocking, cleansing language . . . invites us to see the malignancy of our world and still hope."

100 WOLFE, LINDA. "Woman of Letters Rummages among Her Life's Writings." *Philadelphia Inquirer*, 1 April, p. P5.

Wishes for a smaller, more selective *Second Words*, for all Atwood's readers, not just the scholarly ones. Her rummagings, and introductory dislike of writing criticism, make the reviewer uneasy. "There is simply too much filler here": college-magazine and over-enthusiastic reviews of insignificant books, a torturous academic study of H. Rider Haggard's "Superwoman," and a long polemic rebutting a *Survival* critic. But there are also excellent, insightful, cunning essays and speeches: "An End to Audience?" "Witches," "Writing the Male Character," and some "truly illuminating book reviews," including "Timothy Findley: *The Wars*" and "Reaney Collected."

1985

1 ADACHI, KEN. "Atwood Takes a Chance and Wins." *Toronto Star*, 13 October, p. E1.

Interviews Atwood in her new Toronto home, after "a wave of rave reviews" for *The Handmaid's Tale*: Atwood discusses writing *The Handmaid's Tale*; its links to history, Orwell's *Nineteen Eighty-Four*, Aldous Huxley's *Brave New World*, and Swift's *A Modest Proposal*; its handmaid's nun-like, limiting habit; her novel's compulsory sex and birth scenes; the optimism of Orwell's Newspeak section and of her

["Historical Notes"], Offred's survival, and the underground dissidents. Atwood bears witness from her Amnesty and P.E.N. International work, and spreads the CanLit gospel, as in her last year's course on southern Ontario Gothic.

2 ____. "Atwood's 'Futuristic Fiction' Intense, Compelling." *Toronto Star*, 29 September, p. G11.

Celebrates *The Handmaid's Tale* as disturbing, authoritative, realistic, compellingly "impossible to lay aside," and Atwood's most audacious book. The suspense of this grim narrative is mesmeric; the technique flawless; its surprises are never melodramatic. Perhaps a feminist theological novel, it is didactic, mythic, historic, evoking Swift's *A Modest Proposal*, Genesis, Orwell's *Nineteen Eighty-Four*, and Doris Lessing's satires of totalitarianism. But above all *The Handmaid's Tale* is a pleasurably, furiously engaging novel that never forgets the here and now, the flowers shimmering against the grim violence. The wry "Historical Notes" does not dispel the book's "prophecy and warning."

3 ____. "Budding Essayists Get Crack at Grants." *Toronto Star*, 7 October, p. B5.

Describes *The Handmaid's Tale*'s launching party, and reports that Atwood will edit a CanLit cookbook to benefit the Canadian Centre of International P.E.N. and the Writers' Development Trust.

4 "Atwood Signs Three-Book Contract with Houghton." *Publishers Weekly* 228, no. 5 (2 August), p. 34.

Reports that Atwood has left Simon & Schuster and signed a contract for *The Handmaid's Tale*, a collection of short stories, and one of poetry. Nan Talese, who edited Atwood's last four novels at Simon & Schuster, is now Houghton's editor-in-chief.

5 BAILEY, BRUCE. "NFB Looks at Master Sellers." *Gazette* (Montreal), 30 April, p. B9.

A two-film review, of Barry Greenwald's *Pitchmen* and Michael Rubbo's forthcoming *Margaret Atwood: Once in August*. Rubbo tries too hard to probe Atwood, who says, on-camera, in one of the film's best moments, that his problem is that he treats her as a mysterious problem. Atwood's "'family'" also tease Rubbo, by filming "themselves doing mock interviews with bags over their heads." Though Rubbo ends modestly, feeling he's seen Atwood only through binoculars, most audiences will find satisfying insights.

6 BARBOUR, DOUGLAS. "Canadian Poetry Today." *Landfall*, no. 154 (June), pp. 196-201 passim.

Finds Atwood's popularity deserved, and her generation still creating the most exciting and experimental poetry, as in her cool ironic poems, and in *Murder in the Dark*'s fragmented prose poems that question narrative convention. An overview of Canada's flourishing poetry scene, from one who has reviewed more than 300 poetry books in the past two years.

7 BLACK, BARBARA. "Mustn't Let Down Guard Atwood Warns Women in *The Handmaid's Tale*." *Gazette* (Montreal), 24 October, p. B9.

Interviews Atwood in Montreal: Atwood talks about writing *The Handmaid's Tale*, censorship, enforced parenthood, Blaise 1985.9, Marcel Masse's resignation as minister for communications, being president of P.E.N., teaching southern Ontario gothic literature, and her travels and travel writing.

8 BLAIN, JOANNE. "Watch Out, Women! Return to Child-Bearer Role Isn't Far-Fetched, Atwood Insists." *Vancouver Sun*, 15 October (sic 1984), p. B1.

Interviews Atwood in Vancouver: Atwood talks about declining North American birth rates, and incentives versus penalties for childbearing; *The Handmaid's Tale*'s realism; Canada's quality legislation for women versus the United States' defeated Equal Rights Amendment; and writing novels.

9 BLAISE, CLARK. "Atwood Fires Poisoned Valentine at U.S. Males." *Gazette* (Montreal), 5 October, p. B7.

Reacts against *The Handmaid's Tale* as a poisoned valentine to American male lust and vanity. Though the whole book is "powerfully appropriate to its circumstances," and the narrator is credible and insightful, "Fred and Serena Joy are oafs," and the apparatus of oppression is unworthy of the modern state. Men who could take over the United States and imprison its women would be much more terrifying than these "Reagan Kitchen-aides" and "Moral

1985

Majoritarians." Though every perversion here exists, and right-wing millenialists do put down women thus, *The Handmaid's Tale's* adolescent picture of masculinity and inadequate villains keep it from Orwell's company, and from this slightly chauvinistic reviewer's appreciation. The witty ["Historical Notes"] is the most frightening part, for it shows that no lesson or redemption is permanent.

10 BLAU DuPLESSIS, RACHEL. *Writing Beyond the Ending: Narrative Strategies of Twentieth-Century Women Writers*. Everywoman: Studies in History, Literature, and Culture, edited by Susan Gubar and Joan Hoff-Wilson. Bloomington: Indiana University Press, pp. 110-12.

The "Circe/Mud Poems" use two revisionary, decolonizing strategies: their basic displacement moves towards delegitimation, the creation of an unexpected story. The man bears only the Homeric plot; the woman oscillates between the dominant, unstoppable Homeric plot and the inarticulate, muted plot. *Survival's* victim positions one and two correspond to displacement; three and four, to delegitimation. Delegitimation is still, as Atwood's [1981 "Midnight Birds," reprinted in *Second Words*] review of black American women writers suggests, a dialogue between margin and center, Gauls and Romans.

11 BLOOM, HAROLD, ed. "Margaret Atwood." In *Twentieth-Century American Literature*. Vol. 1. New York: Chelsea House Publishers, pp. 258-64.

After a brief biographical sketch, excerpted from: Piercy 1973.72; Lecker 1981.64; Mandel 1983.84; DeMott 1973.21; Stone 1980.129; Guédon 1983.58; McCombs 1981.66; Gioia 1982.67; Woodcock 1983.147; reprinted from Grosskurth 1973.33; and reprinted in part from Woodcock 1981.111, pp. 236-41.

12 BRADY, ELIZABETH. Review of *Bluebeard's Egg. Fiddlehead*, no. 144 (Summer), pp. 88-90.

Appreciates *Bluebeard's Egg's* new celebration and wonder, in its two parental stories; and the revealing, realistic, accomplished stories of Atwood's own estranged generation. "Significant Moments in the Life of My Mother," with its double narrators, stories, exegesis, and commentary, is "about the fabrication of fictions – in life and art"; and about the secure, rooted, rural family world of the mother, versus the fractured world the daughter inherits. "Unearthing Suite" elaborates the grown writer's alienation and her two parents' vital, harmonious, reverential celebrations of Nature. "Bluebeard's Egg" typifies the other ten stories of estranged relationships, despairing and mostly middle-class, middle-aged, urban women and men; this title story uses fairy tale story-telling as a unifying device, and point of view wittily and ironically as a theme; the shift from medieval romance to contemporary realism mirrors Sally's shift in consciousness. Atwood's dependent but responsible women and exploitative men are generic, not stereotypic.

13 CAMERON, ELSPETH. "Famininity, or Parody of Autonomy: Anorexia Nervosa and *The Edible Woman*." *Journal of Canadian Studies* 20, no. 2 (Summer):45-69.

Though *The Edible Woman* preceded general knowledge of *anorexia nervosa*, its hero Marian comes uncannily close to *anorexia*, exhibiting symptoms of "enmeshment" with the parental Peter, ineffectiveness, disgust with pregnancy and fat, a longing for autonomy, etc. Duncan may also be anorexic. The three-part structure represents three stages of the disease: predisposing causes; diet restriction, with mind/body split; and spontaneous resolution. *The Edible Woman* is a psychodrama of autonomy, and uses madness as a unifying "poetic device."

14 CARPENTER, DAVID. "The Literature of Abandonment in Canada." *Mosaic* 18, no. 2 (Spring):111-23.

Upholds geopiety – the reverence for the ancestral land – in *Surfacing* and in Rudy Wiebe's Indian stories, and critiques the flawed or abandoned geopiety of most Canadian literature. *Surfacing*'s heron signifies, in Taoist thought, the mode of seeing called *kuan*, where there is no seer/seen duality. Like other Canadian women protagonists, *Surfacing*'s narrator has relied too much on the archetypal masculine logos, too little on the feminine eros; like them she returns, after her geopious vision of earth and ancestors, "to so-called reality." Contrasts the genteel fallacy, elitism, and failed geopiety of Hugh MacLennan's *Each Man's Son*; discusses the flight from home to city in most prairie fiction; and concludes that Canadians need to learn to love their earthly home.

1985

15 CHANG, TING. "Margaret Atwood." *Scrivener* 6, no. 1 (Winter):31, 33.

Interviews Atwood, who talks about writing, ["Happy Endings,"] and what makes a story; self-expression and biographical criticism; the co-creating reader and computer technology; and grants for artists.

16 CHASE, K. Review of *Murder in the Dark*. *World Literature Today* 59, no. 1 (Winter):101.

Praises, in a short review, Atwood's deliberately disturbing, unusual yet characteristic *Murder in the Dark*, which has games, cynicism, grim pessimism and pitiless realism, but also fun and sadness and gleeful satire and much more. Atwood "sees too much, feels too much, and knows too much for comfort"; reading this probing artist and catalytic seer changes you, for better or worse.

17 COLLINS, ANNE. "Prisoners in Sexual Cages." *Maclean's* 98, no. 39 (30 September):62-63.

Praises *The Handmaid's Tale* as serious, satiric, and Atwood's most poetic and intense novel. Gilead is the society that right-wing, "'Christian,'" pro-family activists deserve; Offred is the perfect narrator for Gilead's contortions. Atwood brilliantly imagines how "one tiny area of power–giving birth–obsesses the powerless." *The Handmaid's Tale* is as much about human policing and betrayal as about courage. Offred's tale ends with effective ambiguity; but the unsuccessful parody of the "Historical Notes" undermines the novel's lingering effect.

18 CONKLIN, JAMIE. Review of *The Handmaid's Tale*. *Quill and Quire* 51, no. 11 (November):22-23.

Praises Atwood's important anti-Utopian satire; its perfectly suited, sympathetic narrator; its controlled emotion, where tense, bleak sentences suddenly twist, making the reader wary, and sympathetic to the narrator; but finds that the bemused tone of the ["Historical Notes"] undermines the novel's sustained tension.

19 CORBEIL, CAROLE. "Writers Get Wires Crossed in Nuclear-Age Discussion." *Globe and Mail*, 25 October, p. D8.

Reports on a lively and confused panel discussion on "The Writer in the Nuclear Age," where two of the panelists, Atwood and Ursula Le Guin, agreed on the writer's responsibilities in the nuclear age, and shared a speculative joke about getting rid of the White House, which a member of the audience misunderstood.

20 CRITTENDEN, YVONNE. "Novel Vision of a Dark Future." *Sunday Sun* (Toronto), 27 October, p. CL13.

Praises *The Handmaid's Tale* as a "fascinating, wonderfully written and disturbing cautionary tale." Atwood brilliantly outlines a patriarchal society that plausibly extends current realities, such as Christian fundamentalist Rev. Jerry Falwell and anti-feminist Phyllis Schafly. Her captive female society produces "sisterly bonds and female rituals," as for childbirth.

21 DELBAERE-GARANT, JEANNE. "Decolonizing the Self in *Surfacing, Bear,* and *A Fringe of Leaves.*" In *Colonisations: Rencontres Australie-Canada.* Edited by X. Pons and M. Rocard. Travaux de l'Université de Toulouse-Le Mirail, ser. B, vol 7. Toulouse: Université de Toulouse-Le Mirail Service des Publications, pp. 67-78.

Compares, following Kroetsch 1974.18, these three Conradian quest novels whose female protagonists decreate or decolonize the self as they break away from patriarchal structures. *Surfacing,* Marian Engel's *Bear,* and Patrick White's *A Fringe of Leaves* all depict a separation from the mainland and a journey to a wilderness island where the initially fragmented protagonists explore the self's extreme limits and are reborn with new insights. Because their quests take place in a desacralized Judeo-Christian world, they revert to older beliefs. Each achieves a partial victory; their ambiguous returns to ordinary reality are affirmative.

22 DUFFY, DENNIS. "The Rejection of Modernity in Recent Canadian Fiction." *Religion/Culture: Comparative Canadian Studies.* Canadian Issues/Thèmes canadiens, vol. 7. Ottawa: Association of Canadian Studies, pp. 260-73.

Atwood's 1972 *Surfacing,* Marian Engel's 1976 *Bear,* and Timothy Findley's 1977 *The Wars* continue the rejection of modernity theme of Leonard Cohen's Dionysian 1966 *Beautiful Losers.* All three 1970s novels share a mysterious, irrational ambience that seems more suited to animals and to the non-human; starkly defined oppositions and enemies (*Surfacing*'s mythological Americans and evil modernity); and a sad, loveless sexuality. All three end weakly, with personal, solitary revelations, not with the social celebration and commitment of Jack Hodgins's 1977 *The End of the World*.

23 EADY, ROBERT. "Bucking a Trend." *Books in Canada* 14, no. 9 (December):41.

Questions, in a letter to the editor that refers to Owen 1985.81, whether *The Handmaid's Tale*'s forced childbearing is really a trend, when there are 4,000 abortions a day in the United States? and forced abortion and birth control in totalitarian Communist China? Perhaps Atwood, whose *Survival* extensively quoted George Grant, has not read his new book, *English-Speaking Justice*, that warns against dangerous liberal trends like denying the rights of the unborn.

24 FABRE, MICHEL. Review of *Second Words*. *Afram Newsletter* (Paris), no. 21 (June), p. 33.

In French. Questions why Atwood has published the uneven *Second Words*, which contains nothing new; and why the dissuasive preamble? The essays are interesting, but some are too long; and one, that hedges concerning Northrop Frye's influence, is weak. The best piece is the precise review of *Midnight Birds*. Yet *Second Words* can delight and enlighten, especially if read as a form of autobiography.

25 FINK, THOMAS A. "Atwood's 'Tricks with Mirrors.'" *Explicator* 43, no. 2 (Winter):60-61.

The five sections of "Tricks with Mirrors" extend patriarchal tropes to reveal their absurdity: the woman becomes a mirror, literally; she calls attention to the limits of her non-reflecting frame; she emerges as an active, crafty subject, even though repressed by her lover's self-orientation; she protests the entrapping metaphor; finally she warns her Narcissus lover of its dangers.

26 FITCH, DAISY. "Women in Atwood's Books Have Sense of Humor, Lively Minds." *Times* (Trenton, N.J.), 5 May, pp. BB1, 12.

A report on Atwood's Spencer Trask public lecture and discussion at the University of Princeton that quotes Atwood on her men and women characters, her common-law and hence two-pension marriage, her forest childhood, and her popularity.

27 FITZGERALD, JUDITH. "Atwood: Fight for Power in Fiction and Reality." *Citizen* (Ottawa), 5 October, p. C3.

Interviews Atwood at home with her family in Toronto: Atwood talks about *The Handmaid's Tale* and critics' responses to it, her media image, and her commitment to political and cultural organizations. Gail Geltner's striking cover collage hangs in Atwood's studio.

28 _____. "A Necessary Allegory." *Canadian Forum* 65 (October):30-31.

Praises *The Handmaid's Tale* as a needed, complex, compelling allegory, and disagrees with Waelti-Walters 1984.98. *The Handmaid's Tale* shows our world horribly metamorphosed: we must act now. Gilead's women may have more power, but its men have the most. Humanity thirsts for power; love, individuals, "societies come and go"; oppression goes on. The narrator's condensed, powerful language sometimes overloads. The characterizations are memorable; the "'human'" institutions and costumes unforgettable.

29 FRASER, WALTER WAYNE. "The Dominion of Women: The Relationship of the Personal and the Political in Canadian Women's Literature." Ph.D. dissertation, University of Manitoba.

Examines the connections between nationalism and feminism in fifteen English Canadian novels and works of non-fiction: *The Edible Woman*, *Surfacing*, *Lady Oracle*, and Margaret Laurence's *The Stone Angel*, *The Fire-Dwellers*, and *The Diviners* explore Canadian 1960s and 1970s nationalism in the context of the rising Women's Liberation. See *Dissertation Abstracts International* 46:3356A.

30 FRENCH, WILLIAM. "New Works by Atwood, Callaghan This Fall." *Globe and Mail*, 2 July, p. M7.

Describes *The Handmaid's Tale*, due in September from McClelland and Stewart, as a satire and dire warning that is radically different from Atwood's previous work. Houghton Mifflin will publish it in the United States, Jonathan Cape in Britain.

31 _____. "Pessimistic Future." *Globe and Mail*, 5 October, p. D18.

Finds *The Handmaid's Tale* not entirely successful, not from any flaw, but because Atwood warns us against too many things, implausibly interacting–American religious fanaticism, pollution-caused infertility, and feminist extremes that could cause a repressive male backlash. Still, *The Handmaid's Tale* is an honorable dystopia, and all these dangers are very real now. Offred's laconic account highlights the chilling terror of Atwood's male-dominated police state. Unfortunately, the pessimistic story gives little room for Atwood's wit. The whimsical postscript ["Historical Notes"] is clever parody, and fills in narrative gaps. Atwood seems to say that our present excesses are better than no freedom.

32 FULFORD, ROBERT. "Atwood Puts Her Own Generation's Experience to Work." *Toronto Star*, 28 December, p. H5.

Enjoys Atwood's perhaps-classic *The Handmaid's Tale*, and compares it to Y.I. Zamyatin's germinal *We*, Aldous Huxley's *Brave New World*, and George Orwell's *Nineteen Eighty-Four*. A strange, pleasing nostalgia, for our time of "a thousand individual freedoms taken for granted," rises from its pages, and makes the reader see with fresh gratitude. Atwood's anti-Utopian satire, like Zamyatin's, Huxley's, and Orwell's, should be read not as prophecies but as reflections on our own time. Gilead shows an extreme of 1980s male dominance that "legitimizes itself by perverting" women's concerns: natural childbirth becomes a sinister ritual, and "women's hatred of pornography" an excuse for puritanical fascism. Of course Gilead uses women as tools – and this echoes 1980s alliances of anti-pornography feminists and Christian fundamentalists. As in Zamyatin and Orwell, the central character's rebellion is sexual. *The Handmaid's Tale* is chillingly convincing, powerful, and often astonishingly moving.

33 GARVIE, MAUREEN McCALLUM. "Nightmares in Gilead." *Whig-Standard* (Kingston, Ont.), 26 October, Magazine sec., p. 17.

Interviews Atwood, who is in Kingston to promote *The Handmaid's Tale*: Atwood discusses its sales, realism, and how she wrote it; America's real violence, as in her 1961 Cambridge, Massachusetts, residence; male identity and happiness; and human responses and our largely illusory "'freedoms'" as vulnerable to social control, especially through computers.

34 ____. "Thoroughly Atwoodian." *Whig-Standard* (Kingston, Ont.), 12 October, Magazine sec., p. 18.

Praises *The Handmaid's Tale*, whose imposed title, as the "Historical [Notes]" sardonically reveal, is partly a sexist joke. The narrator's tough, funny, feminist activist mother is our contemporary; the narrator is a "generational about-face," conservative and unassertive. Created from "paternalism, fundamentalism and computerization . . . by men tired of being obsolescent," Gilead uses isolation, ignorance, and threats of violence to control. Atwood shows "humankind's extraordinary ability . . . to find the ordinary," even in extreme circumstances, and survive. Offred conceals to protect others. The shreds of hope and charity are powerful affirmations.

35 GERVAIS, MARTY. "Atwood Says Novel Not Future 'Blueprint.'" *Windsor Star*, 23 November, p. C7.
    Interviews Atwood at her new Toronto home: Atwood discusses writing *The Handmaid's Tale*, which she calls "'speculative fiction'"; her scrapbook of evidence for it, and its United States parallels; her fear that it might be used as a guide; and society's attitudes to fertility.

36 _____. "Atwood Takes a Disturbing, Eloquent Look at the Future." *Windsor Star*, 5 October, p. C7.
    Praises *The Handmaid's Tale* as Orwellian, near-prophetic, and Atwood's best novel. Offred is a woman victimized by a repressive, fanatically fundamentalist Gilead that has destroyed feminist practices and meaningful relationships. Partly Atwood is conjecturing, and partly just describing the declining North American birth rate and the rise of fundamentalism and conservatism. She isn't proselytizing, though the Jerry Falwells might find certain elements useful.

37 GIBBS, ROBERT. Review of *Second Words*. *English Studies in Canada* 11, no. 1 (March):113-17.
    Appreciates the humourous, earthy, intelligent *Second Words*, whose carefully arranged chronological divisions reflect Atwood's finding her vocation, and becoming a writer engagé. As in "The Curse of Eve," Atwood faces her critics unflinchingly, "parries the monstrous with laughter," and uses her personal experience to make impersonal points. The first section reveals her realism, dry wit, distrust of labels, and reversals of sexual and national stereotypes. The second section reaffirms the writer's calling, at the end of the 1973.2 Mathews polemic, and the writer as "'I-witness,'" as in the tribute to Adrienne Rich. "An End to Audience," which is central in place and theme to the third section, links reading and freedom.

1985

38 GINGELL, SUSAN. "The Animals in Atwood's Country." In *Glimpses of Canadian Literature*. Edited by Wendy Keitner, C.D. Narasimhaiah, and C.N. Srinath. [Bangalore, India: *Literary Criterion*], pp. 125-37.
Reprint of 1984.30.

39 GODARD, BARBARA. "The Language of Difference." *Canadian Forum* 65 (June-July):44-46.
Compares the subversive poetics of English Canadian and Quebec women writers. Atwood's poetic is romantic and archaeological, not deconstructive; her work retreats from logos and word to sensation and prelinguistic gesture or ritual. Here language begins: "the embryonic Word is gestated and, incarnate, moves out from an organic female centre–for all Atwood's fictions end with symbolic births. . . . [W]omen come to know themselves" through this symbolically conveyed language of origins. Reprinted, revised: 1985.40 (below).

40 ____. "Writing and Difference: Women Writers of Québec and English-Canada." In *In The Feminine: Women and Words / Les femmes et les mots*. Conference Proceedings, 1983. Edited by Ann Dybikowski, et al. Edmonton: Longspoon Press, pp. 122-26 passim.
A revised reprint of 1985.39 (above) that omits the claim that "all Atwood's fictions end with symbolic births." Women "retreat" to a symbolically conveyed language of origins.

41 GODDARD, JOHN. "Lady Oracle." *Books in Canada* 14, no. 8 (November):6-8, 10.
Interviews Atwood in her Toronto home: Atwood discusses her travels, including publicizing *Bodily Harm* in Germany and a term at the University of Alabama; her marriage or non-marriage; writing *The Handmaid's Tale* and fearing that it was too crazy; its plausible U.S. setting and her Cambridge, Massachusetts, studies and ancestors; its scrapbook of evidence; its realistic "'women acting against women'"; democracy, birth control, atmospheric toxification, declining birth rates, and feminism. Atwood sees *The Handmaid's Tale* as "'a comment on power structure rather than a comment on feminism.'" A cover profile. See Gingell 1986.93.

42 GOETSCH, PAUL. "Margaret Atwood's *Life Before Man* as a Novel of Manners." In *Gaining Ground: European Critics on Canadian Literature*. Edited by Robert Kroetsch and Reingard M. Nischik. Western Canadian Literary Documents Series, edited by Shirley Neuman, vol. 6. Edmonton: NeWest Press, pp. 137-49.

Discusses *Life Before Man* as a novel of manners and a psychological novel. Like Jane Austen's novels, *Life* focuses on the discrepancy between surface and interior behavior, and on the rules for relationships between the sexes. Though *Life*'s new rules promote rather than prevent sexual affairs, basically they ensure civilized behavior; the characters repress and hide their feelings and thoughts, and avoid discussing problems. But, as the interior monologues show, even the liberal 1970s code cannot impose order on feelings, passions, and relationships. Without religion and traditional values, the characters ask too much from love and sex. Atwood sympathizes with the victims, but sides with those who struggle and survive, as Elizabeth does.

43 GOLDIE, TERRY. "Folklore, Popular Culture, and Individuation in *Surfacing* and *The Diviners*." *Canadian Literature*, no. 104 (Spring), pp. 95-108.

Compares *Surfacing*'s complete rejection of mass and popular culture to the acceptance of some contemporary popular culture in Margaret Laurence's *The Diviners*. Both women narrators search for identity and are inspired by a mystical knowledge that *Surfacing* finds only in the past and isolation, but that in *The Diviners* involves the present also, and "'significant others.'" Photography, which may be seen as mass or popular culture, is always feared in *Surfacing*; but in *The Diviners* photographs are part of self-discovery and socialization. In *Surfacing*, "[m]ass culture perverts" the narrator's perceptions, her later, socialized notebooks, the bowdlerized *Quebec Folk Tales*, local Quebec culture, and images of fertility and sex. Only the deity scrapbook and the Indian paintings are truly visionary.

44 GOTLIEB, PHYLLIS. "In the Future, a Nightmare for Women." *Citizen* (Ottawa), 5 October, p. C3.

Finds *The Handmaid's Tale* continuously engrossing, but has difficulty believing its sometimes silly satire on the subjugation of women; wonders whether the tough, scrappy Moira should tell this tale. Atwood's novel is extrapolative science fiction and social criticism. The depiction is the plot; little happens to Offred; the end is a [Frank R. Stockton] *Lady-or-Tiger*; the society's dynamic is not much detailed. The narrator, who symbolizes demoralized womanhood, lacks any courage or rebellion, but her memories of husband and child are painfully moving.

45 GOVIER, KATHERINE. "Margaret Atwood: 'There's Nothing in the Book That Hasn't Already Happened.'" *Quill and Quire* 51, no. 9 (September):66-67.

Interviews Atwood in Toronto: Atwood discusses writing *The Handmaid's Tale*, fearing it was too crazy, and finding it "'horrible fun'"; *The Handmaid's Tale* as a collective nightmare, where the society is crazy, and as a dystopia or negative utopia, based on a "logical extension of current trends" like keeping women unequal and outlawing abortion, and on her travels to countries like Iran and Afghanistan; freedom, powerlessness, and population control; the optimism of the novel's resistance and, as the ["Historical Notes"] imply, Gilead's end; its use of women to control women; its Boston setting and her Puritan ancestors; its feminist mother-daughter differences; Atwood's scrapbook of evidence; her travels, two abandoned novels, and finding time to write; and growing up in no set place and envying Alice Munro.

46 GRABHER, GUDRUN M. "Das Wohnen in der Sprache: Eine Gegenüberstellung von Margaret Atwoods *Surfacing* und Margrit Irgangs *Min* auf der Grundlage des Heideggerschen Sprachdenkens." In *Beiträge zu den Sprach-und Literaturwissenschaften: Reader*. Edited by Hans-Alfred Herchen. Frankfurt am Main: Haag & Herchen Verlag, pp. 25-43.

Finds Heidegger's philosophy of Being and language a significant common element in *Surfacing* and *Min*. The novels uncover the inherent danger in language, the tendency to obscure rather than illuminate truth and reality. Betrayed by the unreliability of language, *Surfacing*'s protagonist retreats to a state of pre-speech. After she has de-languaged her world, the protagonist comes to recognize the necessity of communication, and she can return to using language. *Min* illustrates the absence of language; discourse is reduced to monologue. The protagonists in both novels experience intensity or emptiness of feeling that is accentuated through language. Language is a house of Being, and conversation opens the doors that enable movement from house to house.

47 GRANT, YVONNE BROOKS. "Madness as a Means to Unity: *The Golden Notebook* and *Surfacing*." In *Woman's Place: Selected Proceedings of the University of South Dakota's First Annual Women's Research Conference*. Edited by Karen Hardy Cárdenas, Susan Wolfe, and Mary Schneider. [Vermillion]: University of South Dakota, Women's Research Conference, pp. 30-37.

Argues, following Phyllis Chesler's *Women and Madness*, that *Surfacing* and Doris Lessing's *The Golden Notebook* show their artist heroines' "'madness'" as a discarding of patriarchal society's "'false'" selves that leads to a reintegration of their "'true'" selves. Compares the novels' fragmentary structure and style, that reflect the heroines's fragmentation; the confused identities of Lessing's multiply named heroine and Atwood's nameless heroine; their descents into aqueous, unconscious dreams and visions; and their journeys from alienation to Lessing's personal and political commitment, and to Atwood's natural solution of pregnancy. Both heroines can guide contemporary women.

48 HANSEN, ELAINE TUTTLE. "Fiction and (Post) Feminism in Atwood's *Bodily Harm*." *Novel* 19, no. 1 (Fall):5-21.

Explicates the feminist consciousness-raising of *Bodily Harm*'s narrative structure. *Bodily Harm* answers the "'post-feminist'" 1980s by radicalizing Rennie, who learns, through Lora, that the female oppression stories of the 1960s and 1970s are still true. The narrative moves between a third-person present-tense story and past-tense flashbacks in a loose "'stream of consciousness'" linked by "'free association.'" The introductory third-person sentences of Parts I-IV, which do not confirm a prison-cell setting for all parts, "stand outside the spatio-temporal 'consensus of the body of the narrative.'" Taken cumulatively, these sentences subvert conventional assumptions of the novel, of therapeutic analysis, and of individual identity: by linking Rennie's stories to Jocasta's and Lora's stories, they are raising consciousness by understanding the individual through collective sexual politics. The subplot of Rennie and her doctor demystifies masculine authority; Rennie is liberated from regressive feminine fantasies and radicalized, through a fear much greater than her "retrospectively minor" breast cancer; she reappropriates, for Lora, the mythic, maternal, female powers of healing. But, whether or not Rennie will be released from prison, her therapeutic "'transforming experience'" depends on the silenced Lora's suffering and possible death: the feminist consciousness of victimization thus remains divided, not collective, not Utopian.

49 HATCH, RONALD B. "Letters in Canada, 1984: Poetry." *University of Toronto Quarterly* 54, no. 4 (Summer):347-50.

Features *Interlunar* and discusses Atwood, Michael Ondaatje, and Roo Borson as the year's strongest poets of anecdotal experience and modified colloquial line. The anecdotal "Snake Poems" engage with irony and wit. Because "Atwood's wit resembles a snake striking, . . . she has truly become a 'snake woman,'" emulating its speed, precision, and beautiful self-containment. Ultimately, as Atwood's flat, cool voice leads us through the garden, the snake incarnates Heidegger's "'otherness.'" The quite different "Interlunar" series, which exemplifies "what Eli Mandel calls the 'Circe' poem of transformation," begins confessionally but soon becomes an alienation where images float free, and a tour of modern sexual politics, with Orpheus and Euridice retold. ["Heart Test with an Echo Chamber"] goes beyond irony to unite flesh and insight; the world becomes a "'quiet shining.'" But the too-passive voice can only partly make the new persona or "'otherness'" real, can only partly yoke the anecdotal tone and mythic materials. See 1985.50 (below).

50 ____. "Towards Transcendence: The Poetry of Judith Fitzgerald, Margaret Atwood, and Ted Hughes." *West Coast Review* 19, no. 4 (April):47, 50-56.

Prefers, in a three-book review, Ted Hughes's explosively alive, substantial, transfiguring vision to the fine *Interlunar*'s passive language and cautious voyage of initiation that reaches only the borders of vision; but *Interlunar*, which is really two books, is Atwood's most resonant poetry since *The Journals of Susanna Moodie*. In "Snake Poems," Atwood's flat, gravelly monotone, adapted from Anne Sexton and Sylvia Plath, captures the reader in the cool grip of the snake's "'otherness.'" Her affirmation of nature's invaluable, "'not human'" otherness recalls [E.J.] Pratt's shark. "Quattrocento" captures both the medieval grotesque and "the modern comic pastiche" of the Eden myth. ["The Blue Snake"] recalls poems by [Archibald] Lampman and [Irving] Layton. The triadic "Interlunar" poems, which follow Plath's initiation and rebirth, confess what cannot be a biographical powerlessness, but is rather a floating, schizophrenic powerlessness, disconnected from the world. Section II varies the old futile, repressive dialectic of power between men and women. Section III's "Heart Test with an Echo Chamber" begins ironically, but ends with a sudden transformation, so that the poet later finds the world "alive in its 'quiet shining.'"

51 HEATON, JOAN VanSICKLE. Review of *Bluebeard's Egg*. *CM* 13, no. 4 (July):159.

Recommends *Bluebeard's Egg* for senior students, as Canadian literature, as an Atwood book, and as about women's rights. The Ontario and Toronto settings are densely and mythically evoked. Woman's changing role is positively developed throughout, starting with the model of her mother, and going from childhood to death's earliest shadows. Traditional roles betray women; men are as pitiable; only the child, who can chose freely, emerges admirably.

52 H[OOPER], B[RAD]. Review of *The Handmaid's Tale*. *Booklist* 82, no. 7 (1 December):514.

Finds *The Handmaid's Tale*'s obvious didacticism about the United States' excesses and conservatism trying, despite the impassioned *cri de coeur* and adept style; predicts many sales, based on Atwood's previous successes, and many disappointed readers. Excerpted: 1987.53.

53 HOWELLS, CORAL ANN. "Worlds alongside: Contradictory Discourses in the Fiction of Alice Munro and Margaret Atwood." In *Gaining Ground: European Critics on Canadian Literature*. Edited by Robert Kroetsch and Reingard M. Nischik. Western Canadian Literary Documents Series, edited by Shirley Newman, vol. 6. Edmonton: NeWest Press, pp. 121-36.

Traces contradictory discourses of realism versus fantasy in *Surfacing*, *Bodily Harm*, and Alice Munro's *Lives of Girls and Women* and *Who Do You Think You Are?*; and finds that the discontinuities between these discourses generate new, multiple meanings and a new, transforming language. In Munro's Gothic landscape, realism and

1985

fantasy co-exist in mutual, supplementary contrariety; in Atwood's didactic, feminist, humanist fiction their relationship is contradictory and mutually exclusive. The optimistic *Surfacing* affirms woman's possible "self-forgiveness and self-revision"; the pessimistic, Gothic *Bodily Harm* "shows that disengagement and escape may be possible only in fantasy." Revised: 1987.62.

54 JACKSON, MARNI. "Showtime." *Chatelaine* 58, no. 10 (October):4.
Praises *The Handmaid's Tale* as a grim, brilliant fable that brings out Atwood's best – "moral vision, biting humor and a poet's imagination." Though Gilead is a patriarchy, the enemy is tyranny, not men.

55 JAMES, WILLIAM C. "Religious Symbolism in Recent English Canadian Fiction." *Religion/Culture: Comparative Canadian Studies*. Canadian Issues/Thèmes canadiens, vol 7. Ottawa: Association of Canadian Studies, pp. 246-59.
An essay on the movement from the traditional otherworldly eternity to a this-worldly transcendence in Canadian fiction; discusses *Surfacing* as an archetypal female narrative of rebirth into an underlying, transcendent reality. Transcendence, like survival, is not uniquely Canadian; perhaps the Canadian consciousness is that of the marginal, ironic watcher.

56 JEWINSKI, ED. Review of *Second Words*. *University of Windsor Review* 19, no. 1 (Fall-Winter):78-80.
Compares, in a two-book review, *Second Words* to a garage sale, offering junk mixed with jewels. Only time organizes this book. The first part is least satisfactory; like girlhood haircombs, these awkward essays are held together with plastic reviewer's phrases. But there are excellent essays, on [Gwendolyn] MacEwen, nationalism, and Al Purdy; the latter should be required reading in every CanLit course. The second part proves much more tedious. There women writers are encouraged with the "judiciously evasive evaluation" once given early Canadian literature. The good insights on John Newlove show what Atwood should have done with the women's reviews. Pummeling Robin Mathews [1973.2] does nothing to improve *Survival*. The third section is most worthwhile: here Atwood becomes admirably "intelligent, expansive, brooding, wise, comic, serious." What *Second*

Words lacks is subjectivity: it is only a "cool, distant, rigorous presentation of ideas" – nothing from "the home of her own mind."

57 JOHNSTON, JUDITH L. Review of *Second Words*. *Magill's Literary Annual*. Edited by Frank N. Magill. Vol. 2. Englewood Cliffs, N.J.: Salem Press, pp. 785-89.

A detailed appreciation: Atwood's lucidly analyzed, witty, enlightening *Second Words* can be read as literary and cultural history, and as intellectual autobiography. The earliest essays, on Canadian literature and nationalism, and James Reaney, show her discriminating analysis. Her belief in the interdependence of writer and society unites part two, whose diverse essays include her 1973.2 response to Robin Mathews's 1972.26 attack; her clear-eyed, creative criticism of women writers; and "On Being a Woman Writer," which names and classifies reviewers' sexual biases in order to reclaim the writer's imagination and language. Part three's major essays, "Witches," "An End to Audience?" "Canadian-American Relations," and "Writing the Male Character," "demonstrate her essential good humor, analytic and synthetic intelligence, and passionate" commitment to writing.

58 KAMBOURELI, SMARO. "Dialogue with the Other: The Use of Myth in Canadian Women's Poetry." In *In the Feminine: Women and Words / Les femmes et les mots*. Conference proceedings, 1983. Edited by Ann Dybikowski, et al. Edmonton: Longspoon Press, pp. 105-9 passim.

Includes Atwood with mythic critics and with those Canadian women poets who deconstruct traditionally distorting myth and social mythologies to reveal the feminine self, as Mary Daly's *Gyn/Ecology: The Metaethics of Radical Feminism* urges.

59 KEITH, W.J. *Canadian Literature in English*. Longman Literature in English Series. London and New York: Longman, pp. 99-102, 162-64.

Appreciates Atwood's mythopoeic, deeply Canadian, and uniquely laconic, double-edged poetry. From the early, formal mythopoeic poems through the accomplished, archetypal *The Circle Game* and the climactic *The Journals of Susanna Moodie*, Atwood draws on Canadian literature – especially Jay Macpherson and James Reaney – geography, and history. Her binary structures and imagery link her work; her pared-down language creates the Atwood tone. The later books of poetry are less surprising than the dazzling early ones.

Praises Atwood's poetically subtle, cogent novels of contemporary stress. *The Edible Woman* is a witty comedy of manners that artfully critiques our consumer society. *Surfacing* is a tantalizingly ambiguous novel on "lying, madness, guilt, and the" elusive past. The sombre but most compassionate *Life Before Man* ends ambiguously.

60 KLEIN, CARROLL. "A Fertility Tale." *Broadside* (Toronto) 7, no. 3 (December-January):13.

Praises *The Handmaid's Tale*'s bizarre, chillingly possible, nightmare world of Gilead. Everything here comes from the 1980s: the American Christian fundamentalist right combats individual choice, women's liberation, minority rights, sexually transmitted diseases, pornography, and prostitution; nuclear accidents and infertility have spread. The intelligent, educated, formerly apolitical Offred is the daughter of a disappeared feminist. Atwood tantalizingly peels back the layers of story and history.

61 LeBOW, DIANE. "Selfhood in Free Fall: Novels by Black and White American Women." Ph.D. dissertation, University of California, Santa Cruz, 222 pp.

Traces a "'free fall'" process of casting off traditional female patterns to form new ones in Atwood and ten other novelists. These female protagonists see themselves as nontraditional; they gain strengths, and are survivors. Often they are considered outsiders, pariahs, even insane. That these stronger female selves seem to be exiting from cultures that won't assimilate them is a new development in the *bildungsroman*. See *Dissertation Abstracts International* 46 (1986):3034A.

62 LECKIE, BARBARA, and O'BRIEN, PETER. "An Interview with Margaret Atwood." *Rubicon*, no. 6 (Winter), pp. 111-29.

Interviews Atwood 19 November 1984 in Montreal: Atwood discusses writers and politics in Canada, the United States, and elsewhere, citing Jane Austen as a political writer; the voice of the lyric poem as heard, and perhaps plural; writers and language, citing a Welsh conference "Women and Language" workshop where both radical feminists and older women rejected what each called language;

animal language; chairing P.E.N. International Canadian Centre, Anglophone; artists versus ideologies and censorship; semiotics; Canadian women writers; and Scots Canadian versus Irish American attitudes to success and failure. Reprinted: 1987.84.

63 LeCLAIRE, JACQUES. Review of *The Handmaid's Tale*. *Études canadiennes* (Talence), no. 19, pp. 265-66.

Enjoys Atwood's irony and compares her science fiction style to Doris Lessing. The story is demurely lucid and full of passion. *The Handmaid's Tale* is a masterpiece in a unique genre of fiction.

64 LOWEY, MARK. "Poetry: Good, Bleak Unsatisfying, Attempted." *Calgary Herald*, 14 April, p. E7.

Finds *Interlunar* bleak, in a four-book review that prefers Al Purdy's good poems: as Atwood's title implies, "the poet is lost in transit," and also preoccupied with death, and buffeted by nature's harsh indifference. "Snake Poems" has some of *Interlunar*'s best images, and Atwood's usual flawless lines, but occasionally overdoes the human-snake connection. *Interlunar*'s nightmares are personal, in contrast to *Two-Headed Poems* and *True Stories*, whose probing of man's brutality often made the reviewer squirm.

65 McDUFF, DAVID. Review of *The New Oxford Book of Canadian Verse in English*. *Stand Magazine* 27, no. 1 (Winter):79-80.

Appreciates, in a group review, *The New Oxford Book of Canadian Verse in English* as a thoroughly successful and unusually entertaining, varied, and moving anthology; quotes from Isabella Valancy Crawford's serene Canadian poetry; and approves Atwood's selections and introduction, concluding with her "most apt characterization" of English Canadian poetry as unique, spiky, and vital.

66 McGOOGAN, KENNETH. "Atwood Rates Six on Obnoxiousness Scale." *Calgary Herald*, 20 November, p. D1.

Reports on Atwood's speech as the ninth Bob Edwards Award winner and first woman so honored. Atwood's shameless flogging of her new novel, subtle jibes at politicians, and feminist quips, which brought standing applause, were nonetheless judged "'only half as obnoxious'" as the speeches of previous winners like Andy Russell and Alan Fotheringham.

67 ____. "Varied Images Melded in Grim Look at Future." *Calgary Herald*, 9 October, p. F7.

Reports on Atwood's standing-room-only reading of *The Handmaid's Tale* and her remarks at Central Library Theatre: Atwood discusses her novel's plausibility, given "the declining birth rate, increasing pollution and creeping censorship"; pornography and feminism; describes *The Handmaid's Tale*'s two germinal images, of white-hooded bodies hanging from a wall like Harvard University's, and of hooded or Old-Dutch-Cleanser-bonnetted women walking in pairs; her socio-biology readings, newspaper evidence, and social structure for *The Handmaid's Tale*; and its optimistic ["Historical Notes"] that show, like Orwell's *Nineteen Eighty-Four* postscript, that Gilead has ended.

68 McGRATH, JOAN. Review of *The Handmaid's Tale*. *Canadian Book Review Annual*:138.

Praises *The Handmaid's Tale*: "This chilling vision of a sterile dystopia is at moments frightfully convincing, at others painfully–very painfully–funny." It warns the complacent and self-righteous–who, alas, aren't likely to listen.

69 McGREGOR, GAILE. *The Wacousta Syndrome: Explorations in the Canadian Langscape*. Toronto: University of Toronto Press, 473 pp., passim.

Builds on and critiques *Survival* to define a Wacousta syndrome in Canadian painting, literature, and culture, where, as in Major John Richardson's *Wacousta*, a feminized garrison recoils from patriarchal authority and from a wilderness that is hostile, gothic, and masculine, rather than warm and maternal. Canadian literature's death orientation is not necessarily victimizing. Our female isolates are strong, stronger than our male isolates, and not always old. *Survival* simplifies but reveals the Canadian family as trap. Canadians do identify with animal victims, not hunters; but these animals teach us positively about life, suffering, and mortality. Canadian heroes are not simple noble losers, but irrational, violent, or magicians. As *Survival* says, any accurate map is better than none; Canadians do draw straight lines on nature's curves. *The Edible Woman*'s Marian exemplifies the facsimile, ostensibly non-creative artist figure. *Lady Oracle*'s Joan is the prototype of the disguised artist figure. *Surfacing*, with its quest for the lost, dead Canadian baby, is a prototypical parable of the wounded artist. *Surfacing* is also a prototypical personal time-quest; its young woman travels out from civilization and back into her past. Does she break through, given the anomalous end? *The Circle Game* shows that nature is deadlier than order.

70 MALLINSON, JEAN. "Margaret Atwood." In *Canadian Writers and Their Works: Poetry Series*. Edited by Robert Lecker, Jack David, and Ellen Quigley. Vol. 9. Toronto: ECW Press, pp. 15-81.
    Reprint of 1984.60.

71 MANION, EILEEN. Review of *Bluebeard's Egg* and *Murder in the Dark*. In *Glimpses of Canadian Literature*. Edited by Wendy Keitner, C.D. Narasimhaiah, and C.N. Srinath. [Bangalore, India: *Literary Criterion*], pp. 259-63.
    Reprint of 1984.62.

72 MEESE, ELIZABETH. "An Interview with Margaret Atwood." *Black Warrior Review* 12, no. 1 (Fall):88-108.
    Interviews Atwood in April at the University of Alabama: Atwood discusses her critics and controversies; growing up in Canada before feminism; politics at the Jewish [Camp White Pine]; her practical political commitment and the writer's freedom to write versus political fanaticism; men's privileged, abstract theories versus feminism and the Canada-India Village Aid Association; Rennie's taking responsibility and human rights in *Bodily Harm*; life's limited choices; and *Surfacing*'s parents.

73 MILOT, LOUISE. "Margaret Atwood et Nicole Brossard: La question de la représentation." *Voix et images* (Montréal) 11, no. 1 (Autumn):56-62.
    Compares Atwood's and Nicole Brossard's writing styles. Atwood in *Bodily Harm* combines a conventional writing style and a standard plot with the power of referential illusion to arouse emotions. Brossard's more avant-garde style, in *Sold Out* and *Picture Theory*, attempts an ambitious transformation through the power of words.

1985

Atwood's realist discourse and Brossard's utopian discourse show different degrees of feminist engagement; and similarities, particularly in their dominant use of the referential. Brossard, who is associated with new writing and feminist themes, sometimes heads for a dead end in her fictive discourse. Atwood's writing works to say something through fiction; Brossard's writing works to make fiction.

74 MOFFET, PENELOPE. "Canadian Writer Who Can Go Home Again." *Los Angeles Times*, 24 March, pp. 92-93.
Interviews Atwood, who "does not waste words": Atwood talks about writing, teaching, the realistically mixed lives of her women characters, politics, responsibility, and self-development.

75 MURRAY, HEATHER. "The Synthetic Habit of Mind: Margaret Atwood's *Surfacing*." *World Literature Written in English* 25, no. 1 (Spring):89-104.
Foregrounds *Surfacing*'s "interaction of language and land" and analyzes how her prose style supports this theme. "Atwood's *Surfacing* posits a hierarchy of myth, rings of increasing wildness of land accompanied by a furthered freedom of language, radiating out from the individual center." This structure molds story and philosophy; its sustained, unquestioned hierarchy involves "literary ordering and religious faith, a narratology recapitulating teleology." This language/land hierarchy contributes to *Surfacing*'s other systems of "doubling/splitting/mirroring" and of "lying/duplicity/undermining"; and creates problems of narrative that the prose style tries to answer.

76 MYRDEN, JUDITH. "Atwood Optimistic Book Program Still On-Stream." *Halifax Chronicle Herald*, 28 September, p. 46.
Quotes Atwood's strong support for a federally financed payment-for-public-use book program that Marcel Masse, who has just resigned as federal communications minister, was to have got funding for.

77 ____. "Futuristic Society Described in Atwood's Book." *Halifax Chronicle Herald*, 5 October, p. 48.
Interviews Atwood, who is in Halifax promoting *The Handmaid's Tale*: Atwood talks about its realism, declining birth rates and societies' extreme responses; Canada as a less likely setting than the United

States for Gilead; and writing *The Handmaid's Tale*. The interviewer finds its first few chapters confusing, but its plot very well developed thereafter; as in Orwell's *Nineteen Eighty-Four*, the main character leads a depressing life, and disappears.

78 NICKS, JOAN. "Michael Rubbo's *Margaret Atwood: Once in August*." *Cinema Canada*, no. 115 (February), p. 25.

Admires and critiques Rubbo's National Film Board documentary. "Its theme is the art of life, with Atwood the found resource on her family's summer island." Rubbo plays visual anthropologist and "would-be voyeur as voyageur," but his male fantasies and cinematic pretenses exclude him. Merrily Weisbord, Rubbo's go-between, forms an ironic feminist alliance with Atwood; they chat spontaneously. The Atwood island, with her parents and daughter, signifies an order of mutual respect; all the Atwoods are islands, touching. Despite his constrained, binocular vision, Rubbo has shown an ideal Atwood: a natural woman, respected offspring, committed parent, protective writer, and autonomous mate.

79 OSTRIKER, ALICIA. "Being Nobody Together: Duplicity, Identity, and Women's Poetry." *Parnassus* 12, no. 2 / 13, no. 1 (Spring-Winter):206-8.

Reads "This Is a Color Photo" as an ironic version of Walt Whitman's "'look for me under your bootsoles,'" and as part of an invisible woman tradition that goes back to Wordsworth's Lucy ["A Slumber Did My Spirit Seal"] and to Emily Dickinson's "Nobody" and "I died for Beauty." Reprinted, slightly revised: 1986.185, pp. 63-65.

80 ____. "The Thieves of Language: Women Poets and Revisionist Mythmaking." In *The New Feminist Criticism: Essays on Women, Literature, and Theory*. Edited by Elaine Showalter. New York: Pantheon Books, pp. 316, 322.

Reprint of 1982.123. Discusses "Circe/Mud" as revisionist mythmaking, and Circe as angry but quite powerless; reprinted on pages 212 and 222 of 1986.185, within a chapter that revises this article.

81 OWEN, I.M. "Back to the Future." *Books in Canada* 14, no. 7 (October):13-14.

1985

Reads *The Handmaid's Tale* with delight, the first time through; but without surprises and with effort, the second. The book's great glory "is its technique of gradual revelation," dazzlingly sustained throughout. But its elaborate, ingenious machinery comes close to dominating the book. Atwood extrapolates mostly from anti-feminist trends, but with even-handed justice, showing women's movement activists as book burners. "The one important technological innovation is all too alarmingly close"–the computerization of money. *The Handmaid's Tale* remains, on second reading, a valuable contemporary tract; its details are brilliantly developed. See Eady 1985.23.

82 PLATNICK, PHYLLIS. *Canadian Poetry: Index to Criticisms (1970-1979). Poésie canadienne: Index de critiques (1970-1979)*. [Ottawa]: Canadian Library Association, pp. 7-12.

Lists for Atwood, under bibliographies, Horne 1974.15 and 1977.34; lists alphabetically by author 28 items under general, which includes criticism, interviews, and M.A. theses; lists 78 items alphabetically by author under 8 books of poetry. Some items are listed under general and under books of poetry; items listed are mostly Canadian, with a small number from elsewhere.

83 QUICKENDEN, ROBERT. "Poems Are Unforgettable." *Winnipeg Free Press*, 7 September, p. 56.

Appreciates *Interlunar*'s strong, cohering, unforgettable poems of death and blessing, power and powerlessness, love and fear, mythology and landscape. "The Words Continue Their Journey" "is a harrowing vision" of doomed word-seekers. The final poems, of an apparently threatening moonlit darkness that hides nature's life, pull together the book's themes, as in "Interlunar."

84 REEVES, GARLAND. "Reality as She Sees It Is Visiting Novelist's Goal." *Birmingham News*, 11 April. Newsbank 1984-1985, 100:B8-9.

Interviews Atwood at the University of Alabama; intersperses quotes from three of her novels and a review with her comments on writing, feminism, marriage, an albatross she saw on a family trip to the Galapagos, her childhood, and Canadian writing.

85 Review of *The Handmaid's Tale. Jim Kobak's Kirkus Reviews* 53, no. 24 (15 December):1333-34.

Finds Atwood's dystopia "a chillingly specific, imaginable nightmare"; though "short on characterization . . . and long on cynicism," *The Handmaid's Tale* is viscerally scary and, if tinny, still a detailed, "impressively steady feminist vision of apocalypse."

86 RICE, PATRICIA. "Author Margaret Atwood Tells Tales Out of School." *St. Louis Post-Dispatch*, 4 May, p. D3. Newsbank 1984-1985, 109:F14-G1.

Quotes Atwood, who recently read in the River Styx PM Series in St. Louis, on realism, evil, and wimps in her women and men characters; on her overseas sales as indicators of women's progress; on problems of translation; and on writing poetry versus fiction.

87 ROOKE, CONSTANCE. Review of *The Handmaid's Tale*. *Malahat Review*, no. 73 (December) [sic January 1986], p. 120.

Explains how Atwood's harrowing novel is remarkably pleasurable as you watch the situation and ideas develop, and the language compels you to watch. The most obvious, and perverse, satisfaction is your identification with the Handmaid, trapped in that future, concentrating on understanding what happened and how to escape; you are alert, huddling up to Atwood's warmest heroine in this cold, warmth-enhancing surround, as if you were her [Conradian] secret sharer. *The Handmaid's Tale* is also a deadly serious warning.

88 RUBENSTEIN, ROBERTA. "Pandora's Box and Female Survival: Margaret Atwood's *Bodily Harm*." *Journal of Canadian Studies* 20, no. 1 (Spring):120-35.

"Margaret Atwood's *Bodily Harm* (1981) is a feminist, existential study of the relation between women and patriarchy. Having recently undergone a partial mastectomy, the protagonist Rennie Wilford is vulnerable and disaffected. . . . The narrative is structured through parallels in event and symbol, including doubled figures of doctors and grandmothers. Hands and 'faceless strangers' are other important images of both connection and alienation between people. Cancer functions as a scourge of the body and a metaphor for such diseases of the body politic as violence, pornography, and sadism. Through these doublings as well as allusion to the mythical Pandora, Atwood establishes correspondences between female guilt, power, victimization, and moral responsibility. Ultimately, Rennie discovers her complicity in female victimization and transcends her crippling self-contempt."

Rescuing her darker double, Lora, Rennie saves herself; returning home as a "'subversive,'" she has reason to rejoice. Reprinted: 1988.45. Revised: 1987.134.

89 St. ANDREWS, B.A. "Dissonance in Harmony: Some Notes on Margaret Atwood and Adrienne Rich." *Interpretations* 16, no. 1 (Fall):21-25.

Though Rich's feminism is separatist and Sapphic, and Atwood's feminism is resignedly, bleakly heterosexual, both "Two-Headed Poems" and Rich's *Dream of a Common Language* envision a shared, redemptive language. Both writers are rational prophets of this atomic age, foreseeing our increasing mechanization and calling for our individual reassessment and rehumanization. Both *Surfacing* and Rich's *Diving Into the Wreck* depict female heroic quests, with descent and surfacing metaphors of watery rebirth.

90 SCHIEFER, NANCY A. "A Baleful Look at the Folly of Self-Righteousness." *London* (Ontario) *Free Press*, 1 November, p. A17.

Praises *The Handmaid's Tale* highly, as speculative fiction like Doris Lessing's, or Aldous Huxley's *Brave New World*; Atwood's baleful look at fundamentalism and self-righteousness is biting and lyric; her poetry pervades and lifts her moral feminist and humanist vision beyond her tamer, earlier work. *The Handmaid's Tale* will chill, caution, and perhaps challenge our assumptions.

91 SCHLOZ, GÜNTHER. "Schön kühl gehaltene Frauen." *Frankfurter Allgemeine*, 5 October, Bilder und Zeiten sec., p. [5].

Atwood's books are of interest to both men and women. Although her work addresses the problems of the "New Woman" from a female perspective, it also shows the futility of categorizing women's literature as a purely female aesthetic. *Die eßbare Frau (The Edible Woman)* and *Lady Orakel*, recently released in Germany, were two of Atwood's first novels in the English-speaking world. These early novels use satire to show desperate women who have broken out of traditional behavior to find they can not flee from everyday life. Once they are on the run as independent women, there is no going back; they are not free, just alone.

92 SCHWARZKOPF, MARGARETE von. "Hier liegt die Wahrheit im Kuchen . . . ." *Welt* (Hamburg), 10 August, Geistige Welt sec., p. 5.

Recommends *Die eßbare Frau*, the recent German translation of *The Edible Woman*. This fifteen-year-old artistic and entertaining novel may be less polished than Atwood's later fiction, but still shows great originality and spontaneity. Quotes Atwood on the source of the title, *The Eatable* [sic] *Woman*, which came to her in front of a pastry shop displaying little marzipan piglets. *The Edible Woman* took the idea of woman as object one step further – to woman as edible object.

93 S[COBIE], S[TEPHEN]. Review of *Interlunar*. *Malahat Review*, no. 70 (March), pp. 160-61.

Briefly compares Atwood to Pablo Picasso, whose fame went on after his early and greatest work, done in collaboration with Braque; Atwood has yet to surpass her "'collaboration' with Susanna Moodie." Is impressed most by *Interlunar*'s sheer efficiency of craft, image, and aphorisms; but vaguely senses a desperate searching for subjects, as with Picasso. Though the familiar Atwood animals, torture, and victims emerge, only occasionally is there the galvanic surprise of "The Light" or the splendid "The Saints." Mostly an oddly "'patriarchal'" rhetoric is in too-firm control.

94 SHEARD, SARAH. "Captives and Keepers." *Brick*, Fall, pp. 24-26.

Celebrates *The Handmaid's Tale* as a realistic, prophetic, exquisitely executed, totally delightful prison book, in the genre that ranges from the Madeline series to [Dickens's] *Oliver Twist* to [Solzenitsyn's] *One Day in the Life of Ivan Denisovich*. The reviewer, who is a prison book addict, suspects that Atwood must be one, too. Why are prison stories so compelling? The delicious minutiae, of a gesture or a cigarette, expands into a heightened clarity and significance. Everyday things become precious. Imagined tests restore the reader's self-confidence. Atwood must have had wicked fun inventing her Game, costumes, passwords, and moves. Her all-too-realistic Righteous Fundamentalist Right outlaws civil freedoms, women's equality, and love; she does not over-dramatize the danger. Yet individual heroism eventually triumphs, although the narrator may not be identified. The reviewer complains only that Atwood did not write 300 pages more.

95 SHERMAN, KENNETH. "The Survival of *Survival*." *Idler*, no. 5 (June-July), pp. 25-30.

Argues, as a Jewish-identified Canadian writer, that *Survival* oversimplifies identity, nationalism, victims, and survival. Writers like Gwendolyn MacEw[e]n may identify with foreign landscapes; great writers like Kafka may reflect our century's rootlessness. All poets are exiles who write from longing; but *Survival* reduces A.M. Klein's universal "Portrait of the Poet as Landscape" to a statement on Canadian culture. *Survival* is not unique to Canada. Comparing White, affluent Canadian victims to those in Black and Asian undeveloped countries is absurd; comparing Canadian victims to those of the Holocaust, as Atwood's 1973.2 does, is almost obscene. Her survival theme is reductive; for Jews, survival is not nationalism, but values beyond survival; we need to see man's affirmations, humanity, and love.

96 SIGURDSON, NORMAN. "Atwood Offers a Bleak View." *Winnipeg Free Press*, 12 October, p. 63.

Sympathizes with Offred, but concludes that *The Handmaid's Tale* is disappointing, dispiriting, and politically simplistic. "Her unrelentingly pessimistic portrayal is splendidly written and compellingly realized, but the author's didactic purposes ultimately overwhelm her literary skill. . . . Ms. Atwood's dystopia is frightening indeed – her narrator's terror and helplessness are palpable and moving – but it is never really believable." Atwood tries more to attack the extremes – the Moral Majority and militant feminism – that viciously polarize our society, than to create a plausible world. Her liberal middle-class attack is ultimately irrelevant. The banal dog-Latin talisman is as empty as the book's philosophic core. The "Historical Notes" appendix fills in some gaps and reassures us that Gilead ended. Atwood should have probed fascism and oppression's attractions more deeply.

97 SLAWSON, TABBY. "Margaret Atwood Talks Fame, Fiction, and Feminism." *Birmingham Post-Herald*, 12 April, Kudzu Magazine sec., pp. 4-5, 8.

Interviews Atwood in Tuscaloosa: Atwood discusses her literary life, writing habits, childhood, feminism, and bird watching. Quotes several academics and one student on Atwood as writer and teacher.

98 SMITH, ROWLAND. "Margaret Atwood and the City: Style and Substance in *Bodily Harm* and *Bluebeard's Egg.*" *World Literature Written in English* 25, no. 2 (Autumn):252-64.

Appreciates *Bodily Harm*'s satiric comedy, its ironic double-takes, and its satirized yet sympathetically vulnerable Rennie. City values are trendy, stultifying, and counterfeit in Atwood's fiction. Unlike the protagonists of the first three novels, Rennie changes in perception and understanding, not by a final act: she can do very little, in gaol, except ineffectually cradle Lora. The end is optional, because the way out is unimportant; what matters is her changed compassion. *Bodily Harm*'s "special charm lies in its macabre humour," comedy, and pathos. Atwood's satire involves us in double-takes: we readers are trapped, with Rennie, into making conventional judgments, then trapped into denying their core truths. Jocasta's views are comic, and partly true. *Bluebeard's Egg* similarly depicts suspicious and susceptible protagonists, who change in perception rather than action, as in the marvelous title story.

99 SPECTOR, JUDITH A. "The Fatal Lady in Margaret Atwood's *Lady Oracle.*" *University of Hartford Studies in Literature* 17, no. 3:33-44.

Interprets, from a Jungian perspective, Joan as both femme fatale and contemporary suicidal woman poet, or professional; a descendant of John Keat's "La Belle Dame sans Merci" and a sister to Sylvia Plath's "Lady Lazarus." Sexually hostile to men, and hostile to herself as a woman, Joan has "to stand up to her animus," and face her creativity that is blocked by men "who want her to fail." Like many contemporary women, Joan fears, with cause, that her triumphs will displease men. Her real mother is a destructive, potentially both murderous and suicidal femme fatale; Alfred Lord Tennyson's suicidal femme fatale, the Lady of Shalott, is her literary "'mother.'" At the end, Joan abandons both her femme fatale and her ladylike behavior, and acts with strength and understanding.

1985

100 SPRIET, PIERRE. "L'indétermination dans les nouvelles de Margaret Atwood (*Dancing Girls*)." *Journal of the Short Story in English*, no. 4 (Spring), pp. 95-108.

A overall theme of violent duality runs through Atwood's poetry; similarly, her short stories have their own identity and a discursive constant. *Dancing Girls*'s fourteen different stories represent the banal and everyday. Each story uses a simple narrative form to propose a transformation, but never offers a narrative resolution to achieve that transformation. The constancy lies in the purely negative withholding of logical closure and the continual lack of spectacular and dramatic events. Information always comes from the point of view of one character who restricts the field of vision and of knowledge by imposing an internally focused account on the reader. The omnipresent not-knowing manifests itself in the absence of an outcome. "Giving Birth" depicts the dilemma of only being able to gain knowledge through words. The heroine in "Lives of the Poets" claims that writers know they do not know, and that is why they write. The *Bluebeard's Egg* stories are similarly enigmatic and ambiguous. An Atwood story communicates what affirms uncertainty, and pronounces with words the defeat of all discourse.

101 [STEINBERG, SYBIL]. Review of *The Handmaid's Tale*. *Publishers Weekly* 228, no. 24 (13 December):45.

Hails *The Handmaid's Tale* as Atwood's most daring work, "a bitter, all-too-plausible vision" of Western discontent, and a gripping story. Finds the American-rooted Gilead chillingly revealed, and the narrator particularly complex and fascinating; finds both warning and hope in the ambiguous end. Concludes: "In this astonishing novel, Atwood has achieved a high level of social and artistic discourse. It deserves an honored place on the small shelf of cautionary tales that have entered modern folklore – a place next to, and by no means inferior to, [Huxley's] *Brave New World* and [Orwell's] *1984*."

102 STROMBERG, KYRA. "Gefährliche Seiten." *Süddeutsche Zeitung* (Munich), 9 October, Literatur sec., p. 8.

Admires the prose pieces of *Die Giftmischer: Horror-Trips und Happy-Ends* (*Murder in the Dark*) as skilled literary exercises, or linguistic finger exercises, that lie somewhere between the novel and the poem. As usual, Atwood effectively presents fearless insights, humor next to terror, and the oppressive as if it happened incidentally. Even "Happy Endings," with its good sense of humor, has a creepy quality. Anna Kamp's translation maintains Atwood's variations in tone.

103 ____. "Symbolischer Kuchen." *Süddeutsche Zeitung* (Munich), 18-19 May, p. 132.

    Die eßbare Frau, the recent German translation of *The Edible Woman*, reveals the twenty-four-year-old Atwood's surprisingly well-developed talent for dark comedy. Events are precisely and intelligently portrayed against the backdrop of a cold, grey Canadian winter. Chaos is contrasted with the clean, calm world of the middle class. Atwood has a sharp eye for reality and draws decisive conclusions. The change to the third person, to signify Marian becoming a stranger to herself, is unconvincing. Waldhoff's translation is close to the original text.

104 THOMAS, GILLIAN. "Atwood's Novel Vision." *Atlantic Provinces Book Review* 12, no. 4 (November-December):26.

    Appreciates *The Handmaid's Tale*, whose speculative fiction returns to the nineteenth-century novels of political ideas. Though the falling birth-rate premise is questionable, given developments like embryo transplants, the completely convincing takeover of women's money dispels all questions. Offred's fate is deliberately not told. The ["Historical Notes"] appendix shows a 1980s-like pedantic, sexist academic conference: Gilead's oppression and overthrow have changed nothing.

105 TREMBLAY, ANNE. "Canadian Authors Find Paris Can Be a Closed Shop." *Gazette* (Montreal), 10 August, p. C3.

    Cites Atwood as one of the major Canadian writers, English and French, whose work is mostly unknown in Paris; quotes Atwood's former publisher Yves Berger on *Surfacing*'s failure in France, and Matt Cohen on the problems of its translation and of French anti-feminism.

106 van HERK, ARITHA. "Atwood Cuts through Ice of Contemporary Society." *Calgary Herald*, 9 October, p. F7.

    Celebrates *The Handmaid's Tale*: our cautious literati should find the courage to give Atwood her long-deserved Governor-General's award for fiction. Atwood "cut[s] through the congealing ice of contemporary society" to reveal the terrifying potential of human beings and of extreme ideas. *The Handmaid's Tale* is speculative fiction, fable, and allegory of what could happen. Its world is plausible, immediate, and frightfully ordinary; its central metaphor is hunger – for touch, for love, simple human hunger. "Offred embodies the human longings that will always differentiate the person from the state. . . . Few readers will emerge unscathed" from seeing the dangers of our own small fanaticisms.

107 VanSPANCKEREN, KATHRYN, ed. *Newsletter of the Margaret Atwood Society*, no. 2, [6] pp.

Contains information on the Atwood Society's aims, officers, proposed by-laws, and its annual meeting at the 1985 Modern Language Association Convention; a brief description of the 1985 MLA Atwood Session, with an abstract of Rowland Smith's paper there [see 1985.98]; news of primary and secondary Atwood books, articles, theses, and lectures; and Atwood's teaching, reading, and lecture schedule.

108 VERDUYN, CHRISTL. "From the 'Word on Flesh' to the 'Flesh Made Word': Women's Fiction in Canada." *American Review of Canadian Studies* 15, no. 4 (Winter):449-64 passim.

Cites Atwood in discussing both phases of women's writing in Québec and English Canada in the past twenty-five years: the search for self; and the writing on language and writing. As *Survival* suggests, women become their own jailkeepers. Rennie's out-of-body experiences, in *Bodily Harm*, are discarnation, the extreme negation of inner and outer self. *Lady Oracle* shows that women's mind/body alienation can be comic. As *Surfacing*'s protagonist senses, women "'must stop being in the mirror.'" *Murder in the Dark*'s third eye, which is "'the eye of the body,'" suggests a consciousness of mind/body.

109 WALKER, SUE. "Interview with Margaret Atwood." *Negative Capability* 5, no. 3 (Summer):51-67.

Interviews Atwood, who currently holds the Endowed Chair in Creative Writing at the University of Alabama, in February at Mobile Bay: Atwood discusses her writing habits for fiction versus poetry; learning to write as a student and a student editor; her future novels, which include rewriting a 1968 try; marriage, parenting, and biography; political writing and the literary scene in the United States versus Canada; and recommends that young writers get Lewis Hyde's *The Gift* and a waterproof bicycle bag for manuscripts, and learn to budget their time and money.

110 WHITEWAY, DOUG. "Atwood Tale Looks into Future." *Winnipeg Free Press*, 8 October, p. 34.

Atwood discusses the politics and optimism of *The Handmaid's Tale* in Winnipeg 7 October: its grim scenario projects the worst tendencies of contemporary North American society–religious fundamentalism, anti-feminism, censorship, and pollution–to their logical conclusion. *The Handmaid's Tale* is a cautionary tale, not a solution. Societal changes for the worse can be bizarre, and come quickly, as with the Spanish Inquisition, the McCarthy period, and Nazi Germany. But Atwood isn't necessarily pessimistic: even Gilead has resisters, and does end, as the ["Historical Notes"] post-script shows. "'Some people would say this is a wildly optimistic book because it doesn't end with atomic bombs blowing everybody up.'" Atwood leaves Canada to write, because she has to help in so many causes when she's here.

111 WILSON, SHARON R. "Turning Life into Popular Art: *Bodily Harm*'s Life-Tourist." *Studies in Canadian Literature* 10, nos. 1-2:136-45.

Discusses *Bodily Harm*'s literal and metamorphic camera images, and Rennie's metamorphosis. Like other Atwood characters, Rennie is "an unseeing or mirror eye and a pseudo-self, . . . packager/photographer/victimizer as well as photo/product/victim." She sees existence like a film strip, and packages it for popular consumption. Rennie must shed her distancing, fragmenting camera vision, as well as her literal camera, in order to change. *Bodily Harm*'s background camera imagery is revolutionary, aesthetically and politically. Rennie is reborn when she can touch and feel. In the paradoxical, unresolved end, Rennie breaks out of the frame photograph, and other layers and filters, in a political, personal, and profoundly radical metamorphosis. Revised: 1987.171.

112 WONG, CHRIS. "Atwood and the 'Spark from Heaven.'" *Vancouver Sun*, 4 November, p. B6.

1985

Describes Atwood's "Blood and Thunder" talk for the Vancouver Institute, which drew an overflow audience of about 2,000. Atwood, who feels like a "'cultural Fuller brush person'" on book tours, said "Plod and Wonder" would more accurately describe writing. Writers, when not writing, wait for the "'spark from heaven' to ignite their work." She often procrastinates, as with *The Handmaid's Tale*, but books that want to be written keep intruding, like ghosts; you write them or get haunted. Atwood is now working on the Can. Lit. Cookbook, to benefit P.E.N.

113 WOODCOCK, GEORGE. "Canadian Poetry: The Emergent Tradition." *Yearbook of English Studies* 15:239-52.
Approves Atwood's good selections and modest, sensible introduction to *The New Oxford Book of Canadian Verse in English*; acclaims A.J.M. Smith's pioneering, definitive anthologies. Atwood's brisk, but shrewd, winnowing of Smith's earlier poets reflects posterity's tastes. Discusses Canadian voice and sense of place, from the Confederation poets through Al Purdy and Patrick Lane; the Montreal modernists, with their British and American influences, especially Ezra Pound's early Imagism and later Cantos; the myth-oriented 1960s poets; the 1960s and 1970s flowering; and a few omitted poems. Commends Atwood's assessment of P.K. Page and Al Purdy, and William Toye's selection of Atwood's own tough, varied, vital poems. Reprinted, slightly abridged: 1987.174.

114 ____. "Horizon of Survival." In *Towards a Canadian Literature: Essays, Editorials, and Manifestos.* Edited by Douglas M. Daymond and Leslie G. Monkman. Vol. 2, *1940-1983.* Ottawa: Tecumseh Press, pp. 425-27.
Reprint of 1973.106.

115 ____. Introduction to *Canadian Writers and Their Works: Poetry Series.* Edited by Robert Lecker, Jack David, and Ellen Quigley. Vol. 9. Toronto: ECW Press, pp. 1-14.
Places Atwood in the second generation of Canadian modernists; and finds that Mallinson 1985.70 undervalues Atwood's increasingly visual orientation, as in "You Are Happy," and committed moralism, as in "Beyond truth.'" The latter is discussed in Woodcock's own 1975.52, which Mallinson's formal, technical essay has overlooked.

116 WOODCOCK, JOHN. "Science and Survival in Margaret Atwood's *Life Before Man*." *Publication of the Society for Literature and Science* 1, no. 1 (November):9.

    Abstract of 1986.266.

117 WORTH, CHRISTOPHER. "Mapping the Boundaries: Margaret Atwood's *Surfacing*." *World Literature Written in English* 25, no. 1 (Spring):145-51.

    Surfacing sharply foregrounds language and national identity, as with David's secondhand Americanism. "Boundaries abound . . . : city/country, north/south, culture/nature, good/evil, life/death," and Canada/America. Human boundaries must exclude, as the father's fences do. The characters see themselves as non-Americans. The narrator withdraws from her literal and linguistic otherworldly immersions not, as Lecker 1981.64 suggests, to parody the rebirth journey, but to show the human need for boundaries. *Surfacing* is not only a participle, but also a gerund, of the boundaries of surface tensions. *Surfacing* is Canadian in its complex, ironic recognition of human differentiation, survival, and identity.

118 WYMAN, MAX. "Atwood: New Work Is Plainly a Warning." *Province* (Vancouver), 13 October, p. 56.

    Interviews Atwood, who now sees *The Handmaid's Tale* as more like [Aldous Huxley's] *Brave New World* than like [Anthony Burgess's] *A Clockwork Orange*, and as feminist, in the basic sense of are all souls equal? *The Handmaid's Tale* is partly warning, partly didactic; "'a working out of possibilities,'" not a prediction. Despite the horror and the handmaid's enigmatic escape, the novel seems optimistic, and Atwood agrees: "maybe she gets out. . . . [W]e haven't blown ourselves up with atomic bombs. And" Gilead ended, as shown by the ["Historical Notes"]. Though *The Handmaid's Tale* seems to attack religious extremists, Atwood points out its altruistic religious opposition. Atwood reads the Bible in an "'absolutely fundamental'" way, by putting Christ's public words, "the Golden Rule and the Beatitudes," first.

119 YALOM, MARILYN. "Margaret Atwood: *Surfacing*." In *Maternity, Mortality, and the Literature of Madness*. University Park and London: Pennsylvania State University Press, pp. 71-88; [and 90-92].

1985

Like Sylvia Plath's *The Bell Jar*, *Surfacing* depicts an alienated protagonist who moves through bizarre acts "to the brink of normality"; but Atwood's Conradian inner journey is more imaginative, complex, and mythic. *Surfacing*'s mother has been emotionally absent for her daughter. Though the narrator's weird acts are certainly psychologically mad, they yet have the logic of a psychotherapeutic regression; and they also suggest primitive initiations, ritual sacrifice to call the dead, and the primitive "separation, transition, and incorporation" rites for pregnant women that Arnold Van Gennep's *Rites of Passage* describes. Atwood revises Christian myth with a female return to nature that could lead to "personal and social rebirth," and with the scrapbook drawing of a mother/daughter icon. "Giving Birth" also links "maternity, madness, and reborn self"; its mysterious other woman is Atwood's "female Christ figure" and "mythic helpmate."

1986

1 ABLEMAN, PAUL. "After the Revolution." *Literary Review* (London), no. 94 (April), pp. 35-36.

Finds *The Handmaid's Tale* implausible, uninteresting, and humourless, except for its ["Historical Notes"]. We're asked to believe that modern America could have a fundamentalist resurgence like Iran's, that radioactive waste and additives could make most women infertile, and that a bizarre handmaid system, contrary to "erotic and emotional imperatives," could be institutionalized. Offred does little but copulate and shop. Atwood's "flowing, slightly mannered prose" sweeps the reader, but not the critical intelligence, along. Orwell's *Nineteen Eighty-Four* "never seemed plausible either," but it anatomized present trends and told an exciting story. Almost all women authors lack the technological and political grasp of the best male futurists, and "the blood-lust indispensable for imagining a historical nightmare."

2 ABU-JABAR, DIANA. "North of the Border." *Belles Lettres* 1, no. 5 (May-June):2.

Uses *Survival*'s idea of the "symbolic parallel of woman and land" to introduce *Surfacing* and books by four other Canadian women writers. *Surfacing*'s nameless narrator reenters the wilderness, "submerges herself in the womblike" lake and earth, and allows her woman's self and fertility to reemerge. The masculine figure and the "'Americans'" are identified with "intellect and 'progress'"; the female figure with emotion and body.

3 ADACHI, KEN. "All the Old Definitions Seem Broken Away." *Toronto Star*, 20 December, p. M4.

Finds, in a three-anthology review, Atwood's and Robert Weaver's selections for *The Oxford Book of Canadian Short Stories in English* discerning and wide-ranging, if familiar. Their avowedly historical book is a "handy and honorable," if conventional, guide to many of our best short stories.

4 ____. "Atwood, Callaghan Share Literary Prize." *Toronto Star*, 27 October, p. D1.

Reports that the much-lauded writer and civil liberties campaigner, Atwood, and the poet and *Exile* editor Barry Callaghan, share this year's Philips Information Systems prize for outstanding contributions beyond their own work to Canadian letters. Each receives an Indian sculpture and a Philips word processor and software worth about $15,000; the $5,000 cash award is shared. Few will quarrel with these choices – but why has this award gone only to Toronto writers so far?

5 ____. "Governor-General's Award Was a Surprise to Atwood." *Toronto Star*, 4 June, p. F1.

Quotes Atwood: "'I've been shortlisted several times for the Governor-General's fiction award. I thought I would have to wait much longer, judging by the strong short list this year.'" Atwood could not attend yesterday's Montreal ceremony because of a prior Toronto commitment to receive the Canadian Jewish Congress's Humanitarian Award for her Amnesty International and P.E.N. civil rights work. Some may carp that Atwood, who got $605,000 from Fawcett for the American paperback rights, does not need the $5,000 Governor-General's prize; but few would deny her novel's brilliance. Jurors H.R. Percy, Helen Weinzweig, and Rudy Wiebe chose *The Handmaid's Tale* over Sharon Butala's *Queen of the Headaches*, Keath Fraser's *Foreign Affairs*, and David Adams Richards's *To the Stilt House* – but Robertson Davies's *What's Bred in the Bone* was unaccountably not shortlisted.

1986

6 ____. "Poetic Rewards." *Sunday Star* (Toronto), 23 November, p. A24.

Reviews two excellent books: Atwood's intricate, self-concealing, political *Selected Poems II* and Dorothy Livesay's lyric, openly affirming *The Self-Completing Tree*. Atwood's best work "frees one's perceptions drastically," through ironic surfaces and sudden, brilliant images of baleful reality. "Her poems are steeped in politics, sexual and political. . . . There isn't much room for hope, charity or communication." She expresses the anxieties and cruelties of our century. "If you can stand the unrelentingness, this is indeed a powerful collection."

7 ADDINGTON, FRAN. "Atwood's Gilead Tale: Everywoman's Worst Fear." *Minnesota Women's Press* 2, no. 9 (August 19-September 1):3.

Welcomes *The Handmaid's Tale* as a psychological cautionary tale that spells out our worst fears. Though the other characters lack Offred's distinct, single identity, the powerful message more than compensates. The last ["Historical Notes"] chapter, which says what "sociology professors will always say," makes fascist Gilead "seem more frightening than the Third Reich" by accepting and gridding Gilead's excesses. This important book, coming when "the women's movement seems at low ebb," gave the reviewer new perspectives on issues.

8 ADLER, CONSTANCE. "Canadian Club." *Philadelphia Magazine* 77, no. 3 (March):67, 71-72.

A three-book review that appreciates *The Handmaid's Tale* and Timothy Findley's *Not Wanted on the Voyage* and criticizes Robertson Davies's *What's Bred in the Bone*. Both Atwood and Findley worry about men's present misuse of power; both create societies that become fascist to survive, and heroes who struggle to preserve intuition and pity. Atwood's masterfully understated, exquisitely controlled style is perfect for her cautionary story. *The Handmaid's Tale* shows Atwood as an agile theorist of social roles; it is frightening, heartfelt, ideological, superbly told, and her best novel.

9 AHOLA, SUVI. "Margaret Atwood ie kadehdi Nobelia toiselta kirjailijalta: 'Palkinnot tekevät meistä kerran vuodessa sankareita'" [Margaret Atwood does not envy another writer the Nobel Prize: Prizes make us heroes once a year]. *Helsingin Sanomat*, 17 October, p. 27.

1986

In Finnish. Interviews Atwood on the day Nigerian author Wole Soyinka is announced as the Nobel Prize winner. Atwood, who approves the choice, discusses the value of literary prizes; Canadian literature's international recognition, early Canadian literature, and the current second renaissance; and the realities in *The Handmaid's Tale*.

10 ALATON, SALEM. "Atwood Wins Governor-General's Award." *Globe and Mail*, 4 June, p. C5.
Reports on this year's Governor-General's Literary Award winners and on the ceremony, which Atwood was unable to attend. Her futuristic *The Handmaid's Tale* won for English-language fiction.

11 ALLEN, BRUCE. "In Brief." *Saturday Review* 12 (May-June):74.
Is finally very disappointed by *The Handmaid's Tale*: Atwood's detailed, dystopic horror of victimized protagonist and savage Puritanism is first exhilarating, then thin, then tiresome linguistic tricks and predictable ironies. But Offred's memories have "real substance, and suspense," as does the chilling irony of the concluding "Historical Notes." Excerpted: 1987.53.

12 ALLEN, DICK. "The Eye Which Cannot Help but See." *Crosscurrents* (Westlake Village, Calif.) 6, no. 3:10-19.
Values Atwood's protean, even-handed, empathetic realism. Her transitional generation sees both sides of pre- and post-1960s roles, as in *Power Politics*. A major, popular, and serious writer, Atwood bases her work on the transformation of relationships. Everything and "every life matters deeply"; like her characters, we struggle to survive life's changes. Her intense, oblique poetry is strong in narrative, with shifting line-lengths and tones; and often directed to a "'you,'" as in *Power Politics*'s surreal transformations. *Murder in the Dark*'s powerful prose poems and *True Stories*'s lengthened lines merge with her prose. The sad, true "Betty" and the pornography scene in *Bodily Harm* show "how humans use one another, and particularly how women are victims": we cannot passively ignore this, or escape into Absurdity or black humor. Atwood sees men and women struggling against stupid, entrapping roles; she movingly portrays the bewildered Nate of *Life Before Man* and the longing Edward of "The Resplendent Quetzal." We must begin, over and over, Atwood insists. Accompanied by a selection of Atwood's poetry and fiction.

1986

13 AMSTER, BETSY. "A Vision of Future Shock for Women." *Plain Dealer* (Cleveland), 16 February, p. P12. Newsbank 1985-1986, 71:C1.

Like Orwell's *Nineteen Eighty-Four, The Handmaid's Tale* is "a fully imagined negative utopia"; and compelling, if not literally plausible. There's irony here, and sharply subversive humour. Though you may resist Atwood's harsh inventions, these "strong, angry images . . . of fascism masquerading as freedom, and of hope under duress" will disturb you long after you leave Gilead.

14 ANDERSON, LINDA. "Editorial." *Writing Women* (Newcastle upon Tyne) 4, no. 2:3-4.

The Handmaid's Tale's narrator struggles to survive isolation, and imagines a "'you'" for whom to write. If we women write not for a rejecting censor, but for a "'you'" that is "'us,'" we transform our writing. Atwood, in an empowering gesture at her Newcastle reading from the novel, had us bring our chairs "close to her and to each other."

15 ANDREWS, PAUL. "Ever-Surprising Atwood." *Seattle Times*, 2 March, p. K6.

Finds *The Handmaid's Tale* effective, portentous, and satirical, but depressing and hard to relate to: it evokes pity and horror, not empathy. "We resist standing in the narrator's shoes": she lacks an emotional life to identify with, understanding, and a rebellious will, so we can't cheer her on, as we do Winston Smith in *Nineteen Eighty-Four. The Handmaid's Tale* may be good for you, but it isn't sweet.

16 ____. "A 'Feminist *1984*'? No, but Canadian Author Is Sounding a Warning." *Seattle Times*, 17 March. Newsbank 1985-1986, 89:C6.

Interviews Atwood, who is in Seattle to promote *The Handmaid's Tale*: Atwood discusses its "feminist *1984*" label, the consequences of assumptions, declining Western birth rates, and other real bases for Gilead, including the group that held a "funeral for bottled embryos discovered in a laboratory," and was congratulated by President Reagan.

17 "Atwood Adjusts to U.S. Enthusiasm." *Toronto Star*, 28 February, p. D19.

Atwood warned, in her Centre for Inter-American Relations speech to Canadian publishers and American literary agents, that border-crossing Canadian authors, used to qualified Canadian responses, may have difficulty adjusting to American enthusiasm. *The Handmaid's Tale*, which has been lavishly praised in the United States, is the third Canadian book on the *Publishers Weekly* bestseller list this year. Atwood recalled that in 1973, when *Surfacing* was published in the United States, being a Canadian writer was "'a social handicap.'" Reprinted in part: 1986.253.

18 "Atwood: Canada 'Rates a Nine.'" *Globe and Mail*, 17 January, p. C9.
At a P.E.N. conference session that discussed censorship in the United States and Canada, Atwood gave Canada a nine out of ten rating on censorship, but cited Canadian customs officials who increasingly intercept United States books sent to Canadian homosexual and feminist bookstores.

19 "Atwood's Tale Wins Award." *Halifax Chronicle Herald*, 4 June, p. E2.
Reports on the 1985 Governor-General's Literary Awards: Atwood's bleak, Orwellian *The Handmaid's Tale*, which is her first United States best seller, won for English-language fiction.

20 "Atwood's Vision of Woman in the Future." *Vancouver Sun*, 23 August, p. C2.
Briefly describes Atwood's mordant, disturbing, quasi-Orwellian satire, *The Handmaid's Tale*, which is now a Seal paperback.

21 BAKER, JOHN F., and SYMONS, ALLENE. "'Publishing in Canada' Draws Over 300, Results in Many Deals." *Publishers Weekly* 229, no. 12 (21 March):17.
Describes Atwood's witty luncheon speech to the publishing symposium. Atwood recalled her early publishing and publicity, and contrasted the United States's critical vocabulary of "'magnificent' and 'stupendous'" to Canada's "'flawed but interesting.'"

22 BARRON, NEIL. "A Dark, Eloquent Vision." *Fantasy Review* 9, no. 8 (September):20.
Highly recommends *The Handmaid's Tale*'s "disquieting chronicle." Atwood's plot elements are familiar; her prose is spare yet eloquent and poetically resonant; Offred's perceptive but limited "vision illuminates our world" and hers.

1986

23 BARTKOWSKI, FRANCES. "A Fearful Fancy: Some Reconsiderations of the Sublime." *Boundary 2* 6, no. 2:23-32.

Concludes a tracking of "the textual discourse of the sublime," from Longinus and Sappho through Edmund Burke and Freud on the uncanny to Roland Barthes on bliss, by reading "Hand," from *Murder in the Dark*, as a "text of bliss that exhibits the turn of disintegration and verbal reconstitution of the body," transforming fear to *jouissance*, and internalizing the parental illuminating structures to create an inclusive *I*.

24 BATTIATA, MARY. "Atwood's Nightmare New World." *Washington Post*, 6 April, pp. G1, 6.

Interviews Atwood at the Canadian chancery: Atwood discusses *The Handmaid's Tale*'s realism, citing fundamentalist Catholic handmaidens in New Jersey, an abortion consent law in Canada, compulsory pregnancy testing in Romania, *Time*'s Pat Robertson cover story, and "'Boy, this could really happen here'" reactions; the fundamentalist right as the most likely flag for a United States Gilead, contrary to McCarthy 1986.150; fear and caution in repressive countries; Gilead's religious and partly fundamentalist opponents; and feminism, social disease, pornography, and Western women's freedoms. Describes and excerpts from Atwood's Gilead; describes Atwood as "a pale-eyed Cassandra," guarded, priestly, humorous, and "sure enough of her opinions for two people and then some." Reprinted, barely cut: 1986.25 (below).

25 _____. "A Canadian Cassandra." *Winnipeg Free Press*, 20 July, p. 9.

Reprint of 1986.24 (above), very slightly cut.

26 BEAUDRY, ALBERT. "Conte de la servante." *Relations* (Montréal), no. 520 (May), pp. 123-24.

The Handmaid's Tale [sic] is an astonishing political fiction that extrapolates the dangers and tendencies existing in North America. Atwood's carefully composed parable has characters as complex as ourselves. Paradoxically, Gilead's oppression is based on a reinvention of the Biblical hopes of the poor.

27 BELLING, MICHELE. "Big Brother Gets His Utopia." *Body Politic*, no. 127 (June), p. 35.

Celebrates *The Handmaid's Tale* as "entertaining science fiction, thrilling romance, lively" and very scary realism, and "incisive and immaculate feminism [that] dissects the strange grey domain where militant feminists and right-wing Christians overlap and merge. Gilead, in fact, meets many feminist demands." Its women are completely protected from male advances; pornography is outlawed; birthing is a female-only ritual; the handmaids are taught to hate men, and occasionally given a live one to pull apart. Atwood bases the action on the "protection from vs freedom to" that underlies the pornography debate and left/right dissonance. Her humanist "feminism is based not on hatred and separation but on love and understanding." All the characters are humanly real, including the woman-identified feminist activist mother, and the lesbian "buddy Moira, a canny, cynical, street-tough politico whose inspiring macho heroics play" brilliantly against Offred's outward passivity. Atwood's everyday details make Gilead terrifying and funny; her innuendoes, like All Flesh, speak volumes. Her novel pinpoints why the quarrelsome left should start working together.

28 BENDER, EILEEN T. "The Woman Who Came to Dinner: Dining and Divining a Feminist 'Aesthetic.'" *Women's Studies* 12, no. 3 (March):320-21.

Briefly mentions, in a discussion of modern women artists' and writers' treatment of food, that *Surfacing* both fears and exalts nurturance. *The Edible Woman*'s cake effigy saves Marian from starvation and the cannibalistic world; it lets her swallow society's distorted vision, and emerge with a different feminine self-image.

29 BENNETT, DONNA. "Naming the Way Home." In *A Mazing Space: Writing Canadian Women Writing*. Edited by Shirley Neuman and Smaro Kamboureli. Edmonton: Longspoon/NeWest, pp. 228-45 passim.

Categorizes Atwood and Audrey Thomas as covert mythic structuralists, like Northrop Frye, who seek the hidden, benign, powerful source of language, in contrast to the sceptical deconstructionists who see language as a closed, self-referential system, in an inset essay, "What Is Feminine Writing?" The latter critiques language theories and Freudian-based Lacanian female erotics, and proposes an aesthetics of female erotics based on female orgasm's

1986

double vortices. "Naming the Way Home," which is thought, written, heard, read, and spoken during an English Canadian feminist literary critics' flight on the Naming Express, contains a journal called "Progress: Feminist Social Darwinism," a CBC broadcast on "Anglophone Women Critics of Canada," the inset essay, and a sermon on women's identity, "The Naming Paradox."

30 BEST, ANDREW. "Probing Ambiguities." *Country Life* 179 (3 April):893.

The Handmaid's Tale's totalitarian state recalls Orwell's *Nineteen Eighty-Four*, as *Bodily Harm*'s plot and setting recalled V.S. Naipaul's *Guerillas*: Atwood gives us the woman's view of male territories. Gilead is male-dominated, full of spies and torture, and not the "'women's culture'" that Offred's feminist mother wanted. Offred, who remembers and loves, "can still (alas) submit." Offred's is the poet's solitary, fastidious ego, probing ambiguities, as women must do, and "severely and eloquently" questioning the male principle.

31 BLACK, LARRY. "Of Atwood and the U.S. Glitterati." *Vancouver Sun*, 22 February, p. D4.

Describes Atwood's new United States literary stardom: cover stories for *The Handmaid's Tale* in eight major book reviews, high praises in ten national magazines, and a second printing. The *New York Times* 1986.143 accolades sound like excerpts for the book's next printing. Only Mary McCarthy, who has resided in Paris the last several years, found *The Handmaid's Tale*'s religious fundamentalist rulers incredible; but the day after her 1986.150 review, *Time*'s cover story was Pat Robertson running for president in 1988. Quotes Atwood on the United States's history of repressive Puritans and revolution; she and her publisher, Houghton Mifflin, are pleased with her novel's success. Atwood brought her file of clippings for Gilead-like events to last month's New York P.E.N. conference. An abbreviated, anonymous version appears as 1986.32 (below).

32 [BLACK, LARRY.] "Warm U.S. Welcome for Atwood's Novel." *Globe and Mail*, 15 February, p. D14.

An abbreviated, anonymous version of 1986.31 (above) that omits the discussion of McCarthy and Pat Robertson.

33 BLOTT, ANNE. "Journey to Light." *Fiddlehead*, no. 146 (Winter), pp. 90-95.

Appreciates *Interlunar*'s cyclic process of "encounter, descent, and re-emergence," in the three-part "Interlunar" poems, which partly reshape the myths of Orpheus, Euridice, and Persephone. The introductory "Snake Poems" are a sardonic naturalist's guide to "myths, truths, and lies" about snakes. As in Atwood's evocative [watercolour] cover, and "A Boat," all things belong to a continuum of life, death, and rebirth. Like the child-parent poet, the Buddhist's moon, and Heraclitis's river, things are constant, one, and changing. A power that manifests itself in "control, destruction, and creation" links the poems. Atwood evokes "a *frisson* of the skull beneath the skin," as in the ironically titled "Harvest" and the nuclear winter "A Holiday." Some of "Interlunar I" focuses on mortality, children, and parents; some on bleak male-female struggles and postures. "Interlunar II" presents nightmare isolation and the nadir of male-female relations. "Interlunar III" returns to the light, accepting death and life, affirming change and darkness in the title poem. Reprinted: 1988.4.

34 BOERS, ARTHUR. "No Balm in Gilead: A Frightening View of Present Trends." *Sojourners* (Washington, D.C.) 15, no. 10 (November):45, 47.

Finds *The Handmaid's Tale*, which soberly envisions our possible future, "more conceivable – and more horrifying," despite the uneasily hopeful end, than George Orwell's *Nineteen Eighty-Four*. Life in the supposedly Bible-based Gilead "is cruel, horrifying, and mundane." Offred "is completely controlled and always watched"; no superhero, she perceives honestly her coerced choices and Gilead's corruption. All of Gilead's cruelties have happened; we often see injustices, like the oppression of women, as normal, and "fail to see" the victims. This disturbing book will stay with you.

35 BOLAND, MAURA. "Woman [sic] Are 'Cattle' in This Future." *Philadelphia Daily News*, 25 February, pp. 42, 45.

Praises *The Handmaid's Tale*'s skillful narrative and superb social critique. Atwood's more personal novel may be less terrifying than Orwell's *Nineteen Eighty-Four*, because all of it has already happened somewhere, and because we in the late twentieth century

1986

can't be shocked. Even Atwood's goriest scenes are slyly satirized. Gilead is a women's culture that few of us would like.

36 "Booker's Half-Dozen." *Economist* 301 (18 October):96.

Briefly reviews the six books short-listed for Britain's Booker Prize: praises *The Handmaid's Tale*, Kingsley Amis's *The Old Devils*, and Robertson Davies's *What's Bred in the Bone*; finds faults in Paul Bailey's *Gabriel's Lament*, Kazuo Ishiguro's *An Artist of the Floating World*, and Timothy Mo's *An Insular Possession*. *The Handmaid's Tale*, which is Atwood's best book, is wry, "polished, ingenious – and terrifying." Offred's story is "a secret record of atrocities [in police-state, Genesis-ordered Gilead], and of what happens when her Commander breaks the rules" to see her.

37 BORAWSKI, WALTA. Review of *Handmaid's Tale*. *Gay Community News* 13, no. 38 (12 April):B4.

Praises Atwood's harrowing cautionary tale, where white male radical right Christians persecute women, feminists, and gay men; rape and pornography are gone; now there are hangings and women tearing to pieces an alleged rapist. "Anyone who was not intimidated by Dean Wycoff's $3 million campaign to bring about capital punishment for homosexuals is urged to read this book. The rest of us" will find it beautifully records "our worst night (and day) mares."

38 BRADY, CHARLES A. "Puritan Anti-Utopia Envisioned." *Buffalo News*, 23 February, p. E6.

Finds *The Handmaid's Tale* a vividly realized "female-aligned 1984"; admirably balanced – men are not all monsters; and a dazzling anti-Utopia. The "Historical Notes" epilogue cleverly compresses the political analysis. Gilead, which borrows from Cromwellian Puritanism, nineteenth-century Mormonism, and the Ayatollah's Iran, is an entire state turned Malvolio [in Shakespeare's *Twelfth Night*], forbidding cakes, ale, and uncontrolled sex. "This latter deprivation is Offred's greatest travail." One hopes that Atwood is not an infallible prophet; Orwell has not been.

39 "British Author Wins Booker Prize." *Winnipeg Free Press*, 23 October, p. 42.

1986

Kingsley Amis's *The Old Devils* won Britain's highest literary award, the Booker Prize of [£]15,000 [sic], edging out Robertson Davies's extraordinary *What's Bred in the Bone* in the final choice between the two. Atwood's *The Handmaid's Tale* was one of the six finalists. Five judges, led by Anthony Thwaite, chose from 127 entries from past and present Commonwealth countries. Paul Bailey's *Gabriel's Lament*, Kazuo Ishiguro's *An Artist of the Floating World*, and Timothy Mo's *An Insular Possession* were also shortlisted.

40 BRODHEAD, JAMES E. Review of *The Handmaid's Tale. American Atheist* 28, no. 7 (July):45, 48.

Hails Atwood's witty, chilling, and very plausible futurist fable. Gilead's seeds are planted and sprouting now: "the growing militancy of right-wing religious fundamentalists; pandemic pollution . . . ; sexually-transmitted incurable diseases;" declining white birth rates; media-hyped violence; and many Americans willing to sacrifice freedom for security. "Gilead is a fundamentalist, white, Christian theocracy" that "Jerry Falwell, Ed Meese, Phyllis Schafly, or Ronald Reagan" might dream. Offred is an entrancing, gutsy survivor who "carries the hope that civilization itself will" survive Gilead's savage zealotry. Offred's detached musings, lyricism, intelligence, and wordplay leaven what might be unbearably claustrophobic. Atwood deliciously skewers American religion, as in the Soul Scrolls; and gloriously, triumphantly manages to satirize even contemporary religion.

41 B[ROSNAHAN], J[OHN]. Review of *Bluebeard's Egg and Other Stories. Booklist* 83, no. 2 (15 September):82.

Briefly praises Atwood's understated, hilarious, shocking stories, that beautifully probe the inner and outer worlds of their characters.

42 BUNKE, JOAN. "There's No Balm in This Gilead." *Des Moines Register*, 20 April. Newsbank 1985-1986, 98:C6.

Praises *The Handmaid's Tale*'s concise irony, taut mystery, diabolically hilarious women's dress codes, "almost Orwellian power and gallows humor," and its "thumpingly ironic" ["Historical Notes"] finale. Atwood's "chilling story of a male-dominated theocracy . . . will freeze the spine of any independent 1980s woman who" thinks her

1986

freedoms safe. Offred, an oppressed surrogate mother, waits, schemes, remembers, and takes risks, but is ground down.

43 BURGIN, RICHARD. "A World without Love." *St. Petersburg Times*, 9 March. Newsbank 1985-1986, 78:C3.

Commends *The Handmaid's Tale*: "unlike Gilead, it considers human life first and ideology second." Atwood meets the challenge of creating serious social criticism, set in the future but illuminating our present, without "degenerat[ing] into mere political prophecy." A compelling storyteller and an almost flawless stylist, "Atwood always entertains before she tries to teach," in mordant, witty dialogue and Offred's tender, ironic reflections. Though there are early moments of too much 1980s detail, we give ourselves over to Offred's story once Atwood does so. Totalitarian rulers who suppress citizen's – here, women's – rights suppress love and, ultimately, themselves. Offred's fate is open, but Gilead falls, as we learn from the "Historical Notes," a "hilarious spoof on academia" and superbly ironic comedy.

44 CALDWELL, GAIL. "Making Do in the World They Found." *Boston Globe*, 16 November, pp. B116, 118.

Appreciates the haiku-like "intricate character studies and diminutive explosions" of *Bluebeard's Egg*. Atwood's "emotional middle ground" and "'ordinary-looking wreckage,'" make "Hurricane Hazel" more than a coming-of-age story. These women often have trouble escaping what "the world (read: men) assigned them," as in "Uglypuss" and "Loulou." Yet some hard-earned victories are real: the most engaging, infernally energetic 73-year-old mother sweeps roofs; and, in "The Sunrise," the solitary, quirky life of the artist, Yvonne, has seasoned integrity. The bored, half-lonely Sally of the title story realizes, in a strange Bluebeard metaphor, that she has lost her man. But "Spring Song of the Frogs" and "Scarlet Ibis" can't transcend their selfish protagonists.

45 ____. "Weeping for an Imperfect World." *Boston Globe*, 2 February, pp. A11-12.

Values Offred most: though much of *The Handmaid's Tale*'s coup and rule by "the Phyllis Schaflys and TV preachers of today . . . seems didactic, or at least inconceivable, . . . [Atwood's protagonist] is so convincing that even her wretched way station in Gilead seems credible." The characters–the mildly pathetic Commander, the awful Serena Joy, the aging feminist mother, the best friend, Moira–and Offred's snatched, tortured memories make the novel evocative, despite its anti-Utopian limits. Hope lives; Offred's story survives. "The empathy Offred elicits," through her humor and angst, even includes her keepers. "Offred eventually resists; no one this gently defiant could do otherwise." The end is brittle and ironic. Details expose evils, of cruel matriarchy and of censorship. Offred "revere[s] our freedoms even while mourning their decadent legacies."

46 CAMPBELL, CHARLES. "Canada Becomes More than a Writers' Novelty." *Chicago Tribune Bookworld*, 26 January, pp. 37-38.
    Interviews Atwood, who talks about *Survival*; women writers in Canadian, English, and American literature; and *The Handmaid's Tale*, a Canadian best seller that has been highly praised there. Atwood believes in "'the orneriness and diversity of the American people,'" as in Gilead's civil war. Reprinted: 1986.47 (below).

47 _____. "Women Helping Put Canadian Literature on the Map." *Macon Telegraph and News*, 23 March, p. D10, 15.
    Reprint of 1986.46 (above).

48 CARLSON, KRISTINA. "Margaret Atwood Kirjoittaa Naisen Ehdoilla" [Margaret Atwood writes on a woman's condition]. *Suomen Kuvalehti* (Helsinki), 31 October, pp. 42-43.
    In Finnish. Begins an interview with Atwood by praising *The Handmaid's Tale*. In the utopian tradition of Orwell and Huxley, Atwood's Bible-based totalitarian future state warns us about the present. Her novel succeeds by combining moral suffering with an exciting story that is based on real situations. Atwood discusses women's limitations versus their freedoms; the need for a history, beyond dates and wars, written primarily by women about how people have really lived; how having a baby instantly changed her own public image; the effect of colonialism on Canadian literature and culture; the universal common ground of women; and the use of the term genius to describe men rather than women.

49 CARPENTER, MARY WILSON. Letter to the editor. *Women's Review of Books* 3, no. 12 (September):5.

1986

Argues that the "Historical Notes" appendix, not mentioned in Greene's excellent 1986.100, "redefines the entire [*Handmaid's*] tale (tail) by repositioning it," with devastating accuracy and wit, in a largely masculine discourse; thus reenacting "the valorization of patriarchal history and the denigration of such 'crumbs' as women's texts supply." The male Keynote Speaker, Professor Pieixoto, makes the tale an object of his sexist wit, focuses at tedious length on identifying the male Commander, and trivializes the handmaid's documentation of patriarchal oppression and sexism. When the Speaker ends by calling the handmaid's tale "'eloquent'" and "'mute,'" he is being spoken by feminist theory, which sees women's history as a blank but more eloquent page. Appropriately, a blank space follows his last words.

50 CARRINGTON, ILDIKÓ de PAPP. "Demons, Doubles, and Dinosaurs: *Life Before Man*, *The Origin of Consciousness*, and 'The Icicle.'" *Essays on Canadian Writing*, no. 33 (Fall), pp. 68-88.

Analyzes the romance structure, demonic doubles, and Jaynesian theories that underlie *Life Before Man*'s realistic surfaces. *Life* should have a third epigraph, from Julian Jaynes's *The Origin of Consciousness in the Breakdown of the Bicameral Mind*: Elizabeth's auditory hallucinations, and the persisting voices of the dead in Sinyavsky's fantastic "The Icicle" (in a paragraph not quoted in *Life*'s second epigraph), are linked to Jaynes's thesis of pre-conscious, bicameral man's right-hemisphere hallucinations of the ancestral dead, who were heard as gods. *Life*'s title alludes to life before Jaynes's conscious, left-hemisphere, god-severed, cut-off man. Like Atwood's four other novels, and certain stories, *Life*'s structure follows the first half of Frye's romance pattern, the quest and descent. The ironic *Life* questions identity, as dead ancestors become demonic, destructive doubles that haunt the death-bound living. Elizabeth manifests Jaynes's schizoid, vestigial relapses into bicamerality; she and Lesje become doubles of each other, and of their internalized, demonic dead ancestors. Life is meaningless, because social structures and religion have receded. Lesje's need for living gods is religious, not regressive; her need for the voices of her dead is Jaynes's "quest for authorization.'" Lesje's pregnancy is not creative nor responsible, but "a very bitchy act of survival." Both Elizabeth and Lesje experience the fantasies of Sinyavsky's narrator. The final paradisial posters recall

Jaynes on Marxism as a substitute for divine authority, and on Marx's lost paradise. Reprinted: 1988.12. Revised as part of 1987.22.

51 CARTER, NANCY CORSON. "Tales and Their Tellers." *St. Petersburgh Times*, 21 December, p. D7.

Appreciates *Bluebeard's Egg*. As in "Significant Moments in the Life of My Mother," Atwood's characters go from familiar to strange worlds and return, changed by the stories they remember and tell. "Loulou," with its most cartoonish title character, plays with the idea that "we create each other through words." The complex "Bluebeard's Egg" ends disturbingly. Nature does not heal in "Spring Song of the Frogs." The setting of the nostalgic, seemingly autobiographical "Unearthing Suite" recalls *Surfacing*; the story's ending epitomizes the collection's mood and theme. Though Atwood exposes human eccentricities, she prizes the sometimes successful search for "grace in a world too often entropic and sad."

52 CHEUSE, ALAN. "Margaret Atwood Stumbles on Science Fiction." *USA Today*, 7 February, p. D4.

Finds *The Handmaid's Tale* disappointingly boring. In this weird theocracy, Offred does little but sleep, shop, and get ceremonially raped. Because there's too little action and too much of Offred's *longueurs*, the reviewer "wanted to escape from the book."

53 CLOUTIER, GUY. "Pour découvrir la littérature du Canada anglais." *Soleil* (Québec), 10 May, p. D7.

Atwood's writings, especially *Bluebeard's Egg*, exceptionally translated by Hélène Filion, are prime examples of a true English Canadian literature. The stories of *L'Oeuf de Barbe-Bleue* are severe, yet glow with humor; each ends with a moral. They portray women of all ages; Loulou, Betty, Sally, and Yvonne worry about relationships, mainly how to reconcile their need for freedom with their desire for affection from men. Atwood's feminism here is effective without being ideological or militant.

54 COLE, THOMAS. "Two Poets Who Are Equally Adept at Short Stories." *Baltimore Sun*, 16 November. Newsbank 50:A14.

Recommends two excellent, contemporary collections, *Bluebeard's Egg* and Josephine Jacobsen's *Adios, Mr. Moxley*. Only

Atwood's funny-sad "Loulou," "Uglypuss," and "Bluebeard's Egg" have traditional plot constructions with characters in conflict. "Two Stories about Emma" and "The Salt Garden" are not Atwood's best.

55 COLLISON, ROBERT. "Margaret Atwood Takes N.Y.C." *Chatelaine* 59 (June):64-65, 99-100.

Profiles Atwood's New York City literary stardom: she revised the script for a fictive underground-in-Gilead radio broadcast last March to promote *The Handmaid's Tale* in a "vintage Atwood" takeover, "[w]ielding her pen like a surgeon's scalpel" while everyone deferred. Her bleak Gilead has been a mainstream best seller here, though McCarthy 1986.150 dissented. Atwood has become a crowd-attracting New York literary fixture overnight. She and other women writers had a literary brawl with P.E.N. conference organizer Norman Mailer when they protested the lack of women panelists. Atwood says, bizarrely, that her success is resented in Canada – but how could Canada "give her *more* acclaim?"

56 "Confessions of a Booker Judge." *Punch* 291 (15 October):57.

Very briefly describes the six short-listed Booker Prize novels and gives Ladbrokes odds for each. Finds *The Handmaid's Tale* ridiculous feminist nonsense (Ladbrokes:5-1); Robertson Davies's *What's Bred in the Bone* long-winded and boring (3:1); Timothy Mo's *An Insular Possession* unreadable for Melvyn Bragg (6:1); Kingsley Amis's *The Old Devils* most deserving (2:1); Paul Bailey's *Gabriel's Lament* depressing but also first-rate (5:1); and Kazuo Ishiguro's *An Artist of the Floating World* a nice change (9:2).

57 CONN, MELANIE. "Speculative Fiction." *Kinesis* (Vancouver), October, p. 32.

Reviews three novels of resilient heroines in horrifyingly oppressive future worlds; finds *The Handmaid's Tale* plausible, powerful, and subtle; loves its spare style and tangible experiences; but is disappointed with its women's class-line collusion and its heroine's increasing dependency on men. Cites a radio interview where Atwood said that Gilead's only invented scenario – "the funeral for a foetus" – appeared in a newspaper clipping someone recently sent her.

58 C[OOKE], J[UDY]. Review of *The Handmaid's Tale. Fiction Magazine* 5, no. 2 (Spring):2.

Atwood's witty, angry novel "satirises the wilder forms of sexual politics and religious fundamentalism flourishing in America today. . . . As a novel of ideas it is provocative and ingenious and as an adventure story– . . . Offred may contact the rebels and escape–it is narrated with pace and nerve."

59 COSSTICK, RUTH. Review of *The Handmaid's Tale. CM* 14, no. 1 (January):12-13.

Praises *The Handmaid's Tale*'s word play, satire, humour, intriguing ["Historical Notes"], message, extraordinary plot, and horrifying acuity. Atwood depicts an anti-social, anti-sexual future revolution at a time of environmental destruction and an alarmingly low birth rate. The Aunts' inculcations are bluntly horrifying. Recommends *The Handmaid's Tale* for grades 12 and up, as an urgent warning against misuse of our environmental and human resources.

60 COUSINS, P. Review of *Handmaid's Tale. Choice* 23, no. 9 (May):1384.

Unreservedly recommends Atwood's "magnificently crafted and understated" *The Handmaid's Tale* as an important feminist novel that rivals Orwell's *Nineteen Eighty-Four*. In a repressive U.S. theocracy, women are enslaved, but impregnated like queen bees. Offred slowly and matter-of-factly pieces together an entire nightmare society, "a horror world so muffled and enclosed that" an anachronistic "'hello'" sends chills "down the reader's spine."

61 CRAMER, SIBYLLE. "Aus frostigen Gegenden." *Zeit* (Hamburg), 3 October, Literatur sec., p. 12.

Prefers Atwood's novels to *Unter Glas*, the German translation of *Dancing Girls and Other Stories*. These overstuffed and overstretched short stories make it clear that Atwood is a novelist through and through. Some read like aborted novels, and seem cut short. "Betty" is pressed into a feminist mold. "Polarities," one of the most impressive stories, reads like a fugue for two voices. "The Grave of the Famous Poet" is a romantic still life that resembles a cut-out picture from a novel. The stories are uncomplicated, and often funny, but not experimental. Atwood, like Joyce Carol Oates and Doris Lessing,

1986

belongs with those honorable and prolific English language writers who
protect and expand narrative tradition without changing it.

62 DAVEY, FRANK. "Alternate Stories: The Short Fiction of Audrey
Thomas and Margaret Atwood." *Canadian Literature*, no. 109
(Summer), pp. 5-14.

Compares the secret and inherited "'other' stories in *Dancing
Girls* and *Bluebeard's Egg* with those in Audrey Thomas's *Ladies &
Escorts*, *Ten Green Bottles*, and *Real Mothers*. Both authors separate
the "culturally 'received'" stories, that Atwood's characters consciously
follow, from "other potentially more authentic stories"; both authors
use inherited romance stories – Atwood uses the gothic romance of
fairy tale and melodrama that she links to Mary Shelley's story of
technological hubris. Atwood's "main characters are inarticulate about
their personal stories . . . . [that] have an 'alternate' wordless language
of symbol and aphoristic gesture," as in "The Resplendent Quetzal,"
where well, crèche, and bird reveal the stories Sarah and Edward hide.
"Scarlet Ibis" and "Bluebeard's Egg" similarly contrast mechanical
bourgeois life and relationships to mysterious symbol. "The alternate
story is nearly always implicit, iconic, and only marginally understood
by the characters," as with the mother's unknown god in "Unearthing
Suite." Atwood's characters trivialize iconic events in clichés, as the
mother does in "Significant Moments in the Life of My Mother." Both
Atwood and Thomas implicitly discredit Northrop Frye's archetypal
romance structure, by suggesting other gardens than Adam's or
Bluebeard's, and other stories.

63 DAVIDSON, CATHY N. "A Feminist *1984*: Margaret Atwood Talks
about Her Exciting New Novel." *Ms.* 14, no. 8 (February):24-26.

Interviews Atwood and praises *The Handmaid's Tale* as her best
and most controversial work. Atwood's speculative fiction follows
Huxley and Orwell, but "eerily resembles our present, and . . .
concentrates on what happens to women" in a fascist, misogynist, racist,
anti-Semitic, Moral Majority Gilead. "A latter-day Anne Frank, Offred
defiantly witnesses and records what she cannot overtly protest." What
makes Gilead so terrifying is that it "is and is not the world we know,"
as with the [Phyllis] Schafly-like Serena Joy. Atwood discusses *The
Handmaid's Tale*'s realistic historical motifs, PCB pollution, the Bible,
repression, pornography, censorship, the revolutionary United States

as "'humanity's testing ground'" of conflicting ideas, Gilead's resistance, the Puritans, and the politics of speculative fiction.

64 DAVIS, ROBERT I. "Stereotypical, Tedious." *Greensburg* (Penn.) *Tribune Review*, 13 April. Newsbank 1985-1986, 98:C8.

Rejects *The Handmaid's Tale* as tedious, limited, depressing, and stereotyped; wants Orwell's rebellious Winston Smith and encompassing *Nineteen Eighty-Four*. Though totalitarian societies are tedious, so is Atwood's novel, frequently; and it depends entirely on a wildly implausible "assumption of imminent widespread genetic failure." The reviewer "got some laughs out of the satirically described 'ceremony,'" but found most of the book dreary. Offred's understanding of her society is too limited, and her passivity is unsatisfying and depressing. The other characters are little more than "a feminist's worst suspicions come true," for the males; or a male chauvinist's, for the females.

65 DESAI, BINDU T. "Anti-Utopia." *Indian Express* (Bombay), 6 July, Express Magazine sec., p. 5.

A mixed review of *The Handmaid's Tale*. The ["Historical Notes"] section brilliantly parodies academia; "[t]hrough Pieixoto we get an idea of the historical and social conditions that" led to Gilead. "The novel eerily echoes the shallow, selfish[,] arrogant rhetoric heard in the west today"; Atwood has cited "British Prime Minister Margaret Thatcher's repeated declarations that 'a woman's place is in the home.'" But the historically based Gilead is not explored in depth; the main characters, Offred and the Commander, do not seem believable; and the latter's appalling attempt to make his slave his mistress leaves the reader unmoved. Yet *The Handmaid's Tale* is worth reading: "We are all [in India and elsewhere] closer to our own Gileads than we care to acknowledge."

66 DIXON, MICHAEL F. "Letters in Canada, 1985: Fiction 2." *University of Toronto Quarterly* 56, no. 1 (Fall):12-13.

Complains that Canada's first team of literature – Atwood, Barry Callaghan, Robertson Davies, Mavis Gallant, and Hugh Hood – had a stale season of "doing competently what they did better before" – why should *University of Toronto Quarterly* supplement their widespread, enthusiastic coverage in the popular media? Gives one sentence to *The*

1986

Handmaid's Tale: "Atwood dresses her usual dance team of victim and victimizer in unusual costumes against unexpected settings, . . . but their intricate steps move to the familiar Atwoodian gavotte of solemn polemic."

67 DOOLEY, D.J. Review of *Handmaid's Tale*. *Canadian Churchman* 112, no. 2 (February):25.

Finds *The Handmaid's Tale* brilliant, skillfully narrated, and a story that sweeps us up into its nightmare world – but if we stand back we see that this novel is based on an absurd hypothesis of a fundamentalist coup in the United Sates quickly creating "a so-called Christian nation . . . [that has] no hope or charity." Atwood has apparently "swallowed all the [media] propaganda against religion," and based her gripping story on a lie.

68 DUDAR, HELEN. "No Balm in Atwood's Gilead." *Wall Street Journal*, 12 February, p. 28.

Interviews Atwood, who has brought her scrapbook of clippings for *The Handmaid's Tale* to the New York P.E.N. International Congress: Atwood talks about pessimism, writing *The Handmaid's Tale*, her Puritan inheritance, *Surfacing*, and feminism. *The Handmaid's Tale* "is mesmerizing, manipulative, scary and, for female readers, sometimes viscerally painful." Atwood, like her literary style, is cool, opinionated, sometimes dogmatic, but also spunky and sneakily humorous.

69 EDGERTON, CATHI. Review of *The Handmaid's Tale*. *VOYA* 9, no. 5 (December):212.

Finds Offred's testament powerful and utterly believable; we need to know, from the ["Historical Notes"] appendix, that Gilead ended. This nightmare begins in our myth of invulnerability. Should teenagers read this adult book? Yes, "if the future is to be theirs." Atwood's speculations, though fearsome, urge youth to imagine consequences as they recognize today's repressions; perhaps they will value and protect freedom, so that their own future high school children will be free to read *The Handmaid's Tale*, when it is their required reading. Highest (5) quality rating; broad general (4) young adult appeal; for seniors, grades ten to twelve.

70 "Editors's Choice: The Best Books of 1986." *New York Times Book Review*, 7 December, p. 3.

Recommends *The Handmaid's Tale* as one of seven of the year's best fiction books, and describes it as a cautionary tale of "postfeminist future shock" whose Gilead is based on "our present problems run amok" and on Puritan history. Atwood's "deft sardonic humor makes much" of *The Handmaid's Tale*, which is "funny and ominous at the same time."

71 EHRENREICH, BARBARA. "Feminism's Phantoms." *New Republic* 194, no. 11 (17 March):33-35.

Considers *The Handmaid's Tale* an absorbing novel and intra-feminist polemic. As in Orwell's *Nineteen Eighty-Four*, love seems the only really subversive force – the Commander's love for Offred, Offred's for Nick. Atwood's fantasy of masochistic regression is both seductive and repellent. Though her boring and grim dystopia is at times a coloring-book version of Orwell's, and Offred "a sappy stand-in for Winston Smith," perhaps Atwood warns us not only of the religious right, but of repressive feminism. For Gilead, superficially patriarchal, is also a utopia of militant cultural, or radical, feminism: no pornography; women's birthing circles and freedom from male abuse; and males reduced to stud service. Antifeminists' "strident female supremacist literature," like Phyllis Schafly's *The Power of the Positive Woman*, partly converges with these militants. Atwood's sadistic Aunts remind us of women's historic anti-women complicity. We must do better than Offred's passive back-turning. Reprinted, slightly cut: 1987.53.

72 ELIAS, MARILYN. "Author's Version of Church and State as One." *Los Angeles Times*, 9 May, p. E8-9.

Interviews Atwood, who visited Los Angeles on promotional tour: Atwood talks about *The Handmaid's Tale*'s success, plausibility, and the clippings that confirm its realism; and about her writing and mothering.

73 FEINSTEIN, ELAINE. "After Feminism Had to Stop." *Times* (London), 13 March, p. 15.

Features *The Handmaid's Tale* in a two-book review, and confirms its disturbing theme. Atwood's post-feminist, male-dominated science fiction shows "what we always knew about feminism. Not only is it" permanently threatened, but women will willingly collaborate in its demise. The novel's thriller-like power comes from the questions posed: how were women's rights so easily removed, why do the women "knuckle under so readily," and not resist? The heroine lives only in her memories and longings, but is not totally defeated. The novel depends on "imagining womb and ovaries as a key national resource, . . . [rarely] intact after some great catastrophe." Almost 20 years ago, *The Edible Woman* wittily exposed some weak links in sisterhood.

74 FELSKI, RITA. "The Novel of Self-Discovery: A Necessary Fiction?" *Southern Review* (Adelaide) 19, no.2 (July):131-48 passim.
Cites *Surfacing* and other 1972-85 women's novels in an analysis of the "'feminist'" or "'women-centred'" novel of self-discovery, whose protagonists search for transforming self-knowledge, reject society's male-defined roles, and redefine themselves as active subjects. As in *Surfacing*, female alienation is a lack of self-identity and language; the heroine may move from city to wilderness; nature may become a refuge; withdrawal from society may end in return and social engagement. *Surfacing* belongs not with the biographical, dialectical, and historical feminist *Bildungsroman* of the United States; but with the second kind of female self-discovery novel, the neo-Romantic, mythical "'awakening' to an essential female self" of Canada and West Germany. In the latter kind, as in *Surfacing*, the heroine quests for a lost paradise; civilisation is rejected; liberation means discovering "her own natural instincts"; and language fragments and alienates, while speechlessness is authentic. Though "feminist literary theory and cultural politics" debate the self-discovery genre, it serves "a historically important cultural need."

75 FERLAND, ISABELLE. Review of *Les danseuses*. *Nuit blanche* (Québec), no. 25 (September-November), p. 24.
The fourteen *Dancing Girls* stories are similar; all raise the question of what is banal. Applauds Atwood's ability to present ordinary situations, free of extravagance, with the exciting lure of an adventure story; but finds the avoidance of final resolutions frustrating. Quotes Atwood on how authors write to understand what everyone else knows about human nature.

76 FISHER, ANN H. Review of *The Handmaid's Tale*. *Library Journal* 111, no. 2 (1 February):91.

Highly recommends Atwood's powerful and memorable novel to most libraries. Gilead carries "far-right Schafly/Falwell-type ideals" to extremes, creating a feminist's nightmare.

77 FLOWER, DEAN. "Fables of Identity." *Hudson Review* 39, no. 2 (Summer):318-19.

Rejects *The Handmaid's Tale*: Atwood's novel fizzles because her "'what ifs'" are so embarrassingly implausible, though her story is otherwise human and disturbing. Alas, she hides her sarcastic wit to keep this nightmare solemn. The only politics here are sexual: men seem powerful but are really "lost, self-estranged, and choiceless, while females are powerful but divided against themselves, authoritative but vulnerable." Offred laments her lost freedoms, but why does Atwood think these losses imminent?

78 FRASER, LAURA. "A Tale of Gender Treachery." *San Francisco Bay Guardian* 21, no. 6 (19-26 November):23-24.

Praises *The Handmaid's Tale*: "Imagine a world where the Phyllis Schaflys and the Pat Robertsons got their way. Completely." Serena Joy sheds light on the Far Right's contradictorily crusading women. Atwood's absorbing, "imaginative comment on feminism and anti-feminism in the Age of Reagan. . . . goes beyond early feminist preoccupations of self"; *The Handmaid's Tale* is matter-of-fact and universally appealing. Though sentence-by-sentence it doesn't seem beautiful and profound, "it keeps you up at night with its frightening vision." The almost plausible plot, of invalidating women's bank cards, is the most chilling part.

79 FREELY, MAUREEN. "Picking Up the Pieces." *Observer* (London), 16 March, p. 25.

A five-book review that finds *The Handmaid's Tale* "the ultimate feminist nightmare" of women's lost liberties. Its success owes less to its sketchy politics than to the suffocating girls' boarding school atmosphere that makes its bizarre rituals plausible, and to its schoolgirl intimation that petty vice is the way to salvation. Offred is a partly brainwashed handmaid. Though chauvinist males supposedly run Gilead, at home women rule.

1986

80 FRENCH, WILLIAM. "Atwood Is Reunited with Susanna Moodie." *Globe and Mail*, 2 September, p. C7.

Appreciates and excerpts from Atwood's introduction to the Virago Press reissue of Moodie's complete *Roughing It in the Bush*. Atwood's long affinity for Moodie includes *The Journals of Susanna Moodie*, a television play based on a murder in Moodie's *Life in the Clearings*, and ["Days of the Rebels"], a social history of Upper Canada, 1815-40. Atwood's graduate-student dream of a Moodie opera sent her to Moodie's books, and their gaps and tensions led to Atwood's own poems. Atwood also compares women writers in Canada and the United States in Moodie's time and now.

81 ____. "Authors Will Split $5,000 Cheque." *Globe and Mail*, 27 October, p. D9.

Two versatile polymaths, Atwood and Barry Callaghan, will share the Philips Information Systems Literary Prize for outstanding general contributions by Canadian literary figures under 50. Atwood and Callaghan will share the $5,000 cheque, but each will receive a Philips personal computer with trimmings, and an original stone sculpture by John Thomas of the Six Nations Reserve. Atwood, who lost the Booker Prize, is a multi-genre, internationally established writer and a human rights activist; Callaghan is a translator, writer, and *Exile*'s founding editor. Greg Gatenby, Patricia Hluchy, and Paul Farnell judged the Philips.

82 ____. "The Hot Stories." *Globe and Mail*, 29 November, p. E21.

Praises both *The Oxford Book of Canadian Short Stories in English*, edited by Atwood and Robert Weaver, and *86: Best Canadian Stories*, edited by David Helwig and Sandra Martin. Weaver, the world's expert on the Canadian story, has contributed greatly, as *Tamarack Review* editor and as CBC "Radio Anthology" producer, to its current flourishing. As Atwood's introduction points out, the writers included are mostly still alive, increasingly women, and increasingly from Western Canada. There are familiar, even classic, stories here, along with favorite new stories. One can always quibble; John Metcalf, for example, was inexcusably excluded.

83 ____. "Ottawa's 'Punitive Fees on Publishers' Attacked." *Globe and Mail*, 11 February, p. C9.

Reports on the opposition to a new federal policy of excessively high permissions fees, and on "Margaret Atwood month in New York," which includes a dinner, reading, reception, lunch, and McCarthy's 1986.150 *New York Times Book Review* front-page but lukewarm praise of *The Handmaid's Tale*.

84 FULFORD, ROBERT. "Souvenirs: The Price of Fame." *Toronto Star*, 16 August, p. M5.

Describes the Letters (Toronto) bookstore catalogue of 136 Atwood items that includes a December 1960 Victoria College Epicoene [sic] program autographed by the student who designed its cover and played Lady Haughty; Charles Pachter's high-ticket portfolio of *The Circle Game* and his *Speeches for Doctor Frankenstein*; secondary material, even a *Herstories* calendar; and first, autographed, and international editions.

85 GARDAM, JANE. "Nuns and Soldiers." *Books and Bookmen*, no. 365 (March), pp. 29-30.

Features Atwood's terrible and beautiful *The Handmaid's Tale* in a two-book review. Unlike the freedom-seeking heroines of *The Edible Woman* and *Surfacing*, Offred is an unwilling "nun in a nightmare nunnery," cut off from her marriage, child, and all physical freedom. Monastic ideals are imposed horrors in Gilead; Offred is conditioned to be a breeding machine for the state. Gilead's terrible world is partly our present, though it may lack the dread eternal grey of Orwell's *Nineteen Eighty-Four* – can one believe that the American woman's power could be removed overnight? Yet Atwood creates a strangely beautiful and dreamlike landscape that echoes Browning's tulips and Tennyson's poems. "There is even a horrible beauty in the heroine's plight" – her reverie, dignity, sorrow, and courageous rationing of her memories. Even horrors are depicted in pure, clear, but complex prose. The "Historical Notes" postscript reassures us that some nightmares end. Excerpted: 1987.53.

86 GARDNER, MARILYN. "Atwood's Tale of Future Shock – Feminist Style." *Christian Science Monitor*, 24 February, p. 22.

Finds *The Handmaid's Tale* challenging: "part political tract, part suspense thriller, part cautionary tale. Call it future shock, feminist-style. . . . Some details of Atwood's bizarre anti-Utopia are at least as

1986

repellent as those in" Aldous Huxley's *Brave New World* and George Orwell's *Nineteen Eighty-Four*, which are now seen as fiercely moral warnings – will Atwood's widely praised novel be so accepted? She does most persuasively show women's subjugation as a symptom of a politically and environmentally poisoned world. Offred's imagination and her will to survive help keep her sane.

87 GAUL, JOAN. "*Handmaid* an Engrossing Tale of a Grim Future." *Macon Telegraph and News*, 23 March, p. D10.
    Recommends Atwood's best-selling *The Handmaid's Tale* as a strong, engrossing story that "should be read," despite its excesses and questionable satire. Atwood's nightmare world differs from Orwell's and Huxley's in its focus on birth rates and women's place. Offred almost accepts her lot. *The Handmaid's Tale* is about power, love, and loss.

88 GAYLOR, ANNIE LAURIE. "It Can't Happen Here?" *Freethought Today* 3, no. 5 (June-July):1, 3.
    Celebrates *The Handmaid's Tale* as courageous, prescient, complex, and disturbing speculative fiction, with a marvelously empathetic Offred. Atwood dares ask "'What if?'" our "muscular Christian thugs," political fundamentalists like Pat Robertson, and religious-right theorists like the wealthy, patriarchal Chalcedons, combined, unchecked by our Constitution? Because women's status measures liberty, and religionists attack women's rights, the woman's point of view fits here. Atwood's suspense novel reveals what happened piecemeal. Her beautiful prose and "strong underlying humor" grace her grim scenario. The Tammy Faye Bakker/Phyllis Schafly Wife is homebound, speechless at last. Offred "is at once a passionate, educated, twentieth century post-feminist and a timeless prototype of the theocratic victim . . . ."

89 GERTLER, GAYLE. "Atwood Backs Away from Her Grim Vision." *Providence Journal*, 23 February. Newsbank 1985-1986, 78:C11.
    Finds *The Handmaid's Tale* gripping, horrifying, haunting, and painful – but then ruined by its witty ["Historical Notes"]. Atwood's novel has the claustrophobic narration and grim near-future scenario of *Nineteen Eighty-Four*, but not its courage. Gilead's sterile inhumanity is mind-boggling. Atwood's lush, compelling prose may

obscure the lack of context in the first 100 pages. "But reducing Gilead to an academic exercise cheats the reader who has traveled with Offred through her wrenching memories"–should we question her veracity? laugh at the professors? see the failure to probe despotism as ensuring its recurrence?

90 GETTY, SARAH. "Miss Atwood's Stories Show Great Resilience." *Sunday Telegram* (Worcester, Mass.), 21 December, p. D10.

Finds a pleasing technical skill, despair, strength, black comedy, and a "dire moral vision" in *Bluebeard's Egg and Other Stories*, as in *The Handmaid's Tale*. Atwood links her two themes of the insecure woman and of our world's fundamental insecurity; the characters' neuroses are accurate responses to reality, as in her brilliantly realistic and surreal "The Salt Garden." The girlhood sketches create fascinating biographical resonances. Lacking her mother's optimism, the narrator responds with dread, as in "Bluebeard's Egg."

91 GIBSON, SHARAN. "Opening Forbidden Rooms: Margaret Atwood's Crystal-Cut People Are Not Afraid to Look behind Closed Doors." *Houston Chronicle*, 28 December, Zest sec., p. 15.

Praises *Bluebeard's Egg*'s varied, unique, and wonderfully real, even though sometimes distanced, characters. "Significant Moments in the Life of My Mother" and "Hurricane Hazel" seem very autobiographical. Sally in "Bluebeard's Egg" must discover the disheartening, forbidden truth about her doctor-husband. The many finely drawn characters include the potter Loulou, the political-theatre activist Joel, and the survivor Emma. Atwood's people dare to open life's forbidden doors.

92 ____. "The Queen Bee: Margaret Atwood Envisions a Terrifying Role for Women in a 'Brave New World.'" *Houston Chronicle*, 19 January, Zest sec., pp. 23, 25.

Acclaims *The Handmaid's Tale*: "What if we woke up one morning" to find that Gilead's scenario had already happened? Atwood stretches contemporary trends to their logical, chilling conclusions. "The narrator is her typically sensitive young woman who sees more than those around her. Being a handmaid is," she sardonically observes, like being a hive's queen bee. The Soul Scrolls, and the housebound Commander's wife who once gave TV speeches on women staying home, provide humor. But the loss of freedom is grim and frightening. "*The Handmaid's Tale* [is] an excellent novel about the direction our lives are taking, and Margaret Atwood's book belongs on the same shelf with *Nineteen Eighty-Four* and *Brave New World*. Read it while it's still allowed."

93 GINGELL, SUSAN. "Power Ploy." *Books in Canada* 15, no. 1 (January-February):40-41.

Protests, in a letter to the editor, the limited thinking of Goddard's 1985.41 Atwood profile. The descriptions of her surroundings and hair are self-indulgent and irrelevant. Though Goddard gives us his and Atwood's comments honestly, he insists that *The Handmaid's Tale* be about limited moral directives, and wants to see fundamentalist anti-feminism as a warning against women moving too quickly. If there is an anti-feminist backlash, the question is how to change the conservatives and the imbalanced power structures, not women's liberation. Atwood's entire work examines power – and that concerns everyone.

94 GIUDICI, GIOVANNI. "Sfogliate Questa Margaret." *Espresso* (Rome), 9 November, pp. 187-88.

Briefly reviews *Lady Oracolo*, the Italian translation of *Lady Oracle*. Atwood, like many authors writing in English today, has a distinct culture-based style. Her cutting novel displays "Canadianness," while confronting American myths of domestic ritual, false open-mindedness, and women's escapist literature. Atwood tells the story beautifully, and moves skillfully between the personalities of the narrator.

95 GLENDINNING, VICTORIA. "Lady Oracle." *Saturday Night* 101, no. 1 (January):39-41.

Finds *The Handmaid's Tale* ingenious and disturbingly believable, but misses the zany humour and comic-sinister, surreal creativity of Atwood's best novel, *The Edible Woman*. Though Atwood ranks with international women and Commonwealth writers, her novels became hyperliterary and academic after *Surfacing*'s female pantheism led to critical debates. "What seems to ignite her talent is fear" – of society's consuming expectations in *The Edible Woman*, of catastrophe in the great "When It Happens" and the futuristic fantasy of *The Handmaid's Tale*. The latter is also a mutant of the past, a nasty *Upstairs, Downstairs*, made oddly believable by myths and memories, especially from Grimm and the Brontës. Like all Atwood's work, *The Handmaid's Tale* is a subtle costume gothic about power and freedom, oppressions and women's connivance. Reprinted: 1987.53.

96   GODARD, BARBARA. "Tales within Tales: Margaret Atwood's Folk Narratives." *Canadian Literature*, no. 109 (Summer), pp. 57-84.

Discusses *Bluebeard's Egg*'s privileging of embedded and frame anglophone Toronto folklore as a breakthrough in Atwood's narrative technique that invites our own communal and family stories; and contrasts *Surfacing*'s and *Lady Oracle*'s distancing of Indian and Québécois narratives and European *märchen*. In *Surfacing*, Americanized Anglo-Canadian language and "fakelore" appropriate and violate real and naturalized Quebec folklore, especially in the narrator's false, imitative illustrations of bowdlerized Quebec folk tales. The *loup-garou* and fanged princess of the embedded narrative point towards the later metamorphoses of narrator, father, and fish. *Lady Oracle*'s self-reflecting embedded *märchen* subversively refract Joan's metamorphoses in the frame plot. Here as in *Surfacing*, Atwood's parodying of fairy tale material is disdainful, not reverential; but *Lady Oracle*'s focus on process moves closer to real storytelling, as her subversion of patriarchal stories and discovery of women's stories suggests. *Bluebeard's Egg*'s title story, with its embedded Grimm and Perrault Bluebeards and its phoenix egg, mimetically represents, in Sally's decoding, the narrative processes of the book. "Images of growth and process," especially in "Unearthing Suite," value organic life and storytelling over fixed art. In "Significant Moments in the Life of My Mother," "mother and daughter, teller and writer" merge to lovingly create the fictions of "identity and community" that make us real. In "Hurricane Hazel," a Toronto local legend becomes a symbol, as the daughter "wreaks havoc in Buddy's life." Much of the *Bluebeard's Egg* portion is reprinted, revised, as 1987.44.

97   ____. "Voicing Difference: The Literary Production of Native Women." In *A Mazing Space: Writing Canadian Women Writing*. Edited by Shirley Neuman and Smaro Kamboureli. Edmonton: Longspoon/NeWest, pp. 87-88.

1986

An examination of oral and written texts by native Canadian women that refers to *Surfacing*'s matrilineal tradition, shamanic initiation, and, contrary to Guédon 1983.58, its final ambiguous transformation to artist-seer.

98 GOODWIN, STEPHEN. "Short Stories: The Art of the Matter." *Washington Post Book World*, 30 November, pp. 3-4.

A four-book review that praises the viscerally exciting *Raven's Wing* stories by Joyce Carol Oates, especially the ones about a man who handicaps races and a young boxer; and finds *Bluebeard's Egg*'s women characters more reflective, self-aware, and concerned with control, as in the title story. Atwood's shocks are mostly intellectual. Men come off poorly, as in "Uglypuss." A woman "subjecting [a man] to a long, careful, disappointed scrutiny" is Atwood's most frequent image.

99 GRAY, PAUL. "Repressions of a New Day." *Time* 127, no. 6 (10 February):84.

Finds *The Handmaid's Tale* overly complicated as a cautionary tale, but extremely and transcendently fascinating as a narrative "of an observant soul struggling against a harsh, mysterious world." Because Atwood's novel warns against too many things – "heedless sex, excessive morality, chemical and nuclear pollution" – it lacks the chilling realism of George Orwell's *Nineteen Eighty-Four* and Aldous Huxley's *Brave New World*. "Yet [the intelligent and curious] Offred's narrative is beguiling in the extreme." Though some will take *The Handmaid's Tale* for a feminist parable, Atwood's more complex vision shows that Gilead happened partly with women's help, as when the feminist mother burned pornography. Excerpts two paragraphs on Women's Salvagings.

100 GREENE, GAYLE. "Choice of Evils." *Women's Review of Books* 3, no. 10 (July):14-15.

Analyzes the feminist politics of *The Handmaid's Tale*'s cautionary dystopia. Atwood's horrifying vision corresponds logically to reality, as she says in the 1986.219 interview. We share Offred's ignorance and disorientation; with her we piece together a picture of Gilead. Offred is more a "'good German'" than a heroic freedom fighter: though she needs to believe in the courage of her friend Moira,

1986

who is a rebel and a lesbian separatist, Offred identifies with those who try to survive by "'ignoring.'" But such "'ignoring'" led to Nazi Germany, and Gilead. Though history does absolve Offred's mother's feminism, feminism is complexly satirized: in Gilead's "'women's culture'" of shared traditional female lives, work, and birth; in the spooky resemblance of its feminist burnings of pornography to the right's book-burnings; and in its cautionary parody of a separatist utopia at "Jezebel's." As with *Nineteen Eighty-Four* and *Brave New World*, this authoritarian future makes us wish for the present – but is our freedom real or sham? Atwood, like Offred, seems to "'want everything back, the way it was,'" over any imaginable planned society. But the reviewer wants – perhaps unfairly – some suggested ideal, some utopian alternative. See Carpenter 1986.49. Reprinted, slightly cut: 1987.53.

101 GRUMBACH, DORIS. "*Handmaid's Tale* Offers a Grim View of Loveless Future." *Chicago Tribune Bookworld*, 26 January, pp. 37-38.

Gives *The Handmaid's Tale* high praise as a real shocker, grim and fascinating, "gripping in its horrendous details, striking in the extensions Atwood makes from" our present to a possible future of repressive, loveless, cultureless puritanism. All the women have terrible, male-subservient names; everyone is a prisoner; there is always someone hanging on the execution wall. Offred's dimming memories make her present even ghastlier. The lack of events and the somewhat ambiguous end do not matter: "the society is the message," and we are held captive by pity and terror.

102 "Ham-fisted Imagery Sinks Moodie Exhibit." *Calgary Herald*, 27 February, p. B5.

Rejects most of Charles Pachter's 1980 *The Journals of Susanna Moodie* portfolio silkscreens, now exhibited at the University of Calgary. Pachter's imagery is broad, crude, clichéd, and harshly colored, a sledgehammer on Atwood's crystalline, evocative poetic structures. Pachter's best, *Death of a Young Son by Drowning* and *1837 War in Retrospect*, use suggestion and air-filled space. Though Pachter and Atwood are old friends, Atwood should have collaborated with an artist of her own rank.

103 HANCOCK, GEOFF. "An Interview with Margaret Atwood." *Canadian Fiction Magazine*, no. 58, pp. 113-44.

1986

Interviews Atwood 12 and 13 December, 1986, in her Toronto home: Atwood discusses interviews as fictions; the Canadian versus the American literary traditions, voices, and *Survival*; expanding the brackets of what is possible in an art form, as with the Mermaid Theatre's visible puppeteers, the visible author of the 1850s and now, and women's material; her own "brain-to-hand-to-pencil-to-paper connection with a page," and her improvisational writing, editing, and reading habits, versus academic abstractions; her parody "Regional Romances, or, Across Canada by Pornograph," for the Writer's Union pornographic project where Marian Engel's *Bear* began; her Maritime roots and English name; her success in getting "words to stretch and . . . [e]xpand the possibilities of the language"; form and shape in the universe; writing *Life Before Man, Lady Oracle, Surfacing, The Edible Woman, Murder in the Dark,* and "Significant Moments in the Life of My Mother"; morality in literature; the acting, more than thinking, Emma character; women, men, drowning, anxieties, and events in her fiction; "'process,'" deconstructionism, post-modernism, and other fashions in literary criticism ("As a theorist, I'm a good amateur plumber"); language as distortion; learning astrology and palm reading in Edmonton; *The Handmaid's Tale*'s circumscribed life, where details "become significant, luminous," and its ["Historical Notes"] epilogue, which is optimistic, like Orwell's. Atwood finds exhilaration and hope not in "'happy endings'" but, as with a well-done *King Lear,* in seeing "what it means to be human, on earth." Reproduces a manuscript page of "A Symposium on Violence." Reprinted: 1987.56.

104 "*Handmaid* Author Demands Independence." *San Jose Mercury,* 2 March. Newsbank 1985-1986, 78:B14.

Interviews Atwood, who is in the Bay area: Atwood discusses her childhood, Puritan ancestors, moral versus immoral uses of power, and men's position in *The Handmaid's Tale*; and describes her novels' character-shaped styles. *Lady Oracle* is baroque, *Bodily Harm* is slangy, *Surfacing* has run-on sentences and "syllogisms with excluded middles," and *The Handmaid's Tale* is pure, tight, and suspenseful, because its narrator must not indulge her emotions.

105 HARRIS, ROGER. "Atwood's Anti-Utopia is a '1984' for Women." *Star Ledger* (Newark), 9 February, sec. 4, p. 12.

Finds *The Handmaid's Tale* a most competent anti-Utopia, with the proper proportion of "horror and ludicrousness"; but doubts its basic assumption. "The true anti-Utopia must satirize or dwell upon some recognizably true social tendency," as George Orwell's *Nineteen Eighty-Four* and Aldous Huxley's *Brave New World* do. If one believed "the repression of women is growing" and leading to such a theocratic dictatorship, then *The Handmaid's Tale* would be "an almost perfect" anti-Utopia.

106 ____. "Short and Sweet." *Star Ledger* (Newark), 7 December, sec. 4, p. 22.

A short review that praises highly the very imaginative, superb *Bluebeard's Egg* stories, which display Atwood's "sure skill and splendid grasp of human situations" throughout. The description of love in "Bluebeard's Egg" is unusual.

107 HARTMAN, DIANE. "Male Chauvinism Is Big Brother in an Engrossing Tale." *Denver Post*, 23 February, p. D19.

Praises *The Handmaid's Tale* as powerful, disturbing, and yet compellingly readable. The believable and bizarre setting is imaginable. Offred is an average, comfortable young woman – a loving wife and mother, with a job she enjoys. "It's as if she falls down a hole and into a slot" whose unbearableness is gradually revealed. For Offred, the Gilead takeover has happened "like a dream. . . . She wants her husband and daughter back and she wants to survive." Atwood's carefully crafted, spare writing and slow action seem "to leave more room. . . for the reader to participate, to wonder, ponder, fill in the blanks. . . [sic] [The reviewer] was right there with" Offred, wanting what she wanted.

108 HEGER, TERESA. "Atwood Fashions Another Feminist Novel." *Daily Iowan* (Iowa City), 24 April, p. B8.

Finds *The Handmaid's Tale* a first-rate feminist novel, with only minor flaws. Atwood artfully combines the mundane with the unbelievable to create a chilling near-future in America, and vividly depicts the narrator's survival instincts, memories, and vague hopes. Like Joan in *Lady Oracle*, and [Marian] in *The Edible Woman*, the handmaid partly defines herself by other's and society's expectations, instead of creating her own self.

1986

109 HENGEN, SHANNON. "'Your Father the Thunder/Your Mother the Rain': Lacan and Atwood." *Literature and Psychology* 32, no. 3:36-42.

Reads *Two-Headed Poems* as a simulated Lacanian "adult mirror stage for Atwood's female speakers," who temporarily ignore powerful men to face each other and question language and power. In Lacan's formative mirror stage, where language begins, a female child's gender identification can inhibit her speech. Atwood's earlier women – Circe, the protagonists of *Surfacing* and *Lady Oracle*, and the isolated, helpless speakers of "Tricks with Mirrors" and "Siren Song" – are disappointingly mute. Now, in "Five Poems for Grandmothers," "A Red Shirt," and "Solstice Poem," Atwood's women "learn to address the world . . . [and] re-experience the mirror stage . . . by confronting" one another. "Night Poem" shows a female child, unharmed by conventional gender identification, free to choose her parents, perhaps the imagined ones of thunder and rain.

110 HERRIDGE, CATHERINE. "Margaret Atwood: Make No Assumptions." *Harvard Advocate* 120, no. 1 (December):37-38.

Interviews Atwood, who discusses her file of clippings for *The Handmaid's Tale*, social progress and regression, individual moral choice and responsibility, and Gilead's freedom and lack of eroticism – "'It's *Playboy*'s nightmare.'" *The Handmaid's Tale*'s totally plausible and terrifying Gilead rouses the reader's conscience.

111 HILL, HEATHER. "Montrealers, Atwood Nab Literary Honors." *Gazette* (Montreal), 4 June, p. F5.

Reports on the Governor-General's Literary Awards ceremony in Montreal: Atwood's Canadian and American best seller, *The Handmaid's Tale*, won the 1985 English-language fiction award, while she was receiving a human rights award in Toronto. Quotes juror H.R. Percy on why Robertson Davies's *What's Bred in the Bone* was not nominated: Percy and perhaps others found it very cerebral, unemotional, and unconvincing.

112 HILL, JANE. "Stories Examine What It Means to Be a Modern Woman." *Atlanta Journal*, 21 December. Newsbank 1986-1987, 57:C11-12.

Praises *Bluebeard's Egg*'s fine stories, that explore contemporary women's conflicts with inherited expectations and illusory independence. Like the narrator of "Unearthing Suite," Atwood's women are motionless and introspective, yet vital and acutely ironic. In "Bluebeard's Egg," Sally's contemplative, business, and familial power "remains as secret as the female power within the grandparents' home" in "Significant Moments in the Life of My Mother." Like her counterparts, Sally is held captive by a man she knows is her inferior; she is empowered, aware, and yet unable to act. Atwood's dry, world-weary humor carries her points. "The narrative presence is strong," not "'minimalist.'" What the narrator of "Unearthing Suite" and her counterparts long for may be the mother's "freedom to believe" in a minor god.

113 HOLLIDAY, BARBARA. "A Blunt Portrait of Women's Primal Fear." *Detroit Free Press*, 26 January, p. E7. Newsbank 1985-1986, 62:C3.

> *The Handmaid's Tale*'s futuristic satire "exposes woman's primal fear of being used and helpless. . . . Despite the outrageous scenario, this novel achieves a chilling authority through a mass of detail and Offred's appealing, intelligent voice." The gradual revelation is "brilliant and Machiavellian"; but the narrative is perforce myopic, and makes egregious shortcuts – Congress, which has a notoriously lax attendance record, couldn't be machine-gunned all at once.

114 ____. "Dissecting Tender Relationships." *Detroit Free Press*, 28 December, p. F7.

> *Bluebeard's Egg* continues Atwood's clinically precise "dissection of the untender relationships between men and women." Ed in "Bluebeard's Egg" seems kind, if bland; Sally broods and watches him obsessively until she finds something. The very different Emma [in "Two Stories About Emma"] is a fearless survivor who falls in love with success-absorbed, married men. "The warmest of these narratives are not stories at all but vignettes of the author's parents," whose joy may counterpoint this collection's malaise. The final ["Unearthing Suite"] reveals something of Atwood's "fascination with the riddles of human nature," and provides "a small glimpse of grace after these tales of the abyss."

115 HOWELLS, CORAL A[NN]. "Canadian Women Novelists of the 1970s and 1980s." *London Journal of Canadian Studies* 3:16-23.

1986

Features Atwood in an introduction to contemporary Canadian women's fiction, and concurs with Parrinder's 1986.188 acclaim. Many women's stories concern a feminised heroism of inner "exploration and survival"; disrupted realism and open endings are frequent. Canadianness can be a strong local identity, as in *Surfacing*'s quest for origins; or Canada can be the unreachable good place, as in *The Handmaid's Tale*. Revised: 1987.61; see 1987.60.

116 HUTCHEON, LINDA. "Margaret Atwood." In *Canadian Writers Since 1960: First Series*. Edited by W.H. New. Dictionary of Literary Biography, vol. 53. Detroit: Gale Research Co., pp. 17-34.

Traces the paradoxical "contrast between dynamic, natural, creative process and static, unnatural, created product" through all Atwood's books, from *Double Persephone* through *The Handmaid's Tale*; summarizes her childhood, education, and controversial, versatile literary career; provides a primary bibliography; and lists interviews and references. Though Atwood's increasingly self-reflexive and morally responsible work includes feminist, nationalist, and human rights themes, her artistic concerns are aesthetic. *The Circle Game*'s games, mirrors, maps, love, and art are safe but limiting human constructs over "dark, chaotic, and creative forces" of nature and the unconscious. *The Edible Woman* is structured as a "'circle game'" around the metaphoric poles of body and mind. *The Journals of Susanna Moodie*'s "archetypal schizoid Canadian" accepts the process/product duality as inevitable, and perhaps positive. The aphoristic *Power Politics* is more pessimistic than anti-male, for women create their victimizers. *Surfacing*'s mythic journey into nature and self explores dichotomies. The controversial *Survival*, which implies living through crises, provides a witty, popular introduction to certain Canadian themes. *Lady Oracle* parodies popular art and Atwood's own work. *Two-Headed Poems*, which like *The Animals in That Country* prefigures *Life Before Man*, explores our personal doubleness, and Canada's. The self-reflexive *True Stories* shares *Bodily Harm*'s analogous sexual and national politics. *The Handmaid's Tale*'s reconstructed fantasy exposes the unreliability of words while satirizing horrors latent in contemporary trends.

117 _____. "'Shape Shifters': Canadian Women Novelists and the Challenge to Tradition." In *A Mazing Space: Writing Canadian Women Writing*.

1986

Edited by Shirley Neuman and Smaro Kamboureli. Edmonton: Longspoon/NeWest, pp. 219-27 passim.

An essay on the "radical critique of totalizing systems and so-called universal Truths" enacted in Canadian women's novels that finds extensive echoes in Audrey Thomas's *Intertidal Life*, of *Life Before Man*'s symbolically similar Halloween setting, verbal play, human relations, and chosen creative birth. Such extensive recall undercuts Romantic notions of originality and single (male) meaning. Susan Swan's *The Biggest Modern Woman of the World*, whose heroine loses her voice and identity after getting engaged, similarly echoes *The Edible Woman*. *Lady Oracle*'s parody of both popular romance and modernist verse democratizes hierarchies and critiques women's destinies. *Surfacing* is a Canadian women's wilderness novel, of cabin or cottage; Atwood and others create a female, small-town Canadian *Bildungsroman*. Reprinted, slightly altered: 1987.64.

118 INGOLDBY, GRACE. "Lives of Quiet Despair." *New Statesman* 111 (28 March):30-31.

A five-book review that finds Atwood's wickedly ironic *The Handmaid's Tale* "far-fetched but not impossible and play[ing] brilliantly on niggling feminist doubts." Offred remembers how women felt they deserved to have their bank accounts frozen and jobs taken.

119 IRVINE, LORNA. "Atwood's Parable of Flesh." In *Sub/version*. Toronto: ECW Press, pp. 39-53; [also pp. 168-69].

Explicates the linguistic, structural, and thematic subversions of women's narratives in *Bodily Harm*; and in other chapters, in fictions by Audrey Thomas, Mavis Gallant, Alice Munro, Sylvia Fraser, and Marion Engel. *Bodily Harm* sees the world through female eyes, thus radically revising John Berger's remark about the "'surveyed female.'" The superficial plot is of passive female victim rescued by males; but covert, fragmented women's stories appear throughout. The superficial themes – of women's victimization, Canadian nationalism, the act of writing – do not explain *Bodily Harm*'s italicized voice, evasive shifts in perspective, unreliable narrative, or radical statement. Uncoding the text leads to ambiguities of time and space; to Northrop Frye's "'Where is here?'"; to Rennie's paranoia; to the death-like claustrophobia of the cell; to the condensed, surreal, recurring images of grave and operating room; to the metaphors of the game of Clue. Text, bodies, and consciousness are split. Splits are joined by touch; and by the rebirth of Rennie, independent and complete, when she and Lora become one. Then, as Hélène Cixous suggests, women's writing becomes "'flying in language and making it fly,'" as the politically subversive Rennie does at the end. *Sub/version* concludes by quoting from "[A] Red Shirt" and "Book of Ancestors" as expressions of the new, subversive feminine ethos. Slightly revised: 1988.24.

120 ____. Review of *Interlunar*. *Journal of Canadian Poetry* 1:2-6.

Appreciates the moving, politically committed, and finally life-celebrating *Interlunar*. In the allegorical "Snake Poems," a female connection with nature works against domination and male violence. The three "Interlunar" sections explore "the poet's political responsibility in an increasingly insane world" on the edge of catastrophe. Hands heal and harm; violence erupts; while poets sing, men murder. The poet struggles and refuses to despair. Though a few poems are too oblique, even Atwood's flatness elucidates her contemporary tensions. The exhilarating conclusion shows "that politics can be lyrical," the private can illuminate the public, and poets can still use prophetic moon imagery.

121 JAMES, CARYN. "The Lady Was Not for Hanging." *New York Times Book Review*, 9 February, p. 35.

A brief interview that accompanies McCarthy.150: Atwood tells the story of her ancestor Mary Webster, who survived being hung for a witch in Connecticut; discusses Puritan intolerance and the co-opting of women's movement goals – "control over birth, no pornography" – by *The Handmaid's Tale*'s repressive regime; and warns against political manipulators – "'What are we being asked to give up?'" but says her novel "'won't tell you who to vote for.'"

122 JENSEN, EMILY. "Margaret Atwood's *Lady Oracle*: A Modern Parable." *Essays on Canadian Writing*, no. 33 (Fall), pp. 29-49.

Beneath its slick surface, *Lady Oracle* is a parable of the professional woman who wants both career and marriage, art and love. What Joan learns is expressed not in the surface plot, but in the offhandedly introduced yet crucial parables. The "literary" parables – the 1948 film *The Red Shoes*, Hans Christian Andersen's "The Red Shoes" and "The Little Mermaid," and Tennyson's "The Lady of Shalott" – identify the woman artist's conflict, and her need for male approval. Joan's own mini-parables, of the Fat Lady and of Felicia, dramatize Joan's fear of men's ridicule and rejection. The men characters act like hero/villains of Gothic romance, rescuing the passive, vulnerable Joan, but behaving destructively to the successful writer Joan.

123 JOHNSON, JOYCE. "Margaret Atwood's Brave New World." *Washington Post Book World*, 2 February, pp. 1-2.

Celebrates the "extraordinarily satisfying, disturbing and compelling" future shock fiction of *The Handmaid's Tale*. Such disastrous-future novels call forth all of a character's courage and ingenuity for survival, and humanity. "Just as Orwell's *1984* gripped our imaginations, so will the world of Atwood's handmaid." Offred's artless, utterly convincing voice is "very close to us"; her "poignant sense of time" empowers the novel. *The Handmaid's Tale* brilliantly illuminates politics and sex, yet avoids doctrinaire writing. Offred is no Superwoman, no militant feminist like her mother, no gay activist like her friend Moira. Offred "is simply a warm, intelligent, ordinary woman who had taken for granted the freedoms she was to lose – the freedom to love, the freedom to work, the freedom to have access to knowledge." Her plight and assertion of needs are always both human and ideological. Excerpted: 1987.53.

124 ____. "Women Protest at P.E.N." *New Directions for Women* 15, no. 2 (March/April):1, 16.

Two hundred women met to protest the lack of women's representation at P.E.N.'s 48th International Congress in New York, January 1986; drafted a declaration; and chose three speakers, Atwood, Grace Paley, and Cynthia MacDonald, to demand that President Norman Mailer apologize and that P.E.N. explain. Despite Mailer's misogyny, the women of P.E.N. are right, and will persist; liberation is an ongoing process.

125 JOLLY, ROSLYN. "Transformations of Caliban and Ariel: Imagination and Language in David Malouf, Margaret Atwood, and Seamus Heany." *World Literature Written in English* 26, no. 2 (Autumn):295-330.

1986

Compares the use of Caliban and Ariel colonial archetypes, from Shakespeare's *The Tempest*, in Malouf's *An Imaginary Life*, Atwood's *The Journals of Susanna Moodie* and *Surfacing*, and Heaney's poetry. Malouf's "Ovid imaginatively transforms himself from a displaced" Caliban to a free, transcending Ariel, from grub to butterfly. Heaney remains a Caliban tensely linked to his English Prospero. Atwood's arrested transformations, complicated by "historical, political, social and sexual" factors, create "hybrid Caliban/Ariel figure[s] of divided consciousness." The isolated, displaced Mrs. Moodie struggles "between tame and original Caliban selves . . . [and] between Caliban and Ariel archetypes." *Surfacing*'s similarly displaced protagonist chooses between American and animal languages, as Caliban chose between Prospero and Ariel, and oscillates between her Caliban and Ariel voices. *Surfacing*'s language becomes more intrusive when it is rejected.

126 JORDAN, SALLY. "Margaret Atwood's *Handmaid's Tale*." *Sojourner* (Cambridge, Mass.), May, pp. 42-43.

Finds *The Handmaid's Tale*'s style chillingly effective and its content "harrowingly believable," though McCarthy 1986.150 did not. As in *Nineteen Eighty-Four* and other dystopias, there is a horrifying future world, and a pivotal figure who joins its resistance and escapes or succumbs. Offred's understated, oblique tone of voice heightens her story's ghastliness; the gradual revelations make "the reader play detective"; the wry humor is welcome. The most frightening parts are Offred's attempted escape with her family, and Gilead's protective, anti-pornography, and women's birthing distortions of feminism. The engaging, unheroic Offred "does pretty much what most of us would do." *The Handmaid's Tale* is important and fascinating, but not enjoyable; the reviewer recommends Jane Austen's *Persuasion* "as an antidote."

127 JUHASZ, SUZANNE. "Renunciation Transformed, the Dickinson Heritage: Emily Dickinson and Margaret Atwood." *Women's Studies* 12, no. 3 (March):251-70.

Emily Dickinson, who in her life and work renounced her womanly, social self, transformed her renunciation by imaginatively repossessing the social self, and even love, in her poetry. Atwood, who has not renounced the world or her social self, charts a similar struggle as poet and woman. Atwood's persona finds her connecting, womanly self consistently refused by her lover, as in "Against Still Life." But where Dickinson commands extravagant figurative language, Atwood distrusts the figurative, as in "More and more"; but the literal prevents connections. The speaker of "Four Evasions" "has renounced her need for connection." In "Small Poems for the Winter Solstice," a woman poet struggles with issues of love and writing, finds a possible transcendence in the "shining," where both literal and figurative are real, but ends with unanswered questions. "Transformation has yet to be effected in Atwood's work."

128 KAKUTANI, MICHIKO. Review of *Bluebeard's Egg and Other Stories*. *New York Times*, 5 November, p. C29.

Appreciates Atwood's "lyrical, meditative tales and wry, crackly satires." As in ["Hurricane Hazel"], "Loulou," and Atwood's novels, identity is elusive and mysterious, made up by others and oneself, imposed or chosen. Men and women play out "the nervous dance of love and mistrust"; and nature is redemptive. Though, as with the dirty eggs of "Bluebeard's Egg," a knee-jerk feminism tries to sneak in, Atwood's emotional ambiguity and gifted language preclude "didacticism or cliché. . . . [T]hese stories are strewn, like a starry sky, with [integral] shimmering images and bright metaphors." Her storytelling is a luminous art that makes sense of the past. Reprinted: 1986.129 (below).

129 _____. "Storytelling Itself Is Subject of Margaret Atwood [sic] Stories." *Los Angeles Herald Examiner*, 21 December, p. F6.

Reprint of 1986.128 (above).

130 KAMBOURELI, SMARO, and NEUMAN, SHIRLEY, eds. Preface to *A Mazing Space: Writing Canadian Women Writing*. Edmonton: Longspoon/NeWest, ix-xi passim.

Explains that, in order to focus on the many-voiced and multicultural range of women's writing, contributors to this book were asked to go beyond the pre-eminent Margaret Atwood and Margaret Laurence; and to go beyond conventional thematics to questions of women's language and of "women's relationship to hegemonic cultural models."

1986

*131 KEARNS, GLORIA. Review of *L'Oeuf de Barbe-Bleue*. *Analyste*, no. 14 (Summer), pp. 78-79.

Finds, in a favorable review of the French translation of *Bluebeard's Egg*, that Atwood treats relationships more gently and more honestly than before. Prefers "Bluebeard's Egg," a story of malaise that reveals the bad side of human nature and the tendency to desire more. One central theme – the constant struggle by individuals for friendship and love – holds this book together.

132 KENDALL, ELAINE. "A Puritanical Future without Love." *Miami Herald*, 23 February, p. C7.

A slightly condensed reprint of 1986.133 (below).

133 _____. Review of *The Handmaid's Tale*. *Los Angeles Times Book Review*, 9 February, pp. 1, 12.

Appreciates Atwood's spirited, engaging narrator, representative American characters, needed and hilarious ["Historical Notes"], and bleak, unnerving, very real and possible Gilead. All these atavistic changes "could be implemented virtually overnight, smoothly and efficiently"; the legislation, communications, and funds for such are already available. Cites Atwood's comments, in a CBC interview, on Canada playing its usual neutral but non-antagonistic role in *The Handmaid's Tale*. Reprinted, slightly condensed, 1986.132 (above); reprinted, with two sentences cut, 1987.53.

134 KLOVAN, PETER. "'They Are Out of Reach Now': The Family Motif in Margaret Atwood's *Surfacing*." *Essays on Canadian Writing*, no. 33 (Fall), pp. 1-28.

From *Surfacing* on, Atwood's fiction examines her protagonists' personality disorders not in isolation, but as a function of their family relationships. *Up in the Tree*, which was written at the same time as *Surfacing*, and which recalls the unpublished "Up in the Air So Blue," shows the importance of "'stairs'" between childhood and adulthood. *Surfacing* is a romance quest where the protagonist penetrates mazes, and moves from hostility to reconciliation. Her three "families' . . . have left her increasingly isolated and desolate": her peculiar, cold family of origin predisposed her to a mental illness that "was intensified by her unhappy 'love' affair and abortion"; and now her surrogate family, of the wretched, sniping Anna and David and the pathetically failed, minimally human Joe, leave her emotionally apathetic. "Perceiving herself as a mutilated victim surrounded by killer 'Americans,'" she turns to fairy tale, Indian myth, and childhood fantasy for a magic transformation. Though enthusiastic feminist critics have failed to see the ironies of her maternity, Atwood and others confirm the ending's ambiguity. The alleged break-through is partly misanthropic, not ecstatic; the heroine remains emotionally detached; and her decision "to return to Joe and have his child" is a problematic, partial accomplishment.

135 KNAPP, CAROLINE. "New Twist in Book Promos: Authors Take to Videos." *Boston Business Journal*, 17 March, p. [6?].

A fifteen-minute videotape interview with Margaret Atwood on *The Handmaid's Tale*, conducted by Matthew Gilbert, is the first of Mark Shasha's "American Bookbox" book promotion tapes, and has been well-received. Publishers help pay for the tapes, which cost far less than promotional tours, and book stores can lease them.

136 KNICKERS, SUZI. "Suzi Knickers' Book Bits." In *The Bumper Book*. Edited by John Metcalf. Toronto: ECW Press, pp. 89-91.

Satirizes the Canadian literary scene. For Governor General's Awards Week, a nine-man cheering squad of Atwoodsmen danced and sang, to a tune from Gilbert and Sullivan's *Mikado*: "Three little handmaids, all unwary, / Raped and strangled in a cemetery." The Canadian Council is considering a mobile robot audience; Atwood, as spokesperson for the Women's Caucus of the Writers' Union of Canada, called for 50% of the robots to be female.

137 KOENIG, RHODA. Review of *The Handmaid's Tale*. *New York* 19, no. 7 (17 February):120.

Rejects Atwood's "rancid, nagging tone. . . . What distinguishes Atwood's [*Nineteen Eighty-Four*-type anti-utopia] is its fear and hatred of men, projected into [sic] a society where there are no legal or moral constraints on the mistreatment of women." Some may claim that Atwood only mildly exaggerates women's current terrors and subjection, "but her response is not a clean, merry hatred or an imaginative transcendence, just a stubborn whine. (Her heroine is passive and the narrative sluggish.)" Atwood "stay[s] with the dull resentment [that statistics] inspire," not art's wider realm.

1986

138 KULP, DENISE. Review of *The Handmaid's Tale*. *Off Our Backs* 16, no. 8 (August-September):21.

Praises Atwood's overwhelming, compelling, and very feminist novel; its vivid images linger, and at the end you need more, and more hope. We radicals and feminists find its right-wing takeover all too real. Though male reviewers have used Offred's comments on "'a women's culture'" to prove *The Handmaid's Tale* anti-feminist, the reviewer could hardly imagine a more feminist novel; Offred's comments recognize that Gilead's "'women's culture,'" which operates solely to benefit men, is not feminism. Offred remembers, grieves, connects with an underground, and fears it may be spies. Now, when the country is moving ludicrously "forward into the past," and there are rudimentary feminist values in the popular culture, *The Handmaid's Tale*'s serious feminism helps us.

139 LACOMBE, MICHELE. "The Writing on the Wall: Amputated Speech in Margaret Atwood's *The Handmaid's Tale*." *Wascana Review* 21, no. 2 (Fall):3-20.

Reads *The Handmaid's Tale* as a woman's fragmentary, subversive palimpsest – an erased and reinscribed medium – of Offred's sexual/textual relations with men and readers. A spiritual autobiography from the other, alien gender, *The Handmaid's Tale* is closer to Virginia Woolf, Sylvia Plath, and Simone de Beauvoir than to male-dominated science fiction. Legitimate speech, writing, memory, and laughter are forbidden in Gilead: Offred subversively finds new mirrors and new cues, yearns for a past innocence that disguises women's infantilization, and decodes the hanged men with allusions to Plath's archetypally female "Tulips." Offred signifies an offered blood-sacrifice; of Fred; off-red, a secret rebel; and off-read or mis-read, by the Commander and by the historian who reconstructs her manuscript. The schoolboy Latin is literally closeted women's writing. Offred can't conceive the child that would perpetuate the new order. Her speech/act text substitutes for daughter and pregnancy. Like all female authors, she must subvert male constructions to re-create herself.

140 LARSON, SUSAN. "Upon This Rock, Atwood Builds a Future of Ice." *Houston Post*, 23 March. Newsbank 1985-1986, 78:C12-13.

Celebrates *The Handmaid's Tale* as Atwood's most daring, flawless, and best work: "This powerful cautionary tale shatters . . .

complacency, poetically renders small freedoms, . . . and celebrates the flickering brightness of the human spirit in the face of a cold dark future." Offred is intelligent, and wryly conscious of the ironies of Gilead's wrong kind of women's culture; her loss and desire are appealing; as she obeys to survive, "the reader cheers on her small rebellions." The dirty-joke Latin becomes a prayer and a command. Atwood's Scheherezade spins her tale "to save her life, for herself and for the reader."

141 LeCLAIRE, JACQUES. "Féminisme et dystopie dans *The Handmaid's Tale* de Margaret Atwood." *Études canadiennes* (Talence) 21, no. 1:299-308.

Discusses the closely linked feminist and dystopian aspects of *The Handmaid's Tale*, briefly comparing Helen Greven's treatment of dystopia in *Formes du roman utopique en Grande-Bretagne (1918-1970)*. Atwood's unique and unmercifully lucid voice never lacks humour, irony, sympathy, and tenderness. *The Handmaid's Tale* portrays most subtly the power of good and bad in both women and men; and illuminates the ultimate consequences of surrogate motherhood. If Atwood shares the feminists' preoccupations, it is with a critical irony and the understanding that absolute liberty carries the seed of its own destruction. Like seminal works by Lessing and MacLennan, *The Handmaid's Tale* abandons realism for fantasy. This transformed work shows that Atwood can address the problems of imagination and writing, and confirms that Canadian literature has come of age.

142 LEHMANN-HAUPT, CHRISTOPHER. Review of *The Handmaid's Tale*. *International Herald Tribune* (Paris), 4 February, p. 14.

A condensed reprint of 1986.143 (below) that omits two paragraphs on language and genre.

143 _____. Review of *The Handmaid's Tale*. *New York Times*, 27 January, p. C24.

Celebrates *The Handmaid's Tale*: because Atwood's bleak, terrifying world, which is not fully revealed till the last pages, is viewed through an "infinitely rich and abundant" sensibility, her anti-Utopian, Orwellian novel succeeds in a genre where most fail. Atwood's well-honed technique reveals gradually and with the utmost drama that Offred is a fertile slave, renamed and incompletely reeducated. Offred

1986

"partly enjoys her oppression, . . . [and partly] feels guilty for submitting. . . . She never stops scheming to escape, ... [and] never gives up her freedom to play with words." Her "sensitivity to language," in a Gilead that forbids women's literacy, "keeps the book alive." Atwood's very best novel is much more than a political tract: it is also a cerebral sado-masochistic fantasy, "a taut thriller, a psychological study, a play on words," offering humor, ambivalence, and possible redemption, for the Handmaid "has written this book," and perhaps survived. Reprinted, condensed: 1986.142 (above). Reprinted: 1987.53.

144 LINKOUS, ROBERT. "Margaret Atwood's *The Handmaid's Tale*." *San Francisco Review of Books* 11, no. 3 (Fall):6.

Rejects Atwood's unconvincing dystopia, hapless Commander and Wife, and dim, monotonous, puerile Offred. Putting together "souvenirs of world oppression" is not necessarily enough. Atwood should not have written this book, and it should not be compared to *Brave New World* or *Nineteen Eighty-Four*. Reprinted, slightly cut: 1987.53.

145 LINTON, MARILYN. "Atwood's New Tale." *Sunday Sun* (Toronto), 2 February, p. CL7.

Atwood discusses, in an interview in her Toronto home, the real bases of *The Handmaid's Tale*'s Gilead: Utopias, Iran, Cambridge (Massachusetts), English seventeenth-century hangings, polygamy, missing children in Argentina – and, after her book was published, a clipping sent her about "'handmaids'" in an American religious sect.

146 LoNANO, MARI. "It's Beautiful, Tender, and Horrifying." *Norfolk Virginian-Pilot*, 9 February. Newsbank 1985-1986, 71:C4.

A rave review of *The Handmaid's Tale*, which is "as scathing a satire as [Swift's] *A Modest Proposal*," as important as Orwell's *Nineteen Eighty-Four*, and Atwood's surpassing work. Gilead is very imaginable in our world.

147 "The Los Angeles Times Book Prize 1986." *Los Angeles Times Book Review*, 19 October, p. 4.

Briefly describes, then excerpts from, *The Handmaid's Tale*, which is one of the books nominated in fiction.

1986

148 LOW, VIRGINIA. "Could It Happen Here?" *New York Times Book Review*, 9 March, p. 35.

Protests, in a letter to the editor, McCarthy's 1986.150 review of *The Handmaid's Tale*. Atwood's novel is more akin to Isabel Allende's *House of the Spirits* than to *A Clockwork Orange* or *Nineteen Eighty-Four*. Offred "is one of us, a thoroughly believable young woman . . . ." Through her we glimpse how Gilead developed from violence against women; from men's lack of feeling, owing to easy sex and pornography; and from nuclear war and pollution – does McCarthy deny these realities? Where has she been, that she doesn't take the Moral Majority seriously? Does she know about the gradual conservative judiciary takeover, the "'adult'" video buildings, the fundamentalist schools, television, and churches? "Miss McCarthy may not be scared, but many of us are. Very."

149 McCABE, STEPHEN. "A Novel for the Complacent." *Humanist* 46, no. 5 (September-October):31-32.

Appreciates *The Handmaid's Tale*'s chilling realism, true message, and sympathetic, reliable narrator. Atwood chillingly and all too believably portrays fundamentalism. Offred "reveals the novel's most important truth: ignoring is different from ignorance" – it takes work. "Hers is a historian's struggle," juxtaposing and comparing past and present to understand. She shows us Gilead in detail. Her unassuming reliability ensures our sympathy. "Only freedom's antitheses exist for her: indoctrination, regimentation, intimidation, and deprivation." Even if *The Handmaid's Tale* "'won't tell [us] who to vote for,'" as Atwood said in the James 1986.121 interview, it does warn us that complacency and acquiescence are the worst enemies of freedom.

150 McCARTHY, MARY. "Breeders, Wives and Unwomen." *New York Times Book Review*, 9 February, pp. 1, 35.

Finds *The Handmaid's Tale* incredible as a cautionary tale: this very readable novel cannot shock or scare. Why should one worry about credit cards (which the reviewer simply avoids) or take the Moral Majority and far right seriously? The reviewer does not fear that "'excesses'" of tolerance will really cause a Gilead here. "Where are the signs of it? A backlash is only a backlash, that is, a reaction. Fear of a backlash, in politics, ought not to deter anybody from adhering to

535

principle; that would be only another form of cowardice." The narrator's doctrinaire feminist mother is absurd. Gilead is a women's world governed by men; but that we aren't told how they govern it strains credibility. Though *The Handmaid's Tale* has several deft touches of sardonic humor, it lacks satire's force. Perhaps Atwood's projections are too carefully drawn. It must be because *The Handmaid's Tale* lacks a fearsome-future language like Orwell's *Nineteen Eighty-Four* Newspeak or Anthony Burgess's *A Clockwork Orange* that Atwood's novel cannot scare. Its generally weak characterization – "the Aunts are best" – make it "a poet's novel – so hard to put down, in part so striking – "that lacks imagination. Accompanied by 1986.121. See Black 1986.31 and Low 1986.148. Reprinted: 1987.53.

151 McCOMBS, JUDITH. "Atwood's Fictive Portraits of the Artist: From Victim to Surfacer, from Oracle to Birth." *Women's Studies* 12, no. 1 (February):69-88.

Traces three patterns, of the artist as Canadian, female, and visionary, from the 1972 *Survival* through the 1977 "Giving Birth," which ends "Atwood's Stage I, the Closed, Divided, Mirroring World." *Survival's* theory of the Canadian "Paralyzed Artist" is an isolated, maimed victim, and male; the one non-paralyzed exception is female. *Surfacing's* victim artist moves "out of Canadian and female paralyses" to reclaim her lost child and, perhaps, her sold-out art. *Lady Oracle's* creative Trickster hero ducks "in and out of Canadian and female victimhoods," high and low art, vision and parody. From *Surfacing* through *Dancing Girls*, the female artist is foregrounded, "with her sexual and artistic creativity linked, most directly in 'Giving Birth.'" The artist as mystic appears covertly in *Survival*; *Surfacing's* shamanic vision is kept separate from the hero's art; overtly visionary writers are portrayed in *Lady Oracle* and "Giving Birth." The sold-out writer of "A Travel Piece" is a Canadian version of Erica Jong's American female tourist writer in "From the Country of Regrets"; Julia in "Lives of the Poets" recalls the bleeding female writer of Jong's "Playing with the Boys." Jeannie (genie, genius) of "Giving Birth" is visionary, maternal, and a serious, successful artist. Fiction and poetry, visual and verbal genres, seem interchangeable in these portraits; but camera vision is false. Female artists are solitary and hardworking; male artists show off to peers. Briefly discusses the Stage II writer's responsibility to bear witness in *Bodily Harm*, the artist parables of *Murder in the Dark*, and the older female artists of *Bluebeard's Egg*.

152 ____. "Atwood's Haunted Sequences: *The Circle Game*, *The Journals of Susanna Moodie*, and *Power Politics*." In *American Women Poets*. Edited and with an introduction by Harold Bloom. The Critical Cosmos Series. New York; New Haven; Philadelphia: Chelsea House Publishers, pp. 311-26.

A reprint of 1981.66 that omits the endnotes and the *Power Politics* cover illustration.

153 MacDONALD, LARRY. "Psychologism and the Philosophy of Progress: The Recent Fiction of MacLennon, Davies, and Atwood: Errata." *Studies in Canadian Literature* 9, no. 2 (1984):i-iv. (Issued with *Studies in Canadian Literature* 11, no. 1.)

Errata to 1984.57. Corrects a quotation concerning Waugh to read "money is not only not the root" at the bottom of page 138; and correctly transposes page 142's first two and one-half paragraphs to the "Conclusion," page 143.

154 McGOOGAN, KENNETH. "Alberta and Atwood, Readings and Deadlines." *Calgary Herald*, 26 January, p. F6.

Briefly reports that *The Handmaid's Tale*, due out in February in the United States, has been previewed in *Publishers Weekly* [1985.101] as Atwood's most daring work, and possibly a breakthrough book.

155 McGRATH, JOAN. Review of *The Oxford Book of Canadian Short Stories in English*. *Canadian Book Review Annual*:127.

Acclaims Atwood's and Robert Weaver's selections: this appealing, "solid-gold collection of some of the best" Canadian short stories, which includes golden oldies, new work, and diverse subjects, "could proudly hold its own with any short fiction published anywhere."

156 MACKENZIE, MANFRED. "'I Am a Place': *Surfacing* and Spirit of Place." In *A Sense of Place in the New Literatures in English*. Edited by Peggy Nightingale. St. Lucia: University of Queensland Press, pp. 32-36.

Suggests that *Surfacing*'s perhaps prototypical ritual divestment and cultural monstrosity are two stages of the post-colonial naturalization of alien place. After *Surfacing*'s cultural exorcist heroine divests herself of "'Americanism,'" offering her clothing to the lake, she becomes transparent to nature, rejects language, "'becomes' the environment," then atones with her parents. An investiture follows as she re-enters "'American'" culture, but with a new sense of Canadian place. A central cultural divestment occurs in Patrick White's *A Fringe of Leaves*; and in Hawthorne's prototypical *The Scarlet Letter*. Cultural monstrosity, as in the "'man-animals'" of *Surfacing*'s father's aboriginal drawings, may be the next stage of naturalization; compare the "'Gothic monsters'" of Hawthorne's "The Maypole of Merry Mount."

157 McLAY, CATHERINE. "The Real Story." *Journal of Canadian Fiction*, nos. 35-36, pp. 130-37.

Appreciates *Bodily Harm*'s broader quest and vision, human lessons, and compassion; but misses the metaphoric richness and more complex structures of earlier Atwood novels. We learn at the end that Rennie, the sole survivor, has brought "'the real story'" back to society, by writing this book. Rennie begins as a trendy journalist, obsessed with surfaces, uninvolved. Her life is changed by a mastectomy, which she sees as dismemberment. The surgery, the Man with the Rope, Jake's games, and the Toronto pornography research, all seem to divide the world into male doers and female victims, as the epigraph from John Berger's *Ways of Seeing* suggests. Lora and Dr. Minnow teach Rennie involvement and compassion; the brutal beating of Lora is necessary, to commit Rennie to action. By the end she has accepted her mission – to report "'the true story'" – and faced her mortality.

158 _____. "Triple Solitaire." *Journal of Canadian Fiction*, nos. 35-36, pp. 122-29.

Appreciates *Life Before Man* as a complex, compelling study of isolation, comparing it to Atwood's three earlier novels. Often bleak and uncomfortable, *Life* is more realistic and compassionate; its deaths and violence are also more real. As before, Atwood's urban Toronto scenes are vivid, cinematic, heightened. All three of *Life*'s lonely characters indulge in fantasies. Images of division and separation again form an underlying pattern, centered on Chris in *Life*; the mood is again claustrophobic, with the three main characters seen first behind glass, and doors closing off or leading away; language and communication are again problematic. Elizabeth's bathtub tap reflection, the underwear man, Chris, the aunt, and the dinner party, are versions of Atwood signatures. Lesje's pregnancy is partly a move, partly an affirmation like *Surfacing*'s pregnancy. Lesje makes a new beginning; Elizabeth and Nate accept, and compromise.

159 MacLEOD, HILARY. "Margaret Atwood: Art and Motherhood." *Canadian Author and Bookman* 61, no. 4 (Summer):2-3.

Profiles Atwood, who hesitated to write her controversial *The Handmaid's Tale* after past media labels and the *Survival* controversy. Atwood, who based *The Handmaid's Tale* on history and sociobiology, discusses the control of women by women, and feminism; women's and men's freedoms; her own daughter's options, toxic pollution, and society's anti-family, anti-children pressures on women. "'Women [like Atwood herself] with good jobs and independence are still anomalies.'"

160 MacLEOD, JACK. "The Importance of Not Being Earnest: Some Mutterings on Canadian Humour." In *The Bumper Book*. Edited by John Metcalf. Toronto: ECW Press, pp. 79-88 passim.

A discussion that finds Atwood's 1974 "What's So Funny? Notes on Canadian Humour," reprinted in her admirable *Second Words*, wrong, or anachronistic, in characterizing Canadian humour as provincial, showing us as self-deprecating victims. Recent Canadian work, including Atwood's, has a cocky confidence.

161 MADRIGAL, ALIX. "Atwood's Latest Fiction Is Slightly Better Than Her Bite." *San Francisco Chronicle*, 11 March, p. 43. Newsbank 1985-1986, 89:C5.

Complains of Atwood's defensive, stern-schoolteacher mien and rejects *The Handmaid's Tale* in an interview at the *Chronicle*: "Her well-reasoned, beautifully parsed arguments had the ring of set pieces; her answers never quite fit the questions." Her claim to logical conclusions implies others are myopic or witless. "But as impressive as Atwood's clippings [for the harshly-reviewed *The Handmaid's Tale*] are, as logical as her conclusions may be, they point to a central weakness": Gilead is a hodgepodge, a "not recognizably Christian" theocracy whose proponents lack fervor. What applies to past or forced revolutions "doesn't ring true in a country that refuses to give up its handguns."

1986

162 MADSEN, ELAINE MELSON. Review of *The Handmaid's Tale*. *Nit and Wit* 7, no. 3 (June):41-42.

Praises highly *The Handmaid's Tale*, which "you can't put down" or forget: Atwood reveals "how terribly fragile" our humanity, individuality, and civilization are. Her heroine adapts to totalitarian Gilead; there is no happy end. The past Third Reich and our present extremist collage of electronic preachers, Phyllis Schaflyites, fatuously anti-homemaker feminists, and "neo-Nazis poised on state ballots all over the country," show how Gilead could happen. A currently proposed Illinois law would alter women's property rights; anti-choice groups pressure the Supreme Court. "If the state owns the inside of a woman's body," why not of a man's, also, as in Gilead? "Like Jonathan Schel's *Fate of the Earth* and Rachel Carson's *Silent Spring*," Atwood's novel warns us.

163 MAJANDER, ANTTI. "Margaret Atwoodin negatiivinen utopia" [Margaret Atwood's negative utopia]. *Helsingin Sanomat*, 31 May, p. 24.

In Finnish. Praises *Orjattaresi*, *The Handmaid's Tale*, which is unaffectedly translated by Matti Kannosto. Atwood always takes a stand and finds shame in silence. Her humble and defiant moral instinct adapts her ethic to situations. Atwood's *Nineteen Eighty-Four*-like dictatorship uses Orwell's newspeak, reversing the meanings of words, and attempting to make certain words disappear. Atwood's science fiction exposes the familiar through the strange, using Offred's situation to reflect contemporary fears. The final section critiques every generation's mistake – trying to understand its forefathers before understanding itself and the present.

164 MANDEL, ELI. "She Cannot Deny Anything Human: Atwood and Technology." *Canadian Journal of Political and Social Theory* 10, nos. 1-2:100-108.

Argues that Atwood's poetry concerns perception, but her existential psychology framework, ironic mode, and focus on what isn't there create misreadings. Her rich imagery of technology hints at extraordinary possibilities, but in the end her art holds back. Grace 1983.54 examines Atwood's dualities and resolutions, but uses poetic examples that imply moralistic hope, not linguistic resolution. In *Surfacing*, "Speeches for Dr. Frankenstein," and "They eat out,"

Atwood's nature/culture, mind/body, technique/instinct dualism, which follows George Grant's neo-primitivist critique of technology, is unresolved. As Cluett 1983.23 says, Atwood's self-willed ikons show us our dehumanized world. But the postmodern poetry of process that punctures the "'spaces between'" is in Christopher Dewdney's dialectical deconstructions, not Atwood's reticences. Reprinted: 1986.165 (below).

165 ____. "She Cannot Deny Anything Human: Atwood and Technology." In *The Family Romance*. Winnipeg: Turnstone Press, 123-34.
Reprint of 1986.164 (above).

166 MARIUS, RICHARD. "Characters in Place." *Harvard Magazine* 88, no. 5 (May-June):76.
Likes *The Handmaid's Tale* as a nice, interesting conundrum, but not for its social message, or its characters, who aren't compelling or profound; identifies specific Harvard settings. Bodies are "hung on the brick wall by the Johnston Gate; handmaids are "hanged on the steps of Widener Library" before an audience on folding chairs in the Yard, as if for Commencement.

167 MASSIE, ALLAN. "Puritan Pleasures." *Scotsman* (Edinburgh), 15 March, Weekend sec., p. 3.
Finds *The Handmaid's Tale* plausible, humanly true, clever, and ingenious; but finds allegory a frivolous and lower form. The fascistic, racist, Puritan Gilead indoctrinates Offred for her repugnant task. The two resistance movements, and the Elite's hypocrisy, show the human spirit persisting, and Gilead's relative inefficiency. "Could Gilead happen?" Permissiveness leads to repression, and feminism probably to a new Puritanism; the Aunts are credible, and the handmaids formalize surrogate motherhood. That "our pleasant vices . . . thwart the moral reformers give[s] the book a human truthfulness that Orwell's vile [*Nineteen Eighty-Four*] Utopia lacked. Nevertheless, *The Handmaid's Tale*" has allegory's fundamental failings: like a game it appeals to intellect and curiosity, not to emotions; there is always some whimsy, and "a certain flatness"– little is seen or sensed.

168 MATHESON, SUE. "An Interview with Margaret Atwood." *Herizons* 4, no. 1 (January-February):20-22.

1986

Interviews Atwood, who performed at a *Herizons* benefit while in Winnipeg on promotional tour for *The Handmaid's Tale*: Atwood explains the novel's realistic scenario of control through credit; its totalitarian control of women, sex, and men; its ruling men who are helped by women; the satiric Ladies Against Women group; Phyllis Schafly's argument that women have more power in traditional roles than in "'liberated'" ones; uniforms and costumes; the handmaids' colour red, which is based on Mary Magdalene, the Whore of Babylon, Hawthorne's *The Scarlet Letter*, and the very visible red that prisoners of war in Canada wore in the winter; Gilead's "salmonistic" fertilisation; the eroticism of the forbidden, as printed pages in Gilead; Nick and the Commander as the forbidden man and the wistfully romantic one; *Pride and Prejudice*'s two sexy, female power scenes; Harlequins and star-crossed lovers; and her schedule. A cover interview.

169 MATHEWS, LAURA. "A Fable for Our Time." *Glamour* 84, no. 2 (February):154.
Praises *The Handmaid's Tale* as a compelling fable: sly, beautifully crafted, powerful, satirical, and sure; part feminist nightmare but more a haunting story of a woman like us, who means to survive. "Margaret Atwood's novels tickle our deepest sexual and psychological fears."

170 ____. "A Splendid Writer." *Glamour* 84, no. 12 (December):186.
Praises Atwood's delectable *Bluebeard's Egg*, which may be another best seller. Reflective, as in "Significant Moments in the Life of My Mother," or satirical and wickedly funny with her quirky, marginal characters, "Atwood is a magnetic storyteller."

171 MAYNARD, JOYCE. "Briefing for a Descent into Hell." *Mademoiselle* 92, no. 3 (March):114, 118, 120.
Celebrates *The Handmaid's Tale*: Atwood's moving story kept the reviewer up all night, and still consumes her thoughts. Atwood creates a whole world with rules, structures, and "a thousand small, odd, harrowing particulars . . . . [It's] like some wonderfully rich childhood game" – and also a twisted but chillingly recognizable fun-house mirror of our own world. Gilead evolves; it begins to corrupt its own rules. Amazing sardonic wit and devilish glee accompany the grim

terrors. Offred, our worthy guide, is "wry, dispassionate, realistic," and sometimes despairing. But should we hear more of her perhaps unbearable feeling for her daughter? *The Handmaid's Tale* makes us examine our own time; never preachy, it warns against both fundamentalist and feminist extremism. Excerpted: 1987.53.

172 MERNIT, SUSAN. "Poets Who Write Fiction: 'What's Your Primary Form?'" *Coda: Poets and Writers Newsletter* 13, no. 5 (June-July):1.

Interviews a number of those who write both poetry and fiction; quotes Atwood on being primarily neither poet nor novelist, but a writer. To write seriously in more than one genre is more accepted in England than in America.

173 MORAN, MARY HURLEY. "The Fiction of Margaret Atwood: A Critique of Popular Culture." *Postscript*, no. 3, pp.7-12.

Describes Atwood's indictment, which critics have overlooked, of the popular culture over-running North America. Marian in *The Edible Woman* sees the media's influence. Anna and David in *Surfacing* are victims of media images and attitudes, removed from their true selves. Joan Foster in *Lady Oracle* is packaged as a celebrity poet. *Bodily Harm*'s Jake, Jocasta, and Rennie all manipulate popular culture. We are a society of image-conscious, passively detached imitators. Film, photography, and "'pop art'" deaden moral sensibility, as do *Surfacing*'s "Random Samples," *Bodily Harm*'s pornographic films and "'visual puns'" sculpture, and *Lady Oracle*'s "'con-create poetry.'"

174 "Munro, Atwood Tops with *Times*." *Halifax Chronicle Herald*, 9 December, p. E1.

Reports that the *New York Times* [*Book Review*] chose Atwood's funny, ominous *The Handmaid's Tale* and Alice Munro's very realistic *The Progress of Love* as two of the year's seven best fiction books. See 1986.70.

175 MURRAY, HEATHER. "Women in the Wilderness." In *A Mazing Space: Writing Canadian Women Writing*. Edited by Shirley Neuman and Smaro Kamboureli. Edmonton: Longspoon/NeWest, pp. 74-83 passim.

Argues that a "city/pseudo-wilderness/wilderness continuum" is the basic structure underlying English Canadian fiction; *Surfacing*'s cabin and its tangled garden exemplify a mediating pseudo-wilderness that is the site of myth, tale, and poetry, even though there is also a real, underwater wilderness. The United States frontier myth, in contrast, excludes women by reinforcing a nature/culture dichotomy that casts woman as other. Is the mediating pseudo-wilderness in Canadian women's fiction "a ground for liberation, or a ghetto?"

176 MUZYCHKA, MARTHA. Review of *The Handmaid's Tale*. *Breaking the Silence* 4, nos. 3-4 (Spring-Summer):27-28.

Appreciates Atwood's terrifying feminist *Nineteen Eighty-Four*, which speaks to and warns all women. "This frightening and insidious story permeates the reader's vision": we recall the sex-identifying "F" on today's forms, the new cash-eliminating debit cards, and surrogate mothers. Gilead's puritanical new Right has co-opted feminism, eliminating women's freedom, individuality, and reproductive freedom along with rape and pornography. Atwood's spare prose excellently depicts her terrifying scenes, as in the formal sexual ceremony. Offred hungers for sisterhood, for the forbidden thrills of conversation and sexual intimacy. We never know whether the "tenuous 'mayday' network" and its limited sisterhood save Offred.

177 NELSON, JOHN S. "*Handmaid's Tale* Is a Disturbing Vision of Future." *Wichita Eagle-Beacon*, 4 May. Newsbank 1985-1986, 98:C7.

Appreciates *The Handmaid's Tale* as a kind of cross between *Nineteen Eighty-Four* and Hawthorne's *The Scarlet Letter*. Offred, "an unwilling surrogate mother," silently resists, like Hester Prynne, the forces tearing at her – from the household, the underground, her friend, and her memories. The end is surprising but, inevitably, not wholly satisfying. Offred is a follower, and apathetic about women's rights, partly in reaction to her mother's activism. *The Handmaid's Tale* is powerful, grim, sometimes humorous – and a most disturbing warning about the Gileadean characteristics underlying our own society.

178 NEW, W.H. "Canada." *Journal of Commonwealth Literature* 21, no. 2:58-59.

Appreciates *The Handmaid's Tale*, in a group review, as a "devastating female version of the future-present," an engrossing speculative fiction, and an enquiry into reality and language. Offred means both of Fred and off red, a rejection of the handmaids' required red colour. Atwood makes it clear that everything here is based on current realities: and reminds us, with the parodic ["Historical Notes"] frame, that all reconstructions, literary as well as bureaucratic, are nonetheless suspect.

179 NICHOLS, JOHN. "Feminist Author Looks at the Future." *Blade* (Toledo), 4 May, p. E3.

Interviews Atwood, who is in Bowling Green to read and to promote *The Handmaid's Tale*. Atwood discusses the real bases of Gilead and its possibility in the States, asking whether Pat Robertson has entered the 1988 presidential race, and noting that Moral Majority leader Jerry Falwell has made 7-Eleven stores drop *Playboy* and *Penthouse*; feminism, pornography as bad for women, and censorship as a worse evil; and the generally positive, politically focussed reactions to *The Handmaid's Tale*.

180 "1986 *Los Angeles Times* Book Prize Winners." *Los Angeles Times Book Review*, 9 November, p. 1.

All these winners deal with oppression; *The Handmaid's Tale*, which won for fiction, celebrates "one woman's struggle to remember freedom after a theocratic coup d'etat in the United States."

181 OBERBECK, ELIZABETH B. "Atwood's Stories are Strong and Strange." *Milwaukee Journal*, 28 December, p. E8.

Praises the finely crafted *Bluebeard's Egg*, which "signals the unknown, the feared," Bluebeard's forbidden room. As in the family home of "Significant Moments in the Life of My Mother," a hidden undertow of "thoughts and feelings constantly washes through the characters' lives," ending with an ironic splash. The British Canadian family stories are the strongest. Intimacy turns into misreadings and tension between mother and daughter in "Significant Moments." The individual portraits are of hard, distanced, solitary characters: the very sardonic successful potter of "Loulou," the self-sufficient protagonist of "Walking on Water," and the smart, aloof, smug but deceived wife of "Bluebeard's Egg."

182 O'BRIEN, KATE CRUISE. "Vermicelli Cord." *Listener* 115 (1 May):30.

1986

A four-book review that finds *The Handmaid's Tale* "moving, vivid and terrifying," and only hopes that its story of a would-be surrogate mother dreaming of her lost daughter "is not prophetic, since" it cuts the "'vermicelli?'"-mother cord of life. Gilead's authoritarian, fundamentalist patriarchy is also indefatigably bourgeois and defiantly genteel. "Wives hate, fear and patronise the women who will bear 'their' children . . . . [T]he final savage irony in a frighteningly painful book" is the brothel that "'stimulates trade.'"

183 O'BRIEN, TOM. "Margaret Atwood's Vision." *Boston Globe*, 4 February, pp. 11-12.
Interviews Atwood, who discusses *The Handmaid's Tale* as a reality-based "'speculative fiction,'" citing her file of clippings and the diminishing freedom in many societies, especially theocracies; her novel's realistic American setting and the relative optimism of its heroine's possible survival and of its "Historical Notes," contrasting American enthusiasm to Canadian caution and survival mentality; and describes her own scientific, wilderness childhood, Harvard graduate studies, and present relationship with Graeme [Gibson].

184 _____. "Siren's Wail." *Commonweal* 113, no. 8 (25 April):251-53.
Likes *The Handmaid's Tale* less than Atwood's other novels. As she points out, the outlandish Gilead is based on realities, including Philippine "'salvagings'" and Cambodian and Vietnamese "'re-education centers'"; its dire warning is valuable; Offred's always real, lyric or laconic voice "makes us feel keenly [her] conflict and suffering"; and humor helps her survive. But weaknesses offset these pleasures: Gilead's industrial production, and the national and international scene, are skimped. Having mastered the realistic interpersonal novel, Atwood has tried to enlarge her scope. The reviewer remembers being stunned by Surfacing's necessary and apt "'refus[al] to be a victim.'" That Gilead nightmarishly excludes such moral wisdom may be what disturbs the reviewer.

185 OSTRIKER, ALICIA SUSKIN. *Stealing the Language: The Emergence of Women's Poetry in America*. Boston: Beacon Press, pp. 63-65, 149-63, 212, 222, and passim.
Reads "This Is a Color Photo" as an ironic version of Walt Whitman's "'look for me under your bootsoles,'" and as part of an

invisible woman tradition that goes back to Emily Dickinson's duplicitous "I'm Nobody!" and now includes Joyce Carol Oates's *Invisible Woman*, Marge Piercy's radical intellectual "in the men's room(s)," Robin Morgan's institutionalized "Invisible Woman," and others. Discusses "Circe/Mud" as revisionist mythology, and Circe as angry but quite powerless. Pages 63-65 reprint and slightly revise 1985.79; pages 149-63 revise 1984.73; and pages 212 and 222 reprint 1982.123.

186 PALMER, CAROLE L. "Current Atwood Checklist." *Newsletter of the Margaret Atwood Society*, no. 3, insert, pp. 1-5.

Provides an alphabetical, partly annotated checklist of primary and secondary work for 1986. Lists under Atwood's works four books and 61 reviews of them; two cassette tapes; 17 poems, articles, stories, excerpts, and translations; and nine interviews. Lists under secondary sources 15 articles, with succinct annotations.

187 PANNILL, LINDA. Review of *The Handmaid's Tale. Courier-Journal* (Louisville, Ky.), 16 March. Newsbank 1985-1986, 78:C4.

Though Gilead, whose real bases include American television evangelists, Right-to-Lifers, and censorship, is very worth reading about, Offred's numbed passivity weakens interest. Offred seems to forgive men in advance, as does Atwood, since these males are so benign. The reviewer wants fiercer characters, "both worse and better," in a fable: "If there is no Wolf to our 'Little Red Riding Hood,' we may not listen to the warning."

188 PARRINDER, PATRICK. "Making Poison." *London Review of Books* 8, no. 5 (20 March):20-22.

Celebrates *The Handmaid's Tale*, the science-fiction fable Atwood has long hinted of. The recognisable Atwood heroine "is wry, observant, resourceful—and frightened," and puritanically brought up. As in *Survival*'s Rapunzel Syndrome, Offred is imprisoned by the Commander, his household, and Gilead, and escapes momentarily through the Rescuer; her tale, at least, survives. Atwood triumphantly captures Offred's eerily static, minute sensations, intensified by her waiting and fear. Offred really means Afraid—and Not Afraid, since it's not her real name—more than Offered or Off-red. *The Handmaid's Tale* is sharply etched, and "full of subtle but irrepressible verbal play."

1986

Gilead ironically fulfills Women's Movement objectives "of separatist culture and female autonomy." The authoritarian Aunts, like the sinister Auntie Muriel in *Life Before Man,* are puritanical parental figures. *The Handmaid's Tale* leaves political questions unanswered, like many utopias; it is, like other "contemporary women's fiction . . . a tale of the oppressed, and not of the oppressors; and the oppressed" are denied knowledge. Atwood is now "the most distinguished novelist under fifty" writing in English.

189 PARSONS, ANN. "The Self-Inventing Self: Women Who Lie and Pose in the Fiction of Margaret Atwood." In *Gender Studies: New Directions in Feminist Criticism.* Edited by Judith Spector. Bowling Green, Ohio: Bowling Green State University Popular Press, pp. 97-109.

Both *The Edible Woman* and *Lady Oracle* examine women's subterfuges and the social forces that stunt women's growth; both novels explore how women may gain by conniving at their own oppression, or may, painfully, realize and end their complicity. *Surfacing* also explores women's growth, but less fully. Trying to control reality, Marian creates a sedate, camouflaged self that then controls her; *The Edible Woman* ends with her precarious but real victory. *Lady Oracle* goes further in showing the extraordinary chameleon self, Joan, both as an insecure, self-defeating neurotic and as a self-creating artist – and both activities grow from the same source. Even Joan's escapes from self are sometimes life-enhancing and exuberantly creative. Learning to tell the right lies about their selves empowers both Marian and Joan.

190 PECK, LUCINDA ANN. Review of *Bluebeard's Egg and Other Stories. Library Journal* 111, no. 19 (15 November):109.

Highly recommends Atwood's entertaining, excellent, vividly characterized, and finely crafted stories. Her impressive range includes the gentle satire of the growing-up stories, the grief and fear of "Bluebeard's Egg," and the despair of characters trying to save or begin relationships. Many stories are like spoken tales.

191 PETERSON, LESLIE. "Canadians Battling for Booker Prize." *Vancouver Sun,* 21 October, p. E6.

Kingsley Amis's *The Old Devils* is favored 2-to-1 to win the $30,000 [sic] Booker award; Robertson Davies's *What's Bred in the*

Bone is a close second, and would be Canada's first winner. Or the four-woman, one-man jury might choose Atwood's *The Handmaid's Tale*. Quotes Atwood, now in London, on her chances as "'not really too good'" but possible, and on jury chairman Anthony Thwaite's indiscreet letter to someone not on the short list. Paul Bailey's *Gabriel's Lament*, Kazuo Ishiguro's *An Artist of the Floating World*, and Timothy Mo's *An Insular Possession* are also contenders. *The Handmaid's Tale* has just won the *Los Angeles Times*'s Book Prize for fiction.

192 PHILIPS, DEBORAH. "Telling Tales." *Women's Review* (London), no. 7 (May), pp. 14-15.

Atwood discusses *The Handmaid's Tale*: "'A Woman's Place is in the Home'"; the Religious Right; women's money; the defensible Harvard setting; Gilead's patriarchy that contains a matriarchy; its "'freedom from'" versus our "freedom to"; its resistance; its alarming plausibility – "If you think Reagan's bad – just wait'"; and its speculative fiction, dystopias, and utopias, citing Charlotte Perkins Gilman's *Herland*, Ursula Le Guin's science fiction, and George Orwell's male-oriented *Nineteen Eighty-Four*.

193 PINARD, MARY. "A Cautionary Tale." *New Directions for Women* 15, no. 3 (May-June):15.

Confirms *The Handmaid's Tale*'s disturbing vision of our logical near future, which could happen if we continue to ignore our country's wars, corruption, pollution, and injustice. Offred's non-linear, journal-like narrative gradually and eerily reveals, as in a compelling mystery, that her past is our present. Atwood's prose is taut, specific, and ironic. Offred's recovered narrative proves "that true language means survival." The delightful, disconcerting ["Historical Notes"] section implicates us. Excerpted: 1987.53.

194 POSESORSKI, SHERIE. "A Grim Vision Sees Hope." *Boston Herald*, 26 October, pp. 61-62.

Appreciates the riveting, unsettling, socially grounded *Bluebeard's Egg*. Alma in "The Salt Garden" is a quintessential Atwood heroine, hyperacutely aware of self and social context; we are locked into her suffocating life as its tensions build to a crescendo. Atwood's central subject, "the wary and warring relationships between women

1986

and men," achieves moral urgency because her "self-limited characters are–despite their efforts–" caught in history's pressures. The desperate comedy of "Uglypuss" "is hilarious and hurtfully true." Like [the father] in one of the recollection stories, Atwood has "reconciled her grim vision of life with her undoubted enjoyment of it."

195 PRESCOTT, PETER S. "No Balm in This Gilead." *Newsweek* 107, no. 7 (17 February):70.

Celebrates Atwood's splendid visionary fiction: *The Handmaid's Tale* belongs with Wells's *The Time Machine*, Huxley's *Brave New World*, and Orwell's *Nineteen Eighty-Four*–"yet Atwood is a better *novelist* than they," for she creates a nuanced character. Her more limited dystopia is as fully horrifying as theirs, and without special effects; human brutality and electric cattle prods suffice. The visionary novel's formula of acceptance, rebellion, rumors of resistance, unexpected sex, then doom or escape for the protagonist works here: because it follows Atwood's theme of women's survival in a male-dominated world, and because Atwood cruelly amplifies our present potential for totalitarianism, as Huxley and Orwell did. There's also the pervading irony of Gilead's men-designed but women-controlled slave society; and Offred's new and beautifully modulated voice. Excerpted: 1987.53.

196 REEFER, MARY M. "Political Novel Deprives Women of Identities." *Kansas City* (Missouri) *Times*, 23 February. Newsbank 1985-1986, 78:C5-6.

The Handmaid's Tale is a political, not a feminist, novel, and as horrifying as Orwell's *Nineteen Eighty-Four*. In Gilead as in Kafka's works, no one knows who the powerful and the accusers are, or what exactly the crime is. Atwood's earlier nature imagery gives way "to darker icons of scaffolds, walls and military uniforms." The weak, compliant, fantasizing but never rebelling Offred is superbly depicted. The male characters are shadowy. Though Atwood's predictions of a religious extremist takeover here are no more likely than Orwell's have been, *The Handmaid's Tale* is a savagely compelling novel.

197 Review of *Bluebeard's Egg and Other Stories. Jim Kobak's Kirkus Reviews* 54, no. 18 (15 September):1388.

Finds these twelve stories dull. Atwood subjects familiar types of people "to the vicissitudes of contemporary domestic relationships." "Spring Song of the Frogs," which follows a fellow who has trouble with relationships and "bring[s] out the anorexic in" women, is the best. Atwood's feminist "angst and alienation" runs through most of these; the occasional humor mostly misses its mark.

198 REYNOLDS, STANLEY. "O Canada." *Punch* 290 (26 March):61.
   A three-book review that finds *The Handmaid's Tale* "a very easy read" but lacking sparkle. Like Robertson Davies, Atwood shows signs of coming from remote Canada. Her American satire shows the United States taken over by primitive fundamentalist Christians, who create a depressive Nazi-like Gilead that is worse for feminism than are pornography and women's role as man's toy.

199 RIGNEY, BARBARA HILL. "Dystopia." *Canadian Literature*, no. 111 (Winter), pp. 143-44.
   Welcomes *The Handmaid's Tale* as a female revision of Orwell and Huxley, "a new element in feminist literature," and Atwood's characteristic and strongest political work. The villain is not Big Brother, or "'patriarchy,'" but humanity's potential for fanaticism. The near-future "Gilead has poisoned itself with" religious and political ideology as well as nuclear waste. "A profoundly immoral majority has gone be[r]serk," and individuals collude in ceremonial atrocities. Perversion is institutionalized; sex is obscenely and grotesquely confined to procreation. Gilead's women have lost their identities, some of their memories, all of their civil rights. But, for Atwood, though women are more often victims, they are not "necessarily more innocent or more noble": the Aunts use cattle prods, torture, and brain-washing; the radical feminists had begun the book burnings. Offred's ironic understatements contrast with the horrors. As before, Atwood studies power, but also "'forgiveness'" and sane survival "in a schizophrenic world." Offred surfaces with self-control at least, and with a recognition of human political responsibility. Revised: 1987.129.

200 RILE, KAREN. "The Threat of Some Overpowering Force." *San Francisco Chronicle*, 21 December, Review sec., pp. 1, 11.
   Welcomes *Bluebeard's Egg*: its best stories, the autobiographical-seeming "Significant Moments," "Hurricane Hazel," "In Search of the

Rattlesnake Plantain," and "Unearthing Suite," have a moving, memorable honesty and love. The strong-willed, maverick Anglo-Canadian family spring into sharper focus with every glimpse. The narrator, "presumably the artist-to-be," is obliquely rendered. The other, core stories, like "Loulou" and the title story of self-deluding Sally, are cool, elegantly analytical psychological dissections. The unifying theme, if there is one, is "the threat of some overpowering elemental force," thermonuclear or watery. Though the mood is dark, there is humor.

201 RINZLER, CAROL E. "Atwood at Work." *Cosmopolitan* 200, no. 2 (February):28, 34.
   Interviews Atwood, who talks about her writing habits; the social purpose of the novel; *The Handmaid's Tale*'s logical extensions of traditional and feminist pronouncements on women; and the persisting images [behind] its two initial scenes, which come from nineteenth-century Canada, where "they hanged people with white bags over their heads," and from women "in full purdah with little netted windows over their eyes," seen in Afghanistan.

202 _____. "The Future Is Now." *Cosmopolitan* 200, no. 2 (February):28.
   A rave review of *The Handmaid's Tale*: a plausible and chilling Gilead; an extraordinary narrator-heroine whose story "unwinds inexorably, obliquely/directly, moving back and forth in time"; superbly controlled; amazing craft and content; and the best of the many novels the reviewer has read in the last three years.

203 ROBERSON, HARRIETT. "Remembering Times to Come." *Dallas Times Herald*, 20 April, p. C12.
   A rave review of *The Handmaid's Tale* as an uncannily convincing, frightening kind of feminist anti-utopia. Almost everything here has happened already, especially in Nazi concentration camps. Atwood's story "is transparently polemical and yet intensely private, scathingly funny, achingly poignant and densely," sweetly ironic. Serena Joy is a wickedly funny four-way allusion: to Marabel Morgan of *Total Woman* and *Total Joy*, Phyllis Schafly's speeches, and Tammy Bakker's tears – and Serena Joy's real name, Pam, is a baking spray. Though *The Handmaid's Tale* is Atwood's most openly political novel, its protagonist is a spiritual cousin of *Surfacing*'s; both must reinvent

themselves and reconstruct their worlds; and both novels end in studied ambiguity.

204 ____. "Stories Feature Atwood's Fine Descriptions." *Dallas Times Herald*, 23 November, p. E13.

Admires *Bluebeard's Egg*'s "near-perfect slices of invented characters and lives" that, as in "Hurricane Hazel" and "Bluebeard's Egg," startle us into acute awareness of the characters' dilemmas. Most of these characters "have no idea what to do with their lives; some see little reason to do anything at all. Even the seemingly invincible protagonist of 'Two Stories about Emma' is" less an actor than acted on. Yet the characters' psychic journeys are arduous, and they awaken to an irrevocably altered, hauntingly beautiful landscape, as in "Hurricane Hazel."

205 ROSENBERG, JEROME. "In a Future World, New Puritans Rule and Women Suffer." *Philadelphia Inquirer*, 9 February, pp. P1, 8. Newsbank 1985-1986, 71:C2-3.

Praises *The Handmaid's Tale* as a most alarming, "clearly plausible cautionary tale" and a powerful, poignant assertion of humanity. Gilead's radical Christian fundamentalist rulers are both pathetic and powerful, zealous and hypocritical; like the earlier Puritans, they err in imposing a rigid utopia on a free people. The story ends ambiguously, with Offred carried off by "the vicious Eyes" or the underground. The appended set of "Historical Notes" delightfully parodies academic pretensions, glosses Offred's story, and affirms the human spirit's need "for community, for love. . . . Atwood deals in epiphanies, in small yet essential affirmations . . . ." Though ennui and gratuitous wit occur, Atwood's Compubank dystopia is worthy of Huxley's test-tube procreation *Brave New World* and Orwell's television-surveillance *Nineteen Eighty-Four*. The reviewer recalls the television news story on two fire-bombed Cincinnati abortion clinics, heard the day he began this review, and an abortion foe's newspaper letter that warned pro-choice marchers: do we have the communal love, wisdom, and common sense to avoid Atwood's terrifying future?

206 ROSENTHAL, PAM. "The Future of Sexual Freedom." *Socialist Review*, nos. 87-88 (May-August), pp. 151-56.

Analyzes the sexual and feminist politics of Atwood's very impressive but flawed dystopia, *The Handmaid's Tale*. Gilead sexually represses everyone and subjugates women; its sexual objectification and color-coded costumes echo, with bleak irony, the oscillation of sex and power in *The Story of O* and Sade's *Justine*. Atwood superbly depicts "late-feminist single-mindedness and post-feminist confusion," but not anti-feminist certitudes. Because showing only a feminist pornography-burning "suggest[s] that radical feminists are leading us to costumed theocracy," we should see a right-wing book-burning also. Gilead's neo-Puritanism is not enough like our pop Protestant, huckster right-wing evangelism. Atwood avoids the frightening truth that fascism can be fun for many ordinary people; her stagey public rituals are more like solipsistic pornographic fantasy than like the Reagan popular fantasy. Offred's honest memories, and her belief in love between equals, are more compelling than Gilead.

207 ROSS, CATHERINE SHELDRICK, and DAVIES, CORY BIEMAN. "An Interview with Margaret Atwood." *Canadian Children's Literature*, no. 42, pp. 9-16.

Interviews Atwood as a children's author, 20 January 1983, at the University of Western Ontario. Atwood discusses her childhood reading, from children's classics, fairy tales, comic books, origin stories, adult books, and Canadian animal stories and [L.M. Montgomery's] *Anne of Green Gables*; happy endings, national content, and nonsense in children's literature; writing and illustrating *Up in the Tree*; and co-authoring *Anna's Pet* with her aunt. Ann Blades illustrated *Anna's Pet*, and Nova Scotia's Mermaid Theatre has made it into a children's puppet show.

208 ROSS, MALCOLM. *The Impossible Sum of Our Traditions: Reflections on Canadian Literature*. With an introductory essay by David Staines. Toronto: McClelland and Stewart, pp. 133-35, 140-41, 173-75, 184-90, 193-96.

Condemns *Survival*, in a reprint of 1976.86 that terms Frye's "'garrison mentality'" "myth without belief" or commitment: Atwood "flattens the mythopoeic mode into a one-dimensional fiction of fear and failure in Canadian writing." She fails to understand the positive, sacrificial "acceptance of suffering from which flows the water and blood of life," and the larger hopes of the Canadian tradition. Unlike

D.G. Jones's *Butterfly on Rock*, which transfigures Frye's mythopoeic theory through dynamic commitment, *Survival* offers only "the latest popular myth of Frye's new metropolitan garrison[;] . . . a rhetoric, not a poetic." Quotes, in his 5 December 1982 Inaugural Lecture at Canada House, London, "Backdrop addresses cowboy," as a biting satire of Canadian resistance to the American cultural and economic invasion. Argues, in his 18 November 1982 Inaugural Address at the Centre of Canadian Studies, University of Edinburgh, against the titillating and not necessarily Canadian mythology of Northrop Frye's terror of nature and his garrison mentality, in *The Bush Garden*; his disciple Atwood's negative proclamations, in *Survival*; and John Moss's lurid solaces of *Sex and Violence in the Canadian Novel*. *Survival* fairly explains the positive conclusion of Adele Wiseman's *The Sacrifice*, which exemplifies Canada's accepted, recovered, and transcendently re-invented traditions.

209 ROTHSTEIN, MERVYN. "No Balm in Gilead for Margaret Atwood." *New York Times*, 17 February, p. C11.

Interviews Atwood at Houghton Mifflin's offices: Atwood discusses *The Handmaid's Tale*'s realism, mentioning the handmaids in a "Catholic charismatic spinoff sect"; her novel's "examination of character under certain circumstances" and playing with hypotheses, rather than taking good-bad political positions; its men against women and religious right as the form a takeover could plausibly assume in the Puritan-founded United States; her own Puritan ancestors; Orwell's *Nineteen Eighty-Four* Newspeak section, which implies that the regime has ended; and *The Handmaid's Tale* as not wholly bleak or pessimistic, because Offred gets out, Gilead ends, and Offred's "'little message in a bottle has gotten through to someone–which is about all we can hope, isn't it?'" Reprinted: 1986.210 (below).

210 ____. "No Balm in Gilead for Margaret Atwood." *New York Times Biographical Service* 17, no. 2 (February):254-55.

Reprint of 1986.209 (above).

211 RUBENSTEIN, ROBERTA. "Anatomy as Destiny." *Belles Lettres* 1, no. 5 (May-June):2.

Appreciates *The Handmaid's Tale* as "a stunning fable of gender and power politics in the tradition of *1984*." Gilead's fundamentalist theocracy is brilliantly imagined. "Because we learn only what Offred (whose name means 'Property-of-Fred') knows, we identify with her disorientation, fear, and loss." Offred is a politically inactive Everywoman; her story is poignant, horrifying, at times funny, finally hopeful, and "an achievement of psychic survival": that Offred risks telling this story, and takes other risks, is a triumph of human nature over repression. The ironic ["Historical Notes"] coda cautions us.

212 _____. Review of *Bluebeard's Egg and Other Stories*. *Chicago Tribune Books*, 28 December, p. 4.

Praises Atwood's masterfully controlled, acerbic contemporary portraits. Her characteristically bemused narrator describes "the dissonances and near-misses of relationships" that her men and women cannot alter. In "Bluebeard's Egg" the surreal ultrasound heart image exposes the shallow relationship. In the reminiscent sketches, "a narrator confronts her almost-mythologized views of her parents. . . . In the haunting 'Unearthing Suite,' the speaker's inertia is counterbalanced by her parents' intimate, inarticulate rootedness." Many stories implicitly concern survival. Atwood's vulnerable characters struggle; her stories "glow with enigmatic, penetrating light."

213 RUSCONI, MARISA. Review of *Lady Oracolo*. *Espresso* (Rome), 19 October, p. 221.

Praises *Lady Oracolo*. Atwood has shed the influences of the United States and England to become one of the most original contemporary Canadian authors. In *Lady Oracolo*, Atwood's most astounding novel, woman is no longer a powerless victim, but a transformed heroine who adapts to crisis through metamorphosis.

214 SAGE, LORNA. "Projections from a Messy Present." *TLS*, 21 March, p. 307.

Finds *The Handmaid's Tale*'s middle-America dystopia mostly well-synthesized. One gradually puts together Offred's picturesque nightmare world. Atwood's polemic concerns the feminist separatism and matriarchal nostalgia that could combine with "'back to Nature'" conservation, and that in turn could join with right-wing "'traditional values.'" Atwood handles Offred's ambivalence and survivalist mythologies well. *The Handmaid's Tale* praises the messy present, where we still have our individual freedoms. Except for the "Historical

Notes," this isn't hard-core futurology; and there are loose ends, like handmaid Moira's tied tubes. Atwood's "familiar supportive side-kick," Moira, who is "gay in every sense (sceptical, irreverent, funny, 'dirty'),'' exemplifies non-separatist sisterhood. To make the Commander "a puzzled, mildly perverse ex-market-researcher" is too '"understanding.'"

215 St. ANDREWS, B[ONNIE] A. "The Canadian Connection: Frye/Atwood." *World Literature Today* 60, no. 1 (Winter):47-49.

Celebrates *Surfacing*'s beautiful translation of Frye's theories of Canadian literature and identity: the nostalgic but fearful return to the Canadian bush; the Canadian Indian animistic unity of the animal and human, the living and dead; the Canadian pastoral myth of "responsibility and reverence for life," in contrast to the American conquest of Nature; and the vast, purifying, life-giving waters. Though Atwood's "Northrop Frye Observed," in *Second Words*, "eschews any exact literary 'influence' by Frye," *Survival* and *Surfacing* are positively influenced by him; and Frye keenly praises both in 1976.27. Expanded: 1986.216 (below).

216 St. ANDREWS, BONNIE [A]. "Quest for Unity: Margaret Atwood's *Surfacing*." In *Forbidden Fruit: On the Relationship between Women and Knowledge in Doris Lessing, Selma Lagerlöf, Kate Chopin, Margaret Atwood*. Troy, N.Y.: Whitston Publishing Co., pp. 84-110.

Traces Northrop Frye's theories of Canadian identity, and fairy tale and social elements, in Atwood's consummate modern Canadian novel, *Surfacing*, which Frye 1976.27 declared '"extraordinary.'" *Surfacing*'s isolated, Edenic island, its isolated narrator's quest for identity, and her Indian animism, follow Frye. The fairytale princess/pin-up Anna is "victimized by her own socially-inculcated narcissism"; the fairytale prince/playboy David is a '"second-hand American'" who "loves nothing alive." David and Anna, who refuse adulthood and fear time, represent our sad, dangerous technological generation. Joe seems a '"*loup-garou*'" figure. As Sullivan 1976.98 points out, *Surfacing* defines a Canadian supplication of nature against an American male dominance of it. *Surfacing*'s "archetypal yet singular" hero, whose namelessness suggests Everyone, or Everywoman, becomes reliable; her spiritual quest is also a Canadian, social quest. Expands 1986.215 (above).

1986

217 St. PIERRE, P. MATTHEW. "Envisioning Atwood." *Cross Currents* 36,
no. 3 (Fall):371-73.
    Praises *The Handmaid's Tale*: "Atwood rigorously diagnoses the
female dimension of God as much as the female component of society.
Her novel is a triumphant humanitarian testament, unrestricted by
feminist polemic and patrilineal bias alike, an originally provocative
case for the common primacy of woman and man," and an essential
"satire on the abuse of religion . . . [that celebrates] the
inextinguishable religious spirit and" the world where God still exists.
Offred herself seems to represent "the remnant of Christianity: . . . .
Her tale is no less than the gospel of a prophet of a persecuted church."
Her uncertain survival points to her essential spiritual dimension, and
perhaps apotheosis. The "Historical Notes" appendix depicts academics
smugly distancing themselves from injustice. Atwood's "most
imaginatively idiosyncratic" novel draws on Chaucer's *The Canterbury
Tales*, Swift's *Gulliver's Travels* and "A Modest Proposal," Orwell's
Nineteen Eighty-Four, Burgess's *A Clockwork Orange*, and perhaps on
Doris Lessing and Janet Frame.

218 SAINT-MARTIN, LORI. "L'infini servage de la femme." *Spirale*
(Montréal), no. 66 (December), p. 8.
    Praises *The Handmaid's Tale*, Seal Book edition, as a woman's
story of survival that highlights women's fragile situation in
contemporary society. The nightmarish, repressive Gilead is justified as
the alternative to a past when women lived in fear of rape. Women's
bank accounts are frozen and feminist activism against pornography
backfires. The narrative's greatest impact comes afterwards, when
current news reports contain fragments of Gilead. In the ["Historical
Notes"] epilogue, women's experience is still denied. Although *The
Handmaid's Tale* can be didactic, Atwood opens our eyes with this
good, urgently told, and undoubtedly very important book.

219 SCHREIBER, LE ANNE. "Female Trouble." *Vogue* 176, no. 1
(January):208-9.
    Interviews Atwood, who is a parent, celebrity, political activist,
and long-time "deconstructionist of female identity." Atwood discusses
her north woods and city upbringing; *The Handmaid's Tale*'s
sociobiology; its every detail's logical correspondence to some reality in
her file of clippings; and its beginnings in two scenes, "'of women

1986

walking down a street in long, red dresses and white, face-concealing bonnets, and a second scene of a public execution, with hooded figures hanging on a wall.'" Atwood had thought "'Pogo, the mother frog who wheeled her tadpole around in a jar,'" was the "'unconscious source'" for the bottled embryo's funeral; but then a clipping came about a California ceremony. Atwood prefers byways to the mainline social novel of *Life Before Man*: "'I'm interested in edges, undertows, permutations, in taking things that might be viewed as eccentric or marginal and pulling them into the center.'" Accompanied by an excerpt of chapter 23 and part of 24 of *The Handmaid's Tale*.

220 SCHULTE, JEAN. "Seeing Brave New World of Religious Fanaticism." *Columbus Dispatch*, 9 March. Newsbank 1985-1986, 78:C10.

Praises *The Handmaid's Tale*'s mesmerizing plot, shrewd social comment, suspense, and keen irony. Biblical phrases are chillingly twisted. The brilliantly characterized Serena Joy is a furiously housebound Phyllis Schafly. Though shadowed by the bleak utopias of *Brave New World* and *Nineteen Eighty-Four*, *The Handmaid's Tale* charts its own unsettling dimensions, by combining the hateful extremes of religious fanaticism "with the bloated backlash of feminist dogma."

221 SCHWARTZ, AMY E. Review of *The Handmaid's Tale*. *Washington Monthly* 18, no. 3 (April):59-60.

Values Atwood's undoctrinaire political novel, that "vividly and rendingly" shows us how Gilead's oppression of women feels. Little happens to Offred, who is numb with shock. What matters is that Gilead, though sketchily detailed, illuminates "the sometimes overlooked relationships between political and sexual power; between cultural determinism . . . [which includes 'women's culture' feminists] and dehumanization; between loss of individual identity and loss of will. The most chilling oppressors" are Wives and Aunts; the creepiest thing is Offred's "unconscious acceptance of some" rules, as when she does not name her mother or her daughter. Atwood warns us not just of guns, spies, and religious fundamentalists, but of our own natures.

222 SEILER, ROBERT M. Review of *Selected Poems II: Poems Selected and New, 1976-1986*. *Canadian Book Review Annual*:87-88.

1986

Finds *Selected Poems* fascinating, disturbing, and great poetry, if sometimes gloomy. These strikingly controlled poems trace Atwood's vision of "mythology and its role in everyday life." Her "colloquial vigor and sardonic wit" are unmistakable; her mastery of line and image recalls Robert Frost and T.S. Eliot. Wearing many masks, she explores many subjects, including the inner and outer self. The *Two-Headed Poems* persona reflects on "'creating'" as a mother and poet. The laconic poet of *True Stories* "presents her poem to the world." *Murder in the Dark* glances at art and life. *Interlunar* explores "renewal through transformation." The new poems return to metaphors of language and geography.

223 SKENAZY, PAUL. "Atwood and *Handmaid*: Fiction's Future Tense." *In These Times* 10, no. 18 (2-8 April):13.
  A reprint of 1986.224 (below) that omits several paragraphs' worth of appreciation.

224 ____. "Desperation of Home Life Mirrors State Terror in 21st Century." *San Jose Mercury News*, 2 March. Newsbank 1985-1986, 78:C1-2.
  Praises *The Handmaid's Tale* as a "vivid, frequently moving vision of a future world gone horribly wrong"; and recognizes its sources in Puritan theocracy, credit cards, and the Moral Majority. Centered on home life as seen by an enslaved woman, *The Handmaid's Tale* lacks the political and cultural detail of Orwell's *Nineteen Eighty-Four*. Gilead is profoundly, if sentimentally, condemned in the "extraordinary, frequently unbearable passages in which Offred remembers" her sacrificed husband, friend, mother, and daughter. Like much of Atwood's work, *The Handmaid's Tale* is solipsistic, which flattens other characters; it is also a bit too long; and the ["Historical Notes"] ending is inept and silly. "But its several faults duly noted, [the reviewer] cannot praise this book highly enough; it is an important, often moving story that will fascinate and educate." Reprinted with significant cuts: 1986.223 (above).

225 SLONCZEWSKI, JOAN L. "A Tale of Two Handmaids." *Kenyon Review*, n.s. 8, no. 4 (Fall):120-24.
  Compares Atwood's dystopic *The Handmaid's Tale* and May Sarton's celebratory *The Magnificent Spinster*. Both novels deal with the

expression and repression of sexuality; and both use horn imagery, as in the handmaids' horn-shaped caps. Atwood's more clearly feminist novel "critiques patriarchal domination," but lacks strong women characters, except for the Aunts and Moira, whose escape fails. Does Atwood recommend or critique our complacent, sexually liberated present? Her satire of conservative American Christianity is unconvincing, as in the bizarre handmaid rituals. Sarton's strong women dominate throughout, but is her affirmation of American society true, or a lulling nostalgia? Both novels lack active males, and focus on female friendship. Both are magnificent, in their different ways.

226 SLOPEN, BEVERLEY. Review of *The Handmaid's Tale*. *Toronto Star*, 26 January, p. B6.

Characterizes *Publishers Weekly* 1985.101 as a review "that a writer would kill for," and quotes its concluding sentences: "'In this astonishing novel, Atwood has achieved a high level of social and artistic discourse. It deserves an honored place on the small shelf of cautionary tales that have entered modern folklore – a place next to, and by no means inferior to, *Brave New World* and *1984*.'" Other accolades are imminent. *The Handmaid's Tale* has sold over 30,000 hardbacks in Canada since September; Houghton Mifflin plans a U.S. 50,000 copy print-run. Also reports on a New York Canadian Consulate party for Atwood and others during P.E.N.

227 SMITH, GITA MARITZER. "Econowives and Handmaids: A Chilling View of the Future." *Atlanta Journal*, 23 February, p. J8.

Finds *The Handmaid's Tale* irresistible, "a marvel of survival-by-small-increments," as Offred learns the tiny signals of possible freedom. Who can resist science fiction braced with chilling political prophecy? Pre-Gilead is right now. In 2195, the ["Historical Notes"] section reveals, a university symposium will examine "a valuable archeological find" – Offred's tapes of fundamentalist, ultraconservative Gilead.

228 SMITH, WENDY. "A Scary Scenario of Lost Freedom." *Plain Dealer* (Cleveland), 16 February, pp. P1, 4.

A slightly condensed reprint of 1986.229 (below).

1986

229 ____. "Writers at Work: Margaret Atwood." *Chicago Sun-Times*, 9 February, Show sec., p. 25.

Interviews Atwood in New York City after P.E.N.: Atwood discusses the scrapbook of clippings and the totalitarian Puritans behind *The Handmaid's Tale*'s realism, the concealed "'you'" who Offred talks to, and events that test characters; tells the story of her ancestor Mary Webster, who survived being hung for a witch; and explains that if Offred had been more heroic, she would not have survived to get out and make her tapes. The interviewer finds *The Handmaid's Tale* a frighteningly plausible near-future. Reprinted, slightly condensed: 1986.228 (above).

230 SNITOW, ANN. "Back to the Future." *Mother Jones* 11 (April-May):59-60.

Appreciates *The Handmaid's Tale* as a philosophical disquisition on history, freedom, and hope, "disguised as an intense good read, almost a game or a puzzle"; Atwood's coldness braces, and she keeps getting better. Offred had passively inherited the women's freedoms won by her mother's generation; now, a prisoner of sex, she becomes "a mental time traveler" and a historian craving knowledge. Opposites sag close over time; Gilead's Birth Ceremony is a mockery of "'a women's culture.'" Offred's conflated memories show that "a bombing is a bombing." Offred longs for lost love and *Vogue*'s female mobility, is reminded of freedom's problems, and finally rejects Gilead's either/or dualities. Gilead teems with possibilities–does Offred escape? The ["Historical Notes"] symposium sets Gilead in a larger frame; but its academics are pompous, falsely objective, and sexist–like ours. We readers, whose freedoms might be taken like Offred's, know her better. Reprinted, slightly cut: 1987.53.

*231 "Sociedad esclavista basada en la reproducción." *Vanguardia* (Barcelona), 27 March.

Finds the *The Handmaid's Tale*'s Gilead, a Genesis-based society devoted to the act of reproduction, more real than the utopias of Wells, Huxley, and Orwell. Atwood's religious government employs older women who use corporal punishment to prepare the handmaids: pregnancy will bring privilege; failure means banishment to the radioactive labor camps. That the narrator longs for the past and her weak, ordinary husband, adds irony to this Chaucerian, feminist story.

1986

Values Atwood's statement of the dangers to the individual in our society.

232 SOMERVILLE-LARGE, GILLIAN. "No Balm in Gilead." *Irish Times* (Dublin), 22 March, p. 14.

Hails Atwood's exceptional *The Handmaid's Tale* in a four-book review: her lucid, icy, engaging prose puts her grim fable beside George Orwell's [*Nineteen Eighty-Four*]. Like Iran, Gilead has "become a murderously efficient theocracy where women are chattels. . . . [The] images are precise and horrible. The theme is red and white. The ritualised violence and the horror" are intensified as Offred matter-of-factly details women's decline.

233 STAINES, DAVID. "Dark Future of Today." *Dallas Morning News*, 16 March, p. C10.

Finds *The Handmaid's Tale* "truly brilliant," because it creates an easily imaginable future that too logically extends many "disturbing aspects of the present, . . . [such as] the contemporary atrocities depicted in J.M. Coetzee's South African fiction. Perhaps only a Canadian, a neighbor as well as an outsider to the United States, could create such an unsettling vision of the American future. . . . *The Handmaid's Tale* is one Handmaid's valiant and perhaps vain attempt to make sense, if sense there be, of Gilead." Atwood's valiant, apocalyptic warning is not only a fictional story.

234 ____. "Home Word." *Canadian Literature*, no. 109 (Summer), pp. 103-4.

Compliments Atwood's poetic talents, acute perceptions, sardonic humour, and increasing compassion in the *Bluebeard's Egg* stories of unhappy modern men and women, who drift and struggle against their crippling loneliness. Like Joel of "Uglypuss," these characters are homeless, and suffering deeper anxiety and pain than the characters of *Dancing Girls* suffer. Like Sally [in the title story], they are traumatized by meaningless existences; relationships and marriage are loveless and unsatisfying. "Significant Moments in the Life of My Mother" and "Unearthing Suite" contrast the narrator's joyful, innocent childhood to her present life. Atwood's bored, inert characters should reach out, as at the end of ["The Sin Eater"].

1986

235 [STEINBERG, SYBIL]. Review of *Bluebeard's Egg and Other Stories*.
Publishers Weekly 230, no. 15 (10 October):76.

"Unfortunately, the author's arch cleverness and cool
understatement anesthetize ... [these] conversations and gloomy
relationships. . . . Symbols abound, and some . . . are strained," as in
"Uglypuss." But the affecting "Bluebeard's Egg," whose egg "aptly
symbolizes the protagonist's premonitions" about her doomed
marriage, somewhat redeems the collection.

236 STEWART, ROBERT. "Short Stories, the Beginning of Canadian
Writing, Have Become the National Specialty." *Gazette* (Montreal), 20
December, p. B7.

Atwood and Robert Weaver, "the godfather of Canadian letters,"
have co-edited an indispensable treasure, *The Oxford Book of
Canadian Short Stories in English*. As Atwood's introduction points out,
short stories are a major and historically-rooted genre here, in which
women writers are increasingly prominent. A disproportionate number
of writers selected are Western Canadian, or born outside Canada.
Apparently the criterion was not Canadian content or current
residency, which explains including Bharati Mukherjee's "The Lady
from Lucknow," a choice made more puzzling by the exclusion of
Elizabeth Spencer's Montreal stories and John Metcalf's Canadian
stories. But there are marvelous inclusions, such as James Reaney's
"The Bully," and Atwood's macabre, masterful "The Salt Garden,"
along with golden oldies, new work, and styles ranging from
conventional to experimental.

237 STIMPSON, CATHARINE R. "Atwood Woman." *Nation* 242, no. 21
(31 May):764-67.

Appreciates *The Handmaid's Tale*'s feminist dystopia and
Atwood's political writings. Gilead's totalitarian, pro-natalist patriarchy
is *Bodily Harm*'s "Griswold gone wild." Commander Fred, a market
researcher who packages ideology, is Gilead's Michael Deaver.
Offred's tale interweaves the protest and the psychological novel with
the bedroom farce. The characteristic "Atwood Woman is young,
educated, white, middle class, invariably heterosexual," employed, and
urban; fleeing her daily life, she discovers what survival means. Atwood
Woman is flanked by her often noisier or bolder contemporary, and by
her reactionary, manipulative, morally indecent elder. Gilead's Aunts,

whose repressive morality Atwood links with radical feminism, are both sinister and satirized petty female bosses. Since the 1960s, Atwood has explored how victims resist men's and American domination; since the mid-1970s, she has critiqued repression and, now, the patriarchal state; Canada in *The Handmaid's Tale* returns fugitives to Gilead. Like Adrienne Rich, Atwood hones and distrusts language. The surprising ["Historical Notes"] parody shows Gilead fallen, but "pompous, sniggering academics" still labeling reality. Atwood insists "that the writer bear 'witness,'" as the returning Rennie will do, and as Offred does.

238 STOVEL, NORA FOSTER. "Reflections on Mirror Images: Doubles and Identity in the Novels of Margaret Atwood." *Essays on Canadian Writing*, no. 33 (Fall), pp. 50-67.

Traces the development, in Atwood's first five novels, of the literal and figurative mirrors that symbolize self-definition and reveal her increasingly affirmative conclusions. *The Edible Woman*'s mirror images in spoon, faucets, dolls, roommate, the heroine's dolled-up self, and the doll-like cake, are distorted self-images that the heroine finally exorcises. *Surfacing*'s narrator rejects mirrors and cameras, finds her elemental reflections in the lake and the eyes of her alter egos, confronts her mirror self, and achieves survival and salvation, returning to civilization with her new created life. *Lady Oracle*'s literal triple mirrors and reflecting alter egos symbolize the protagonist's multiple personality; Atwood's "self-reflecting mirror becomes a window onto the spirit world," and then a door through which Joan's double, her mother, "draws her into identity." *Life Before Man*'s two couples are mirroring alter egos; Atwood's glass disappears, "revealing a gaping hole in space" though which Elizabeth's double, Chris, pulls her towards the void; after facing her mirror self, Elizabeth finally affirms life through maternity, as does Lesje. *Bodily Harm*'s rope metaphorically reflects sexual, medical, and political harm; Rennie sees humanity and herself through the prison window, and draws her alter ego, Lora, through the hole in space to life, thus saving both, and flying home, in Atwood's most creative affirmation.

239 STRATFORD, PHILIP. "The Uses of Ambiguity: Margaret Atwood and Hubert Aquin." In *All the Polarities: Comparative Studies in*

1986

Contemporary Canadian Novels in French and English. Toronto: ECW Press, pp. 82-95.
A slightly altered reprint of 1983.130.

240 SUTHERLAND, FRASER. "Frisking Laura Secord." In *The Bumper Book*. Edited by John Metcalf. Toronto: ECW Press, pp. 14-25.
Critiques *Survival* and its popularity. Cultural nationalism peaked in 1972 and *Survival*; Atwood's "Authorized Version" became "the key manifesto of its generation," and has now sold an extraordinary 80,000 copies. Takes issue with Atwood 1982.11, and quotes James Polk on *Survival*'s "assemblage." *Survival*'s popularity came from its lists, its copious acknowledgments, its widespread ideas, its wit, range, energy, and popularizing, and its author's "triple threat" successes, which made her "the spokesperson for a generation." *Survival*'s great virtue was its "vigorous sense of discovered terrain . . . of *hereness*"; its great vice was not its thematic method, but an authoritarianism latent in liberal humanism and implicit in ideological structures.

241 ____. "The Unterrorized Poet at Home." *Globe and Mail*, 15 November, p. E1.
Finds pervasive menace, "exquisite poise and icy confidence" in *Selected Poems II*: "The unterrorized poet is at home with terrors." The misjudgments – an undermining flash of wit in "Eating Snake," an odd Hemingway echo in "True Stories" – are too few to count. Mostly these photographic poems are finely focused and exposed, with a perfect matte finish, as in "One Species of Love." Atwood's world "is a morgue, the poems coroner's reports or anatomy lessons," of blood, bones, and skin, as in "The Page" and "'the tree bleeding'" of "Daybooks II." *True Stories*'s politically inspired horrors extend the poet's metaphors. Nature is a violated Eden. Survival is ironic, guilty, temporary, as in "Reading a Political Thriller." A tenuous courage and tentative love surface in "Solstice Poem" and "Variations on the Word Sleep." A selection from two decades would have served readers better.

242 TANENHAUS, SAM. "Short Stories Find New Life – in Two of Three Collections." *Chicago Sun-Times*, 14 December, Show sec., p. 27.
Praises *Bluebeard's Egg* most in a three-book review, comparing it to "a grand hotel suite – capacious, opulent, exquisitely appointed. Atwood ranges over genres and styles, from affectionate girlhood

reminiscences to acid" literary satires and even an updated, ironic Bluebeard story of "marital deception and self-deception. . . . [R]azory intelligence and cool Anglo wit" compensate for the sometimes too stiff feminism. Atwood "measures the world with a level, amused gaze, even when" revisiting adolescence in "Hurricane Hazel."

243 TAYLOR, LINDA. "Spoiling the Dream." *Times* (London), 23 March, p. 51.
     Features *The Handmaid's Tale* in a three-book review. The twentieth century races to its doom, and "the dream is spoiled" even in the United States. Under the widespread infertility explained in the ["Historical Notes"], a totalitarian, puritanical, sterile Gilead prizes babies and persecutes and hangs adults. What interests the reviewer is how women (or a failed feminism) cause Gilead's aggressive matriarchy, through the [A]unts. If women keep working against each other, they will pay with disassociation. The handmaids are "crimson sterile flowers like the tulips that . . . [symbolize] defunct female sexuality" with their brilliant, chilling emptiness.

244 THEODORE, LYNN. "Return to a Future of Female Exploitation." *St. Louis Post-Dispatch*, 16 February, p. G4.
     Praises *The Handmaid's Tale* as a gripping "novel in free verse" that "beautifully and intelligently confronts" universal issues of time, sorrow, and beauty. Offred, significantly 33, finds ironic contrast and, somehow, courage, in the beauty of flowers; she hoards her sanity, and begins to take risks. "Finally she risks everything, not for her '"sisters,"' but for an unexpected love": so *The Handmaid's Tale* can't be dismissed as feminist polemic. Like Offred, "[w]e are all refugees from the past."

245 THOMA, PAM. Review of *The Handmaid's Tale. Colorado Review*, n.s. 13, no. 2 (Spring-Summer):81-83.
     This realistic social commentary succeeds in "'pulling [the eccentric or marginal] into the center,'" as Atwood said in the 1986.219 interview. From the beginning to the satiric "Historical Notes" epilogue, Atwood temptingly reveals Offred's tale and the New Right religious fundamentalist Gilead. "Offred's commander commits the heinous crime" of getting involved with her. *The Handmaid's Tale*,

1986

which is more than a feminist or woman's identity novel, "is about the cycles of civilizations," for Gilead's struggles are internal.

246 THOMPSON, JAMES J., JR. "Bashing the Bible-Thumpers." *The World & I*, May, pp. 438-42.

Protests *The Handmaid's Tale*'s ignorant misrepresentation of American fundamentalists. Fundamentalist women do hold jobs, and speak out publicly now. "Love and lifelong commitment can do wonders for one's sex life," far more than frenetic copulation; see Marabel Morgan's *The Total Woman*. Gilead's rulers don't attend church, do smoke, drink, and practice infanticide; they lack the Religious Right's moral fervor and often-strident patriotism; and, incredibly, these rulers are fighting the Baptists! Man-hating radical feminists will disapprove of Gilead's "'women's culture'" and its "'butch paradise'" at Jezebel's. Today's real Left and Right extremists "hate freedom and diversity." American Puritans would have liked Gilead. Prohibition, like Gilead's pornography ban, was supported by Left and Right. But Atwood's fundamentalist Gilead fails to horrify like Orwell's Stalinist *Nineteen Eighty-Four*; Offred's "personality remains intact," hoping and despairing. Atwood's best seller will win the right accolades because it gives leftists another weapon for pummeling the Religious Right, and it confirms feminists' fearful fantasies.

247 TILLY, NANCY. "Margaret Atwood's Tale of Freedom Lost." *News and Observer* (Raleigh, N.C.), 2 March. Newsbank 1985-1986, 78:C8-9.

Finds *The Handmaid's Tale* extraordinary, riveting, moral, and compassionate. We must read between the lines to grasp the enslaved Offred's extreme despair; we want her "to beat the odds in this dystopia." The conservative feminist Serena Joy has also lost her freedom. Atwood follows our society's ideas to extremes, and creates a paradoxical world "of female domination and female powerlessness." Pregnancy in Gilead is a pyrrhic victory. The Scrabble game redefines pornography. Atwood makes clear our moral involvement. "Fiction helps us survive, spiritually, in a world" that encroaches on and warps us.

248 TOWERS, ROBERT. "Old-Fashioned Virtues, Bohemian Vices." *New York Times Book Review*, 23 November, p. 11.

Finds the unmatched stories of *Bluebeard's Egg* entertaining and interesting. The engaging, gentle, and apparently autobiographical parental stories show a British Canadian family with old-fashioned, Protestant "self-reliance, plain living and respectability, . . . humor and affection." Their daughter's evocations can rise to visionary eloquence, as in ["Significant Moments"] and ["Unearthing Suite"]. The distanced, psychologically astute fictional portraits offer little affection, but plenty of "clear-eyed and sardonic amusement as the author anatomizes her subjects," as in "Loulou" and the dark but deadly accurate "Uglypuss." Both sexes' "follies, insecurities and self delusions" are shown with perfect even-handedness, as in "Bluebeard's Egg."

249 TRITEL, BARBARA. "A World of Slave Women." *San Francisco Chronicle*, 2 February, pp. 1, 10.

Extols Atwood's best book, *The Handmaid's Tale*, whose power lies partly in its gradual revelations. That Offred's past is so close to our 1980s makes right-wing Gilead more alarming. Offred's freedom, family, and name have been stolen; she is defined as a possession only. Atwood's *Surfacing* and *Life Before Man* "explored the relationship between fecundity and power/lack of power" that *The Handmaid's Tale* ambivalently, and somewhat paranoidly, develops. Atwood excels at showing the transcendence of the ordinary; her "hard, elegant prose" completely assimilates her poetry.

250 TYLER, ANNE. "Margaret Atwood's Chilling New Tale of a Future America." *Chicago Sun-Times*, 2 February, Show sec., p. 28.

Praises *The Handmaid's Tale*. Everything in this "eerily inhuman story" has happened somewhere, sometime. Offred tells us, quietly and directly, of her non-life in Gilead. Two questions create considerable suspense: what will happen to Offred finally? and, even more pressingly, what has happened to her already? The reader's curiosity grows; the chilling past emerges, bit by bit. Small details make Gilead and Offred's past, which is our present, with freedom and its dangers, real to us. "The only false note" is the final revelation that Offred's present-tense, seemingly diary account was recorded later. But the novel's essential, vivid immediacy matters more: *The Handmaid's Tale*, which lacks a memoir's reflective distance, "could be taking place at this moment."

1986

251 UPDIKE, JOHN. "Books for Christmas." *American Spectator* 19, no. 12 (December):29.

Briefly recommends *The Handmaid's Tale* and two other books that "deal with violence, yet share a certain poetry and calm intelligence as well."

252 _____. "Expeditions to Gilead and Seegard." *New Yorker* 62, no. 12 (12 May):118, 121-23.

Appreciates *The Handmaid's Tale* as a bemused, spirited Canadian caricature of the United States and as a feminist liberal's "lovely subversive hymn to our ordinary life," in a two-book review of Atwood's novel and Iris Murdoch's *The Good Apprentice*. Though many details of Gilead seem droll, this serious anti-Utopia is "a living checklist of a feminist liberal's bugaboos – rampant pollution, the Christian fundamentalist New Right, sexism, and racism," with foreign and historic allusions. But what American would take the New Right, or falling Caucasian birthrates, so seriously? Yet the poet in Atwood creates an offhand, dreamlike, gradually compelling narrative, not a tract. "What saves *The Handmaid's Tale* from [the futuristic novel's] instant fustiness is" its intimate hymn to woman's customary life, "intensified and darkened" in Gilead. Offred learns to tolerate the generalized Fred like a prostitute, but falls recklessly into heterosexual love with someone else – which turns out to be her shrewdest possible move. Unlike Orwell's death-clouded *Nineteen Eighty-Four*, Atwood's Gilead is pitifully human, with possibilities everywhere, and her heroine is irrepressively vital.

253 "U.S. Praise Hard to Deal with, Atwood Says." *Winnipeg Free Press*, 28 February, p. 35.

Atwood warned, in her Centre for Inter-American Relations speech to Canadian publishers and American literary agents, that border-crossing Canadian authors, used to qualified Canadian responses, may have difficulty adjusting to American enthusiasm. *The Handmaid's Tale*, which has been lavishly praised in the United States, is the third Canadian book on the *Publishers Weekly* bestseller list this year. Reprinted in part from: 1986.17.

254 [VanSPANCKEREN, KATHRYN, ed.] *Newsletter of the Margaret Atwood Society*, no. 3, 4 pp.; 5 pp. insert.

Contains a detailed description of the 1986 Modern Language Association Atwood Session, on "Social Criticism in Margaret Atwood's Novels," especially her quasi-feminist dystopia *The Handmaid's Tale*; information on the Atwood Society's annual meeting at the 1986 MLA Convention and a secretary-treasurer's report; primary and secondary Atwood books, with abstracts of Mendez-Egle 1987.103, McCombs 1988.28, and VanSpanckeren and Castro 1988.52; news of articles and conference papers on Atwood, a slide presentation of her art, and a proposed Atwood session; Atwood's teaching and reading schedule; and the first annual Carole L. Palmer 1986.186 primary and secondary checklist.

255 VERDUYN, CHRISTL. "*Murder in the Dark*: Fiction/Theory by Margaret Atwood." *Canadian Fiction Magazine*, no. 57, pp. 124-31.

Murder in the Dark's experimentation, self-conscious theorizing, "unmitigated assault on patriarchy," and use of the body move towards a theoretical fiction or "'fiction théorique.'" In "Autobiography," "Murder in the Dark," "Raw Materials," and throughout, a banal or oppressive reality is presented, "the writer/liar/murder unsettles the scene, deconstructs the reality, writing/creating a new one." Sections three and four "explode patriarchal settings" and "illustrate the constraints of language" in "Simmering," "Liking Men," and "Iconography." The feet, the body's third eye, and "the senses of touch and smell" concretely if clumsily deconstruct misrepresentations and lead to new, female inscriptions.

256 VINCENT, EMILY. Review of *The Handmaid's Tale*. *Best Sellers* 46, no. 3 (June):83.

Finds *The Handmaid's Tale* compelling: how Offred copes, balancing fear and boredom in dismal Gilead, is a powerful, imaginative, and ironic story. While Offred's despair envelops us, her tale's survival fans hope. Offred's purdah makes her "vague about men's activities."

257 VINCENT, SALLY. "Just Like a Woman." *New Society* 76 (11 April):28.

The Handmaid's Tale's future is a morality tale of our past and present. Surrogate mother Offred is dressed up like a bloodied nun. Everyone mouths platitudes. The witty Atwood is "much more ruthless

1986

than Orwell or Huxley–there is no Big Brother," it's all a habit. Poor Offred is doomed from the beginning. "Just like a woman, [she is] never happy with the way things are."

258 WALL, JAMES M. "The Human Spirit as Machine." *Christian Century* 103, no. 37 (3 December):1083.

Approves *The Handmaid's Tale*'s prophetic message. Like an Old Testament prophet, Atwood does not predict the future but warns of the present–of fundamentalist theocratic desires and of efforts to control pornography, sex education, and free-thinking Catholic priests. Offred's anguished story slowly reveals her handmaid role. Gilead, which limits sexuality to reproduction, is not a literally accurate picture of fundamental Protestant or conservative Catholic reactions; Atwood's deeper concern is "with what society does to itself" when it consolidates authority and forces "on modern women a tribal demand to reproduce." As Garrison Keillor's stories also tell us, "the human spirit needs privacy," and creative love.

259 WARNER, MARINA. "Stepford Revisited." *Guardian* (Manchester), 20 March, p. 20.

Finds *The Handmaid's Tale*'s near-future chillingly convincing, but its characters flat, and wants to be sure what Atwood warns us against most. Women's political prescriptions, once disguised as prophecy and vision, are now science fiction; Atwood's novel is what Ursula Le Guin calls a thought-experiment of cautionary tale-telling and an Orwellian dystopia where women are chattels. The grotesque fucking scene captures the essence of denatured Gilead. In her sexual politics terrain, Atwood attacks not only "Right-to-Lifers, anti-ERA campaigners, born-again Christians, and Stepford Wives, but also" feminist puritans and essentialists who celebrate sisterhood. Offred's character is flattened by her deadening days; and her disappeared husband and unlikely lover, Nick, are shadows.

260 WARREN, CATHY. Review of *The Handmaid's Tale. Charlotte Observer*, 9 March. Newsbank 1985-1986, 78:C7.

Atwood's chilling and exquisitely crafted account "warns of a future constricted by a past built on excess." Females have helped shape Gilead's male-dominated, sinister theocracy. Gilead bars all pleasurable sex, indoctrinates and controls its handmaids, and displays its hung misfits. At night Offred remembers and reconstructs; by day she measures her life carefully, while others fare worse.

261 WAUGH, HARRIET. "Love and Death at Sea." *Illustrated London News* 274 (May):90-91.

A three-book review that finds *The Handmaid's Tale*'s forceful science-fiction fantasy horrifying and fascinating, but not enjoyable. Her American theocracy is a very nasty police state. "Ironically, women themselves, the wives, have colluded with men to enslave their fellow women as red-robed Handmaidens," Marthas, or Unwomen. Atwood warns us "how easily all freedom, but particularly . . . [women's], can be taken away"; one wants to dismiss her world as paranoid fantasy, but it exists, in Iran, Russia, and Reagan's bible belt. Atwood brilliantly conveys captivity, boredom, and horror; but her novel lacks plot, excitement, and climax.

262 WEXLER, JOYCE. Review of *The Handmaid's Tale. America* 155, no. 1 (5-12 July):16-17.

Atwood's cautionary moral tale haunts, rather than harangues, the reader; she warns us of unwanted consequences of our desires, but embeds the issues in the narrator's vividly aware life. Offred's name indicates her dependent status, and perhaps an "'offered'" sacrifice. Atwood redistributes "'pro-life' and 'pro-choice'" arguments to show how using force nullifies both. . . . [C]ontemporary theories of discourse" underlie this reconstructed, postprint novel to an unknown audience. Near the end, Offred's victim's testimony changes to a confession of her "sin of adjusting to an unjust order." *The Handmaid's Tale* recalls Deuteronomy's "'Therefore choose life that both thou and thy seed may live.'"

263 WILSON, SHARON R. "Bluebeard's Forbidden Room: Gender Images in Margaret Atwood's Visual and Literary Art." *American Review of Canadian Studies* 16, no. 4 (Winter):385-97.

Examines the sexual politics of Atwood's visual and literary images, which resonate with fairy tale, myth, and gothic stories. The 1970 "Death as Bride," an archival watercolor reproduced here, expresses Atwood's central and evolving Bluebeard motif, which derives from Grimms's "Fitcher's Bird," "The Robber Bridegroom," and "Little Red-Cap." Though these Grimm tales are generally read as traditional cautionary tales, they show that heterosexual relationships are dangerous for women who cannot use their imagination, cunning, and art; "Fitcher's Bird" presents multiple, complex gender roles for the wizard and the third sister. Like these tales, Atwood's work abounds with mutilation, dismemberment, and sexist violence, as in *True Stories*. The sexual politics of "Fitcher's Bird" are embedded in "Hesitations Outside the Door." Sally in "Bluebeard's Egg" "casts herself and Ed in multiple, contradictory roles drawn from" "Fitcher's Bird," "The Robber Bridegroom," and other Grimm tales, Hans Christian Andersen's "The Snow Queen," popular culture, epics, and ballads. Atwood's male/female images are inextricably tied and frequently doubled. See 1988.55.

264 WINTER, HELMUT. "Unter Glas." *Frankfurter Allgemeine*, 20 September, Bilder und Zieten sec., p. [5].

Atwood's poems and novels mirror Canada. *Unter Glas*, Helga Pfetsch's smooth translation of *Dancing Girls* into German, reflects Atwood's artistic use of imagery and her anti-Americanism, but lacks the intensity and originality of her poems and novels. These stories are about women in crisis, and their tensions and polarities. The best story, "Giving Birth," excellently portrays birth as a metaphor of the creative process. The open endings are sometimes irritating.

265 WOLITZER, HILMA. "A Future in Which Love and Lust Are Criminal." *Newsday* (Long Island), 2 February. Newsbank 1985-1986, 71:B14.

Finds *The Handmaid's Tale*'s theme seriously political and convincing, and its characters successfully imagined. Patriarchal, puritanical Gilead limits sex to reproduction, and forbids love and lust. Offred recalls her vanished nuclear family, her mother, and her friend; her story is suspenseful, witty, and touching; the reader trusts this plucky, unquelled heroine. Even alone, Offred comforts herself with words and their meanings; one thinks of silenced writers now, Orwell's *Nineteen Eighty-Four*, Huxley's *Brave New World*, and Shirley Jackson's "The Lottery."

266 WOODCOCK, JOHN. "Science and Survival in Margaret Atwood's *Life Before Man*." *Annals of Scholarship* 4, no. 1 (Fall):122-32.

1986

Discusses *Life Before Man*'s pervasive use of science in theme, images, "character, setting, and narrative point of view." *Surfacing*'s narrator sees science as destructive; *Life Before Man* is more sympathetic, but still subtly critical of science. The socially uneasy Lesje, who came to science as a refuge from a difficult upbringing, is a serious, realistic, and representative scientist, though not the exemplary scientist C.P. Snow wanted in literature. Extinction pervades the museum and the modern life outside it. Life consistently associates the three main characters' losses of meaning and vitality with "the language, reductionism, and depersonalized point of view of science." Individual intuition, not science, provides their tentative hopes. Abstract: 1985.116.

267 YORK, LORRAINE M. "Lives of Joan and Del: Separate Paths to Transformation in *Lives of Girls* and *Women and Lady Oracle*." *University of Windsor Review* 19, no. 2 (Spring-Summer):1-10.

Compares Alice Munro's and Atwood's *bildungsroman* heroines: at crucial moments, each rejects Tennyson's isolated heroine, of "Mariana" or of "The Lady of Shalott." Both reject, but later empathize with, their mothers. Realism and fantasy clash within both heroines, in remarkably similar episodes of traumatic childhood theatrics; of religion, from which each heroine salvages some creative aspect; and of sex, which is linked to violence for each. Though Del is the more realistic artist, and Joan the more Gothic, both books end with a baptism of sorts, not a Tennysonian death.

268 ZEIDNER, LISA. "Can Her Republic Happen Here?" *Philadelphia Inquirer*, 5 March, pp. E1, 4.

Interviews Atwood, who discusses *The Handmaid's Tale*'s "'stupendous'" reception here—25 of 26 reviews were positive, and, contrary to [McCarthy 1986.150], a minister has just confirmed that evangelical radio already sounds like Gilead; Gilead's historic and contemporary bases, including the American Puritans, Iran, and sociobiology's walrus-like harems; Canadian versus American politics, writers, female writers, and attitudes to women; and the optimism of Gilead's end.

1987

1 AITKEN, JOHAN LYALL. "Towards a New Mythos." In *Masques of Morality: Females in Fiction*. Toronto: Women's Press, pp. 138-57.

Discusses *Surfacing* at the beginning and end of a chapter devoted to the artist as heroine in Alice Munro's *Who Do You Think You Are? Surfacing*, which evoked many women's repressed feminism, shows the "necessity of the journey back into order to move forward to a new mythos of self and soul . . . . While we are pushed under again and again, it is to no small degree our own choice – to drown or to surface." Rejecting false stories, male morality, and victimization, the empowered protagonist chooses her new pregnancy.

2 ALLEN, GINA. Review of *The Handmaid's Tale*. *Humanist in Canada* 20, no. 2 (Summer):3, 37.

A rave review: "*The Handmaid's Tale* is a must read for Humanists, . . . a marvelous read," and a terrifying classic – "Right up there with George Orwell's *1984*." Atwood shows what the United States will be like "when Pat Robertson becomes President, when Jerry Falwell is Secretary of State and Phyllis Schlafly is Secretary of Education. . . ." There are purgatories for barren Handmaids, and for men. Former abortionists, homosexuals, freethinkers, and evolutionists are publicly hung. "[Offred's] life is regimented, lonely and loveless. Fred's life is no picnic either." *The Handmaid's Tale* happens here, where people have been gullible, and fundamentalists are grabbing power.

3 ARGÜELLES, IVAN. Review of *Selected Poems II: Poems Selected and New, 1976-1986*. *Library Journal* 112, no.18 (1 November):113.

Atwood's new collection should support her reputation as one of Canada's finest writers. Her thematically complex poetry goes beyond categories: the Canadian "Four Small Elegies" transcends the regional, and her feminism may not evoke pacifism. As in "She," Atwood discovers implicit violence in human nature. Her fatalistic, mordant diction might be post-modern, but is not experimental or obscure.

4 "Atwood among *Ms*. Women of the Year." *Winnipeg Free Press*, 14 January, p. 41.

Reports that Atwood read from her works at a New York ceremony honoring *Ms.* magazine's 13 Women of the Year.

5 "Atwood Blasts Park 'Ransom.'" *Calgary Herald*, 21 June, p. C7.
    Quotes Atwood on British Columbia's request for "almost $200 million to stop logging a potential national park," designated a United Nations World Heritage site, "in the South Moresby region of the Queen Charlotte Islands." Atwood calls the demand "'environmental hostage-taking'" and proposes a public fund, which she would start off with $1,000.

6 BABINEAU, GUY. "Kanada: The Miniseries." *Canadian Forum* 66 (February):41-42.
    Describes the first episodes of *Kanada*, on CanIt, the Canadian International Network (formerly the CBC): after an American takeover of Canada, freedom fighter Margaret Atwood, played by Sigourney Weaver, has escaped from a Quebec prison labour camp, and now crashes a session of the House of Commons, whose members are played by American stars, and threatens them with a huge bazooka and Farley Mowat, played by Kenny Rogers. Next week Atwood and Joan Collins will mud wrestle.

7 BADER, ELEANOR J. "Each of Atwood's Stories Is an Alluring Feminist Gem." *Guardian* (New York) 39, no. 22 (11 March):17.
    Praises *Bluebeard's Egg* highly–great and varied tales, unsurpassed language, "a terrific read," moods so palpable they make us experience the situations and characters. The diverse characters include the aging mother [of "Significant Moments in the Life of My Mother,"] the unsure 14-year-old [of "Hurricane Hazel,"] and the potter [of "Loulou"], whose self-sacrificing makes her a 1980s overwrought housewife. Relationships are wonderful or hateful; some characters choose to be alone. The overtly political stories portray activists negatively, perhaps defensively, but recall leftists we've known and probably hated.

8 BAINES, ELIZABETH. "Prisons of Fiction." *PN Review* 14, no. 1:57-58.
    Praises *The Handmaid's Tale* highly, in a review of it and Elizabeth Wilson's *Prisons of Glass*. Atwood's first-person, present-

tense narrations brilliantly re-create experience, facilitating the reader's close identification, and profoundly understanding our shared obsessions and very contemporary fear of acknowledging feeling. *The Handmaid's Tale* goes even further: Offred is virtually a prisoner in the police state of Gilead. Her survival strategy, of refusing to hope, further restricts her world; as she submits to feeling, fantasy and possibility flood in. Atwood brilliantly dissects the dangers of "our own linguistic codes and ways of thinking" in this alienated future. But the ["Historical Notes"] context reduces "the acute subjective experience of Offred" and Atwood's nightmare myth.

9 BARSTOW, JANE M. "*Surfacing.*" In *Masterplots II: British and Commonwealth Fiction Series*. Edited by Frank N. Magill. Vol. 4. Pasadena, Calif. and Englewood Cliffs, N.J.: Salem Press, pp. 1643-48.

Discusses *Surfacing*'s profoundly disturbed narrator, who searches for her father and self-discovery; the thinly drawn Joe, who is the opposite of the fake husband/lover; the hypocritical David, and the vulnerable Anna. After recovering and understanding her childhood paradise, the narrator can return to civilization. The plot is psychological symbolism; the underlying loss, quest, and rebirth are mythic. The presumed purity of the wilderness is used to judge civilization's corruption. Hailed in Canada and the United States as a modern classic, *Surfacing* is considered Atwood's best work; the best-selling, visionary *The Handmaid's Tale* may succeed it.

*10 BAYLES, MARTHA. "Atwood Puts Ideology Aside for Explorations of the Heart." *Washington Times*, 9 February, p. M6. Newsbank 1986-1987, 69:B14.

Review of *Bluebeard's Egg*, B14-? All copies obtained appear to be incomplete.

11 BEMROSE, JOHN. "Orphans in a Harsh Land." *Maclean's* 100, no. 9 (2 March):51.

Praises the real poetry, power, economy, tragedy, and plotting of *Heaven on Earth*, a two-hour CBC television drama by Atwood and director Peter Pearson, despite its lapses into the sentimental and plebeian. *Heaven* follows five of the more than 125,000 Home Children sent from Britain between 1867 and 1914 to caring or cruel Canadian homes.

12 BERAN, CAROL L. "George, Leda, and a Poured Concrete Balcony: A Study of Three Aspects of the Evolution of *Lady Oracle*." *Canadian Literature*, no. 112 (Spring), pp. 18-28.

Examines three revisions of the *Lady Oracle* manuscripts which raise questions of our perceptions of fiction and reality. Having Joan address the reader, rather than, as in the earlier drafts, her fantasized husband George (later renamed Arthur), makes *Lady Oracle* a fictionalized celebrity autobiography, and a fictional spiritual autobiography; *Lady Oracle*'s gothic elements also question genre conventions. The late addition of Leda Sprott, with her mythological name, her Spiritualism, and her reappearance, raises further questions of reality and fantasy, life and art. The reworking of the first paragraph with multiple, realistic (poured concrete), and gothic details that are dispersed into the first chapter, has similar effects. Ultimately, *Lady Oracle* asks not what fiction is, but what reality – as shaped by our fictions – is.

13 BERRYMAN, CHARLES. "Atwood's Narrative Quest." *Journal of Narrative Technique* 17, no. 1 (Winter):51-56.

Surfacing can combine the Persephone myth of descent and rebirth with the modern realistic novel because it follows Frye's archetypal patterns of comedy and romance which are dramatized, with some realism, in Shakespeare's *A Midsummer Night's Dream* and *The Tempest*. *Surfacing*, *Midsummer*, and *The Tempest* all move into a Frygian "'green world'" that represents the irrational and romantic. *Surfacing*'s four characters often resemble Midsummer's young lovers; Atwood's talismanic rock paintings and imagined divine commands, like *Midsummer*'s fairies and Puck, are comedy's supernatural interventions; *Surfacing*'s end, where the narrator and Joe are closer, fulfills the comic marriage pattern. *Surfacing* largely fulfills the romance pattern seen in *The Tempest*, with its emphasis on father-daughter relationships, evil, and shaping a brave new world. Atwood's narrator descends into nature, "gain[s] her father's knowledge of evil and death," and returns able to love. The imagined new world is described in *Survival*.

14 BLAKE, PATRICIA. "Life Studies." *Time* 129, no. 2 (12 January):74.

Praises *Bluebeard's Egg*'s rapid, telling characterizations, especially of men, as in "Scarlet Ibis" and "Bluebeard's Egg." Atwood's stories are like life studies against her novels' "large, symbolic canvases." Formidably disciplined, she "keeps her characters at a distance." Like the artist in the finest story here, "The Sunrise," Atwood sketches imperfect, rained-on people who are alive.

15 BOREN, LYNDA S. "Paper Heads and Zero at the Bone: Margaret Atwood's Unclaimed Territory." In *Women's Studies and Literature: Neun Beiträge aus der Erlanger Amerikanistik*. Edited by Fritz Fleischman and Deborah Lucas Schneider. Erlanger Studien, edited by Detlef Bernd Leistner-Opfermann and Dietmar Peschel-Rentsch, vol. 73. Erlangen: Palm & Enke, pp. 212-228.

Discusses Atwood's geography of the female body as symbol and analogy of the Canadian region. *Survival*'s English island is significant for the Atwood heroines who long for islands of repose. Canada offers only survival, and "a dialectic between polarities – past, future; America, England; man, woman; illusion, reality – which works itself out in the consciousness of a female protagonist" and marks her body. The feminist writer tries "to reclaim the female body as symbol . . . . [T]he voice that guides us through bodily regions impishly seeks" anonymity in "A Paper Bag." *Lady Oracle* shows us "the collective unconscious of a Canada that is indistinguishable from that of America." Blocked from her past, *Surfacing*'s unnamed heroine works through identity problems. The physical and emotional scars of Atwood's heroines portray Canada's struggling survivors, as in "Polarities" and *Bodily Harm*.

*16 B[OUVIER], L[UC]. Review of *Meurtre dans la nuit*. *Apropos* 5, no. 2:92-93.

Appreciates *Meurtre dans la nuit* (*Murder in the Dark*). Atwood unifies the themes of relationships between men and women, the act of writing, and childhood by playing masterfully with perception. *Murder in the Dark* connects writer, reader, and book to create a new reality. Recognizing the multiplicity of the universe, Atwood's content evokes multiple perceptions, and her form serves multiple functions.

17 BRODSKY, NAOMI R. "Stunning Stories from Atwood." *Providence Journal*, 11 January, p. I7. Newsbank 1986-1986, 57:C14.

Praises *Bluebeard's Egg*'s rich, diverse, well-crafted, funny, and haunting stories. In this enigmatically titled book, Atwood reveals the foibles, inner lives, and multi-level relationships of her colorful characters, as in "Loulou." Sally and Ed of "Bluebeard's Egg" typify her multi-faceted, fragmented modern characters.

18 BROOKNER, ANITA. "A Girl's Best Subject Is Her Mother." *Spectator* 258 (6 June):37.

Praises *Bluebeard's Egg*'s expert, simple, straightforward style, in a two-book review featuring Atwood; but finds her material insubstantial – such gifted writers should do more. Canadian women writers seem to do their mothers effortlessly. The first and last autobiographical stories have Atwood's best style. The parents inhabit "a world of innocence and virtue"; the other stories are mildly sleazy, with Yvonne [of "The Sunrise,"] who picks up men, the dreadful Sally of "Bluebeard's Egg," who satirises her lover, and the fed-up title character Loulou. Atwood's odd feminism has feral women and "sneaking sympathy for men," like Joel [of "Uglypuss."]

19 BROWN, ROSELLEN. Review of *The Handmaid's Tale*. *Radcliffe Quarterly* 73, no. 1 (March):46.

Acclaims Atwood's harshly and brilliantly inventive novel; Radcliffe readers will recognize the narrator's poignantly remembered past world as the Cambridge we know. In her present world of Gilead, sexual fundamentalists categorize women by function, like barnyard animals; affection, autonomy, and spontaneously formed families are gone. Yet even in this chilling, stratified Gilead, Atwood triumphantly creates the women: gossiping, consoling, colluding, or rebelling, like Offred. Offred "is our surrogate, bearing memories like ours into a world made terrible and strange. Though it is a far more poetic and sensually exact guide to the unspeakable than Orwell's," Atwood's all-too-plausible novel belongs with his *Nineteen Eighty-Four*.

20 BYATT, HELEN. "New Novels." *Books*, no. 3 (June), p. 25.

A review of *Bluebeard's Egg* and other books. Atwood's stories slip down with deceptive ease, "their kick masked by" her cool, comfortable storytelling, as in "Betty." Assumptions are dangerous; Bohemia [in "Loulou"] is like other domestic situations, if you're female. "The Sunrise" is bleaker, with less wry comedy. In "Bluebeard's Egg" the ignorant "wife patronisingly but tragically jokes about her husband's stupidity," and Atwood drops in the terrifying chopped-up women while dinner is prepared. "Happy domesticity with a dash of doom."

21 CARMEAN, KAREN. Review of *The Handmaid's Tale*. In *Magill's Literary Annual*. Edited by Frank N. Magill. Vol. 1. Englewood Cliffs, N.J.: Salem Press, pp. 371-75.

Finds *The Handmaid's Tale* fascinating, chilling, and a deadly serious challenge to readers. Gilead's repressive patriarchy denies women's freedoms, even its handmaids' names. Offred's limited movements restrict the action. Her "flat, almost emotionless prose" is really numb; "she is a grim survivor" who gradually takes the few risks possible. *The Handmaid's Tale* is also about women's conflicts, mistrusts, and control of other women. This "extremely self-conscious narrative" turns out to be reconstructed, unauthenticated, and equivocal. That Atwood's irony can be hilarious could be the novel's only flaw.

22 CARRINGTON, ILDIKÓ de PAPP. "Margaret Atwood." In *Canadian Writers and Their Works: Fiction Series*. Edited by Robert Lecker, Jack David, and Ellen Quigley. Vol. 9. Toronto: ECW Press, pp. 25-116.

Analyzes the Frygian romance structure, questions of identity, and doubles in Atwood's novels and stories. Each of her five novels uses "an obsessive metaphorical network to dramatize her protagonists' developing consciousness. . . . One of the major metaphors is always some form of controlled or uncontrolled locomotion – running, journeying, diving, dancing, or falling . . . . Her moving protagonists are always accompanied by characters who function as ghosts, doubles, and/or guides," and thus signal inner conflicts of protagonists and creator. The climax always "follows arrival at the same kind of oracular place" – ravine, lake, maze, Elizabeth Schoenhof's imagined "*caves of ice*," or prison cell. The journey, "which follows the first half" of Frye's romance pattern, is always "a search for a unifying vision of identity"; that question is variously framed but, because of the ambiguous ascents, ironically answered. *The Edible Woman* asks "'What is a woman?'" and "'Who am I going to be?'" *Surfacing*, which is cognate with Howard O'Hagan's *Tay John* and P.K. Page's *The Sun and the Moon*, asks "'What is a human being?' and 'What is a Canadian?'" *Lady Oracle* asks "'What is an artist?'" and "'What have I become?'" These three protagonists define their identities by positive locomotion and by separating from their ghosts, doubles, or guides. Two childbirth stories, "Giving Birth" and "The Resplendent Quetzal," "continue the romance pattern of the first three novels." *Life Before Man* and *Bodily Harm* show "a deepening confusion about identity," and an emphasis on human evil. *Life* asks "'What *is* identity?' . . . [T]he objective, triple point of view complicates, and finally negates, identity." Locomotion becomes falling; the protagonists fuse "with each other and with their demonic doubles" in the descent's climax. *Bodily Harm* asks "'How can identity be accurately perceived?' and 'What is a writer's moral responsibility?'" *Bodily Harm*'s major themes and romance structure reappear in *Murder in the Dark*, in the misperceptions of identity in "Bluebeard's Egg," and in the affirmative ascent of "Scarlet Ibis," where the guide is a fat angel in disguise. Provides a detailed literary biography, a discussion of literary tradition, a detailed review of the major secondary work, and a selected primary and secondary bibliography. Condenses and revises 1982.34, 1983.21, and 1986.50. [Reprinted] 1987.22 (below).

*22a ____. *Margaret Atwood and Her Works*. Toronto: ECW Press [1987?], 92 pp.
   [Reprint of] 1987.22 (above).

23 ____. "A Swiftian Sermon." *Essays on Canadian Writing*, no. 34 (Spring), pp. 127-32.
   Reads *The Handmaid's Tale* as an impassioned cautionary satire whose narrator, like Rennie in *Bodily Harm*, "prefer[s] to ignore evil." The Sufi epigraph criticizes those readers who prefer stones to the serious moral and political literature *Second Words* advocates. Like Swift's *A Modest Proposal*, Atwood's novel ironically pushes assumptions to logical conclusions; like "Simmering" it extrapolates to warn us. Gilead's sterile theocracy makes a scripture-based surrogate motherhood into law. Offred's name means "'offered' and 'afraid'" as well as Of Fred. "The painful history Offred secretly and reluctantly records on her tapes is full of parallels to the facts that she, like Rennie, has failed to pay attention to": assassinations, concentration camps, killing Jews, a male backlash that begins, like the Holocaust, with taking women's jobs and bank accounts, a Commander whose mistress thinks him "'not a monster . . . .'" The satirical "Birth Day" and climactic "Salvaging" dramatize Atwood's warning most powerfully.

1987

Though the "Historical Notes" satirize feminists and tell us of Offred's fate, they are a didactic anticlimax.

24 CAVEN, PATRICIA. "Trying Too Hard to Write Canadian SF." *Ottawa Citizen*, 26 December, p. C2.

Praises Atwood's detailing of the potential effects of new social diseases as one of the four stories that are the blazing diamonds of *Tesseracts2*, edited by Phyllis Gotlieb and Douglas Barbour. Other stories range from good to unreadable; the anthology gets only a qualified recommendation.

25 CHAMBERLAIN, TIMOTHY. "Food and Drink." *Books in Canada* 16, no. 9 (December):27.

Enjoys *Margaret Atwood's [sic] CanLit Foodbook*, which benefits P.E.N. International and the Writers' Development Trust. *Foodbook* could be dangerous: imagine Aunt Martha asking for more Yuletide guests/ingredients after reading "Eating People is Wrong – Cannibalism Canadian Style.'" Or the *Foodbook* could control pests, with Farley Mowat's "Creamed Mice" and Michael Ondaatje's "Rat Jelly." Recipes reveal personalities – is Graeme Gibson's "Potroast with Chocolate" utilitarian-exotic? Paulette Jiles's "Scrambled Pig's Brains with Fried Green Tomatoes" – better let be. J. Alfred Prufrock could have used Timothy Findley's "Summer Peaches."

26 CHARMAN, JANET. Review of *The Handmaid's Tale*. *Broadsheet* (Auckland, N.Z.), no. 152 (October), pp. 44-45.

Critiques *The Handmaid's Tale*: this "sanitised feminist" novel has a cynically commercial ending. The reviewer stayed up late to finish it. "Its themes are fascinating. . . . To her credit, Atwood keeps [the sex] banal," never prurient. "If Sally Miller Gearhart's *The Wanderground* was a pattern of post-holocaust-feminist-heaven: [sic] *The Handmaid's Tale* is a kind of hell, . . . [offering] institutional rape, mass hysteria, concubinage, and domestic slavery. Perhaps [the reviewer] could have given Atwood more credit if she'd sent her heroine to the wall, but a copout ending in a book which so cleverly echoes the miserable reality of many women's lives, leaves [the reviewer] feeling cheated."

27 CHOA, CAROLYN. Review of *The Handmaid's Tale*. *Everywoman* (London), June, p. 31.

1987

Has mixed reactions to *The Handmaid's Tale*. In Gilead's sexist, hierarchical, racist theocracy, the Handmaids are forced to be surrogate mothers. Though Atwood's potent language evokes an alien yet familiar world, "the book is long, depressing, claustrophobic," and sickening at times. But there is hope, for the human spirit does grow back, the heroine finds a kind of love, and the ["Historical Notes"] shows Gilead is gone. But, contrary to the chilling Professor, we must censure: "Gilead must never happen."

28 CLUTE, JOHN. "Embracing the Wilderness." *TLS*, 12 June, p. 626.

Appreciates Canadian and *Survival* elements in *The Oxford Book of Canadian Short Stories in English* and *Bluebeard's Egg*. Most of Atwood's and Robert Weaver's fine, claustrophobic tales show Canadians surviving, mostly in solitude and in cities near the American border. Arranging the stories not by date of publication but by their authors' birth dates produces strange results. The wilderness is omnipresent text or subtext, as if to counteract the scarcely mentioned United States. Though few stories are happy, about a dozen "are superbly artful," including Atwood's "The Sin Eater."

Bluebeard's Egg, which replaces "The Sin Eater" with two other stories, is not happy either, but is often hilarious. Atwood varies her stories at will. "Significant Moments in the Life of My Mother," "Hurricane Hazel," and "In Search of the Rattlesnake Plantain" share a Canadian "fragility and airlessness. The empty northern wastes inform 'Unearthing Suite' . . . and 'The Salt Garden,' which dazzlingly conflates the void and nuclear holocaust." The calm "Spring Song" and "Bluebeard's Egg" are tales of a terrifying loss of control. As in the Oxford anthology, the United States is scarcely mentioned; for Atwood, Canada means survival, face to the void.

29 "A Conversation with Margaret Atwood." In *Margaret Atwood: Reflection and Reality*. See Mendez-Egle, 1987.103, pp.172-80.

Interviews Atwood November 1983 at Pan American University. Atwood advises beginning writers to read and write a lot; and discusses her "'pre-feminist'" fiction; the realistic brutality of "Notes Toward[s] a Poem That Can Never Be Written" and the human responsibility to bear witness; becoming a successful Canadian writer; writing *Bodily Harm* and *Surfacing*; her non-autobiographical and realistic, not supermen, men and women characters; Elizabeth of *Life Before Man* as

585

1987

her best creation and Joan Foster of *Lady Oracle* as her most amiable; "When It Happens" and our present "sense of impotence in the face of evil"; and stories and poems that prefigure *Lady Oracle* and *Bodily Harm*.

30 COX, YVONNE. "People." *Maclean's* 100, no. 46 (16 November):64.
    Quotes Atwood on her just-published *Can[L]it Foodbook*, which benefits P.E.N. and the Writers' Development Trust: "I could have done sex, but then it would be less likely that Aunt Millie would give it to her nieces for Christmas.'"

31 CRAIG, PATRICIA. "Getting the Measure of Modern Women." *Times* (London), 7 June, p. 56.
    Features the exhilarating *Bluebeard's Egg* in a four-book review. The more than evocative "Significant Moments in the Life of My Mother" and "Loulou" show how we hold onto our images of others. The title story, with its modern entanglements and benign Bluebeard, is enriched by the fairytale, and by a hint of Katherine Mansfield's "Bliss." Significant, connecting, sometimes tonic emblems appear, as in ["Scarlet Ibis" and "The Salt Garden"].

32 CREAMER, BEVERLY. "Book Talk with Margaret Atwood." *Honolulu Advertiser*, 21 September. Newsbank 1987, 36:D7.
    Interviews Atwood, who is here with Jess and Graeme Gibson to read from her award-winning *The Handmaid's Tale* at the University of Hawaii. Atwood talks about her novel's plausibility, citing women's rights, credit cards, and Oliver North; the forthcoming film of *The Handmaid's Tale*; and writing habits and bird-watching for herself and Graeme Gibson.

33 CULP, KRIS. "Reconstructing the Church: 'The Handywoman's Tale.'" *Criterion* 26, no. 3 (Autumn):9-12.
    Concludes a 1987 theological speech on reconstructing a feminist redemptive community by citing *The Handmaid's Tale*. "Atwood's novel reminds us powerfully that the creation and preservation of a just and inclusive human community is an ongoing struggle." This possible, necessary reconstruction "is not a handmaid's tale, but rather the Handywoman's Tale." Atwood's dystopia warns us against passivity, victimism, and forgetting the sufferings and struggles of others.

34 DAVID, CATHERINE. "Les fous de l'Éternel." *Nouvel Observateur* (Paris), no. 1197 (16-22 October), p. 62.

Welcomes *La Servante écarlate*, the French translation of *The Handmaid's Tale*, comparing it to an apocalyptic "Little Red Riding Hood." Atwood's Anglo-Saxon, extreme fundamentalist society is created from the germ of actual events; her story focuses on women's sensibility and diversity. As in "Giving Birth," maternal protectiveness is a major theme. For Atwood, descendant of Noah [sic] Webster, writing tries to protect the world.

35 "De Faulkner à Atwood: Une question d'ambiance." *Circuit* (Montréal), no. 17 (June), p. 3.

Interviews Hélène Filion, who translated *Murder in the Dark* and *Survival* into French. Filion discusses the different usages of language among French-speaking countries and her use of Canadianisms in translations, instancing problems in the translation of *Surfacing*.

36 DEER, GLEN GEORGE. "Rhetoric, Ideology, and Authority: Narrative Strategies in Six Innovative Canadian Novels." Ph.D. dissertation, York University. See *Dissertation Abstracts International* 48 (1988):2631-A.

Studies "the relationship between narrative strategies (or rhetoric) and ideology in six innovative or experimental English-Canadian novels," from 1959 to 1985, including *The Handmaid's Tale*.

37 DICAPRIO, LISA. "Bleak Future Envisioned for Women." *Guardian* (New York) 39, no. 22 (11 March):17.

Finds *The Handmaid's Tale* "not pleasurable or inspiring," but, with the celebrative 1970s feminism now blunted, not outlandishly pessimistic. Offred's "tale is intensely subjective," and her spare language emphasizes her limited understanding of Gilead. The futuristic male coup against women uses existing racism and sexual puritanism, including the antipornography movement, which Atwood earlier supported. Gilead's historical precedents include "Nazi exaltation of women's 'biological destiny'. . . . Offred is no heroine," but a "'post-feminist.'" The ["Historical Notes"] epilogue parodies the "'disengaged'" historical scholarship that often rationalizes women's oppression. Though Atwood implausibly singles out women and progressive men as targets, certain trends do suggest a punitive sexual climate emerging under Reagan.

*38 Di IORIO, LYN. "Of Feminists and Fairy Tales." *Harvard Crimson*, 21 January.

A two-book review of *Bluebeard's Egg* and Angela Carter's *Saints and Strangers* that praises Carter's vibrant, "flagrantly original voice," and rejects Atwood's always complaining feminism in *Bluebeard's Egg* and *The Handmaid's Tale*. *Bluebeard's Egg*'s condescending women, typified in "The Sunrise," all "meld together into one composite character, . . . the Atwood bitch." *The Handmaid's Tale*'s Biblical handmaids and weak men are quite unbelievable and tiresomely pessimistic.

39 DOUD, KATHERINE. "[A Woman's Place:] Future: *Handmaid's Tale*." *Kalamazoo* (Mich.) *Gazette*, 15 February, pp. G1-2. Newsbank 1986-1987, 82:B5-6.

"Give women enough rope and they'll hang themselves," Atwood's bleak tale suggests. Her religious right takeover of the United States seems extreme at first. When Offred's life becomes unbearable, she escapes, and is helped along the underground "Femaleroad." "Frightening stuff? You bet."

Quotes Atwood's written statement, made a year after *The Handmaid's Tale*'s publication, on its frightening plausibility; Canadian media reactions of "'could it happen here?'"; and United States reactions of "'how long have we got, and how can we prevent it?'". . . Hardly anyone thought this scenario was entirely fabricated.'"

40 FAGAN, CARY. "The Reel Stuff." *Books in Canada* 16, no. 4 (May):3-4.

Wonders, after reading that *The Handmaid's Tale*'s film rights have been sold to a New York company, and Harold Pinter will write the screenplay, whether novelists should let their books become films; and advises people to read the book first, because a film cannot contain the voice, vision, and meaning of the novel.

41 FELDMANN, BETTY H. "Antidote to the Heat: Chilling Summer Reading." *From NOW On* (Rockville, Md.), July, p. 9.

Recommends *The Handmaid's Tale* highly, as gripping, shocking, and far-sighted. Gilead "becomes breathtakingly real as Offred's tale unfolds. Given the misogyny, racism and anti-Semitism which abound today, it is not difficult to imagine the consequences of a Moral Majority-like group holding the reins of government. . . . Read it while you're still allowed!"

42 FREUD, VERA. "Margaret Atwood." *Humanist* 47, no. 5 (September-October):5-6.
Introduces Atwood at the presentation of the 1987 Humanist of the Year Award; praises her literary work and her powerful, courageous voice in "defense of Mother Earth, human dignity," freedom, women's status, and humanism.

43 GAGNON, LYSIANE. "Margaret Atwood, la grande plume de l' 'autre Canada.'" *Presse* (Montréal), 6 June, p. E1, 4.
In an interview, Atwood discusses criticism of her work, and university literary criticism; the difference between French translations from Québec and France; the interdependence of French Canada and English Canada; and reading as an inspiration for her writing. Atwood is an Anglo-Canadian nationalist who is anti-free trade, anti-America, pro-peace, and pro-ecology.

44 GODARD, BARBARA. "Palimpsest: Margaret Atwood's *Bluebeard's Egg*." *Recherches Anglaises et Nord-Americaines* (Strasbourg), no. 20, pp. 51-60.
A revised reprint of the *Bluebeard's Egg* portion of 1986.96 that explores Atwood's recontextualization of the oral tale in "Bluebeard's Egg," "Unearthing Suite," and "Significant Moments in the Life of My Mother," to illuminate their *"mise en abyme* and embedding."

45 ____. "Telling It Over Again: Atwood's Art of Parody." *Canadian Poetry*, no. 21 (Fall-Winter), pp. 1-30.
Examines Atwood's early writings to argue that her parody both valorises and challenges traditional texts, creating alternate readings from Canadian and feminist perspectives, and also exhibits postmodernist reflexion and reflection. *Synthesia*, an operetta performed by a 1956 Leaside Highschool [sic] Home Economics Class, demonstrates Atwood's fundamental and characteristically ludic parody. *Double*

Persephone's parody alters the matriarchal Demeter story of encroachment on the Great Mother's creative power, to emphasize the rape and threatening underworld, thus exorcising the young writer's fear of entering a patriarchal tradition. "The Triple Goddess" poem for voices, a refunctioning of Robert Graves's *The White Goddess*, tells "over and over again the story of the women's captivity in domesticity." The "Avalon Revisited" suite of poems ironically parodies and inverts the Arthurian male epic into women's lyric art, self-reflexively foregrounding the inversion. "The Idiot Boy" and the "Mad Mother" poem series, which parody Wordsworth's "The Idiot Boy" and other poems, foreground the Boy's kinship with nature, relocate nature in the Canadian prairies, and show the Boy's mother as a mad Mother Nature crone or witch. "The Trumpets of Summer" libretto for John Beckwith's choral suite parodies and satirizes Shakespeare, the Ontario Stratford, school readers, and literary criticism, using a Mikhail Bahktinian carnivalesque dialogic technique. "The Poetry of the People," "Anglo-Saxon and I," and "The Expressive Acts," by Atwood as Shakesbeat Latweed in *Acta Victoriana*, are self-parodies and complex parodies within parodies of Canadian and literary culture.

46 GODFREY, JOHN. "Loony Tunes and Merry Melodies." *Financial Post* (Toronto), 9 November, p. 18.

Ridicules Atwood's arguments against the free trade deal with the United States as essentially sexual, inaccurate, overconfident about predicting the future, and profoundly irrational. *Survival's* Victim Position One brilliantly describes her own situation.

47 GRAY, FRANCINE du PLESSIX. "Margaret Atwood: Nature as the Nunnery." In *Adam and Eve and the City: Selected Nonfiction*. New York: Simon & Schuster, pp. 291-95.

A slightly condensed reprint of 1977.28 that replaces Lisa Alther and Marge Piercy with Margaret Drabble and Alice Munro as examples of social quest novelists, and omits Carol Christ's and Judith Plaskow's names from the *Signs* discussion.

48 GREEN, MARY JEAN. "Tradition as Mother: Women's Fiction and the Canadian Past." *CEA Critic* 50, no. 1 (Fall):41-56.

Examines the distinctly feminine and profoundly Canadian mother-daughter relationship, that searches for autonomy and connectedness, and affirms continuity, in Sheila Watson, Margaret Laurence, Alice Munro, and Atwood. *Surfacing*'s daughter's quest is "for reunion with the mother"; *Lady Oracle*'s daughter seeks "autonomy within an oppressive mother-daughter relationship"; both proceed through "identification and understanding." *Surfacing*'s unusual mother is not passive or oppressive, but strong; the narrator's "choice to become a mother herself" affirms her own strength and creativity. *Lady Oracle*'s mother is oppressive; Joan's rejection of her, Joan's disguises, conforming goals, fantasies, faked suicide, and anger at men, all parallel or resemble her mother. Joan's final self-acceptance lets her be reconciled with her mother.

49 GREENE, GAYLE. "Margaret Atwood's *The Edible Woman*: 'Rebelling Against the System.'" In *Margaret Atwood: Reflection and Reality*. See Mendez-Egle 1987.103, pp. 95-115.

Atwood's misunderstood but witty and original novel combines Dickensian social satire, black comedy, and a Marxist feminist view "of male-female relationships in consumer capitalism." *The Edible Woman*, whose end breaks with the conservative "'two-suitor convention,'" follows Joanna Russ's lyric structure: analogous images of hunting and sex radiate out from Atwood's central conceit of digestive and socio-economic consumption. "Like Dickens, Atwood renders the objectification of people and animation of things" as reflecting social processes. Marian, who fears both entrapment and dissolution, moves from alienating work to more alienating sexual objectification. Only the shape-shifter, Duncan, counters the alienating processes. The therapeutic cake lady succeeds "as a symbol of Marian's control over processes which have been controlling her," but Marian evolves only "from prey to predator."

50 GROSSUTTI, JUDITH. Review of *The Oxford Book of Canadian Short Stories in English*. *Canadian Catholic Review* 5, no. 11 (December):425-26.

Compliments Atwood's and Robert Weaver's satisfying anthology. The Canadian public will find pure pleasure, as in the stories by Hugh Hood, W.P. Kinsella, and Alice Munro. The academic will appreciate the birth-date order, index, and insightful biographies; and the educator will appreciate the judicious selections, as of the stories by Mordecai Richler and Timothy Findley. But the inclusion of stories set in Europe, by Norman Levine and Mavis Gallant, and from writers Bharati Mukherjee and Jane Rule, who were born elsewhere, is questionable.

51 HALES, LESLIE-ANN. "Genesis Revisited: The Darkening Vision of Margaret Atwood." *Month*, 2d n.s. 20, no. 7 (July):257-62.
Where Atwood's first three novels treated the individual journey, descent, and rebirth with humour, irony, and optimistic ends, the transitional *Bodily Harm* and the metafictional *The Handmaid's Tale* treat society with anger and pessimism. *Bodily Harm* spirals down into cynicism and alienation; "Rennie's sickening revelation . . . [that men are really frightening] destroys the illusion that society is a safe place to return to." Where the first three novels ended with the narrator tacitly accepting a man, Rennie categorically rejects the man on the plane back to Toronto; she will report to women, not to the male enemy.
Though the "Historical Notes" epilogue self-reflexively exposes *The Handmaid's Tale*'s fictional illusion, it is distressingly real, and not a dismissable story, as Atwood's file of clippings from the real world shows. Offred does not control the end of her story; we never learn if she escapes or dies. Like most of us, women in pre-Gilead society fail to see, until too late, what is happening. Offred cannot surface and return to society, "because society itself, as *Bodily Harm* implied would happen, has become the very hell of descent." Though Gilead does end, the historians' smug objectivity is morally appalling – and not "a redemptive or hopeful conclusion."

52 ____. Review of *Bluebeard's Egg*. *Month*, 2d n.s. 20, no.12 (December):481.
Appreciates these sobering stories: Atwood "*cares* about the [nuclear-threatened] world" that shapes these vulnerable, sometimes mundane or cruel, often unsympathetic characters and their relationships. Almost every character has trouble communicating. The problem is that, like Alma in "The Salt Garden," they know not to show too much fear of the nuclear threat. The implicit question is, "what happens to people" when neither God nor government (neither is directly mentioned) can prevent nuclear destruction? Yvonne's suicide preparations, in "The Sunrise," are despair "just barely masked as reason." If characters like Will in "Spring Song of the Frogs" are confused, Atwood's ironic anger is clear about our responsibility for

these psychological casualties of the nuclear threat. The lighter "Hurricane Hazel" and the tender "Significant Moments" and "Betty" are also moving; but "The Sin Eater" seems cynical.

53 HALL, SHARON K., ed. *Contemporary Literary Criticism Yearbook*. Vol. 44. Detroit: Gale Research Co., pp. 145-62.

Summarizes the critical success of Atwood's chilling dystopia, quoting her on its historical precedents; provides an excerpt from the novel and an illustration of its U.S. hardback cover; and provides reprints and excerpts from one Canadian essay, two reviews from English critics, and 13 U.S. reviews. Reprinted from: Glendinning 1986.95, Lehmann-Haupt 1986.143, and McCarthy 1986.150; reprinted, slightly cut, from: Kendall 1986.133, Ehrenreich 1986.71, Snitnow 1986.230, Greene 1986.100, and Linkous 1986.144; and excerpted from: H[ooper] 1985.52, Johnson 1986.123, Prescott 1986.195, Gardam 1986.85, Maynard 1986.171, Pinard 1986.193, Allen 1986.11, and Malak 1987.93.

54 HALLIDAY, DAVID. "On Atwood." *Waves* 15, no. 4 (Spring):51-54.

Rejects the much-honoured but empty *The Handmaid's Tale* – is that crazy? The main character was dull before Gilead and is dull now, as are all her indistinguishably bland friends. Only the lonely commander is interesting. Atwood's totalitarianism is silly – the appeal of the rising U.S. and Canadian evangelism is due to boredom, not religion. "What does this book tell us about the present except that Atwood (and apparently the award givers) have a great anxiety about conservatism, Christianity, and traditional female roles." Atwood uses clichés – the Utopia novel, women's suffering, totalitarianism, and conservative theology – as if they were truths, without irony or humour. The media glorying in her New York and London recognition strike the reviewer as part of the "Canadian inferiority complex."

55 HALLIGAN, MARION. "Style, and a Sharp, Dissecting Intelligence." *Canberra Times*, 29 August, p. B4.

Enjoys Atwood's expertise and celebrates her superb style in *Bluebeard's Egg*: "One is absorbed into the other world of her prose, immersed in it, seduced by its rhythms, lulled by its wisdom, tickled by its wit, amused by its deflations, delighted by the quick flash of images." Atwood can get away with length; "more is more" in the nicely ironic, minutely detailed "Bluebeard's Egg." The narrator "often seems to be Atwood," or her persona, a character or friend who dissects her subjects, even patronising Emma. The growing-up and family stories are elegiac, "sometimes sentimental, and moving, with a slightly awful humour . . . . Atwood here is the writer-vampire," celebrating and exploiting her family. The nuclear war and conservation themes of "The Salt Garden" and "In Search of the Rattlesnake Plantain" are woven into ordinary life without any didacticism. Only "Uglypuss" seems too long and unpleasant.

56 HANCOCK, GEOFF. "Margaret Atwood." In *Canadian Writers at Work: Interviews with Geoff Hancock*. Toronto: Oxford University Press, pp. 256-87.
Reprint of 1986.103, without the manuscript page.

57 HATCH, RONALD B. "Letters in Canada 1986: Poetry." *University of Toronto Quarterly* 57, no. 1 (Fall):35-36.
Selected Poems II, which contains selections from three poetry books and *Murder in the Dark*'s weaker prose poems, "is, if anything, even better than the highly praised *Selected Poems* of 1976." As before, Atwood satirizes sexual-political relationships and elegiacally presents individual alienation. "Ageing Female Poet Sits on the Balcony" begins with satire but ends with mortality. Her recent books show "a note of affirmation . . . [in] the dark side of the modern sensibility." *Interlunar*'s materialist perspective on man as interstellar dust no longer stops her from seeing a possible transcendence, "an 'approach' to others which enables one to 'shine.'" The new poems also show how the world becomes more life-giving as the ego's stranglehold relaxes.

*58 "Heaven on Earth Triggers 'Twinning' Talk." *Winnipeg Free Press*, 7 February, p. 20.
Heaven on Earth, written by Atwood and Peter Pearson, portrays the hardships of the orphans sent to what social workers called a "Heaven on Earth" in Canada. This two-hour TV movie is twinned or paired with a World War I film, *Going Home*; both are co-produced by Canadian and British film companies. Twinned productions can share markets and funding. Canadians R.H. Thompson and Fiona Reid star in *Heaven on Earth*; Welsh actors Sian Leisa Davies and Huw Davies play orphans.

59 HINZ, EVELYN J. "The Religious Roots of the Feminine Identity Issue: Margaret Laurence's *The Stone Angel* and Margaret Atwood's *Surfacing*." *Journal of Canadian Studies* 22, no. 1 (Spring):17-31.

Explicates *Surfacing*'s pervasive Judaeo-Christian and archetypal religious allusions. The narrator's identity crisis goes back to eighteenth-century anti-religious Rationalism; her primitivism is not solely feminist. Although *The Stone Angel* and *Surfacing* are central to understanding

> "the relationship between women's identity and religious issues, both works . . . [question the] contentions of feminists like Mary Daly. Both works do quarrel with 'God the Father,' but both also emphasize the need for religious support systems and locate the cause of contemporary sexism and alienation in the decadence of traditional religious symbolism and authority. Both works present the monotheism of the Judaeo-Christian tradition and the non-ritualistic aspects of Protestantism as the key"

problems for women.

60 HOWELLS, CORAL ANN. "Canadianness and Women's Fiction." In *Private and Fictional Words: Canadian Women Novelists of the 1970s and 1980s*. London and New York: Methuen, pp. 11-32.

Examines national and gender characteristics in Atwood's and other Canadian women's fiction. As in "True Stories," multiple codes and disrupted realism occur. From the nineteenth century on, Canadian women have consistently feminized the national wilderness myth, as in *Surfacing*, where the deeply symbolic wilderness provides a rehabilitating respite from civilized city life. Atwood's urban fiction, and *The Journals of Susanna Moodie*, update the wilderness myth in Toronto; the latter's "Afterword" strikingly elaborates Virginia Woolf's "'As a woman, I have no country.'" The coincidence of nationalist and feminist identity problems, which *Surfacing* explicitly links, helps make Canadian women's writing visible. The prison narratives of *Bodily Harm* and *The Handmaid's Tale* show women's fictions defying power, and creating a space for self-revision. Yet Atwood sometimes sees writing, which conflicts with feminine decorum, as an illegitimate exposing, as in the heart machine scene of "Bluebeard's Egg."

1987

61 ____. Introduction. In *Private and Fictional Words: Canadian Women Novelists in the 1970s and 1980s*. London and New York: Methuen, pp. 1-10 passim.

A revision of 1986.115 that cites Atwood on Susanna Moodie's "'inescapable doubleness of vision'" in discussing the parallel questioning of inheritance by Canadians and women; mentions Atwood's rewriting of popular genres to expose their fallibilities; and concurs with Parrinder's 1986.188 acclaim for Atwood as "the most distinguished novelist under fifty currently writing in English.'"

62 ____. "Margaret Atwood: *Bodily Harm, The Handmaid's Tale*." In *Private and Fictional Words: Canadian Women Novelists of the 1970s and 1980s*. London and New York: Methuen, pp. 53-70.

Like all Atwood's fiction, these two didactic, feminist, humanist novels revise inherited texts. *Bodily Harm* minimally transforms traditional female gothic's pervasive threats to and final incarceration of the heroine, astutely analyses her "fears of sexual assault and her hopes of rescue by a hero," and exposes "female gothic as a lie which . . . [limits women's] perceptions of themselves as morally responsible human beings." Rennie's release from prison is a fantasy to distance herself; yet in her "one truly generous gesture," for Lora, Rennie herself may be morally reborn. The Aunts' patriarchal-delegated matriarchal power over other women may be "the most disturbing feature" of *The Handmaid's Tale*'s nightmare dystopia. Offred's "refusal to believe in biological reductionism . . . gives her the power to resist Gileadean ideology" and tell her story. *The Handmaid's Tale* is "surprisingly lyrical and erotic . . . . Forgiveness, love and trust are" Offred's alternative, transforming powers; heterosexual love continually subverts Gilead's absolute authority, and enables Offred's escape. The final question of the supplementary ["Historical Notes"] challenges present readers. The *Bodily Harm* portion revises 1985.53.

63 HUGHES-HALLETT, LUCY. "Heroine of the Feminist Outerworld." *London Evening Standard*, 4 June, p. 29.

Interviews Atwood, whose *Bluebeard's Egg* and paperback *The Handmaid's Tale* are being published this week. Atwood, who grew up in the Canadian wilderness, talks about Canadian and female identity, how totalitarians come to power, and her peripatetic adult life, which includes sojourns in London, Edinburgh, and Norfolk. *The Handmaid's*

Tale shows how feminist ideas, like natural childbirth, "can be used to limit women's freedom."

64 HUTCHEON, LINDA. "Shape Shifters: Canadian Women Novelists Challenge Tradition." *Canadian Forum* 66 (January):26-32 passim.

A slightly altered reprint of 1986.117 that omits the notes and a passage on *Intertidal*'s uses of entomologies, including indecorous ones.

65 INGERSOLL, EARL G. "Evading the Pigeonholers: A Conversation with Margaret Atwood." *Midwest Quarterly* 28, no. 4 (Summer):525-39.

An updated transcript of a videotaped 13 September, 1979, interview at the State University of New York College at Brockport. Atwood discusses color imagery in "You Begin"; Linda Rogers's 1974.38 cover photo and chill arguments; Atwood's own aural poetry and its formative Canadian influences; line-length and structure in formal and free verse; the novel's social characters and its basic unit – "blocks of imagery that connect with other blocks – character, plot"; and her politics as a Canadian writer who is not limited to feminism. Atwood comments that her "first three novels comprise a unit, and *Life Before Man* is the first of another unit of three."

66 INGOLDBY, GRACE. "Multiple Echo." *New Statesman* 114 (3 July):29.

Briefly reviews *Bluebeard's Egg* as one of six of the best collections of short stories. Atwood's voice lingers on. She studies women like a species. If her relaxed confidence lets "the stories unravel just that bit too much, the striking pictures" echo on, as with the heart image and the hugged, humming fridge in "Bluebeard's Egg."

67 ISRAELSON, DAVID. "Atwood Takes Up Her Pen in Bid to Save Wilderness." *Toronto Star*, 2 May, p. A2.

Interviews Atwood in Toronto: Atwood argues that building two new logging roads in the Temagami wilderness area will drive out tourists, fishers, and hunters; and that short-term, destructive logging should not be favored over the growing tourism industry, which cannot relocate. Atwood, who grew up near Temagami, has written Environment Minister Jim Bradley, will write Premier David Peterson, and will take a five-day canoe tour there this summer, along with historian Ramsay Cook, former federal cabinet minister Judy Erola, and writers M.T. Kelly and Graeme Gibson.

68 JAIDEV. "Into the Motherland." *Times of India* (New Delhi), 29 November, Sunday Review sec., p. 4.

Praises *The Handmaid's Tale* as a haunting, painful nightmare of apocalyptic fiction. The computerised, Bible-invoking Gilead treats the handmaids as merely biological national resources. The hair-raising ritual [Ceremony] is bizarre, like all of Gilead. The retrospective analysis of how our present realities led to Gilead is terrifying; the lesson – that human individualism, dignity, love, and resistance can be crushed – is even more terrifying.

69 JOLLEY, ELIZABETH. "A World without Love." *CRNLE Reviews Journal*, no. 1, pp. 23-26.

This near-future historical novel, *The Handmaid's Tale*, is a haunting, moving, frightening picture of a loveless world. Gilead is extremely puritanical, and cruelly repressive. The resistance movement is vague, the affair with the Commander very curious, and the affair with the chauffeur more ordinary. Details are unrealistic – where Offred can hide her manuscript is a problem, but irrelevant. Gilead parallels Khomeini's Iran, but not China or Western Australia in the Depression, when relief was given for children.

70 KADRMAS, KARLA SMART. "Owen Barfield Reads Margaret Atwood: The Concepts of Participatory and Nonparticipatory Consciousness as Present in *Surfacing*." In *Margaret Atwood: Reflection and Reality*. See Mendez-Egle 1987.103, pp.71-88.

Reads *Surfacing* as a literary corollary of Owen Barfield's 1957 *Saving the Appearances*. Barfield distinguishes the participatory, communal, totemic consciousness of early humans who imaginatively and figuratively perceived "themselves and nature joined"; versus the nonparticipatory, scientific consciousness of contemporary humans who, through logic and language, see nature as separate. *Surfacing's* narrator sees persons who are separate from nature, themselves, and humanity, as figuratively mechanical Americans. What Barfield would call "receptiveness of heart" makes her unlike them. She blames logic for her own separations, recognizes nature's language "as her own," and prepares to immerse herself in Barfield's participatory consciousness;

by the end, she "exists in a web of connection . . . with self, nature, and others."

71 KEITH, W.J. "Apocalyptic Imaginations: Notes on Atwood's *The Handmaid's Tale* and Findley's *Not Wanted on the Voyage*." *Essays on Canadian Writing*, no. 35 (Winter), pp. 123-34.

Though the dust-jacket misleadingly calls *The Handmaid's Tale* "*A Clockwork Orange* as seen by women,'" Atwood's novel is more imaginative and complex, but without Burgess's linguistic inventiveness. Like Swift's *Gulliver's Travels* and *A Modest Proposal*, Atwood's satiric trap presents a seemingly fantastic world that mirrors the contemporary one, and logically extends existing policies. Her double satire not only warns against a future rightist, fundamentalist takeover, but crushingly indicts our present. Beneath the popular sex and suspense, and the serious satire, are "post-modernist and self-reflexive modes" of storytelling. The fully realized, sympathetic Offred maintains her individuality, and survives to tell her tale, at least; the ["Historical Notes"] epilogue "implies that the human race is still somehow muddling through." Both Atwood and Timothy Findley write modern, quasi-allegorical, feminist-oriented political critiques. Though both use qualified post-modern techniques, both rely on traditional absorbing plots and conventional sympathetic characters: this "continuity within change" characterizes recent Canadian fiction.

72 KELLMAN, STEVEN G. "Atwood Scoffs at Sexual Stereotypes, Happy Endings." *San Antonio Light*, 16 February, p. C5.

Reports on Atwood's Trinity University reading, of "Women's Novels," which she called "'a seven-part oratorio,'" "Men at Sea," "Happy Endings," and a section of a novel-in-progress [*Cat's Eye*], about a nine-year-old's theological speculations in a Toronto Sunday School. In the question-and-answer period, Atwood talked about becoming a writer, *The Handmaid's Tale* and its Harold Pinter screenplay, and the tyranny of our now-ubiquitous images.

73 KILDAHL, KAREN A. "Margaret Atwood." In *Critical Survey of Short Fiction: Supplement*. Edited by Frank N. Magill. Pasadena, Calif. and Englewood Cliffs, N.J.: Salem Press, pp.13-19.

Discusses, after a short literary biography, four stories from the 1977 *Dancing Girls* and three from the 1983 *Bluebeard's Egg*. "The Man from Mars" is "a comic and satiric look at" shallow liberalism, with some final pathos. "Dancing Girls" and "Polarities" examine xenophobia and alienation. The most complex, "Giving Birth," concerns language, fiction, and reality; the birth of an infant, of successive selves, and of a literary work.

Though Atwood's sexual power struggles can verge on insanity, "Bluebeard's Egg," which reverses stereotypes by having Sally see Ed as dumb and beautiful, is less bleak. The seemingly autobiographical and atypically mellow "Significant Moments in the Life of My Mother" and "Unearthing Suite" are loving but unsentimentally realistic. Though it is easy to overstate Atwood's pessimism, one should remember the "human strength and tenacity" also, and the affirmation of writing in this negative age.

74 KINGSTONE, HEIDI. "A Writer's Road from Wilderness to Wealth." *Independent* (London), 6 February, p. 12.

Interviews Atwood in her Toronto home. Atwood talks about becoming a successful female and Canadian writer; her recent *Ms.* "Woman of the Year" award, *Los Angeles Times* fiction prize, and Booker Prize shortlisting; living in England, where she wrote *Surfacing* "under a duvet" in a Parson's Green flat in 1970; writing *The Handmaid's Tale*, whose scenario is unlikely for Canada or Britain; and women as individuals, not WOMEN.

75 KINGSTONE, JAMES. Review of *The Oxford Book of Canadian Short Stories in English*. *CM* 15, no. 2 (March):63.

Welcomes Atwood's and Robert Weaver's selections of stories set mostly in Canada, which show imperilled living and "an engaging, heroic ordinariness." The stories' usual brevity disguises their fiercely compressed richness and complexity. There are perennial favourites to delight older readers; work from "our middle generation of celebrity-authors," Atwood, Munro, Richler, and Findley; and from strongly talented younger writers, several apparently influenced by Margaret Laurence. With most of the selected writers still alive, as Atwood's introduction points out, the Canadian short story is young and promising.

76 KIRTZ, MARY K. "The Thematic Imperative: Didactic Characterization in *Bodily Harm*." In *Margaret Atwood: Reflection and Reality*. See Mendez-Egle, 1987.103, pp. 116-30.

Explores *Bodily Harm*'s didactic and often triadic characterization. A victim among killers, Rennie becomes the "'third thing'" of Atwood's 1973.27 interview, a reporter bearing witness. Didactic art may also be the "'third thing'" when, as St. Antoine's religious-political slogans indicate, politics and religion have decayed. Bodily harm stands for Rennie's body and the body politic. The central hand imagery pairs characters as healers, manipulators, or connectors, and marks Rennie's spiritual progress. Dr. Minnow, who represents the artist's voice in society; the deaf mute, who represents the voiceless masses; and Paul, the pivotal "'connection,'" are Rennie's three guides, and represent her inner needs and progress. The names reinforce themes; Renata means born again and renewal. Jocasta "represent[s] the erudite middle class feminists and Lora stand[s] for the uneducated, abused mass of" poor women. Rennie's handshake with the deaf mute connects them, as feminism must connect with broader social solutions. Luck, and humanism, are also "'third'" things.

77 KNAPP, MONA. Review of *Bluebeard's Egg and Other Stories*. *World Literature Today* 61, no.4 (Autumn):629.

Praises Atwood's unique, wryly understated, sensitively characterized stories, but misses the gripping human vulnerability of *The Handmaid's Tale* (and *Bodily Harm*). The lack of first publication dates makes evaluation more difficult. The four quasi-autobiographical stories have elementary plots: childhood, the Canadian wilderness, the first boyfriend, the vital, individualistic parents. The other stories, of frustrating marriages and affairs, have protagonists resigned to perpetually deficient communications between the sexes. "Bluebeard's Egg," which describes a third wife's inner fears through the fairytale, the black humor "Uglypuss," and "Two Stories about Emma" are outstanding.

78 KRIEGER, ELLIOT. "*Handmaid's Tale* Underestimates America." *Providence Journal*, 22 March, p. I7. Newsbank 1986-1987, 91:D5-6.

Finds *The Handmaid's Tale* disconcerting, powerful, and successful, at least as gripping fiction, despite many flaws. Though this award-winning, bestselling novel lacks superficial popular appeal, the handmaid's lifeless, flat storytelling is just right. Compared with *Nineteen Eighty-Four* and *Brave New World*, Atwood's anti-Utopia is the most circumscribed and the most ominous, because its narrator is so restricted and passive. Atwood's future is "primitive, almost tribal," with paralyzing near-zero birth rates, and handmaids rather than high-tech responses from the government. This surreptitious report almost convinces you, till you step back and see how inconceivable and preposterous it is for Americans. This Canadian writer's polemic ludicrously overestimates the religious right, sees Americans as "sheepish, malleable, easily duped," and sees women as contemptibly helpless.

79 LAIRD, SALLY. "The Frogs Fall Silent." *Literary Review* (London), no. 108 (June), pp. 34-36.

Appreciates *Bluebeard's Egg*: Atwood's virtuoso key-changes evoke her characters' entire worlds and their inner changes. Under the coldly hilarious ritual and coping is "a deep sense of [mysteries that] cannot be coped with," as when the mother's comic cat-piss story [in "Significant Moments in the Life of My Mother"] reaches into space. Dread "'seeps into things'"; characters ignore it, seek formulae, are trapped "in the obsessive present tense of their own thoughts," and are unable to penetrate others' surfaces, as in ["Bluebeard's Egg" and "Scarlet Ibis."] The artist [of "The Sunrise"] reduces her world till only the chilly new light "'reaches'" her. Women, the world, the frogs recede from the man [in "Spring Song of the Frogs"]. People "who constantly renew their contact with earth and moisture may still be granted grace," as in the marvelous final parable, "Unearthing Suite." Yet the central theme holds real pathos: the narrator's perceptiveness irreparably estranges her from her mother's world.

80 la MOTTE-SHERMAN, BRUNHILD de. "Frauen Tauchen Auf." *Sinn und Form* (East Berlin) 39, no. 3 (May-June):662-69.

Surfacing and *Bodily Harm* assume an economic and political understanding of feminism that is not generally accepted in writing in the German language. Atwood is part of a contemporary English tradition that includes Doris Lessing, Margaret Drabble, Valerie Miner, and Zoe Fairbairns, who analyze women's position in society. The narrator in *Surfacing* exists in a world where only men's values are considered. The theme of abortion – a female problem that affects all of society – reflects imperialism and internalization. *Bodily Harm* takes a more constructive position, focusing on the female injuries resulting from men's psychological and physical violence. Atwood proves that the feminist novel need not be narrow or anti-male.

81 LANCHESTER, JOHN. "Dying Falls." *London Review of Books* 9, no. 14 (23 July):24, 26.

Enjoys most of *Bluebeard's Egg* in a four-book review. Perhaps Atwood's liberal Canadianness helps her combine "feminist ideas with an essentially traditional aesthetic," the usual relationships with parents and men, and constantly self-interpreting narrators. "The point about 'Significant Moments in the Life of My Mother'" is that now such moments can be significant. The talented Atwood "has a particular gift for aperçus which combine sympathy," insight, and ironic humour; and for "rationalisation and minor deceit," as in "Loulou; or, The Domestic Life of the Language." But her pleasing comedy may come too easily; lapses occur. She is at her best in the rich, ironic, genre-adapting "Bluebeard's Egg."

82 LANGER, BERYL DONALDSON. "Women and Literary Production." In *Australian-Canadian Literatures in English: Comparative Perspectives*. Edited by Russell McDougall and Gillian Whitlock. Melbourne: Methuen Australia, pp. 133-50.

A reprint of 1984.50 that incorporates the latter's endnotes into the text.

83 LARSON, JANET KARSTEN. "Margaret Atwood's Testaments: Resisting the Gilead Within." *Christian Century* 104 (20-27 May):496-98.

Celebrates *The Handmaid's Tale*: Atwood's two testaments, of Offred and the "Historical Notes," together "give us back the lost or muted voices of some scriptural women, while demonstrating how they were silenced by" the patriarchal textual politics of the Bible, theology, and historical-critical scholarship. Even after the Third Reich, Atwood's modern dystopia darkly mirrors "the earthly grounds for hope." Atwood both caricatures and subtly satirizes Gilead's nazified theocracy with hidden, outrageous allusions and jokes. The "Night" chapters chillingly echo Wiesel, Nietzsche, and Job. Gilead's rigid, legalistic, faithless theocracy erases "the life-affirming themes of

Israel's covenant." Gilead's greensward, and the forbidden hand lotion that the Handmaid longs for, recall the Old Testament Gilead and its medicinal balm. Like Rachel smuggling the family gods, and Israel in exile, the exiled Handmaid smuggles words and tells the tales that are her resistance and hope. Her Everywoman's story gathers a vast sisterhood of women's indirect, muffled, or lost stories. Yet, as the Genesis epigraph reveals, the Handmaid idea came from a woman. That the Handmaid's story keeps its power even after the insidious authoritarian sexism of the historical-critical notes is a parable for feminist reconstruction of our empowering biblical past.

84 LECKIE, BARBARA, and O'BRIEN, PETER. "Margaret Atwood." In *So to Speak: Interviews with Contemporary Canadian Writers*. Edited by Peter O'Brien. Montreal: Véhicule Press, pp. 175-93.
    Reprint of 1985.62.

85 LEDGER, BRENT. "Story Anthologies: The Tried, the True, and the Best of the New." *Quill and Quire* 53 (January):29.
    Praises *The Oxford Book of Canadian Short Stories in English* in a three-anthology review: its expert editors, Atwood and Robert Weaver, have given us the cream, and almost three-quarters of it was first published after 1960. The earlier stories are indeed poor; but the last 300 pages, from Helen Weinzweig's unsettling "Causation" on, are extraordinarily high in quality, with delights from CanLit establishment writers Mavis Gallant, Alice Munro, and Margaret Atwood, and superb and wacky surprises from Bharati Mukherjee and Gloria Sawai.

86 LeNORMAND, VÉRONIQUE. Review of *La Servante écarlate. Marie Claire* (Paris), no. 422 (October), p. 384.
    Declares, in a rave review, that *La Servante écarlate* (*The Handmaid's Tale*) is "as fantastic as Orwell's *1984*." Atwood's brilliant use of positive irony works as a language coup. This impertinent political speculation is also a scholarly investigation of the psychology of women and the relations between men and women.

87 LOEB, CATHERINE R.; SEARING, SUSAN E.; and STINEMAN, ESTHER F. *Women's Studies: A Recommended Core Bibliography, 1980-85. Littleton, Col.: Libraries Unlimited, pp. 158, 238-39.*

1987

Annotates *Bodily Harm* as a novel of the body politic and a passive woman forced by crises to confront the sources of her powerlessness. As in *Dancing Girls* and *Life Before Man*, Atwood evokes an astonishing range of women's lives.

Annotates *Two-Headed Poems* as thematizing love, dualisms, history, memory, and women's relationships. *True Stories* questions consensual truth; includes the brutal, the lyric, and the oracular; and manipulates "conventional imagery in startling ways." *Second Words* sketches Atwood's development as writer and critic. Recommends Grace 1980.47, Arnold E. and Cathy N. Davidson 1981.23, and Jerome H. Rosenberg 1984.81.

88 LUTZ, HARTMUT. "Anglo-Canadian Women Writers and Canadian Female Identity." In *Anglistentag 1986, Kiel: Vorträge*. Edited by Rudolf Böhm and Henning Wode. Tagungsberichte des Anglistentags Verbands deutscher Anglisten, vol. 8. Giessen: Hoffmann Verlag, pp. 520-35.

Critiques *Surfacing*'s ideology; affirms Anna Brownell Jameson and the truly Canadian female "courage, open-mindedness and freedom" of Morag Gunn and Pique Tonnerre Gunn in Margaret Laurence's *The Diviners*. *Surfacing*'s combined French- and Anglo-Canadian strands, quest for identity, and landscape would make it a Canadian national novel; but it deliberately invites Jungian and Frygian archetypal and myth criticism; and its "use of Native 'shamanism' [for a personal, demented vision quest] is highly controversial," unsatisfactory, and ideologically insensitive. Atwood's perhaps feminist blood imagery and earth mysticism disregard "German misuses of the blood and soil mystique." Like Marian Engel's *Bear*, the consciousness-raising *Surfacing* offers a personal, individualist solution for an Anglo-Canadian middle-class woman.

89 LYONS, BONNIE. "An Interview with Margaret Atwood." *Shenandoah* 37, no. 2:69-89.

Interviews Atwood 13 February 1987 in San Antonio. Atwood discusses being a woman writer, a writer from an ex-colony, teaching, and mothering; her enlightened family, who did not socialize her in sexist or racist ways; *The Handmaid's Tale*'s plausible U.S. setting, Puritanism, and Harold Pinter screenplay; writing poetry and novels; transformations in entomology, women's bodies, and the unexpurgated

Grimm, which has active princesses and the passive prince; the non-supernatural, claustrophobic *Life Before Man* as homage to the middle-everything *Middlemarch*; food and hands; and politics and art.

90 ____. Review of *Bluebeard's Egg and Other Stories*. *Studies in Short Fiction* 24, no. 3 (Summer):312-13.

Values *Bluebeard's Egg* as autobiographical revelations, and as excellent Atwood stories. Apparently the rabbit cookie anecdote, in "Significant Moments in the Life of My Mother," portrays the artist as a young girl. "Significant Moments," "Hurricane Hazel," "In Search of the Rattlesnake Plantain," and "Unearthing Suite" reveal the family independence and closeness to nature that nurtured Atwood's exact observation, naming, and other strengths. Other stories evoke modern dangers, and the struggles between the sexes and the generations. The best stories, like the realistic Bluebeard story, "Bluebeard's Egg," "are interesting simply as stories."

91 McKINSTRY, SUSAN JARET. "Living Literally by the Pen: The Self-Conceived and Self-Deceiving Heroine-Author in Margaret Atwood's *Lady Oracle*." In *Margaret Atwood: Reflection and Reality*. See Mendez-Egle 1987.103, pp. 58-70.

Reads *Lady Oracle* as "Joan's confessional tale of her growth as heroine and writer, her *kunstlerroman* disguised as female Gothic and *bildungsroman* . . . . For Joan, and her readers, female Gothics celebrate protective female cunning. . . . But, like her heroines, Joan becomes trapped in the maze of romantic vision. She cannot [continue to] be both controlling author and victimized heroine," both independently imaginative and conventionally passive. She loses control of her dual identities, and finds others' dual selves frightening. Fiction's conventions – not its imagination – are dangerous to heroines. The happy ending celebrates "the female imagination as Joan resurrects herselves [sic] into new stories."

92 McLUHAN, MARSHALL. Letter to Margaret Atwood. In *Letters of Marshall McLuhan*. Selected and edited by Matie Molinaro, Corinne McLuhan, William Toye. Toronto; Oxford; New York: Oxford University Press, p. 457.

Congratulates Atwood, 22 November 1972, on *Survival*, which answers a question McLuhan has been asking for years: "'Why do

North Americans, unlike all other people on this planet, go outside to be alone and inside to be with people.' . . . You provide the answer in *Survival* when you indicate the North American crash program for conquering nature." Atwood replied 27 November: "'One wonders about the Eskimos especially in mid-winter but I suppose they do not go outside to be alone but rather to hunt which is quite different.'"

93 MALAK, AMIN. "Margaret Atwood's *The Handmaid's Tale* and the Dystopian Tradition." *Canadian Literature*, no. 112 (Spring), pp. 9-16.

Atwood's landmark dystopia, *The Handmaid's Tale*, recreates the major dystopian features of Yevgeny Zamyatin's *We*, Huxley's *Brave New World*, and Orwell's *Nineteen Eighty-Four*, and "offers two distinct additional features: feminism and irony. Dramatizing the interrelationship between power and sex, the book's feminism, despite condemning male misogynous mentality, upholds and cherishes a man-woman axis; here, feminism functions inclusively rather than exclusively, poignantly rather than stridently, humanely rather than cynically. The novel's ironic tone . . . [skillfully secures] the reader's sympathy and interest." Contrary to Sage 1986.214, *The Handmaid's Tale* does not praise the present, but aims to wrest "an imperfect present from a horror-ridden future: it appeals for vigilance," tolerance, compassion, and "women's unique identity." Even Gilead's oppressors are victimized. The sympathetic Offred progresses, as in *Survival's* "'basic victim positions,'" from helpless victim to "sly, subversive survivor." The hilarious, climactically ironic ["Historical Notes"] epilogue satirizes critics who circumvent issues and thus condone evil; and shows us misogynous features persisting in a distant future. Excerpted: 1987.53.

94 MANGUEL, ALBERTO. "A Literary Smorgasbord." *Maclean's* 100, no. 47 (23 November):54B. (Not available in all editions.)

Atwood's unique, entertaining *Canlit Foodbook*, which benefits the Writers' Development Trust and P.E.N., balances the best of two worlds, literature and food. The cannibalism chapter includes *The Edible Woman*'s cake-woman, Leonard Cohen's Iroquois customs, and Timothy Findley's boiling of Noah's son. The recipes from Graeme Gibson and Audrey Thomas "are mouth-watering"; those from the refined Constance Beresford-Howe and the prolific Pierre Burton

1987

match the writers' styles. "'Eating is our earliest metaphor,'" Atwood's introduction says; her *Foodbook* can be read like travel books.

95 MANSUR, CAROLE. "Going for Growth." *Punch* 292 (24 June):63-64.
    A two-book review that prefers Rose Tremain's *The Garden of the Villa Mollini* to Atwood's *Bluebeard's Egg*. In "Significant Moments in the Life of My Mother," the lethargic, coffee-drinking daughter seems not to have inherited her mother's knicker-rescuing agility, but perhaps Margaret was absorbing "Personal Relationships" data for her stories. Atwood deliberately and artfully constructs significant moments, often of "people who make a profession of their sensitivity"–the potter, painter, and actress [in "Loulou," "The Sunrise," and "Uglypuss"], whose audacious acts spring from a terrible or funny desperation. Sally in "Bluebeard's Egg" is the most confident; perhaps her final hallucination comes from indigestion, or the author's early coffee drinking.

96 "Margaret Atwood: 1987 Humanist of the Year." *Humanist in Canada* 20, no. 2 (Summer):3.
    Atwood, whose writing career reflects a concern for improving life on earth, "will receive the 1987 Humanist of the Year Award . . . June 27, 1987 at the Joint Conference of the American Humanist Association and the Humanist Association of Canada" in Montreal. Reviewing her best-selling *The Handmaid's Tale* for *The Humanist*, McCabe 1986.149 wrote that "'Atwood places the blame precisely where it should be: on those who allowed totalitarianism, repression, and ignorance to gain a toehold and grow. . . . With the new right's growing ascendancy, the images in Atwood's mirror on the world are both all too familiar and all too alarming.'"

97 MARIN, RICHARD T. "Atwood at Work." *American Spectator* 20, no. 1 (January):35-37.
    Characterizes Atwood's literary career as that of a "'queen bee,'" doted on by academic drones, writing "trenchant feminist tracts" about women victims. Her mordant, laconic, but equally ideological poetry is "always much better than her" best-selling, macabre, Mc-generation Gothic prose. Her "institutional power" culminated in the sycophantically praised, tendentious, brutally dull *Survival* that made her queen of CanCrit as well as CanLit. She made demands concerning

[1973.103 [Wigle]] and interviews. *The Handmaid's Tale*, the most explicit victimology of her nightmares, lacks imagination, as McCarthy 1986.150 perceived. Now the icy hue of her melancholic *Bluebeard's Egg* blights her prose; even the humor is grim. "By insisting on a programmatic male-female dualism, Atwood cramps the imagination" and misses the erotic. See Shook 1987.141. Reprinted: 1987.98 (below).

98 MARIN, RICHARD [T]. "CanLit's Queen Gets One Cold Shoulder from U.S." *Gazette* (Montreal), 31 January, p. B7.
    See Shook 1987.141. Reprint of 1987.97 (above).

*99 MARRA, NELSON. "La ambición negativa." *Pais* (Barcelona), 26 March.
    Enthusiastically welcomes *El cuento de la criada*, the recent Spanish translation of *The Handmaid's Tale*, to a country where Atwood has been unknown. This original, feminist work predicts the destiny of women by smoothly combining science fiction with contemporary allegory. Like the negative utopias of *A Clockwork Orange, Brave New World*, and *Nineteen Eighty-Four*, Atwood's speculative fiction warns women that "what we have been in the past, we can be again." The novel, structured by its nightmarish fantasy and language, is starkly logical, yet violent and ironic, awakening passion in the reader.

100 MEEK, MARGARET. Review of *The Handmaid's Tale. School Librarian* 35, no. 3 (August):278.
    Celebrates Atwood's acclaimed, splendid, unsettling, allegorical satire: "girls doing GCSE literature" need this liberating book. Atwood brilliantly catches the born-again fundamentalist; the women's roles are harrowing, but never gratuitously so. "The question of what do we do when nothing can be done is met with this modest [Swiftian] proposal . . . . We are to remember the past when, clearly, it has been destroyed, and confront the future with clear-eyed hope when hope has, apparently, gone." Atwood skillfully sets the tale in the ["Historical Notes"] context.

101 MENDEZ, CHARLOTTE WALKER. "Loon Voice: Lying Words and Speaking World in Atwood's *Surfacing*." In *Margaret Atwood: Reflection and Reality*. See Mendez-Egle 1987.103, pp. 89-94.

1987

Surfacing's echoing loon voice, which like its end recalls Wordsworth's "The Prelude," foreshadows its "questioning of human" language and its search for truth. The narrator rejects language as destructive, sexist, and mechanical; David especially represents corrupt language. "The worst lies" are about love. The narrator moves towards "the wordless language of nature" and seeks "genuine ritual and true magic," especially in secret, coded, non-verbal messages from her parents. Gradually she, like *Surfacing*'s fairy-tale "king who talks to animals after eating a magic leaf," learns nature's other, truer language. Nature, and the loon, mutely accept her; she regains self, power, truth, and love.

102 MENDEZ-EGLE, BEATRICE. Preface to *Margaret Atwood: Reflection and Reality*. See Mendez-Egle 1987.103, pp. v-vii.
Briefly describes the book's diverse essays, which all concern "the journey from confusion and insecurity to self-discovery." As *Survival* points out, literature reflects realities; so do Atwood's characters.

103 ____, ed. *Margaret Atwood: Reflection and Reality*. Living Author Series, edited by James M. Haule, no. 6. Edinburg, Tex.: Pan American University, 182 pp.
Contains Mendez 1987.102, VanSpanckeren 1987.160, Rainwater 1987.124, Wilson 1987.171, McKinstry 1987.91, Kadrmas 1987.70, Mendez 1987.101, Greene 1987.49, Kirtz 1987.76, Peterson 1987.119, Simmons 1987.142, Walker 1987.165, Conversation 1987.29.

104 MONAGHAN, CHARLES. "Year of the Reader." *Washington Post Book World*, 20 September, p. 19.
When, during the Library of Congress's Year of the Reader, Atwood and three other Ballantine/Del Rey/Fawcett paperback authors were asked for "750-word essays on the one book 'that made a difference' in their lives," Atwood cited "Beatrix Potter, *Alice in Wonderland, Robinson Crusoe, Swiss Family Robinson*," and Grimms's *Fairy Tales*, which she defended against charges of sexism, arguing that traits were evenly spread between men and women.

*105 MORRERES, JOSEP M. "La angustia del futuro extrapolado." *Vanguardia* (Barcelona), 24 August.

Appreciates *El cuento de la criada* (*The Handmaid's Tale*). This timely, unpleasant story successfully demonstrates that Puritan attitudes toward reproduction are absurd when abortion, surrogacy, and "in vitro" fertilization are leading contemporary issues. Atwood's futurist novel presents a militarized society where sexuality is outlawed and speech is considered subversive. Through the narrator, the novel focuses on memory, interior discourse, and internal personal resistance to oppression.

106 MUSTE, JOHN M. "*The Edible Woman.*" In *Masterplots II: British and Commonwealth Fiction Series.* Edited by Frank N. Magill. Vol. 1. Pasadena, Calif. and Englewood Cliffs, N.J.: Salem Press, pp. 432-36.

Discusses *The Edible Woman*'s late 1960s social realism plot, feminist critique of women's roles in male-dominated society, deliberately ordinary protagonist, and type characters. "Atwood is pessimistic about social change" in women's lives, and "shows little sympathy for" her men characters. Though she deliberately sacrifices reader interest for social message, Atwood very considerably overcomes the hazards this creates.

107 ____. "*The Handmaid's Tale.*" In *Masterplots II: British and Commonwealth Fiction Series.* Edited by Frank N. Magill. Vol. 2. Pasadena, Calif. and Englewood Cliffs, N.J.: Salem Press, pp. 690-94.

Atwood's feminist anti-utopia warns that suppressing women's rights, as some Protestant Fundamentalists and Phyllis Schafly advocate, would repress everyone. Because Atwood imagines Gilead in detail, characters are not strongly individualized. Offred, who had been ordinary before the religious revolution, now has little to do but shop and remember. Sexually reawakened by Nick, she tries to escape, with his help. The Commander, who "becomes more human" when he offers Offred forbidden intimacies, will be purged. Serena Joy, who used to lecture on women's subservience, is "cruel to Offred," and bitter. The ["Historical Notes"] show that Offred did escape, long enough to record her story at least; and Gilead did end.

108 MYERS, GEORGE, Jr. "Atwood Picks Up after *Handmaid.*" *Columbus Dispatch*, 5 April, p. G8.

A telephone interview that quotes Atwood on success, *The Handmaid's Tale*, Canadian literature, and becoming a writer. *The*

1987

Handmaid's Tale started with a "What if?" question as to whether it could happen here, not as Russian-style communism, or Hitler's Germany, but as another form of curtailing freedom. Atwood describes Gilead's distorted, Bible-based suppressions; her file of clippings for *The Handmaid's Tale*, that includes the 1940s Old Dutch Cleanser "woman with a face-concealing hat," on which the handmaids' costumes are based; and her own fears that the novel was paranoid – or an accurate prediction.

109 NADELSON, REGINA. "Eating Out with Atwood." *Guardian* (Manchester), 18 May, p. 10.

Interviewed in Toronto, Atwood talks about deadpan Maritime humour, feminism, *The Handmaid's Tale*'s sales and the Baby M surrogate mother case, food, shopping, and her current book on food in Canadian literature for P.E.N.; and gives the interviewer a copy of *Bodily Harm* and Atwood's mother's recipe for calla lily cookies. The interviewer, who recalls food in "The Sunrise," "Loulou," "Uglypuss," and other *Bluebeard's Egg* stories, praises Atwood's unmistakable funny, ironic voice and her unequalled specificity, of clothes and interiors, that make her characters so real.

110 NEUFELD, ALICE. "Tales of Gutsy Women." *New Leader* 70, no. 3 (9 March):18-19.

Appreciates *Bluebeard's Egg*: "Atwood's deadpan humor lightens the troubles [of today's bristling women-men relations] that darken her stories"; she anatomizes and helps dispel our contemporary melancholies. Her gutsy, smart, independent women "make the best of their lives." "Significant Moments in the Life of My Mother" reveals the mother's and the daughter's secrets. "Hurricane Hazel" focuses on 1950s teenagers. "'Loulou; or the Domestic Life of the Language' is a tour de force about the needs of modern day woman, a battle-of-the-sexes update." A successful potter, the poets' muse, and sexually independent, Loulou sustains her household, and herself.

111 NICHOLSON, MERVYN. "Food and Power: Homer, Carroll, Atwood, and Others." *Mosaic* 20, no. 3 (Summer):37-55.

Mentions *The Edible Woman*'s anorexia, movement from "'edible'" powerlessness to power, and substitute cake-woman offering, *Lady Oracle*'s rebellious overeating, and *The Handmaid's Tale*'s "food as a metaphor of power/control," in an essay that explores the conservative use of "food as the medium of power" in the *Odyssey*, and the subversive use of it in *Alice in Wonderland* and *Through the Looking Glass*.

112 NIELSON, KATHLEEN BUSWELL. "Comedy in Twentieth Century Fiction: *The Ambassadors, A Passage to India, To the Lighthouse,* and *Surfacing*." Ph.D. dissertation, Vanderbilt University, 319 pp.
    Studies these four twentieth-century novels in detail as comedies. Each has a central woman who embodies comedy's life force. Comic patterns and themes occur: movement to a less ordered, less controlled place; "experience of chaos and darkness;" and emphases on society as life-sustaining, on sexuality as vital, and on "words as tied to" comedy's fragmentation and magic flow. See *Dissertation Abstracts International* 48:648A.

113 NISCHIK, REINGARD M. "Back to the Future: Margaret Atwood's Anti-Utopian Vision in *The Handmaid's Tale*." *Englisch Amerikanische Studien* (Munster) 9, no. 1:139-48.
    Praises highly the extrapolations of current trends, the ingenious plot, and the condensed, eloquent style of Atwood's fascinating dystopia, which may well become a *Nineteen Eighty-Four* of the 1980s. The extraordinary and colourful rendering of this dismal right-wing fundamentalist theocracy partly relieves the reader's possible depression. Because Atwood's futurism is of social relationships, not technology, *The Handmaid's Tale* is not strict science fiction. In this dismal world, ordinary things and human communication, warmth, resourcefulness, and resistance become precious; Nick risks his life to see his Commander's Handmaid, who is probably rescued by the "'Underground Femaleroad.'" Not a simple feminist or anti-religious tract, *The Handmaid's Tale* warns against any absolutist system. Reading it is "'horrible fun.'"

114 NIZZI, CAROLYN. "Explosive Prose." *San Antonio Light*, 8 February, pp. J1, 4.
    A telephone interview: Atwood, who will read at Trinity University, talks about *The Handmaid's Tale*'s survival humor, sales, and the first critical reaction of "'Can it happen? Is it going to happen? Oh, my gosh, it's already happening'"; feminism; and human rights. The

interviewer, who cites *Second Words* and *Lady Oracle*, "suspect[s] that Atwood has had to create a public self to keep the private one" for writing.

115 PAHL, EILEEN. Review of *The Handmaid's Tale* and *The Good Mother*, by Sue Miller. *Harvard Women's Law Journal* 10 (Spring):335-40.

Atwood's haunting cautionary tale for feminists, who are now caught between allying with conservatives on traditional female roles and insisting on gender neutrality, shows "the horrors of a world in which women's highly valued role enslaves them. . . . As long as men define the terms and apply the laws," both Atwood's surrogate mother and Miller's protagonist are trapped. Both novels challenge panaceas of

> "current feminist legal theory. *The Handmaid's Tale* highlights the flaws in difference feminism. Separate is rarely equal, and the ideology of separatism constrains individual expression and choice. . . . Offred's small defiances are the heroics of the concentration camp. Even her possible escape . . . [is] an ambiguous social *deus ex machina*."

116 PALMER, CAROLE L. "Current Atwood Checklist, 1987." *Newsletter of the Margaret Atwood Society*, no. 4, pp. [4-9].

Provides an alphabetical, descriptively annotated listing of primary and secondary work for 1987 and for those 1986 items not included in the previous annual checklist, 1986.186. Lists under Atwood's works 19 primary items, including some excerpts, reprints, and interviews, with brief explanatory annotations; five other interviews are listed with the secondary work. Lists 73 reviews, alphabetically by author, under five Atwood books and one translation. Lists under secondary sources 49 articles, alphabetically by author, with succinct annotations. Foreign-language primary and secondary material is included.

117 PECK, DAVID. "*Life Before Man*." In *Masterplots II: British and Commonwealth Fiction Series*. Edited by Frank N. Magill. Vol. 2. Pasadena, Calif. and Englewood Cliffs, N.J.: Salem Press, pp. 959-64.

Criticizes *Life Before Man* as a modern novel of manners with a cleverly structured but quite thin domestic realism plot; pervasively sad relationships and characters – a strong but intolerant Elizabeth, weak Lesje, ineffectual Chris and Nate; and themes of the past, paleontology, and modern marriage that are not totally clear. Perhaps Atwood's 1979 novel illustrates Christopher Lasch's 1979 *The Culture of Narcissism*. *Life Before Man* may recall modern novels by Saul Bellow, Marilyn French, and others; but its 1960s and early 1970s attitudes, "from which many men and women have been trying to free themselves," seem amusingly dated.

118 PELLETIER, FRANCINE. "Atwood Keeps High Profile among Québécois Readers." *Gazette* (Montreal), 26 May, p. D9.

Interviews Atwood in Montreal, and describes her promotion tour for the just-published *Meurtre dans la nuit* (Murder in the Dark). Atwood, who has nine books translated into French, and who is the only Canadian writer well-known here, credits Pierre Turgeon's 1987.158 interview, and comments on Montreal, Marie-Claire Blais, federalism, the monarchy, and her French translations – Robert Lafford [Laffont?] in Paris has the French rights to *The Handmaid's Tale*. Quotes Atwood's fans, *Meurtre*'s publisher Rachel Bédard, and its translator, Hélène Filion, who has translated four other Atwood books, and who argues that North Americans should translate North Americans.

119 PETERSON, NANCY J. "'Bluebeard's Egg': Not Entirely a 'Grimm' Tale." In *Margaret Atwood: Reflection and Reality*. See Mendez-Egle 1987.103, pp. 131-38.

Compares "Bluebeard's Egg," Charles Perrault's "La Barbe Bleue," and Grimms's "Fitchers Vogel" to show how Atwood transforms the latter to modern realism, using a not necessarily reliable narrator. Perrault's Bluebeard attracts women through wealth; his wife's siblings save her; the key to the forbidden room gets bloodied. The Grimms's wizard casts spells on women; the clever, curious third wife keeps her egg unbloodied, revives her sisters, saves herself, and burns the wizard. Atwood's Ed is a heart doctor who casts the spell of romantic love; Sally "does not revive Ed's previous wives, but she does raise their children." Self-sufficient Sally is in Ed's control, until she sees, in the keyhole desk scene, that he may be replacing her. The egg,

1987

which as in "True Romances" symbolizes the ego and the whole person, "merges with the heart [imagery] only when" Sally can regain control. Atwood shows "that curiosity–leading to painful insight–can transform a woman's life."

120 PIETREK, KLAUS W. Review of *Der Report der Magd*. *Science Fiction Review* (Hamburg), August, pp. 24-25.

In German. *Der Report der Magd* (*The Handmaid's Tale*) is fascinating, and perhaps a classic like Orwell's *Nineteen Eighty-Four* and Huxley's *Brave New World*. Atwood's masterfully depicted, emotionless Gilead warns us that without love we will die. Offred comes to understand the need to resist, and slowly gains the strength to react. The strongest scenes describe the tension between the tortured spirit and the powerful oppressors, as in the degrading sexual intercourse ritual. The ending is left open to despair or triumph; but Offred is lost to the historians who in a later era debate the authenticity of her story.

121 PIOFFET, MARIE-CHRISTINE. Review of *Essai sur la littérature canadienne*. *Nuit blanche* (Québec), no. 30 (December-January), p. 68.

Briefly praises the recent French translation of *Survival*, that is the answer to the question: can one talk about Canadian literature as one would talk about French or American literature? Canadian literature focuses on a quest for identity; it examines the existential crisis of a colonized, disseminated society situated in an immense territory. It is unfortunate that it took fifteen years for this translation of *Survival* to be published.

122 PRATT, ANNIS. "Medusa in Canada." *Centennial Review* 31, no. 1 (Winter):1-32.

Analyzes the Medusa archetype in Canadian male and female poetry. In contrast to British and American poets, Canadian poets, as Frye and others note, see nature as neither human nor subordinate to human anthropomorphism. Explicit Medusa poems are rare; Canadian poets typically foreground an unnamed Medusa power merged into a nonhuman, rocky, sometimes feminized landscape. Canadian male poets range from hostility to sympathy and assimilation of indigenous stone powers; George Bowering's "Desert Elm" endows the father with stone's qualities. Canadian women poets make lovers into stone, "escape from male lovers into nature, . . . [and] approach stone females as 'terrible' or 'good' mothers. . . . [T]he petrified woman is a vehicle for rebirth." Both men and women emphasize relating to rocks as much as to the other sex; and often use stone imagery of "a paradoxically petrified and potent intercourse or . . . linguistically inspiring elixirs." Atwood uses metaphoric and metamorphic stone imagery in "Progressive insanities of a pioneer," "Resurrection," and "Some Objects of Wood and Stone"; the latter, like Pat Lowther's "A Stone Diary" and many other Canadian poems, assimilates an empowering Native Canadian animism. Canadian critics also shift from Western superiority to a cautious appreciation of nature; this may be, as Frye and *Survival* suggest, an identification with the victim; it may also reflect French Canadian influences not explored here.

123 "Prix Hemingway: Margaret Atwood en nomination." *Devoir* (Montréal), 24 February, p. 7.
     Reports that *The Handmaid's Tale* is one of three novels nominated for the Ritz-Paris-Hemingway award.

124 RAINWATER, [MARY] CATHERINE. "The Sense of the Flesh in Four Novels by Margaret Atwood." In *Margaret Atwood: Reflection and Reality*. See Mendez-Egle 1987.103, pp. 14-28.
     The narrators of *The Edible Woman, Surfacing, Lady Oracle*, and *Bodily Harm* suffer from what psychologists call severe body-boundary disturbances, which are "extreme feelings of psychological and physical vulnerability owing to a vaguely defined" self and "'other.'" Their boundary conflicts involve sexist and other social stereotypes, and language. All these narrators go through a four-stage physical and psychological metamorphosis: first, "increasingly destructive attitudes and behavior" toward the body and food; second, "attempts to become 'invisible'"; third, regression or atavistic retreat into a more primitive, physical, nonlinguistic state; and fourth, emergence with a new, though tentative, "orientation toward self, world and words."

125 READ, MIMI. "Canadian Writer Delights in City's Sights and Smells." *Times-Picayune* (New Orleans), 17 February, p. B1-2.
     Interviews Atwood, who will read at Tulane, in New Orleans. Atwood talks about *The Handmaid's Tale*'s success, its realistic sources, the screenplay by Harold Pinter, and holding odd jobs while

becoming a writer; and praises New Orleans's flavors and colors. *The Handmaid's Tale* is a chilling, starkly poetic reverse utopia.

126 Review of *Selected Poems II: Poems Selected and New, 1976-1986.* *Booklist* 84 (1 November):429.
    Urgent, incisive sensuality and "fiercely didactic fabulism" empower Atwood's poetry. The additional new poems insist we take to heart her hard lessons, "projecting human into animal consciousness, as in 'Porcupine Tree' and 'Porcupine Meditation,'" and dissecting angry, dangerous fantasies, as in "Werewolf Movies" and "Machine. Gun. Nest." As before, Atwood's lessons concern "the difficult dichotomies of love and violence, male and female," and are pithy and hallucinatorily intense.

127 Review of *The Handmaid's Tale. Kliatt Young Adult Paperback Book Guide* 21, no. 3 (April):20.
    Recommends *The Handmaid's Tale* very highly for young adults concerned about women's role, the Moral Majority, ecological disaster, and other urgent social issues; and as "a riveting story of a totally believable woman and her struggle for personal freedoms," which ends in breathtaking "resistance and escape." Atwood's grim, haunting future in the ritualized religious tyranny of Gilead recalls *Brave New World* and *Nineteen Eighty-Four* "because it convincingly describes what might be the future outcome of our present way of life."

128 RICE, DOUG. "Characters in *Bluebeard's Egg* Push against the Grain." *Pittsburgh Press*, 26 April. Newsbank 1986-1987, 103:E12.
    Praises Atwood's closely linked, subtle, traditional, daring stories, that mythically explore early influences and "passages 'leading elsewhere.'" Like the storytelling narrator of "Unearthing Suite," Atwood's listening, remembering characters "travel great distances without moving their feet." As in "In Search of the Rattlesnake Plantain," they work hard for their epiphanies. The "Bluebeard's Egg" woman learns to fear emergent lives, not forbidden rooms. The artist of "The Sunrise" freezes men's stories on her canvases.

129 RIGNEY, BARBARA HILL. *Margaret Atwood.* Women Writers, edited by Eva Figes and Adele King. Totowa, N.J.: Barnes and Noble,

1987

146 pp. Houndmills, Basingstoke, Hampshire and London: Macmillan Education.

Atwood's increasingly political, feminist, and radically humanist work sees the writer as responsible for bearing moral witness. All her heroines "are, in varying degrees, failed artists [who must] recognise their complicity in ... power and victimisation. Writing out of *Survival*'s victim tradition, linking fertility myth to creativity, Atwood turns myth and archetype into human realities. *The Edible Woman*'s anorexic, Alice-in-Wonderland Marian is a word manipulator who rejects her maternity, creativity, and humanity, seeing herself as a powerless child, animal, or object, and projecting subjective realities onto others. Though making the doll-like cake is her one creative act, "Marian will remain a Diana," not a Venus. *Surfacing*'s protagonist is a failed artist and failed mother who moves from an "Under Glass"-like refusal to feel or commit, *through* madness and myth to a psychological, not religious, rebirth to sanity and human responsibility. *The Journals of Susanna Moodie*'s speaker remains a failed artist and divided Canadian female ancestor. *Lady Oracle*'s schizophrenic, protean "'escape artist,'" Joan Foster, never escapes from her false, self-deluding fictions and roles, which she adopts from "Snow White," mirrors, Moira Shearer in *The Red Shoes*, the Lady of Shalott in Tennyson's poem and perhaps in Pre-Raphaelite paintings by William Holman Hunt and John William Waterhouse, goddess myth, Disney films, and gothic romances. *Life Before Man*'s Nate and Alice-Lesje are failed, self-pitying artists who remain children; the domineering, spiteful Elizabeth "is the only adult," a survivor who makes a home in an uninhabitable world. *Life* inverts Atwood's fertility myth; Lesje's pregnancy is an ironic mockery of creativity. *Bodily Harm*, like "A Travel Piece," points out our human guilt and responsibility. Rennie begins as a failed artist and uninvolved, truth-avoiding human; by the end, she may or may not get out of prison, but she does give birth to her own humanity in a redemptive, secular pietà with Lora. *The Handmaid's Tale* shows how a society's uninvolvement can lead to slavery. Offred envies the courageous Moira, but "sacrifices her own integrity" to survive. Yet, as in *True Stories*, love persists; and Offred does report and warn. *Survival*, though criticized and quibbled over, outlines politically significant victim positions for Canadians, women, and others. *Second Words*'s best essays critique injustices and propose alternatives. Critics have misread Atwood's irony, and complained of her male characters and pessimism.

130 _____. Review of *Bluebeard's Egg and Other Stories. Journal: The Literary Magazine of Ohio State University* 11, no. 2 (Fall-Winter):46-48.

Discusses Atwood's Bluebeard theme: all her anti-heroines, here and earlier, are failed artists who choose a psychological dismemberment. For Atwood, "one must always enter the secret room" of art, self-knowledge, and sexual knowledge. "Too many women, Atwood scolds repeatedly, abdicate their human responsibility to confront reality and to create art by escaping into the role of art object," becoming like the paper dolls of "Scarlet Ibis." Each story considers some escape from reality: a Caribbean island in "Scarlet Ibis," an illusorily safe marriage in "Bluebeard's Egg," or, in "The Salt Garden," a fantasy world, during premonitions of nuclear war. Atwood's juxtapositions and cynical humor "shock us into awareness"; her fairy tale adaptations show women silencing and victimizing themselves and other women.

131 ROSENBERG, J[EROME] H. Review of *Bluebeard's Egg and Other Stories. Choice* 24, no. 10 (June):1549.

Recommends Atwood's subtle, modern Jamesian stories. "Hurricane Hazel" and "Scarlet Ibis" anatomize soured relationships. Atwood's often bizarre or farcical, but always deadpan, humor appears in "Scarlet Ibis," where a Mennonite missionary plugs a leaking boat with her buttocks. Though Atwood's stories, here and in *Dancing Girls*, are less important than her novels or poetry, they do have the latter's epigrammatic sharpness. The casual reader will find these stories worth experiencing; the Atwood student and scholar, and libraries, will find them necessary.

132 ROSENBERG, JEROME, and VanSPANCKEREN, KATHRYN, eds. *Newsletter of the Margaret Atwood Society*, no. 4, [10] pp.

Contains news of the Atwood Society's annual meeting at the 1987 Modern Language Association Convention and an election slate of officers; recent and forthcoming primary and secondary Atwood books, essays, and conference papers and sessions; an update on Atwood's travels and activities; and the Carole L. Palmer 1987.116 primary and secondary checklist.

133 ROYER, JEAN. "'Pourquoi tous les adultes ne sont-ils pas des artistes?'" *Devoir* (Montréal), 20 June, p. D1, 8.

Admires the ironic treatment of identity, language, adult dreams, and children's games in the poems and stories in *Meurtre dans la nuit* (*Murder in the Dark*). Quotes Atwood on why adults lose the artistic talents of childhood, on the function of the artist in society, and on her definition of feminism.

134 RUBENSTEIN, ROBERTA. "Escape Artists and Split Personalities: Margaret Atwood." In *Boundaries of the Self: Gender, Culture, Fiction*. Urbana and Chicago: University of Illinois Press, pp. 63-122.

Analyzes "boundary, union, and separation" in Atwood's first six novels. As in her recurrent image of paradoxically joined yet separate Siamese twins, identity is individual and also Canadian. All the central characters of the first five novels experience internal divisions, which the sixth ironically recasts as female roles. Distorted self- and body-images often manifest "unresolved psychological issues." *Surfacing*'s narrative shifts, characters, and boundary images reflect the narrator's self divisions. Recurrent allusions to Lewis Carroll's *Alice in Wonderland* and *Through the Looking Glass* and Frank Baum's *The Wizard of Oz* dramatize boundary issues in *The Edible Woman*, *Lady Oracle*, and *Life Before Man*. As Nancy Chodorow explains, female identification with the mother complicates ego boundaries and individuation. "In Atwood's fiction, mothers or their stand-ins are narratively absent . . . , dead or missing . . . , and/or overwhelming. . . . [F]athers are notably absent." *Lady Oracle*'s Joan fears becoming her internalized "'bad mother'"; the three narrators of *Life Before Man* are made vulnerable by problematic mother or substitute-mother relationships. Boundary issues of the mother-daughter and other relationships become anxieties about "ingestion and/or maternity, . . . drowning or engulfment," especially in the first three novels; "experiences of invasion, violation, and existential panic; and the desire" to escape these threats. In more explicitly feminist and deeply existential *Bodily Harm* and *The Handmaid's Tale*, boundary issues broaden to emphasize personal and political correspondences of male power and "female passivity and complicity"; the protagonists struggle for self-preservation in a world of oppressive "corporal and political" boundaries; human touch and reciprocal connection are the opposite of boundary transgression. That Atwood's novels, and most of Penelope

Mortimer's similar narratives, conclude without resolution, reflects both modernism and women's internally and externally stunted growth. Revises part of 1985.88.

135 RUBIN, MERLE. "Fiction on Nuclear War and Other Themes." *Christian Science Monitor*, 22 January, p. 22.

A two-book review that finds *Golden Days*, by Carolyn See, distressing, because its ego-tripping World War III survivor trivializes nuclear war; and praises *Bluebeard's Egg*'s salient "sense of responsibility." Alma, in "The Salt Garden," fantasizes about surviving nuclear war, and doesn't want to keep others out of her imaginary overcrowded shelter. Like the wife in "Bluebeard's Egg," Atwood's characters try to analyze their lives. Praises Atwood's cool understatement, quiet humor, and shrewd, detached, compassionate insights; but finds some stories insufficiently explored, or uninterestingly "'ordinary,'" or forced. See 1987.139.

136 SCARCE, RIK. "Genesis Resurrected." *Futures* 19, no. 4 (August):488-90.

Commends *The Handmaid's Tale*: Atwood's finely crafted dystopia, which follows *Nineteen Eighty-Four* and *Brave New World*, also poignantly addresses today's problems. Her nightmare USA mixes alternative futures that recall Jim Dator's "'continued growth' scenario" of conservatism and fundamentalism, and his "'decline and collapse'" of liberties and women's rights. Cloistered in a new-fascist theocracy, Offred struggles to keep her humanity and identity. Atwood shows liberties undermined both by abuses of technology, as through computerized "books and monetary exchanges," and by feminist burnings of pornography. Our apathy today may lead to "a severe backlash against those who have recently claimed their share of society's freedoms." Atwood challenges each of us to take responsibility for the world we are making.

137 SCHULTE, JEAN. "Collection of Stories Full of Magic." *Columbus Dispatch*, 25 January, p. J8.

Praises *Bluebeard's Egg*'s tremendous range of settings and characters, from the Trinidad of "Scarlet Ibis" to the northern birch forest of "In Search of the Rattlesnake Plantain." "Atwood's most dazzling spell is cast by" her vulnerable, perceptive characters and what

1987

she lets them see in situations they can't leave, as in "Bluebeard's Egg" and ["Loulou."] "Bullets of strident feminism . . . zing in and out," but never fix on a target. Atwood's very unsettling characterization "scratches away at the soft underbelly of our own psyches."

138 SCIFF-ZAMARO, ROBERTA. "The Re/membering of the Female Power in *Lady Oracle*." *Canadian Literature*, no. 112 (Spring), pp. 32-38.

Claims that Joan's quest, for the real self hidden in her split identity, is epitomized by the novel's recurrent Great Mother archetype. As Robert Graves remarks in *The White Goddess*, the ancient, three-phased Great Mother was eclipsed by patriarchal societies. Joan's attributes and stages recall all three phases of the White Goddess – Diana, Venus, and Hecate. Joan's mother is a Hecate with Diana and Venus trapped inside, as described in *Survival*. Women's knowledge has been buried in dark caves, and partly lost, as Gilbert and Gubar comment, in *The Madwoman in the Attic*: Joan's descent to the Sibyl's cave, symbolized in her automatic writing, recovers scattered words and confused myths. Although the novel is open-ended, Joan's quest does represent the woman writer's quest for a new artistic identity.

139 SEE, CAROLYN. "Hatching Family Histories and Fears of the Holocaust." *Los Angeles Times*, 12 January, sec. 5, pp. 4, 6.

Bluebeard's Egg's remarkable "stories, despite their bleak content, are filled with a combination of love, curiosity, speculation." The sweet mother of "Significant Moments in the Life of My Mother" tells personal tales. Her grown daughter's very different stories bear "'news of a great disaster,'" the upcoming nuclear holocaust of "The Salt Garden" that makes the mother's stories obsolete. Though the exhausted and peevishly agreeing reader may ask what's new about possible planetary death, Atwood's answers are fresh. As "Bluebeard's Egg" hints, the egg may hatch; the mother [in "Unearthing Suite"] wants to live to see what happens. See 1987.135.

140 SHAW, VALERIE. "And the Moral of *That* Is. . . ." *Listener* 117 (11 June):29.

Features Atwood's superb *Bluebeard's Egg*, which shows her profound understanding of how every human story meets the teller's and the listener's unspoken needs, in a four-book review. For the mother in "Significant Moments in the Life of My Mother," every story has its "'proper construction'"; the questioning narrator sees how we invent our inescapable and precious mythologies of each other. Her perception shapes all these diverse relationships, as in the fable-like "Bluebeard's Egg," "Loulou," and "Uglypuss." The man and nature relationship is also edgy. Real integrity seems possible only, as in "The Sunrise," "between the artist and her work"; Atwood uncovers what's behind the faces, yet keeps her strong objectivity, "without being cold or indifferent."

141 SHOOK, KAREN. "Work Like Atwood's to Endure." *Gazette* (Montreal), 23 February, p. B2.
      Protests, in a letter to the editor, Marin's 1987.98 attack on feminism and Atwood's work. Twentieth century literature is often negative; and great art often shocks, instead of pandering to prejudices like sexism. Marin praises Irving Layton and Norman Mailer, accepting their male-centred egotism, while finding in Atwood's critique of male-female relationships a pathological misanthropy. As for Atwood's earthiness and scatology, Marin should reread his undergraduate copy of Jonathan Swift.

142 SIMMONS, JES. "'Crept in upon by Green': Susanna Moodie and the Process of Individuation." In *Margaret Atwood: Reflection and Reality*. See Mendez-Egle 1987.103, pp. 139-53.
      Reads *The Journals of Susanna Moodie* as a Jungian journey of individuation, of the integration of Moodie's "societal English self (her conscious) and her Canadian wilderness self (her unconscious)." An ill-prepared immigrant, Moodie reluctantly explores her unknown wilderness unconscious, and gradually begins to assimilate it. "Belleville is a middleground, . . . neither London nor the wilderness," and a midpoint in Moodie's attempted synthesis. Her three dreams, of the Edenic "Bush Garden," of her animus "Brian the Still-Hunter," and of "Night Bear Which Frightened Cattle," are "unconscious reaction[s] to halting the individuation process." Though Moodie never achieves individuation in life, Atwood celebrates her struggle, and her rebirth as "Canada's timeless unconscious," urging individuation, and getting through, to Atwood's unconscious, dream, and poems.

143 SINGH, SUSHILA. "Joyce Carol Oates and Margaret Atwood: Two Faces of the New World Feminism." *Panjab University Research Bulletin: Arts* (Chandigarh, India) 18, no. 1 (April):83-93.

Compares the stark feminine realism of the American Oates's *Them* and the female self-analysis of the Canadian *Surfacing*. Atwood's distraught, grieving narrator fabricates a marriage, divorce, and child story to cover pain she can't accept. *Surfacing* pioneered in understanding the trauma of abortion when its legality was still debatable. Though the word abortion is never used, its Latin root meaning, of "*ab* (from) and *oriri* (arising)," is evoked when the narrator feels her lost child "'rising from the lake where it has been prisoned for so long.'"

144 SMITH, MICHAEL. Review of *The Oxford Book of Canadian Short Stories in English*. *Review: Latin American Literature and Arts*, no. 38 (July-December), pp. 92-94.

Appreciates Atwood's and Robert Weaver's anthology, commending Weaver's essential support of the genre, which few of the writers included specialize in. The chronologically arranged stories evolve as Canada has, from wilderness melodrama and frontier survival to urban, modern angst; compare Hugh Garner's simpler "One-Two-Three Little Indians" with Margaret Laurence's more complexly sensitive "The Loons." Most of the writers born after 1930 focus more on character than on plot. Some emphasize the style of telling over the story told; George Bowering succeeds. Gloria Sawai is the freshest discovery. These Canadian stories "seem obsessed with death"; and, except for Bharati Mukerjee's scarcely Canadian story, curiously unsexy, although they talk of lovers, including homosexual ones. John Metcalf should have been included, as Alice Munro and Hugh Hood have publicly stated.

145 STABLEFORD, BRIAN. "Is There No Balm in Gilead? The Woeful Prophecies of *The Handmaid's Tale*." *Foundation* (London), no. 39 (Spring), pp. 97-100.

Atwood's feminist dystopia, which won the first Arthur C. Clarke Award for the best 1986 science fiction novel published in Britain, recalls Jeremiah's lamentations; and "the policing of thought, the rewriting of sacred texts," the cathartic hate sessions, and the "ironically bitter pessimism" of George Orwell's classic *Nineteen Eighty-Four*.

"There is nothing forgiving about *Nineteen Eighty-Four*, but for a feminist work, *The Handmaid's Tale* is surprisingly easy on its male characters." We see the Commander being pathetic, not evil; we see women behaving badly. Like the pusillanimous Janine, the heroine lapses into self-effacing capitulation to her oppressors, and comes close to "losing her moral indignation" and forgiving. We should not endorse the historians' avoidance of censure [in the "Historical Notes"]; but, the novel asks, how much should we, and modern feminists, forgive?

146 STEELE, CHARLES R. "Canada's New Critical Anthologists." *ARIEL* (Calgary) 18, no. 3 (July):77-85.

A review-essay on Canadian poetry anthologies that finds *The New Oxford Book of Canadian Verse in English* responsibly and carefully edited, and judiciously selected, though occasionally questionably weighted. Atwood's introduction and selection do reveal personal preferences and "the apparently endemic hierarchicalism of anthologizers" in terms of poems and space: the most favoured include D.C. Scott, E.J. Pratt, and Al Purdy; "Irving Layton [is] at the very peak of the pyramid," over Birney, Atwood (chosen by William Toye), Purdy, and others conventionally considered more primary. Contemporary poets, and "Jay Macpherson and Phyllis Gotlieb are overrepresented while Daphne Marlatt is underrepresented." Atwood aims to represent the range of "Canadian poetry to the uninitiated at home and abroad."

147 STRAUSS, JENNIFER. "'Everyone is in Politics': Margaret Atwood's *Bodily Harm* and Blanche d'Alpuget's *Turtle Beach*: Being There, Being Here." In *Australian/Canadian Literatures in English: Comparative Perspectives*. Edited by Russell McDougall and Gillian Whitlock. Melbourne: Methuen Australia, pp. 111-19.

Compares these two national, realistic, humanist novels that confront the Third World to examine Canadian or Australian consciousness. Both protagonists are "educated, articulate and comfortably off" women journalists, "'liberated'" but defined and remade by men. That both protagonists experience "themselves simultaneously as central and peripheral . . . provide[s] a metaphor for their countries": affluent but "'not English,'" Australians and Canadians often see themselves as guiltless sharers in a British and American civilization that claims superiority to the Third World. Both novels satirize the home countries; Atwood tellingly evokes "dutiful Griswold, trendy Toronto," and sweet Canada. Atwood's much better, profoundly moral and political novel ends with an unambiguous, "uncompromising 'This is what will happen'"; Rennie's rejection of the temptation to deny what she saw needs to be made after her release. But Rennie's promising subversion is vague, and she loses Canadian representativeness in the conclusion. See Tiffin 1987.156.

148 STROBEL, CHRISTINA. "'It's Time To Like Men Again': Ueber Margaret Atwood." In *Women's Studies and Literature: Neun Beiträge aus der Erlanger Amerikanistik*. Edited by Fritz Fleischman and Deborah Lucas Schneider. Erlanger Studien, edited by Detlef Bernd Leistner-Opfermann and Dietmar Peschel-Rentsch, vol. 73. Erlangen: Palm & Enke, pp. 229-243.

In German. A six-part essay on the feminine "I" and its perspective on the relationship between men and women in Atwood's poetry. Part one, "'I probably am a feminist,'" recognizes Atwood's feeling of kinship with women, despite her refusal to be attached to the feminist movement. Part two, "'You fit into me,'" reveals man and woman as opposites: man, at the center of the world, constantly tries to force nature into his straight lines, while woman observes the error of his ways. Part three, "'Weary distances,'" explores *The Circle Game* and *Power Politics*, where love is a deadly game between the man and the woman, each playing oppressor and oppressed, perpetrator and victim. Part four, "'Breaking the circle'" of oppression, explores the possibility of closeness and the hope for a better future in *You Are Happy*. Part five, "Marrying the Hangman," considers, as in McCombs 1981.66, society as the "'ornamental scene'" where the struggle between men and women takes place; society also dictates the rules of the game. Part six, "'It's time to like men again,'" examines the dilemma of women trying to like men in *Murder in the Dark*. Atwood's poetry humorously and courageously describes the behavior of both sexes, but offers no solutions.

149 STROBL, INGRID. "Der Report de Atwood." *Emma* (Cologne), April, pp. 48-49.

Der Report der Magd (*The Handmaid's Tale*), which created a sensation in the United States and Canada, is a negative utopia based on fact. Atwood's Gilead, a primitive, fundamentalist patriarchy that maintains authority through technology and terror, is based on past and current realities, such as the Puritans, the Iranian theocracy, and the U.S. Christian Right. Like all religious fundamentalists, the rulers of Gilead are woman-haters who completely eliminate women's self-determination and use female accomplices to enforce patriarchal rule. The protagonist, who risks her life for love rather than liberation, may be less a heroine than Moira, her lesbian feminist friend.

150 SULLIVAN, ROSEMARY. "The Forest and the Trees." *Brick*, Winter, pp. 43-46.
    Revision of conclusion of 1977.90: after a summer in the wilderness, the critic finally understands that, after *Surfacing*'s trial of evolutionary regression, Atwood sees nature as its own fact, "which makes us fact," and as our place, where man belongs but does not dominate. "Atwood has brought us full circle, back to the first" wilderness encounter, to warn us that its dark pines are our own. Objectifying and destroying the wilderness, we objectify and destroy ourselves.

151 SUSSEX, LUCY. Review of *The Handmaid's Tale*. *Australian Science Fiction Review*, 2d ser., 2, no. 3 (May):31-33.
    Though *The Handmaid's Tale* "is probably the nastiest female dystopia outside the Gor novels of John Norman," it lacks the power of *Nineteen Eighty-Four*. The narrator Offred, who is too obviously Everywoman, suffuses her dispirited resignation. Moira, who is "sassy, blood-minded and unbowed until almost the very last," would have told a much more interesting tale – one close to "Joanna Russ at her fire-spitting best, mean, misandrist and thoroughly angry." Atwood's disturbing lack of anger does not make a powerful polemic. How could women lose their jobs and money without economic chaos? The puerile humour and "academic smartarse" of the "Historical Notes" jar. The odd, wry touches, like the Commander's scrabble perversion, are the best.

152 SYMONS, JULIAN. "Tales and Stories." *Sunday Times* (London), 21 June, p. 57.
    A two-anthology review that finds *The Oxford Book of Canadian [Short] Stories in English*'s Canadian homogeneity and directness very attractive. Though, as Atwood's introduction points out, there is no

"'essence of Canada,'" and the writers may follow European models, still a national – not provincial – flavour pervades the book. Most of the stories, including those by Timothy Findley, Norman Levine, and Alice Munro, are recognisably Canadian products, affected by the national life, even if indirectly. Atwood and Munro may be the major talents here, "but the level is high."

153 TENNANT, EMMA. "Margaret Atwood in Conversation with Emma Tennant." *Women's Review* (London), no. 21 (July), pp. 8-11.

Atwood, in Britain for her new *Bluebeard's Egg* and re-published *The Handmaid's Tale*, discusses with Scots novelist Emma Tennant women's writing, including Doris Lessing's *The Golden Notebook*, and the older Jean Rhys and her *Wide Sargasso Sea*. Atwood jokes about men's studies; compares Britain's smaller landscape, longer human time, and pervasive class structure to Canada; and praises Tennant's class-conscious *The Last of the Country House Murders*. Tennant praises *The Handmaid's Tale*'s brilliant dystopia, which Nawal El Sa'adaawi's *Woman at Point Zero* confirms, and the portrait of the writer's necessary torpor in "Unearthing Suite"; and discusses the female double in her own *The Bad Sister*.

154 _____. "Nature of the Beast." *Guardian* (London), 19 June, p. 15.

Appreciates *Bluebeard's Egg* and briefly praises *The Oxford Book of Canadian Short Stories* [*in English*]. Atwood skillfully juxtaposes real and metaphoric worlds, the long Canadian childhood summers and the nervy, urban stories. "Unearthing Suite" and the mosaic "Significant Moments in the Life of My Mother" show the naturalist father and extraordinary mother. The funniest urban story, "Loulou; or, The Domestic Life of the Language" does more than attack men's reifying of women; Loulou, after attempting an affair, settles for good-humoured polyandry, and "lives happily ever after." The historic present tense works triumphantly as Yvonne's cutting edge in "The Sunrise," which is the most controlled, terrifying urban story.

155 THEODORE, LYNN. "Stories Locked Inside Characters' Heads." *St. Louis Post-Dispatch*, 4 January, p. D5.

The *Bluebeard's Egg* stories, which lack the extraordinary conditions of *The Handmaid's Tale*, are superbly written and occasionally beautiful, but claustrophobic and boring as a whole. Only in the loving, funny, beautifully nostalgic "Significant Moments in the Life of My Mother" does Atwood's introspective technique catch fire. Most stories are about what a poet in "Loulou" calls non-events; as in "Bluebeard's Egg," the reader is "locked inside the heads of too many troubled, puzzled, self-conscious people." "The Salt Garden" is a marvelously sensitive description of a woman who hallucinates nuclear war; but a bookful of marvelous sensitivity will cure insomnia. Even the frequent sex "is a non-event," as in "Uglypuss."

156 TIFFIN, HELEN. "'Everyone is in Politics': Margaret Atwood's *Bodily Harm* and Blanche d'Alpuget's *Turtle Beach*: Voice and Form." In *Australian/Canadian Literatures in English: Comparative Perspectives.* Edited by Russell McDougall and Gillian Whitlock. Melbourne: Methuen Australia, pp. 119-32.

   Critiques *Bodily Harm*'s universalist perspective, aesthetic, and form; and argues, against Strauss 1987.147, that *Turtle Beach* is the better post-colonial novel, more politically radical, and "more radically experimental . . . [with] techniques appropriate to cross-cultural material." Rennie's controlling consciousness, which is far more self-aware and self-consciously ironic than Brydon 1982.31 suggests, leaves little room for other irony, voices, or perspectives. Minnow's voice matters for "Rennie's conversion to an undefined 'commitment' and subversion. . . . Minnow speaks regretfully of colonialism, but in terms of the novel's 'representation' of that subject he is politically silent." That the judgment-making Rennie remains the novel's focus and voice "implicitly undermines the explicit criticism that the novel makes of the imperial-interpreter role." Integrating the sexual and political themes disturbingly "glosses over any sense of qualitative difference . . . [and reduces] real engagement with the 'other' culture." Like Conrad's *Heart of Darkness*, Atwood's novel insufficiently adapts traditional, monocultural form and aesthetic to cross-cultural material.

157 TROWELL, IAN. "Purdy a Poet without Peer in Canada: Atwood Struggles to Hold Poetic Individuality." *London* (Ontario) *Free Press*, 2 January, p. A11.

   Acclaims *The Collected Poems of Al Purdy*, predicting a Nobel Prize nomination for him, and finds faults in Atwood's *Selected Poems II*. Atwood, who in "Notes Towards a Poem That Can Never Be Written" writes of saying what you wish but not being listened to, is

1987

"heeded in Canadian literary circles, if not much beyond," though "she may mortify most" readers. With so many Canadian poets now writing the shockingly gruesome and unpleasant, she must wonder how she can "hang on to her poetic individuality." The theme underlying many poems is hackneyed. "Atwood does have a wonderful way with language." She could write nobly – somebody should.

158 TURGEON, PIERRE. "Coup de foudre pour Margaret Atwood." *Châtelaine* (French ed.) 28, no. 2 (February):33-34, 36, 40.

Opens an interview with Atwood by asking why this widely recognized English-Canadian author is not more popular in Quebec. Atwood discusses the physical and cultural relationship between Quebec and English Canada; men as creators of political rules and writers of history; feminism; Canadian men; family history; background research on *Bodily Harm*; and the sane and creative artist versus the anguished artist.

159 Van GELDER, LINDSY. "Margaret Atwood." *Ms.* 15, no. 7 (January):49-50, 90.

Interviews Atwood in her Toronto home, and praises her internationally lauded *The Handmaid's Tale* "as a page-turning thriller," a powerful political "articulation of our scariest nightmares," and an exquisite, surgically detailed work. Atwood discusses Canada's one-way knowledge of the United States ("'the maid knows what's in the master's bureau drawers'"); Canadian stability and Catholicism, English class and Anglicanism, and the monarchy in both, as counterforces to religious extremism; her Bible-reading and early churchgoing; *The Handmaid's Tale*'s non-militant, postfeminist narrator; and the protest against the dearth of women panelists at the P.E.N. 1986 international congress, which could have been settled with an apology.

160 VanSPANCKEREN, KATHRYN. "Magic in the Novels of Margaret Atwood." In *Margaret Atwood: Reflection and Reality*. See Mendez-Egle 1987.103, pp. 1-13.

Atwood's first three novels use particular forms of Western magic – "[f]ood sacrifice, alchemy and mediumship" – as transformational themes and structural figures. *The Edible Woman* is an inverted Cinderella or Sleeping Beauty story, of escaping the prince;

1987

and a comic, modern anti-sacrifice that ends with Marian becoming herself. Devouring and ironic ritual feasts abound; a substitute man eats the substitute cake woman. *Surfacing*'s island and cabin, and its protagonist's body and self, are forms of athanor, the alchemists' oven. Alchemy's seven-part "chemical cycle of death, purification and rebirth" can be traced in *Surfacing*'s transformations. Atwood's underwater descriptions of heightened perception recall the aklahest, the universal solvent. *Lady Oracle*'s mediumship involves the "raising of ghosts (necromancy) and crystal- or mirror-gazing (crystallomancy)"; Joan's seven-step transformations are each multiply fragmented. "Aunt Lou is the [warm, parody] psycho-pomp who initiates Joan into . . . sex and magic." Joan's cold, vampirish mother is finally seen as a sad victim. Atwood's magic is resonant and psychologically true.

161 VANSTONE, ELLEN. "Prize Writer." *Toronto Life*, March, pp. 10-11.
Reports on Atwood's very impressive 1987 and 1986 awards: Humanist of the Year and a *Ms*. Magazine Woman of the Year in 1987; and, in 1986, her well-publicized P.E.N. Congress attack on organizer Norman Mailer for including too-few foreign women writers; *The Handmaid's Tale*'s international raves, bestseller lists, Governor General's Award, and Booker Prize short list; and the Ida Nudel Humanitarian Award from the Canadian Jewish Congress, the shared Philips Information Systems Literary Prize, and an inaugural Toronto Arts Award.

162 VERDUYN, CHRISTL. "No Tongue in Cheek: Recent Work by English Canadian Poets Daphne Marlatt, Lola Lemire Tostevin, and Margaret Atwood." *Canadian Woman Studies* 8, no. 3 (Fall):60-62.
In *Murder in the Dark*, Daphne Marlatt's *Touch to My Tongue*, and Lola Lemire Tostevin's *Colour of Her Speech*, the tongue motif is central to women's linguistic and/or sexual expression. The tongue amputations in "Simmering" and in a chillingly clinical Tostevin poem signal the urgency of woman's "'difference,'" as in Julia Kristeva's writings, not her Otherness. All three poets see the mouth as vulnerable yet resisting; all three would change patriarchal reality by undoing its language. "Saying the unsaid . . . , *naming*, in a woman's language that is linked to the body," challenges patriarchy, as in Marlatt's "'musing with mothertongue,'" Atwood's "'third

632

eye' – significantly 'of the body,'" and Tostevin's seeing tongue and speaking eye.

163 VOISARD, ANNE-MARIE. "Margaret Atwood: Un regard lucide posé sur le monde." *Soleil* (Montréal), 23 May, p. C5.
     An interview. Atwood, who speaks French beautifully, discusses xenophobic tendencies toward speakers of foreign languages, and language/culture problems between French and English Canada; the impact of the conservative right and the abortion issue on women; and recent anti-pornography legislation.

164 WAGNER-MARTIN, LINDA W. "Epigraphs to Atwood's *The Handmaid's Tale.*" *Notes on Contemporary Literature* 17, no. 2 (March):4.
     The Handmaid's Tale is dedicated to Mary Webster, Atwood's ancestor who survived being hung as a witch, and to Perry Miller, who studied our Colonial witchhunt. Atwood's science fantasy of a brutal, horrifying, anti-sexual culture "may well come to equal" Orwell's *Nineteen Eighty-Four*. Readers familiar with Colonial America will find Atwood's "understatement and all-too-germane analogy" thoroughly convincing.

165 WALKER, CHERYL. "Turning to Margaret Atwood: From Anguish to Language." In *Margaret Atwood: Reflection and Reality*. See Mendez-Egle 1987.103, pp. 154-71.
     Atwood's poetry begins with a Modernist anguish, but in *Two-Headed Poems* and *True Stories* goes "very far beyond Modernism" to a post-modern sensibility. Modernism sees poetry as a "'sign manifest,' a bridge joining signifier and signified, bringing news of an absolute . . . ." "You Are Happy" has a Modernist emphasis on an essential vision of the image. "'There are two islands'" recalls Hart Crane's "'evidence of experience of a recognition,'" albeit elusive. In *The Journals of Susanna Moodie* "life gives way at last to an entry into a world beyond language." Contrary to Grace 1980.47, *Two-Headed Poems* undermines subject/object and language/reality distinctions. The title sequence, especially in its sixth poem, plays with post-structuralist theories of language; its final duet between deaf singers "is what the post-modern poet has instead of a bridge." *True Stories*'s political and love poems share Michel Foucault's historical contexts and post-structuralist

attitudes to "self" and language. "Last Day" contradictorily wants existence to have the old, devalued meaning.

166 "Warnung vor Gilead." *Spiegel* (Hamburg) 41, no. 23 (1 June):210, 212-13.

Approves *Der Report der Magd*, the German translation of *The Handmaid's Tale*, a speculative fiction based on existing realities. Like Orwell and Huxley, Atwood aims to warn people who carelessly assume that such things could not happen to them. Gilead's ideology is a hybrid of extreme fundamentalism and radical feminism dedicated to combating the falling birth rate. The sarcastic, imaginative description of the handmaid's joyless life contrasts with the humor of the final "Historical Notes" to reverse the meaning of the story. Some U.S. reviewers disliked the play between feminist and anti-feminist points of view. Atwood began writing *The Handmaid's Tale* in West Berlin while on an exchange program at Deutschen Akademischen Austauschdienstes.

167 WEBB, JANE. "CanLit in the Kitchen and Food to Keep You Fit." *Quill and Quire* 53, no. 11 (November):24.

A four-book review that finds the *Canlit Foodbook* an entertaining "cornucopia of recounted meals and odes" and recipes. Chapters range from the "Preprandial Prologue: Food as Metaphor" to "Eating People is Wrong: Cannibalism Canadian Style." Some recipes, like Graeme Gibson's pot roast with chocolate and Farley Mowat's noisome Creamed Mice, are fanciful. This good read supports the good causes of the P.E.N. International Writers in Prison Programme and the Writers Development Trust. Reprints Atwood's "Canadian Tea Angel à la Johnston" illustration.

168 WEGNER, MATTHIAS. "Kasernierte Frauen." *Frankfurter Allgemeine*, 18 May, p. 30.

A mixed review of *Der Report der Magd* (*The Handmaid's Tale*), which follows Huxley and Orwell in its "speculative fiction." Atwood based *The Handmaid's Tale* on the inhumane acts of groups like the Puritans, Iranian religious fundamentalists, and Nazis. Her fascinating feminist account of the female psyche should be read by men, not just women. Although Atwood is not yet a first-rate stylist, *The Handmaid's*

Tale is well done. It confronts the reader's political conscience, and recognizes that even the courageous are vulnerable.

169 WEISS, ALLAN. "Sins of Omission." *Books in Canada* 16, no. 1 (January-February):21-22.

Atwood's and Robert Weaver's selections for *The Oxford Book of Canadian Short Stories in English* seem eclectic, with established and newer writers, classics and weaker work, and a good balance of realism, fantasy, and metafiction. But where are Ernest Buckler, Alistair MacLeod, and Alden Nowland? Almost every story comes from a book; apparently periodicals were not searched. Atwood's introduction bases her statistics on her own selections; neither she nor Weaver explain their principles of selection. Though their anthology is not representative, most of its stories are very good, and many are excellent.

170 WHITEMAN, BRUCE. "Victims of a Bleak Universe." *Books in Canada* 16, no. 1 (January-February):22-23.

A three-book review that finds in almost all of *Selected Poems II* an "astonishing precision and assuredness," a most recognizable voice, and a mastery of line equal to Laforgue and Creeley; but finds Atwood's vision of the world as a rarely illumined, hellish landscape "both troubling and troublesome." One senses a detached negativity, an Upper Canadian Presbyterian focus on a post-lapsarian, irredeemable world. "The claim for bleakness . . . is irrefutable," though one may turn aside from an occasional rote horror.

171 WILSON, SHARON R. "Camera Images in Margaret Atwood's Novels." In *Margaret Atwood: Reflections and Reality*. See Mendez-Egle 1987.103, pp.29-57.

Discusses the four functions of literal and metaphoric camera images, which critics have not completely recognized, in Atwood's first five novels: "as 'neutral' recorders of experience, instruments of attack or invasion, external validators, and vehicles of transformation." All five novels move from fragmentation towards transformation, without resolution. Metaphoric camera images include commercial and non-commercial art, mirrors, images seen through binocular and other lenses, and mental and moving pictures. Marian in *The Edible Woman* acts as camera and photograph, partly fragmenting herself. *Surfacing's* narrator rejects existence as camera or photograph, and begins "to develop the third eye of love" by the end. *Lady Oracle*, whose Joan must destroy her own and other's dehumanizing photographs, is itself "a lens which focuses and distills the narrator's growth." *Life Before Man*'s three fragmented characters mentally frame themselves and others, but progress somewhat toward metamorphosis. *Bodily Harm*'s narrator "is again a packager/photographer/victimizer as well as the photo/product/victim." Background "photographs, pictures, and products," such as the cut-open melon that depicts Rennie and all women, may seem insignificant, until the boundaries blur. Though she may not leave the cell, Rennie is reborn in touching Lora; without camera or passport, she breaks out of her fragmenting camera vision, "protective layers, and distorting filters." Revises 1985.111.

172 _____. "Deconstructing Text and Self: Mirroring in Atwood's *Surfacing* and Beckett's *Molloy*." *Journal of Popular Literature* 3, no. 1 (Spring-Summer):53-69.

Argues that both *Surfacing* and *Molloy* "subvert conventions of genre, plot, structure, usage, and punctuation in shaping texts which question their own existence." Both present self-conscious, fragmented, metamorphosing "narrators of uncertain identity" who feel lost in a "'foreign'" inner landscape and obsessively name and unname their stories. "*Surfacing* also parodies the illusion of reality, heroic quest, and journey/return conventions." Though less radical in its self-conscious questioning, "*Surfacing* is anti-fiction, or at least closer to it than 'straight' or traditional fiction." Though *Surfacing* comes closer to an end than Molloy, neither of these fundamentally linguistic artist quests can be resolved.

173 WITHIM, PHILIP. "'Packing It in Salt': Form in Atwood's *Surfacing*." *CEA Critic* 50, no.1 (Fall):67-73.

Appreciates form as powerfully interconnected patterns and structures of narrative, images, language, and "even of themes" in the most distinguished *Surfacing*; after concurring with Frank Davey's 1983.31, unannotated parts of Paul Stuewe's 1984.91 book, and William Butler Yeats's "'all that is personal soon rots; it must be packed in ice or salt'" on the importance of form over theme. *Surfacing*'s very strong and arching narrative structure "moves from an anaesthetized beginning, through a painfully awakened middle," to the concluding rite of initiation and courageous decision. *Surfacing*'s "images of borders, dividedness, entanglement, pictures, journeys, and metamorphosis coalesce" to show a unified human life, both organic and mental. As Cluett 1983.23 shows, *Surfacing*'s radically retrenched language "parallels the narrator's" retreat from the ornately civilized. The most important themes, "of guilt, of quest for the true self and true nature, of metamorphosis, and of necessary mortal limitations," form an interconnected structure.

174 WOODCOCK, GEORGE. "Canadian Poetry: The Emergent Tradition." In *Northern Spring: The Flowering of Canadian Literature*. Vancouver and Toronto: Douglas & McIntyre, pp. 181-95.

Reprints, slightly abridged and with a new preface, 1985.113.

175 _____. Introduction to *Canadian Writers and Their Works: Fiction Series*. Edited by Robert Lecker, Jack David, and Ellen Quigley. Vol. 9. Toronto: ECW Press, pp. 5-21.

The fiction of Margaret Atwood, Matt Cohen, Marian Engel, Margaret Laurence, and Rudy Wiebe is a modernist imaginative realism that tends to develop native myths; freed from self-conscious Canadianism, these five novelists project "the inner reality of Canadian life." Atwood, who is also an unusually powerful poet, is in fiction "an ironically didactic realist" and a master of literature's games. Her Gothic strain, subtly combined with Jungian psychology and animism, impels *Surfacing*, which may be her best novel. Her serious social criticism novels are becoming more realistic, and hence more pessimistic.

176 _____. "Metamorphosis and Survival: Notes on the Recent Poetry of Margaret Atwood." In *Northern Spring: The Flowering of Canadian Literature*. Vancouver and Toronto: Douglas & McIntyre, pp. 266-84.

Appreciates the stronger affirmations and the powerful Ovidian theme of metamorphosis in *You Are Happy, Two-Headed Poems, True Stories*, and *Interlunar*, in an essay that reprints 1983.147, slightly abridged, with a new preface and *Interlunar* section. The latter, which may be Atwood's most serene book, reflects on the indifference of the universe to human cruelty. One senses "an almost animist pushing to the edges of human consciousness," as in *Surfacing*. "Snake Poems" considers the creature in nature and myth. The "half worlds of death-life, flesh-spirit" are marvelously evoked in the Orpheus and Euridice poems. Atwood masterfully "draw[s] out the numinous from the normal, as in "Heart Test with an Echo Chamber" and "Interlunar."

177 "Writer's Writers." *Books in Canada* 16, no. 1 (January/February):8.
   Asks 25 Canadian writers what they are reading this winter, and what they think of the present state of Canadian literature. Atwood lists five books, emphasizing Alice Munro and Timothy Findley; and finds CanLit flourishing, but the economy endangered–is the government trying to "wipe out Canadian culture" so it can sell Canada out for free trade?

178 YEOMAN, ANN. Review of *The Handmaid's Tale. Canadian Woman Studies* 8, no. 1 (Spring):97-98.
   Finds Atwood's novel compellingly suspenseful on first reading, but questions its credibility on second reading. "Atwood refuses to present Gilead as a satiric inversion of our own world or as an hermetically-sealed 'alternate' world." The coldly factual ["Historical Notes"] Epilogue totally lacks compassion, and entirely misses Offred's reason for telling her tale. "Offred craves communion" with others and the world; she risks her life for love, and escape. "Atwood gives us hope when she shows that Offred's faith in human love enables her to endure; she chills us when" the Epilogue's academics don't even notice that essential quality.

1988

1 ATWOOD, MARGARET. "[Review of *Second Words*.]" In *Critical Essays on Margaret Atwood*. See McCombs 1988.28, pp. 251-53.
   Reprinted from 1982.12.

2 BAER, ELIZABETH R. "Pilgrimage Inward: Quest and Fairy Tale Motifs in *Surfacing*." In *Margaret Atwood: Vision and Forms*. See VanSpanckeren and Castro 1988.52, pp. 24-34.
   Analyzes the transformations of motifs from Quebec's *loup-garou* (werewolf) and from the Grimms's "Fitcher's Feathered Bird" in *Surfacing*. Atwood inverts the traditionally male *loup-garou* with a female protagonist, who is forbidden to eat, rather than compelled to devour; most radically, Atwood inverts the protagonist's primal, animal

side to one essential for full humanity. *Surfacing* and "Fitcher's" are both quest stories, "of a journey into the woods, of a young woman who is split apart and then made whole, of transformation into an animal state . . . to achieve vision and triumph." *Surfacing*'s father represents the sorcerer Fitcher as kidnapper and murderer; the lover who insisted on abortion represents the sorcerer as murderer. The narrator, who puts her missing pieces back together and effects a transformation (the new child), is "a version of the three sisters"; both narrator and fetus can represent the egg. *Loup-garou* and "Fitcher's" motifs most strongly influence the narrator's destruction of her conventional self and her transformation into an animal. Ellen Moers links women's bird imagery to becoming a free adult; so it is with "Fitcher's" sister disguised as bird. The narrator's quest for her parents is even more for her mother, who "is a kind of phoenix." See 1981.3.

3 BARBOUR, DOUGLAS. Review of *Two-Headed Poems*. In *Critical Essays on Margaret Atwood*. See McCombs 1988.28, pp. 208-212.
    Reprint of 1979.8.

4 BLOTT, ANNE. "Journey to Light. In *Critical Essays on Margaret Atwood*. See McCombs 1988.28, pp. 265-79.
    Reprint of 1986.33.

5 BRANS, JO. "Using What You're Given." In *Listening to the Voices: Conversations with Contemporary Writers*. Dallas: Southern Methodist University Press, pp. 125-47.
    A slightly revised reprint of 1983.14, with a new preface on Atwood's successes through the brilliant, militant *The Handmaid's Tale*, her scientific family background, and her vision of power and survival.

6 BREWSTER, ELIZABETH. "Powerful Poetry." In *Critical Essays on Margaret Atwood*. See McCombs 1988.28, pp. 35-36.
    Reprint of 1971.2.

7 BROMBERG, PAMELA S. "The Two Faces of the Mirror: *The Edible Woman* and *Lady Oracle*." In *Margaret Atwood: Vision and Forms*. See VanSpanckeren and Castro 1988.52, pp. 12-23.

1988

"Both *The Edible Woman* and *Lady Oracle* exemplify [Luce] Irigaray's ideas; their plots subvert patriarchal literary conventions and their language deconstructs traditional specular metaphors." Both novels identify touch with potential female "wholeness and escape from the 'dominant scopic economy.' . . . [Atwood] suggests that female narcissism" comes from internalizing the male gaze and the self's imprisonment in objectifying roles. Specular metaphors tell the first novel's counterplot; as Marian's marriage nears, her image acquires "power and her subjective self nearly disappears." The woman/cake "deconstructs Peter's image of" Marian, and specular language; by consuming the cake, Marian heals the mirror's split. Marian experiences Duncan through touch – but will he devour her? *Lady Oracle* "again uses mirror symbolism" and extends Atwood's "concepts of doubling"; Joan, who is divided by her mother's rejection, invents new identities for various men; "a countermovement toward wholeness . . . is mediated through touch." Both novels end ambiguously, with conditionally freed protagonists.

8 BROWN, RUSSELL [sic]. "Atwood's Sacred Wells." In *Critical Essays on Margaret Atwood*. See McCombs 1988.28, pp. 213-29.
An abridgment of 1980.13.

9 BUCHBINDER, DAVID. "Weaving Her Version: The Homeric Model and Gender Politics in *Selected Poems*." In *Margaret Atwood: Vision and Forms*. See VanSpanckeren and Castro 1988.52, pp. 122-41.
Follows Itamar Even-Zohar's polysystem theory to decode *Selected Poems* as an intertextual discourse on gender politics. The Homeric model, of the *Odyssey* and related, non-Homeric myths, provides three kinds of ambiguously subordinate yet powerful female roles, and a male Other. Atwood's duplicitous Siren and transforming Circe are each passive victimizers and island-isolated victims, trapped in predictable temporal loops. The unnamed, implicit Penelope is an active victor who appears in Circe's slanted poems and in the last seven poems of *Selected Poems*. In "There Is Only One of Everything" she values the mundane, provisional present. In "Book of Ancestors," the final poem of transformation and resolution, the active, experienced speaker adopts a male approach, while the passive, virginal man becomes female. Like the *Odyssey*, *Selected Poems* can also be read as a discourse on fidelity; metonymically, Atwood's duplicitous Siren is a

1988

betraying Helen, her yearning Circe a Nausicaa, her Penelope an Athene who provides temporary but satisfying resolutions. The first poem in *Selected Poems*, "This Is a Photograph of Me," covertly presents the Homeric model, with its Siren-like voice, "metamorphosis, verbality, confusions of tense, and duplicity of signification."

10 CAMERON, ELSPETH. "In Darkest Atwood." In *Critical Essays on Margaret Atwood*. See McCombs 1988.28, pp. 254-56.
   Reprint of 1983.19.

11 CAMPBELL, JOSIE P. "The Woman as Hero in Margaret Atwood's *Surfacing*." In *Critical Essays on Margaret Atwood*. See McCombs 1988.28, pp. 168-79.
   Reprint of 1978.16.

12 CARRINGTON, ILDIKÓ de PAPP. "Demons, Doubles, and Dinosaurs: *Life Before Man*, *The Origin of Consciousness*, and 'The Icicle.'" In *Critical Essays on Margaret Atwood*. See McCombs 1988.28, pp. 229-45.
   Reprint of 1986.50.

13 CASTRO, JAN GARDEN. "An Interview with Margaret Atwood 20 April 1983." In *Margaret Atwood: Vision and Forms*. See VanSpanckeren and Castro 1988.52, pp. 215-32.
   A corrected reprint of 1984.11 that adds a paragraph on the game of Dictionary, and an interchange on American big-dish television and acid rain in Canada.

14 "A Conversation: Margaret Atwood and Students, Moderated by Francis X. Gillen." In *Margaret Atwood: Vision and Forms*. See VanSpanckeren and Castro 1988.52, pp. 233-43.
   In response to questions at the University of Tampa, 25 January 1987, Atwood discusses her writing habits and favorite authors, politics and art, Amnesty International, Cuba, civil liberties in the United States, Lewis Hyde's *The Gift*, poetry in Canada, and writing versus self-expression.

1988

15 DAVEY, FRANK. "Atwood's Gorgon Touch." In *Critical Essays on Margaret Atwood*. See McCombs 1988.28, 134-53.
    Reprint of 1977.12.

16 DAVIDSON, ARNOLD E. "Future Tense: Making History in *The Handmaid's Tale*." In *Margaret Atwood: Vision and Forms*. See VanSpanckeren and Castro 1988.52, pp. 113-21.
    Analyzes the sexist, racist, history-creating implications of the "Historical Notes," which raise ominous questions of scholarly " – male, of course – " authority over "a woman's eyewitness account" and of dehumanizing "'objectivity.'" How much does the assembling of the text create a fiction? Offred's gender-cliché passivity is "underscored by Professor Pieixoto's" gender distinctions; Gilead's grotesque transformation of women becomes, grotesquely, his "silly sexist jests." Such academic texts condition readings of society. Pieixoto's pre-Foucault, pre-de Beauvoir "objective" historical criticism shows "little awareness that context itself is a construct." As Carpenter 1986.49 points out, the professor trivializes the handmaid's document "because he trivializes women's role" in Gilead and his own society; his racist, sexist jokes marginalize the handmaid and the chairwoman/charwoman. But "our reading of his reading can authenticate Offred's account" differently, and reveal his insidious gender prerogatives.

17 FOSTER, JOHN WILSON. "The Poetry of Margaret Atwood." In *Critical Essays on Margaret Atwood*. See McCombs 1988.28, pp. 153-67.
    Reprint of 1977.22.

18 FREIBERT, LUCY M. "Control and Creativity: The Politics of Risk in Margaret Atwood's *The Handmaid's Tale*." In *Critical Essays on Margaret Atwood*. See McCombs 1988.28, pp. 280-91.
    Analyzes how Atwood's novel satirizes Western phallocentrism and tests French feminist theory. The Chaucerian and anatomical pun on *Tale* sets up multiple ironies. The first, biblical epigraph, of Rachel, Jacob, and Bilhah, which instances the pervasive Israelite custom of using handmaids for progeny, foreshadows the novel's central "violation of individual autonomy" and its inner "female envy and male/female enmity . . . ." The prayer sessions and the impregnation and birthing rituals are hilarious burlesques at which no one dares

laugh. The second epigraph predicts Atwood's Swiftean exaggerations of present ideological conflicts, that indict inhumane simplistic solutions. The third, Sufi epigraph counterpoints human survival and Gilead's outrageous legalism. Offred demonstrates, "in terms of *écriture feminine*, . . . that women, able to take risks and to tell stories, may transcend their conditioning, . . . [claim their identities, bodies, and voices,] and reconstruct the social order." A sympathetic and credible "voice crying in the desert," Offred conflates traditional images of women. Shaking with fear, she takes the greatest risks, and breaks through "to her courageous sexual self . . . with Nick." Her tale may precipitate Gilead's end. Atwood as realist questions the ultimate success of the French feminists; the satirized small-minded academics of the "Historical Notes" are not an ideal society. Still, *The Handmaid's Tale* achieves Hélène Cixous's goal for a feminine text; it subversively shatters institutional frameworks, and "'break[s] up the truth with laughter.'"

19 GRACE, SHERRILL E. "In Search of Demeter: The Lost, Silent Mother in *Surfacing*." In *Margaret Atwood: Vision and Forms*. See VanSpanckeren and Castro 1988.52, pp. 35-47.

Follows Elaine Showalter's feminist model of "'double-voiced discourse'" to read *Surfacing* as a "'muted' story of Persephone's successful search for Demeter within a 'dominant' story of an equally successful wilderness quest for a father." In the long-silenced and distorted myth of the "awesome goddess of vegetation," Demeter, Persephone's rebirth and life's renewal depend on their ecstatic, speech-restoring reunion; and Demeter, Persephone, and Hecate ally against the males to win back two-thirds of the year together. Though many American and French feminists distrust *Surfacing*'s woman-nature conflation and childbearing, the ancients celebrated childbirth and Persephone's appearance with a Dionysus-reborn son. *Surfacing*'s Eleusian ritual mating, destruction, and deeper ecstatic dive "carry the narrator" and hoped-for god/baby past language and all boundaries to union. The nature-joined, sustaining mother-vision shows the narrator what to be; the father-vision warns her. As in the Demeter-Persephone myth, *Surfacing*'s males "embod[y] a death principle"; the impregnated narrator can be reborn only through the mother's life-bringing power. As in Atwood's other work, both principles are essential for rebirth and wholeness; the controversial baby symbolizes that knowledge and the reconceived "powerful female self." That *Surfacing*'s Persephone is the searcher may indicate an alternate myth, realism, the mother's call, or women's loss of Demeter's power in Western culture. "A Stone" transforms Demeter's evil medusa aspect into comfort, and reverences the powerful mother.

20 GRAY, FRANCINE du PLESSIX. "Nature as the Nunnery." In *Critical Essays on Margaret Atwood*. See McCombs 1988.28, pp. 131-34.
   Reprint of 1977.28. See also 1987.47.

21 GREENE, GAYLE. *"Life Before Man: 'Can Anything Be Saved?'"* In *Margaret Atwood: Vision and Forms*. See VanSpanckeren and Castro 1988.52, pp. 65-84.
   Though Atwood 1986.219, Grace 1980.47, and others have complained of its claustrophobic grey realism, *Life Before Man* is partly modernist; external events are minimal and adventures internal. The characters' minds "roam time and eternity" as, despite the past, they change, imperceptibly, constantly, and profoundly. Both structure and title call attention to time. Though Elizabeth, Lesje, and Nate see humanity as psychologically, evolutionarily, or historically determined, each does change, and attain the "freedom and dignity" that Nate's mother and Atwood believe in. The novel's "long view of time . . . reduces human life," yet expands the imagination. Nate and Lesje move from limiting to liberating relationships; Elizabeth is liberated from Nate, and her compassion and imagination are reborn with Auntie Muriel and in her final vision of a communal ideal. Lesje initiates an adult, creative pregnancy, and learns compassion. The shallower Nate, who changes the least, learns to see his mother as a person, returns to political work, and becomes protective and hopeful. But these late 1970s personal changes cannot change society.

22 GROSSKURTH, PHYLLIS. "Survival Kit." In *Critical Essays on Margaret Atwood*. See McCombs 1988.28, 66-70.
   Reprint of 1973.32.

23 HELWIG, DAVID. Review of *The Animals in That Country*. In *Critical Essays on Margaret Atwood*. See McCombs 1988.28, pp. 32-33.
   Reprint of 1969.5.

24 IRVINE, LORNA. "The Here and Now of *Bodily Harm*." In *Margaret Atwood: Vision and Forms*. See VanSpanckeren and Castro 1988.52, pp. 85-100.
A slightly revised version of 1986.119.

25 LARKIN, JOAN. "Soul Survivor." In *Critical Essays on Margaret Atwood*. See McCombs 1988.28, pp. 48-52.
Reprint of 1973.46.

26 LAURENCE, MARGARET. Review of *Surfacing*. In *Critical Essays on Margaret Atwood*. See McCombs 1988.28, pp. 45-47.
Reprint of 1973.47.

27 LILIENFELD, JANE. "Circe's Emergence: Transforming Traditional Love in Margaret Atwood's *You Are Happy*." In *Critical Essays on Margaret Atwood*. See McCombs 1988.28, pp. 123-30.
Reprint of 1977.45.

28 McCOMBS, JUDITH, ed. *Critical Essays on Margaret Atwood*. Critical Essays on World Literature, edited by Robert Lecker. Boston: G.K. Hall & Co., 306 pp.
Contains: Introduction 1988.29, Ondaatje 1988.36, Helwig 1988.23, Skelton 1988.47, Brewster 1988.6, Stevens 1988.48, Purdy 1988.40, Newman 1988.35, Laurence 1988.26, Larkin 1988.25, Piercy 1988.39, Grosskurth 1988.22, Onley 1988.37, Woodcock 1988.56, Sullivan 1988.49, Mandel 1988.34, Lilienfeld 1988.27, Gray 1988.20, Davey 1988.15, Foster 1988.17, Campbell 1988.11, MacLulich 1988.31, Rosowski 1988.43, Barbour 1988.3, Brown 1988.8, Carrington 1988.12, Mandel 1988.33, Atwood 1988.1, Cameron 1988.10, Redekop 1988.41, Rubenstein 1988.45, Blott 1988.4, Freibert 1988.18, and a Primary Bibliography.

29 _____. Introduction to *Critical Essays on Margaret Atwood*. See McCombs 1988.28, pp. 1-28.
Provides a detailed bibliographic guide to Atwood criticism in Canada and the United States, 1967-87, and some British work, based on over a thousand English-language reviews and essays, four books, and four other collections of essays on Atwood. Traces the earliest and major critical focuses on themes and patterns of social criticism,

feminism, women's literature, Canadian literature, Gothic and other genres, re-enacted or transformed myth, mysticism, and folklore; the less frequent linguistic, formal, structuralist, and postmodern approaches; and the just-beginning studies of Atwood's manuscripts and watercolors. Assesses the development of Atwood's reputation as poet, fiction writer, and critic, comparing national, gender, and political differences among critics. Discusses the Canadian New Critical appreciation of her first book, *The Circle Game* poems; Canadian ambivalence towards her "exciting, controlled, but disquieting and rather cold poetry," from *The Animals in That Country* on; the earliest acclaim for *The Edible Woman*; *Surfacing*'s triumphs among Canadian and United States literary, feminist, and theological critics; controversies over *Power Politics*, the highly influential *Survival*, and Atwood's emergence as English Canada's foremost writer; assumptions of increasing "warmth, equality, and love" in Atwood's poetry; and recognition of the realism, Julian Jaynesian elements, and overt Amnesty International and feminist liberal politics of Atwood's second stage, from *Two-Headed Poems* through *The Handmaid's Tale*.

30 _____. "Politics, Structure, and Poetic Development in Atwood's Canadian-American Sequences: From an Apprentice Pair to "The Circle Game" to "Two-Headed Poems." In *Margaret Atwood: Vision and Forms*. See VanSpanckeren and Castro 1988.52, pp. 142-62.

Explicates Canadian literary and political allusions, Jaynesian allusions, structure, and poetic development, in two unpublished poems and two title sequences. "The Idea of Canada" and "America as the Aging Demon Lover," which depict Canada as a "self-imprisoned Rapunzel Crone and America as Metal Man," belong to Atwood's apprentice period, with their allegorical personifications, Gothic grotesques, and echoes of James Reaney. "The Circle Game," which is concentrically structured, enacts mirror, orphan, garrison, and map games that correspond to gender and national power scenarios; it belongs to Atwood's "Stage I, the closed world of mirroring, female Gothic elements." Stage II, "the open world," subordinates Stage I elements to "realistic, transnational, human ends"; "Two-Headed Poems" is "embryonic (or misborn) Stage II." Its Siamese twins go back to an apprentice image, and dramatize the late-1970s English versus French Canadian separatist language conflicts. Its concentric structure attempts, following Julian Jaynes's theories in *The Origin of*

1988

Consciousness, "a palentology of Canada's two left-brained national consciousnesses," and three transcendent oracles, of sun-spelling, claiming the dead, and a dreamed-of, bicameral song. For Atwood, after Jaynes, language becomes the wider human territory, and our Great Mother tongue.

31 MacLULICH, T.D. "Atwood's Adult Fairy Tale: Levi-Strauss, Bettelheim, and *The Edible Woman*." In *Critical Essays on Margaret Atwood.* See McCombs 1988.28, pp. 179-97.
    Reprint of 1978.58.

32 McMILLAN, ANN. "The Transforming Eye: *Lady Oracle* and Gothic Tradition." In *Margaret Atwood: Vision and Forms.* See VanSpanckeren and Castro 1988.52, pp. 48-64.
    In Gothic fantasy, the heroine's transforming eye simultaneously perceives the potential hero and transforms him into a hero. *Lady Oracle,* like Jane Austen's *Northanger Abbey,* is mixed Gothic fantasy and Gothic naturalism; both heroines begin by imitating the fantasy heroines, and narrowly escape the dismal naturalism fates. In both Atwood and Austen the transforming eye is transitional, and provides opportunities for the heroine's "maturation and insight." Joan's transforming eye envisions each man as a rescuing hero, then as a non-rescuing villain; and creates the fear that "incites her to escape" her unglamorous aspects, which then haunt her. Motivated by guilt, Joan finally learns to face the ghosts; following the transforming eye, she injures a complete stranger, and that "at last frees Joan from her self-created maze" of transformation and escape. In the ambiguous, hopeful end, the unreliable Joan may, however, let "her transforming eye cast yet another man as her savior."

33 MANDEL, ANN. Review of *True Stories.* In *Critical Essays on Margaret Atwood.* See McCombs 1988.28, pp. 245-51.
    Reprints the Atwood portions of 1982.110.

34 MANDEL, ELI. "Atwood Gothic." In *Critical Essays on Margaret Atwood.* See McCombs 1988.28, pp. 114-23.
    Reprint of 1977.52.

1988

35 NEWMAN, CHRISTINA. "In Search of a Native Tongue." In *Critical Essays on Margaret Atwood*. See McCombs 1988.28, pp. 43-45.
    Reprint of 1972.30.

36 ONDAATJE, MICHAEL. Review of *The Circle Game*. In *Critical Essays on Margaret Atwood*. See McCombs 1988.28, pp. 29-32.
    Reprint of 1967.5.

37 ONLEY, GLORIA. "Power Politics in Bluebeard's Castle." In *Critical Essays on Margaret Atwood*. See McCombs 1988.28, pp. 70-89.
    Reprint of 1974.33.

38 PALMER, CAROLE L. "Current Atwood Checklist, 1988." *Newsletter of the Margaret Atwood Society*, no. 5, pp. [5-11].
    Provides an alphabetical, descriptively annotated listing of primary and secondary work for 1988 and for those 1987 items not included in the previous annual checklist, 1987.116. Lists under Atwood's works 14 primary items, including some excerpts, reprints, and interviews, with brief explanatory annotations; 14 other interviews are listed with the secondary work. Lists 41 reviews, alphabetically by author, under five primary books and five translations. Lists under secondary sources 78 articles, including three books on Atwood, alphabetically by author, with succinct annotations. Foreign-language primary and secondary material is included.

39 PIERCY, MARGE. "Margaret Atwood: Beyond Victimhood." In *Critical Essays on Margaret Atwood*. See McCombs 1988.28, pp. 53-66.
    Reprint of 1973.72.

40 PURDY, A[L] W. "Atwood's Moodie." In *Critical Essays on Margaret Atwood*. See McCombs 1988.28, pp. 38-42.
    Reprint of 1971.14.

41 REDEKOP, MAGDALENE. "Charms and Riddles." In *Critical Essays on Margaret Atwood*. See McCombs 1988.28, pp. 256-58.
    Reprint of 1984.78.

42 ROSENBERG, JEROME, ed. *Newsletter of the Margaret Atwood Society*, no. 5, [12] pp.

Contains news of the Atwood Society's annual meeting and the Atwood Session at the 1988 Modern Language Association Convention; minutes of the 1987 annual meeting; primary and secondary Atwood books for 1988-89, with abstracts of McCombs 1988.28 and VanSpanckeren and Castro 1988.52; a list of seven audio-visual Atwood items; an update on Atwood's travels and activities; notes and queries concerning current and forthcoming Atwood publications, conference papers, and theses; and the Carole L. Palmer 1988.38 primary and secondary checklist.

43 ROSOWSKI, SUSAN J. "Margaret Atwood's *Lady Oracle*: Fantasy and the Modern Gothic Novel." In *Critical Essays on Margaret Atwood*. See McCombs 1988.28, pp. 197-208.

Reprints an earlier version of 1981.86, from a paper delivered at the Midwest Modern Language Association Convention, Minneapolis, 3 November 1978, which did not have the 1981 article's first two paragraphs on Canadian social mythology.

44 RUBENSTEIN, ROBERTA. "Nature and Nurture in Dystopia: *The Handmaid's Tale*." In *Margaret Atwood: Vision and Forms*. See VanSpanckeren and Castro 1988.52, pp. 101-12.

Analyzes the multiple inversions and violations of nature and nurture in Atwood's fablelike sixth novel. Female anxieties toward "fertility, procreation, and maternity [evident in her first three novels] are projected as feminist nightmare and cultural catastrophe." Anatomy becomes destiny for the sexually indentured handmaid, Offred, whose name means "'offered'" and "'Of-Fred.'" "From the central issue of procreation to the [substructure of] language and imagery," bodies are objectified, dismembered, and mutilated. Gilead perverts normalcy; "distinctions between 'natural' and 'unnatural,' between human and non-human, are grotesquely inverted or reduced." Animal references often "suggest the debased" human body, and are often repugnant; the handmaids as prize or trained pigs recalls Orwell's *Animal Farm*. Smell, taste, and hunger are "assaulted by the unnatural . . . ." "'Nature'" is invoked to justify male sexual dominance. After the ambiguous, Kafka-like rescue or capture, the ironic "Historical Notes" coda briefly parodies the narrative's inverted nature imagery.

1988

45 ____. "Pandora's Box and Female Survival: Margaret Atwood's *Bodily Harm*." In *Critical Essays on Margaret Atwood*. See McCombs 1988.28, pp. 259-75.
> Reprints 1985.88. Revised 1987.134.

46 SCHLUETER, JUNE. "Canlit/Victimlit: *Survival* and *Second Words*." In *Margaret Atwood: Vision and Forms*. See VanSpanckeren and Castro 1988.52, pp. 1-11.
> Discusses Atwood's critical analyses of Canada and women. Like *Surfacing*, *Survival*'s "Basic Victim Positions" reveal a collective Canadian victim mentality. Though *Survival* soon became Canada's most widely read literary criticism, knowledgeable critics defended Canlit against Atwood's literary negativism and liberal politics; Atwood's 1973.2 defended *Survival*'s accuracy and commitment. *Second Words* reveals Atwood's developing vision of Canlit, from her 1960s college reviews and Harvard experiences; through the essays on Canadian monsters and Canadian humour, which confirm *Survival*; to the latest criticism, which "endorses and broadens her *Survival* thesis." Atwood's criticism of feminism, literature, and women writers goes beyond Canadian boundaries to gender victimization. *Survival*'s women chapter develops Robert Graves's Diana-Venus-Hecate model, in *The White Goddess*, for Canadian literature.

47 SKELTON, ROBIN. Review of *The Journals of Susanna Moodie* and *Procedures for Underground*. In *Critical Essays on Margaret Atwood*. See McCombs 1988.28, pp. 34-35.
> Reprint of 1971.17.

48 STEVENS, PETER. "Dark Mouth." In *Critical Essays on Margaret Atwood*. See McCombs 1988.28, pp. 37-38.
> Reprint of 1971.18.

49 SULLIVAN, ROSEMARY. "Breaking the Circle." In *Critical Essays on Margaret Atwood*. See McCombs 1988.28, pp. 104-14.
> Reprint of 1977.90.

50 VanSPANCKEREN, KATHRYN. Introduction to *Margaret Atwood: Vision and Forms*. See VanSpanckeren and Castro 1988.52, pp. xix-xxvii.

1988

Describes Atwood's status as a foremost Canadian writer, widely discussed in and writing about the United States, and her national and international cultural diplomacy, genres, and concerns; and introduces the book's fourteen essays, interview, and conversation.

51 ____. "Shamanism in the Works of Margaret Atwood." In *Margaret Atwood: Vision and Forms*. See VanSpanckeren and Castro 1988.52, pp. 183-204.

Follows Mircea Eliade and others to explicate Atwood's pervasive Arctic and Amerindian shamanism: the shamanic orientation to death, descents to the spirit realm, journey-songs, tutelary animals, magical vision, mirrors, and primal images of animals, bones, teeth, plants, rocks, fire, earth, air, and water. "Procedures for Underground," which comes from a Northwest Bella Coola legend, identifies "a dreamlike shamanic descent" to the world of dead spirits with the artist's descent to the creative unconscious. From *Double Persephone* on, death "is a wellspring of creativity." *The Circle Game*'s orphic poems seem to come from a watery Inuit spirit realm, and end with a shamanic speaking skeleton. Descents pervade *Two-Headed Poems* and *Interlunar*, whose "Snake Poems" celebrate the Great Goddess's sacred snake/python. *You Are Happy*, which celebrates a transformative death, includes shamanic magical sight, the tutelary animal spirits of "Songs of the Transformed," and a shamanlike Circe who recalls the Inuit Mother of Sea Beasts, Takánakapsâluk. Circe, the *Surfacing* protagonist, *Lady Oracle*'s Joan, *Life Before Man*'s Elizabeth, and *Bodily Harm*'s Rennie are their own shamans, descending to cure themselves; they learn human self-sufficiency. Lora resembles the Mother of Sea Beasts, crippled by men; Rennie's shamanic return and true story will purify the larger community. *The Journals of Susanna Moodie* may be Atwood's best shamanic imagery, death-wisdom, and magical song. Atwood's shamanism is regenerative, female, and universal.

52 VanSPANCKEREN, KATHRYN, and CASTRO, JAN GARDEN, eds. *Margaret Atwood: Vision and Forms*. Ad Feminam: Women and Literature, edited by Sandra M. Gilbert. Carbondale and Edwardsville: Southern Illinois University Press, 269 pp.

Contains: Introduction 1988.50, Schlueter 1988.46, Bromberg 1988.7, Baer 1988.2, Grace 1988.19, McMillan 1988.32, Greene 1988.21,

1988

Irvine 1988.24, Rubenstein 1988.44, Davidson, A. 1988.16, Buchbinder 1988.9, McCombs 1988.30, VanSpanckeren 1988.51, Wilson 1988.55, Castro 1988.13, Conversation 1988.14, **and a Margaret Atwood Chronology.**

53 VOGT, KATHLEEN. "Real and Imaginary Animals in the Poetry of Margaret Atwood." In *Margaret Atwood: Vision and Forms*. See VanSpanckeren and Castro 1988.52, pp. 163-82.

Discusses the animals in Atwood's poetry from *Double Persephone* through *Two-Headed Poems*. Atwood movingly depicts the victimization of animals in "Dream 2: Brian the Still-Hunter," "Dreams of the Animals," and her 1975 Toronto zoo article, "Don't Expect the Bear to Dance." Where animals are reduced to objects, so are people, as in "'You want to go back.'" But victimization can also mean being taken over by animal selves, or a hostile wilderness. The maggot-nourishing dog of "The Double Voice" expresses the actual; Frank Davey 1977.12 indicates Atwood's static versus kinetic tension. The carved animals of "Some Objects of Wood and Stone" mediate between self and other; the eel of "Fishing for Eel Totems" proclaims its reality in life and as sacramental food. As in "Digging," transcendent metamorphosis becomes less possible in Atwood's later poems. *Two-Headed Poems*'s totems "are of the eel kind," not carved; natural process is sacramental in "All Bread." Atwood insists that our individual space is shared with "trees, sky, hawks, and humankind"; her actual animals may express themselves, or, metaphorically, humans. Like the *Surfacing* protagonist, Atwood affirms both the human and the other.

54 WALL, KATHLEEN. "Surfacing: The Matriarchal Myth Re-Surfaces." In *The Callisto Myth from Ovid to Atwood: Initiation and Rape in Literature*. Kingston and Montreal: McGill-Queen's University Press, pp. 155-70.

Explicates the Callisto myth in *Surfacing*, citing Hinz and Tuenissen 1979.54 and Pratt 1981.82. As in *Jane Eyre*, *The Scarlet Letter*, and *Lady Chatterley's Lover*, the narrator "has two relationships, one which violates her integrity and one which is renewing." Both nature and human emotions, of the narrator and her friends, are wastelands. The teacher's seeming godliness disguised him; that destructive relationship, and the abortion he chose, amounted to the narrator's allowing a rape. As Callisto sought Diana's help, so the narrator seeks the help of her natural, powerful mother, who had saved the childhood pictograph of the pregnant Great Mother that guides the narrator's initiatory renewal with Joe. The narrator seeks the sacred in a forest exile, becomes animal-like, and then returns to society, with the mediator Joe, having reclaimed her sexuality, motherhood, and autonomy. See 1984.29.

55 WILSON, SHARON R. "Sexual Politics in Margaret Atwood's Visual Art." In *Margaret Atwood: Vision and Forms*. See VanSpanckeren and Castro 1988.52, pp. 205-14.

Discusses the sexual politics of Atwood's book covers and archetypal watercolors, quoting Atwood's comments on them, and interprets the eight archival-labeled watercolors reproduced here. The 1970 "Death as Bride," whose Grimms's "Fitcher's Bird" elements are discussed more fully in 1986.263, prefigures Atwood's later Bluebeards, visual and literary. The 1969 pair, "Lady and Sinister Figure" and "Lady and Executioner with Axe," picture Anne Boleyn or Mary Stuart, and resemble "Marrying the Hangman." Two 1970 watercolors, "Man Holding Woman's Body" and "Mourners at Woman's Bier," evoke Mary Shelley's *Frankenstein*, Atwood's "Speeches for Dr. Frankenstein," and questions of creation, self, and murder. The Tarot-based 1970 "Hanged Man," which is the original for *Power Politics*'s cover, shows man and woman as timeless victims/victors. The undated "Insect in Red Gown with Bouquet" is a fertility figure illustrating Atwood's "Termite Queen" series of poems. The 1974 "Atwoods as Birds" satirizes bitch-harpy and chick ideas of women.

56 WOODCOCK, GEORGE. "Margaret Atwood: Poet as Novelist." In *Critical Essays on Margaret Atwood*. See McCombs 1988.28, 90-104.
Reprint of 1975.52.

Author Index

ABBEY, MARILYN R., 1982.1
ABLEMAN, PAUL, 1986.1
ABLEY, MARK, 1981.1; 1983.1;
    1984.1
ABRAMS, ALAN, 1982.2
ABU-JABAR, DIANA, 1986.2
ADACHI, KEN, 1977.1-2; 1981.2;
    1982.3-4; 1984.2; 1985.1-
    3; 1986.3-6
ADAMS, JAMES, 1983.2
ADAMS, PHOEBE-LOU,
    1980.1; 1982.5
ADAMSON, ARTHUR, 1980.2
ADCOCK, FLEUR, 1983.3
ADDINGTON, FRAN, 1986.7
ADLER, CONSTANCE, 1986.8
AGER, SUSAN, 1982.6-7
AHOLA, SUVI, 1986.9
AITKEN, JOHAN LYALL,
    1987.1
ALATON, SALEM, 1986.10
ALLEN, BRUCE, 1986.11
ALLEN, CAROLYN, 1977.3;
    1978.1
ALLEN, DICK, 1972.1; 1986.12
ALLEN, GINA, 1987.2

ALLEN TOTH, SUSAN, see
    TOTH, SUSAN ALLEN
ALMÉRAS, DIANE, 1982.8
ALSOP, KAY, 1972.2
ALTMAN, PETER, 1973.1
AMABILE, GEORGE, 1975.1
AMEY, LARRY, 1978.2
AMIEL, BARBARA, 1976.1;
    1979.1-3
AMSTER, BETSY, 1986.13
ANDERSEN, MARGRET,
    1975.2
ANDERSON, J.L., 1971.1
ANDERSON, LINDA, 1986.14
ANDREWS, B.A. St., see St.
    ANDREWS, B.A.
ANDREWS, PAUL, 1986.15-16
ANTONELLI, MARYLU, 1979.4
APPELBAUM, JUDITH, 1983.4
APPENZELL, ANTHONY,
    1983.5
ARGÜELLES, IVAN, 1987.3
ASHENMACHER, BOB, 1982.9
ATHERTON, STANLEY S.,
    1982.10

Subject Index

Subjects discussed in criticism, interviews, and reviews are indexed most fully, by country of publication, under the titles of Atwood's books. Time, place, and development of the major subjects in secondary Atwood work may be traced by following her titles in chronological order. The few items published in more than one language, or simultaneously in more than one country, are indexed by subject for each language or country. Work reprinted in another country, however, is indexed by number only, not subject.

Criticism, which means essays in whole or in part, is indexed selectively, by major subjects and treatments; essay work not indexed by subject is listed first. Interviews concerning specific Atwood books are indexed under those books; more general interviews appear under Interviews. Reviews are indexed in their total number first, so that coverage may be compared, then indexed by subject.

A small number of key concepts are indexed outside Atwood's titles. Criticism on multiple books of Atwood's poetry or prose, and on several genres of her work, is indexed under Poetry and/or Prose, as well as under the specific Atwood titles. Material focused on Atwood's achievements, media images, and activities is indexed under Atwood.

The Literary Introduction provides a more detailed guide.

Abortion, 1974.41; 1976.2; 1977.51-52; 1981.52; 1986.205; 1988.34, 54. *See also* Birth

Adler, Renata, *Speedboat*, 1977.68

Aesthetics, 1977.12; 1978.20; 1980.47; 1983.19, 27, 29, 54; 1988.10, 15

Affirmations, resolution, 1975.43; 1977.51-52, 99; 1981.64; 1984.81; 1987.134;

-biographical sketches, 1975.18;
1981.42; 1983.20; 1984.6;
1986.116
-catalogue of items, 1986.84
-correspondence, 1977.76;
1981.113; 1984.81
-film of, 1985.5, 78
-images by. *See* Art, visual;
Imagery
--self-portrait, doll, 1968.5;
1982.142
-images of. *See* Awards; Status
--Canadian commentary,
criticism, and reviews,
1974.6, 20, 23, 28, 35, 38;
1975.1, 32; 1976.90;
1977.16, 26, 69, 75, 82;
1978.99; 1982.85;
1983.104; 1984.75;
1986.83; 1987.6, 98, 141
--Canadian interviews, 1975.13,
29-30, 47; 1976.58, 93;
1977.43, 80
--United States interviews,
1977.44; 1978.70
--United States reviews,
1978.15, 103; 1987.97
-literary activism, 1974.9;
1975.14; 1982.142;
1987.46. *See also Survival;
The New Oxford Book of
Canadian Verse in
English; The Oxford Book
of Canadian Short Stories
in English; CanLit
Foodbook*
--P.E.N., 1986.5, 18
-women writers' protest,
1986.55, 124; 1987.159,
161
--Writers' Union, 1977.25;
1978.70; 1982.58. *See also*
1985.76

-photographs of, 1974.38;
1977.81; 1980.108
-poems, fiction, and collage for,
1977.81
-politics, Canadian nationalism,
feminism. *See also
Second Words; Survival*
--Amnesty International,
1978.28; 1979.43; 1981.43-
44, 112; 1982.2, 76;
1986.5. *See also Bodily
Harm; True Stories*
-pseudonyms, pseudonymous
work, 1976.58, 101;
1978.70; 1987.45
-readings of her work, 1975.13;
1980.67, 123; 1982.13;
1983.127; 1984.61;
1987.72
-speeches, lectures, 1973.24;
1980.127; 1982.167;
1985.26, 66, 112; 1986.17,
21, 253
--panels, 1983.126; 1985.19
-status, success, 1969.16-17;
1972.40; 1973.20, 99;
1974.4, 6, 19-20, 23;
1975.12, 14, 52; 1976.26;
1977.82, 91, 98; 1979.56,
104; 1980.59, 72, 148;
1981.24; 1983.55; 1984.8,
60; 1985.70; 1986.84, 130;
1987.103; 1988.22, 29, 50,
56. *See also* Critical
books
--in Australia, 1983.67; 1984.50;
1987.82
--in Britain, 1986.95, 1988.115;
1987.53
--in Quebec, 1987.118
-works by. *See* Poetry; Prose;
specific titles
Atwood Papers, 1977.76; 1984.81

Breeze, Claude, 1977.49 Brewster,
　　Elizabeth, *It's Easy to*
　　Fall on the Ice, 1978.49
British Columbia literature,
　　1982.133
Brontë, Charlotte, *Jane Eyre*,
　　1976.63; 1978.82; 1988.54
Brontës, 1975.47
Brooke, Frances, *The History of*
　　Emily Montague, 1980.82
Brophy, Brigid, 1980.27
Brossard, Nicole,
　　-*Picture Theory*, 1985.73
　　-*Sold Out*, 1985.73
Brown, Edward Killoran, 1974.22
Bruce, Phyllis, *15 Canadian Poets*
　　plus 5, 1980.144
Buckler, Ernest, 1975.42
　　-*The Mountain and the Valley*,
　　1974.27
Burgess, Anthony, *A Clockwork*
　　Orange, 1985.118;
　　1986.150; 1987.71
Burgos, Jean, *Pour Circle*, 1976.76
Butler, Joan, 1982.10
Byron, Lord, 1972.20

Callaghan, Barry, 1986.4, 66, 81
Callaghan, Morley, 1973.32;
　　1977.50; 1983.23; 1988.22
Camera images, photographs,
　　1969.9; 1985.43, 111;
　　1987.171. *See also*
　　Surfacing; "This Is a
　　Photograph of Me"
Cameron, Elspeth, 1983.128
Campbell, Joseph, 1980.13;
　　1981.25; 1988.8
　　-*The Hero of a Thousand*
　　Faces, 1976.88; 1977.28;
　　1978.16; 1987.47; 1988.11,
　　20
Camus, Albert, 1978.53

Canadian feminist literary
　　criticism, general, 1986.29
Canadian identity, literature, and
　　nationalism. *See The*
　　Journals of Susanna
　　Moodie; *Surfacing*;
　　Survival
-Canadian and Australian
　　identity, literature,
　　1980.122; 1984.50;
　　1987.82
Canadian literary scene, satires of,
　　1976.58, 101; 1977.25;
　　1978.70; 1983.135;
　　1986.136; 1987.6. *See also*
　　Lady Oracle
Canadian Literature, 1973.106,
　　1985.114
"Canadian Monsters," 1981.11
Canadian poetry, general, 1981.1;
　　1983.126; 1985.6, 113;
　　1987.122. *See also The*
　　New Oxford Book of
　　Canadian Verse in
　　English
Canadian short story, general. *See*
　　The Oxford Book of
　　Canadian Short Stories in
　　English
Canadian women's writing,
　　general, 1985.108;
　　1986.115, 117, 130;
　　1987.60, 64
CanLit Foodbook
　　-Canadian reviews, 1987.25, 94,
　　167
　　-interviews, statements,
　　1987.30, 109
Cannibalism, 1967.5; 1969.16-17;
　　1975.52; 1987.94; 1988.56
Cardinal, Marie, *Les Mots pour le*
　　dire, 1978.30
Carr, Emily, *Klee Wyck*, 1978.85

under Poetry; specific
Atwood titles
Conrad, Joseph, 1985.21
-*Heart of Darkness*, 1976.88;
1977.29; 1984.9; 1987.156
-"The Secret Sharer," 1982.34
Consumer society. *See* Popular
culture; *The Edible
Woman*
Crane, Hart, 1987.165
Creative development. *See Second
Words*; *Selected Poems*;
Selected Poems II
-capillary links, resonances,
1972.40; 1975.52; 1980.13,
148; 1988.8, 56
-Siamese-twin genres, 1969.16-
17
Creative stages, 1980.47; 1983.16;
1986.151; 1988.30
"Creatures of the Zodiac, The,"
1971.10
Crews, Harry, *The Hawk is Dying*,
1973.65
Critical books on Atwood,
1980.47; 1984.18, 81;
1987.129
-essay collections on Atwood,
1977.81; 1981.23; 1983.56;
1987.103; 1988.28, 52
Criticism, guides to, 1979.56;
1980.59; 1984.60; 1985.70;
1987.22; 1988.29
Criticism, obtaining from Canada,
1984.56
"Crow Song," 1976.62

d'Alpuget, Blanche, *Turtle Beach*,
1987.147, 156
Daly, Mary, 1987.59
"Dancing Girls," 1981.49.

Dancing Girls, 1977 Canadian
collection. *See also
Dancing Girls*, 1982
-Canadian criticism, 1980.47;
1981.49, 95
--comparative, 1986.62
--iconic stories, 1984.18,
1986.62
--mass culture and sacred
depths, 1980.13
-Canadian reviews, 1977.2, 6, 9,
18, 20, 23, 31, 32, 60, 63,
65, 67, 70, 71, 73; 1978.6,
27, 49, 64, 66-68, 88, 92;
1980.148
--Canadian WASPs, 1977.31;
1978.64
--comedy and slapstick tragedy,
1977.32, 65
--*doppelgängers*, 1978.67
--lacks love and cheer, 1977.23;
1978.64
-United States criticism,
1984.81; 1988.8
-United States reviews,
1978.15; 1987.73
Dancing Girls, 1982 United States
and British collection.
See also Dancing Girls,
1977
-Australian review, 1983.25
-British reviews, 1982.35, 65,
68, 147, 157; 1983.15, 38,
86, 89; 1984.15, 83
--Laingian sanity and madness,
1982.65
-Canadian review, *en français*,
of *Les danseuses*, 1986.75
-French criticism, 1985.100
-German reviews, of *Unter
Glas*, 1986.61, 264
-India, review from, 1984.35

Double Persephone
  -Canadian criticism, 1980.47;
    1984.18
  --Demeter, Gorgon, 1977.12;
    1978.20; 1983.29; 1987.45
  --form, style, 1977.12, 83
  --influenced by Jay
    Macpherson, 1981.28;
    1984.60; 1985.70
  -Canadian interviews, 1977.80,
    87
  -Canadian reviews, 1962.1-3
  -French criticism, 1976.76
  -Italian criticism, 1978.17
  -United States criticism,
    1984.81; 1986.116;
    1988.15, 53
  --death and creativity, 1988.51
Doubles, 1978.67; 1982.34;
    1986.50, 238; 1987.22;
    1988.12. *See also* 1975.17;
    Lady Oracle
"Double Voice, The," 1983.109;
    1988.53
Doyle, Arthur Conan, *The Lost
    World*, 1984.77
Drabble, Margaret, *Jerusalem the
    Golden*, 1984.45
  -*Realms of Gold, The*, 1983.63
"Dream: Bluejay or
    Archeopteryx," 1977.42
"Dream 1: The Bush Garden,"
    1987.142
"Dream 3: Night Bear Which
    Frightened Cattle,"
    1987.142
"Dream 2: Brian the Still-Hunter,"
    1979.50; 1987.142;
    1988.53
"Dreams of the Animals," 1988.53
Dualities, dichotomies, double
    vision, 1977.12, 51-52;
    1980.47; 1983.54, 84;

1984.18, 81; 1986.116;
    1988.34. *See also* Doubles
Duncan, Sara Jeannette, *Cousin
    Cinderella*, 1980.82
  -*The Imperialist*, 1979.86
"Dwarf, The," 1977.55

Early work, 1980.47; 1984.60, 81;
    1985.70; 1987.45. *See also
    Double Persephone*; "Up
    in the Air So Blue"
"Eating Fire," 1975.50
Écriture feminine. See Feminist
    literary criticism
Edible Woman, The
  -Australian criticism, 1978.12
  -bibliography, annotated in,
    1976.24
  -British criticism, heroism,
    myth, responsibility,
    1979.15; 1981.81;
    1987.129
  -British interview, 1970.14
  -British reviews, 1969.8, 11, 13;
    1980.24, 61. *See also*
    1986.95
  --consumer society, 1969.13
  -Canadian criticism, *en
    français*, 1970.24; 1976.52;
    1980.73
  -Canadian criticism, in English,
    1975.33; 1984.27; 1987.22
  --anorexia nervosa,
    cannibalism, 1975.52;
    1980.148; 1985.13
  --characterization, 1974.4;
    1980.93; 1982.126;
    1983.104; 1984.75
  --children's story and fairy tale
    elements, 1973.19;
    1977.61; 1978.58
  --comedy, anti-comedy,
    1973.19; 1974.33; 1977.55,

84; 1980.29, 47; 1981.64,
69; 1983.30; 1984.18
--comparative, 1978.44; 1983.66
--consumer society, 1974.34;
1975.3; 1978.51; 1983.79
--descent, structure, 1981.69;
1983.66, 82
--doubles, Duncan, 1973.19;
1982.34; 1983.82
--introduction to paperback
edition, 1973.19
--introductory, brief, 1973.17;
1974.4, 21; 1977.101;
1978.36; 1981.76; 1985.69;
1986.117; 1987.64, 94, 111
--ranked highly, 1975.52;
1980.148; 1986.95
--self and normalcy, 1977.78;
1978.53, 60; 1979.28;
1986.238
--self, woman's, and feminine
identity, 1974.38; 1975.2-
4; 1977.92; 1978.44, 58;
1980.82
-Canadian interviews, in
English, 1975.17, 29;
1977.80
--anorexia nervosa, 1983.46
--anti-comedy, 1973.27; 1977.87
-Canadian reviews, in English,
1969.1-2, 9, 16-17;
1970.12, 23, 25, 29-30, 34,
36-47; 1973.7
--anorexia nervosa and camera
terror, 1969.9
--Canadian elements, 1969.9;
1973.7
--emotional cannibalism, social
novelist, 1969.16-17
--women's issues, 1970.12, 25
-dissertations, Canadian,
1977.66; 1985.29
-Finnish review, 1980.78

-French criticism, 1974.44;
1980.112
-German criticism, 1984.31
-German reviews, of *Die
essbare Frau*, 1985.91-92,
103
-India, criticism from, 1972.40
-Italian criticism, 1978.17, 31;
1981.18
--mention of *La donna da
mangiare*, 1977.95
-screenplays, by Atwood,
1970.20; 1972.22; 1982.72
-United States criticism,
1984.81; 1986.116;
1988.31, 37, 56
--anorexia, body/boundary
issues, 1981.16; 1987.124,
134
--fairy tales, myth, 1981.81;
1987.160
--introductory, brief, 1978.22;
1981.57; 1986.28, 173;
1987.106
--language, perception,
metaphors, 1979.34;
1980.49; 1987.171; 1988.7
--self in consumer society,
1973.72; 1982.130;
1987.49; 1988.39
--self, responsibility, 1975.19;
1986.189; 1987.129
--structure, deconstructions,
1987.49; 1988.7
-United States interviews and
statements, 1973.46;
1978.70
-United States reviews, 1970.1-
2, 5, 11, 25, 32-33, 35;
1971.16; 1972.24; 1976.48
--truth-telling dementia, 1970.5
--women's issues, 1970.5, 25

Frank, Anne, 1986.63
Fraser, Sylvia, 1977.36
French, Marilyn, *The Bleeding
  Heart*, 1983.63
-*The Women's Room*, 1980.39
Friedan, Betty, 1975.47
Frye, Northrop, 1972.26; 1974.22,
    44; 1975.43; 1976.17, 61,
    96; 1977.35; 1978.17, 25,
    94; 1983.31; 1984.39, 91;
    1986.50, 215-16; 1987.122;
    1988.12
-*Anatomy of Criticism, The*,
    1979.25
-archetypes, archetypal
    criticism. 1983.8, 132-33
-*Bush Garden, The*, 1978.93;
    1986.208
--culture/nature, 1973.63
--fictional modes, 1973.66
--garrison mentality, 1973.11,
    80; 1975.42; 1976.49, 86;
    1977.66, 90; 1981.27;
    1983.8; 1984.81; 1986.208;
    1988.49
--influence on Atwood, 1978.17
--quest, romance pattern,
    structure, 1975.43;
    1977.88; 1981.64, 69;
    1986.62; 1987.13, 22
--thematic criticism, 1973.17;
    1983.131
--where is here?, 1972.30;
    1986.119; 1988.24, 35
Fuentes, Carlos, 1982.152

Gallant, Mavis, *Home Truths*,
    1982.44; 1986.66
"Game After Supper," 1970.3, 10
Games, 1973.52; 1979.24; 1985.94;
    1986.230
-circle game, 1968.6; 1974.38;
    1977.90; 1983.12; 1988.49

Gearhart, Sally Miller, *The
    Wanderground*, 1987.26
Geddes, Gary, *15 Canadian Poets
    plus 5*, 1980.144
Gerrard, Bart. *See* Atwood,
    Margaret
Gibson, Graeme, 1975.8, 29, 47;
    1981.81, 106; 1987.32
-*Five Legs*, 1970.29 Giguere,
    Diane, 1982.10
Gilbert, Matthew, 1986.135
Gilbert, Sandra M., *The
    Madwoman in the Attic*,
    1987.138
Gilman, Charlotte Perkins,
    Herland, 1986.192
"Gingerbread Man, The," 1978.58;
    1988.31
"Giving Birth," 1979.61; 1980.13,
    47; 1981.49; 1983.177;
    1985.119; 1986.151;
    1987.22, 73; 1988.8
Glassco, John, 1973.103; 1977.69
-*Fetish Girl*, 1983.135
Godfrey, Dave, 1973.32; 1988.22
-*Read Canadian*, 1973.92
Goldmann, Lucien, 1979.18
Goldsmith, Oliver, of Halifax,
    "The Rising Village,"
    1983.72
Goluska, Glenn, 1984.59
Gothic, 1971.17; 1972.25; 1974.25,
    31; 1977.51-52; 1978.19,
    31; 1980.25, 62; 1981.66;
    1983.26, 84; 1986.152;
    1987.62; 1988.34, 47. *See
    also* 1977.80, 87; 1978.71;
    Interviews; *Lady Oracle*
"Gothic Letter on a Hot Night,"
    1976.19; 1977.51, 52;
    1988.34
Gotlieb, Phyllis, *Tesseracts2* [sic],
    1987.24

Grace, Sherrill E., 1987.165
"Grace Marks," 1980.45
  -Margaret Atwood: Language,
    Text, and System, 1983.40,
    146
Grant, George, 1972.26; 1984.57;
  1986.164, 165
"Grave of the Famous Poet, The,"
  1974.32; 1981.95
Graves, Robert, "To Juan at the
  Winter Solstice," 1982.46
  -White Goddess, The 1976.96;
    1980.47; 1987.45, 138;
    1988.46
Gray, Francine du Plessix, *Lovers*
  and Tyrants, 1979.13
Great Mother, Great Goddess,
  1982.143; 1987.45;
  1988.51, 54. *See also*
  Demeter; Graves, Robert
Greenwald, Barry, *Pitchmen,*
  1985.5
Greven, Helèn, *Formes du roman*
  utopique en Grand-
  Bretagne (1918/1970),
  1986.141
Grey Owl. See Belaney, Archibald
  Stansfeld
Grimm Brothers, *Fairy Tales,*
  1977.80; 1987.89, 104
  -"Fitcher's Bird," 1984.32;
    1986.263; 1987.119;
    1988.2, 55
  -"Little Red-Cap," 1978.58;
    1986.263; 1988.31
  -"Robber Bridegroom, The,"
    1986.263
  -"Snow White," 1987.129
Grove, Frederick Philip, 1978.36
  -"Snow", 1974.27
Gubar, Susan, *The Madwoman in*
  the Attic, 1987.138

Gustafson, Ralph, *Fire on Stone,*
  1974.40
Gutteridge, Don, *Riel,* 1973.34

Haggerty, Jean, 1975.48
Haley, Albert, *Exotic,* 1982.94
"Hand," 1986.23
Handmaid's Tale, The
  -Australian reviews, dystopia,
    realism, 1987.69, 151
  -awards and honours
  --Canadian coverage, 1987.161
    -Booker Prize short list,
      1986.39, 191
    -Governor General's
      Award, 1986.5, 10, 19,
      111
    -Humanist of the Year,
      1987.96. See also 1987.2
    -Los Angeles Times Book
      Prize, 1986.191
    -Ms. Magazine Woman of
      the Year, 1987.161
  --British coverage.
    -Arthur C. Clarke Award,
      1987.145
    -Booker Prize short list,
      1986.36, 56. *See also*
      1987.74
  --United States coverage,
    1986.70
    -Humanist of the Year,
      1987.42. *See also*
      1986.149
    -Los Angeles Times Book
      Prize, 1986.147, 180
  -British criticism
  --editorial, 1986.14
  --introductory, brief, 1986.115;
    1987.60
  --Offred's courage, love,
    1987.62, 129
  --realism, pessimism, 1987.51

fox"; "Owl Song";
"Procedures for
Underground"; "Some
Objects of Wood and
Stone"; "Instructions for
the Third Eye," 1984.11,
36; 1988.13. *See also*
"Forehead Eye," 1973.38
Interlunar. See Snake Poems,
1984.59
-Canadian criticism, 1984.18;
1987.176
-Canadian reviews, 1984.2, 4-5,
17, 20, 41, 66, 68, 74, 88,
95-96; 1985.49-50, 64, 83,
93; 1986.33, 120
--absurdist, existential, 1984.68
--autobiographical, 1984.4
--Canadian gothic, 1984.41
--"Interlunar" poems, 1985.49-
50; 1986.33
--mortality, rebirth, 1984.41, 88;
1986.33
--myths, transcendence,
1985.49-50; 1986.33
--politics, woman and nature,
1986.120
--"Snake Poems," 1985.49-50
-United States criticism,
descents, "Snake Poems,"
1988.51
-United States review, 1988.4
"Interview with a Tourist," 1980.77
Interviews. *See* Specific titles
-Australian interviews, 1982.66,
119
-British interviews, 1982.80, 83;
1984.85
--food, 1987.109
--politics, feminism, writers,
1979.21, 33; 1984.75;
1987.153

-Canadian interviews, *en
français*
--art, children, poetry, 1975.47;
1987.133
--criticism of Atwood's work,
1987.43
--French and English Canada,
politics, feminism,
1975.20; 1976.46; 1987.43,
133, 158, 163
--French translations of
Atwood's work, 1983.7;
1987.43
-Canadian interviews,
Atwood's statements, in
English, 1975.13, 36;
1977.43; 1978.74; 1979.62;
1981.106; 1982.165;
1983.2; 1985.15; 1987.118
See also Canadian
profiles
--aesthetics, literary theory,
1972.20; 1976.91; 1977.80;
1986.103; 1987.56
--anorexia, eating, 1983.46;
1987.94
--biographic details, biography,
1970.20; 1974.47; 1975.29-
30; 1979.44; 1981.6
--Canadian literature,
mythology, 1973.27;
1986.103; 1987.56. *See
also The New Oxford
Book of Canadian Verse
in English*; *The Oxford
Book of Canadian Short
Stories in English*;
Survival
--censorship, 1979.16; 1986.18
--children's author, childhood
reading, 1986.207
--conditions of interviews,
1975.6-9, 22, 41

--creative methods, images,
metamorphosis, 1972.2;
1977.80; 1979.98;
1985.109; 1986.103-04;
1987.56. *See also* 1982.12
--criticism, reactions, reviews,
1975.8, 13, 17; 1976.91;
1977.87
-from Canada and United States,
1977.80; 1986.17, 253
-from women and men,
1973.46; 1976.91; 1988.25
-on women and women
writers, 1969.12; 1972.5;
1975.47; 1976.43, 93;
1982.106
-York University class
study, 1975.48; 1980.3
--ethics, 1973.27; 1981.43-44
--feminism. *See* Politics;
Women
--French translations of her
work, 1987.118
--genres, 1973.27; 1975.48;
1977.80, 87
--language, 1979.50; 1985.62;
1986.103; 1987.56, 84
--new mother, 1976.43, 58, 93-
94
--poetry, influences on her
poetry, 1972.20; 1976.91;
1977.80, 87; 1980.142
--poetry-reading tours, 1983.42
--politics, feminism, 1975.18,
29-30; 1977.49, 80;
1980.39; 1981.43-44;
1985.62, 76; 1987.5, 67,
84, 177. *See also* Amnesty
International
--religion, Bible, Christ,
1975.18; 1981.43-44;
1982.2, 62; 1985.118;
1987.159

--screenplays by Atwood, films
of her works, 1970.20;
1972.22; 1974.9; 1979.52,
68; 1982.72. *See also*
1987.40; Screenplays
under United States
interviews
--success, 1973.27; 1975.47;
1985.62; 1987.84
--women and men writers,
1972.20; 1975.47;
1986.103; 1987.56. *See
also* criticism
-Canadian profiles
--celebrity-writer, 1972.22;
1975.8; 1976.58; 1981.97;
1986.55
--film profile, 1985.5, 78
--mother, 1976.58, 94; 1977.41;
1978.97; 1979.16
--nationalist, 1972.3; 1973.93
--revue organizer, 1977.25
--self-profile, 1982.70
--writer, 1970.20; 1975.29-30;
1979.68; 1981.91
-Danish interviews, 1979.80;
1984.63
-Finnish interview, literary
prizes, 1986.9
-French interview, in English,
Canadian literature,
feminism, women's
writing, and critics,
1978.77
-German interview, 1979.88
-Italian interview, Americans,
Canadians, and literature
as Goliath, David, and
slingshot, 1977.30
-Norwegian interview, 1979.48
-United States interviews,
Atwood's statements.
1975.37; 1978.89;

1982.146; 1983.9; 1985.74;
84, 97. *See also* United
States profiles
--advice to young writers, early
writing and publishing,
1978.87; 1983.37;
1985.109
--biographical, 1978.35;
1984.77; 1987.89
--Canadian, Caribbean, and
United States politics and
writing, 1976.38; 1983.70;
1984.11; 1985.109;
1986.21; 1988.13-14. *See
also* Politics
--Canadian images of Atwood,
1977.44
--Canadian nationalism,
1978.70-71
--creative habits, imagery,
edges and center,
1978.70; 1982.6; 1986.219;
1987.65
--fiction and poetry, 1985.109;
1986.172
--novels, 1983.70; 1987.29, 65
--poetry, as lens, Canadian
elements, reviews,
1978.71; 1979.50;
1983.126; 1987.65
--politics, feminism,
pornography, 1981.39;
1985.72. *See also*
Amnesty International
--readings of other authors,
1978.70-71; 1979.50;
1984.11; 1987.104;
1988.13
--screenplays of Atwood's
works, 1980.19, 80;
1987.72, 89, 125. *See also*
Screenplays under

Canadian interviews, in
English
--success, overseas sales,
translations, 1983.127;
1985.86
-United States profiles, poetry,
novels, screenplays,
1979.50; 1980.80
Introduction to Catherine M.
Young's *To See Our
World*, 1980.16, 100
Introduction to Susanna Moodie's
Roughing It in the Bush,
1986.80
Irgang, Margrit, *Min*, 1985.46
Irigaray, Luce, 1983.53; 1988.7
Ishiguro, Kazuo, *An Artist of the
Floating World*, 1986.36,
39, 56, 191
"Is/Not," 1975.43

"Jack the Knife," 1977.25
Jacobsen, Josephine, *Adios, Mr.
Moxley*, 1986.54
Jacobus, Mary, 1983.63
James, Henry, 1973.27; 1977.80;
1980.149
-*The Ambassadors*, 1987.112
Jameson, Anna Brownell, 1977.22;
1978.98; 1984.77; 1987.88;
1988.17
Jaynes, Julian, *The Origin of
Consciousness in the
Breakdown of the
Bicameral Mind*, 1979.85;
1983.142; 1984.81;
1986.50; 1988.12, 30
Jeremiah, 1987.145
Johnson, Judith. *See* Sherwin,
Judith Johnson
Johnson, Pamela Hansford, *The
Holiday Friend*, 1973.16

--self, individuation, 1980.31; 1987.142

--wendigo, shamanic elements, 1982.107; 1988.51

--woman and nature, 1982.107; 1984.33

-United States reviews, 1970.18; 1971.1, 3; 1972.12; 1974.42; 1988.40, 47

Journals of Susanna Moodie, The, 19[80] Charles Pachter, artist's book, 1980.40; 1984.64; 1986.102

"Journey to the Interior," 1975.24; 1978.57; 1980.49; 1983.83

Jung, Carl G., 1976.4, 88; 1981.82-83; 1984.57

Kaczender, George, 1970.20; 1972.22

Kamp, Anna, 1985.102

Kanada, 1987.6

Kannosto, Matti, 1986.163

Kaplan, Johanna, 1980.50

Keats, John, "La Belle Dame sans Merci," 1985.99

Keillor, Garrison, 1986.258

Kernberg, Otto, 1982.176

Kesten, Steven, 1974.9

Kidder, Margot, 1979.52

King, Mackenzie, 1976.94

Kizer, Carolyn, 1973.96

Klein, A.M., 1972.20

Kriesel, Henry, 1975.31

Kristeva, Julia, 1987.162

Kroetsch, Robert, 1978.36; 1985.21

-*Badlands*, 1984.94

-*What the Crow Said*, 1984.39

"Kultchur Komix," 1976.58, 101; 1978.70

Lacan, Jacques, 1986.109

Lady Oracle

-Australian review, 1982.50

-Austrian review, of *Lady Orakel*, 1984.54. *See also* German reviews; Swiss reviews

-awarded 1976 City of Toronto Book Award, 1977.1

-British criticism

--artist, 1987.129

--comic gothic, 1983.137

--Demeter and female heroic myth, 1979.15; 1981.81

-British reviews, 1977.15, 39, 56-57, 100; 1982.14, 154

--fake drowning, precedent for, 1977.57

--picaresque, 1982.14

-Canadian commentary, on reviews and sales, 1977.1

-on satire, *roman à clef*, 1976.29-30; 1977.4

-Canadian criticism, 1979.69; 1980.27; 1981.10; 1983.135; 1984.27; 1987.22

--artist, art and love, 1978.21; 1980.114; 1986.122; 1987.138

--comparative, 1983.53; 1986.267

--fairy tales, parables, 1980.47; 1986.96, 122

--genres

-comedy, 1980.29; 1981.94; 1983.30; 1984.18

-gothic, 1978.19; 1980.47, 81; 1983.26, 137; 1987.12

-humourist, 1978.5

-picaresque, 1982.57

-romance, 1980.114; 1981.64

709

--camera images, specular
metaphors, 1987.171;
1988.7
--comparative, 1977.13;
1979.13; 1988.32
--fairy tales, magic, 1984.32;
1987.160
--fake drowning, precedent for,
1976.63
--genres
-*bildungsroman,
Kunstlerroman,* 1979.13;
1987.91
-comedy, satire, 1977.13;
1980.25
-gothic, 1976.63; 1980.25;
1981.86; 1988.32, 43. *See
also* 1978.70
-orphan tradition, 1976.63
--introductory, brief, 1978.22;
1980.63; 1981.16, 57;
1986.116
--mother/daughter
relationship, 1978.46;
1979.95; 1982.176;
1984.81; 1985.99; 1987.48,
134, 160
-Demeter-Persephone-
Kore myth, 1979.15
--popular culture, social
mythology, 1980.25;
1981.86; 1986.173;
1988.43
--self, 1982.176; 1986.189;
1987.91, 124
-United States interviews,
1977.44; 1978.70; 1980.19;
1987.29
-United States reviews, 1976.3,
5, 9, 11, 15, 22, 39-40, 42,
51, 55, 60, 66-67, 75, 77,
79-82, 84, 87, 92, 95, 100,
102-03, 105; 1977.5, 46,

62, 68, 72, 89, 96; 1978.15,
73
--artists, 1978.15
--bulimia, 1976.95
--feminine, feminism, 1976.15,
55, 75
--gothic comedy, gothic
romance, 1976.92;
1977.46
--parody of *Surfacing,* 1977.46
Lahr, John, *The Autograph
Hound,* 1973.49-50
Laing, R.D., 1973.66, 101; 1974.33;
1975.45; 1982.65; 1988.37
-*The Divided Self,* 1975.24;
1978.57; 1983.83
-*The Politics of Experience,*
1983.84
Lalonde, Michèle, *Fiancée,
Geôles,* "La mère patrie,"
1979.73; 1983.94
"Landcrab I," 1984.30, 1985.38
Lane, Patrick, 1980.144; 1981.1
-*Old Mother,* 1982.63
-*Poems New & Selected,*
1978.12
Language, 1975.43; 1976.7;
1977.94; 1982.126;
1983.142; 1984.69;
1987.165
--and colonized, 1974.18;
1975.16; 1983.78
--and women, 1975.16; 1976.37;
1979.59; 1985.108;
1986.29; 1987.162. *See
also* 1979.50
Lasch, Christopher, 1982.176
"Last Day," 1987.165
"Late August," 1974.35; 1975.27,
43; 1978.59
Latweed, Shakesbeat. *See*
Atwood, Margaret

92, 95, 97, 102, 104-05,
109-11, 113, 116-17, 120,
129, 132-33, 136-38, 140,
143, 145-46; 1981.11, 65,
88; 1983.4
--dreams, images, 1980.138;
1981.65
--ethics, 1980.41, 140, 146
--promotion, reviews, 1979.6;
1981.88
--*Survival* themes, 1980.92
--tragicomedy, 1980.75-76
Livesay, Dorothy, *The Self-
Completing Tree*, 1986.6
"Lives of the Poets," 1982.87;
1986.151
"Looking in a Mirror," 1977.8
"LouLou; or the Domestic Life of
the Language," 1987.110
Love. *See* Affirmations; Poetry;
specific titles, especially
Power Politics; *You Are
Happy*
-affirmed as realistic, 1971.2;
1975.33; 1979.24; 1981.86;
1982.110; 1984.60;
1985.70; 1986.33, 85;
1988.4, 6, 33, 43
-critiqued as insufficient,
1967.3; 1969.5; 1970.36;
1971.14; 1974.38; 1977.12,
75; 1988.15, 23, 40
-debated, 1970.38; 1973.46;
1977.14, 55; 1984.81;
1988.25
-inversions and transformations
of love, 1973.52; 1974.33;
1977.45; 1988.27, 37
-overview of debate, 1988.29
Lowther, Pat, "A Stone Diary,"
1987.122
Lukács, György, 1978.16, 17, 22,
24

McAulay, Sara, *Choice*, 1982.81
McCarthy, Mary, 1986.24-25, 31,
148
McClure, Michael, 1974.33;
1988.37
-"Revolt," 1973.66
McDonald, Ross, 1978.10
MacEwen, Gwendolyn, 1976.35;
1981.111
-*The Drunken Clock*, 1962.1, 3
McKinney, Jim, 1977.49
MacLennan, Hugh, 1978.36;
1984.57
-*Each Man's Son*, 1985.14
-*Return of the Sphinx*, 1974.27
MacLuhan, Marshall, 1974.33;
1988.37
McNeil, Florence, 1977.86
Macpherson, Jay, 1962.1; 1972.20;
1980.47; 1982.46; 1984.60;
1985.70
-*Boatman, The*, 1981.28
"Mad Mother," 1987.45
Maeterlinck, Maurice,
Ariane et Barbe Bleue,
1984.32
Magic, 1983.84; 1987.60. *See* Fairy
tales; Shamanism
Mahon, Derek, 1983.34
Mailer, Norman, 1986.55, 124;
1987.161
Malouf, David, *An Imaginary Life*,
1986.125
"Man from Mars, The," 1978.70;
1982.168
Mandel, Eli, 1980.81
Mansfield, Katherine, "Bliss,"
1987.31
-"The Garden Party," 1970.25
Margaret Atwood Society. *See*
Atwood Society
Newsletter

-British reviews, 1987.28, 152, 154

--Canadian and *Survival* elements, 1987.28

-Canadian reviews, 1986.3, 82, 155, 236; 1987.50, 75, 85, 169

--criteria questioned, 1986.236; 1987.50, 169

-United States review, 1987.144

"Owl Song," 1977.22; 1988.17

Ozick, Cynthia, *Bloodshed and Three Novellas*, 1976.105

Pacey, Desmond, 1974.22

Pachter, Charles, 1968.5; 1980.40; 1981.97; 1982.2

-*Circle Game, The*, 1966.1; 1977.76; 1986.84

-*Journals of Susanna Moodie, The*, 1980.40; 1984.64; 1986.102

-*Speeches for Doctor Frankenstein*, 1967.4; 1974.14; 1986.84

Page, P.K., 1972.20; 1974.17

-*The Sun and the Moon*, 1987.22

Paley, Grace, *The Little Disturbances of Man*, 1980.61

Pannell, Raymond, 1977.64

"Paper Bag, A," 1987.15

Parrinder, Patrick, 1986.115

Patterson, Nancy-Lou, *Sugar Bush*, 1970.22

Pearson, Peter, 1981.97

-*Heaven on Earth*, 1987.11, 58

-*Snowbird*, 1980.96

Peck, John, *The Broken Blockhouse Wall*, 1979.45

P.E.N., 1986.5, 18

-women writers' protest, 1986.55, 124; 1987.159, 161

-Writers in Prison Programme benefit. *See CanLit Foodbook*

Perrault, Charles, "Barbe Bleue," 1984.32; 1987.119

Persephone. *See* Demeter-Persephone-Kore myth; *Double Persephone*

Pfetsch, Helga, 1986.264

Photographs. *See* Camera images

Piercy, Marge, 1980.67; 1986.18

-*Braided Lives*, 1982.81

-*Moon Is Always Female, The*, 1980.123

-*To Be of Use*, 1973.69

-*Vida*, 1980.123

Pinter, Harold, 1987.40, 72, 89, 125

Pirandello, Luigi

-*It Is So, If You Think So*, 1978.5

-*On Humour*, 1978.5

Plath, Sylvia, 1970.13; 1972.20; 1975.46-47; 1976.37; 1984.60; 1985.50, 70

-*Bell Jar, The*, 1973.20, 28; 1975.45

-"Lady Lazarus," 1976.63; 1985.99

-"Tulips," 1986.139

Poe, Edgar Allen, 1972.10

Poetic development. *See Second Words*; *Selected Poems*; *Selected Poems II*

Poetry. *See* specific titles

Poetry, multiple Atwood books

-British criticism, 1975.46; 1982.114; 1983.132; 1985.59

"Polarities," 1974.33; 1978.6;
1979.61; 1981.49, 95;
1984.31; 1987.15; 1988.37
Politics and feminism. *See Second Words*
Polk, James, 1981.106
Popular and mass culture,
1974.14; 1977.11; 1978.19;
1980.13, 25; 1983.26;
1985.43, 111; 1986.173;
1987.171; 1988.8. *See also The Edible Woman*
Porter, Katherine Anne, 1984.51
Postcolonial, colonial, and
commonwealth themes,
1975.25
-*Bodily Harm*, 1982.31;
1987.147, 156
-in Commonwealth curriculum,
1980.88, 122
-interviews, 1976.38; 1983.70
-*Surfacing*, 1974.18; 1975.16;
1978.32; 1980.122; 1984.9,
26; 1985.21; 1986.125. *See also* 1981.7
Postmodern, modernist, 1983.77;
1986.262; 1987.71, 165;
1988.21
Potter, Beatrix, 1972.2
Power Politics
-Atwood's cover design,
1973.52; 1981.66;
1986.152; 1988.55
-border ballads allusions,
1974.28
-British criticism, 1975.46;
1982.114
-Canadian criticism, 1973.99;
1975.52; 1977.22;
1980.148; 1983.12;
1984.18, 60; 1985.70

--gothic, *Frankenstein*
elements, 1974.32;
1981.66
--love, sexual politics, fertility,
1972.38; 1974.32-33, 38;
1975.33; 1977.55; 1981.9,
52
--modular style, 1977.83
--negative persona, 1973.17;
1977.12; 1978.20; 1983.29
--social mythology, 1974.32-33
-Canadian reviews, 1971.2, 4, 6,
8-9, 11-12, 19-21; 1972.6-
7, 18
--characters, love as struggle,
1971.2; 1972.6, 18
--surreal, 1972.7
-India, criticism from, 1972.40;
1983.96
--survival poetic and ethic,
1972.40
-interviews, Atwood's
statements, 1973.96;
1975.29; 1976.63; 1977.80
--on women's and men's
reactions, 1973.46;
1976.91; 1988.25
-United States criticism,
1973.96; 1974.17, 24;
1981.28, 53; 1982.13;
1984.81; 1986.12, 116,
152; 1988.15, 17, 37, 56
--comparative, 1984.73
--feminist, demythicizing,
gender struggles, 1973.72,
96; 1976.62; 1979.59;
1980.77; 1982.130;
1984.73; 1988.39
--*Frankenstein* elements,
1974.14
--love, games, personae,
1973.52

720

Robertson, Pat, 1986.24-25, 31,
179; 1987.2
Rogers, Linda, 1987.65
Rohmer, Richard, *Balls!*, 1980.101
Rooke, Leon, 1983.25
Rosenblatt, Joe, 1968.4; 1969.7
Ross, Alexander, 1975.9
Ross, Sinclair, 1975.42
Roszak, Theodore, 1974.33;
1988.37
-*Sources*, 1973.66 Roth, Philip,
Portnoy's Complaint,
1976.11
Roy, Gabrielle, 1975.31; 1984.33
-*Bonheur d'occasion*, 1978.72
-*Cashier, The*, 1977.29
Rubbo, Michael, *Margaret
Atwood: Once in August*,
1985.5, 78
Rukeyser, Muriel, "Ajanta,"
1977.42
Russ, Joanna, 1987.49, 151
Ryga, George, 1978.36

Sade Comte Donatien Alphonse
François de, [Marquis de
Sade], *Justine*, 1986.206
"Salt Garden, The," 1987.52
Salutin, Rick, 1983.54
Sarton, Mary, *The Magnificent
Spinster*, 1986.225
"Scarlet Ibis," 1986.62; 1987.22
Schafly, Phyllis, *The Power of the
Positive Woman*, 1986.71
Schell, Jonathan, *The Fate of the
Earth*, 1982.106
Schlesinger, John, *Marathon Man*,
1976.53
Schwaiger, [Brigitte], 1981.107
Schwaiger, Brigitte, *Marie-toi, ma
fille*, 1978.14

Science fiction, 1970.14; 1974.14;
1986.188, 259; 1987.136,
145; 1987.24; 1988.40
Scott, F.R., "Lakeshore," 1981.28
Screenplays by Atwood, films of
Atwood's works, 1970.20;
1972.22; 1974.9; 1979.52,
68; 1980.19; 1982.72;
1987.40, 72
Sears, Dennis Patrick, 1978.36
Second Words. *See* 1981.11
-Australian review, 1984.67
-British criticism, feminism,
humanism, politics,
1987.129
-Canadian reviews, *en français*,
1983.122, 139
-Canadian reviews, in English,
1982.3, 12, 25, 54, 64, 89,
108, 117, 148; 1983.11, 17,
40, 48, 62, 73, 75, 88, 99,
101, 116, 125, 136;
1985.37, 56
--Atwood as critic, *Survival*,
1982.12; 1983.73
--self-made feminism, 1983.88
-French review, in English,
1985.24
-United States criticism
--feminism, politics, 1984.81;
1987.129; 1988.46
--in women's studies
bibliography, 1987.87
--*Survival* elements, 1988.46
-United States interview,
1983.114. *See also*
1982.12
-United States reviews,
1983.100, 111-12; 1984.22,
24, 49, 52, 55, 65, 80, 82,
87, 92-93, 100; 1985.57;
1988.1

--distance versus concern, 1984.65

See, Carolyn, *Golden Days*, 1987.135

Selected Poems
  -Canadian criticism, 1979.89; 1981.104; 1982.177
  -Canadian interview, 1977.87
  -Canadian review, *en français*, 1976.41
  -Canadian reviews, in English, 1976.6, 8, [14], 16, 25, 28, 32, 35, 45, 56, 71, 90, 97, 106; 1977.10, 16, 38, 75, 88
  --craft, 1976.35
  --for Canadian students, 1976.32
  --mythopoeic, quest-romance, 1976.106; 1977.88
  --personae, 1977.75
  --woman and nature, 1976.90
  -United States criticism, 1979.103
  --Homeric model, gender politics, 1988.9
  -United States interview, 1978.96
  -United States reviews, 1978.9, 26, 34, 42, 47-48, 54, 83, 101-02; 1979.60, 72
  --wilderness, madness, civilization, 1978.26, 101

Selected Poems II, 1976-1986
  -Canadian reviews, 1986.6, 222, 241; 1987.57, 157, 170
  --affirmations, negations, 1986.241; 1987.57, 157, 170
  -United States reviews, 1987.3, 126
  --didactic fabulism, 1987.126

Self, identity, 1973.72; 1977.22, 78; 1978.60; 1982.130; 1987.22, 134; 1988.17, 28, 39
  -characters, personae, 1977.12; 1980.93; 1984.18, 81; 1986.237; 1987.129; 1988.15
  -concept of self, 1980.47
  -unreliable narrator, 1972.13; 1980.47
  -victim-thesis characters, 1974.4; 1983.104; 1984.76

Service, Robert, "The Cremation of Sam McGee," 1970.9

Seton, Ernest Thompson, 1974.27; 1978.94

Sexton, Anne, 1975.47
  -"Jesus Papers, The," 1984.73

Sexual politics, 1972.38; 1974.32-33; 1975.19; 1979.59; 1984.18; 1986.12, 263; 1988.37, 55. *See also* Gothic; "Circe/Mud Poems,"; *Power Politics*

Shakespeare, William, 1987.45
  -*Midsummer Night's Dream, A*, 1987.13
  -*Tempest, The*, 1986.125; 1987.13

Shamanism, 1976.98; 1977.90; 1978.85; 1980.115; 1983.58; 1988.49, 51. *See also* "Procedures for Underground"

Shearer, Moira, in *The Red Shoes*, 1987.129

Shelley, Mary, 1979.49
  -*Frankenstein*, 1974.14; 1977.80; 1981.66; 1986.152; 1988.55. *See also Speeches for Doctor Frankenstein* (1966);

1983.23; 1984.9; 1985.75,
117; 1986.125
--mass culture, modernity,
technology, 1980.13;
1985.22, 43; 1986.164-65
--modern, postmodern,
poststructuralist, 1978.24;
1983.77; 1984.9
--nature, earth, land, 1974.33;
1975.24; 1976.98; 1977.40,
90; 1978.55; 1983.142;
1985.14, 75; 1986.175;
1987.150
--Quebec and French Canadian
elements, 1975.31;
1976.36; 1986.96
--self, 1975.24; 1977.59, 78;
1979.51; 1978.57, 60;
1980.47, 93; 1983.83;
1986.134, 238
--theological perspectives,
1981.55; 1985.55
-Canadian interviews, in
English, on *Surfacing*'s
ghost story, fake
marriage, narrator,
religious elements, and
being censored, 1973.27;
1975.29, 48; 1977.80, 87;
1979.16; 1982.62;
1985.105
-Canadian reviews, *en français*,
of *Faire surface*, 1978.30,
72; 1980.73
-Canadian reviews, in English,
1972.8-11, 13, 17, 19, 23,
27-28, 30, 32-33, 36, 41;
1973.3, 5-6, 15, 18, 30, 33,
38, 47, 54, 57, 59, 81, 90;
1974.7, 13, 18, 26;
1975.28; 1983.78

--archetypal quest, female
Odysseus, 1972.27-28;
1973.47
--breakthrough, sanity, 1973.47;
1974.18; 1983.78
--Canadian nationalism,
demythologizing, 1972.19,
30; 1974.18; 1983.78
--original title, "Forehead Eye,"
1973.38
--*Survival* intrusions, 1972.8;
1973.38
--unreliable narrator, boring
WASPs, female pain,
1972.13; 1973.30, 54
--woman-led, French-Canadian
northern quest, 1974.26;
1983.93
-Danish interview, 1984.63
-dissertations, Canadian, in
English, 1977.66; 1984.7,
29, 39; 1985.29
-dissertations, United States,
1978.79; 1980.32; 1981.3;
1983.59; 1987.112
-East German criticism, in
English, of *Surfacing*,
feminism, 1987.80
-East German review, of
Strömung, 1981.77
-Finnish review, of *Up till ytan*,
1980.78, 89
-French criticism, *en français*,
1974.44; 1975.11
-French criticism, in English,
1975.16; 1977.29, 74;
1985.21. *See also*
1985.105
--colonizing, decolonizing,
minority literature,
1975.11, 16; 1985.21
--comparative, 1975.11;
1977.29; 1985.21

--Northern or Canadian quest, 1977.29, 74; 1985.21

-French reviews, *en français*, of *Faire surface*, 1978.3, 14

-French reviews, in English, of *Surfacing*, 1973.50

-German criticism, in English, 1987.15

--comparative, 1985.46

--earth mysticism, 1987.88

-German criticism, in German, ecological themes, 1984.31

-German interviews, on *Der lange Traum*, 1978.81-82

-German reviews, of *Der lange Traum*, 1979.31, 40, 87

-India, criticism from, 1983.123

--comparative, 1987.143

--sexual colonialism, 1978.32

-Italian criticism, 1978.31; 1981.13

-Norwegian review, of *Gjenkjennelsen*, 1979.97

-screenplay, film, 1974.9; 1979.52; 1982.72

-Swedish criticism, in English, postcolonial identity, 1984.86

-Swedish reviews, in Swedish, of *Up till ytan*, 1979.10; 1980.53

-United States criticism, 1986.116, 173; 1988.11, 34, 37, 49, 56

--abortion, maternity, Callisto, Grieving Mother, hierogamy, 1974.41; 1976.2, 44, 74, 88; 1979.54; 1980.125; 1985.119; 1988.54

--artist, 1975.10; 1986.151; 1987.129

--Canadian versus American, 1976.2; 1979.14; 1986.215-16

--comparative, 1975.10; 1976.4; 1978.1, 40-41; 1983.63; 1985.47; 1987.13, 172; 1985.54. *See also* 1978.70

--daughter/mother, 1978.46; 1979.95; 1987.48

--deconstruction, double-voiced discourse, 1987.172; 1988.19

--Demeter-Persephone-Kore myth, 1976.83; 1988.19

--fairy tale, gothic, *doppelgängers,* alchemy, 1978.80, 82; 1986.216; 1987.160; 1988.2

--images and themes, 1987.171, 173

--introductory, brief, 1976.68; 1977.42, 97; 1978.22; 1979.49; 1980.35; 1981.53, 57; 1983.20; 1986.2; 1987.9

--language, 1978.1; 1980.49; 1981.30; 1983.22; 1987.101

--nature, 1976.88; 1982.143, 1986.215-16

  -woman and nature, 1976.13, 74; 1977.28; 1980.17; 1982.107; 1987.47, 60; 1988.20

--on promotion, publication, reviews, 1976.2; 1981.46; 1984.11; 1988.13

--primitivism, participatory consciousness, 1978.40-41; 1987.70

--quest

  -archetypal, heroic journey, 1976.88; 1977.28;

--Canadian survival and victim
themes debated, upheld,
1973.2, 66, 106-07;
1974.22; 1975.52; 1976.27;
1977.90; 1980.47, 148;
1981.111; 1982.11, 60;
1985.114
--cartoons, 1973.64; 1976.58
--commentary on popular and
critical responses, 1973.2,
43; 1982.11; 1983.8;
1986.240
  -individual responses,
1973.99; 1977.33
  -as Western film shoot-out,
1974.22
--compared with Australian
and British Columbia
literature, 1981.14;
1982.133
--editorial, 1973.106; 1981.111;
1985.114
--gothic, ghost story,
sadomasochistic,
shamanic, 1973.66;
1974.25; 1977.51-53;
1983.8, 84
--influenced by Frye, 1973.66;
1976.17, 49, 86; 1978.25;
1983.8, 31, 133-34;
1986.208
--influence on Canadian
criticism, 1978.36, 93;
1985.69
--interpreted for feminist
criticism, 1975.2
--liberal, bourgeois (Marxist
critiques), 1973.11;
1974.8; 1976.61; 1978.18,
24, 62, 94
--pre- and proto-Marxist,
1977.79; 1983.54

--themes in Atwood's other
work, 1972.8; 1973.38;
1975.24, 33; 1977.40, 66;
1978.36, 57; 1982.161;
1983.41, 73, 83, 104;
1984.18, 27, 75
-Canadian interviews,
Atwood's speech,
statements on, 1973.2, 24;
1976.58; 1977.80; 1982.11
-Canadian review, *en français*,
of *Essai sur la littérature
canadienne*, 1987.121
-Canadian reviews, *en français*,
of *Survival*, 1973.25, 44
-Canadian reviews, in English,
1972.14-16, 21, 26, 29, 31,
35, 37, 42; 1973.26, 34-35,
39, 40-41, 63, 68, 70-71,
80, 82, 84-85, 92, 97, 105;
1974.43, 46
--Canadian community and
struggle, 1972.26;
1973.34-35, 71
--nature, 1973.68
-East German review, 1979.30
-French criticism, in English,
themes in Atwood's
work, 1974.44
-German criticism, in English,
1987.15
-German review, in English,
1973.31
-German review, in German,
1973.67. *See also* 1979.30
-India, criticism from, animal
victims in Atwood's
poetry, 1984.30; 1985.38.
See also 1972.40
-"Survival II anthology,"
1973.17, 82